S0-BSN-384

Operational Excellence

Series on Resource Management

Montante Family Library
D'Youville College

Operational Excellence

Using Lean Six Sigma to Translate Customer Value through Global Supply Chains

James William Martin

Auerbach Publications
Taylor & Francis Group
New York   London

CRC Press is an imprint of the
Taylor & Francis Group, an **informa** business

Auerbach Publications
Taylor & Francis Group
6000 Broken Sound Parkway NW, Suite 300
Boca Raton, FL 33487-2742

© 2008 by Taylor & Francis Group, LLC
Auerbach is an imprint of Taylor & Francis Group, an Informa business

No claim to original U.S. Government works
Printed in the United States of America on acid-free paper
10 9 8 7 6 5 4 3 2 1

International Standard Book Number-13: 978-1-4200-6250-2 (Hardcover)

This book contains information obtained from authentic and highly regarded sources. Reprinted material is quoted with permission, and sources are indicated. A wide variety of references are listed. Reasonable efforts have been made to publish reliable data and information, but the author and the publisher cannot assume responsibility for the validity of all materials or for the consequences of their use.

Except as permitted under U.S. Copyright Law, no part of this book may be reprinted, reproduced, transmitted, or utilized in any form by any electronic, mechanical, or other means, now known or hereafter invented, including photocopying, microfilming, and recording, or in any information storage or retrieval system, without written permission from the publishers.

For permission to photocopy or use material electronically from this work, please access www.copyright.com (http://www.copyright.com/) or contact the Copyright Clearance Center, Inc. (CCC) 222 Rosewood Drive, Danvers, MA 01923, 978-750-8400. CCC is a not-for-profit organization that provides licenses and registration for a variety of users. For organizations that have been granted a photocopy license by the CCC, a separate system of payment has been arranged.

Trademark Notice: Product or corporate names may be trademarks or registered trademarks, and are used only for identification and explanation without intent to infringe.

Library of Congress Cataloging-in-Publication Data

Martin, James W. (James William), 1952-
Operational excellence : using lean six sigma to translate customer value through global supply chains / James William Martin.
p. cm.
Includes bibliographical references and index.
ISBN 978-1-4200-6250-2 (alk. paper)
1. Business logistics. 2. Production management. 3. Six sigma (Quality control standard) 4. Customer relations. I. Title.

HD38.5.M375 2008
658.5'03--dc22   2007045043

Visit the Taylor & Francis Web site at
http://www.taylorandfrancis.com

and the Auerbach Web site at
http://www.auerbach-publications.com

HD 38.5
.M 375
2008

Contents

PART 1 ADAPTING STRATEGIES FOR GLOBAL COMPETITIVENESS

AUG 1 1 2008

v

PART 3 OPERATIONS PLANNING, MANAGEMENT, AND CONTROL

PART 4   COLLECTING, ANALYZING, AND SHARING INFORMATION ACROSS A GLOBAL SUPPLY CHAIN

PART 5 GLOBAL SUPPLY-CHAIN MANAGEMENT INTEGRATION AND CONTROL

Foreword

My goal, in writing this book, is to provide a practical reference of tools, methods, and concepts to improve operations across the world. More than several hundred key tools, methods, and concepts are contained in this book. These have been collected from 30 years of experience teaching graduate courses in operations management, economic forecasting, operations research, leading Lean and Six Sigma deployments, consulting, and basic work experience in engineering and operations. I have also attempted to consolidate the information into 110 key concepts that will help an organization translate the voice of the customer (VOC) through its global supply chain to improve organizational productivity and shareholder economic value added (EVA). To accomplish these goals, this book has been divided into five major sections. These sections focus on adapting strategies for competitive organizations in today's world; the translation of customer needs and value expectations into products and services; the planning, management, and control of operations; the collection, analysis, and sharing of information; and the management, integration, and control of a global supply chain.

In my opinion, competitive failure is often self-induced through poor leadership coincident with an inability to form a coherent strategic vision and effectively execute it. In operations management parlance, *leadership* is equivalent to ensuring that an organization's activities are effective (working on the right things) and *execution* is the efficiency of achieving strategic goals and objectives (doing the right things well). As an example, it is especially important to get the VOC right the first time (effective and efficient translation of the VOC) when we create product and service designs. Aligning operations with the VOC to improve organizational productivity and shareholder EVA are critical goals throughout the 20 chapters comprising this book. As a result, many of the tools, methods, and concepts discussed in this text are designed to improve productivity and EVA through strategic and tactical alignment of operational goals and objectives with the VOC, because, in our opinion, these form the operational foundation of a competitive organization. Of course, there are numerous external factors that may impact operational efficiency, but from our viewpoint, organizations can and must do more to improve their internal operational efficiencies to successfully compete in today's world. After all, many organizations thrive in today's competitive world while others, in the same market space, fail.

This book was written from a viewpoint that many organizations can do much more to increase their global competitiveness, vis-à-vis a "flattened world" (Thomas L. Friedman), and improve their tactical execution, vis-à-vis "how to execute strategy" (Larry Bossidy and Ram Charan). This can be accomplished by applying leading-edge tools, methods, and concepts that are found in Lean, Six Sigma, design excellence, and other leading-edge initiatives. A second premise of this book is that an organization's financial, operational, and resultant productivity and shareholder EVA metrics are directly correlated with operational performance as well as its level of geographical, cultural, technological, and economic isolation. A third premise of this book is that noncompetitive organizations often neglect the basics of operations management, engineering, and other fundamental business competencies, exacerbating their noncompetitive position except in protected environments. In other words, organizations can increase their global operational competitiveness using basic and proven tools, methods, and concepts currently found in the field of operations management, economic forecasting, operations research, Lean and Six Sigma, and related disciplines. This implies that value-adding activities are not isolated to any one country or region and do not always depend on being the lowest cost producer.

In summary, *Operational Excellence: Using Lean Six Sigma to Translate Customer Value through Global Supply Chains* is a practical and hands-on reference written for people who need a concise and practical source of information to improve their manufacturing or service operations anywhere in the world. The 20 chapters comprising this book contain more than 450 figures, tables, and road maps covering a range of practical topics, from translating the VOC to product and process design, including design for Six Sigma (DFSS) methods, product forecasting, Lean concepts, financial and productivity analysis, capacity management, process scheduling, inventory control, supply-chain design, Six Sigma concepts, conducting of operational assessments, and project management, as well as the deployment of information technology across a supply chain to support operational goals and objectives. Understanding these diverse topics and their interrelationships will help ensure that an organization's operational systems meet or exceed customer needs and expectations.

I must thank my editor, Mr. Raymond O'Connell, for encouraging me to publish this book, as well as the reviewers of the book, who made constructive comments that changed its direction to a more practical and hands-on approach. Along this line of thought, the book has been expanded to include many practical tips for the identification and analysis of projects to improve operational efficiency. In fact, the entire focus of the book is to allow someone with little knowledge of leading-edge management concepts, such as creation of product and service designs, creation of process designs, and deployment of Lean and Six Sigma, to "quickly come up to speed," to improve the effectiveness and efficiency of operational workflows. Finally, I thank my family, clients, and Providence College graduate students, who have provided the inspiration for this book.

Introduction

It has been my experience that many organizations in diverse industries across the world can improve their productivity using currently available tools, methods, and techniques. However, the diverse subjects of operations management economic forecasting and operations research are scattered across many books and references. This makes it difficult to piece together the sequence of tools, methods, and concepts necessary to systematically improve organizational productivity from the voice of the customer (VOC) back through an organization and its supply chain in a practical and efficient manner. A major premise of the book is that many noncompetitive organizations neglect basic principles associated with marketing research, design engineering, process engineering, and operations management, as well as other fundamental business competencies. This causes them to become noncompetitive except in protected environments or situations in which they are geographically, culturally, technologically, and economically isolated from competitive pressures. Organizations could do much more to increase their relative global competitiveness if they effectively applied and efficiently used tools and methods already in existence. In other words, lost market share is caused not only by low wages and similar economic factors, but also by an organization's culture and its inability to execute its strategies at an operational level.

The fact that we are in an increasingly competitive world can be seen in the growing list of products and services exchanged across the world. Global transactions occur because, from a customer's viewpoint, there is a higher per unit value created by these exchanges. As organizations attempt to maximize the relative value content of their products and services, the degree of insourcing and outsourcing of work will accelerate over time. Also, boundaries between suppliers and their customers will continue to diminish in favor of collaborative and flexible workflow systems designed to deliver products and services at higher quality levels and lower cost. To increase relative competitiveness, an organization must identify its core competencies and create operational systems that amplify these competencies. By understanding customer needs and value by market segment, in the context of a culturally diverse global marketplace, organizations can align their process workflows to meet customer value expectations through the design of their products and services. Customer value will be defined in subsequent chapters as a composite of price and convenience.

Organizations continue to struggle with the question of where and how to add value to their products and services. The solution of value maximization for many leading-edge organizations is to outsource or insource work wherever the highest value can be added to their products or services. It is also apparent, based on purely economic considerations, that outsourcing and insourcing cannot be effectively slowed or mitigated by any individual country without adversely impacting customer value at a local level. This implies that organizations throughout the world, which lack one or more forms of competitive protection, must develop competitive strategies to add value to their products and services or experience erosion of their market share and profit margins. The practical result is that an organization that wants to avoid erosion of productivity and shareholder economic value added (EVA) must either maintain high local operational efficiency or move work elsewhere to remain competitive. Doing work where it has the highest value content is "hybrid decentralization." In hybrid decentralization, organizations determine where to outsource or insource work based on where its value content is highest. As an example, an organization might have its call centers located in India, its product design team scattered across the world near its major markets, its manufacturing in China to minimize standard costs, and its human resources operations located within its home country.

Organizational competitiveness is also related to a country's political and economic environment. In other words, every country has a different competitive advantage vis-à-vis other countries. As an example, some countries can easily compete on price due to low hourly wages. Other countries are competitive because their laws and regulations facilitate business transactions. Still other countries have significant educational and other infrastructures that facilitate commercial activities. Putting geopolitical and macroeconomic considerations aside, there is a long list of ways in which organizations can effectively level or "flatten" their competitive playing field. This can be accomplished along the dimensions of technology, the regulatory environment, organizational design, product and service design, workflow design, and workforce management. These characteristics differentiate inherently competitive from less competitive organizations. From an operational viewpoint, there are many tools, methods, and concepts that enable organizations to increase their productivity and EVA. These will be discussed in the next 20 chapters.

This book has been written to help operations managers and process improvement experts such as Lean experts and Six Sigma "belts" in manufacturing and service organizations to improve their organizational productivity by bringing together leading-edge tools, methods, and concepts to provide anyone involved with operations management with a one-source reference to immediately improve his or her organization's quality, productivity, and customer service operations. Major themes of the book include the alignment of operational strategy with business goals and objectives, the design of systems to meet customer needs and expectations, management of system capacity, and continuous improvement of system performance over time using Lean and Six Sigma methods. My goal has been to provide a concise and practical reference of modern operations management, based on my experience teaching graduate courses in operations management, economic forecasting, and operations research, as well as deploying Lean and Six Sigma initiatives within Fortune 500 and smaller companies across the world. As an example, this book contains over 450 figures, tables, and checklists to increase organizational productivity. Its 20 chapters lead a reader through the latest tools, methods, and concepts currently used in the fields of operations management, economic forecasting, operations research, Lean manufacturing, Six Sigma, product and service design, and supply-chain management across diverse industries such as manufacturing and financial services. These leading-edge methods, tools, and concepts are also currently used by best-in-class lean supply chains and will enable an organization to immediately identify and execute process improvements.

Chapters 1 to 3 have been organized under the section "Adapting Strategies for Global Competitiveness." We begin our discussion in Chapter 1 by laying the groundwork for why increasing productivity is important to effectively compete in the global economy. An important goal of Chapter 1 is explaining why organizations, which are admittedly not very efficient at a local level, are able to survive very well in protective environments, but begin to fail when they are exposed to external competitive forces. Also explained is why knowledge industries such as copy editing, publishing engineering design, and software development can now be done anywhere in the world at low cost and high quality or with an increased value content. However, the fact that organizations have competitive weaknesses does not imply that they cannot effectively compete on a global scale, but only that they must develop marketing and operational strategies that promote and augment their core competencies. In other words, they must compete based on their core competencies within market niches in which they are major players. The discussion in Chapter 1 also brings together several important concepts relevant to the strategic deployment of operations and their effective execution. In Chapter 2, we discuss modern change initiatives currently deployed in leading-edge organizations across the world. This discussion focuses on defining organizational change and how to execute it in diverse organizations, and focuses on specific initiatives, such as building high-performance work teams and the deployment of Lean, Six Sigma, design excellence, supply-chain excellence, and information technology excellence. The major success and failure characteristics of change programs will be discussed relative to these initiatives. VOC is discussed in Chapter 3. Understanding the VOC is a major competitive advantage in a global economy. In particular, the ability to mass customize products and services to satisfy local customer needs and value exactions is a major competitive strength. This allows small companies to dominate their market space or niche and compete with larger and more established organizations. In these situations, current investment and infrastructure may not even be a significant competitive factor. Thus, to provide a firm foundation on which to discuss the more technical aspects of operations management, we must understand how to translate the VOC through our products, services, and process workflow systems.

Chapters 4 to 7 have been organized into the section "Translating Customer Value into Products, Services, and Workflow Systems." Chapter 4 begins the discussion of VOC translation from the external customer back into the design of products and services using best-in-class design methods. These design methods include concurrent engineering (CE), design for manufacturing (DFM), and the tools, methods, and concepts used to create, design, prototype, pilot, and launch new products and services. The concepts of risk assessment and product life cycle issues are also discussed in Chapter 4. Expanding on the DFM concepts, mass customization is discussed from the perspective of increasing operational flexibility and productivity. Additional topics include design for Six Sigma (DFSS), developing design standards, reduction in product proliferation, and design outsourcing. Chapter 5 continues the discussion of product and service design, but from an operational or process perspective. This is because once a product or service has been designed, a transformation process must be created to produce the new product or service design for customers. Chapter 5 also discusses process modeling, simulation, queuing analysis, linear programming, and work simplification and standardization. Value stream mapping, operational analysis, bottleneck management, and operational balancing are key topics of Chapter 6, as well as other important Lean tools and methods. Productivity and EVA are the subjects of Chapter 7. Chapter 7 shows how to calculate productivity ratios and EVA and its impact on operational effectiveness. The information discussed in Chapter 7 is important to an operations manager or process improvement specialist, such as a Lean expert or Six Sigma "belt," because these tools and methods serve as a basis on which to measure organizational effectiveness and efficiency as measured by productivity and shareholder EVA in subsequent chapters of this book.

The third section of the book is entitled "Operations Planning, Management, and Control." It includes Chapters 8 to 14. Once products and their associated transformation processes, workflows, and operations have been designed, organizations must plan, schedule, manage, control, and improve them to increase productivity. Chapter 8 discusses demand management concepts because they impact capacity decisions, resource allocations, and production schedules. This discussion ranges from a basic to advanced level and includes simple time series analysis and multiple linear regression methods. At the end of Chapter 8, the demand management discussion is focused on using point-of-sale (POS) and related methods to obtain real-time information of customer demand. Chapter 9 discusses capacity management from the viewpoint of creating capacity to meet customer demand. In this discussion, capacity is discussed from a systemwide perspective, including the insourcing and outsourcing of work as proven methods to increase capacity and system flexibility. The risks associated with insourcing and outsourcing are also discussed in Chapter 9. Chapter 10 discusses facility location and management. These include analyzing demographic factors, the underlying political and economic infrastructure, and other important criteria that may impact facility location decisions. Several quantitative methods used to evaluate facility location decisions are also discussed in Chapter 10. These include ad hoc methods, the Pugh matrix, decision tree analysis, and regression analysis. Chapter 11 discusses the sales and operations planning (S&OP) functions within an organization. Chapter 12 discusses scheduling methods and rules based on the S&OP as well as workflow design. Chapter 12 also discusses pull production and kanbans, and shows why they are very effective scheduling systems. Chapters 13 and 14 cover the efficient flow of work through a system using best-in-class tools, methods, and concepts. These systems include master requirements planning (MRPII), modifications of MRPII systems that incorporate various elements of pull scheduling, production activity control (PAC), and inventory management.

Chapters 15 to 18 are contained within the fourth major section of this book, which is entitled "Collecting, Analyzing, and Sharing Information across a Global Supply Chain." Chapter 15 discusses the deployment of major information technology (IT) systems and their impact on the design of workflow management (WM) systems in manufacturing and service industries. Chapter 15 also discusses business process management (BPM), business process modeling and analysis (BPMA), business intelligence (BI), business activity monitoring (BAM), and enterprise application integration (EAI). It ends with a discussion of agile project management (APM). Continuing the theme of data collection, analysis, and information sharing, Chapter 16 discusses Six Sigma methods and how they are integrated with operational strategy. The discussion ranges from a basic to very advanced level, including experimental designs. Operational assessments are discussed in Chapter 17. In particular, their usefulness is discussed relative to collecting and analyzing process information to identify ways to increase productivity and EVA. Chapter 17 uses many of the tools, methods, and concepts discussed in previous chapters. Finally, in Chapter 18, project management is discussed relative to deployment of the improvement projects that have been identified during an operational assessment. Also, Chapter 18 discusses team formation, Gantt charts, the program evaluation and review technique (PERT), and risk analysis.

The last major section of this book is "Global Supply-Chain Management Integration and Control." Chapter 19 discusses important supply-chain functions, including software systems. In addition, key operational and financial metrics are discussed as they apply to global supply-chain management. Chapter 20 covers many of the integrative standards impacting today's organizations around the world. These include the Supply-Chain Operations Reference (SCOR®) model, International Standards Organization (ISO), Financial Accounting Standards Board (FASB), Occupational Safety and Health Administration (OSHA), Food and Drug Administration (FDA), Automotive Industry Action Group (AIAG), and the Malcolm Baldrige Award. Metric dashboards are also discussed in the context of implementing effective process controls within process workflows.

This book is intended to provide operations managers, process improvement specialists, Lean experts, Six Sigma black belts, green belts, and champions, and consultants with information useful to analyze and improve process workflows within their global supply chain that are relevant to improving productivity and EVA. As the various tools, methods, and concepts necessary to increase operational effectiveness and efficiency are discussed, we will use the term *organization* rather than *corporation* because our discussion is focused broadly on for-profit as well as not-for-profit organizations. Also, we will use the term *product* to mean manufactured goods or services because almost all the tools, methods, and concepts discussed in the next 20 chapters are analogous, regardless if the transformation system is for materials or information.

About the Author

James W. Martin is president of Six Sigma Integration, Inc., a Lean Six Sigma consulting firm, located south of Boston, and the author of *Lean Six Sigma for Supply Chain Management: The 10 Step Solution Process*. As a Lean Six Sigma consultant and master black belt for ten years, Mr. Martin has trained and mentored more than 1,500 black belts, executives, deployment champions, and green belts in Lean Six Sigma methods, including supply-chain applications, and led successful Lean Six Sigma assessments across Japan, China, Korea, Singapore, Malaysia, Thailand, Australia, North America, and Europe. This work included organizations in retail sales, residential and commercial service, banking, insurance, financial services, measurement systems, aerospace component manufacturing, electronic manufacturing, controls, building products, industrial equipment, and consumer products. He has also served as an instructor at the Providence College Graduate School of Business since 1988. He instructs courses in operations research, operations management, and economic forecasting, as well as related quantitative subjects, and counsels M.B.A. candidates from government organizations and leading corporations. He holds an M.S. in mechanical engineering, Northeastern University; M.B.A., Providence College; and B.S. in industrial engineering, University of Rhode Island. He also holds several patents and has written numerous articles on quality and process improvement. He is a member of APICS and has certifications in production and inventory management (CPIM) and integrated resource management (CIRM). He is a member of the American Society for Quality (ASQ) and is a certified quality engineer (CQE).

ADAPTING STRATEGIES FOR GLOBAL COMPETITIVENESS

1

Chapter 1

Enhancing Global Competitiveness

Competitive solution 1: Increase productivity and competitiveness using modern operations management tools, methods, and concepts.

Overview

Competitive pressures on organizations have increased over the past several decades due to the convergence of several major trends. These include geopolitical changes in Eastern Europe, Asia, and elsewhere, improvements in technology such as the Internet, and changes in workflow structure and management. These convergent trends have been discussed by several authors, including Thomas L. Friedman in his book *The World Is Flat.* According to Friedman, in the last several decades, several accelerating trends have changed the way in which we view the workflow management associated with the production of products and services. These trends included expansion of the World Wide Web, making information readily available, improvements in workflow and software management, the standardization of technology, international collaboration, outsourcing and insourcing of work, changes in the geopolitical environment, and offshoring of work across the world. These trends recently converged and contributed to the creation of production systems in which organizations may dominate not by virtual of their size, but rather on their organizational core competencies and other competitive strengths applied to niche or newly created markets.

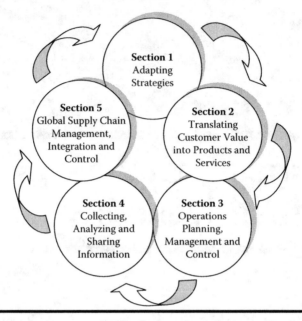

Figure 1.1 Developing operational solutions for today's world.

Current Trends in Operations Management

Although the world has become more competitive, there are many steps that organizations can take to become more competitive in the new global economy. The premise of this book is that an organization can increase its relative competitive position by understanding and successfully using basic tools, methods, and concepts found in the field of operations management. Some examples include understanding customer needs and value elements to more clearly focus product development efforts, deploying technology to align and improve workflows, and taking many other actions, at an operational level, to improve productivity through the efficient use of labor, materials, and capital. These actions, if properly executed, will increase the relative competitiveness of an organization.

Our discussion of operations management, as it applies in today's world, will be presented using the five solution categories shown in Figure 1.1. Each category contains several chapters as well as hundreds of important tools, methods, and concepts that will show how to design and produce products and services for your customers. These categories are:

■ Adapting strategies
■ Translation of customer value elements and needs into products and services
■ Planning, management, and control of process workflows

- Collection, analysis, and sharing of information across an organization's supply chain
- Management, integration, and control of that global supply chain

Through the tools, methods, and concepts presented within the 20 chapters of this book, we will discuss how an organization can increase its operational efficiency to become more competitive in today's world.

How the Competitive Environment Transforms Operational Strategy

Marketing strategy follows the voice of the customer (VOC) and voice of the business (VOB), and operational strategy follows marketing strategy. This is a basic tenet of operations management. Prior to the advent of the current competitive environment, an organization's operational strategy was relatively simple. It was determined by an organization's available technology, its logistical systems, and competitive threats on a regional or, at worst, national level. Customer preferences and the technology used to create the products and services to satisfy customer preferences changed very slowly over time. As an example, the product life cycle in consumer appliances was measured in years or decades. However, in today's world, the life cycles of many products and services are measured in months. The proliferation of consumer choices in today's world corresponds to an increase in purchasing alternatives created by newly created production systems. Whereas several decades ago an organization's operational strategy was stagnant, in today's world it changes dynamically in response to marketing and sales requirements, which are driven by customer needs and value expectations at a local market level. This new competitive environment requires flexible process workflow systems and management methods. In other words, organizations must understand what products and services customers want and provide them within very short cycle times, but at high quality and low per unit cost.

To ensure the efficient translation of strategic goals and objectives throughout an organization, its goals and objectives must be mapped using a strategic flow-down methodology similar to that shown in Figure 1.2. Figure 1.2 shows how organizational goals and objectives are mapped through successive organizational layers to ensure that, from a process perspective, downstream process outputs are fully linked to upstream long-term strategic inputs. In other words, an organization's operational strategy and the execution of that strategy should correspond to its strategic goals and objectives. In particular, its operational systems should be designed to execute marketing strategies. As an example, several years ago, the operational strategies of Burger King and McDonald's were obviously different. If we had compared and contrasted them, we would have found that Burger King had a customization strategy based on its marketing promise of "Have it your way." To support

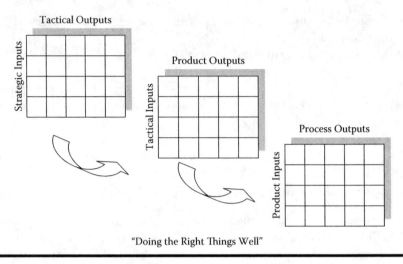

Figure 1.2 **Mapping strategic goals to process inputs.**

this marketing strategy, its operational design allowed customers to customize their orders. When customers visited Burger King, their food was processed through a "flame broiler." This operational strategy was based on a batch-and-queue process workflow system in which the flame broiler set the throughput rates of the system on a batch-by-batch basis for each customer order. So when customers arrived at Burger King, they expected to wait for their customized food for a longer period of time than they would at McDonald's, which was highly standardized based on its marketing strategy. There was a higher variation of waiting time in Burger King's batch-and-queue system because the waiting time was impacted by the length of the waiting line as well as the types of orders processed through the system. In summary, at Burger King, customers received customized food, but expected to wait longer than they would at McDonald's. In contrast to the operational strategy of Burger King, the operational strategy of McDonald's was to provide fast and standardized service. Customers arriving at McDonald's would find food products designed in a more standardized way to improve the process workflow efficiencies. McDonald's also maintained a small inventory of food, i.e., finished-goods inventory that was ready to sell to its customers on demand. The types and quantities of food were determined by historical customer demand patterns by the time of day. Although McDonald's and Burger King targeted different market segments, they were successful businesses. This simple example shows that an organization's operational strategy should be aligned with its marketing strategy relative to the types of customers expected to be served by the process workflow. In either restaurant system, it is important that customer expectations are met on a day-to-day basis. In fact, in its simplest form, customer satisfaction is determined by how well an organization keeps its marketing promise. To the extent that an organization's process workflows fail, customer satisfaction and organizational productivity deteriorate.

In summary, an operational linkage with marketing strategy is necessary to ensure operational systems are available to meet customer needs and value expectations.

Operational linkage must be achieved through both the design of the process workflow and its day-to-day management and control. Also, there must be a clear line of sight between resource allocation within a process workflow and anticipated business benefits in terms of its productivity and shareholder economic valued added (EVA). This is especially important in larger and more complex systems in which many interrelated process workflows exist and several initiatives have been deployed to improve organizational effectiveness and efficiency. Table 1.1 shows how "enabler" initiatives are aligned in best-in-class organizations to improve operational efficiencies and productivity. As an example, if the rolled throughput yield (RTY) of a process workflow is low, Six Sigma methods can be applied to identify, analyze, and eliminate the root causes of low process yields. To the extent that process yields are increased, scrap and rework percentages will decrease. This situation will result in material and direct labor cost savings as well as reductions in workflow cycle time, which will increase productivity. In the second example, shown in Table 1.1, an inventory turns ratio is increased by applying Lean tools and methods to reduce the lead time for a hypothetical product. Inventory turns is a ratio of the annual cost of goods sold (COGS) divided by the average on-hand monthly inventory investment. As an example, if COGS is $12 million annually and the average inventory investment necessary to maintain operations on a month-to-month basis is $1 million, then the inventory turns ratio is 12. The business benefits realized through a reduction in inventory investment include increases in cash flow, reductions in the interest expense required to purchase and maintain the inventory in a warehouse, and reductions in warehousing costs. In summary, all operational activities within an organization should be strategically linked with higher-level organizational goals and objectives to increase operational efficiencies and productivity.

As the world becomes more integrated and geographical barriers to free trade are systematically eliminated, an organization's marketing strategies continue to evolve to serve culturally diverse customer needs and value expectations through globally deployed workflow systems. This evolution has been accelerated by technology

Table 1.1 Operational Linkage to Financial Metrics

Measurable Improvement	Enabler	Productivity Opportunity	Productivity Linkage
Reduce scrap percentage	Use Six Sigma methods	Reduce scrap expense	A reduction in direct labor and materials
Increase inventory turns	Apply Lean methods to reduce forecasting error or lead time	Lower inventory investment	Increase cash flow and reduce inventory holding costs

improvements, changes in the geopolitical and macroeconomic environments, and increasing sophisticated and diverse operations management tools, methods, and concepts. In fact, the information available to organizations through the World Wide Web has leveled the playing field relative to the ability of organizations to keep in touch with their customers and productive workflow systems across the world to increase the exchange value of per unit value in products and services. The increased availability of information-related demand and supply has enabled customers to satisfy their specific needs and wants rather than relying on products and services designed for other people and cultures. This situation has enabled organizations to compete broadly across the world, by market segment, based on value elements related to price, speed, utility, and functionality through the mass customization of products and services. Mass customization is also focused through understanding customer needs as determined through Kano analysis. In Kano analysis, customer needs are described using three categories: basic needs, performance needs, and excitement needs. Basic Kano needs include product or service characteristics expected by the customer. Basic needs are common to every product and service regardless of the industry. As an example, when a person rents an automobile, he expects it not to break down during normal usage. He does not get excited if the automobile takes him where he needs to travel. On the other hand, performance needs differentiate one supplier from another based on relative performance exceeding basic levels. As an example, if a person is routinely upgraded by an automobile rental service, provided free navigation systems, or given a lower rental price, then she would differentiate this supplier as superior to others who do not provide these additional service features with the automobile rental. Excitement needs include product or service features that are initially unexpected by a customer, but once experienced create a "wow" effect. An example of an excitement need relative to renting an automobile would be giving free fuel or collision insurance, or perhaps the rental vehicle has a rear-view camera to help the driver back the car up. The competitive differentiation is significant when excitement needs are satisfied by a supplier.

In recent years, collaboration within global supply chains has accelerated. This has reduced the cycle time of order to receipt for products and services across diverse industries. In large part, this situation has been accelerated through aggregation or desegregation of process workflows across global supply chains. As an example, the marketing research for a product or service may be done in several countries or regions across the world, and the product might be designed in Taiwan, manufactured in China, and then distributed throughout the world. Also, as organizations build diverse work teams to interact within the globally deployed process workflows, the number of available ideas and unique solutions rapidly increases. In fact, when properly facilitated, collaboration within a diverse team increases, because team members tend to ask questions from several different perspectives rather than immediately moving off in a predetermined direction, which may yield a suboptimum solution. As an example, many years ago I was asked to join a forecasting improvement team because I taught a graduate course in economic forecasting. This team consisted of about 20 people at management and director levels. The team had been meeting for two years in an attempt to improve forecasting accuracy. In fact, during the proceeding two-year time interval, it had mapped the entire forecasting process, but had never initiated any real process improvements. As an outsider, I recognized that there was a problem with the team dynamics. This situation occurred because the team was led by people who had already focused the team on the forecasting modeling process and formed a process improvement team around this predetermined process workflow. However, the team found out only after a long period that its product forecasting error percentages were in line with those of similar industries and various benchmark statistics. It became clear that the team was formed under an incorrect assumption that significant improvements to the forecasting models were in fact possible. The reason the team had made little improvement to its demand management process was that it had gone off on a tangent by focusing on the wrong process workflow, i.e., forecasting models. The team should have asked: How can we improve the demand management process? Focusing attention on identifying and managing customer demand by market segment based on customer demographics would have provided the team with a much larger range of improvement options, including some related to forecasting models. Another important fact is that 50 percent of the organization's sales were due to only ten top retailers. Also, several of these retailers collected demand information in real-time as the supplier's products were scanned across their checkout counters. The balance of the organization's customers were represented by approximately 1,500 smaller warehouse distributors whose demand had to be aggregated by product group and forecast. An additional complicating factor was that this organization initiated periodic promotional campaigns that distorted product demand patterns. In summary, the organization could improve demand management on many levels, but a failure to build a diverse team resulted in failure. This simple example shows that by carefully defining the practical questions to be answered by a team, the number of available options for any business problem increases and solutions become more apparent. As they say, a problem well defined is half solved. Effective team formation is a competitive strength organizations can create to ensure that the right questions are asked, but many organizations do not take advantage of this competitive tool.

It has been shown that time and again organizations neglect the basic principles of operations management, effective marketing and sales methods, customer service requirements, or other critical competencies to their own detriment. On the other hand, best-in-class organizations consistently outperform their competitors across diverse countries and markets. In these situations, the competing organizations may even use the same labor, materials, and other resources. In effect, the differentiating competitive advantages among organizations usually are due to differential process workflow designs and more efficient process management. In other words, they use the same labor, materials, capital, and infrastructure, but exhibit differential levels of productivity and EVA. Toyota is a good example of this phenomenon in that it executes the basics of operations management well, as opposed to many of its competitors who use similar resources. The Toyota success story has shown that low cost is not the only differentiating factor in gaining market share in automobile manufacturing. However, there are islands of competitive excellence scattered across the world in which the cost structure is very low, such that competitive threats do exist for an organization, but these situations do not always fully explain the apparent relative differences in organizational competitiveness and productivity. As a result, in my opinion, organizations cannot continue to ignore state-of-the-art technology and best-in-class operational methods if they are to successfully compete in today's world.

Developing Adapting Strategies to Enhance Operational Capability

In his book entitled *The Transformation Imperative*, Thomas E. Vollmann states that organizations must dominate or die. However, the strategies and tactics that an organization uses to dominate its marketing space have radically changed over the last few decades. It used to be the case that organizational size and available capital would help ensure market share and allow an organization to adapt slowly to changing market conditions. In these older and bureaucratic systems, even if newly developed technologies were deployed by competitors, organizations often had sufficient time to reverse engineer the new systems, independently develop similar versions, or buy out the competitive organization to remain dominant in their market. Consumer preferences were also relatively stable several years ago. This was because technology evolved more slowly, which allowed organizations to easily manage customer value expectations and meet customer needs. In these relatively static environments, operational strategies were also often stagnant. The appliance industry is an example of an industry that was previously characterized by product designs that evolved very slowly over time. However, in response to competitive pressures, this industry rapidly adopted best-in-class process workflows and manufacturing systems. This allowed it to reduce product development time and standard cost and increase quality. Several decades ago, dominance of a market was facilitated by the ability of large organizations to set industry standards and deploy capital-intensive barriers that prevented new market entrants. However, in today's world, smaller organizations can effectively dominate their market space and eliminate larger and historically more entrenched organizations through increased learning rates and the creation of flexible and, in many situations, virtual process workflows. These operational strategies allow scalable responses, permitting smaller organizations to compete against larger ones.

In their book entitled *Blur*, Stan Davis and Christopher Meyer provide a list of 50 ways to blur an organization. Their book was written several years ago, at a time in which the Internet had just become popular and before eBay and similar Web-based e-commerce systems became commonplace. As I wrote this book, it occurred to me that the 50 blurring strategies are more true today than they were ten years ago. In many ways, when redefined appropriately, they correlate to several of the major trends discussed by Thomas L. Friedman. Some of these blurring strategies include:

- Make speed your mindset.
- Connect everything with everything.
- Grow your intangibles faster than your tangibles.
- Be able to do anything, anyplace.
- Put your offer online.
- Make your offer interactive.
- Customize every offer.

There are 40 other great ideas in their book. The 50 ways to blur your organization enable an organization to become more competitive in today's world because new entrants can effectively blur their organizations and become dominant players in their markets. In this book, these and similar concepts are integrated to show how process workflow designs have evolved over the last several decades.

Unfortunately, having great ideas is not the same as executing them well. Process workflow systems must be designed, deployed, and actually work the way they were intended in order to deliver products and services coincident with customer value expectations and create the productivity levels necessary for an organization to meet its commitments to shareholders. In their book entitled *Execution: The Discipline of Getting Things Done*, Larry Bossidy and Ram Charan discuss the importance of strategic execution. I worked at AlliedSignal from 1982 to 1997 (with some time spent elsewhere) and observed firsthand its transformation from a bureaucratic and lethargic organization to a faster-moving one due to the many strategic initiatives initiated by Larry Bossidy's leadership team. When I left AlliedSignal ten years ago, there were still organizational issues, but based on my perceptions, the new AlliedSignal was heads above the previous one relative to its ability to execute strategy through process performance improvements.

In John Kotter's book entitled *Leading Change*, he puts forth an eight-stage process to create major change within an organization. In my consulting practice, which is focused on the deployment of Lean and Six Sigma initiatives, I often reference Kotter's book to show why change initiatives fail or succeed. Kotter's eight characteristics of effective change are:

1. Establishing a sense of urgency
2. Creating a guiding coalition
3. Developing a vision and strategy
4. Communicating the change vision
5. Empowering a broad-based action

6. Generating short-term wins
7. Consolidating gains and producing more change
8. Anchoring new approaches in the culture

The ability of an organization to change its organizational structure, work habits, and systems to meet competitive threats is dependent on its culture. In other words, technology deployment is often easier than cultural change within an organization. However, culture is the driving force behind an organization's competitiveness. Competitive organizations know that their strength lies in the quality of their people and culture.

Linking Operational Strategy to Strategic Goals and Objectives

According to the book *Execution: The Discipline of Getting Things Done*, "execution has to be in the culture." This means it must be embedded into the reward system of an organization as well as organizational norms related to group and individual success or failure. Effective execution requires doing the right things efficiently and according to schedule to achieve strategic and tactical goals and objectives. As an example, when I was at AlliedSignal, the top-level financial goal of the organization was return on equity (ROE), which was set at approximately 30 percent at that time. This top-level ROE target was successively delayed at every level of the organization to improve financial and operational metrics that were clearly linked with each other. As an example, the metric layer just below the ROE target consisted of sales, cash flow, and operating income targets. The next lower metric level consisted of year-over-year productivity targets. The concept was that if these second, third, and lower-level metrics were improved over their original baselines to achieve planned targets, the higher-level organizational ROE target would be achieved according to plan. To systematically improve these metrics, it was necessary to deploy operational initiatives such as Lean, Six Sigma, preventive maintenance programs, supply-chain improvements, information technology (IT) deployments, and others. Deployment of enabling initiatives helps drive improvements to lower-level operational metrics such as inventory investment, cost reductions, gross margin improvements, and other productivity drivers. These concepts are shown in Figure 1.3, in which the VOC is integrated with the voice-of-the-business (VOB) through a ROE metric, and eventually with the voice-of-the-process (VOP) through enabler initiatives and their operational metrics. Figure 1.3 shows that the planning process is top-down, whereas the project execution activities occur at a process workflow level and are bottom-up, but integrated with strategic goals and objectives.

Over the past ten years, I have worked with many organizations throughout the United States and the world. It has been interesting to note that diverse organizational cultures, even within the same industry, may approach strategic

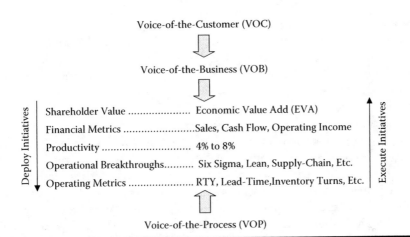

Voice-of-the-Customer (VOC)

Voice-of-the-Business (VOB)

Deploy Initiatives

Shareholder Value .... Economic Value Add (EVA)

Financial Metrics ....Sales, Cash Flow, Operating Income

Productivity .... 4% to 8%

Operational Breakthroughs.......... Six Sigma, Lean, Supply-Chain, Etc.

Operating Metrics .... RTY, Lead-Time,Inventory Turns, Etc.

Execute Initiatives

Voice-of-the-Process (VOP)

Figure 1.3   Strategic execution of business goals.

goal deployment using different execution strategies, but compete very success-fully against each other using their specific underlying core competencies. As an example, the organizational culture of one financial services organization I worked with was consensus based and employee centric. At the end the first year of their Six Sigma deployment, after training 200 black belts, only a small number of projects had been successfully executed by the organization. In contrast, a second financial services organization that had a more execution style culture completed more than 50 projects within 90 to 120 days of their inception. The second organization also generated almost 20 times the cost savings in one third the cycle time with about 40 percent less deployed resources. The difference in execution style between the two organizations was their culture and leadership. However, in subsequent conver-sations with people who had worked for the first organization, I found they had suc-cessfully closed their projects and caught up with the second organization. Being a consensus-based organization resulted in the first organization taking a longer cycle time to execute its projects. However, both organizations have been very success-ful over the past several years, although their operational execution strategies were different. Execution is critical in successfully competing in today's world, but goals and objectives must be attained by an organization in a balanced way.

However, many organizations do not know how to execute their strategies. This is why productivity statistics range from negative to weakly positive across many organizations. In his book *The Transformation Imperative*, Vollmann states that organizations must develop effective initiatives to execute their strategies through the development of core competencies. Core competencies may include best-in-class process workflows in finance, marketing, sales, customer service, product develop-ment, operations, and other functional areas within an organization. Another way to think about Vollmann's core competency argument is that an organization must develop the required process workflows necessary to deliver the key customer value elements related to cycle time, selling price, and product or service functionality. An implicit assumption is that an organization has already stratified customer Kano needs by market segment. As an example, some organizations compete based on their product development or marketing competencies, others compete based on their operational and supply-chain efficiencies, while still others compete based on quality and customer service.

The current competitive environment leaves no room for error relative to the ability of an organization to execute its strategy. Over the past several years, I have observed firsthand many organizations that exhibited one or two core competencies, but were subpar performers in other competitive areas. This is because having one or more competitive competencies allowed them to succeed in their market space to the detriment of process workflow improvement in noncore competency areas. As an example, one large international organization is well known for its new product development and marketing processes but, unknown to many people, it is one of the lowest rated suppliers by its customers due to poor quality and on-time delivery. However, as a consultant I could see a huge potential for productivity improvement if this organization were running on all "six cylinders." Effective execution means that every part of an organization must execute well. To compete in today's world, it is not an acceptable situation to rely on just one or two core competencies, even though financial performance may be very good at the moment. In fact, it is often the situation that currently successful organizations may be inefficient when they must compete globally. The days of being able to stay level because your organization is protected from competitors by geopolitical or other competitive barriers have ended for the foreseeable future. However, this argument assumes no significant changes in the current geopolitical environment that increase protectionism or disrupt global supply chains. Furthermore, even protectionists measures, if they should be implemented by individual countries, must be short-lived in today's world because increases in relative per capital economic advantage are facilitated by free trade.

At a macroeconomic level, a country's standard of living can be measured on a per capita productivity basis. Per capita productivity is comprised of three components: labor, capital, and factor productivity. Factor productivity is the efficiency of capital and labor utilization. Countries have mixtures of each of these three components. As an example, some countries may have a large capital and labor base, but factor productivity may be small. In these situations, resources will not be utilized efficiently. Prior to 1995, smaller organizations, relative to their larger competitors, lacked all three of these productivity components. But after the development of the World Wide Web, small organizations could be big in presence with little labor or capital. In fact, over the past several years, the relative importance of capital and labor has been deemphasized in favor of factor productivity. In fact, the ability of an organization to increase its factor productivity is now on par with that of much larger organizations due to technological convergence. This means that not only has the competitive playing field among organizations been leveled in recent years due to technological convergence, but also the result has been an increase in per capital productivity in smaller organizations, increasing their competitiveness relative to larger organizations. However, major components of factor productivity external to organizations include infrastructure, the regulatory environment, organizational culture, and technology. Thus, in some cultures, the impact of technological convergence has not been fully realized due to geopolitical and other constraints external to an organization. The productivity differentiators in today's world will become more people or knowledge dependent. This is especially true for products and services requiring high customer contact and information exchange, as opposed to back-office operations, which have already migrated to lowest-cost areas. However, this trend must be facilitated by a reduction in barriers to free trade.

Global Metrics and Operational Maturity

Metrics are used to define, measure, control, and identify metric performance gaps for improvement in the process workflows characterizing organizational systems. Table 1.2 shows that metrics have several important characteristics. First, it is important that they are aligned with high-level strategic goals and objectives and link across an organization. As an example, a high-level strategic goal might be to reduce warranty expense across an organization. As a first step, warranty expense should be clearly defined, including the informational components used to calculate its value. This is because, at an organizational level, warranty expense represents an aggregated amount of all lower levels within an organization. This aggregated expense can be delayed or disaggregated level by level down through the organization to ensure linkage, as shown in Figure 1.4. Strategic disaggregating ensures alignment of the metric throughout an organization. Metric alignment is also important to ensure that resource allocations are made within those areas of an organization that will provide the greatest productivity opportunities. This is important because high productivity drives high ROE and EVA for shareholders. Alignment of metrics also ensures that they are linearly additive level by level

Table 1.2 Metric Characteristics

1. Aligned with strategic goals and objectives
2. Links across organizational functions
3. Helps improve performance
4. Easy to use every day
5. Controllable by people who are responsible for its performance
6. Tough to manipulate and may require compensating metrics

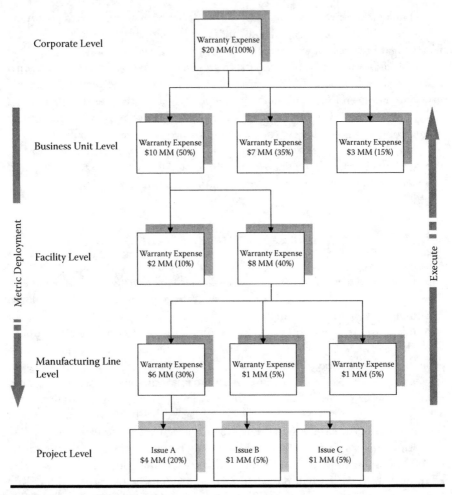

Figure 1.4 Strategically aligning metrics.

throughout an organization. As an example, warranty expense is clearly linear because its unit of measure is in dollars, as shown in Figure 1.4. Time is also a linear metric. However, at a local operational level, there may be specific operational metrics that must be improved to reduce warranty expense. These metrics are often seen at a project level and must be correlated to higher-level financial metrics. A second important concept of metric definition includes its data collection, analysis, and presentation. A third important consideration is the display of metrics using automated and visual displays of their status to ensure real-time dissemination within an organization. As an example, in modern call centers, process workflow status is displayed in real-time using visual display boards. These visual display boards show the number of calls per unit time within a call center by function, including incoming call volumes, average call durations, and other operational and service metrics throughout the call center. These automated and visual systems allow real-time process measurement and control by call center personnel. This discussion of metric display will be expanded in Chapter 15. A fourth important characteristic of metrics is that they are actionable by the people using them. As an example, if a material planner is assigned responsibility to control inventory investment for his product groups, then he must also be able to control product lead times and demand variation or forecasting error because these drive inventory investment at a target unit service level. Of course, lead time and demand variation cannot usually be controlled by material planners. This means inventory investment metrics must be clearly defined to specify inventory investment within a range of lead time and variation of demand or forecasting error. Once a metric is clearly defined, reasonable, and actionable, it is very difficult to manipulate or distort over time.

Metrics can also be classified in several ways relative to their organizational impact and specific format. Organizational impact can be broken into the categories of time, cost, and quality. Within these categories each organizational function develops and uses metrics specifically designed to measure, analyze, control, and continuously improve process performance. Table 1.3 lists several common metrics used by organizational functions to measure and control workflows across their global supply chain. Admittedly, this is a small and arbitrary metric listing because there are literally thousands of specific metrics used throughout the world. However, they fall into the three higher-level categories of time, cost, and quality. As Figure 1.5 shows, metrics can also be broken into four categories based on their format: business, financial, operational, and compensating metrics. Business metrics are used by an organization to linearly deploy metrics throughout the organization to enable their aggregation. As an example, business metrics can be aggregated at an organizational, local business unit, or local process workflow level. Business metrics are typically measured on a percentage-of-total basis. Examples include percentage of recordable accidents, percentage of equipment uptime, percentage of forecasting accuracy, percentage of on-time delivery, warranty cost as a percentage of sales, and scrap and rework as a percentage of cost. There are many other metrics that can be measured at a local level and aggregated throughout an organization. Financial metrics are directly correlated to business metrics and show the impact of the business metric on organizational financial performance and productivity. Referencing Figure 1.4, the financial metric "warranty expense" is correlated to the business metric "warranty expense as a percentage of sales." Figure 1.4 is a useful example, showing where warranty expense is incurred on a percentage basis throughout several organizational levels, as well as its business impact. However, at a local process workflow level, operational metrics are used to measure, analyze, improve, and control local operations within the process workflow. As one example, warranty expense at a facility level might be due to three different types of defects. These defects might include a dimensioning problem, an off-color product, or damaged packaging. The operational metrics corresponding to these defects would be defined in units of inches, color coordinate using an instrument to measure color, and the

Table 1.3 Commonly Used Metrics

Financial	Quality	Customers
Sales	First-pass yield	Customer satisfaction
Income	CPk	% New customers
Cash flow	% Warranty	% Customer retention
Productivity	% Returned goods	% International sales
		% Export sales
R&D	*Process*	*People*
% New products in last 3 years	Lead time	% Employee diversity
Product development life cycle	% On-time delivery	Training hours per employee
% Engineering change requests	% Schedule attainment	% Employee turnover
% R&D costs of sales	% Machine uptime	% Employee satisfaction
Materials	*Suppliers*	*Environmental*
% Forecasting accuracy	% On-time delivery	Energy costs to sales
% Schedule changes	% Supplier satisfaction	
% Overdue backlog	Number of improvement suggestions	
% Data accuracy	Total business benefits	
% Material available		

tear strength of the packaging. These local operational metrics must align and be translatable into the warranty expense metric. Compensating metrics are used to balance the impact of business and project metrics on the process workflow operations. As an example, reducing lead time to reduce inventory investment would require a compensating metric such as maintaining the customer service-level target. Reducing internal scrap and rework without increasing external warranty expense is another example of a compensating metric.

Metrics are important because they require resources to develop, deploy, and use very day. Also, important decisions are made based on their performance levels. For these reasons, organizations should carefully develop their metrics using the information listed in Table 1.2 as a minimum. Best-in-class metrics are characterized by their focus on customer value, how well an organization designs its process workflow systems to meet its customer needs and value expectations, the speed of product or service delivery, the flexibility of its systems to increase or decrease available capacity, the ability to foster continuous process improvement, and the ability to increase productivity and align operational performance with an organization's strategic goals and objectives. These characteristics can help today's organizations enhance their relative competitiveness. Table 1.4 lists 20 key competitive metrics that enable best-in-class organizations to compete in their global supply chains. Many of the metrics listed in Table 1.4 measure improvements to the metric over

Table 1.4   20 Key Competitive Metrics

1. Customer satisfaction by market segment
2. Percentage new customers in last 12 months
3. Percentage customer retention in last 12 months
4. Percentage of international sales
5. Percentage of new products in last 12 months
6. Sales growth by market segment
7. Employee satisfaction
8. Employee cultural and global diversity
9. Month-over-month productivity
10. Month-over-month percentage cycle time reduction
11. Month-over-month first-pass yield
12. Month-over-month safety index
13. Order fill rate
14. Delivery to request
15. Delivery to promise
16. Sales, general, and administrative (SG&A) cost
17. Delivery cost
18. Manufacturing cost
19. Working capital
20. Income from operations

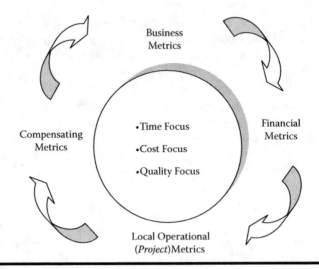

Figure 1.5 **Linking the four key metric types.**

time and impact customer satisfaction, organizational productivity, or employee empowerment. This is a small subset of metrics currently used by organizations.

Relative competitiveness depends on many factors, but at an operational level (neglecting the effectiveness of strategy), it can be represented in matrix format as operational efficiency as measured by productivity versus the degree of competitive transparency. But productivity and transparency vary by industry, so they must be evaluated relative to mutual competitiveness within a particular product or service marketing space. In Chapter 7, productivity will be discussed from the viewpoint of a ratio of outputs to inputs, or sales to costs. In other words, productivity will be shown to depend on how efficiently an organization satisfies year-over-year customer demand. In Figure 1.6, competitive transparency is broken down by regional, national, and international levels. Higher competitive transparency occurs when competitors are able to sell within an organization's market space due to geographical transparency, have an ability to provide similar technology and performance to customers, or enjoy comparative marketing advantages relative to the political and cultural environment. Operational efficiency or productivity can be broken into low, medium, and high levels using readily available benchmarking data from numerous studies over the past few decades. Figure 1.6 is a qualitative representation that argues that productivity must be high to prevent market erosion for any organization that has significant competitive pressures. As an example, when I was an employee of AlliedSignal, its year-over-year productivity was in the 6 to 8 percent range. This was considered best in class at the time. I have also worked for a smaller, privately held organization that had both unique proprietary positions based on technology and relative geographical isolation because the weight of its product protected it from international competition due to high transportation

	Low-Regional	Medium-National	High-International
High (>4%)	Highly Competitive Regionally	Highly Competitive Nationally	Highly Competitive Internationally
Medium (0–4%)	Erosion of Regional Market Share	Erosion of National Market Share	Loss of National Markets
Low (<0)	Erosion of Regional Market Share	Loss of National Markets	Not Competitive Nationally or Internationally

Operational Efficiency-Productivity

(Geographical/Technical/Political/Cultural)
Degree of Competitive Transparency

Figure 1.6   Competitive evaluation table.

costs into U.S. markets. This company had a productivity level in the range of 1 to 2 percent. A third organization I worked with was in bankruptcy protection. Its productivity level was 1 percent. I have observed that organizations that exist in low competitive transparency environments tend to have lower operational efficiencies and productivity levels, whereas organizations having low competitive transparency tend to have high productivity levels, or they cease to exist. The real question is: Where is your organization relative to productivity today? Also, what is your productivity level relative to your competitors'? Organizations have two choices when they design and manage their operations. Either they can manage their operations with high effectiveness and efficiency regardless of the geographical, technical, or other factors that impact the degree to which they must compete, or they can become inefficient and eventually lose their market share to more productive competitors as their relative isolation evaporates. Now some organizations may argue that the reason they are losing market share is because competitors have lower labor costs. This may very well be true, but the complaining organizations must then find other ways to lower their operational costs or find niche markets that enable them to charge higher prices based on customer perceived value. Of course, there are situations in which the products or services are so highly driven by labor costs that low labor costs dictate who will be in the market space. Finally, availability of information through the Internet has increased competitive transparency across major supply chains in today's world. This has created a situation in which inefficient organizations lose their market share. In the absence of artificial competitive barriers, this trend will accelerate over time as consumers demand high per unit transaction value.

Internal and External Benchmarking

Internal benchmarking is conducted across similar organizational functions within the same organization or within a single function based on operational assessment and analysis. An example would be comparing the key performance metrics of several distribution centers across a logistics network. In this analysis, inventory turns could be compared for each distribution center, with some facilities having higher or lower turns ratios than other facilities. If a facility has similar operations, products, and sales volumes, then internal benchmarking of inventory turns ratios might be appropriate. In this situation, the poorer-performing facilities could learn from those performing at higher levels. However, if the distribution centers have different operational designs or customers, then a benchmarking comparison may be useless. In fact, it might even be detrimental to the organization because those facilities that may appear to be performing more poorly would be forced to take action, causing a possible deterioration in other important performance metrics. In contrast, an organization should benchmark itself against *entitlement* performance levels developed through internal operational assessments. If necessary, it could then extend its benchmarking activities to external process workflows within other organizations. Entitlement is a concept used to understand how much a process can be improved relative to its original design intent. The entitlement concept implies that there will be limitations to how far an organization can improve its process workflows because of design limitations. However, the first step in a benchmarking study should be to understand how well your processes currently perform, what you can reasonably accomplish through process improvements given current system constraints, i.e., design limitations, and what might be possible if the process workflows were completely redesigned by your organization. Entitlement will be discussed in the context of product and service design in Chapter 4, as well as the design of workflow systems in Chapter 5. Chapter 16 will continue the discussion of entitlement from a *capability* analysis perspective. Capability is how well a process performs to customer requirements. (In Chapter 16, a more formal definition will be provided using tools and methods found in Six Sigma programs.)

In contrast to internal benchmarking or entitlement analysis, external benchmarking is a simple process used by many organizations to baseline their performance by comparing their internal workflows to best-in-class external systems. This helps organizations improve their performance relative to key financial and operational metrics. In addition, it may also be useful for organizations to externally benchmark current process workflows against those from completely different industries. As an example, some package delivery organizations recently created a new business model wherein information is e-mailed rather than transported via physical format. This type of benchmarking across industries and technologies may lead to greater productivity improvement for an organization than if it emulated competitors of similar industries. However, there are right and wrong ways to undertake an external benchmarking study. As an example, Table 1.5 shows

Table 1.5   10 Key Benchmarking Activities

1. Determine benchmarking goals and objectives.
2. Form a cross-functional and diverse team.
3. Create a project plan.
4. Develop data collection strategy.
5. Collect data in a standardized manner.
6. Analyze data to understand best-in-class performance.
7. Develop plans to change the process.
8. Communicate the proposed process changes.
9. Change the process.
10. Continually review and expand the benchmarking methodology.

that benchmarking studies should identify the goals and objectives of the external benchmarking study, how it should be performed, the expected analysis of the collected data, and how the benchmarking analysis will be used to improve the internal process workflows. An important goal of an external benchmarking study is to provide data in the form of financial and operational metrics, and to use this information to improve process performance. Using these basic concepts, many organizations employ external benchmarking studies across diverse organizational functions.

External benchmarking involves comparing organizations in the same industry sector, i.e., competitors or completely different business, but doing similar functions. As an example, competitive benchmarking may be done through industry associations or third-party research organizations. In those studies it is very important to ensure that there is an apples-to-apples comparison between the workflows being compared. What this means is that the competitors being benchmarked should in fact have process designs similar to those of the organization conducting the benchmarking study. In situations in which benchmarking is conducted with organizations outside an industry, the benchmarking organization may be able to gain insights into how radical changes to their product or process designs might improve internal operating performance. As an example, Federal Express Corporation (FedEx) evaluated the Internet technology explosion of the mid-1990s and began to offer transfer of information through e-mail. In other words, they partially redefined themselves as an information courier. Also, United Parcel Service (UPS) and FedEx have migrated all over the world, similar to other international organizations, and simultaneously integrated with organizations such as Kinko's, Staples, and other consumer sales outlets where customers can drop off packages. External benchmarking studies allowed UPS and FedEx to grow beyond their initial service offerings.

However, it is important to carefully plan the benchmarking project to ensure that relevant information is collected, analyzed, and will be useful for improving the process workflow under evaluation. The first step in the process is to clearly establish the goals and objectives of the benchmarking study, including the information that must be collected to answer the relevant benchmarking questions for an organization. A second important question is: Where will the benchmarking information be collected and from whom? A third consideration is: Who will be collecting the information and in what form? There are many other questions that the benchmarking team must answer as part of its workflow comparison activities. After the benchmarking information has been collected, it is important to determine the analytical tools and methods required to answer these questions. The team must also consider how the benchmarking information will be communicated to the organization and its eventual impact on internal process workflows. To ensure these important benchmarking activities are accomplished, the organization must bring together a cross-functional and diverse team to undertake the benchmarking activities. The people supporting the benchmarking team should also have the required analytical skills to successfully quantify their analysis.

The team should begin the benchmarking process by reviewing the project's goals and objectives and creating a project charter. The project charter acts as a guide as to where the benchmarking study will begin and end. After the team has verified its project charter and key milestones, these milestones must be broken into key activities and work tasks. A project plan is created using this information. The project plan is a time-sequenced listing of required milestones, activities, and work tasks, as well as the resources required to accomplish all work tasks. Benchmarking also implies that metrics will be compared across several business entities and their process workflows. This work will involve either internal organizational functions or external organizations. The team should plan to collect the benchmarking data in a consistent manner under standardized conditions to ensure its benchmarking analysis can be extrapolated across the various internal process work flows that are part of the study. An integral part of this detailed process analysis includes building a quantified process map to develop a clear understanding of every work task, including its operational definitions, work sequences, and methods, as well as inspection procedures. It is also important to have other team members "walk" the process to ensure all the required information has been correctly collected for analysis. After the data has been collected, the benchmarking team must ensure that the correct statistical analysis is conducted to reach unambiguous conclusions. As an example, if we had collected inventory turns ratios for several distribution centers and found that one center was better than the others, we could prove this statement with a certain confidence level given that we used sample data to calculate the inventory turns ratio. We could use this statistical analysis to say that the better-performing facility was in fact statistically different from other facilities. To summarize, internal and external benchmarking are very useful in identifying ways to dramatically improve your process workflows in a very short period.

Table 1.6   Key Concepts to Improve Operational Efficiency

1. Map strategic goals and objectives through your organization to a project level to ensure alignment.
2. Every project should be defined relative to the four major metric classifications of business metrics, financial metrics, compensating metrics, and project or operational metrics.
3. Understand how metrics are linked, including the underlying relationships, and, ideally, be able to create process models to understand how metrics change in response to changes in workflow inputs.
4. Internally benchmark workflows to identify productivity opportunities, then externally benchmark other organizations that are similar or completely different, but understand the goals and objectives of the benchmarking study.

However, you should not underestimate the required resources or the complexity of the benchmarking project activities. These concepts have been summarized in Table 1.5 as ten key benchmarking activities.

Summary

The focus of this chapter is "Enhancing Global Competitiveness" in response to the major technological, operational, political, and macroeconomic trends currently taking place throughout the world. In this context our discussion was on the effective and efficient use of operations management methods, which are evident in major improvement initiatives such as Lean and Six Sigma, as well as the important operational principles that are known to increase organizational productivity and EVA for your organization's shareholders. This chapter can be summarized by the four key concepts listed in Table 1.6.

The balance of the book will present specific tools, methods, and concepts to increase your organization's efficiency in today's world.

Suggested Reading

Giovanni Arrighi. (2006). *The Long Twentieth Century*. Verso, London and New York.
Larry Bossidy and Ram Charan, with Charles Burck. (2002). *Execution: The Discipline of Getting Things Done*. Crown Business.
Stan Davis and Christopher Meyer. (1998). *Blur: The Speed of Change in the Connected Economy*. Addison-Wesley, Reading, MA.
Thomas L. Friedman. (2006). *The World Is Flat*. Farrar, Strauss and Giroux, New York.

John P. Kotter. (1996). *Leading Change.* Harvard Business School Press, Boston.

Michael E. Porter. (1990). *The Competitive Advantage of Nations.* The Free Press.

Thomas E. Vollmann. (1996). *The Transformation Imperative.* Harvard Business School Press, Boston.

Martin Wolf. (2004). *Why Globalization Works.* Yale University Press, New Haven and London.

Chapter 2

Organizational Change in a Competitive World

Competitive solution 2: Create an adaptable organizational culture by deploying initiatives to improve core competencies.

Overview

In their book entitled *Corporate Culture and Performance*, John P. Kotter and James L. Heskett came to the following conclusion: corporate culture can significantly affect an organization's performance. Also, an organization's culture, either positive or negative, is difficult to change. Why don't organizations want to change? It is a simple question with a simple answer. There is often not a clear reason to change. The problem with asking successful organizations to change is that they have achieved success based on their current paradigms and culture. Unless an organization can see real value in changing its way of doing things, it will not undertake a major change initiative. To complicate and worsen matters, the most successful people in an organization are often the most isolated from information showing the necessity of change. Also, in some organizations, those who control the organizational power structure and resources usually stand to lose the most from a dramatic change within their organization. This situation, if it exists, may place the proponents of change on the defensive. According to Kotter and Heskett in *Corporate Culture and Performance*, slowly changing and reactive organizational cultures often fail to realize their full market potential, but in today's competitive environment, problems with launching new products, getting to market late, and

Table 2.1   Competitive World Metrics: Organizational Change

1. Percentage of the organization converted to and practicing the new behaviors
2. Cumulative net business benefits by improvement category, project types, location, and organizational level
3. Key success factors of the various initiatives as well as plans to reinforce them
4. Key barriers preventing full deployment of initiatives and plans to remove them from the deployment
5. Organizational satisfaction level for each initiative, including its relevant organizational demographics

other aspects of poor strategy and strategic execution can put an organization out of business.

Change is difficult to implement in any organization. But according to John Kotter in his book *Leading Change*, as well as in similar studies, there are key characteristics that indicate that a change initiative is succeeding within an organization. In fact, in *Leading Change* Kotter lists eight key characteristics associated with a successful change initiative. In Table 2.1 I have listed five key metrics that are commonly used by organizations to manage and evaluate the effectiveness of their initiatives. The most obvious metric is the percentage of people actually using the new toolsets and methods of an initiative. However, a simple percentage conversion as measured by the number of people trained or using a system may not fully measure the effectiveness of an initiative. In situations in which initiatives are deployed, but create no observable business benefits, initiative effectiveness degrades and usually falls in general disuse within an organization. For this reason, it is important to also measure the cumulative net business benefits of an initiative by improvement category, project, and location across an organization. In other words, the deployment of an initiative should create business benefits in excess of the initiative's cost. The general categories of business benefits include revenue enhancement, cost reduction, asset conversion, cost avoidance, and increases in customer, supplier, or employee satisfaction. Business benefits should be measured at a project level and aggregated up through an organization to show where an initiative is working or failing to achieve its goals and objectives. Business benefits will be discussed in more detail in subsequent chapters and specifically in Chapter 7. Another useful approach in measuring initiative effectiveness is to identify its key success factors and the organization's tactical plans to reinforce these success factors. Key barriers preventing the full deployment of an initiative should also be identified, as well as the tactical plans necessary to remove these barriers. It is important to measure

Figure 2.1 Competing factors that may impact change.

organizational satisfaction levels for an initiative to look for ways to improve and accelerate its deployment. Finally, to the extent senior management takes a hands-off approach to the deployment of an initiative, it will fail.

Figure 2.1 shows several competitive characteristics of successful versus unsuccessful organizations. There are many studies available that show how these contrasting organizational structures develop, as well as the impact of organizational culture on competitive performance. One of the most important change characteristics of successful organizations is the ability to develop and execute their strategic vision at a tactical level through one or more core competencies. Integration of operational capability across an organization is facilitated by effective leadership through an empowered and diverse workforce. This is called an execution culture. An important characteristic of these execution cultures is their ability to set and achieve year-over-year strategic goals and objectives. Successful organizations dominate their market space. They also effectively manage all aspects of their enterprise, including sales, marketing, customer service, R&D, engineering, and operations. In contrast, unsuccessful organizations fail to efficiently articulate or align operational systems behind their strategic vision. In effect, they are unable to coordinate operational resources to successfully achieve their strategic goals and objectives. These organizations become losers in today's world unless they are protected by a unique technological advantage such as intellectual property, laws and regulations, geography, or societal culture and norms.

What Is Organizational Change?

Organizational change occurs when a majority of people within an organization consistently practice a new behavior. However, to practice a new behavior, individuals within an organization must be convinced the new behavior provides value. It should also be recognized that a new behavior may have either a positive or negative impact on an organization. In other words, not all behaviors are beneficial to an organization. In summary, the key conclusion behind studies of successful change initiatives is that a new behavior must be consistently practiced prior to adoption by the majority of an organization.

There are different levels and types of cultural change that can take place within an organization. In fact, in some situations, the resultant change could be very dramatic due to internal or external situations that threaten an organization. Examples include a bankruptcy, a forced merger with another organization, downsizing of a product line, productive capacity, or workforce, or a spin-off of a business. However, in most situations, cultural change within an organization is incremental and unfolds over an extended period of time. This transition period may last between 5 and 20 years or more, depending on the organization and industry. In situations in which successful change has occurred, the organizational changes evolved most likely through either the execution of myriad strategically linked tactical projects or a major shift in strategic direction. In either situation, execution cultures tend to be more successful than others.

Understanding Organizational Values

There is a saying: "What gets rewarded gets measured, and what gets measured gets done." Execution cultures effectively align rewards and punishments with strategic and tactical goals and objectives. There is also an accountability for effective and efficient execution of goals and objectives. In an execution culture, achieving goals and objectives is the normative behavior and gets rewarded on a continuing basis. These organizations usually compete well in today's world if their strategy is aligned to customer needs and values; otherwise, they will execute the wrong initiatives and projects. In other words, they will be very efficient at executing the wrong things.

Building Organizational Capability

Simply telling people they should change without providing them the vision, tools, and methods necessary to successfully create the required change results in frustration and demoralization. In contrast, developing a coherent vision and strategy enables effective change through deployment of appropriate initiatives. An initiative is an enabler that ensures that relevant strategic goals and objectives are executed at every level of an organization. An initiative provides tools, methods, and concepts that enable people to define, measure, analyze, and implement the correct change to the process workflows. Figure 2.2 shows that there are four key conditions that must exist for an organization to successfully change: a correct strategic vision, relevant core competencies that can execute the strategy, initiatives that will reinforce or create new core competencies, and an ability to execute strategic goals and objectives using the initiative. In fact, from my viewpoint, operational initiatives are a good way to provide the tools and methods necessary to understand both

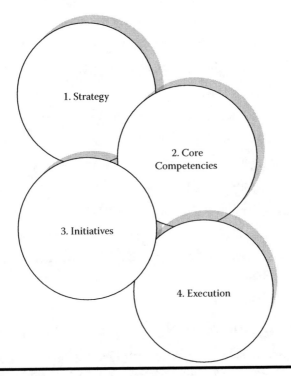

Figure 2.2 How to create organizational change.

how major process workflows work and how they should be changed to improve an organization's competitive position. Figure 2.3 shows how operational initiatives link over time an organization's strategy to improve its ability to execute projects at a tactical level. In summary, initiatives are important tools that enable strategic execution at a tactical level. Also, as they are executed, the behavior of an organization's workforce is modified through training and the application of the tools and methods associated with the initiative. We will discuss how to identify, develop, and deploy important initiatives within an organization in the the section entitled "Integrating Operational Initiatives."

Another important aspect of an effective change program is communication of its status throughout an organization. As an example, although people may have different perceptions of what needs to be changed or how the proposed changes should be managed and executed, they will have a greater tendency to agree on what the problems are, and what needs to be changed within their process workflows if unbiased facts and analyses are used to show why the change is necessary. These change activities require soft skills such as building diverse teams, developing team consensus, and presenting important findings to the organization in an easy-to-understand format relative to key characteristics of the proposed changes to workflows.

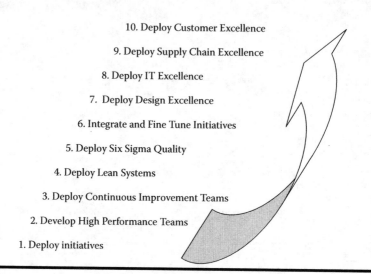

10. Deploy Customer Excellence

9. Deploy Supply Chain Excellence

8. Deploy IT Excellence

7. Deploy Design Excellence

6. Integrate and Fine Tune Initiatives

5. Deploy Six Sigma Quality

4. Deploy Lean Systems

3. Deploy Continuous Improvement Teams

2. Develop High Performance Teams

1. Deploy initiatives

Figure 2.3   How initiatives evolve.

Managing Organizational Change

Managing organizational change begins with developing a strategy for why an organization needs to change and how it should be changed to achieve its goals and objectives. The link between strategic goals and objectives is made through the various organizational initiatives deployed at an operational level through process improvement projects. These projects are designed to improve key operational metrics. As an example, if product development cycle time is too long, projects can be created to reduce this cycle time. If machines break down unexpectedly, causing missed manufacturing schedules, preventive maintenance projects can be deployed to eliminate breakdowns. An organization's operational competency or ability to execute strategy will increase over time as it completes hundreds or even thousands of improvement projects. However, these projects must be strategically linked to ensure that an organization increases its productivity and economic value added (EVA) in a systematic and sustainable manner. Over time, the process of project identification, analysis, and execution will change an organization.

Integrating Operational Initiatives

At any one time, an organization might have several major initiatives in progress to improve its diverse competencies. As an example, initiatives may be deployed to improve the performance of diverse functions related to marketing, sales, finance, research and development (R&D), engineering, manufacturing, and the supply chain. Initiatives consist of tools, methods, and concepts that an organization uses to execute its strategic goals and objectives. In this context, initiatives are deployed in a hierarchal manner across an organization. Also, organizational resources are assigned relative to the anticipated business benefits each initiative offers an organization. In this context, initiative deployment leaders are required to ensure the correct prioritization of resources across an organization so that initiatives are effectively utilized to execute strategic goals and objectives.

Deploying Initiatives across an Organization

Figure 2.4 lists the three common operational initiatives of Six Sigma, Lean, and Total Productive Maintenance (TPM). When properly defined, prioritized, and deployed, these initiatives work synergistically to increase an organization's productivity and directly impact its long-term competitive success. A key step in a deployment process is to create an organizational steering committee consisting of the leaders from the functions that will be impacted by the initiative. The steering committee helps ensure alignment of deployed resources relative to organizational goals and objectives. Another important step or activity in a deployment process is communication of an initiative throughout the organization using a simple and consistent message. Effective communications will describe why the initiative is important to the organization as well as the major characteristics differentiating it from current initiatives. In addition to ensuring effective communication, the people who will become part of the new initiative must be trained in its tools and methods because these will be necessary to execute the applied projects. A fourth important

Productivity = Yield × Uptime × Speed

Yield	•Six Sigma Methods
	•Metrics
	•Database Tools
	•Statistics
	•Team Building
	•TPM
× Uptime	•Ergonomics
	•Improve Set-Up Efficiency
	•Mistake Proofing
× Speed	•Lean Techniques
	•Cycle Time Reduction
	•Pull Systems
= Value	•Profit Increase
	•Sales Increase
	•Stock Appreciation
	•Higher Earnings per Share
	•Customer Satisfaction

Figure 2.4   How several initiatives can increase productivity.

element of initiative deployment is development of tracking metrics to integrate the process improvements across the process workflows of an organization.

Organizational learning and competence are directly related to the successful deployment of an initiative. These skills are gained through practical application of an initiative's tools and methods. For this reason, applied projects are critical to ensuring that an initiative meets its goals and objectives. However, not all projects require the same set of tools and methods, hence the need for more than one operational initiative. For this review, it is important to understand an organization's performance gaps and the types of projects that will be required to close those gaps. As an example, there are several different types of projects, including "just do it" projects, capital expenditure projects, Lean projects, projects utilizing Six Sigma tools and methods, and others, that require specialized technology such as preventive maintenance tools and methods or the application of engineering technology. Finally, major reengineering programs or modifications in strategic direction may dramatically change significant portions of an organization's infrastructure. Each of these major productivity enablers has unique tools, methods, and concepts that can be used to identify and execute applied projects.

Figure 2.4 shows that Six Sigma, Lean, and TPM have their own unique toolkits. Six Sigma increases operational yields through root cause identification and analysis using simple or complex data analysis tools. Lean tools and methods map customer value through a process workflow to simplify, standardize, and mistakeproof it and to pull value through the improved process workflow based on external customer demand. It should also be noted that there are overlaps in tools and methods between these operational initiatives. As an example, there is a commonality relative to the use of process maps, brainstorming, and simple analytical tools and methods. However, the Six Sigma initiative pushes the sophistication of analytical tools and methods to a higher level than Lean. Also, Lean tools and methods are often used to ensure effective and sustainable process control by the countermeasures that are implemented to execute Six Sigma process improvements. In summary, both the Six Sigma and Lean initiatives reduce operational cycle times and improve quality to meet customer demand. TPM ensures machines are available when needed to sustain a process workflow. TPM is analogous to ergonomic philosophies in that the ergonomics ensures tools and methods are used within a process workflow to make certain that people are available to do work. Also, ergonomic methods ensure that people perform their work safely without injury over extended periods of time. Figure 2.4 shows these initiates work together synergistically. TPM enables an operation to produce more and more by increasing resource uptime or availability. Six Sigma enables an organization to increase yield, i.e., make an operational output better and better. Lean enables a process to produce faster and faster. The combined result is higher organizational productivity.

Table 2.2 shows ten basic steps necessary to deploy an initiative. The first critical step is to ensure the initiative has tools and methods that will be useful to an organization. At any point in time, an organization has performance gaps that need

Table 2.2 10 Key Steps to Deploy Initiatives

1. Ensure the initiative has tools and methods that will be useful to organization.
2. Develop models showing how and where the initiative would be useful to the organization.
3. Obtain support from senior management.
4. Form an executive steering committee to guide deployment of the initiative.
5. Train senior management in the initiative structure, organizational impact, and schedule.
6. Train middle management to identify business improvement opportunities and align organizational resources at their level.
7. Finalize the deployment goals and objectives.
8. Finalize the deployment schedule.
9. Select and train key people throughout the organization to begin the project implementation process.
10. Track and measure initiative process against key deployment milestones and make changes where necessary.

to be closed by deployment and execution of tactical projects. However, the specific tools and methods necessary to close a performance gap vary from project to project. For this reason, an organization must ensure it has properly aligned the productivity opportunity with the toolset that will be required to identify the root causes for the performance gap and to ensure a successful project closure. An important part of this evaluation process is assessing where the initiative will be applied as well as creating financial and operational models showing why it will be useful to an organization. Using financial and operational models, such as those discussed later in this book, will allow proponents for the initiative to make a business case for its deployment and create a high probability of obtaining the support of senior leadership. After review of the business case and approval by senior management, an executive steering committee can be formed to guide deployment of the initiative. As mentioned above, the executive steering committee should be representative of the major organizational functions that will be impacted by the initiative. The purpose of the executive steering committee is to coordinate project selection, participant selection, and training activities to align the initiative with organizational norms and culture. This will improve the probability that an initiative's goals and objectives are met on schedule. Once the executive steering committee has been formed, it is trained on the specifics of a deployment structure and its anticipated organizational impact and schedule. At this point in the deployment process, middle management is selected and trained to identify business improvement opportunities within their process workflows through formal process assessments. In addition, they are trained in the specifics of alignment of organizational resources against the identified projects. After process workflows have been analyzed and the project identification process has been completed through the operational assessments, the specific people who will execute the identified projects are selected and trained in use of the tactical tools and methods characteristic of the initiative. The deployment goals, objectives, and schedule are finalized at this point. As the root causes for the projects are identified and eliminated, process improvements and business benefits are tracked against key deployment milestones, goals, and objectives. Modifications are made as necessary to increase deployment effectiveness over time. The balance of this discussion will focus on several common initiatives currently deployed by organizations across the world to improve their productivity.

Building High-Performance Teams

High-performance work teams are no accident. It has been shown that there is a very structured and proven methodology to building these teams. The team-building process includes ensuring that the team has a defined project objective as well as the resources necessary to achieve its objectives. Also, the people comprising the team should represent the portion of the process workflow that will be investigated and improved by the project team. The team should also be diverse and consist of people having a range of skills. It is also important to ensure the team is properly facilitated using standardized team-building and meeting management methods and techniques. Proper facilitation will ensure everyone on the team fully contributes to it, and that they will reach agreement on the actions necessary to move projects from their initial identification through to a successful completion. In addition to proper team facilitation, teams must go through an evolutionary process involving various degrees of group consensus or disagreement. However, application of proper team-building methods will help develop a high-performance work team, which will be a tremendous asset for your various organizational initiatives.

Table 2.3 shows ten basic steps necessary to develop a high-performance work team. The first step is to develop the team's project charter. The project charter embodies the business justification for a project, including its benefits and required resources. The project charter is also a communication vehicle showing an organization where a team will work within a process, what problems it will investigate, and the specific impact expected from elimination of a problem. The project charter contains a list of the project's team members and other information relevant to the project coordination. Project charters will be discussed in more detail in Chapter 7, and a common format is shown in Figure 7.9. Project charters typically contain four metrics. These include the business and financial metrics showing senior management the positive impact the project will have on their organization. A second set of balancing metrics is also incorporated into the charter to ensure a

Table 2.3   10 Key Steps to Develop High-Performance Teams

1. Develop the team's project charter.
2. Select the team.
3. Understand team dynamics.
4. Facilitate the team.
5. Manage the four stages of team growth.
6. Use a sequenced improvement methodology.
7. Train the team in the proper tools and methods of problem identification, data collection, analysis, and changing the process.
8. Manage team conflict.
9. Continuously improve team performance.
10. Celebrate success.

team does not drive the primary business metric to an extreme. As an example, if the business metric is to increase inventory turns, i.e., reduce inventory investment at a constant sales level, then customer service levels should be incorporated into the project charter to ensure there is enough inventory to satisfy customer demand. As the project team works though the root causes of the problem, it may create specific project-focused metrics. As an example, inventory investment is usually increased by long lead times. Long lead times may be due to several different causes, such as large lot sizes or scheduling misses due to poor quality, maintenance issues, or other process breakdowns. When the project team gets down to these lower-level process issues, the project metrics must be created to continue the root cause analysis. In these situations, the project charter must be updated to reflect the new metrics as well as their current performance levels and required targets. Also, the team must make extra effort to ensure there is direct alignment among all four types of metrics so the organization can clearly see the interrelationships. As an example, as the project team improves the lower-level operational or project metrics, senior management should be able to clearly see the improvements in higher-level financial and business metrics without a deterioration in compensating metrics. Important to the development of a high-performance work team is its team member selection. The team should be selected from the functional areas comprising the process workflow under evaluation, as well as those immediately before or after it.

In addition, team members should be experienced with their portion of the process workflow to ensure they fully contribute to the team. It is also important to understand team dynamics and facilitation. It has been suggested that high-performance work teams undergo four stages of team evolution: forming, storming, norming, and performing. In the team formation stage, the team begins its discussion relative to the project's scope and objectives. During this stage, there may not be very many disagreements among team members. However, disagreements usually caused by differing interpretations or perspectives of available information will eventually occur within a team. However, through proper facilitation methods, a team can usually quickly move past the storming stage, through to the norming and performing stages, and begin to work effectively together to a point where they mutually respect one another and very efficiently coordinate their project activities.

A high-performance work team uses a structured methodology to analyze a project charter's problem statement and objective to eventually identify the root causes for a process breakdown. The identification of root causes contributing to a process breakdown may require the tools and methods associated with a specific initiative. But regardless of the initiative, a root cause analysis is applied in a sequential manner to define the problem and eventually arrive at a solution. Common methodologies to improve operational performance include Six Sigma's define, measure, analyze, improve, and control (DMAIC); Deming's Wheel, i.e., plan, do, check, act; and Lean's "understand value, create a value stream map, eliminate process waste, etc." The team must also be trained in the elimination of process waste and the root causes of poor process performance. These tools and methods include problem identification, data collection and analysis, and the specifics of changing a process. Specific analytical techniques include brainstorming, process mapping, and similar tools and methods. In summary, it is very important that the team leader and the team itself manage team conflict through proper facilitation. As part of this facilitation process, it is important to identify ways to continuously improve team performance and celebrate success.

Deploying Continuous Improvement Teams

Thirty years ago, organizations used continuous improvement teams to analyze and make improvements to their local processes based on the use of simple quality tools and methods. The training was usually focused on improvement projects within the team's functional area. It was subsequently found that teams aligned with an organization's strategic goals and objectives were more successful relative to project selection and closure than nonaligned teams. As a result, the projects of nonaligned teams were not adequately resourced by their organizations, resulting in poor project selection and execution. As a result, continuous improvement activities fell into general disuse within many organizations during the mid-1980s and 1990s. In these nonaligned deployments, improvement activities generally fell under the direction of the human resource, training, or quality functions, as opposed to modern operational improvement programs that are deployed throughout organizations and managed at a high level across diverse functions.

The problem with early change initiative was not in the concept of continuous improvement. After all, many organizations were very successful using the simple tools and methods characteristic of continuous improvement deployments. The problem was that in many organizations, the people assigned to the initiative either were not properly trained or were so far down within an organization that they could not get the necessary organizational alignment for their projects. In these situations, the resultant business benefits were low or nonexistent and caused senior management to distance them from the continuous improvement initiative. In retrospect, the continuous improvement initiatives helped lay the foundation for Lean and Six Sigma deployments, in that organizations understood the terminology of continuous improvement and how to build teams that accelerated the deployment of Lean, Six Sigma, and related operational initiatives in the mid-1990s to the present time. Most recently, the concept of continuous improvement has been reinvigorated by the Lean and Six Sigma initiatives.

In summary, understanding business goals and objectives is a critical aspect of a continuous improvement process because a team's resources must be aligned with projects that will increase productivity and shareholder economic added value (EVA). Table 2.4 lists ten key steps that are useful in deploying a continuous improvement team. These steps mirror those described in Table 2.2.

Table 2.4   10 Key Steps to Deploy Continuous Improvement Teams

1. Understand business goals and objectives.
2. Develop executive steering committee to develop the deployment plan and schedule.
3. Develop performance evaluation and incentive systems to reinforce the initiative.
4. Deploy the business goals level by level throughout the organization.
5. Provide a consistent message throughout the organization.
6. Develop team project charters to execute the deployment strategy.
7. Select and train team members in process analysis and improvement tools such as graphical analysis, statistical analysis, brainstorming, process standardization, and project management basics.
8. Execute projects throughout the organization with the majority within local work teams.
9. Communicate team success and share lessons learned.
10. Review the continuous improvement process relative to what worked well and how it could be improved in the future.

Deploying Lean Systems

As mentioned above, continuous improvement teams started to run out of steam in the mid to late 1980s. About this time the automotive industry was under tremendous competitive pressure from Toyota to improve its quality performance and reduce cost. As a result, organizations emulated several of Toyota's operational systems embodied under the general term Lean. Lean systems are characterized by simple processes that have been optimized over time to eliminate the waste related to defects, unnecessary motion, job setups, and unnecessary movement of materials, waiting, and transportation of materials and jobs. In addition, high quality and low costs were additional benefits that relied on mistake-proofing strategies, and highly flexible cross-trained workers, to name just a few characteristics of Lean. The reason Lean tools and methods are very effective in process improvement is that everyone from the front office to the factory floor can get involved with improvement projects because they use simple tools and methods that can be applied to the analysis of any process workflow. These tools and methods include work simplification, standardization, cleaning local work areas, throwing out unneeded materials, value stream mapping, and mistake-proofing. These actions fall under the general category of 5-S, an acronym for sorting, simplifying, sweeping (cleaning the work area), standardization, and sustaining process improvements. Also, because people become involved in the team meetings, process analysis, and projects' resultant process changes, they see the power of teamwork as well as the application of fact-based methods to process improvement. The value of Lean applications in process improvement has been very well documented and can yield significant productivity improvements. This makes it easy to gain senior management's support for a Lean initiative. Lean tools and methods are also the basis for other initiatives because Lean simplifies and standardizes workflows, which facilitates subsequent process analysis and improvement. We will discuss Lean is more detail in Chapters 5 and 6.

Table 2.5 lists ten important steps that will move an organization toward an integrated Lean system. Under the direction of an executive steering committee, the first step is to organize local problem-solving groups. Organizing local problem-solving groups allows an organization to develop continuous improvement strategies that are aligned with local work cell activities. This enables workers to learn how to more efficiently operate and maintain their machines and work operations within their local works cells. Second, they are trained to identify process improvement opportunities and analyze process breakdowns using simple quality tools and methods that facilitate continuous improvement activities. Integral to the success of any initiative, including Lean, is the development of system performance metrics to monitor, control, and identify improvement opportunities. Metrics were discussed in detail in Chapter 1 and will be an important subject throughout this book. Standardization of processes is another major characteristic of Lean systems. This is because a stable process is required to meet external customer demand based on a system's required takt time — the amount of time in which one unit of production

Table 2.5　10 Key Steps to Deploy Lean Systems

1. Organize problem-solving groups.
2. Develop system performance measurements and metrics.
3. Eliminate unnecessary activities.
4. Standardize processes using 5-S.
5. Reorganize physical configuration.
6. Upgrade quality through mistake-proofing and design modifications.
7. Implement Total Productive Maintenance (TPM) and Single Minute Exchange of Dies (SMED).
8. Level the facility load using mixed-model scheduling and other methods.
9. Introduce Kanban quantities and standardized containers and other visual controls.
10. Develop supplier agreements and networks.

must be completed to meet total daily demand for all production units. An example would be having a daily demand of 100 units and 500 minutes available per day to produce the units. The takt calculation would be one unit every five minutes. Takt time will be discussed in Chapter 6. As mentioned above, 5-S consists of five major activities designed to ensure the workplace is orderly and standardized, and its process workflow status is easily seen at a glance. Application of 5-S methods to a process workflow also improves its quality because there will be fewer mistakes within work operations. Lower error rates have an added advantage of reducing cycle time and cost.

At a higher level, a process workflow can be analyzed using value stream mapping (VSM). VSM shows the interrelationships of operations within a process workflow, as well as its rework loops and other non-value-adding work tasks within operations. Non-value-adding work tasks are commonly associated with the movement of materials, setup of jobs, processing of work, inspection of work, storage of information or materials, and similar activities. It should be noted that process workflows that move information rather than materials are analogous. After the VSM has been analyzed relative to those workflow operations that either add or do not add value, the non-value-adding operations and their associated work tasks are eliminated from the process workflow. In summary, using a VSM has the practical effect of simplifying a process and its workflows. Process simplification reduces costs and operational cycle times and improves quality. Reorganizing the physical configuration of a process to increase its throughput is another important Lean method. Bringing operations in closer proximity reduces unnecessary material movement between work stations and facilitates the real-time communication between work stations. As an example, using a particular operational layout called U-shaped work cells allows easy balancing of the workflow because workers can simply turn around to complete one or several work tasks. Also, as the work volume fluctuates (with the takt time recalculated in these situations), it is easier to expand or contract the workforce size. As the process is simplified and standardized, mistake-proofing and design modifications are also successively applied throughout a process. This has the effect of ensuring high quality throughout a process using very inexpensive error warning and control systems. Total Productive Maintenance (TPM) and Single Minute Exchange of Dies (SMED) methods are also implemented within a process to further ensure stabilization relative to its takt time. In addition to takt time stabilization, the external demand on a system can also be level loaded using mixed-model scheduling and other methods useful in creating a common product, process, or scheduling system. Once a Lean system is stabilized and optimized relative to its constraints, Kanban quantities and standardized containers can be used to control the process workflow. Kanban systems are useful in maintaining stable inventory levels and controlling the process workflow. The application of Lean methods also enables fast responses to unexpected process changes. Finally, development of supplier agreements and networks is integral to the long-term success of a Lean system. These Lean concepts, tools, and methods will be discussed in more detail in Chapters 5 and 6.

Deploying Six Sigma Quality

Six Sigma is a quality initiative that attempts to make breakthrough process improvements as opposed to the more gradual improvements characterizing a continuous improvement initiative. The Six Sigma quality initiative began at Motorola in response to competitive threats to its consumer electronics business from Japan. However, by the early 1990s the Six Sigma deployment was more of a continuous rather than breakthrough improvement program. In response to a need to significantly improve productivity, Richard Schroeder, a former Motorola executive, and Larry Bossidy, the CEO of AlliedSignal, reinvigorated Six Sigma and deployed the program in late 1994. I became a part of the AlliedSignal deployment in January 1995 in Dallas, Texas, along with Erik Lawson, Kevin Rucinski, and Peter Behmke. The Six Sigma program, Lean, and Total Productive Maintenance (TPM) quickly became top productivity drivers at AlliedSignal, contributing approximately 2 to 4 percent year-over-year productivity on top of other improvement initiatives, such as purchasing price reductions and reengineering activities. These three operational initiatives were quickly folded into AlliedSignal's Operational Excellence initiative in late 1995. In 1996, the Six Sigma program was also deployed at General Electric (GE). By 1997, several major organizations also began to deploy Six Sigma, and the program diffused across the world. The effectiveness of the program is indisputable to those who have been part of successful deployments, but many organizations often develop ineffective versions of the program, and it falls into disuse for many reasons.

The Six Sigma deployment success factors include:

- Complete alignment of the program with an organization's strategic business goals and objectives
- Control of the program at a high level by senior executives in the form of an executive steering committee
- Identification of applied projects that will increase productivity between 1 and 2 percent per year
- Selection of full-time and high-caliber belts who are trained to execute the identified project portfolio

A successful Six Sigma and Lean deployment for organizations over $1 billion should provide productivity increases in the range of 2 to 4 percent. If your organization is not driving productivity at this level, then something is wrong with your deployment strategy and project execution.

Six Sigma is characterized by five sequential phases. These are described by the acronym DMAIC. The DMAIC methodology is applied by green belts and black belts to complete aligned projects. The DMAIC phases are *define* the project, *measure* the process key metric, also called the key process output variable (KPOV), *analyze* collected data, *improve* the KPOV by changing one or more key process input variables (KPIVs), and put the process into *control*. The initial Six Sigma deployment followed a MAIC methodology, which resulted in many false starts relative to project identification. GE inserted the define phase into the program as well as the concept of the voice of the customer (VOC) to ensure the projects were focused on customer satisfaction issues as well as the voice of the business (VOB). A Six Sigma initiative starts after executives have been trained in its basic concepts and deployment strategy. This process is usually initiated by external consultants. After executive training, project champions are trained to select projects and guide the program's deployment through their organization. The champions also help select the "belts" that will be trained to work the DMAIC methodology using applied and aligned projects. These belts will use DMAIC tools and methods to investigate the root causes for process breakdowns and develop countermeasures to eliminate them.

Table 2.6 lists ten steps an organization must take to develop and deploy a successful Six Sigma initiative. The first and most important step is to execute the actions listed in Table 2.2 and Table 2.4 regarding organizational alignment, executive engagement, and deployment of the initiative. No initiative can be successful without organizational alignment. After organizational alignment, the Six Sigma initiative is deployed at successively lower levels of an organization. Once the

Table 2.6   10 Key Steps to Deploy Six Sigma Systems

1. Execute the actions listed in Table 2.2 and Table 2.4 regarding organizational alignment, executive engagement, and deployment of the initiative. In addition, select and train project champions to assess project opportunities throughout the organization.
2. Develop project charters for the black belts and green belts. Select and train the belts to execute the projects using the information contained in Table 2.3 and Table 2.5.
3. Refine the project's problem statement, objective, and key process output variables (KPOVs), i.e., output metric baselines relative to the voice of the customer (VOC) and voice of the business (VOB). Develop a high-level map of the process showing inputs, outputs, and how the process works.
4. Ensure the KPOVs can be accurately measured and performance gaps have been calculated, i.e., process capability on the KPOVs, or Y's. Recalculate business benefits.
5. Brainstorm all possible input variables (X's) that may impact the KPOVs, develop a data collection plan, and collect data on the X's and Y's.
6. Analyze data to identify the root causes for the process breakdowns (KPIVs), eliminate trivial inputs (X's), and select key inputs (X's) to build the process model $Y = f(X)$.
7. Experiment and test the model $Y = f(X)$ under controlled conditions, i.e., process pilot and scale up the solution.
8. Develop countermeasures to the root causes and build an integrated control plan on the inputs (X's) using tools and methods such as 5-S, failure mode and effects analysis (FMEA), modified work instructions and training, mistake-proofing, elimination of unnecessary operations, and related improvement activities.
9. Verify business benefits.
10. Identify lessons learned and develop translation opportunities.

executive steering committee has been selected and is operative, champions are selected and trained to guide the tactical aspects of the Six Sigma deployment. Deployment champions guide the initiative at a divisional level, ensuring that the selection process for projects (through the project champions) and belts remains on target. Project champions provide organizational support to the belts project-by-project to ensure projects are closed on schedule and the business benefits are properly assigned by the organization to the initiative. The development of project charters has been discussed above in the section "Building High-Performance Teams." Project selection, i.e., charters, is a good foundation on which to build the success of any initiative. The specific business opportunities, i.e., projects, determine the selection of the belts who will execute the applied projects.

After a belt has been assigned to a project, the project team refines the project's problem statement and objective. This process involves analyzing and refining the project's KPOVs. These are output metrics related to the VOC and VOB. Integral to this evaluation process is development of a high-level map of the process showing inputs, outputs, and how the process works. As the team enters the measure phase of the project, a second important task is to accurately measure the performance gaps of the KPOV variables using various process capability tools and methods. The project's business benefits are verified at this point. In other words, the team now has quantitative data showing the current process performance baseline of each KPOV versus the original project goals and objectives. At the conclusion of the measure phase or beginning of the analyze phase, the team will brainstorm all potential causes for the poor performance of the KPOV. These potential causes are called input variables (X's). Through data collection and analysis, one or more of these input variables may be found to significantly impact the project's KPOVs. After the team develops a list of potential input variables, a data collection plan is created to gather the required process data.

In the analysis phase of the project, analytical tools and methods are used to identify the major root causes for the process breakdowns. These are called the key process input variables. These KPIVs are used to build the famous Six Sigma model $Y = f(X)$. This relationship shows the output (Y), or KPOV, is driven by the interrelationships among the process inputs (X's), or KPIVs. In the improve phase of the project, the project team experiments with various levels of the KPIVs and evaluates their joint impact on the KPOV. This process experimentation is conducted under controlled conditions called a process pilot. Once the project team understands the levels of the KPIVs that will optimize the KPOV, countermeasures tied to the root causes of the problem are developed and integrated within a project control plan using tools and methods such as 5-S, failure mode and effects analysis (FMEA), modified work instructions and training, mistake-proofing, elimination of unnecessary operations, and related improvement activities. After the process pilot is completed, the best or optimum solution to the problem is selected for implementation. At this point, a cost–benefit analysis is made to determine the business impacts of the project on the organization. Finally, the team identifies the lessons learned from the project and leverages the solution opportunities through the organization.

Integrating and Fine-Tuning Initiatives

Initiatives need to be periodically evaluated after they are deployed to determine how to make them more effective in the future. A common problem with initiatives is that they are often deployed independently of other initiatives and begin competing for scarce resources. Also, they may have overlapping tools and methods, which creates confusion within an organization. To avoid competition and confusion among initiatives, it is common to link them under an umbrella initiative, such as Operational Excellence, to coordinate resources and prioritize improvement projects. In this content, in Operational Excellence, Lean, Six Sigma, and Total Productive Maintenance (TPM) are integrated in a way that their toolsets and methods reinforce each other. As an example, Lean simplifies and standardizes a process. TPM ensures all machinery (or in an ergonomics sense, all people) are available as necessary. After a process has been simplified and standardized, and the machines (and people) are available to do the work, Six Sigma can be applied to the process to increase process yields.

Deploying Design Excellence

Product and process design drive an organization's cost structure and long-term productivity. A simple design will take less time to build and have higher quality and lower cost than a more complicated one. This will make it more competitive from a global perspective. As an example, many years ago I worked for a European manufacturer of direct current (DC) motors that turned the read–write head of computer disc drives. Our competitors were in Japan and the United States. Each competitive organization had developed differing product designs to meet customer requirements. This resulted in different competitive positions for each supplier. The European manufacturer's motor design had a plastic cooling fan glued to one end of the motor. The U.S. version had the fan screwed on to the end of the motor. However, the Japanese left the fan off the motor entirely. Also, a braking mechanism was applied to the outside of the motor to slow it down. The European manufacturer's design could not meet the surface finish (surface roughness) requirements required of the outside motor housing. This required the manufacturer to sand the outside of the motor housing, creating a situation that contributed to rusting over time. It should be noted that the U.S. and Japanese manufacturers met the original surface finish requirements of the customer, and their products did not require refinishing of the motor housing. The relative quality was highest for the Japanese motor design, with the European manufacturer having the poorest overall quality. The Japanese also had the lowest-cost motor, while the European manufacturer had the highest. Eventually, the European manufacturer was forced out of the market and the Japanese dominated it over time. In retrospect, I believe the problem can be attributed to poor communication within the European manufacturer's organization, as well as a failure to understand the VOC. In fact, we later found that there were actually three versions of the European manufacturer's design floating around the system. The European manufacturer had the latest motor design, the customer had an earlier version, and our assembly operation had an even earlier one. This situation was completely unnecessary because the European manufacturer was first to market with the DC motor. This example shows the advantages of design simplicity and listening to the VOC. In fact, just using the basic engineering design principles, discussed in Chapter 4, will go a very long way toward making any organization competitive. Proper product or service design is important because much of the total life cycle cost is committed at the design stage of a product or service's life cycle. In addition, the expected profitability of a product or service may be higher in some industries for an organization that arrives to market first. As an example, it has been claimed that in high-technology electronic manufacturing, the first organization to market quickly builds approximately 70 percent market share for the life of the product, with the other 30 percent market share going to the competitor arriving to market later.

As another example, I was also involved in a program to develop a high-volume manufacturing application of a specialty adhesive. This adhesive system eliminated several manufacturing operations and components. However, the actual purpose of the new adhesive system was to develop a unique and exciting modification to our current product design to increase our market share. The basic idea was great, but the technology was so revolutionary and expensive that by the time the organization had developed its manufacturing prototypes, it found that the product performance in the field was only marginal, and at a cost higher than the old system. However, due to organizational politics, the new product design and its manufacturing process were deployed in several manufacturing facilities. The project came to a screeching halt after just four hours, when the product could not be removed from the molds. It was later found that under manufacturing conditions, the adhesive could not be removed from its mold due to the higher than expected production temperatures. This situation necessitated that the older design be immediately rolled back into place and the project halted because the performance and cost targets could not be achieved in practice. This is an example of how not listening to the external VOC and organizational politics may result in groupthink. I have seen many similar situations over the years within other organizations. The conclusion we can derive from these and similar examples is that by not employing basic design principles, an organization can drive itself into a noncompetitive position. The world may be becoming more competitive, but many organizations are falling victim due to their internal failure to identify a correct design strategy and effectively execute it through production. In Chapters 4 and 5, we will discuss strategies to effectively use product and process design tools and methods to increase organizational competitiveness. Our belief is that if organizations do the design basics well, their competitive position will be greatly enhanced in today's world.

Table 2.7 lists ten key steps an organization can take to improve its design excellence. These concepts will be discussed at a high level in this chapter and in more detail in Chapter 4. The first step in creating design excellence is to integrate the findings from the quality function deployment (QFD) matrix relative to the VOC and VOB. This includes incorporating all key design features and characteristics that are related to form, fit, and function of the product or service design. These

Table 2.7   10 Key Steps to Deploy Design Excellence

1. Integrate the results from the quality function deployment (QFD) matrix, including the voice-of-the-customer (VOC) and voice-of-the-business (VOB).
2. Develop a high-performance work team using concurrent engineering (CE) methods.
3. Develop CE metrics and measures relative to VOC and VOB to meet marketing goals and objectives.
4. Select design alternatives using effective brainstorming and prioritization methods such as the analytical hierarchy process (AHP) and Pugh matrix methods.
5. Use design for manufacturing (DFM) tools and methods to simplify and mistake-proof designs throughout their intended life cycle, i.e., from manufacturing, through product testing and serviceability, to eventual disposal.
6. Develop robust designs that will optimally perform under all expected environmental and usage conditions based on experimental design methods and parameter simulations.
7. Characterize the optimum design alternative using failure mode and effects analysis (FMEA) and reliability testing.
8. Modify the design as required to create an optimized version.
9. Verify design and process capability based on voice-of-the-process (VOP) and VOC.
10. Verify design intent as well as VOB metrics and formally transfer the design to manufacturing using the CE process.

characteristics directly impact a design's reliability, maintainability, serviceability, ease of assembly and disassembly, customer usability, ease of installation at a customer's location, upgradeability, availability, disposability at the end of its life cycle, and ability to recycle, if necessary. In the second step of the design process, a high-performance work team is brought together and managed using concurrent engineering (CE) methods. Integral to management of the design team and execution of the entire design process is development of key CE metrics and measures relative to the VOC and VOB. This is the third step in the deployment of design excellence. CE metrics allow the design team to meet marketing goals and objectives on schedule and within budget. The fourth step in the design process is to select design alternatives using effective brainstorming and prioritization methods such as analytical hierarchy process (AHP) and Pugh matrix methods. These prioritization tools and methods will be discussed in Chapter 4. The final design alternative is the one that embodies the best features and characteristics of several of the better initial designs. Integral to the development of design alternatives is the design for manufacturing (DFM) tools and methods listed in step 5. DFM tools and methods are used to simplify and mistake-proof product designs throughout their anticipated life cycle, i.e., from the time they are manufactured, used by the customer, serviced by field technicians, and eventually disposed of. DFM will be discussed in Chapter 4. Step 6 of Table 2.7 shows that the final product or service design must be tested under expected customer usage conditions using experimental design methods. Experimental design methods change the levels of a design's KPIVs to evaluate the best combination of variable levels to ensure the product's KPOVs remain on target with minimum variation. This methodology ensures that the final design configuration will optimally perform under all expected environmental and customer usage conditions. The concept of experimental design is based on several advanced statistical tools, methods, and concepts, including parameter simulation. These subjects will be discussed in Chapter 16.

Step 7 requires that the final design be evaluated against the VOC using failure-mode-and-effects-analysis (FMEA) methodology as well as reliability testing. FMEA is a structured brainstorming methodology that evaluates the ways in which a product or service design can fail in use. In an FMEA, KPOV failure modes, effects and their causes are methodically listed and rated or ranked. Countermeasures are placed against each failure cause to reduce its occurrence and improve the ability of a measurement system to detect the failure cause if it should occur in practice. Reliability testing is also used to ensure that a design will meet its design functions throughout its life cycle. After full-performance evaluations, steps 8 and 9 show that a design should be modified, as necessary, to ensure it meets its form, fit, and functional requirements with high probability. At this point in the product development process, the product should have been designed to perform at a Six Sigma capability level. This translates into a 2 parts per billion failure level. (Note: Some people believe this translates into 3.4 parts per million over a long period, but this concept has been widely disputed by quality professionals.) After the capability of a design has been verified, Step 10 shows that it should be formally transferred to manufacturing or operations using a concurrent engineering (CE).

Deploying Information Technology Excellence

Information technology (IT) is integral to any organization. As the complexity of an organization increases, its IT infrastructure becomes increasingly important in improving organizational productivity. In nonmanufacturing organizations, IT is the principal process design function in that it executes process workflow designs of various forms across an organization's supply chain. In industries having major supply chain functions, IT integrates the entire business enterprise and is a major factor in determining the relative competitiveness of a supply chain. Our discussion, in Chapter 15, will be from the latter perspective in a context of enabling and improving an organization's relative global competitive position through process workflow design, monitoring, and control.

Table 2.8 lists ten steps necessary to develop IT excellence within your organization. The specific details of each step as well as related concepts will be discussed in Chapter 15. In many ways, IT functions are similar to those used to design products. As a result, IT design and development activities must begin with the VOC and VOB to ensure they are aligned with organizational goals and objectives. This concept is clearly shown in the first step of Table 2.8, which requires integration of the results and findings from the QFD matrix, including the VOC and VOB, to develop specifications for IT projects. Many of the VOC concepts, including QFD, are discussed in Chapter 3, and an example of a QFD matrix is shown in Figure 3.4.

Table 2.8   10 Key Steps to Deploy IT Excellence

1. Integrate the results from the quality function deployment (QFD) matrix, including the voice of the customer (VOC) and voice of the business (VOB) to develop IT projects.
2. Develop a high-performance work team using Agile Project Management (APM) and Scrum Master methods.
3. Develop CE metrics and measures relative to business VOC and VOB to meet marketing goals and objectives.
4. Release software code as a series of process batches to obtain immediate user feedback relative to performance.
5. Iterate software development over many cycles to incorporate the latest learning from process performance evaluations.
6. Ensure customers prioritize system features for development and release.
7. Create self-organizing teams around immediate requirements and schedules and share work tasks in groups of 2–3 programmers to enhance collaboration.
8. Work backwards from the VOC into critical-to-quality characteristics and specifications to design software code.
9. All work tasks must be completed prior to closing an activity, and all activities must be completed prior to closing a project milestone.
10. Everything is kept simple and is changed to meet new project requirements.

The second step shown in Table 2.8 is to develop a high-performance work team using Agile Project Management (APM) and Scrum Master (SM) methods. Agile Project Management is described by Sanjiv Augustine in *Managing Agile Projects*. APM and SM methods use the best practices of Lean and concurrent engineering to ensure IT software is developed based on the VOC and VOB in an efficient manner. The concepts of APM will be discussed in more detail in Chapter 15. The third step in deploying IT excellence is the development and use of metrics to manage its process workflow activities. CE metrics and methods ensure that an IT design will meet an organization's VOC and VOB goals and objectives. Step 4 requires that software code be released as a series of small process batches (called transfer batches in manufacturing) to obtain immediate user feedback relative to software performance. This feedback enables faster feedback on design features, which allows more software iterations, as described in step 5. Software development proceeds faster using APM because the latest learning from process performance evaluations can be incorporated into the software design. Step 6 requires that customers prioritize system features of the new design for its development and release. This task is also part of the initial VOC discussion, but at this point in the development cycle, as new information is learned about the product design, customer prioritization is useful to focus the team on revisions to design features. Step 7 requires that the APM development team create self-organizing teams around immediate customer requirements and schedules (as they were prioritized in step 6) and share work tasks in groups of two or three programmers to enhance team collaboration. Step 8 requires that the APM team work backwards from the VOC into the product's critical-to-quality characteristics and specifications to design software code. In fact, this is an organizing theme throughout the APM development process. Step 9 requires that all work tasks be completed prior to closing an activity, and that all activities be completed prior to closing every project's milestone. Throughout the design process, activities must be kept simple, and should be changed as necessary, to meet new project requirements as described in Step 10 of the IT excellence deployment recommendations.

Deploying Customer Excellence

Customer excellence is a subject on which everyone has an opinion. Many studies have been conducted to understand its numerous interrelated characteristics. In its simplest form, customer excellence is about keeping promises to your customers. This implies that an organization's strategic goals and objectives are well defined and are efficiently executed against those goals and objectives. Also, integral to customer excellence is the necessity that your products and services be designed to meet customer expectations. Expectations are conveyed to the customer by marketing and advertising as well as through other customer touch points. This implies that customer needs and perceived value elements have been well defined, as shown in Figure 3.1 to Figure 3.5. It is also important that the process and operational design at the organizational–customer interface must reliably deliver value. This does not imply that an organization must do everything a customer asks if there is not an implied or explicit promise to do so; however, declining customer requests should be very carefully considered by an organization. Also, process workflows should be designed to satisfy customers by market segment and based on their expected value.

Table 2.9 shows ten key steps that are necessary to deploy customer excellence. The first step is for the senior management of an organization to develop a strategy consistent with the long-term goals and objectives of their organization. A second, and often poorly executed, next step is to proactively obtain information on customer needs and value elements by market segment and translate these into internal specifications using translation tools and methods, including prioritization matrices. Translation tools and methods include various types of surveys to capture the VOC. A common prioritization matrix includes the quality function

Table 2.9   10 Key Steps to Deploy Customer Excellence

1. Develop an organizational strategy to deploy customer excellence with senior management.
2. Proactively obtain information on customer needs and value elements by market segment, and translate these into internal specifications.
3. Meet all basic needs, become best in class for all performance needs, and discover excitement needs.
4. Design systems to provide services and products as promised without defects, on time, and at target costs.
5. Ensure the process design embodies the VOC at every step. This includes all procedures, policies, and training.
6. Measure both the VOC and internally related specifications, and continuously improve all metrics.
7. Understand the difference between customer service and customer relations, and be good at both.
8. Hire the right people who are customer-friendly.
9. Provide people with tools, methods, and training to be successful.
10. Continuously increase customer value by increasing convenience and reducing cost.

deployment template, which is often called the house of quality. The third critical step is to actually meet the basic and performance needs expected by the customer. After these two needs have been met, an organization can determine the customer's excitement needs to truly deliver an exciting and differentiated customer experience. Step 4 of Table 2.9 requires that an organization's operational systems are capable of providing products and services as promised without defects, on time, and at target cost levels. Unfortunately, many organizations poorly design their delivery systems or fail to monitor and control them, and hence fail Step 4. At every step, the process design must embody the VOC. This includes all procedures, policies, and training. Step 7 requires that the VOC be quantitatively measured both externally and internally, and continuously improved over time. Organizations must also understand the difference between customer services and customer relations and be good at both because they require different execution systems. Step 8 requires that organizations hire people who are customer-friendly. Entire books have been written on this subject. Suffice it to say, service workers must know their customers and how to satisfy their needs, meet value expectations, and enjoy working with customers. Step 9 requires that people be provided with the training, tools, and methods to be successful. Finally, step 10 shows that it is important to continuously increase the perceived value of your products and services. Value can be increased by reducing cost and cycle time and improving the utility, functionality, and quality of your products and services over time.

Summary

Operational improvements depend on making changes to process workflows. This implies that new systems must be deployed through the various workflows within a process, and people must be trained to use new tools and methods to change the way they complete their work tasks. However, change is very difficult, at both an organizational and personal level, for many reasons, ranging from cultural barriers within an organization to individual perceptions and behavior. It has been found through numerous studies that successful change initiatives have key success factors. These have been well documented and discussed by John P. Kotter and other researchers. Several of the key concepts of this chapter are listed in Table 2.10. The first success factor includes the identification of financial and operational performance gaps to make a business case for process improvement. It is easy to gain support for an initiative that directly increases organizational productivity. Second initiatives and their toolsets should be matched to business opportunities. In other words, initiatives should be resourced differentially by an organization based on strategic considerations and anticipated business benefits. It is also important that initiatives be directed and managed by senior executives in the form of an executive steering committee. Operational initiatives should follow

Table 2.10 Key Concepts to Accelerate Organizational Change

1. Identify financial and operational performance gaps to make a business case for process improvement.
2. Determine the required initiatives that must be deployed as well as their toolsets to close the performance gaps.
3. Form an executive steering committee to guide initiative deployments to ensure goals and objectives are met and resources are aligned to business opportunities.
4. Deploy at an operational level using Lean, Six Sigma, and Total Productive Maintenance (TPM) and at strategic levels through design, IT, human resources, and the customer, but prioritized and sequenced as necessary.
5. Align reward and recognition systems, including the organization's bonus and incentive systems, to achieve the initiative's goals and objectives.
6. Develop communication systems to promote change at every level of the organization.
7. Train people to use appropriate toolsets to analyze and improve process workflows at an operational and work task level.
8. Complete projects on a continuing basis and according to schedule to build momentum for change by showing business benefits.
9. Make modifications to the deployment based on new information.

a well-recognized format that has a well-documented deployment history. As an example, Lean, Six Sigma, and Total Productive Maintenance (TPM) and similar initiatives have a long history of success as well as failure, which can be studied by an organization to increase the probability of its initiative's success. It is also important that reward and recognition systems, including an organization's bonus and incentive systems, are aligned in a way to achieve an initiative's goals and objectives. Simple and consistent communications should be made of an initiative relative to its deployment status at every level of the organization. People must also be trained to use appropriate toolsets to analyze and improve process workflows at an operational and work task level. Nothing promotes change as well as success. For this reason, it is important that projects be completed on a continuing basis and produce business benefits according to schedule to build momentum for organizational change. Finally, as in any set of activities, it is important to make modifications to the deployment based on new information.

Suggested Reading

Sanjiv Augustine. (2005). *Managing Agile Projects*. Prentice Hall, Englewood Cliffs, NJ.
Rosabeth Moss Kanter. (1983). *The Change Masters: Innovation & Entrepreneurship in the American Corporation*. Simon and Schuster, New York.
John P. Kotter. (1996). *Leading Change*. Harvard Business School Press, Boston.
John P. Kotter and James L. Heskett. (1992). *Corporate Culture and Performance*. The Free Press, New York.
Tom Peters. (1999). *The Circle of Innovation*. Vintage Press, New York.

Chapter 3

Understanding the Voice of the Customer (VOC)

Competitive solution 3: Translate customer's needs and values into new product and service designs.

Overview

If there were one major concept above all others that could help organizations compete effectively in today's world, it would be to understand and create systems that consistently meet customer needs and value expectations. Understanding the voice of the customer (VOC) is critical in today's world. As an example, competition in many industries in today's world occurs within increasingly narrowly defined market segments where organizational size becomes irrelevant. In these situations, narrowly focused market segments enable smaller organizations to successfully compete against larger ones if they arrive to market earlier and with products or services that match or exceed customer expectations. Understanding and translating the VOC also allows organizations to develop exciting new solutions to old problems, or to completely redefine older problems in terms of new paradigms and solutions. As an example, understanding key customer value elements such as time, price, utility, and function often allows immediate and substantial improvements to process workflows because nonessential operations or process waste can be easily identified and eliminated using value stream mapping (VSM) and similar Lean methods to map customer value through a process workflow. Subsequent improvement activities reduce cycle time and cost and improve quality. Understanding customer needs and value perceptions also drives organizations to identify and align their resources behind core competencies. Alignment also acts as an impetus to outsourcing, insourcing, developing new supply-chain designs, and focusing attention on necessary improvements and modifications to process workflow design.

Unfortunately, few organizations really understand how to obtain the VOC to effectively and efficiently design their workflows to deliver the required customer value. As a result, there may be significant differences between what customers need and value and what an organization actually provides to them. A failure to effectively translate the VOC through process workflows may result in lost customers and increased operational costs due to breakdowns at the organization–customer interface. These breakdowns appear as warranty issues, returned goods or customer credit, and poor customer retention. Also, there is often constant friction with customers and organizations over expected versus actual performance. In the most severe situations, an organization may lose customers to the point where it ceases to exist. Although obtaining the VOC is a complex process requiring strategies to identify relevant market segments and their major customers, it is critical to an organization's productivity and shareholder economic value added (EVA). Integral to the VOC process is collecting, quantifying, and analyzing VOC information. Once the VOC information has been analyzed by market segment, the marketing team can translate the information into actionable goals and targets. This VOC information may also prompt the development of new product or service designs or modifications to current systems. However, in many organizations VOC work is never done or is left to poorly trained people lacking the necessary education and quantitative skills. Improvements in marketing capabilities can help organizations to more effectively compete in today's world.

How does an organization know it is meeting the VOC? Table 3.1 lists several metrics that can be used to measure and improve an organization's marketing performance vis-à-vis its market share percentage, revenue growth by segment and customer, margin percentage and growth by segment and customer, percentage

Table 3.1   Competitive World Metrics: VOC

1. Market share percentage and growth by segment and customer
2. Margin percentage and growth by segment and customer
3. Percentage customer retention by segment and customer
4. Customer returns as a percentage of sales by segment and customer
5. Warranty cost as a percentage of revenue by segment and customer
6. Acquisition costs by segment and customer
7. Customer satisfaction by segment and customer

customer retention by segment and customer, customer returns as a percentage of sales by segment and customer, warranty cost as a percentage of revenue by segment and customer, acquisition costs by segment and customer, and customer satisfaction by segment and customer. There may be other metrics, used by specific organizations, to ensure marketing activities are successful. The metrics listed in Table 3.1 were developed based on several simple considerations. If an organization is increasing its market share in a profitable way and customer satisfaction is high, then the organization is performing well in its market space. However, leading-edge organizations develop strategic plans to grow their businesses organically by increasing market share and margins year to year.

Marketing's Influence on Internal Operations

Marketing strategy should influence the design of an organization's internal operations. The product and process influence of marketing strategy is usually easy to see because marketing information, whether right or wrong, is necessary to manufacture a product or provide a service. This situation may also exist in systems not designed to meet customer needs, although having a very high customer interface. On the other hand, competitive organizations evaluate how, when, why, and where customers use their products and services. An organization must understand the VOC and translate the VOC into internal design requirements for use by its operational systems and various process workflows. Unfortunately, some marketing organizations have developed an emphasis on sales (push) rather than VOC (pull). In contrast to a reliance on sales promotions and related push systems, the VOC approach to marketing is one in which marketing actively and methodically solicits information from customers. Using the VOC, customer needs and value elements are quantitatively translated back into the organization to ensure alignment of its operational systems. However, many organizations have shown an inability to sufficiently execute marketing strategies, with the result that today's competitive organizations easily displace them. This situation is exacerbated by global competition and demand for mass customization of products and services due to local customer preferences based on cultural and other demographic factors.

Important Marketing Activities

Figure 3.1 shows, at a high level, how marketing interacts with design engineering and customers relative to their impact on process workflows touching design engineering and other internal operations. Up front in the new product or service planning process, marketing brings into an organization the general requirements that must be met based on the VOC information collected and analyzed by marketing. In parallel, marketing actively works with design engineering to translate the major

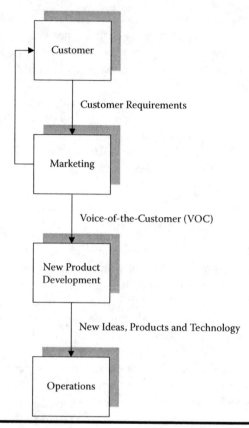

Figure 3.1 How marketing influences internal processes.

themes obtained from the VOC analysis into customer critical-to-satisfaction (CTS) characteristics. These CTS characteristics will be broken down in high-level metrics called critical-to-time (CTT), critical-to-cost (CTC), critical-to-quality (CTQ), and critical-to-safety (CTSF). Design engineering begins the internal translation process by breaking down the CTT, CTC, CTQ, and CTSF metrics into internal specifications through association with the subsystems that will satisfy customer requirements. These subsystems provide functional, dimensional, and aesthetic characteristics as well as other product or service attributes identified through the VOC translation process. Integral to these translation tasks are alpha and beta testing, prior to full-scale commercialization, of various design iterations through focus groups and test marketing. In this process, design engineering is the gatekeeper to ensure that products and services are designed and produced to satisfy customer requirements.

Table 3.2 lists five important marketing research activities. Marketing strategy begins with the goal of executing an organization's high-level strategic goals and objectives to meet sales and revenue projections. Integral to these activities is

Table 3.2   Important Market Research Activities

1. Design of marketing research strategy
2. Development and coordination of test marketing studies
3. Coordination and development of sales forecasting models
4. Ongoing customer surveys
5. Collection and analysis of benchmarking information

the design of marketing research studies to gauge customer satisfaction levels and identify customer preferences and needs for new products and services. Marketing research requires that customer demographic factors are stratified and studied to build models to explain sales potential. After the initial sales models are built, test marketing plans are developed that eventually feed anticipated demand into an organization's sales forecasting models. Forecasting models will be discussed in Chapter 8. In addition to formal studies of market potential, marketing designs ongoing customer satisfaction surveys. It also works with design engineering to develop entirely new products and services based on original concepts. Another important marketing activity is competitive benchmarking of comparative products and services. Competitive benchmarking activities are highly interactive between marketing and design engineering.

Estimating New Product or Service Demand

Estimating new product demand is a methodological process in which data is collected from targeted market segments using experimental design methods. These are also called design of experiments (DOE). DOE will be discussed in Chapter 16. Data collected using experimental designs is used to build sales purchase models. Table 3.3 shows ten basic steps to build a sales purchase or projection model. In the first step, the marketing team brainstorms all potential buyers by market segment and determines Kano needs and value elements for every segment. This brainstorming process requires a multifunctional team. It is very important that the team understand customer demographics and cultural attributes. In particular, it is important that the team know where the new product or service will actually be sold and the relevant sales channels. In Step 2, marketing models are developed based on the key customer demographic factors. These demographic factors vary by product and service offering and market segment. Ideally, an organization will have histories of similar products and services on which to build its models. Relevant factors may include the level of customer real disposable income, their age classifications, their education levels, and similar demographic information describing customers. In the third step of the study, data is collected from customers in the

Table 3.3   10 Key Steps to Estimate Demand for New Products

1. Brainstorm potential buyers and the major demographics variables that determine their purchase intentions, such as Kano needs and value elements.
2. Develop market models using key demographics to set up experimental designs to collect data by stratification variable.
3. Collect data according to the experimental design strategy.
4. Analyze the collected data relative to the major design features, their pricing, and customer demographics versus the expected market share.
5. Develop a life cycle model of the product relative to its introduction, growth, maturity, and decline stages.
6. Estimate market penetration rates for the new product by market segment and related demographics.
7. Estimate sales levels by market segment over the product's anticipated life cycle based on expected advertising and related promotional activities.
8. Test all assumptions on a limited sales basis.
9. Analyze and revise sales projections.
10. Continuously improve the process.

field using a structured methodology. Ideally, this methodology will be quantitatively based on experimental design strategies and statistical analysis. In this data collection and analysis process, the goal is to capture customer buying preferences based on demographic factors known to be statistically relevant to purchase intent by the targeted customers. Data collection is often conducted through several test markets and analyzed to estimate the expected market share for the product or service. In the test marketing phase of the new product or service, some factors, such as pricing, are varied to analyze the impact of various levels on customer purchase intentions. Pricing evaluations are made based on several considerations, with design attributes or features by market segment the most critical. Integral to the estimation of total profit of a new product or service, over its anticipated life cycle, is the estimation of the time duration of each stage within the life cycle. This analysis can be made based on similar products or services that are currently sold in similar markets. Depending on the specific industry, products and services may have different useful lives. As an example, an automobile has an economically useful life of between six and ten years, depending on the type of automobile and its required maintenance. On the other hand, many products have seasonal demand patterns or are fads. These products and services may have useful lives that are measured in weeks. In Step 6, market penetration rates are estimated using customer demographic information and the quantitative studies performed in the field. In Step 7, based on the projected penetration levels, advertising and related promotional activities are developed to ensure targeted sales levels are met in practice. In other words, if the penetration rates and other information indicate lower than expected sales levels, an organization must plan to increase its advertising levels to pull up the projected sales estimates. After, steps 1 through 7 have been completed, the marketing assumptions are tested on a limited basis using test markets. Final sales projections are developed based on the activities of steps 8 and 9. Over time, this demand estimation process is continuously improved using feedback of actual to predicted sales by market segment. These activities will be described in detail in the balance of this chapter.

Using Marketing Information to Estimate Sales

Figure 3.2 shows qualitatively how the initial estimates of market potential are progressively adjusted based on estimated marketing penetration rate. The actual shapes of the growth curves depend on a product or service's industry and market segment. It is usually helpful to analyze the demand curves of similar products and services to build these demand curves. Market penetration is estimated as a percentage of market potential, and the shape of the market penetration rate curve is based on the concept of cumulative adoption. Later in this chapter we will discuss some common market penetration patterns using Figure 3.5. It takes time for a new product or service to be adopted or purchased by customers. This time lag depends on the ability of marketing to inform the customer of the availability of

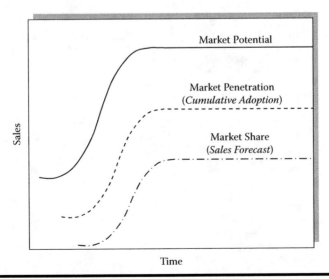

Figure 3.2   Using marketing information to estimate sales.

the product or service and the specific purchasing preferences and behaviors of its customers. As an example, some customers are early adopters and others are later adopters. Early adopters purchase products as soon as they are released to a market based on the features of the product or service. Early adopters will also pay more for new products or services than later adopters. The initial market penetration estimates are also modified based on the market share and sales of similar products and services. Throughout this marketing analysis, it is important that an organization correctly estimate the market potential, penetration rate, and share of its new products or services because sales forecasts will be built using this information. If improperly done, poor marketing and sales estimates will eventually lead to excess or obsolete inventory, on the one hand, or insufficient inventory to meet actual customer demand, on the other. The first situation results in higher operational costs due to numerous process breakdowns. The latter situation results in lower sales and customer satisfaction.

Table 3.4 lists ten steps required to estimate market potential and the size of the potential market. The first step in this estimation process is to define the market segment demand based on the best available information. In this estimation process, the market share demand of similar products and services can be very useful in estimating the market share demand for a new product or service. In the second step, market segments are broken down by demographic factors, i.e., stratification variables and their levels. This latter task is very critical to global organizations competing in a particular market segment across several regions or countries. An example would be defining a market segment as 14- to 18-year-old students who need calculators. The overall market segment may be teenagers, but this segment must be broken down based on customer demographics and local culture to provide

Table 3.4   10 Key Steps to Estimate Potential Sales

1. Defined market segment
2. Local customer demographics
3. Local culture
4. Technology level of local culture
5. Laws and regulations of the country or region
6. Price elasticity
7. Product awareness
8. Product availability
9. Purchasing intention
10. Penetration rate

variations on the basic product design or service. As an example, it may make sense to offer the calculators in different colors, different languages, and with differential functionality. Steps 3 and 4 show that it is also important to estimate the ability of the local culture to be able to use and purchase the new product or service. In other words, they may want the new product or service, but can they actually purchase it or benefit from its use at a local level? Another important consideration is determining which product or service features are important to customers having different cultural values. Laws and regulations are also important considerations in estimating market potential and penetration rate. This is because significant modifications to a product or service design may be required to sell it within a country or region. This is especially true for products or services that may have a significant negative impact on customers, including injury, death, or financial loss. Also, governments may levy tariffs or other taxes on products or services. This would increase the per unit cost to the customer. Higher per unit costs may make products or services uncompetitive in their local marketplace. In Step 6, marketing must evaluate the price elasticity of the product or service relative to its required profitability. In other words, an organization must determine if it would be profitable to sell the product or service to a particular market segment. Integral to estimation of market potential is the current awareness of the new product or service. This is because if the customers do not know about the product or service, then advertising budgets must be increased to meet required sales targets. This will have the result of lowering gross margin. In addition to product or service awareness, it is important to determine how and in which form the product will be distributed to customers at a local level. This is because high distribution costs will also lower gross margin. Finally, in Steps 9 and 10, customer purchase intentions and expected penetration rates for a new product or service are estimated based on customer feedback. This feedback should be obtained from carefully designed studies such as focus groups or surveys. The information should also be based on statistically valid methods to allow extrapolation of the analysis across the market segment under analysis. This marketing information provides the basis for sales estimates, which are used to build an organization's forecasting models.

Figure 3.3 shows that estimation of sales demand is calculated as the multiplicand of market potential, penetration rate, estimated number of customers who will purchase the product or service, number of customers who are aware or could be made aware of the product or service, the sales success, and the anticipated usage rates for the product or service. Figure 3.4 shows that market potential is estimated as the multiplicand of the size of the current customer base times the feasibility of the customer using the product or service, the awareness of the product or service, the availability of the product or service, i.e., the ability of the organization to effectively distribute the product or service to the customer at a local level, and, finally, the intention of the customer to actually purchase the product or service. Marketing and advertising methodology can also be employed to increase the level of customer awareness, product availability, and purchasing intention. Another

$$\text{Sales Demand}_t = \begin{aligned}&(\textbf{Market Potential})_t \\ &\times (\textbf{Penetration Rate})_t \\ &\times (\textbf{Potential Customers} \\ &\quad \textbf{Who Purchase})_t \\ &\times (\textbf{Product Awareness})_t \\ &\times (\textbf{Sales Success Rate})_t \\ &\times (\textbf{Usage Rate})_t\end{aligned}$$

Figure 3.3   How to estimate sales demand.

$$\text{Market Potential}_t = \begin{aligned}&(\text{Customer Base})_t \\ &\times (\text{Feasibility}) \\ &\times (\text{Customer Awareness})_t \\ &\times (\text{Product Availability})_t \\ &\times (\text{Purchase Intention})\end{aligned}$$

Figure 3.4   How to estimate market potential.

important term shown in Figure 3.3 is the market penetration rate, which was discussed earlier in this chapter. Figure 3.5 shows there are several different market penetration patterns that depend on specific products or services as well as the local market segment. These diffusion or penetration patterns are also impacted by advertising, local laws and regulations, available distribution networks, product or service pricing levels, and the relative importance of the product or service to the customer. The market penetration rate can be described in terms of a diffusion model based on the concept of early and late adopters and the uniqueness of the product or service relative to those products and services that can be substituted for the new product or service. These concepts are shown in Figure 3.5 and Figure 3.6. The model shown in Figure 3.6 is the basis for the market penetration graphs shown in Figure 3.5. In this discussion, the description of market penetration is at a very high level, but a summarization would be that the more unique and necessary a product or service is from a customer viewpoint, the faster its diffusion through a market segment, with other demographic factors held constant.

Table 3.5 shows that these concepts can be used to estimate potential sales of a new residential valve. The initial number of new houses to be built in the location and market segment of interest represents the maximum potential market size for the new valve. Assuming the new valve has a unique design, the number of new adopters is estimated at 20 percent. The proportion of these new adopters who will

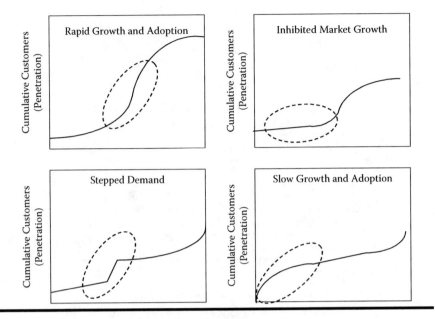

Figure 3.5   Common market penetration patterns.

$$\text{Adoption}_t = C_{\text{Innovation}}(\text{MP-TA}_t) + C_{\text{Imitation}}(\text{TA}_t/\text{MP})(\text{MP-TA}_t)$$

1. $C_{\text{Innovation}}$ & $C_{\text{Imitation}}$ are Estimated from Similar Products (Product Analogies) using Regression Analysis.
2. MP = Market Potential.
3. TA = Cumulative Adopters at Time$_t$.

Figure 3.6   How to estimate a market penetration rate.

actually purchase the new value is estimated at 80 percent based on market research. Their awareness is estimated at 80 percent based on previous advertising of valves of similar design. The sales effectiveness is 50 percent based on the success rate of previous proposals. The number of valves that must be used per house is estimated at 10. Multiplying the various terms together provides a total annual demand of 64,000 valves at the current sales price. However, this demand estimate could be increased by lowering the per unit sales price or increasing advertising levels. But the additional per unit sales must be offset by the increased selling expenses, which impact per unit gross margin and product profitability.

Marketing plays a very important role in helping design engineering obtain the VOC, and in helping operations estimate annual demand for the products or services they must produce. Marketing's impact on operations is particularly felt

Table 3.5 Estimating Product Demand Using a Simple Example

Sales of a new commercial valve must be estimated for the next year. The valve is sold in residential housing in groups of 10.

Number of new houses to be built	100,000
Number of new adopters	20%
Proportion to buy	80%
Awareness	80%
Sales effectiveness	50%
Use per customer	10
Annual demand	64,000

The next step would be to use a decomposition method to allocate annual demand by month.

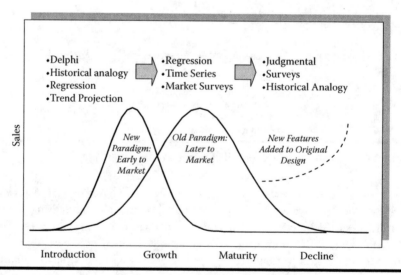

Figure 3.7   How forecasting methods change by product life cycle.

up front, when demand estimates are created to build product or service forecasts. Figure 3.7 shows that demand for a product or service goes through four life cycle stages: introduction, growth, maturity, and decline. Also shown in Figure 3.7 is the fact that the modeling method used to estimate demand varies for each life cycle stage. Prior to the introduction of a new product or service to the marketplace, estimates of demand depend on the amount of available and quantified information relative to sales. This is the reason marketing methods and techniques are important to an organization. In the absence of demand estimates that have been quantified through focus groups, customer surveys, and similar studies, an organization must rely on mathematical methods using data that may have a low correlation with actual sales. In fact, there may be no marketing data available to estimate sales. In these situations, an organization relies on the best judgment of its executives. This may create a situation in which products or services are produced that do not sell or for which there is not sufficient capacity to meet actual customer demand, and thus sales are lost. In addition to the long-term product life cycle impact, products and services may have localized demand patterns based on seasonality, economic cycle, and other related factors. Chapter 8 will discuss the demand management and forecasting models shown in Figure 3.7 in more detail. At this point in our discussion, suffice it to say that marketing's estimates of new product and service demand must be quantified for an organization's operational systems on both a long- and short-term basis. Longer-range estimates of demand are important if the new product or service requires significant expansion of current capacity rather than a simple extension of current product or service offerings.

Understanding Customer Needs and Value

Dr. Noriaki Kano, dean of engineering at Tokyo University, wrote a book describing estimation of customer needs. The premise of this book was derived from work Dr. Kano did with Konica Camera during the 1970s. Konica wanted to differentiate itself from competitors. Initially, it had sought advice from its internal product designers regarding creating new design features for cameras. However, the information gathered from the design engineers was not useful to Konica. Dr. Kano took a different approach in that he went out to ask the customers using the Konica camera as well as the laboratories that developed their pictures what they would like to see in way of camera improvements. As a result of his interviews and on-site visits, Dr. Kano recognized many unspoken customer needs. Based on his analysis, Konica developed several design improvements to Konica's cameras. Dr. Kano developed three categories to classify customer needs, as shown in Figure 3.8. The first Kano need is categorized as *basic*, the second as *performance*, and the third as *excitement*. Basic needs are usually unspoken by the customer. The expectation is that the product or service will satisfy these customer needs at a basic level. It takes methodical research to extract this information from customers because they rarely describe the level at which basic needs must be set in order to be satisfied. Customers do not really notice if the basic need is met because it is an expectation of the value exchange between supplier and customer. Another characteristic of a basic need is that when it is absent, the customer will immediately notice and

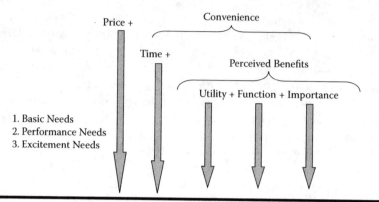

Figure 3.8 Kano needs and value elements.

complain about its absence. An example of basic need is going to a restaurant and receiving the food cooked properly. If the restaurant meets this basic need, i.e., cooks the food properly, the customer does not really notice because this is an expectation by the customer, but the customer will complain if the food is not cooked properly. Customers differentiate one product or service from another based on performance needs related to value elements such as cycle time, price, utility, and functions related to the product or service. Customers will usually be able to state the levels at which performance needs must be set to ensure their satisfaction. Also, there are usually several competitive product or service alternatives available to a customer at a given time. This makes it easy for a customer to compare such things as on-time delivery, product pricing, and other performance characteristics among competitors. In contrast to basic needs, customers will usually pay more for performance features if these are important to the customer. Excitement needs are product or service characteristics that delight a customer. An example would be a situation in which a customer says, "Wow! I didn't know I needed this!" Excitement needs are usually associated with new products and services that delight and excite customers. Relative to excitement needs, customer purchasing behavior is important. This is because some customers will be early adopters of the product or service and pay higher prices than later adopters. On the other hand, late adopters prefer to wait until the purchase cost decreases to a level at which, relative to their perception, the product or service is fairly priced. Over extended periods excitement needs migrate into performance needs, and performance needs become basic needs. Personal computers are an example of this evolutionary process. At any point in their product life cycle, different features of personal computers can be categorized as meeting basic, performance, and excitement needs. At this point in time, examples of basic needs would be the ability to run common Microsoft or Linux operating systems and connect to the Internet. Performance needs might be related to microprocessor speed or other features that improve performance or make a computer easier to use by customers. Excitement needs may be related to the availability of dual processors, video imaging, compactness, and other unique features. Over time, the categorization of these features will change as technology improves and customer value expectations migrate.

A customer's perceived value for a product or service can be broken into the elements of *convenience* and *price*. As an example, in certain situations, some customers may be willing to pay more for the convenience of a product or service. An example is a convenience food store that charges higher prices than other retail stores because it is open 24 hours per day and 7 days per week and is conveniently located for its customers. Convenience can be further broken down into elements of time and perceived benefits. Finally, perceived benefits can be broken down into subelements of *utility, function,* and *relative importance to the customer.* To summarize, there are five value elements of any product and service: price, time, utility, function, and relative customer importance. The relative prioritization of these five value elements will vary by market segment as well as customer purchase behavior regarding adoption of new products and services, i.e., risk evaluation. These value elements can be used in combination with the three Kano needs to obtain useful customer information by market segment.

Market Segmentation

The best market segmentation strategy is to assume, at the outset of the marketing research study, that all customers have differing needs and value expectations. This does not imply that we should not aggregate customers into well-defined market segments, but only that we should not assume customers are similar from a marketing perspective until there is a good basis for making that assumption. There are many ways to stratify customers. Common stratification factors include age, income level, location, job function, other interests, purchasing habits, and other relevant demographic factors. Also, within a market segment there might be direct and indirect customers. As an example, direct retail customers might sell to contractors who sell to home owners. There may also be indirect customers. Indirect customers include regulatory agencies that regulate product codes, as well as other stakeholders. The market segmentation of customers usually proceeds from the general to the specific, resulting in broader marker segments that are successively broken down into narrower segments. Market segments can also be narrowed by asking questions related to who uses the product or service, what they use it for, why they use it, how they use it, as well as when they use it. There may be many other relevant questions that should be asked based on your organization's products or services.

To understand customer's requirements, quantitative and qualitative data, as applicable, is methodically collected for each of the 15 combinations of 3 Kano needs and 5 value elements shown in Figure 3.8. This information is used to obtain the VOC by market segment and translate it into design features directly correlated to the VOC. The next section of this chapter will discuss several VOC data collection methods. In today's world, small companies that understand market segmentation and how to obtain the VOC in terms of Kano needs and value elements will be able to focus their resources on very narrow market segments and be in position to outperform larger organizations that try to broad-brush entire market segments with generic products and services.

Measuring the VOC

Measuring the VOC requires understanding three important concepts: Kano needs, value elements, and market segmentation. Understanding the VOC relative to these three concepts allows an organization to design systems to collect, analyze, and translate the VOC into meaningful internal metrics and targets. This enables organizations to develop new or modified products and services to meet global competitive pressures and maintain high productivity levels. However, collecting VOC information must be done in a systematic manner using standardized data collection tools and methods. In fact, these data collection systems should be fully integrated within an organization's process to ensure continuous improvement of process workflows over time. Figure 3.9 shows several major elements of the VOC data collection system. In addition to high-level market segmentation, organizations have direct and indirect customers. As an example, your organization might

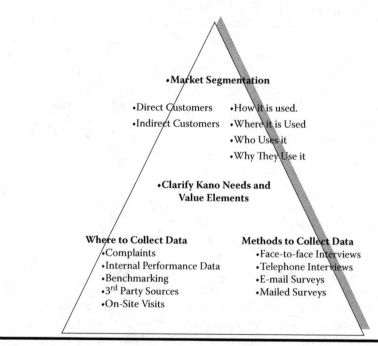

Figure 3.9   How to collect customer information.

directly sell to a major retailer who in turn indirectly sells to another customer. In this type of system, your organization must understand both the retailer's and its customers' requirements in order to design products and services to satisfy the VOC at all levels. A third way to think about market segmentation is relative to the how, where, who, and why your products or services are used by customers. Finally, there may be other stakeholders in an industry, such as regulatory agencies, which review the design, manufacture, and use of an organization's products or services. Figure 3.9 also shows there are several sources of information that can be used to amplify the VOC as well as specific tools and methods that will facilitate collection of the VOC data.

Common sources of VOC information include open sources that are available to everyone, information provided by customers, or that which is actively collected from customers. Open-source information includes data obtained from the Internet, industry benchmarking studies, and similar sources. A key characteristic of open-source data is that it is easily obtainable, but will not provide a competitive edge for an organization because competitors within an industry have access to the same information. However, open-source data may show general industry trends, metrics, benchmarks, and their expected performance levels. Information provided by customers may include warranty data, complaints, returned goods, lawsuits, and similar information. Customer information is useful in bringing your products and services up to the basic or performance need levels. However, this type of information will not show an organization's relative performance against competitors or identify customer excitement needs. Actively collected information includes customer interviews, surveys, and on-site visits at customer facilities. Actively collected information requires up-front planning by the marketing team. It is also more expensive to obtain than other sources of VOC information. However, actively collected information will help an organization identify new performance and excitement needs that may provide it with a competitive edge to move past its competitors.

Customer interviews are one of the important ways to actively obtain customer information. Interviews can be conducted automatically using e-mails and mailings or conducted in person. In either situation, questions should be relevant to the VOC information that must be collected and open ended to obtain unbiased information from customers. It is also important to carefully plan activities prior to collecting customer information to ensure team members understand common definitions and terms as well as the VOC methodology. This is particularly important when framing questions for written or e-mail surveys. As an example, if e-mails and mailings are used to obtain customer information, the survey must be tested using a smaller audience to validate questions relative to clarity and relevance. E-mails and written surveys typically have a very low response rate, but they are relatively inexpensive to conduct and analyze. In contrast, personal interviews will normally provide more information on customer needs and value perceptions, but they are more expensive to deploy. The general format for effective personal interviewing is to probe the customer with relevant and very clearly phrased questions that should be followed up with clarifying statements. At the end of an interview, validation questions should be asked by the interviewer to confirm the customer's responses to prior questions. In-person interviews can also be broken down into one-on-one and focus group interviews. In either situation, the interviewing team should plan the interview to include relevant questions that will be asked, interviewer roles, and the facilitation to be used during the interviewing process. Focus group interviews have an advantage over one-on-one interviews in that group dynamics may increase the availability of new ideas. But focus groups must be properly facilitated by the interviewing team. Finally, if on-site interviews are conducted by the team, it may be useful to gather customer information relative to how a product or service is used at the customer's location, including who is using it, where they use it, why they use it, when they use it, and other relevant information that may identity opportunities to increase performance and excitement features of a product or service.

Each interviewing strategy has advantages and disadvantages, with respect to both the amount of information provided by the interview and its cost. As an example, the greater the interpersonal interaction between the interviewer and customer, the higher the probability that performance and excitement needs will be discovered by the interviewing team. In fact, this is the major advantage of actively obtaining the VOC. However, relative to quantification and extrapolation of the results, surveys may be a better choice of interviewing technique because large sample sizes can be analyzed statistically. However, surveys may not obtain all the relevant information necessary to identify performance and excitement needs.

Figure 3.10 shows that as VOC information is collected from multiple information sources using one or more data collection methods, the cumulative information

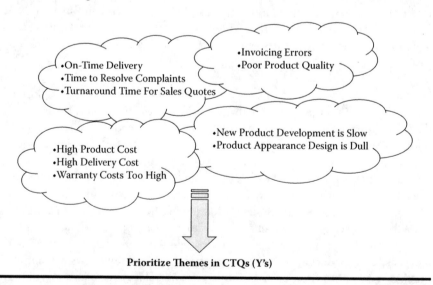

•On-Time Delivery
•Time to Resolve Complaints
•Turnaround Time For Sales Quotes

•Invoicing Errors
•Poor Product Quality

•High Product Cost
•High Delivery Cost
•Warranty Costs Too High

•New Product Development is Slow
•Product Appearance Design is Dull

Prioritize Themes in CTQs (Y's)

Figure 3.10   Organizing VOC information.

must be organized into major VOC themes related to the basic value elements related to price, time, utility, and function. These themes are broken into critical-to-quality characteristics (CTQs). The CTQs are evaluated, organized, and prioritized by the marketing research and design team using a prioritization method such as paired comparisons or the analytical hierarchy process (AHP) method. An overview of the paired comparison method is shown in Figure 4.3, and the AHP method is shown in Figure 4.4. These methods will be discussed in more detail in Chapter 4.

Translating the VOC Using Quality Function Deployment

Collection of VOC data from multiple sources requires aggregation of the collected data and the analysis and prioritization of the major themes that customers identify as necessary to meet their needs and value expectations. Organizing and prioritizing the VOC into themes requires the use of multifunctional teams using brainstorming and prioritization tools and methods. These prioritized themes will become the CTQs or high-level customer requirements that drive the internal specifications corresponding to the key process output variables (KPOVs) necessary to satisfy customers. Gaps in product or process performance require creation of new or modified products and services. Quality function deployment (QFD) is the structured methodology used to correlate CTQs into their specific design specifications, i.e., KPOVs, or Y's. QFD is also used to compare the required CTQs to those of current systems and identify performance gaps. In addition, QFD is useful in helping coordinate the work of a design team across organizational functions and facilitate competitive benchmarking activities. These characteristics ensure linkage of the VOC to an organization's design and workflow systems. The QFD methodology is embodied within the house-of-quality (HOQ) concept, which is shown in Figure 3.11. The HOQ is divided into sections or rooms that summarize data relevant to understanding how customer requirements, i.e., CTQs, are related to system elements of the product or service design. These system elements are summarized in the form of specifications, i.e., Y's, that in aggregate satisfy the CTQ expectations of the customer as well as system key design input variables (KDIVs), i.e., X's, which drive the levels of the Y's in the product or service design. The goal of the CTQ to specification analysis is to ultimately develop quantitative relationships or models between the Y's and their associated inputs, or X's. The HOQ also allows the improvement team to see the interrelationships among several Y's. This is useful when making trade-off decisions between various subsystems of the design. As an example, an automobile may be required to obtain high miles per gallon fuel ratings, but also have a minimum internal cabin volume for customer comfort. The QFD matrix or HOQ would show these interrelationships and allow design

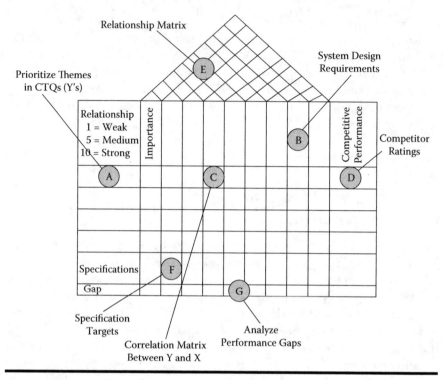

Figure 3.11 House of quality (QFD).

trade-offs to be made by the team relative to weight that correlated to cabin volume. The Pugh matrix is a useful tool to evaluate product or service design trade-offs. An overview of the Pugh matrix method is shown in Figure 4.7. This evaluation method will be discussed in Chapter 4.

Section A of Figure 3.11 is used to list the prioritized CTQs obtained from the VOC analysis. The relative importance ratings are estimated using various prioritization tools, including the AHP method, which will be discussed in Chapter 4. Modifications to these ratings can be made by considering Kano needs and the five value elements by market segment. In QFD literature these CTQs are called the what's. In section B of Figure 3.11, the design requirements necessary to provide the CTQs are listed as clearly defined design specifications and translated into internal Y's. These Y's are often called the how's. Section C of Figure 3.11 shows the correlations between each CTQ and the associated system elements, or the what's as they relate to the how's. A rating system of 1 to 10 is usually used to indicate weak (1), medium (5), and strong (10) correlations between the what's and how's. Competitive benchmarking is also used to aid the design analysis. This is shown in section D of Figure 3.11, in which competitive benchmarking enables a design team to understand how competitive designs meet the CTQ. Section E is used to evaluate relationships between one or more design elements, i.e., the how's, because

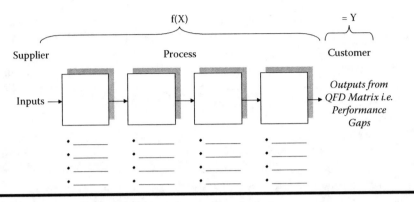

Figure 3.12   How to use a SIPOC to translate the VOC.

there may be conflicts among CTQs of different design elements, as mentioned earlier in the automobile example. The rating scale is 1 to 10. A 10 rating implies a high correlation between design elements, which could be positive or negative. Section F lists the specifications of each design element, i.e., Y's. Several Y's may be required to satisfy a specific CTQ. In section G, specifications are analyzed versus current design capability to identify performance gaps. Performance gaps may require that one or more projects be deployed to improve system performance. Alternatively, entire new system elements may have to be created by the team to satisfy some CTQs.

Service systems are also designed using the VOC and QFD methodology as well as process workflow models. Figure 3.12 shows a high-level system map called a SIPOC. SIPOC is an acronym representing the phrase supplier–input boundary–process–output boundary–customer. Relative to our current VOC discussion, the SIPOC is used to capture the prioritized list of CTQs for major process workflows. This information is used to correlate the CTQs to key operations and their system elements, i.e., the process and input X's, and define the final process design. As the process design is iteratively created, the SIPOC becomes more detailed and quantified until finally a system model is created to quantitatively describe the relationships of process inputs and outputs, i.e., $Y = f(X)$. In many situations, this system model can be dynamically simulated and analyzed to ensure it meets its original design requirements as specified by the CTQs. These concepts will be discussed in Chapter 5 as well as subsequent chapters.

Exchanging Value in a Competitive World

Value exchange in today's world is a dynamic process involving supply-chain participants across diverse geopolitical regions. Participants are both customers in one sense and suppliers in another. In many situations, buyer–supplier interactions flow both ways between buyer and seller. In their book entitled *Blur: The Speed of*

Change in the Connected Economy, Davis and Meyer argued in 1998 (and ahead of their time) that buyers and sellers should "extract information with every buy and sell" and everyone should "buy while selling," and vice versa. Currently eBay is an excellent example of the exchange in which organizations of every size, throughout the world, use systems of virtual exchange to level buying and selling transactions. In this environment, customer needs, values, and relative relationships constantly change.

Another key consideration, relative to value in today's world, lies in the definition of what should be valued and how it should be valued by suppliers and customers. In *Blur* the authors discuss the concepts of valuation of intellectual and virtual assets in contrast to physical assets. They also discuss the importance of branding in a world full of information, of which much is useless at the moment, i.e., the negative sides of informing, as defined by Thomas L. Friedman in his book *The World Is Flat*. Organizations that accurately define their customer segments and scope their product and service offerings based on brand recognition will dominate any other organization in the same competitive space. Understanding the VOC is one of most effective competitive weapons an organization has in competing in today's world, but this is often left to poorly trained people who lack the skills and experience to do effective VOC translation. This is one of the many reasons for the relatively poor competitive performance exhibited by organizations having lower profit margins than their competitors. Protectionist legislation will make this chronic problem worse; i.e., the automotive and other heavy industries (protected organizations) in the United States and other developed countries will tend not to listen to their customers, but rather "push" their products and services into the marketplace.

Summary

In a globally competitive organization, customer excellence must be understood in terms of the VOC by designing systems that will efficiently transform information or materials into products and services that satisfy customer needs and value expectations. Figure 3.13 captures the overall strategy of our discussion over the next 17 chapters relative to increasing operational efficiency in today's world. Our goal will be to present and discuss the tools, methods, and concepts of operation's management, including product and service design, Lean, Six Sigma, productivity analysis, and other important operational concepts, in an integrative manner to demonstrate how they can be effectively used to increase an organization's operational efficiency in today's world.

Table 3.6 lists the key concepts that will help your organization increase its competitiveness. The first concept recommends using modern marketing research tools and methods to obtain customer information related to customer needs and value elements by market segment. The second concept suggests training marketing and sales people to use efficient and quantitative methods to enable them to

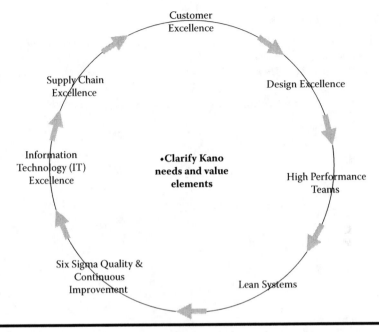

Figure 3.13   Executing marketing strategy through operational systems.

Table 3.6   Key Concepts to Understand the VOC

1. Use modern marketing research tools and methods to obtain customer information related to Kano needs and value elements by market segment.
2. Train salespeople to use quantitative methods to enable them to obtain the maximum amount of information from customers during every interaction.
3. Develop internal systems to gather and quantitatively analyze VOC information, including product forecasts and other systems used to estimate demand.
4. Translate VOC information through the product or service design process.

obtain the maximum amount of information from customers during every interaction. The third concept advocates the development of internal marketing systems to consistently gather and quantitatively analyze VOC information, including product forecasts and other systems used to estimate demand. Finally, the fourth key concept is translating the VOC information through the product or service design process.

Suggested Readings

Stan Davis and Christopher Meyer. (1998). *Blur: The Speed of Change in the Connected Economy.* Addison-Wesley, Reading, MA.

James W. Martin. (2007). *Lean Six Sigma for Supply Chain Management.* McGraw-Hill, New York.

John Tschohl. (1996). *Achieving Excellence through Customer Service.* Best Sellers Publishing, Minneapolis.

2

TRANSLATING CUSTOMER VALUE ELEMENTS INTO PRODUCTS, SERVICES, AND WORKFLOW SYSTEMS

Chapter 4

Designing for Customer Value Using Design for Six Sigma (DFSS)

Competitive solution 4: Design products and services that can be manufactured anywhere in the world at low cost and high quality to meet customer needs and value expectations.

Overview

Product and service design has a direct and significant impact on an organization's operations. Understanding the important tools, methods, and concepts of design will enable an operation's manager to significantly improve operational efficiency. Relative to the organizational impact of design, it is commonly accepted that it drives a significant portion of cost over the life cycle of products and services. These costs may include direct labor, materials, capital equipment purchases, inventory investment, and similar operational costs. It has been widely documented that the deployment of best-in-class design practices results in reductions in total life cycle cost and time to market, and higher quality. Building a core competency in the design of products and services will also help an organization mitigate competitive advantages. These competitive advantages may include direct labor, materials, available capital, and similar advantages. Also, best-in-class design practices are widely known throughout the world, and competitors have access to the tools, methods, and concepts associated with the efficient design of products and services. As a result, organizations located in geographical locations having high direct labor costs have much to gain by using best-in-class design methods such as quality function deployment (QFD), concurrent engineering (CE), design for manufacturing (DFM), failure-mode-and-effects-analysis (FMEA), and design for Six Sigma (DFSS) to ensure their products and services will be competitive in today's world. The purpose of this chapter is to present basic and well-accepted design tools, methods, and concepts for immediate use by your organization. The discussion will be focused on applications to products and services.

How does an organization measure the effectiveness and efficiency of its design activities? In Table 4.1, ten metrics are listed that enable an organization to measure key attributes of its design process and workflows. The first metric is time from concept to market. The ability to quickly and efficiently bring a new concept to market or commercialize it greatly increases an organization's market share because it allows it to be first to market. This is important because in some industries, an organization's market share significantly increases if it is the first to market with a new product or service. A second important metric is the number or changes to the final design after it is released to operations. Getting to market first is important, but if a product or service contains many defects, then its life cycle cost will dramatically increase due to process breakdowns that result in customer complaints. These process breakdowns may cause customers to ask for refunds or additional money for economic losses caused by use of defective products or services. As a result, percentage of warranty cost to revenue is an important metric because it measures

Table 4.1   Competitive World Metrics: Product and Service Design

1. Time from concept to market
2. Number or changes to final design
3. Percentage of warranty cost to revenue
4. Percentage of maintenance cost to revenue
5. Total customer life cycle cost
6. Percentage market share of new products and new products introduced within the past five years
7. Actual standard cost versus target cost
8. Percentage excess and obsolete inventory caused by design changes
9. Design costs as a percentage of total revenue
10. Function-to-cost ratio versus competitive designs

defects in the field. Percentage of maintenance cost to revenue is an important criterion when evaluating the design process because high maintenance costs adversely impact customers. At a higher level, products or services that represent a large monetary investment by customers can be measured using the total customer life cycle cost metric. Total customer life cycle cost is a major competitive weapon for an organization in that, although products may cost more up front, the overall life cycle cost to customers may be less than products or services that are less expensive to purchase. An example is the purchase of an automobile based on energy costs. Automobiles having a higher miles per gallon or liter ratio will normally be more attractive to consumers, all other things being equal — even if the selling price of the more energy efficient automobile is a little higher than that of similar models. If an organization's design function is performing well, then the ratio of new products to old should be higher than that of poorly performing organizations. Also, the relative market share of newly introduced products and services should be higher than that of an organization's competitors. This performance characteristic of a design function can be measured using the percentage market share of new products, or perhaps another metric, such as the percentage of products introduced within the last five years. Metrics that evaluate the cost efficiency of new products and services include the actual standard cost versus target cost, percentage excess and obsolete inventory caused by design changes, and design cost as a percentage of total revenue. Finally, the function-to-cost ratio versus competitive designs is a measure of the value of a product or service relative to competitors'. This metric should be based on an external customer viewpoint.

The process for designing and producing products and services consists of five phases (Figure 4.1):

1. Concept creation and approval
2. Development of alternative designs
3. Prototype development and testing
4. Pilot tests of the new design under actual operating conditions
5. Commercial launch of the new product or service

Integral to these five phases is the use of concurrent manufacturing (CE) methods to manage activities, provide feedback, and enable control among all functions involved in the design process. Referring to Figure 4.1 we see that the planning of a new product or service spans the concept phase. The product and process design activities span the concept, design, and prototyping phases. Finally, product and process validation activities continue into the launch phase. Feedback and assessment of the design process occurs throughout the five phases. CE facilitates a collaborative project management approach in which cross-functional teams work together through the five design phases.

A design process has five unique roles and responsibilities, which are listed in Table 4.2. The first responsibility is the identification and translation of customer Kano needs and value elements into specific design elements to meet

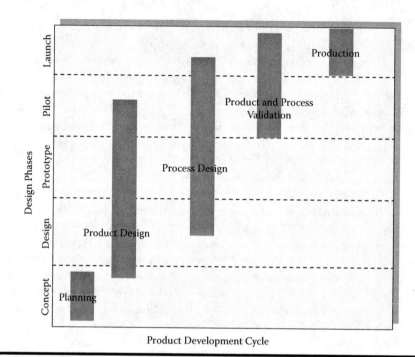

Figure 4.1 Overview of the new product development process.

Table 4.2 Major Design Roles and Responsibilities

1. Translation of VOC into design specifications	Marketing research, quality function deployment (QFD)
2. Gathering information relevant to constructing the design	Concurrent engineering, design reviews, historical performance data, manufacturing and supplier data
3. Continuous improvement of design process to reduce cycle time, reduce costs, and improve quality	Computer-aided design (CAD), computer-aided engineering (CAE), etc.
4. Leveraging technology to increase analytical efficiency	Monte Carlo simulation, finite element analysis (FEA), experimental design, statistical tolerances
5. Project inceptions and management	Design reviews, Gantt charts, etc.

internal specifications. Internal specifications must be calibrated to the voice-of-the-customer (VOC). Typical tools used to execute this responsibility are marketing research tools and methods, quality function deployment (QFD), and target costing. Important marketing research and QFD tools and methods were discussed in Chapter 3, as well several methods used to capture the VOC information. In Chapter 3, marketing research was discussed as an integrated set of qualitative and quantitative methods that help an organization determine customer preferences and value expectations for every design feature. This analytical process also includes estimation of the number of potential buyers of the new product or service, as well as the price they will be willing to pay for various combinations of features. This estimated purchase price, based on a marketing evaluation, is used to estimate the target cost for a product or service. Setting a target cost is important because, at a basic level, the profit margin is the difference between sales price and production cost of the product or service. Using target costing, the CE team can evaluate all components of the new product or service design to ensure that the cumulative cost does not exceed the target cost. However, this does not mean the team should "cheapen" the design at the expense of required product or service functionality. In fact, as mentioned above, the team should look at the total life cycle cost of the new product or service. The next responsibility of the design team is to bring together the diverse information necessary to begin the design of the product or service. This information-gathering process brings together qualitative and quantitative information related to target values for each design feature as well as its target tolerance, as translated from the VOC current technical capability related to design and production. Information from prior versions of the product or service being designed, or similar products and services, is also very useful in the evaluation process. The design team should be managed as a high-performance work team or a set of integrated teams if geographically dispersed. The ability to form high-performance work teams across various countries and cultures is an important enabling characteristic of highly competitive organizations in today's world. Accelerating this team-building and information-gathering process are various technological tools such as computer-aided design (CAD), rapid prototyping, simulation algorithms, computer-aided manufacturing (CAM), statistical tolerance analysis, and many others. Throughout the design process, effective project management tools and methods such as CE are critical to project success as the design project proceeds through the five phases of concept, design, prototyping, piloting, and launch.

Design practices vary by industry as well as the specific product or service designed. As an example, the creativity of the design process is very high when there is little required structure to the design, i.e., few customer or marketing requirements, and the design issues are relatively low. In other words, there are few requirements specified in advance of the design concept. As the design issues become magnified or product and service features are specified in advance by the customer or market, then collaborative teams will be required to work through design issues.

In the case of design changes that are minor or evolutionary, the design issues may be less urgent, but concurrent engineering teams will also be required to efficiently work through the process issues related to the design function.

There are also several ways in which the design process can break down. These situations, when they occur, result in higher product or service design costs. In addition, production costs may be higher, and it may take a longer time to commercialize the product or service. Breakdowns in the design process could place an organization in a noncompetitive position and result in significant economic loss for an organization. One of the most obvious breakdowns would be designing a product or process at the very edge of technical feasibility or organizational capability. Other risks include designing products and services that require high capital investment, variations in customer requirements, or a failure to efficiently use the necessary design tools and methods.

Major Objectives of the Design Process

There are several important objectives that must be considered when designing products or services. These relate to how easy it is to design and produce the product or service throughout its life cycle. Also, the more successfully an organization can execute key design objectives to meet customer needs, the greater will be the perceived value of the product or service to the customer. This implies the product or service will be more competitive vis-à-vis competitive products or services from Kano and value perspectives. Table 4.3 lists ten key design objectives that should be considered by the CE team. The first objective is how easy it is to assemble or

Table 4.3   10 Key Design Objectives

1. Ease of manufacturability or deployment for services
2. Design for manufacturing (DFM) or Lean systems for services
3. Design for assembly/disassembly or configuration flexibility for services
4. Product or service reliability
5. Ability to install or deploy
6. Ability to use
7. Ability to service or ensure operational stability
8. Ability to maintain or use every day
9. Ability to upgrade the product or service
10. Ease of disposal, recycling, or phaseout of the system

build a product or deploy a new service system. As an example, if a product or service design has many complex assembly procedures or components, it will be more costly and take longer to construct than a simpler one. There will also be a greater probability that errors will occur in the handling and assembly of components. The second design objective listed in Table 4.3 is use of design for manufacturing (DFM) methods to simplify the product design. In the case of service systems, it would be the application of Lean methods to simplify the new process. Lean tools, methods, and concepts will be discussed in Chapter 6. The point is that the more simplified the process, the easier it will be for operations to produce the product or service day to day. Operational costs and throughput time will also be lower and quality enhanced by designing the simplest systems that meet customer requirements. Step 3 of Table 4.3 requires that a design be easy not only to assemble or build, but also to disassemble. In other words, it has configuration flexibility. An example would be designing components to "snap-fit" together, rather than relying on adhesive bonding or mechanical fastening systems. This contributes to the concept of minimizing total life cycle costs at the time when a product or service must be disposed of or eliminated from an organization. Once a product or service has been commercialized, it should meet its intended functions over its life cycle. This implies it will perform at a predetermined reliability or availability level. As an example, if an automobile is maintained according to manufacturer's recommendations, then it should be available for use by the customer based on its reliability targets. In other words, its mechanical and electrical functions should perform according to the stated warranty of each subsystem, which is based on initial reliability estimates and expected maintenance practices as determined by design engineering through performance testing. Because customers evaluate a product based on its total cost, including installation, the easier and less costly a product is to install and maintain, the greater will be its perceived value to the customer. In the case of service systems, the easier a new service system is to deploy, use, and maintain, the more likely it will be successfully deployed for customer usage. Steps 5 to 9 show that the ease of use of a product or service should be a key design objective. Customer satisfaction will usually increase if products or services are easy to use. As an example, how many products or services do we encounter every day that are difficult to use or require a significant investment of time to learn how to use them efficiently. In the worst-case scenarios, a failure to use them correctly may result in problems, such as breakage or injury to a customer. An example would be the purchase of an electronic device having many extra features that customers cannot use correctly without a significant investment of time. These additional features may even be confusing to the customer and inhibit easy use of the device's essential functions, resulting in customer dissatisfaction. In contrast, there are many products, such as software, that self-install and, from a customer viewpoint, are invisible. In summary, it is important that once a product or service has been sold, it is easy to service, maintain, and even upgrade by customers. Software is a common example in which upgrades are very easy. Examples include Norton Antivirus and

Windows XP. These software systems are automatically downloaded and either self-install or require a simple click of the mouse to install. Step 10 (Figure 4.3) shows that a major design objective is the design of products and services that are easy to dispose of, recycle, or phase out of a system.

Concurrent Engineering Methods in Design

The ability to develop speed or agility in the design process is enhanced through the simultaneous execution of parallel process workflow tasks in a coordinated manner. In the CE process, team members from diverse organizational functions are organized into high-performance project teams to facilitate communication and collaboration. In addition, there is an emphasis on developing and focusing on core design competencies rather than trying to do everything in one place or by a single organization. Best-in-class CE practices allow Lean agile design teams to offer a variety of design options and reduce time to market for their organization. The CE process is also called Lean Agile Product Design (LAPD). LAPD is characterized by the development of customer solutions rather than incremental performance over competitors. Along this line of thought, the focus in Lean agile product development is on satisfying customer requirements rather than specifications. Close customer relationships are critical to effective execution of LAPD. In addition, the emphasis of CE is on doing the right things and doing them well, i.e., effectiveness and efficiency of the design process.

Important enabling characteristics that help organizations compete in today's world include obtaining accurate VOC information to ensure customers receive the features they need and value. In parallel, an organization must also ensure it is making product or service design a core competency while outsourcing noncore competencies to organizations that flawlessly execute design functions as part of their own core competency. In this context, the VOC implies the development of products and services from a global perspective, if it is applicable. Finally, it is important to use all the available tools and methods to design a product or service so it meets its intended design functions throughout its useful life cycle.

In Figure 4.2, a qualitative representation of the rework aspect of a new product or service design is shown. Best-in-class organizations ensure the design process has the necessary resources and is executed using state-of-the-art tools and methods, such as CE, to achieve the ten key design objectives listed in Table 4.3. If an organization can identify and eliminate design flaws during the concept and design phases of a new product or service, then the overall life cycle costs will be lower than if the design is released and its flaws are found during commercialization by external customers. Various studies have been conducted on the cumulative failure costs of new designs. It is commonly agreed that there is a cost multiplier effect when going from the design to production phases and on to the customer. This concept implies that if a design flaw is caught by an external customer and causes problems such as

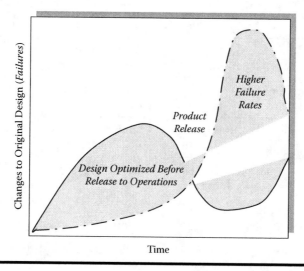

Figure 4.2   Reducing engineering changes (rework).

CTQ	Successful Paired Rankings	Add "1"	Success Fraction	Prioritization Ranking
Reduce Cycle Time	3	4	0.4	1
Improve Reliability	2	3	0.3	2
Easy to Maintain	0	1	0.1	4
Easy Upgrade Installation	1	2	0.2	3
Total	**6**	**10**	**1.0**	

Figure 4.3   Paired comparison prioritization method.

product returns or high warranty costs, the resultant required changes to the design and their impact on production operations may result in significant cost increases, which may exceed the original per unit target cost of the design.

Another important aspect of a new product or service is that the project cost depends on five major factors (Table 4.4): R&D cycle time, the degree of technological risk associated with the new product or service design, the available capital and labor resources, the types and magnitude of the performance gaps that must be closed to commercialize the new product or service, and the technology available to produce the product or service. Relative to R&D cycle time, the longer the cycle time of the R&D design phase, the longer it will take to release the new design to the marketplace. This may have a major negative impact on an organization. In some industries the first organization to market receives approximately 70 percent of the market share for the product's entire life cycle. In these industries, R&D

Table 4.4   Major Factors in New Design Costs

	Current Technology	Pushing State of the Art	Not Feasible
1. R&D cycle time	Cycle time targets met	Some targets not met	Project failure
2. Technology risk	Low risk	Some technology not available	Too high
3. Available capital and labor resources	Cost targets met	Over budget	Complete breakdown in cost projections
4. Performance gaps	No gaps	Some gaps	Significant
5. Available technology	Commercial technology	New technology designed	Not available

cycle time can have a dramatic impact on the new design's profitability. Technological risk, the second factor, implies the more that R&D must be involved in the successful commercialization of a new product or service, the higher the risk to the project because components of the new design must be invented prior to finalization of the optimum design alternative. In contrast, design projects that do not require R&D have less risk because design changes are applications of known technology or simple modifications and extensions to current products or services. These situations pose little technological risk to an organization. However, a new design may pose tremendous risk to an organization if it is positioned at the leading edge of technology. It is extremely important that an organization accurately estimate a design project's technological risk level and its impact on a design project, including its schedule and cost. Poor project planning or long cycle times can greatly increase the expenses of a design project due to increases in material, labor, and tooling costs, as well capital expenditures. As mentioned earlier, market share and revenue may also be adversely impacted by poor project planning. Available capital and labor resources must also be carefully considered by an organization. The fourth factor is related to closing performance gaps identified through the VOC using the new product or service design. In some projects, the required performance targets may exceed anything the organization has accomplished during previous design iterations. Large performance gaps relative to current organizational competencies will also increase the risk that these gaps cannot be closed by the CE team. Finally, if technology is not available to reliably and cost-effectively design and produce a new product or service, then a design project will fail, or if executed, profitability throughout the product or service's life cycle will be lower than the original targets.

Table 4.5 10 Key Concurrent Engineering Benefits

1. Improved communication
2. Fewer misunderstandings among organizational functions
3. Reduced cycle time to commercialize new products or services
4. Increasing productivity of CE team members, resulting in significant reductions in required project indirect labor hours
5. Reduced tooling and other capital expenditures
6. Fewer mistakes and higher quality in the design phase
7. Fewer engineering changes after the design phase
8. Greater organizational competitiveness
9. Best-practice sharing and leveraging new knowledge
10. Improved organizational profitability

CE Benefits

The benefits from using CE have been well documented by its practitioners over the past 20 years. Ten key benefits are listed in Table 4.5. Improved communication is an obvious benefit from bringing together cross-disciplinary teams to focus on new product development. This results in fewer misunderstandings among organizational functions. The result is a shorter cycle time to develop and commercialize new products or services. Depending on the organization, reductions in product development cycle time of between 5 and 50 percent are common. In addition to a reduction in project cycle time, the number of indirect labor hours required to complete a project is often at least 20 percent less than for projects not managed using CE. There are also fewer mistakes and design changes once the new design is transferred to production operations. CE also helps reduce tooling and other capital expenditures because major tooling modifications are not usually necessary during the production phase in CE environments. Finally, sharing of best practices and knowledge leveraging are enhanced through the CE project management process.

Ten Key Steps to Implement CE

Although there are many sources of information regarding how to create and effectively deploy CE teams, several important steps must be taken to enable your organization to begin a CE deployment process. In Table 4.6, ten such steps are listed. The first step is to create the initial CE team to work on a new product or service

Table 4.6   10 Key Steps to Implement CE

1. Create a multidisciplinary CE team.
2. Develop a detailed project plan.
3. Assign project tasks based on project plan.
4. Develop product and process data based on VOC information.
5. Develop design goals, preliminary BOM, preliminary process flowchart, and preliminary list of special characteristics.
6. Evaluate required technology to create and manufacture the product design.
7. Develop the product assurance plan with operations and quality assurance.
8. Validate the new product design through testing and evaluation under controlled conditions (pilot tests).
9. Scale up for product commercialization.
10. Review feedback lessons learned by the team.

design. If this is an organization's first CE project, it would be a good idea to retain consultants or send people to seminars to understand the myriad work tasks required to kick off the CE process in your organization. The CE team should also be highly facilitated to ensure proper team meeting practices are followed throughout the design project. The CE team should also create a project charter describing its assigned work plan. Project charters will be discussed in Chapter 7, and an example is shown in Figure 7.9. The project charter should contain the specific goals and objectives for the new design as well as each of its subsystems, including their required functions, dimensions, and aesthetic features. In addition, the team should build a very detailed Gantt chart to schedule project work tasks and show their interrelationships, time duration, and required resources. Project management is discussed in Chapter 18, and an example of a Gantt chart is shown in Figure 18.4. This project planning process is usually best done using project management software, such as Excel-based templates or Microsoft Project, to facilitate the flow of design information and changes in project status quickly across your organization. Also, works tasks and their required resources can be easily recalculated dynamically by the project management software as conditions change during the project. The CE team should also assign the required project activities and their associated work tasks based on team member expertise.

Once the CE team has been organized and begins to plan its work, a top priority should be development of product and process data based on VOC information.

This information will enable the CE team to identify performance gaps in the current design relative to the VOC. Identification of performance gaps will enable the CE team to modify the current design or develop entirely new subsystems to meet customer requirements. In addition to this discovery process, the CE team develops design goals and objectives that are incorporated into the project's Gantt chart to update the project schedule. Additional information required by the CE includes creating a preliminary bill of material (BOM), process flowcharts, and a list of special characteristics and unique features of the new product or service design based on VOC information. Using this information, the CE team evaluates the technology required to create and produce the new product or service design. Eventually, the various design alternatives are tested and evaluated until a final optimized design has been created that blends the best characteristics of all design alternatives developed during the design project.

In parallel, operations will be developing a new process that will produce the product or service at high quality levels to achieve all target costs, cycle time, quality, and other requirements. Quality assurance also develops, in parallel, the quality control plan for the new product or service. As part of this process, quality assurance works with other organizational functions to develop supporting documentation for the design project. This supporting documentation includes inspection, audit, and similar procedures that reflect the VOC. Finally, as the final design iteration is validated through testing and evaluation under controlled conditions (pilot tests), the new product or service is scaled up for commercialization. Throughout the CE process the design team incorporates lessons learned and best practices into their project work.

Applying Design for Manufacturing Methods

Because design for manufacturing (DFM) with its tools and methods is so important in the development of new products and services, it will be discussed in detail here. Product and process simplification are probably the two most useful concepts in modern process design and improvement. Simplified systems can be developed faster and cost less than more complicated systems. Also, the time to move through a simple system will be less than that for more complicated designs. However, many systems are designed to be unnecessarily complex, which makes it difficult to understand the cumulative impact of incorporating unnecessary components into the new design. The cumulative impact of complexity may not be seen until an extended period has passed and the new product or service is failing. These situations require that improvements be immediately implemented to enhance performance. There are two prevalent methods to reduce design complexity. Design for manufacturing (DFM) is used to reduce design complexity of products, and Lean methods are used to simplify process complexity. There are strong analogies between the two initiatives.

In the mid-1980s, DFM become popularized through the work of Dewhurst and Boothroyd, who were professors at the University of Rhode Island. Their work was a modification of classical value engineering (VE). In VE, a product design is broken into its components and associated assembly operations and elemental work tasks. Using VE, the standard cost of all components, as well as the standard work necessary to produce a product, is estimated for the entire assembly. After obtaining baseline design data, the VE team attempts to reduce product complexity through the elimination or combination of components to reduce assembly time and material costs. In this process, various design alternatives are compared against the current baseline design. The goal is to reduce the number of components and materials and the standard time to assemble one unit, to lower the total per unit cost. Published case studies have consistently shown reductions in component count that exceed 50 percent using DFM methods. Also, there are usually corresponding reductions in standard cost, the number of required suppliers, inventory investment, and new product development time.

Ten Key Steps to Implement DFM

Although there are many sources of information describing DFM, Table 4.7 lists ten common steps that will help an organization implement and realize the benefits of DFM. The first step is simplification of a new product or service design through

Table 4.7 10 Key Steps to Implement DFM

1. Simplify a design through elimination of unnecessary components.
2. Use standardized materials, components, and procedures where possible.
3. Combine several functions into one component.
4. Eliminate of different materials, if possible.
5. Eliminate of screws, fasteners, adhesives, and secondary operations where practical.
6. Ensure components can be easily aligned to allow vertical assembly.
7. Ensure all assembly operations are visible and easy to perform.
8. Mistake-proof assembly operations to prevent misalignment and assembly errors.
9. Ensure products are easy to disassemble, service, maintain, and dispose of.
10. Ensure products are easy to test and analyze.

elimination of unnecessary components and their associated work tasks. There are many ways to accomplish this objective. These include the elimination of unnecessary product or service features, combining functions or components, and reducing the number of assembly and inspection operations. If several product functions can be combined into a fewer number of components, there will be less required assembly operations, resulting in reduced cycle time and cost as well as higher quality. The number of different materials should also be reduced whenever possible to allow aggregation of product functions. As an example, if several components used the same material, i.e., polymer (or plastic), then these components could be combined into just a single part. Because screws, fasteners, adhesives, and secondary operations increase cost and cycle time, they should be eliminated whenever possible. The product or service should also be designed for easy assembly. As an example, components should be aligned to allow vertical assembly by robots or machines. These types of operations reduce cycle time and cost. Standardized materials, components, and procedures should also be used whenever possible. As an example, standardization will allow multiple sourcing of components by purchasing. Standardized components and procedures also enable easier assembly of the product or deployment of the service, resulting in fewer mistakes. Product quality is also improved through DFM. Step 7 of Table 4.7 requires that all assembly operations be visible and easy to perform by workers or machines. As an example, imagine trying to assemble two components together but not being able to clearly see the assembly operation because it is hidden from view. Those assembly operations that remain after implementing Steps 1 through 8 should be mistake-proofed to prevent the occurrence of errors due to component misalignment. Products should also be easy to disassemble and serviced at customer locations or remotely until the end of their useful life. At the end of their useful like, their disposal should be inexpensive and safe. Finally, it is important to ensure that new products and services are easy to test and analyze, both during their assembly and at the customer's location.

Key Tasks of the Design Process

The process of designing products or services follows the 20 steps listed in Table 4.8. These clearly defined steps will bring a new product or service design through the five phases shown in Figure 4.1 and described in this section as the initial design concept, design creation and evaluation, developing prototypes of the final design, pilot and preproduction evaluations under limited operational conditions, and the launch of the new design, including its commercialization. In parallel, the production process is developed by operations using all available design data and information. The tools and methods necessary to design the corresponding process to produce the product will be discussed in Chapter 5.

Table 4.8 20 Key Design Activities

1. Marketing strategy/VOC	11. Prototype build
2. Product/process data	12. Engineering drawings and specifications
3. Product reliability studies	13. Equipment and tooling requirements with manufacturing
4. Design goals	14. Testing requirements
5. Preliminary BOM and process flowchart	15. Packaging specifications
6. Preliminary list of special characteristics	16. Process instructions
7. Design failure mode and effects analysis (DFMEA)	17. Measurements systems analysis
8. Design for manufacturability applications	18. Preliminary process capability study plan
9. Design verification	19. Production trial run with manufacturing
10. Design reviews	20. Customer production part approval

Concept Phase

In Chapter 3 we discussed the steps necessary to identify and translate the voice of the customer (VOC) into internal design specifications. This translation process began with identification of the VOC by market segment. Using various data collection tools and methods, the CE team organized the VOC into the major themes shown in Figure 3.10. A prioritized list of critical-to-quality characteristics (CTQs) is also created from this analysis by aggregating and quantifying the VOC themes. At the next lower level, CTQs are derived from the VOC gathering, aggregation, and analysis and prioritized using one of several methods. As an example, the CE team could use a weighting system in which each CTQ is ranked against several evaluation criteria. The CTQ that ranks highest relative to the evaluation criteria would have the highest ranking. The CE team can also use the paired comparison prioritization method. In the paired comparison method (PCM), CTQs are compared in pair-wise combinations as shown in Figure 4.3. The analytical hierarchy process (AHP), shown in Figure 4.4, is another effective analytical method that can help the CE team prioritize the CTQs for insertion into section A of the house-of-quality (HOQ) matrix shown in Figure 3.11.

CTQ	Reduce Cycle Time	Improve Reliability	Easy to Maintain	Easy Upgrade Installation	Normalized Rankings	Prioritized Rank	Original Paired Comparison Rank
Reduce Cycle Time	1.0	5.0	9.1	9.1	2.3	0.6	1
Improve Reliability	0.2	1.0	9.1	9.1	1.1	0.3	2
Easy to Maintain	0.1	0.1	1.0	0.2	0.1	0.0	4
Easy Upgrade Installation	0.1	0.2	5.0	1.0	0.4	0.1	3
Total	**1.4**	**6.3**	**24.2**	**19.4**	**4.0**	**1.0**	

(1) Same Importance
(5) More Important
(9) Much More Important

Figure 4.4   Analytical hierarchy process (AHP) method.

To demonstrate that these concepts can be integrated, Figure 4.3 shows a hypothetical analysis of paired CTQ comparisons for a software product. The CTQs are listed as reduce cycle time, improve reliability, easy to maintain, and easy upgrade installation. There are four CTQs listed in Figure 4.3. This results in a total of six pair-wise comparisons (4! divided by (4 − 2)! 2! = 6). This pair-wise analysis asks a simple question: Which of the two CTQs should be ranked more important than the other? The paired comparison analysis should be made relative to market segment to ensure the paired comparisons are consistent with the VOC at a market segment level. The paired comparison test is easy to use, but it has low resolution because there is no numerical scale. The relative success fraction of a particular CTQ, in the example, is calculated by dividing the adjusted ranking of each CTQ by the total adjusted ranking of 10. The analysis also shows that "reduce cycle time" is the highest-priority CTQ. This information would be inserted into the HOQ matrix shown in Figure 3.11 or Figure 4.10 in the "Important" column.

Figure 4.4 shows the same example, but presented as an AHP analysis. The AHP method was developed by Thomas Saaty. It uses a quantitative scale to compare CTQs and, as a result, has higher resolution than the paired comparison test. In Figure 4.4, the scale has been set as 1, 5, or 9. However, a higher-resolution scale, such as 1, 2, 3, 9, and 10, can also be used by the CE team. The AHP ranking comparisons are a little more complex than a paired comparison method. In the software example shown in Figure 4.4, each of the CTQs is ranked against the others using the numeric scale 1, 5, or 9. As an example, "reduce cycle time" has a ranking of 5 versus "improve reliability." In other words, "reduce cycle time" is more important than "improve reliability." Similarly, "improve reliability" is much more important than "easy to maintain." In other words, it is ranked as a 9 against "easy to maintain." The AHP method is very useful in practice, and the calculations can be made by computer.

Design Phase

After the CE team has ranked the CTQs, they evaluate current subsystems that impact positively or negatively on the CTQs. These subsystems usually represent product or service designs currently offered to customers. In these situations, the new product or service is usually a moderate improvement to the current design. Alternatively, the new product or service might be a completely new design. If the new design is similar to current ones, existing subsystems are reviewed for their ability to satisfy immediate customer CTQ requirements. However, performance gaps will require that subsystems be modified to improve the current design. On the other hand, completely new products or services will rely instead on the application of basic technological principles to create new features and functions. In this design work, the CE team gathers all relevant data describing the new product and its associated process design. This information includes current performance specifications and data related to the product or service's fit, form, and function, and the ability of operations to produce the design day in and day out. In other words, the CE team requires operational data documenting the ability of the current process to consistently produce the design relative to customer requirements. Process capability information is collected and analyzed by Six Sigma "belts" and other quality professionals. Additional data required by the CE team includes engineering drawings, performance testing, if available, and information related to customer usage in the field. This last information includes ease of installation, ease of maintenance, the serviceability of the product, and how easy it is to dispose of or recycle the product or service. In other words, important characteristics of the current design are evaluated by the CE team prior to determining where the design changes need to be made or systems created to satisfy the VOC.

Design goals are determined by the VOC as well as the technological position of an industry (state of the art). However, some organizations are able to produce more efficient designs than others. An example was given in Chapter 2 in the section entitled "Deploying Design Excellence," in which each of the three manufacturers of the direct current (DC) motors had slightly different product designs, but different quality and cost positions. The Japanese had the simplest and most competitive design. These types of examples consistently show that organizations should use the tools and methods described in this chapter to design their products and services. In other words, my position is that global competitive advantages in many ways are no accident, and organizations have much more control over their relative competitive position than they may believe is possible. Setting correct design goals and objectives is the most important task of design engineering in the sense that all subsequent activities of the product life cycle are impacted by a product's bill of material (BOM) structure, required testing, and production. These all depend on the final product or service design. An organization must get its new products and service designs right the first time. But how can an organization do this? It is important to ensure that the right questions are asked at the start of the design process. As mentioned in Chapter 3, the best place to start the design process is by understanding the VOC. The first step is to bring together a cross-functional team having a clear agenda and proper facilitation to ensure design solutions are not focused in the wrong direction. Brainstorming ways to initiate the project is usually very useful at this point. There are also different levels of brainstorming, ranging from simple idea generation to the use of very structured checklists, such as those used in *The Theory of Inventive Problem Solving (TRIZ)*.

TRIZ will be discussed in more detail because of its direct connection to improving product and service designs. TRIZ is an acronym that translates from Russian as the theory of inventive problem solving. This methodology was invented by Dr. Genrich Altshuller while in a Soviet Union prison camp confined as a political prisoner. During his imprisonment, he analyzed the Soviet Union's patent literature, looking for common themes regarding how products were invented across diverse industries and applications. His hypothesis was that analogous problems across diverse industries had similar solutions that could be reapplied to different problems. In fact, he found that only a small fraction of inventions actually required completely new technology. As he reviewed the patent literature he found that the majority of problems had been solved more than once, but in different industries. In recent years, the TRIZ methodology has been formulated as the four steps of identify the problem, formulate the problem, search for a previously solved problem, and look for analogous solutions to the current problem. Altshuller and his consultants found 39 engineering parameters that can be used to search for previously solved problems. They also found 40 inventive principles to aid in identification of an analogous solution. These are always under active investigation by TRIZ consultants. There are many common examples of where TRIZ has been successfully applied in practice, with the predominance of applications in the design of products and services. Table 4.9 shows the TRIZ methodology applied to brainstorm ways to reduce the cycle time of a product across a global supply chain. The product under analysis was a heavy industrial component manufactured in China and used in the United States. This product had a very long lead time between time to order and delivery, which resulted in excessive inventory investment across the organization's global supply chain. Table 4.9 shows that TRIZ offers several ways to look at the high investment problem that may lead to alternative solutions, which range from not manufacturing the product to manufacturing it at other locations or manufacturing some components in one place and the other components at other locations. The important point is not that all the solutions listed in Table 4.9 are valid, but that many alternative solutions were created using the TRIZ methodology. We will

Table 4.9 TRIZ Applied to Cycle Time Reduction

TRIZ Principle	*Possible Solution*
Segmentation (1)	Divide into different product centers; make some things 100% in different counties.
Take out (2)	Lean manufacturing; eliminate steps and operations in the process.
Local quality (3)	Position casting manufacturing close to customers.
Merging (5)	Bring things together; manufacture product closer to final assembly.
Universality (6)	Design product to perform multiple functions; generic design.
Preliminary action (10)	Complete as many operations in advance as possible.
Beforehand cushioning (11)	Ensure supplier quality and systems are very good to avoid waste.
The other way around (13)	Bring final assembly to China; analyze worst-case supply chain.
Spheroidality/ curvature (14)	Have someone else make the castings; get out of the way.
Partial actions (16)	Complete product partially; move along faster; forget component cost savings to reduce inventory levels and increase cash flow and customer service, i.e., profitability.
Another dimension (17)	View your organization from the outside in using consultants; do not make product.
Periodic action (19)	Transfer batches rather than process batches; decrease lot size.
Feedback (23)	Change magnitude of feedback (metric); move from inventory metric to profitability or customer satisfaction.
Intermediary (24)	Merge on object temporarily with another, i.e., hire consultant to help.
Discarding (34)	Migrate advantages of Chinese manufacture to another location.
Multiple matching (37)	Ensure supplier teams are diverse to eliminate groupthink.
Boosted interactions (38)	Implement risk and revenue sharing partnerships.

not discuss the TRIZ method in more detail because such information is readily available elsewhere, and it is not the focus of this book. However, brainstorming methods such as TRIZ can be very useful to a CE team.

As a product or service is being designed to satisfy the VOC, a preliminary bill of material (BOM) is created for products, or a detailed process map and work instructions are created for service systems. The BOM shows the parts list of a product as well as the hierarchal position of every component and material of the product's design. Also, the process workflows necessary to produce the new product are designed using the product's BOM hierarchal structure. In parallel, process engineering creates the new process workflow and the equipment and other technology required to produce the new product according to the BOM and other information supplied by the design team. The development of process workflows and process engineering tools and methods will be discussed in Chapter 5. However, at this step in the design process, it is important to note that the design team needs to work closely with process engineering and production operations to ensure the design requirements, reflecting the VOC, are met when the product or service is commercialized. An important consideration, at this point of the project, includes the completeness of specifications relative to performance and dimensional tolerances. As an example, small tolerances require that high-precision equipment be used in production operations. This may necessitate the purchase of new equipment to prevent rework and scrap when a product is commercialized. In the case of service systems, the people must be highly trained, and their tools and equipment must be available to provide the required customer service.

Target Costing

A simple definition for standard cost is sales price of a product or service minus required profit margin. It makes no sense to design a product or service at a high standard cost and then simply add a desired profit margin only to see it fail to sell in the marketplace. Best-in-class organizations work through a series of data collection and analysis activities to ensure their products or service are strategically positioned relative to competitive offerings, have the features that customers need and value, and are priced correctly. This target costing concept is shown in Figure 4.5. Due to competitive pressures, it is important the design team set the maximum standard cost of the product or service. To do this, standard cost targets are allocated to every component of the BOM for products, or to the list of work tasks in a service system. The CE team then works through an evaluation of design alternatives and takes other actions to achieve cost targets. Cost targets should also be set relative to the total life cycle costs of a product or service. As part of these cost containment activities, the CE team coordinates the purchase and manufacture of materials and components across the supply chain using the BOM, technical specifications, and related information. Figure 4.6 shows how the house-of-quality (HOQ) matrix is

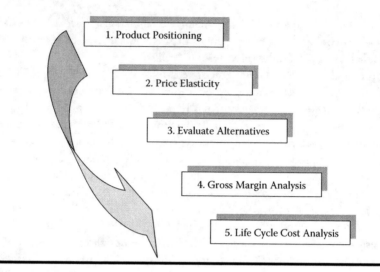

Figure 4.5 Target costing.

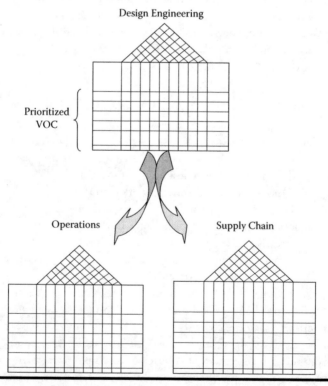

Figure 4.6 Translating VOC and design requirements through an organization.

extrapolated out through the supply chain. Each portion of the supply chain makes detailed plans relative to *what* is required versus *how* it will be done. At this point in a project, the BOM information has not been formally loaded into the materials requirements planning (MRPII) system, so the development process requires coordination by the CE team, which may be manual or electronic.

Prototype Phase

As the CE team works through various design iterations, portions of each design alternative will eventually be incorporated into the final design. In this process, subsystems are tested using specific analytical tools and methods, which are shown in Table 4.11 and will be discussed later in this chapter under the topic of design for Six Sigma (DFSS). The Pugh matrix shown in Figure 4.7 is a useful tool to evaluate several alternative designs during the prototyping phase relative to prioritized CTQs (prioritized using one of the methods previously discussed). The Pugh matrix was developed by Dr. Stuart Pugh to analyze various alternative systems.

CTQ	Importance Ranking (From AHP)	Alternative A	Alternative B	Alternative C (Baseline)	Alternative D	Alternative E
Reduce cycle Time	1	–	+	B	+	–
Improve Reliability	2	+	+	B	+	–
Easy to Maintain	4	–	–	B	+	+
Easy Upgrade Installation	3	+	S	B	–	+
Total +'s		2	2	0	3	2
Total –'s		2	1	0	1	2
Sum of +'s and –'s		0	1	0	2	0
Weighted Total +'s		5	3	0	7	7
Weighted Total –'s		–5	–4	0	–3	–3
Weighted Total		0	–1	0	4	4

Note: Alternatives D and E are superior to the current baseline design. But, the CE team can learn something from each of the alternatives which can be incorporated into the final design.

Figure 4.7   Prioritizing design alternatives using a Pugh matrix.

The usefulness of the Pugh matrix is derived from its analytical basis, which allows evaluation of one of more design alternatives against the current baseline concept. Using this analysis, the best design alternative becomes the CE team's new baseline concept. The best design alternative may also be augmented using characteristics and features derived from other design alternatives to develop a final optimized design. Figure 4.7 shows that each design alternative is evaluated against the prioritized CTQs. These CTQs were prioritized using methods such as the paired comparison method or AHP, as shown in Figure 4.3 and Figure 4.4. Using the prioritized CTQ listing, design alternatives are compared against the current baseline design CTQ by CTQ. The CE team uses a variety of data and information to facilitate the design evaluation process alternative by alternative using the Pugh matrix. This information includes design drawings, flowcharts, capability studies, failure mode and effects analyses, and many other useful sources of data. In Figure 4.7, if the alternative design is superior to the baseline design, relative to a particular CTQ, it receives a +. If it is inferior, it receives a −. If it is equivalent, then it receives an S for "similar." Additional + and − signs can also be used in the analysis. Eventually, these + and − signs are weighted using the prioritization rankings and a weighted total is calculated for each design alternative. The design alternative with the highest positive weighted total score is considered superior to the current baseline design. The goal is to incorporate the highest-ranking characteristics and features from the various alternative designs into the final design. As the final design emerges from this analysis, actual working models of the design are built and tested to ensure they meet the required performance specifications as translated from the VOC. Engineering drawings, the BOM, test and inspection procedures, tooling and other equipment, and packaging specifications are finalized at this point. However, there may still be minor changes to the new design after it is evaluated during the pilot phase.

Pilot Phase

Prior to the pilot phase, process engineering and production operations work concurrently through the CE team to develop process layouts, work and test procedures, measurement systems, and training procedures, and to purchase equipment. These activities will be discussed in more detail in our process engineering discussion in Chapter 5. However, at this point, it is important that the new design can be built according to all original assumptions regarding throughput rates, cost targets, quality levels, and the functional performance of the new product. A carefully controlled trial of the new product is made under actual production conditions at the location at which the new product will be built to verify that these original assumptions can be met in practice. Analysis of the results from this pilot study will help finalize the design requirements and confirm that the product can be built as planned by the CE team to satisfy the VOC requirements.

Launch Phase

In the product launch phase, a new product or service begins its commercialization. Most of the technical issues remaining with the new design will be quickly identified at this phase of the project. However, issues related to actual use by a customer, including usability, serviceability, maintainability, and reliability, will appear after extended usage by customers. However, if a CE team has effectively worked through the design process and incorporated all the information learned during the development of the new product or service, the number of required engineering changes will be small and the new product will be successfully commercialized.

How the Product Life Cycle Impacts the Design Process

In Figure 3.7, we showed the product life cycle from a marketing perspective relative to several forecasting methods used to estimate customer demand. This life cycle discussion, in the context of product or service design, covered the initial release of a new design and minor modifications to it over time based on observed deficiencies. Also, at the end of its maturity stage, significant modifications may be necessary to reposition a product or service based on evolving customer preferences. The impact of a life cycle on a product or service also varies by industry. As an example, in high-technology industries, such as electronics manufacturing, the first organization to market normally receives a majority of the market share throughout the life cycle of the product. This may force an organization to go to market even if its product designs are not optimum because the alternative is a low gross margin for the life of the product. However, organizations need to understand that competing in today's world requires they be first to market and their products and services meet customer expectations. Unfortunately, not all organizations use efficient design methods to commercialize or manage their products and services.

Understanding a product's life cycle is also critical to maintaining customer satisfaction and its target profit margin over time. As an example, it was stated in Chapter 3 that life cycle considerations should begin early during the market research phase of a new design, in which its features and functions are determined based on the VOC information. In this context, it is important that a CE team consider how a new design will be produced, inspected, tested, transported, serviced, maintained, and disposed of or reconditioned at the end of its useful life. Developing products based on these considerations will ensure that customer satisfaction and profit margins will be maintained by an organization over time.

Risk Assessment

In any project there are risks and issues that must be managed by a CE team. A risk is an uncertainty associated with one or more key project deliverables.

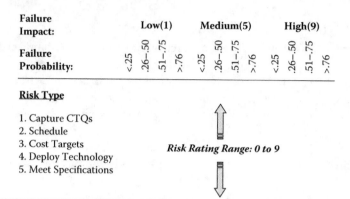

Failure Impact:	Low(1)				Medium(5)				High(9)			
Failure Probability:	<.25	.26–.50	.51–.75	>.76	<.25	.26–.50	.51–.75	>.76	<.25	.26–.50	.51–.75	>.76

Risk Type

1. Capture CTQs
2. Schedule
3. Cost Targets   *Risk Rating Range: 0 to 9*
4. Deploy Technology
5. Meet Specifications

Figure 4.8   Risk assessment.

Major risk factors include accurately capturing customer requirements, meeting the agreed upon project schedule, meeting cost targets, and successfully deploying the required technology related to the product, as well as the process required to produce it, and the functionality of the new product or process design relative to targeted specifications. In addition to risks, there are environmental factors that may impact a design project. These environmental factors include macroeconomic trends and competitive threats. Although the CE team cannot eliminate these environmental factors, contingency plans can be created to mitigate their impact on the project. Project risks are also characterized by an occurrence probability. Figure 4.8 shows how the CE team can manage these project risks by category. Each category of Figure 4.8 has an impact rating as well as a probability of occurrence. The risk scale ranges from 0 to 9. High risks must be managed by the CE team to ensure project success.

The first risk category, i.e., capture CTQs, relates to the fact the CE team must accurately capture the VOC information. Failure to do so will result in a situation in which the new product or service cannot be sold or must be retrofitted at great expense to make it saleable to customers. The tools and methods presented in Chapter 3 will help the CE team avoid this situation. Failure to accurately capture the VOC can result in poor estimation of demand, a failure to consider relevant competitive threats, and a failure to achieve cost, schedule, or quality targets. These situations may result in a diminished demand for a new product or service. However, this type of risk can be mitigated if the team has properly conducted its market research. Alternatively, in situations in which the new product is designed for a few major customers, it is important for the CE team to maintain close contact with these customers throughout the design process to ensure there will be a market for the new product or service. Relative to late entry into the market, it is important the CE team meet its schedule commitments because competitors may be working in parallel to develop similar products and services. As mentioned earlier, in some industries, organizations arriving to market late may experience a significant reduction in potential market share over the life of a new product or service. Finally, issues that impact performance or cost and delay commercialization of a new product or service may make it unattractive to customers when it finally reaches the market.

The second type of major project risk is a failure to achieve the originally agreed upon project schedule. Scheduling risk occurs for a variety of reasons, including unavailable labor, capital, technology, or information, or inefficient coordination of resources. Lack of useful and timely information is another cause of poor schedule attainment. Contingency plans must be made using a risk assessment model similar to the one shown in Figure 4.8. If the project is subject to schedule risk, then all the factors associated with the scheduling risk should be listed and countermeasures applied to reduce their occurrence probability. Scheduling risks must be managed by the CE team throughout a project because the types of risks may change as the team moves through the concept phase to the production phase of a project.

The third project risk category is related to cost issues that negatively impact a project. Scheduling issues will usually have a direct impact on project cost. These costs may vary from their budgeted amount for a variety of reasons, e.g., unexpected raw material cost increases or increased usage of materials and components. An additional reason for a higher than expected standard cost may include a failure to meet expected process yields, due to technical issues, requiring additional labor and materials. Scarce or unavailable materials, labor, or capital may also adversely impact project costs. However, to the extent that costs do not exceed budgeted amounts, a new product or service should be cost competitive based on the original project assumptions.

Technological risks are a fourth major project risk. This is especially true if a project's business justification and assumptions were based on the development and use of leading-edge or "to be developed" technology. In fact, the further an organization moves from its current technology basis toward unfamiliar technology, the greater the risk impact on a project. Organizations should try not to base commercial projects (as opposed to R&D projects) on the development of new technologies. These situations almost always result in a delayed schedule, higher project cost, and lower than expected product performance. Organizations should develop leading-edge technology in advance of a new product or service. However, if new technology must be developed in parallel, the CE team must create contingency plans to mitigate and manage the associated technological risks.

The fifth project risk is a failure to meet performance requirements. Because a new design concept has never been fully evaluated as an entire system, it is not surprising that once the entire system has been built, there may be incompatibilities and issues with performance of the system as a whole. This is especially true for radically new designs, as opposed to variations of current products or services. However, proper design practices as well as the use of optimization and other advanced tools and methods found in DFSS will provide the CE team with the best chance to optimize an entire system relative to all its required inputs and outputs prior to the production phase of the project and full-scale commercialization. Specific issues relative to performance risk may include an inability to scale up the new design concept from the laboratory to full-scale production, a failure to properly analyze a product's performance against customer requirements, inaccurate assumptions relative to the VOC prior to the project inception, or just poor design work during the development process. However, these issues can be prevented or managed by the CE team to minimize their impact on a project.

Design for Six Sigma (DFSS)

Most organizations that I have encountered do not focus on the VOC in a meaningful way. Instead, they discuss their current technical capabilities and develop specifications with customers from an internal perspective. This is not to say there is not an interaction with external customers, but only that customer needs and values are not methodically studied and analyzed using the tools and methods discussed in Chapters 3 and 4. In most organizations, the focus is more on the voice of the business (VOB) than the VOC. In a traditional design approach, a product or service is built component by component in a way in which the higher-level system becomes suboptimized from cost, performance, and time-to-delivery perspectives. In contrast, the Design for Six Sigma (DFSS) approach to product and service design considers the overall product or service system. In particular, models are built to quantify relationships between system outputs (Y's) and their inputs (X's). The inputs impact the outputs by changing their average level and their variation around the average. In DFSS, the interrelationships between the outputs and inputs are also validated using advanced statistical methods. There is also a heavy emphasis on getting the VOC right at the beginning of the design process, and then developing a reliable product or process design to meet the VOC requirements.

The DFSS methodology is characterized by five integrated phases, with the deliverables of each phase shown in Table 4.10. In addition to the major deliverables of each DFSS phase, Table 4.11 lists the key tools and methods used to obtain each deliverable. The first phase is identification of the customer requirements using the VOC. The second phase requires translating the VOC requirements into internal specifications and developing design alternatives. In the third DFSS phase, alternative design concepts are coalesced into a final design that is optimized using statistical models. Optimization ensures that reliability, serviceability, and other required performance of the new product or service design will be met in practice. The fourth DFSS phase requires validation of a new product or service design to meet VOC requirements, under expected environmental conditions and customer usage, at a Six Sigma capability level. In DFSS, the goal is a maximum failure rate for each specification of 2 parts per billion (on a short-term laboratory basis) or 3.4 parts per million over an extended time. This concept is discussed in detail in

Table 4.10   Design for Six Sigma (DFSS) Phases

Identify	a) Identify customer needs, expectations, and requirements (CTQs) using marketing research, QFD, and related tools. b) Establish metrics for CTQs. c) Establish acceptable performance levels and operating windows for each output.
Design	a) Evaluate and translate CTQs into functional specifications. b) Evaluate and select concept designs with respect to design specifications and targets using FMEA, alternative ranking methods, focus groups, and QFD.
Optimize	a) Select important design concepts for optimization using experimental design methods, reliability analysis, simulation, tolerance design, and related optimization tools.
Validate	a) Pilot/prototype according to design specifications. b) Verify that pilots/prototypes match predictions; mistake-proof the process and establish the process control plan for CTQs using capability analysis, mistake-proofing, control plans, and statistical process control.
Incorporate	a) Verify manufacturability and customer requirements are met over time using design reviews and metric scorecards.

Chapter 16 and is shown in Table 16.12. The fifth DFSS phase is incorporation of all lessons learned by the concurrent design team during the development process. We will now discuss each of the five DFSS phases in detail.

Overview of the Five DFSS Phases

In the identification phase, critical customer needs and requirements are determined using market research tools and methods as well as quality function deployment (QFD). These concepts were discussed in Chapter 3. At the end of the identification phase, the VOC requirements should be finalized into internal specifications. This is a critical step of the DFSS process because an organization can obtain a competitive advantage by developing close relationships with its customers. This enables them to create a design that will satisfy customer needs and value at a competitive standard cost. At the end of the identification phase, the project team develops acceptable performance levels for the design's features that are represented as CTQs, and at lower levels by specific Y's and specifications. In the design phase, VOC information will be used to translate customer requirements into specific inputs of

Table 4.11   Design for Six Sigma (DFSS) Tools and Methods

Identify	Market/customer research
	QFD
	CTQ flow-down
Design	Brainstorming, etc.
	QFD
	Robust design
	Monte Carlo simulation
	DFMEA
	Reliability modeling
	Design for manufacturing (DFM)
Optimize	Design of experiments
	Transfer function, $Y = f(X)$
	Design/process simulation tools
	Tolerance design
Validate	Process capability modeling
	Experimental designs (DOE)
	Reliability testing
	Mistake-proofing
	Statistical analysis
	Preliminary quality control plan
	Updated DFSS scorecard
Incorporate	Lessons learned, project transition, and leveraging

the design process (i.e., Y's) and to develop several alternative design concepts and prototypes. In the optimize phase, subsystems of the parent design are optimized relative to expected environmental conditions and customer usage using experimental design methods. Also, the process capability of the new product or service design is established based on the original customer VOC. In the validate phase, the CE team builds prototypes of the final design and moves to preproduction trials under actual production conditions. These activities are used to ensure a new product or service can be produced at high quality levels, i.e., Six Sigma capability under actual production conditions. A preliminary quality control plan is also created in the validate phase to ensure a product or service is produced according to all customer requirements. At the end of these activities, the CE team integrates the lessons learned from the project for use in future design projects. We will discuss the DFSS phases in more detail.

Identify

In the identify phase of DFSS, customer needs, expectations, and requirements (CTQs) are quantified. This information is used to establish internal design specifications as well as acceptable performance levels for every specification. Key tools used in the identify phase include market research, QFD, CTQ flow-downs, and DFSS scorecards. A CTQ flow-down is a method that successively de-layers high-level systems into lower-level ones. Also, DFSS scorecards are used to characterize every component and operation necessary to build a product or service relative to its capability to meet specifications. DFSS scorecards will be discussed in the validate phase section of this chapter. A DFSS scorecard is shown in Figure 4.13. The calculation of specific capability metrics will be discussed in Chapter 16. However, at a high level, capability is a measure of how well a product or service meets customer requirements in the form of specifications. Capability is calculated by comparing the VOC to the VOB.

Design

The subject of this chapter has been the design of products and services. The design phase of DFSS begins with the evaluation and translation of the VOC into CTQs and functional specifications. Using this information, the CE team evaluates and selects design alternatives with respect to how well they meet specifications using a variety of analytical tools and methods. However, to the extent that subsystems exist and provide the required functions and features necessary to satisfy the VOC, they should be incorporated into the new design and not recreated. This will enable a CE team to focus on performance gaps needing subsystem modifications or creation of entirely new subsystems to provide required customer functions and features. In this design process, several design alternatives are often created by the CE team. Eventually, design alternatives may be combined into the final design using a Pugh matrix.

These tools and methods include brainstorming, QFD, robust experimental design evaluations, Monte Carlo simulation to determine optimum tolerances for the input variables, failure-mode-and-effects-analysis (FMEA) to analyze how a design might fail and the causes of failure, reliability analysis to predict the useful life of the product or service in the field under actual usage, and design for manufacturing (DFM). DFM tools, methods, and concepts help to integrate and focus design activities.

Design Failure-Mode-and-Effect-Analysis

Design failure-mode-and-effect-analysis (DFMEA) is used to analyze the ways, i.e., modes, in which a design could fail to meet customer requirements. Countermeasures are developed to prevent or manage identified subsystem failures. Figure 4.9 shows a generic DFMEA, and Table 4.12 and Table 4.13 list important attributes of this DFMEA form. Organizations may also modify the basic DFMEA form relative

Process or Product Name:							Prepared by:		
Responsible:							Date (Orig) ___(Rev) ___		

Process Step/Part Number	Potential Failure Mode	Potential Failure Effects	S E V	Potential Causes	O C C	Current Controls	D E T	R P N

Figure 4.9 Design failure mode and effects analysis (DFMEA).

Table 4.12 FMEA Definitions

Failure mode	Description of a nonconformance or failure for a system
Failure effect	Effect of a particular failure mode on the customer
Severity	Assessment of the seriousness of the failure effect on the customer using a scale between 1 and 10
Failure cause	Describes how the failure mode could have occurred
Occurrence probability	An assessment of the frequency with which the failure cause occurs using a scale between 1 and 10
Detection probability	An assessment of the likelihood (or probability) that your current controls will detect the failure mode using a scale between 1 and 10
Risk priority number (RPN)	RPN = (severity) × (occurrence) × (detection); used to prioritize recommended actions; special consideration should be given to high severity ratings, even if occurrence and detection ratings are low

to the definitions of its various rating scales. The failure mode is a description of a nonconformance or failure of a subsystem. A failure effect is the impact on the customer from the failure mode. The severity is an assessment of the seriousness of the failure effect on the customer. Severity is measured using a scale ranging between 1 and 10; 1 signifies a minor impact on the external customer, whereas a 10 represents a very severe impact on the external customer. The failure cause describes how the

Table 4.13   20 Key Steps to Build an FMEA

1. Assign an FMEA number.
2. Assign a title to your FMEA.
3. Department and person responsible for the FMEA.
4. Customer and product name.
5. Assign FMEA start date.
6. Assign current date.
7. List core team members.
8. List design systems based on hierarchy.
9. List potential failure modes.
10. List potential failure effects.
11. Assign severity to each effect.
12. List potential failure causes.
13. Assign occurrence probability to each cause.
14. List current controls for causes.
15. Assign detection probability to causes.
16. Calculate the risk priority number (RPN).
17. List preventive or corrective actions.
18. Assign responsibility for preventive or corrective actions.
19. Record preventive and corrective actions by date.
20. Recalculate RPN and reprioritize RPNs.

failure mode could have occurred. The occurrence probability is an assessment of the frequency with which the failure cause occurs, using a scale between 1 and 10; 1 represents an infrequent occurrence, whereas 10 represents a frequent occurrence. The current controls relate to the systems in place to prevent the failure from occurring or reaching an external customer. The detection probability is an assessment of the probability that current controls will detect the failure mode using a scale between 1 and 10. In this scale, a 1 means the current controls are effective and a 10 implies they are not very effective in detecting a failure mode. The risk priority number (RPN) is calculated as the multiplicand RPN = (severity) × (occurrence) × (detection). The RPN ranges between 1 (minor) and 1,000 (major) and is used to prioritize recommended countermeasures for each of the failure modes. Special consideration should also be given to high severity ratings, even if occurrence and detection ratings are low.

Reliability Methods

Reliability analysis is a broad field of analysis in which a new product or service design is evaluated under expected operating conditions and accelerated testing. The resultant data is analyzed using specialized statistical methods to determine the probability of failure modes over time relative to environmental and other external conditions that may negatively impact the useful life of the new product or service. Table 4.14 lists ten key methods used to increase the reliability of a product or service. These include the development of sample size plans to determine the number of test units required to calculate reliability percentages for units under test with statistical confidence. A second method is development of specification demonstration plans to verify a maximum number of failures in a predetermined time duration. This information is used to create accelerated life test plans, developed to calculate the number of test units to be allocated to each experimental condition of the experimental design. Accelerated testing allows a product or service to be highly stressed for short periods to predict its performance at lower stress levels for longer periods. An example would be to heat a component at 100°C for 24 hours and use the test results to correlate the failures rates at 50°C for 12 months. A service example would be to use queuing models to analyze high demand on a service system and its impact on customer service levels and system cost. Queuing models will be discussed in Chapter 5. Parametric analysis of repairable systems is used to estimate the mean number of expected repairs to a system over time for units under test by assuming a specific probability distribution. On the other hand, nonparametric analysis of a repairable system is used to estimate the mean number of repairs to a system over time for units under test, but without assuming a specific probability distribution. Distribution assumptions are important in building accelerated testing models of time to failure versus several independent variables. The accelerated testing models are usually based on a particular model structure, such as linear or exponential relationships between time to failure and independent or accelerating variables. However, regression-based testing can be used to build reliability models to predict time to failure versus several independent variables, as well as covariates, nested variables, and variable interactions. Probit analysis is a method used to estimate survival probabilities of test units exposed to an experimental stress condition. Distribution analysis is used to determine the time-to-failure probabilities for particular design characteristics exposed to an experimental stress condition. Finally, all information gathered during reliability testing and analyses is incorporated into the DFMEA. After several design alternatives have been evaluated

Table 4.14   10 Key Methods to Increase Product Reliability

1. Develop sample size plans to determine the number of test units required to calculate reliability percentages for units under test with statistical confidence.
2. Develop specification demonstration plans to verify the maximum number of failures that will occur in a predetermined time duration.
3. Determine accelerated life test plans to calculate the number of test units to be allocated to each experimental condition of the experimental design.
4. Use parametric analysis of repairable systems to estimate the mean number of repairs over time for units under test and assuming a specific distribution.
5. Use nonparametric analysis of a repairable system to estimate the mean number of repairs over time for units under test and without assuming specific distribution.
6. Use accelerated life testing to build models of failure time versus several independent variables.
7. Use regression-based testing to build models to predict time to failure versus several independent variables, including covariates, nested terms, and interactions.
8. Use probit analysis to estimate survival probabilities of test units exposed to an experimental stress condition.
9. Use distribution analysis to determine the time-to-failure probabilities for a particular design characteristic exposed to an experimental condition.
10. Integrate information gained from reliability analyses into the design FMEA.

through reliability testing and a finalized version is selected by the CE team, the project moves into the optimize phase.

Optimize

In the optimize phase, important characteristics of one or several alternative designs are incorporated into the final and optimized design using several key tools and methods. These tools and methods include design and process simulation to build and analyze the transfer function $Y = f(x)$, Monte Carlo simulation, tolerance design, computer-aided design (CAD), and finite element analysis (FEA), which are used to develop tolerances for the important variables, i.e., key process input variables (KPIVs), that impact the Y's, or key process output variables (KPOVs). Monte

Carlo simulation will be discussed later in Chapter 5 relative to process design. Experimental design methodology will be discussed in Chapter 16 in the context of Six Sigma quality improvement tools, methods, and concepts based on the methodology called define, measure, analyze, improve, and control (DMAIC).

Building Transfer Functions to Understand Y = f(x)

Figure 4.10 shows how the house-of-quality (HOQ) concept is used to translate CTQs into Y's and ultimately into the KPIVs that control the variation of the KPOVs, or Y's. In the optimize phase, the CE team builds test plans to vary the levels of the KPIVs and evaluate their combined impact on various KPOVs of subsystems. Statistical models are constructed for each KPOV based on the levels of its KPIVs and their impact on the KPOV. Also, some KPIVs may impact more than

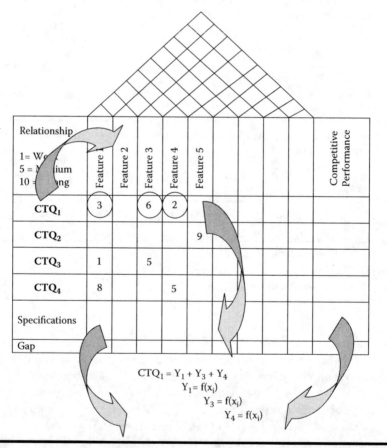

Figure 4.10 Building a transfer function Y = f(X) using experimental designs.

one KPOV, which requires the use of algorithms to simultaneously set the levels of all KPIVs to optimize several KPOVs. The underlying statistical models are regression based, hence the relationship Y = f(x). Multiple linear regression methods will be discussed in Chapter 8.

Statistical Tolerance of the X's

Once the transfer function, Y = f(x), has been established, the KPIVs can be set at levels that will ensure the Y, or KPOV, is at its optimum level. This concept is shown in Figure 4.11. Statistical tolerance refers to a methodology that specifies the range over which a KPIV can vary, but still ensures Y is at an optimized level. Optimized implies the KPOV is on target with minimum variation. A KPOV must exhibit a level of variation small enough such that when a KPIV changes its level, the impact on the KPOV, or Y, is at a Six Sigma performance level relative to the customer specification. Although capability analysis and concepts will be discussed in more detail in Chapter 16, at a high level, Six Sigma performance means there are six standard deviations of the distribution of the KPIV that can be fit within the customer tolerance on both sides of the target value of the Y. In other words, there are 12 standard deviations that can be fit within the tolerance. Complicating the tolerance analysis is the fact that measurement error adds to the

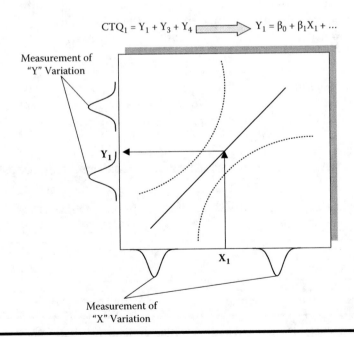

$$CTQ_1 = Y_1 + Y_3 + Y_4 \quad\Longrightarrow\quad Y_1 = \beta_0 + \beta_1 X_1 + \cdots$$

Measurement of "Y" Variation

Y_1

X_1

Measurement of "X" Variation

Figure 4.11   Using design and process simulation tools to tolerance the design.

variation of the KPOVs or KPIVs. In statistical tolerancing, Monte Carlo simulation is used to dynamically change the levels of KPIVs and evaluate their combined impact on the KPOV using capability metrics. Capability metrics will be discussed in Chapter 16.

Validate

In the validation phase, prototypes are carefully evaluated under controlled production conditions. These evaluations are called pilots. Pilot activities are necessary to ensure prototypes of the new design match predicted performance targets. The actual capability of a production process to produce a new product or service is measured at this point in the project. Based on the pilot results, specifications on the KPOVs (Y's) and KPIVs (X's) are finalized by the CE team. Finalization of the measurement methodology and testing requirements is also completed during the validation phase. The DFMEA is updated with the pilot evaluations and is used to implement mistake-proofing strategies and countermeasures to control the KPIVs. This information is incorporated into the preliminary quality control plan shown in Figure 4.12 and into the design and its process based on FMEA analysis. Quality assurance will also include the process FMEA in the quality control plan and finalize the plan to ensure the VOC requirements have been met by the organization. The actual format of the quality control plan varies by industry and organization. However, Figure 4.12 captures the important information.

The balance of the information contained within the quality control plan will discussed in Chapter 16. An integral part of the quality control plan is the DFSS scorecard shown in Figure 4.13. Figure 4.13 represents a final summarization of several lower levels in which product performance by customer requirement, process performance by operation within each process workflow, raw material performance, and purchased part performance are rated using quality metrics. These quality metrics will be discussed in Chapter 16 and include parts per million (PPM),

Product Number: Design Engineer:		Customer: Facility:					Date: Revision:		
Sub-System	Requirements		Specifications		Measurement Method	Testing Procedure	Special Characteristics	FMEA Reference
	Key Outputs (Y)	Inputs(X)	Lower	Upper				

Figure 4.12   Required documentation for the preliminary quality control plan.

Product Scorecard Analysis					
Product Number: Design Engineer: Customer:				Date:	Revision:
Facility: **Performance Category**	Parts-Per-Million (PPM)	Opportunity Count	Defects-Per-Million Opportunities (DPMO)	Normalized Yield	Sigma Score (Zst)
1. Product Performance:					
2. Process Performance:					
3. Raw Material Performance:					
4. Purchased Parts Performance:					
Product Scorecard Summary:					

Figure 4.13   Developing the product design for Six Sigma (DFSS) score card.

opportunity counts, defect per million opportunities (DPMO), normalized yield, and the Six Sigma score, which is also called Z_{st}. At this point in our discussion, it is only important to know that capability metrics are directly correlated to a failure to meet specifications or defect percentages. DFSS scorecards can be modified to measure an entire supply chain.

Incorporate

In the incorporate phase, a CE team incorporates lessons learned from all design activities and uses this information to create design documentation that is communicated to the organization. This information includes detailed drawings of the product or process workflows, specifications, and tolerances of each KPOV, or Y; a list of important design features; and their testing and evaluation requirements. Integral to documentation and transitioning activities is transfer of design knowledge to the process owner and local work team. At this point in the project, final verification of a design is made to ensure it has achieved all cost and performance targets. The DFSS scorecards are also updated to reflect new information.

Design Standards for Global Competitiveness

An extremely important aspect of a new product or service design is ensuring it meets the design standards for the local market in which it will be sold. As a simple example, in Singapore and Britain the steering wheel of an automobile is located on the opposite side from automobiles driven in the United States, Canada, or Germany. This is an obvious example wherein a product must be customized for local customers. Unfortunately, not all customer requirements are as obvious. For this reason, it is critical that the CE team consist of representatives from the appropriate countries and regions in which the new product or service will be sold. But equally

Table 4.15 Design Standards to Increase Global Competitiveness

1. Correlated and adaptable to the local VOC
2. Easy to understand by user community
3. Enable global collaboration on design projects
4. Transferable from one system to another without a requalification
5. Modular design facilitated to enable higher-level system development and control
6. Movement facilitated between systems regardless of their configuration
7. Common interfaces supported to allow a system to interact with disparate and different systems
8. Systems able to be scaled to higher performance levels as technology evolves over time

important, the VOC must be gathered at a local level. In other words, products and services must be designed to ensure they will be purchased by local customers. To achieve this objective, at a minimum, adherence to local design standards is mandatory, but more is required to understand the VOC and satisfy customers. Table 4.15 lists basic attributes of global standards. Global standards should correlate to the local VOC and be adaptable. They should also be easy to understand by their user community and facilitate global collaboration on design projects. Other important characteristics of global design standards are that they are transferable from one system to another without a prequalification program of a product or service. Relative to the design of process workflows, their design should facilitate modularization to enable higher-level system development and control, but also allow local customization to meet customer requirements in niche market segments, i.e., mass customization of the new service offering. Process workflow design should also facilitate movement between locations across the world and different IT systems regardless of their configuration. Common interfaces should be supported to allow a process workflow to interact with disparate and different systems across a single organization or other organizations across the world. The design of process workflow systems should also enable simple scale-up to higher performance levels as technology evolves over time. To the extent an organization can meet or exceed these basic global standards in its product and service designs, its overall competitiveness will be increased across the world. In other words, an organization's competitiveness is directly related to its design competency. This is reflected in an ability to adapt to global standards, but provide products and services at a local level.

Impact of Mass Customization on Design

Having an ability to mass customize a product or service depends on its design and associated production process. Mass customization enables an organization to provide customers with unique styling and features that will meet the needs and value expectations of diverse customers. However, having an ability to mass customize products or services depends on an organization's underlying infrastructure. This infrastructure is related to product or service design commonality, which enables easy changeovers from one product or service to another based on dynamic changes in external customer demand. Having a common design platform allows an organization to continually produce the same product and apply customization toward the end of the product's build sequence. This capability enables an organization to maintain high quality levels and lower costs. However, external customers see their product or service as customized for their usage.

Table 4.16 lists ten key steps an organization can take to mass customize its products or services. Creating this list is easy, but creating common design and process workflows often takes many years of carefully planned capital investment. The first step to build mass customization capability is to analyze product profitability and volume to eliminate unprofitable and low-volume products. Reducing product proliferation is an excellent way to concentrate resources on profitable products and services. A second excellent way to reduce design complexity is to analyze the bill of material (BOM) and eliminate nonstandard materials, components, and processes. In parallel, those materials, components, and processes that are hazardous or require specialized training and maintenance should be candidates for elimination. Remaining components should be modularized and their functions combined into a single subsystem to eliminate components. It is also important to understand dynamic relationships among product materials, components, and subsystems to develop realistic tolerances to achieve quality levels. This reduces rework and production inefficiencies. Also, the design of components, subsystems, and higher-level assemblies should be based on machine and tooling capability and to reduce or eliminate job setups. These activities will enable mixed-model production scheduling and mass customization. Mixed-model scheduling systems will be discussed in Chapter 6, and an example is shown in Figure 6.9. Mass customization is also facilitated if an organization can outsource processes elsewhere at lower cost, lower cycle time, and higher quality. To ensure Steps 1 through 7 are implemented, activities should be integrated using concurrent engineering (CE) and design for manufacturing (DFM) methods. Additional strategies to facilitate mass customization are to postpone final product customization to the latest possible time and deploy a pull production system that is based on actual customer demand. Pull production systems will be discussed in Chapters 6 and 12, and an example is shown in Figure 12.6.

Table 4.16   10 Key Steps to Mass Customize Products

1. Analyze product profitability and volume and eliminate unprofitable and low-volume products.
2. Analyze the bill of material (BOM) and eliminate nonstandard materials, components, and processes.
3. Eliminate materials, components, and processes that are hazardous or require specialized training and maintenance.
4. Modularize and combine subsystem functions to eliminate components.
5. Understand the dynamic relationships between product materials, components, and subsystems to develop tolerances to achieve high capability levels.
6. Design components, subsystems, and products based on machine and tooling capability and to reduce or eliminate job setups.
7. Outsource all processes that are nonproprietary and can be done elsewhere at lower cost, lower cycle time, and higher quality.
8. Integrate concurrent engineering (CE) project management methods and design for manufacturing (DFM) methods throughout the product development process.
9. Postpone final product customization to latest possible assembly time and based on actual customer demand.
10. Deploy a pull production system based on actual customer demand.

Note: Step 6 is the most important attribute of mass customization because it enables mixed-model production scheduling (discussed in Chapter 6 and shown in Figure 6.9). The concept in step 10 will be discussed in Chapters 6 and 12 and shown in Figure 12.6.

Outsourcing Design Workflows

Table 4.17 list several reasons why it might be advantageous for an organization to outsource its design activities. Outsourcing may be advantageous if a design or its subsystems require design expertise that is outside the normal competence of an organization. In other situations, outsourcing may occur because of resource limitations that impact the design project. In these situations it is desirable to outsource design work that can easily be done outside an organization to free up internal resources to concentrate on core competencies. A third situation in which to outsource design activities may be when the design technology, including equipment and work procedures, is hazardous or the necessary equipment is not available internally to an organization. Outsourcing

Table 4.17   Reasons to Outsource Design Activities

1. Unfamiliar technologies obtained
2. Difficulties jeopardizing the project
3. Exceeding design capacity
4. Multidisciplinary requirements
5. Reduction in research costs
6. Joint ventures

may also occur due to joint ventures in which all parties agree to perform certain design functions for the other organizations within the joint venture.

Summary

The major concepts of this chapter are listed in Table 4.18. It is our opinion that applying these concepts will increase organizational efficiency. The first key concept is to use concurrent engineering (CE) principles to manage your design process. Second, design for manufacturing (DFM) principles should be applied to the design of products and services to reduce their complexity to lower cost and improve quality. Design for Six Sigma (DFSS) is also a very useful method to create new products

Table 4.18   Key Concepts to Understand Product or Service Design

1. Use concurrent engineering (CE) to manage your design process.
2. Use design for manufacturing (DFM) to design products and services that are easy to produce for customers.
3. Apply design for Six Sigma (DFSS) methods to minimize variation of products and services.
4. Effectively translate the VOC into design features.
5. Understand how design components interact to provide functions, dimensions, and other product features.
5. Design to global standards to expand marketing and sales opportunities.
6. Apply mass customization tools, methods, and concepts to reduce the order-to-deliver cycle time.
7. Outsource work that can be done more efficiently elsewhere.

and services, and ensures they are optimized and validated so that the VOC is effectively translated into the new design. Also, it is useful to understand how design components interact with each other to provide functions, dimensions, and other product features according to VOC requirements. It is important to design to global standards, but meet local needs and requirements, to globally expand marketing and sales opportunities in culturally diverse markets. The application of mass customization tools, methods, and concepts will make an organization more responsive to diverse customer needs and values. An organization will also become more productive. Finally, design work should be outsourced to locations where incremental value is added and cost, cycle time, and risk are minimized for an organization.

Suggested Reading

David M. Anderson. (2004). *Build-to-Order and Mass Customization*. CIM Press.

Geoffrey Boothroyd and Peter Dewhurst. (2001). *Product Design for Manufacture and Assembly*, revised and expanded. Marcel Dekker, New York.

Biren Prasad. (1997). *Concurrent Engineering Fundamentals*, Vols. I and II. Prentice Hall, Englewood Cliffs, NJ.

Chapter 5

Using Lean Methods to Design for Process Excellence

Competitive solution 5: Ensure process workflows are easily reconfigurable to match inevitable changes in customer needs and values.

Overview

The design of process workflows to build products or deliver services should be based on an organization's marketing strategy. In other words, an organization should design its products and services to meet customer needs and value expectations. However, there are many examples of products and services that have been very well designed from an internal viewpoint, but customers are disappointed when they purchase and use them. In these situations, there may be a feeling that something is missing or should not be present. Examples include higher than expected purchase price, expected features are not present, or there are process breakdowns related to quality and delivery. These situations are unnecessary if an organization applies the concepts discussed in Chapters 1 to 4. In summary, a process workflow design should follow the design of a product or service because it is based on the voice of the customer (VOC) and marketing strategy. This simple concept will ensure that the design of a process workflow is aligned with the VOC and also meets an organization's productivity goals.

Table 5.1 Competitive Metrics: Process Design

1. Throughput time of the workflow
2. Number of changes to final process design
3. Percentage of warranty, scrap failure, rework, or similar costs to standard cost based on process design issues
4. Actual standard cost versus target cost for the process
5. Process engineering costs as a percentage of total revenue
6. Process capability of new equipment

The goal of process workflow design is to create workflows that will dynamically meet external demand, within ranges of capacity and at service levels designed into the process, using a minimum amount of required resources. Some important metrics that enable an organization to measure and manage to this goal are listed in Table 5.1. Reducing the throughput rate or cycle time of a process workflow helps reduce its required resources because the work is migrated toward unit flow production. This will be the subject of Chapter 6. Also, the number of changes that are required to finalize a process workflow design is an indicator of how well the workflow was designed up front by the concurrent engineering (CE) team. The percentages of warranty, scrap, rework, and similar failure costs are also good indicators of how well a process workflow was designed. Failure costs impact direct labor and material usage and, as a result, the standard cost of a product or service. It is important that the new process workflow meet the original standard cost target set by the CE team. For this reason, failure costs must be prevented or minimized in the design of a process workflow. It is also important to measure process engineering costs as a percentage of total revenue. These costs include indirect labor as well as all cumulative project costs of the process engineering team. Finally, if process workflows have been designed properly, the measured process capability of new equipment used in a process should meet customer requirements.

The specific workflow system used by an organization will vary by industry, available technology, and an organization's internal work procedures and controls. Although the design of a product or service will have a major impact on the process workflow design, there are efficient ways to design workflows, which can significantly increase an organization's operational efficiency. However, the exact design of a process workflow depends on the specific products and services an organization produces and the industry. Table 5.2 lists ten major steps necessary to efficiently design process workflows in today's world. The first step coincides with a major theme of this book. This is to align the productive resources of an organization with the VOC based on strategic goals and objectives. In fact, this theme has been a major focus of Chapters 1 to 4. For this reason, it is critical that the VOC is

Table 5.2   10 Key Steps to Design Workflows

1. Ensure the VOC has been effectively and accurately translated into the process design.
2. Ensure the product is designed using best-in-class methods, including design for manufacturing (DFM) and design failure mode and effects analysis (DFMEA) methods.
3. Focus on the key outputs of the process related to utility and functionality.
4. Create the simplest possible process design, ensuring it has high process capability.
5. Create flexible and virtual transformation systems using best-in-class resources from across the world.
6. Ensure the work is organized so all the information necessary to perform it is localized at its source.
7. Ensure first-pass yields are high and the work is done only once, and a process failure mode and effects analysis (PFMEA) is created on the new process design.
8. Balance the system's throughput using the calculated takt time, and ensure the bottleneck and capacity constrained resources meet the takt time requirements.
9. Use visual controls in the process and across the supply chain to ensure everyone has viability to system status.
10. Continuously improve process performance using Lean, Six Sigma, and related process improvement methodologies.

accurately translated into the product or service design in the new process work-flow. This implies process engineering should have been an integral part of the CE team. Also, there is an implication that design engineers have followed best-in-class methods, such as design for Six Sigma (DFSS), through their CE project activities. In other words, they should have executed all design deliverables through the production and commercialization phases of the new product development process, which was shown in Figure 4.1.

An especially important part of the product or service design process is the use of design-for-manufacturing (DFM) tools, methods, and concepts. These were discussed in Chapter 4. DFM was shown to be a critical set of tools in creating easy-to-build, lower-cost, and higher-quality alternatives. Another important concept discussed in Chapter 4 was the use of design-failure-mode-and-effects-analysis (DFMEA). The DFMEA is important in translating the VOC into production operations because it provides process engineers with a clear line of sight to the important design characteristics of a new product or service, including current risks related to fit, form, and function. In addition, a DFMEA provides recommended countermeasures to prevent product or service failures. Process engineering uses the DFMEA and other design and process engineering documentation to design process workflows. Once all the necessary information has been made available to the process engineering group, they will create process workflows to produce a product or service to consistently meet customer requirements.

A process workflow should be designed so it can be deployed across an organization's global supply chain in a way to increase system flexibility and provide sufficient capacity to meet customer demand. In other words, a process workflow should be designed so its work can be performed anywhere in the world and at any time. Another important consideration in the design of a process workflow is that it should be organized in a way in which the information necessary to deploy the process workflow is readily available to those who will use it and at a high reliability and easy maintenance levels. It should also be easily transportable. This means work instructions, testing procedures, and other documentation necessary to perform the work must be translated into local languages and be culturally neutral. Additional considerations are that the documentation of the process workflow be visual and easy to understand without extensive training. Although more complex process workflows will have higher failure risks, these can be mitigated through careful planning by a CE team. In addition, risks will be higher when a new product or service design is pushing the limits of technology.

A process failure-mode-and-effects-analysis (PFMEA) is created by process engineering using the DFMEA. The PFMEA is critical in identifying potential failure points within a new process workflow or where modifications may be required to achieve standard costs and yields. Once a process workflow has been designed using Steps 1 through 7 of Table 5.2, its throughput should be balanced across its operations or workstations based on the required takt time of the system. Takt time is calculated by dividing the available production time by the required number of units that must be produced during the available production time. As an example, if there were 480 available minutes in a day and 60 required units, then the takt time would be calculated as 1 unit every 8 minutes. Bottleneck resources may adversely impact a system's takt time they are not available to produce at the required throughput rates. Although most balancing analyses focus within a single facility or takt time, balancing of workflows across operations or workstations can also be done across an entire system regardless of its location. In other words, if a process is geographically dispersed, then its takt time can be calculated through electronic means and controlled virtually across the system. In this scenario, process measurements and controls should be electronic and allow for easy interpretation of the system's dynamic status anywhere in the world at any time. This information should also be readily available to all supply-chain participants. Finally, it is important to deploy initiatives such as Lean, Six Sigma, Total Productive Maintenance (TPM),

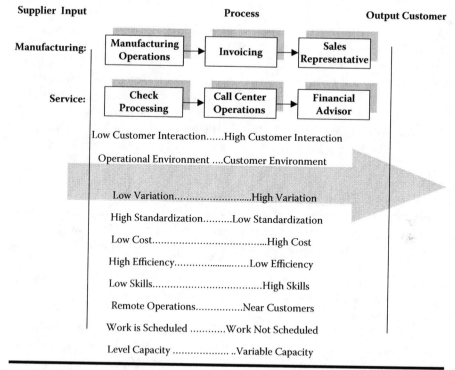

Supplier Input   Process   Output Customer

Manufacturing: Manufacturing Operations → Invoicing → Sales Representative

Service: Check Processing → Call Center Operations → Financial Advisor

Low Customer Interaction......High Customer Interaction

Operational Environment ....Customer Environment

Low Variation.........................High Variation

High Standardization..........Low Standardization

Low Cost..High Cost

High Efficiency............................Low Efficiency

Low Skills......................................High Skills

Remote Operations................Near Customers

Work is Scheduled ....Work Not Scheduled

Level Capacity ....Variable Capacity

Figure 5.1 Process design at the customer interface (old paradigm).

and related process methodologies to continually improve the newly designed process workflow over time.

A paradigm of process workflow design is that the complexity of a process is in many ways dictated by the degree of external customer interface. This paradigm is shown in Figure 5.1, in which a high degree of customer interface requires skills to meet operational requirements as measured by operational complexity at the organizational and customer interface. This implies that high-contact process workflows should be less efficient, less operationally flexible, and more costly than lower interfacial operations, i.e., backroom operations. Although this concept has been true over the past several decades, it has begun to change in some industries due to the convergence of several trends, including increases in technology, offshoring, changes in the global geopolitical environment, and increasing global competitiveness. These convergent trends have created a chronic situation of high labor capacity in areas such as software development, design engineering, call center management, and financial transaction processing. These trends have been enabled by increasingly highly skilled labor pools across the world in countries such as India and China. Also, offshoring has resulted in higher levels of product and process workflow standardization to facilitate the efficient deployment of work across the world. The resultant business benefits are seen as lower per unit transaction costs than previously attainable in locations where material and labor costs have been higher. These trends were summarized in Chapter 1. In fact, it has been found that with enabling technology such as business process management, the operational characteristics of many process workflows can be standardized to a degree unachievable several years ago. Chapter 15 discusses business process management (BPM) and workflow management (WM) from an information technology (IT) perspective. This discussion will include business process modeling and analysis (BPMA), business intelligence (BI), and business activity monitoring (BAM), as well as similar topics. These systems have directly impacted our ability to work anywhere in the world because many process workflows are now virtual.

In conjunction with enabling initiatives such as Lean and Six Sigma, process workflows should be analyzed relative to the VOC and in contrast to systems that exhibit isolated components; permeable systems should be created using business process management concepts to create virtual workflows that allow an entire supply chain to interact with its customers and their suppliers dynamically and virtually, but on a standardized basis. These permeable systems integrate backrooms with customer interfacing operations. As an example, an improvement project was initiated within a call center to reduce average handling time (AHT) of calls from customers. The process was characterized by a long AHT and a low customer service level. AHT is the time an agent spends on the phone providing information to a customer. The AHT also includes follow-up activities that are necessary to close out a customer inquiry. Service level is measured as the quality of the agent and customer interaction as specified by internal call center standards. It should be noted that AHT and service-level targets vary by customer market segment. In this example, the operational standards required that agents be assigned to different market segments based on their skill and experience levels. Also, in the more complicated market segments, customers were expected to ask detailed questions concerning their service package, so the allocated AHT was longer than that in other market segments. The project was focused on one market segment. The historical AHT, for this market segment, based on call center statistics, showed that the AHT was 120 seconds versus the 90-second target. It was found, through data collection and analysis, that the AHT sometimes exceeded 240 seconds for certain agents. It became evident that there were many process breakdowns after mapping and analyzing agent and customer interactions. This situation was caused by a lack of process workflow standardization, training, mistake-proofing, and other issues. As an example, it was found that agents did not have standardized scripts for the customer interaction. This forced them to answer the customer's questions in a nonstandardized manner. This practice increased the length and variation of the customer call. Also, agents did not have easy access to the information necessary to answer the customer questions. This resulted in additional lost time. A third reason for the high AHT was poor training of agents due to high employee turnover at the call center. The solutions included standardizing the process workflows for each market segment through implementation of 5-S (sorting, simplifying, sweeping, standardization, and sustaining) methods and mistake-proofing strategies. These and other Lean concepts will be discussed in Chapter 6. After completion of the project, the AHT was reduced by more than 20 percent. Of course, customer interactions that were more complicated due to their market segmentation would be expected to take longer on average than the simpler interactions, but standards could also be developed for these more complicated process workflows.

Sales force management is another example in which operational standardization could be deployed to increase operational efficiency as well as service quality. As an example, in conjunction with the establishment of sales force goals and objectives, analysis of the process workflows associated with the sales process often shows breakdowns related to time, quality, and cost. The root causes of these process breakdowns can be analyzed to increase the process throughput and quality. As an example, the efficiency of a sales force, as measured by the number and types of its sales activities, can be studied using Lean or Six Sigma DMAIC (define, measure, analyze, improve, and control) methods, root causes for poor performance identified and eliminated, and the process standardized to ensure that a sales organization increases its productivity. Alternatively, the sales process workflow could be designed optimally using a DFSS approach. These simple examples do not imply that operations at customer interfaces are not complicated or can be completely standardized, but only that much more can be done, given today's technology, to improve productivity and service quality and increase organizational efficiency.

Figure 5.2 shows that in today's world, a new paradigm is evolving, in which workflow standardization enabled through technology and process improvement initiatives creates lower process variation, increased flexibility for its users, and higher throughput rates. The resultant systems are characterized by higher operational efficiencies, higher quality, and lower per unit transaction costs. However, there may be limitations to the concept of workflow standardization. As an example, in some industries, a point of customer contact must be user-friendly, as opposed to an environment that is designed from a perspective of operational efficiency. However, depending on the specific market segment, there are increasing examples in which customers serve themselves or purchase in environments that have been designed from an operational efficiency perspective. Sam's Club, Costco, and BJ's are all examples in which customers shop in a warehouse environment. The process workflows, in these environments, are characterized as highly efficient, but still have a high degree of customer interaction. Also, an increasing number of transactions are initiated and completed by customers from their homes. An example is shopping online, in which supplier organizations have entirely automated their sales process workflows to improve operational efficiencies.

Complicating the design of a process workflow is that different products or services are associated with specific production delivery systems based on available technology and cost per unit considerations. As an example, Figure 5.3 shows four basic types of production or transformation systems. These include job shops as well as batch, assembly, and continuous operations. Figure 5.3 breaks down the four

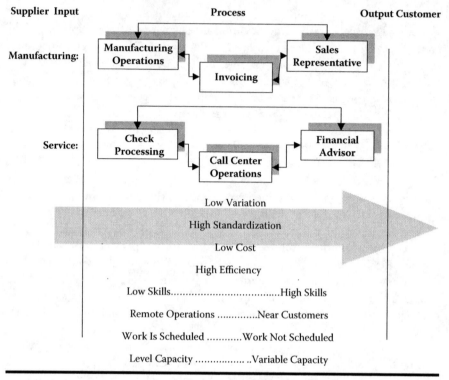

Figure 5.2   Process design at the customer interface (new paradigm).

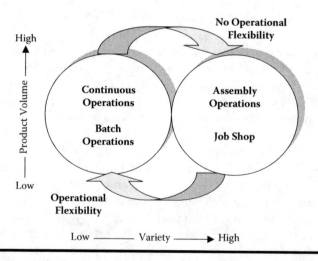

Figure 5.3   Operations strategy based on volume versus variety (old paradigm).

systems into the classic dimensions of volume and variety, as well as a third dimension related to the degree of operational flexibility associated with each system. A job shop-type transformation system is characterized by operations performed by dedicated machines and highly trained people. Products and services that move through a job shop require unique sequencing and combinations of work. This results in a diverse product mix. An example of a job shop would be visiting a hospital and then being moved from department to department based on the type of medical service you received from the system. Another example of a job shop would be the manufacture of a product that has been customized for a specific customer and as a result requires a separate machine setup every time the product is manufactured. Unless the underlying product or service design has been highly standardized using DFM and related methods, customized products or services must be produced using a process workflow based on a job shop design. In batch operations, products or services are produced periodically in batches having similar setups. Examples include short runs of similar products or services. Normally, batching of products or services can be done if they can be grouped into product families having similar design features. "Assembled" products or services are produced on a regular basis. Also, they usually use similar workflows and components, although there may be slight variations in workflows that result in the production of a variety of products or services. The manufacture of automobiles and computers is an example of assembly workflows. In continuous workflow environments, products or services are transformed on a continuous basis, i.e., a unit flow system. Products and services in these workflow systems have a high degree of design commonality up to a point within the process workflow, at which they may become slightly differentiated into different end items or products. Examples include petroleum refining and other types of process industries or high-volume manufacturing or service transaction systems, such as call centers having common process workflows, but slightly different service offerings based on customer segments.

The previous discussion presented the classic breakdown of process workflows based on their volume and variety. However, Figure 5.4 shows that many industries are expanding the technological barriers that have historically constrained their operational efficiency. These industries are migrating toward mass customization of their products or services. In Chapter 4 we discussed tools and methods that increase mass customization through deployment of enabling technologies as well as operational initiatives, such as design-for-manufacturing (DFM), Lean methods, and the other five major tools and methods shown in Figure 5.4. DFM and Lean methods simplify product and service designs to allow the cost-effective production of a variety of products. Greater process workflow and operational flexibility is also enabled by common product and process designs by reductions in the number of job setups. Value stream mapping, bottleneck management, mixed-model scheduling systems, transfer batching, and several other tools and methods that increase operational flexibility will be discussed in more detail in Chapter 6. Figure 5.4 shows that operational flexibility continues to expand to low-volume workflows.

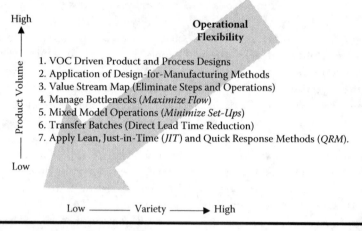

High

Product Volume

Low

Operational Flexibility

1. VOC Driven Product and Process Designs
2. Application of Design-for-Manufacturing Methods
3. Value Stream Map (Eliminate Steps and Operations)
4. Manage Bottlenecks (*Maximize Flow*)
5. Mixed Model Operations (*Minimize Set-Ups*)
6. Transfer Batches (Direct Lead Time Reduction)
7. Apply Lean, Just-in-Time (*JIT*) and Quick Response Methods (*QRM*).

Low ——— Variety ——→ High

Figure 5.4   Operations strategy based on volume versus variety (new paradigm).

Designing Process Workflows

What should a process workflow look like? It should reflect the product or service customers need and value. In manufacturing this concept is embedded within the bill of material (BOM) hierarchy as well as design documentation such as the DFMEA. A BOM is used as the basis on which to design a production system because it shows how a product is constructed at every level of its design. The BOM also shows hierarchal relationships between each level of the design. As a simple example, an automobile has four wheels and each tire has five lug nuts. The BOM associated with this product would include four wheels per automobile and five lug nuts per wheel, each related in a hierarchal manner. This concept also applies to service industries. As an example, McDonald's builds hamburgers. The BOM of a hamburger would specify one roll split in half, one hamburger patty and pickles, as well as other materials to be placed on the hamburger. The engineers designing McDonald's process would build its workflows to include this BOM information. Finally, in the case of financial service organizations, customers who purchase various mutual funds and other financial services would have a product and service portfolio (BOM) created for them to provide their financial advisor with information useful in managing their portfolios.

Table 5.3 lists 20 basic steps necessary to ensure a new product or service can be successfully produced to meet organizational goals and objectives. In addition to the information listed in Table 5.3, process engineers should obtain additional information from the CE team. Several of the 20 steps require documentation from the design phase of the project. This documentation includes a preliminary process flowchart based on the product's BOM, or the service package in the case of a new service. The preliminary process flow diagram is developed by process engineers

Table 5.3   20 Key Steps to Create New Product or Service Workflows

1. Preliminary process flowchart
2. Product assurance plan
3. Design failure-mode-and-effects-analysis (DFMEA)
4. Preliminary quality control plan
5. New equipment, tooling, and facilities requirements
6. Gauges/testing equipment requirements
7. Product/process quality systems review
8. Process flowchart
9. Floor plan layout
10. Process failure-mode-and-effects-analysis (PFMEA)
11. Prelaunch control plan
12. Process instructions
13. Measurements systems analysis
14. Production trial run
15. Preliminary process capability study
16. Production part approval
17. Production validation testing
18. Packaging evaluation
19. Production control plan
20. Quality planning sign-off and management support

who were CE team members. It should include spatial relationships as well as the key inputs and outputs of every operation. To ensure the new design has been fully evaluated relative to its failure points, a DFMEA and preliminary quality control plan should also be available to the process engineers. Process engineering also works with suppliers to design new equipment, tooling, and facilities (if necessary), as well as measurement and testing equipment. A PFMEA should also be created by process engineering as part of its prototyping. The PFMEA is comparable to the DFMEA except that process workflows are aligned with the critical design characteristics at each process step. The prelaunch control plan is built using information from the DFMEA and PFMEA to communicate to the organization important information that is necessary to produce the product or service. Integral to the final process workflow design is creation of work instructions, measurement systems, preliminary process capability studies, and related documentation. This information is used to plan the production trials, whose purpose is to collect samples or other information related to the performance of the new product or service for analysis by design and process engineering. These production validation activities are used to ensure that customer requirements are met by the new product or service under actual production conditions within the new process workflow. If production validation testing is successful, the new production system will be scaled up for full commercialization. In parallel, various components of the packaging design are evaluated to ensure they also meet customer requirements. Finally, the production control plan and all related documentation are updated across all organizational functions. The outputs from these integrated activities are a finalized process flowchart, work and inspection procedures, floor plans, and a project schedule to scale up and commercialize a new product or service. The project schedule includes the balance of the deliverables that are necessary to support the new process workflow.

Workflow Modeling

Developing a capability to model your process workflows allows experimentation of the workflow model offline as well as evaluation of numerous alternative workflow design concepts under varying modeling conditions. But, too often, organizations do not use workflow modeling methodology due to resource limitations, organizational barriers, or a lack of training. The ten key steps as shown in Table 5.4 will allow an organization to successfully implement workflow modeling. The first step is to bring together a group of people who have been trained to build and analyze workflow simulation models. This group should have a strong background in engineering or statistics and preferably at a graduate level. Training provided by workflow software vendors may also be very useful to the team. The second step is to develop a list of applications where the model's methodology can be realistically applied within your organization to create benefits such as reductions in time or cost, or simplification of the workflow design. To facilitate this work, several common modeling methodologies can be used by a team, depending on the type of workflow and questions that need to be answered by the simulation analysis. These methods include simulation, queuing analysis, linear programming, and customized models and algorithms that have been developed for very specific applications.

Once the team has determined the type of required modeling methodology, it can begin the process of researching off-the-shelf software and hardware. Modeling software has been developed for a wide range of applications based on differing workflow assumptions. These assumptions may range from simple to complex. The software that models simpler workflows can be generic and applied to diverse process

Table 5.4 10 Key Steps to Model Workflows

1. Organize a group of people who have been trained to build simulation models.
2. Develop a list of areas in which the model's methodology can be realistically focused.
3. Research and select off-the-shelf modeling software and associated hardware to match expected process applications, i.e., manufacturing, service systems, warehousing, logistics, etc.
4. Develop a library of applications that can be used as examples of applying the model within your process.
5. Develop the underlying model structure, including its goals and objectives, system constraints, and parameter settings.
6. Determine probability distributions and time span of the model.
7. Develop decision rules, including initial and final states of the model.
8. Develop plans to obtain the necessary process data to test the model's accuracy.
9. Analyze the output of the model using statistical tests to determine significance of the model's output.
10. Document and communicate the model's results, and develop plans to implement solutions as practical.

applications, but to the extent generic software models must be customized, they may require much effort to set up and analyze. It is always more efficient to purchase software that has been designed specifically for your workflow application because it will be easier to develop and interpret the model. Also, training will be easier using specialized software. As an example, there are many different types of off-the-shelf modeling software for workflows such as manufacturing processes, financial services, call centers, warehousing, inventory management, distribution networks, and many others. It makes sense to purchase the type of workflow software that is easily configurable to system elements that reflect your workflow rather than create workflow models from the ground up. As part of the process of researching software systems, a modeling team should develop a library of examples that show how their organization's workflows will be modeled. This will help the team communicate the advantages of workflow modeling to its organization.

After the modeling team has selected the necessary software and hardware, it begins to build workflow models. These activities include developing the underlying structure of the workflow model, including its goals and objectives, system constraints, and parameter settings. In addition, probability distributions are

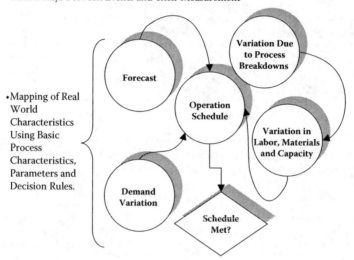

Real World Process Characteristics
- Unknown Process Performance and Inter-Relationships
- Dynamic and Complex Performance of System Components
- Ambiguity and Poor Resolution of Performance
- Time Delays Between Events and Their Measurement

- Mapping of Real World Characteristics Using Basic Process Characteristics, Parameters and Decision Rules.

Forecast

Variation Due to Process Breakdowns

Operation Schedule

Variation in Labor, Materials and Capacity

Demand Variation

Schedule Met?

Virtual World Process Characteristics
- Known Model Performance
- Specified inter-Relationships Between System Components
- Ability to Experiment and Resolve Inter-Relationships
- Ability to Compress Time Between Events

Figure 5.5 Transformation systems are complex and dynamic.

determined and integrated relative to the model's inputs and outputs for the various steps or operations within the workflow. The model's underlying structure and form, the time span of the analysis, and its decision rules are also developed to mirror the key characteristics of the real workflow, including its initial and final states. After the workflow model has been created, the team obtains the necessary process data to test the model's accuracy. In these evaluation activities, the performance characteristics of various workflows are evaluated under simulated conditions. Finally, the various analyses are documented in an appropriate format and communicated to the larger organization in the form of recommendations and practical solutions to improve process workflow efficiencies.

Figure 5.5 shows that workflow models are virtual representations and should correspond to actual characteristics of the process workflow. In real-world situations, the underlying interrelationships of the numerous workflows within a process may initially be unknown or poorly understood by an organization. In particular, the dynamic and complex performance characteristics of workflows cannot usually be fully understood in terms of their theoretical or actual performance without creating models. This is because operational relationships are complicated and not obvious to a casual observer of the process workflow. Also, actual systems are characterized by ambiguity and poor resolution of performance, as well as time delays between the occurrences of events and when events are actually measured by an observer. This makes it difficult to understand the relationships between causes and their effects in actual workflows. Thus, mapping of actual workflow characteristics, including their parameters and decision rules, into a virtual model of the workflow is very useful in improving operational performance. The advantages of using a workflow model are that its structure and the dynamic performance of its operational components are known by an analyst. Also, an ability to experiment on a system and compress the time between workflow events enables an analyst to evaluate numerous alternative workflow designs and identify an optimized version of the process workflow.

Simulation

Simulation methods are useful in modeling a diverse set of process applications. These include analyzing system capacity under various constraints, comparing system performance among several alternative workflow designs, and conducting sensitivity analyses to determine the impact on a system's outputs relative to variations of one or more key process input variables. The major advantage of using a simulation model is that it can be designed in a flexible manner to model a workflow, and its event probabilities can be easily defined by their underlying probability distributions. On the other hand, if your model is goal oriented, such as maximization or minimization of an objective function, and subject to clearly defined and deterministic constraints, then linear programming models might be more useful in modeling a workflow. Queuing models provide additional tools and methods to model process workflows, but the process workflow must fit predefined criteria. We will discuss the application of linear programming and queuing models to workflow analysis later in this chapter.

The first step in creating a simulation model requires identifying the model's goals and objectives as well as its structure and constraints. Specifically, the team should ask: Why is the simulation model being created, and what are the expectations of the analysis by the process owner of the workflow? Other relevant considerations may include the simulation project's budget and schedule. It should be noted that developing simulation models usually takes longer than expected because the model must be modified in an iterative manner to ensure its performance corresponds with that of the actual workflow. The second step in developing a simulation model requires defining the scope of the project relative to the workflows modeled by the team. In other words, where does the model begin and end relative to the workflows under evaluation? The third important step is identifying the underlying functional relationships, i.e., $Y = f(X)$. These functional relationships are the basis

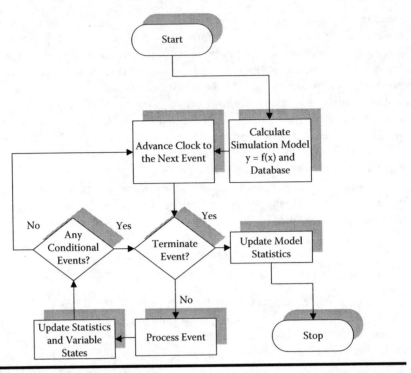

Figure 5.6 Simple simulation analysis.

of the simulation model. In particular, the relationships between Y (i.e., output of a model) and the X's (inputs) must be clearly defined in terms of their transfer functions as well as applicable decision rules and system constraints. The fourth step in the modeling process is collection of process data to aid in development and subsequent analysis of the model. Depending on the model's objectives, these sources of data include process maps, actual process data related to throughput rates, yields including rework and scrap, machine and direct labor cycle times, downtimes, lot sizes, inventory levels, floor layouts, and other relevant operational data. The specific data that is collected and analyzed by a team should correspond to the questions that must be answered by the simulation model.

Although there are many sophisticated off-the-shelf software packages that can be used to build and analyze simulation models, it will be useful to discuss a simple example to show the basic concepts of more complicated simulation models and software. Figure 5.6 shows the basic steps necessary to conduct a simulation analysis. The first step is defining the functional relationships between the model's outputs and inputs, represented by the expression Y = f(X). In Step 2, the system's clock is set to time t = 1, an event is simulated, and the model's statistics are updated by the software. If the model is not at its terminal time period, the clock is advanced to the next time period, t = 2, and the simulation cycle continues until the terminal

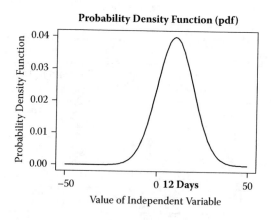

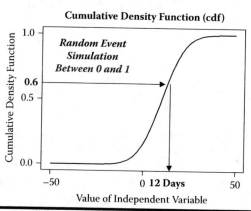

Figure 5.7   How simulation works.

time period has been reached. Statistics are collected based on the specific structure and functional form of the simulation model. The functional form of a model will depend on the workflow modeled as well as the probabilities of the event occurrences at each operation within the workflow. We will discuss two simple examples. These include a single operation and a workflow that consists of three sequential steps or operations arranged in series. In Figure 5.7, a single operation is shown in which the value of an independent variable, such as cycle time, has been assigned probability values over its actual observed range of cycle times. A specific cycle time of 12 days will be discussed by way of an example. Using this model we will generate random numbers having a uniform occurrence probability between 0 and 1. These random numbers will be transformed using the cumulative density function (cdf) of cycle times of the actual observed distribution. The cdf has a range between 0 and 1 based on the original probability density function (pdf). The relationship of a cdf to an independent variable can be discrete or continuous. The functional relationship between cycle time and its occurrence probability has been discretely defined

Table 5.5   How Simulation Works

Value of X	Probability	Cumulative Probability
17	0.0312254	0.758036
16	0.0333225	0.725747
15	0.0352065	0.691462
14	0.0368270	0.655422
13	0.0381388	0.617911
12	**0.0391043**	**0.579260**
11	0.0396953	0.539828
10	0.0398942	0.500000
9	0.0396953	0.460172

Note: If the random number is less than 0.617911 and higher than 0.539828, then the event is 12.

in Table 5.5. In effect, any random number in the range of greater than 0.539828 and less than 0.617911 is defined as a discrete cycle time of 12 days. However, using a continuous cdf, we could map a one-to-one relationship between a continuous random variable in the range of 0 to 1 and a continuous range of cycle times. This concept is shown in the lower portion of Figure 5.7. An example, using cycle time as a continuous variable, will be discussed using Figure 5.8 to Figure 5.11.

Figure 5.8 to Figure 5.10 show three common probability distributions used in simulation applications. There are also many others that are used, depending on the distribution characteristics of the system. Once statistical sampling has shown the pattern or distribution of the metric of the workflow under analysis, which in this example is cycle time, the empirical data is fit as appropriate to a standard probability distribution using goodness-of-fit testing methods. Once the empirical data has been fit to a specific probability distribution, the formula for calculating random deviates from the standard distribution is obtained from one or more of the references listed at the end of this chapter. Recall that this formula is derived using the cdf of the probability distribution. Figure 5.11 shows how these concepts are applied in practice using Minitab software. In this example, the total cycle time through the workflow is estimated by adding the simulated cycle times across its three sequential operations. Operation 1 is uniformly distributed with a minimum cycle time of 10 seconds and an upper cycle time of 30 seconds. These two parameters specify a unique uniform distribution for operation 1. Operation 2 is distributed, as a normal distribution, having a mean cycle time of 60 seconds and a standard deviation of 10 seconds. Operation 3 is exponentially distributed with

Probability Density Function

$$f(x) = \frac{1}{\quad -\quad}$$

$\leq x \leq$

Cumulative Density Function

$$F(X) = \frac{X_i - a}{\quad -\quad} = r_i$$

$\leq x \leq$

Generated Random Number

$$X_i = a + r_i (\quad - \quad)$$

Where: is the mimimum value

and   is the maximum value

Figure 5.8   Uniform distribution.

Generated Random Number

$$X_i = \mu + \sigma \left[\sum_{t=1}^{12} r_i - 6 \right]$$

Where: μ and σ are the mean and standard deviation of the original distribution

Figure 5.9   Normal distribution.

Probability Density Function

$$f(t) = \lambda e^{-\lambda t}$$

t=service time>0
λ=service rate>0

Cumulative Density Function

$$F(t) = 1 - e^{-\lambda t}$$

Generated Random Number

$$t = -1/\lambda (\ln r_i)$$

Figure 5.10   Exponential distribution.

a mean cycle time of 90 seconds. The total cycle time, across the workflow, is the summation of the cycle time of each of the three operations. Statistical analysis of the example shows the median cycle time to be 144.37 seconds, and the distribution is highly skewed right.

Admittedly, there may be easier ways to build simulation models using off-the-shelf software. This example was presented to show the underlying logic behind a simulation model. However, this approach would be tedious to apply to more

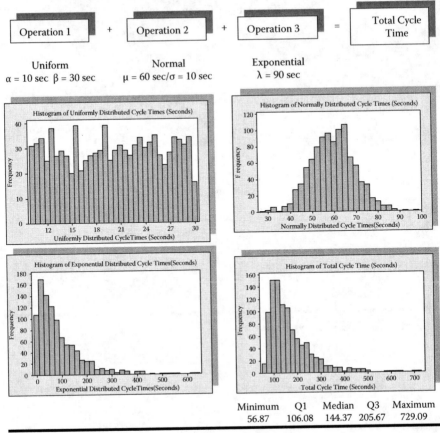

Figure 5.11   Estimating total cycle time across three operations using Minitab.

complicated workflows having more operations, parallel paths, and rework loops. The advantage of using off-the-shelf simulation software is that useful information related to workflow simplification and reconfiguration can be obtained very easily by an analyst. In summary, off-the-shelf simulation models are usually easy to build and reconfigure by an analyst, depending on the goals and objectives of the simulation analysis.

Queuing Analysis

The dynamic characteristics of many systems have been studied over the past several decades by mathematicians, statisticians, and operations research professionals. As a result, tools and methods have been developed to analyze specific process workflow applications based on specific assumptions. Also, in many analytical situations the same practical problem can be solved using more than one analyti-

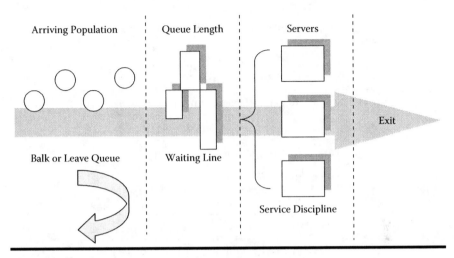

Arriving Population

Queue Length

Servers

Exit

Balk or Leave Queue

Waiting Line

Service Discipline

Figure 5.12 Common elements of a queuing system.

cal technique. As an example, many workflows can be analyzed using simulation, queuing analysis, or linear programming with similar results, depending on the purpose of the analysis. Although simulation is useful in any analyses, queuing analysis and linear programming are more efficient because they have a firm analytical basis. Figure 5.12 shows an example of the various modeling elements that characterize a queuing system. The queuing system described by Figure 5.12 could represent a process workflow of a bank in which customers arrive, are serviced, and then depart. The arrival pattern of customers into the workflow is specified by their average arrival rate. In addition to the arrival rate, the size of the population from which the people arrive (calling population) may be very large (infinite) or small (finite). Depending on the system modeled, arriving customers may not join the workflow if its waiting line is too long (balking) or, once they join the waiting line, may leave it (reneging). The queuing analysis predicts the average number of people waiting in line, how long they wait on average, the average number of people waiting within the workflow (number waiting in line and being serviced), and how long customers wait on average within the workflow (average time waiting in line and being serviced), as well as the utilization of the workflow's servers and other relevant statistics.

Table 5.6 shows several common statistics obtained from queuing models. This table shows that much information can be obtained from a very simple study of a system's queuing characteristics. However, the specific form of the equations providing the information listed in Table 5.6 varies depending on the underlying probability distributions of the queuing system components, which are based on specific characteristics of the workflow modeled. As an example, Table 5.7 shows six major workflow characteristics that help define a queuing model of a process workflow. The distribution of arrivals into the workflow, as well as their behavior

Table 5.6   Questions Queuing Models Answer

1. Arrival rate into system (λ)
2. Average units serviced (μ)
3. System utilization factor (λ/μ) (note: $\lambda/\mu < 1$)
4. Average number of units in system (L)
5. Average number of units in queue (L_q)
6. Average time a unit spends in system (W)
7. Average time a unit waits in queue (W_q)
8. Probability of no units in system (P_0)
9. Probability that arriving unit waits for service (P_w)
10. Probability of n units in the system (P_n)

Table 5.7   Queuing System Characteristics

Arrival distribution	The arrival distribution is specified by the interarrival time or time between successive units entering the system — also, if the unit balks and leaves the line because it is too long (prior to joining the line) or reneges and leaves the queue because the wait is too long.
Service distribution	The pattern of service is specified by the service time, or time required by one server to service one unit.
System capacity	The maximum number of units allowed in the system; in other words, if the system is at capacity, units are turned away.
Service discipline	There are several rules for a server to provide service to a unit, including first-in-first-out (FIFO), last-in-last-out (LIFO), service in random order (SIRO), prioritization of service (POS), and another general service discipline (GSD).
Channels	The number of parallel servers in the system.
Phases	The number of subsequent servers in series within a given channel.

Note: Queuing systems are characterized by the arrival distribution of the calling population, the service distribution, the number of services, the number of phases, the service discipline, and system capacity.

Table 5.8 Modified Kendall's Notation, (a/b/c): (d/e/f)

Arrival and service distributions	M = exponentially distributed
	Ek = Erlang type – k distributed
	D = deterministic or constant
	G = any other distribution
Service discipline	There are several rules for a server to provide service to a unit, including first-in-first-out (FIFO), last-in-last-out (LIFO), service in random order (SIRO), prioritization of service (POS), and another general service discipline (GSD).

Note: Kendall's notation summarizes the modeling characteristics of a queuing system where a = the arrival distribution or pattern, b = the service distribution or pattern, and c = the number of available servers or channels. Other characteristics can also be added to Kendall's original notation, such as those by A.M. Lee (d = the service discipline, e = the system's capacity) and Handy A. Taha (f = size of the calling population, i.e., infinite or finite).

relative to the waiting line, defines the first characteristic of the queuing model. The second characteristic is the distribution of service provided to the arrivals. The third characteristic is the allowable capacity of the system. As an example, some systems cannot accommodate all the arrivals. An example would be a store with a limited amount of parking spaces or a bank drive-up window that allows a finite number of automobiles to wait in line. The fourth characteristic relates to how customers are serviced. Some systems allow first-come-first-served (FCFS) prioritization, whereas others use a different service discipline. The number of channels in the system refers to the total available parallel servers in the model. The number of phases refers to the number of subsequent operations past the first server in a particular channel. Because there are many types of queuing models specified by the characteristics of the system they are designed to model, a concise descriptive notation was developed to make their description easier to understand and interpret by analysts. The classic queuing notation was developed by Kendall and is shown in Table 5.8, along with some modifications to the original notation. Table 5.8 lists some of the more common probability distributions that are used to describe the arrival and service patterns occurring within a workflow. Table 5.9 summarizes our discussion and lists important queuing model characteristics. Once specific quantitative data has been collected relative to the arrival and service rates within the process workflow, as well as its other performance characteristics, a modeling team can build their queuing model. Integral to modeling efforts is building a process map of the workflow according to one of the examples shown in Figure 5.13 or using modified versions of these examples. Once the basic system characteristics have been determined and the process layout has been specified, the team can use off-the-shelf

Table 5.9 Summarization of Queuing Model Characteristics

Calling Population	Service Discipline
1. Infinite distribution	1. Deterministic (constant) service
2. Finite distribution	
3. Deterministic arrivals	2. Distributed pattern of service
4. Distributed arrivals	
5. Balking or reneging allowed?	3. Service rules (FIFO, LIFO, SIRO, POS, GSD)
6. Single channel	4. Single phase
7. Multichannels	5. Multiphases

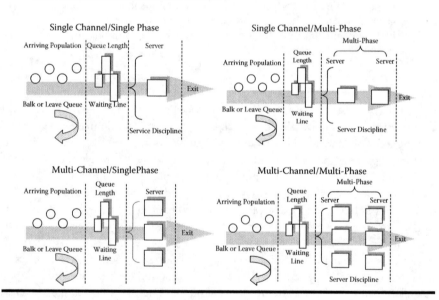

Figure 5.13 Several common queuing systems.

software to quickly analyze the process workflow and obtain the information listed in Table 5.6.

Four common queuing models are shown in Table 5.10. These models are described using simple Kendall's notation. This is the simplified format that is used to succinctly represent the key characteristics of a queuing model based on the underlying process workflow. There are many other types of queuing models that can be constructed to match your particular workflow. A literature search may be the best way to find a queuing model that matches your team's specific requirements. The

Table 5.10 Four Common Queuing Models

Model Type	Process Layout	Arrival Distribution/ Calling Population	Service Distribution/ Service Discipline
(M/M/1)	Single channel	Poisson arrivals/infinite calling population	Exponential service distribution/FCFS
(M/M/k)	Multichannel	Poisson arrivals/infinite calling population	Exponential service distribution/FCFS
(M/G/k)	Multichannel	Poisson arrivals/infinite calling population/ capacity constrained	General service distribution/FCFS
(M/M/1)	Single channel	Poisson arrivals/finite calling population	Exponential service distribution/FCFS

(M/M1) model can be used to analyze workflows that are characterized by Poisson arrival and exponential service distributions, a single channel, and first-in-first-out (FIFO) service discipline. An example would be waiting in line at a ticket office where there is one server. The (M/M/k) models can be used to analyze workflows in which there are several parallel servers. Examples would be waiting lines in supermarkets and banks having several clerks to handle transactions. The (M/G/k) model, if modified with a capacity constraint, can be used to analyze workflows characterized by a finite number allowed in the system. An example would be a Web site designed to handle a limited number of incoming calls. The fourth model, (M/M/1), is classically applied to situations in which the calling population requiring service is small (finite). An example would be a repair shop servicing machines or other equipment.

A simple example of the (M/M/1) queuing model is shown in Table 5.11. The formulas for this model are easy to manually calculate; however, the calculations for other models quickly become complicated and require use of a computer. In this example, customers arrive at the process workflow at an average rate of 20 per hour. It should be noted that this rate fluctuates with some time periods having customers arriving faster or slower than the average rate of 20 per hour. The service rate is 25 customers on average serviced per hour. Again, the average service rate of some time periods will be higher or lower than the average. The variation in arrival and service rates requires that customers periodically wait for service or, alternatively, servers may be idle and wait for customers. A general requirement of all these queuing models is that the average service rate must exceed the average arrival rate.

Arrival and service rates are usually estimated empirically using check sheets or automatically by business activity monitoring (BAM) systems that record customer arrivals and departures from the system. Using this empirical information as well as the other system performance statistics provides useful information relative

Table 5.11 Example of Simple Queuing Model (M/M/1)

Customers arrive at a repair shop at an average rate of $\lambda = 20$ per hour; the average service rate is 25 customers per hour. Assume Poisson arrival distribution/exponential service distribution/a single channel/FCFS service discipline/no maximum on number of systems/infinite calling population.	
1. Arrival rate into system (λ)	$\lambda = 20$ per hour
2. Average units serviced (μ)	$\mu = 25$ per hour
3. System utilization factor (λ/μ) (note: $\lambda/\mu < 1$)	$\lambda/\mu = 0.80 = 80\%$
4. Average number of units in system (L)	$L = L_q + (\lambda/\mu) = 4.0$ units
5. Average number of units in queue (L_q)	$L_q = \lambda^2/[\mu(\mu - \lambda)] = 3.2$ units
6. Average time a unit spends in system (W)	$W = W_q + (1/\mu) = 0.20$ hours
7. Average time a unit waits in queue (W_q)	$W_q = L_q/\lambda = 0.16$ hours
8. Probability of no units in system (P_0)	$P_0 = 1 - (\lambda/\mu) = 0.20 = 20\%$
9. Probability that arriving unit waits for service (P_w)	$P_w = \lambda/\mu = 0.80 = 80\%$
10. Probability of n units in the system (P_n)	$P_n = (\lambda/\mu)^n P_0$

to workflow performance. This information can be used to minimize customer waiting time and cost, or meet established service levels at minimum cost. As an example, a queuing model can be used in conjunction with marketing research information to build into the workflow a predetermined service level or waiting time to ensure customer satisfaction at the lowest possible operational cost. Once a workflow has been analyzed in this manner, many options to improve it will usually become apparent to the team.

Another example that shows the advantages of using queuing analysis to model a dynamic workflow is shown in Table 5.12. Although there are many books recommending that a workflow should have excess capacity, the reason is not always clearly shown. However, Table 5.12 shows why excess capacity may be useful for some systems. As the utilization of the machine increases, the average waiting time for a unit to be serviced by the machine increases rapidly. However, designing a process workflow with low utilization may not be a good alternative. An alternative strategy would be to use low-cost parallel machines that are activated rather than utilized as demand fluctuates instead of utilizing one very large and expensive machine that is inflexible to demand fluctuations. Another example would be using information technology to transfer incoming customer calls to call centers that have excess capacity rather than to a location at its maximum capacity level.

Table 5.12   Queuing Analysis Study of Capacity Utilization

Arrival Rate	Percentage of Capacity	Service Rate	Probability of Zero Units Waiting	Average Units Waiting	Average Waiting Time	Probability of Waiting
10	20%	50	80%	0.05	0.005	20%
25	50%	50	50%	0.5	0.2	50%
40	80%	50	20%	3.2	0.1	80%
45	90%	50	10%	8.1	0.18	90%
49	98%	50	2%	48.02	1	98%

Note: As the system's capacity utilization approaches 100%, waiting time significantly increases. Assumption: Single-channel queue/Poisson arrival rate/ exponential service rate.

Linear Programming

A third class of analytical algorithms useful in designing and optimizing a process workflow is linear programming (LP) and related models. Table 5.13 lists several diverse applications of linear programming models. There are many others in the literature. LP models are characterized by minimization or maximization objectives and the model's objective function limited by one or more system constraints. Typical system constraints relate to resource scarcity, minimum requirements relative to demand or service, and other requirements. The basic characteristics of

Table 5.13   Typical Linear Programming Applications

1. Maximizing service productivity
2. Minimizing network routing
3. Optimizing process control
4. Minimizing inventory investment
5. Optimally allocating investment
6. Optimizing product mix profitability
7. Minimizing scheduling cost
8. Minimizing transportation costs
9. Minimizing cost of materials mixtures

Table 5.14   Linear Programming (LP) Characteristics

What is linear programming?

1. An LP algorithm attempts to find a minimization, maximization, or solution when decisions are made with constrained resources as well as other system constraints. As an example, supply-chain optimization problems require matching demand and supply when supply is limited and demand must be satisfied. An LP problem is comprised of four major components:

   a. Decision variables within analyst's control: when and how much to order, when to manufacture, when and how much of the product to ship.

   b. Constraints placed on the levels or amounts of decision variables that can be used in the final solution. Examples are capacity to produce raw materials or components, specified number of hours production can run, how much overtime a worker can work, a customer's capacity to handle and process receipts.

   c. Problem objective relative to minimization or maximization. Examples include maximizing profits, minimizing cost, maximizing service levels, and maximizing production throughput.

   d. Mathematical relationships among the decision variables, constraints, and problem objectives.

When do we have a solution to a linear program?

1. Feasible solution: Satisfies all the constraints of the problem or objective function.

2. Optimum solution: The best feasible solution, relative to the decision variables and their levels, that achieves the objective of the optimization problem. Although there may be many feasible solutions, there is usually only one optimum solution.

an LP model are shown in Table 5.14. As an example, supply-chain optimization problems require matching demand and supply when supply is limited and demand must be satisfied.

Table 5.14 shows that an LP optimization problem is comprised of four major components. These include decision variables whose levels are within an analyst's control. Examples are decisions relative to when and how much to order, when to manufacture, and when and how much of a product to ship. Constraints are limitations placed upon the system. These include available capacity to manufacture raw materials or components, available production time, available hours, available overtime, and minimum sales. The objective of an LP analysis is to maximize or minimize an objective function. Examples include maximizing profits, minimizing cost, maximizing service levels, and maximizing production throughput. The LP

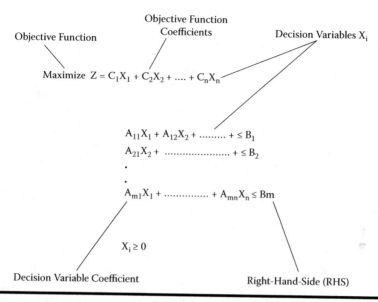

Figure 5.14 Basic LP model formulation.

model is used to evaluate mathematical relationships between decision variables and their constraints relative to the model's objective. An optimum solution will be the best feasible solution, relative to the decision variables and their levels, that achieves the objective of the optimization problem, which is either minimization or maximization, without violating the constraints. Although there may be many feasible solutions, there is usually only one optimum (this may not always be true).

Figure 5.14 shows the basic elements of an LP model. The objective function represents the goal or objective of the optimization analysis. The problem is to determine the specific level or amount of each decision variable that should be used to optimize the objective function. Each decision variable X_i is weighted by an objective coefficient C_i. In many LP problems the objective coefficient is a cost per unit of the decision variable. The optimization of the objective function is limited by the constraints that specify the minimum or maximum amount of resources that can be used in the final solution. Each decision variable in a constraint is weighted by a coefficient that shows its relative contribution to usage of the constraint toward optimization of the objective function. The right-hand side of each constraint can be of three types: less than or equal, equal, and greater than or equal. Finally, in standard LP models, all decision variables are constrained to be positive, i.e., $X_i > 0$.

An example of how the LP concept is applied in practice is shown in Figure 5.15: a simple transportation network consisting of three manufacturing facilities and four distribution centers. This is a special type of LP algorithm called the transportation model. The most common objective of a transportation model is to minimize transportation costs between manufacturing facilities and distribution

Solution Obtained UsingExcel's "Solver"

From/To		DC 1	DC 2	DC 3	DC 4	Supply
	Facility 1	10	20	10	5	100
	Facility 2	5	15	20	30	200
	Facility 3	3	5	20	5	300
	Demand					
		150	200	50	200	

Candidate Solution						Shipped
	Facility 1	0	0	50	50	100
	Facility 2	150	50	0	0	200
	Facility 3	0	150	0	150	300
	Supplied	150	200	50	200	

Cost										
	Facility 1	$	-	$	-	$	500	$	250	
	Facility 2	$	750	$	750	$	-	$	-	
	Facility 3	$	-	$	750	$	-	$	750	
						Total Cost		$	3,750	

$$\text{Min } Z = X_{11} + X_{12} + X_{13} + X_{14} + X_{21} + X_{22} + X_{23} + X_{24} + X_{31} + X_{32} + X_{33} + X_{34}$$

$$X_{11} + X_{12} + X_{13} + X_{14} \leq 100$$

$$X_{21} + X_{22} + X_{23} + X_{24} \leq 200$$

$$X_{31} + X_{32} + X_{33} + X_{34} \leq 300$$

$$X_{11} + X_{21} + X_{31} = 150$$

$$X_{12} + X_{22} + X_{32} = 200$$

$$X_{13} + X_{23} + X_{33} = 50$$

$$X_{14} + X_{24} + X_{34} = 200$$

$$X_{ij} \geq 0 \text{ for } I = 1, 2, 3; j = 1, 2, 3, 4$$

Figure 5.15　Transportation system example.

centers. There are two types of constraints in a transportation model. These relate to the maximum available material that can be shipped from a given manufacturing facility and the required demand by a given distribution center for the material. If the available supply and required demand do not balance, then "dummy" manufacturing facilities or distribution centers are incorporated into the model to balance supply and demand constraints. The right-hand side (RHS) of each constraint also differs in that available supply is less than or equal to the RHS of the supply constraints, and demand is equal to required demand because it must be satisfied by the solution. The problem shown in Figure 5.15 is analyzed using Excel's Solver algorithm, but many operations research books have software that can analyze LP models. The optimum solution is also shown in Figure 5.15. In the From/To matrix, the costs of every facility and distribution center combination are listed. As an example, the cost per unit from Facility 1 to DC 1 is $10. Also, the maximum supply from Facility 1 is 100 units. The demand of each distribution center is shown as DC 1 = 150 units, DC 2 = 200 units, DC 3 = 50 units, and DC 4 = 200 units. The optimum solution is shown in the Candidate Solution matrix. As an example, Facility 1 ships 50 units to DC 3 and 50 units to DC 5. The total cost of the optimum solution is shown in the Cost matrix as $3750. An alternative and more general form of the model is shown at the bottom of Figure 5.15. LP models have proven useful in process workflow modeling and analysis in many diverse fields of business and science.

Process Failure-Mode-and-Effects-Analysis (PFMEA)

In Chapter 4 we discussed the design failure mode and effects analysis (DFMEA) tool, including how to create and interpret it. In a similar manner, the process FMEA is created to ensure a product or service design is produced according to customer requirements as specified by the VOC translation process. VOC requirements should already be incorporated into the DFMEA. Process engineers use the DFMEA to identify critical characteristics and their required targets and tolerances. Workflows are designed to achieve all the design objectives required by the VOC and documented by the CE team in the DFMEA. Finally, quality assurance uses the DFMEA and PFMEA documents and related information to create the quality control plan to ensure the product or service meets the original VOC requirements.

How to Improve the Work Environment

It is important to create a work environment that will support a new product or service. This requires that the people who will become an integral part of a new process workflow be well trained in its operations. This is critical to achieving cost, performance, and quality targets. Creating high-performance work teams to support a new process workflow was discussed in Chapter 2. In this chapter, we will provide additional information to improve team effectiveness. Table 5.15 shows there are ten key steps an organization can undertake to ensure its workforce is performing at levels necessary to increase its global competitiveness. The first step in creating a high-performance working environment is for senior management to provide leadership and set the future direction of the organization in clear and concise terms. This will ensure the organization can easily understand how to prioritize its work and efficiently allocate resources to its various process workflows.

Table 5.15 10 Key Steps to Improve the Work Environment

1. Provide leadership to set future direction and values of the organization.
2. Create strategic goals and objectives 3 to 5 years out to improve productivity and customer satisfaction.
3. Translate goals and objectives to successively lower levels throughout the organization.
4. Communicate change to the organization in a simple and consistent manner.
5. Align resources with the goals and objectives of the organization.
6. Hire and train people who have the organization's core values, but embrace cultural diversity.
7. Ensure incentive systems are coincident with organizational values so organizational behavior reinforces organizational values.
8. Remove organizational barriers to change.
9. Effectively execute strategic goals and objectives to enhance productivity and customer and employee satisfaction.
10. Develop organizational systems to continuously learn and improve all operations over time.

Organizational values should also be promoted in a consistent manner. Consistency in communication is important to minimize misunderstood priorities, such as project selection, execution, and resource allocation. A second key step in creating an improved working environment is to create strategic goals and objectives that show where an organization is going in the next several years and how the workforce will fit into the evolving organization. It is also important to show how employee work efforts, at a tactical level, integrate with the overall strategic plans of an organization. A third step necessary to improve an organization's work environment is to translate organizational goals and objectives down through successively lower levels of the organization in a linearly and straightforward manner. This will ensure goal alignment at an initiative and project level. The fourth step is to communicate change throughout an organization using simple and consistent forms of communication, and integrating communication with organizational norms and cultural values. Resource alignment is also critical to ensuring the workforce has the tools and resources necessary to do their work. A sixth key step is to hire and train people who have the organization's core values and embrace cultural diversity. Having the right people in the first place will tend to minimize the creation of organizational barriers. Employee incentive systems should also be coincident with organizational goals, objectives, and values to reinforce employee behavior.

Removing the barriers to organizational change is necessary to ensure a work environment is positive and necessary change is reinforced at all organizational levels. The ninth step is to efficiently execute strategic goals and objectives to meet productivity targets and enhance customer, supplier, employee, and shareholder satisfaction. Success breeds success and is a powerful motivator for future process improvement. Unfortunately, many organizations do not communicate well nor do they desire to create a work environment in which everyone can succeed in proportion to the value they add to their organization. Finally, it is important to develop learning systems to ensure employees are continuously learning and adapting to changing business conditions. These actions will improve process performance and increase an organization's competitiveness.

How to Develop High-Performance Work Teams

An important and integral part of process workflow design is development of high-performance work teams. It would make no sense to design a new process workflow and expect it to be competitive if its workforce is not provided with proper incentives, and trained and willing to work at target levels of productivity and quality. Deployment of high-performance work teams is essential to an organization. Table 5.16 lists ten key principles necessary to develop high-performance work teams to move an organization toward higher performance levels. The first key step in deploying a high-performance work team is to ensure that the team is

Table 5.16 10 Key Steps to Develop High-Performance Work Teams

1. Ensure the team is formed around common goals and objectives coincident with a work area.
2. The team members should be jointly accountable for success or failure.
3. Ensure the team has a diverse membership and has been trained in proper facilitation methods.
4. All team members should have the required skills to support their team.
5. Ensure the team has adequate resources for its goals and objectives.
6. Clarify team roles and responsibilities.
7. Develop mechanisms to share information in an honest and open manner.
8. Resolve team conflicts in a positive manner.
9. Ensure the team remains on schedule and meets its goals and objectives.
10. The team should remain together for an extended period.

formed around common goals and objectives that are coincident with their work area. The second is that team members should be jointly accountable for the success or failure of the projects assigned to their local work area. This will tend to foster cooperation and collaboration among team members. A third important step is to ensure the team has a diverse and properly facilitated membership. Also, all team members should have the skills required to support their team. The fifth key step is to ensure the team has adequate resources to execute its goals and objectives. The team should also clarify its roles and responsibilities relative to the assignment of its work tasks. The seventh step is to develop systems to share information between all team members in an honest and open manner to encourage cooperation. Also, team conflicts should be resolved in a positive manner using proper facilitation methods. The ninth step listed in Table 5.16 recommends a team remains on schedule and meets its goals and objectives using effective project management practices. Project management will be discussed in Chapter 18. Finally, it is important a team remain together for an extended period to evolve into a high-performance work team. This will increase the probability it will achieve organizational goals and objectives.

In addition to the specific steps required to create a high-performance work team, teams go through a four-stage evolutionary process as they mature. These stages are forming, storming, norming, and performing. In the forming stage, the team meets and begins to develop common goals and objectives. However, there is often much confusion at this point in the team maturation process. Also, productivity is very low in this formative stage. It is during this stage that the team develops basic facilitation tools and methods to achieve its goals and objectives. The team may be focused on a single project or several projects within its local work area. One of the most important facilitation and project management tools, at this point in the team's project, is a project charter. An example of a project charter is shown in Figure 7.9. The project charter specifies where a team will work, the resources required for team activities related to data collection, analysis and work-flow improvements, the specific objectives of its work, and the expected business benefits, both financial and operational. These project objectives include achieving improvement targets according to the project's schedule. In the storming stage of team maturation, there is often a conflict among several team members due to different perspectives on how the team should proceed with its work. External facilitation of the team may be useful during this stage of team maturation. Part of the facilitation process includes development of a team code of conduct to ensure team member disagreements are resolved in a mutually agreeable manner. In the norming stage of the team maturation process, the team's productivity increases, as it resolves team conflicts more effectively than in previous maturation stages. In this maturation stage the team begins to succeed in achieving its goals and objectives relative to the project's milestone activities. Finally, in the performing stage, the team works together to consistently achieve its goals and objectives. High-performance work teams must be methodically developed by an organization because work is best done using the full range of employee skills and capabilities.

An important enabler of high-performance work teams is an organization's reward and recognition systems. These systems should be aligned to recognize teams' contributions to their organization. Individual recognition must also be designed into the incentive system in a balanced manner.

How to Simplify and Standardize Work

Table 5.17 lists ten key steps that will help an organization simplify its work. These are broadly divided into the three categories of (1) not creating the work in the first place, (2) efficiently doing work that must be done, and (3) standardization of the work so it is done the same way every time regardless of the person doing it. Work simplification begins in the product or service design phase. This is the first step in Table 5.17, which states, "Simplify the product or service design first." The fewer the components or assembly operations a design has, the less work that will be required to produce it day to day. This concept is embodied in the design

Table 5.17   10 Key Steps to Simplify and Standardize Work

1. Simplify the product or service design first.
2. Design the process as simply as possible using automatic systems where practical to minimize the percentage of manual activities, and mistake-proof the process.
3. Balance workflow between operations based on the required takt time (time allowed to produce one unit). This will be discussed in Chapter 6.
4. Break the work of each operation into its elemental tasks either empirically through observation and work sampling or micromotion study, or using predetermined time standards.
5. Set time standards by work task within each operation.
6. Develop a sequential strategy to do the work tasks the "best way" to minimize time and unnecessary motions using tools, methods, and fixtures that will mistake-proof the work.
7. Ensure work tasks are combined or broken into parallel activities that will not exceed the takt time.
8. Ensure work procedures are standardized, easy to understand, and visual in nature with examples of good and poor workmanship.
9. Ensure people are trained to perform, measure, and continuously improve their workmanship.
10. Continually evaluate and improve the work system.

for manufacturing (DFM) concepts listed in Table 4.7. The second key step of Table 5.17 recommends simple automation and mistake-proofing of work operations to minimize the percentage of manual activities within a process workflow. This will reduce the direct labor requirements necessary to produce a product or service and reduce errors. Once the required operational sequences have been determined by process engineering, the flow of work across the work operations is balanced according to the system's takt time — the time allowed to produce one unit. An example would be having a production schedule of 80 units and 8 hours (480 minutes) of available manufacturing time. This would require a takt time of one unit every six minutes throughout the eight-hour shift. Takt time and other Lean tools, methods, and concepts will be discussed in Chapter 6. Once the takt time has been calculated, the sequence of work tasks within each operation is aggregated or formed into operations or workstations consisting of one or more work tasks. The cumulative completion time of all work tasks, within an operation, must be less than or equal to the system's takt time. In other words, if the takt time is one unit every six minutes, then the maximum cycle time for every operation or workstation must be six minutes or less. To achieve this takt time, work tasks may be aggregated together or broken into smaller groups, as shown in Figure 5.16. To do this, the work tasks must be studied to determine the best way and time to complete each work task. Common methods for studying work tasks are work sampling, micromotion studies, or predetermined time standards. Work sampling involves studying a work task over a period of time and determining the best way to accomplish the task. Micro motion studies are similar to work sampling, but are more precise in determining work task time duration than simple work sampling methods. This is because cameras are used to record every motion related to completing the work task. This allows the motions associated with a work task to be studied over and over. Also, time duration can be measured to a microsecond level of precision. Predetermined time standards can be applied up front to a new workflow design and later validated through work sampling or micromotion studies. Alternatively, they can be created using these methods. Time standards are used to design the manual portion of new process workflows, and with similar analyses of machine cycle times to balance the flow of work across the process workflow to achieve the required takt time.

Figure 5.17 shows how data from more detailed time and motion studies can be summarized to determine what major components of time are allowed within a process. A baseline analysis is conducted of an operation's work tasks, and the time required to complete each task is calculated but at a work task level of detail. An analysis is made of each work task and its time duration to identify and eliminate wasted time elements. Next, time standards are calculated for each work task, similar to the standard method shown in Figure 5.17. This data collection form also enables collection of time durations that are related to the use of specific tools, materials, and fixtures. The tasks are further categorized as setting up a job, inspecting the work, actually doing the work, moving the work, or waiting for materials

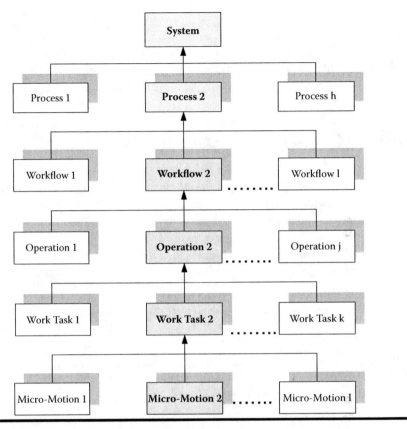

Figure 5.16   How to identify lower-level work tasks.

Department:	Date:
Process:	Operator:
Workflow:	Takt Time:
Operation Number:	Required Production:
Product Identification:	

Time In Minutes (Change Scale as Required)

Major Time Component (Contine analysis to work task level)	1	2	3	4	5	6	7	8	9	10		Average	Percent
Set-up													
Inspection													
Process													
Transport													
Waiting													
Etc.													
Total:													

Figure 5.17   How to develop time standards.

or information. As part of this analysis, unnecessary work tasks are eliminated and the remaining work tasks are mistake-proofed. Finally, employees who actually do the work are trained on how to use the new work methods, tools, and inspection and measurement systems. Visual examples of good and poor workmanship are also frequently used to control and improve work methods.

How to Develop an Effective Training Program

Employee training is critical to any new process. Table 5.18 lists ten key steps to build an effective training program. The first step is to ensure the training is focused on business and individual needs, and the goals of the training are clear. Goal alignment and clarity will ensure training is beneficial to both an organization and its employees. Also, the greater the degree of alignment and clarity, the stronger will be the senior management commitment for training. Second, it is important to measure the effectiveness of training with testing or other quantitative

Table 5.18   10 Key Steps to Improve Training Effectiveness

1. Ensure training is focused on business and individual needs, and its goals are clear.
2. Ensure its effectiveness is measured with testing or other quantitative metrics directly related to its goals and objectives.
3. Design training to appeal to different learning styles, i.e., somatic (touching), auditory, visual, and intellectual.
4. Create a positive training environment where participants feel free to learn without distractions.
5. Ensure presentation of training is most conducive to learning using online learning, workbooks, and presentation materials tied together through combined instructor and participant presentations.
6. Encourage participant feedback to improve the training process.
7. Have participants practice what they learn in their work environments through project applications.
8. Develop posttraining materials to reinforce the training concepts.
9. Provide coaching and mentoring to help clarify and reinforce the training concepts.
10. Ensure the training process is continuously improved using the latest methods and theories.

metrics directly related to its goals and objectives. We want to avoid situations in which the number of people put through a training program is the only measure of its success. The training should also be designed to appeal to different learning styles, i.e., somatic (touching), auditory, visual, and intellectual, to increase its effectiveness at an individual level, and by extrapolation to the group level. Blended learning models, such as those listed in suggested reading at the end of this chapter, are particularly helpful in increasing training effectiveness.

During the training it is important to create a positive environment where participants feel free to learn without distractions. Also, it is important to ensure that the presentation of training is most conducive to learning. This can be accomplished using a blended learning approach in which online learning, workbooks, and presentation materials are used by participants and tied together through combined instructor and participant presentations. In a blended learning training model, participants study training modules prior to class. The instructor and participant interactions represent a greater proportion of the class time. To continuously improve the training process, participant feedback is critical. Immediate application of training is another important consideration. Participants should practice what they learn back at their jobs through applied projects. Effective training should also generate business benefits that can be measured by an organization. To aid in this process, posttraining materials should be developed to reinforce the training concepts, and coaching and mentoring should also be provided to help clarify and reinforce the training concepts. Finally, the training process should be continuously improved using the latest training methods and theories.

Summary

The design of a process workflow should correspond to the product or service design it must produce. For this reason, process engineering must work closely with design engineers from the CE team to design workflows. Once the workflows have been designed and the relationships between all operations have been quantitatively established, it is useful to quantitatively model process workflows to understand their dynamic relationships. The information gained from workflow modeling will help reduce process variation, and ensure goals and objectives are met by the new product or service design. Modeling of process workflows will reduce cost and improve quality. In addition, it is important to create a work environment that reinforces organizational change and learning. In this context, high-performance work teams will also be required to manage and improve workflows over time. All work tasks within each operation must be standardized based on the design of the process workflow. Finally, people must be trained to properly use tools and methods, and follow work and inspection instructions. These key concepts are summarized in Table 5.19.

Table 5.19   Key Concepts for Effective Workflow Design

1. Use information from the CE team to design your process's workflows.
2. Quantitatively model your workflows to understand dynamic relationships.
3. Create a work environment that reinforces change and continual learning.
4. Create high-performance work teams to manage and improve your workflows.
5. Standardize work to reduce process variation.
6. Train people to properly use tools and to follow work and inspection instructions.

Suggested Reading

Sanjiv Augustine. (2005). *Managing Agile Projects*. Prentice Hall, Englewood Cliffs, NJ.

Richard B. Chase, F. Robert Jacobs, and Nicholas J. Aquilano. (2006). *Operations Management for Competitive Advantage*, 11th ed. McGraw-Hill, New York.

Paul Harmon. (2003). *Business Process Change: A Manager's Guide to Improving, Redesigning, and Automating Processes*. Morgan-Kaufman, San Francisco.

Averill M. Law and W. David Kelton. (1991). *Simulation Modeling and Analysis*, 2nd ed. McGraw-Hill, New York.

Dave Meier. (2000). *The Accelerated Learning Handbook*. McGraw-Hill, New York.

Lou Russell. (1999). *The Accelerated Learning Fieldbook*. Jossey-Bass Pfeiffer.

Chapter 6

Making Value Flow through a Process

Competitive solution 6: Align process workflows, using Lean tools and methods, to deliver customer value without wasting resources.

Overview

Mapping customer value through a process is a powerful way to identify areas to improve workflows. Once properly mapped and analyzed, customer value elements help identify work tasks that are aligned with customer value and, by extension, are important versus those that are not aligned and should be eliminated from the workflow. In Chapter 3, the concepts of the voice of the customer (VOC) based on the three Kano needs and five value elements were shown to be critical factors for strategic alignment of the VOC within an organization. Also, in Chapters 4 and 5, the VOC was shown to be an integral part of the design of products and services and their process workflows. In this chapter, we will expand our discussion of process workflow analysis. In this discussion, an assumption will be that either workflows are poorly designed relative to the VOC or the VOC migrated over time causing nonalignment between the VOC and the process workflow. As an example, over time, organizations often add unnecessary work tasks to their operations that are not related to the VOC. In this chapter we will show how the concept of customer value and the application of Lean tools and methods will enable an organization to create simpler workflows having higher quality and lower cycle time and cost.

The application of Lean tools and methods has been shown to consistently enable organizations to realize significant operational benefits relative to improvements in on-time delivery and increased material and information throughput. However, an integrated approach to a Lean deployment is required to fully realize all its potential benefits. This is because a Lean system must have several operational components, each functioning together, as an entire system, before significant improvements become visible within a process workflow. As an example, an organization cannot standardize its takt time if quality and maintenance are poor or work has not been standardized and mistake-proofed. However, improving quality, ensuring equipment and machines are properly maintained and available for use, standardizing work, mistake-proofing, and utilizing the many other tools and methods characteristic of a Lean deployment require an in-depth understanding of each specific toolset. But, these toolsets must also be integrated. Additionally, there is a natural sequence for the implementation of the various Lean system components and their toolsets. As an example, maintenance improvements, work standardization, and mistake-proofing usually precede takt time stabilization and quality improvements. In fact, to transform an organization into a Lean enterprise requires a great deal of practical learning over time through the application of Lean tools, methods, and concepts. Table 6.1 lists five key metrics Lean organizations continuously improve: reductions in order-to-delivery cycle time as measured by higher material or information throughputs, high asset utilization efficiencies, including inventory, an increased percentage of value added (VA) to total process workflow cycle time, lower per unit transaction costs, and a higher first-time yield. In this chapter, we will discuss several aspects of Lean systems that enable organizations to continuously improve these five metrics.

Ten common benefits of a Lean deployment are listed in Table 6.2. The first key benefit listed in Table 6.2 is higher customer on-time delivery (schedule attainment). A simple and standardized system will tend to execute its delivery schedule more consistently than one that is more complex and exhibits a high degree of process variation. Value stream mapping (VSM) is a very useful tool in identifying work tasks that do not have value. This information is used to eliminate the relative percentage of non-value-adding work within a process workflow. The elimination of non-value-adding (NVA) work tasks will increase the percentage of

Table 6.1 Competitive World Metrics: Value Flow

1. Order-to-delivery cycle time or throughput
2. Asset utilization efficiency, including inventory
3. Percentage value to total time
4. Per unit transaction cost
5. First-time yield

Table 6.2   10 Key Benefits of a Lean Deployment

1. Higher customer on-time delivery (schedule attainment)
2. Higher value added time/total time
3. Higher throughput of materials or information
4. Faster machine or job changeover (especially at bottleneck resource)
5. Higher machine uptime (available time)
6. Higher quality of work (scrap/rework/warranty/returns)
7. Less floor space utilized
8. Lower system inventory
9. Higher supplier on-time delivery
10. Lower overall system cost

value-adding (VA) to NVA time in a workflow. Also, a higher throughput of materials or information can be achieved as a process is simplified, standardized, and mistake-proofed. Throughput is also positively impacted by reductions in overall cycle time and inventory. Using a VSM to identify operations that constrain the flow of materials or information through a process, i.e., bottlenecks, allows a VSM team to focus Lean tools and methods to increase the available time of a system's bottleneck. These Lean improvements are usually seen as faster machine throughputs, or less time for job changeovers (especially at the system's bottleneck resource), higher machine uptime (available time), and higher quality of work (reduced scrap, rework, warranty, and returns). Additional benefits of Lean deployments are less floor space utilized, lower system inventory, and lower overall system cost.

What Is a Lean System?

A Lean system consists of the ten operational components listed in Table 6.3. These components also have sets of tools and methods that are necessary to fully implement a Lean system. A truly Lean organization will have each of these components and perhaps others more specific to the industry. Unfortunately, some organizations implement just a few of the components. As a result, they do not obtain all the advantages of a fully implemented and integrated Lean enterprise. The first key component of a Lean system is system performance measurements. Key performance measurements are listed in Table 6.2. Performance measurements show an organization where to focus its Lean improvement efforts. Measurements are important because a Lean implementation may take several years. The second key

Table 6.3   10 Key Components of a Lean System

1. System performance measurements
2. JIT/stable system
3. Standardized work (5-S)
4. Mistake-proofing
5. High quality
6. Total Productive Maintenance (TPM)
7. Single Minute Exchange of Dies (SMED)
8. Visual workplace
9. Container design (packaging)
10. Supplier agreements

component of a Lean system is implementation of just-in-time (JIT) and a standardized workflow. JIT implies that raw materials and components are delivered to the process just when they are needed for production. This increases system flexibility, and raw material and work-in-process (WIP) inventory can be kept at very low levels. However, demand and lead time variation must also be decreased to implement JIT and reduce system inventory. Variation reductions imply that work tasks have been standardized and demand is presented to the system at a constant rate with minimum variation. To achieve JIT, several of the other Lean system components listed in Table 6.3 must also be successfully implemented by an organization. As an example, Lean systems require that the work tasks be standardized or done the same way all the time. However, work tasks can be standardized only after they have been studied to the level of detail shown in Figure 5.16 and Figure 5.17. Important characteristics of work standardization include written work and inspection instructions as well as employee training to use them effectively. Mistake-proofing is another important way to standardize work tasks. It begins early in the design of products or services using design for manufacturing (DFM) and other design tools and methods. If correctly implemented, only the simplest design is released for production based on DFM principles. Quality increases as the key components 3, 4, and 5 of Table 6.3 are implemented within a workflow.

As a Lean deployment evolves, the tools and methods associated with Total Productive Maintenance (TPM) and the Single Minute Exchange of Dies (SMED) are implemented within process workflows. These are the key components 6 and 7 of Table 6.3. TPM includes the study and deployment of preventive and corrective maintenance practices. These practices ensure machines will not unexpectedly break down, disrupting the workflow. SMED is a set of tools and methods that study how jobs are set up. The goal is to reduce setup time and cost to increase the available number of setups for the system. This provides increased scheduling flexibility. In addition, the quality and reliability of job setups are increased by using SMED tools and methods. In SMED, a key concept is to separate a job setup into those operations that can be done externally or offline versus those that must be done internally or online. The concept is that if key work tasks associated with a setup can be done offline, then resources can be applied to complete these offline work tasks according to a schedule that has little impact on the actual online job setups. Also, modifications to online setup tooling and fixtures, as well as the application of mistake-proofing strategies, will help reduce the time required to complete online setups. SMED concepts will be discussed later in this chapter based on Table 6.7 and Table 6.8.

Integral to the communication process within and between workflows is deployment of visual controls in several formats. These are used to create a visual workplace. In a visual workplace, the status of a process workflow and its operations and their work tasks can be seen at a glance, i.e., they are visible. Creation of a visual workplace within a Lean system allows the status of key workflow metrics to be readily seen and controlled by the local work team. The key steps necessary to implement a visual control system will be discussed later in this chapter based on the information contained in Figure 6.10. Additional supporting components of a Lean system include rules governing the flow of standardized amounts of material or information (service industries) based on the concept of Kanban containers and supplier agreements. The concept of Kanbans will be discussed in Chapter 12 under the topic of scheduling operations. Long-term supplier agreements are also an integral component of Lean systems. Finally, long-term cooperative supplier agreements ensure suppliers have access to customer demand information and work jointly to improve the efficiency of process workflows between the two organizations.

Table 6.4 summarizes ten proven methods to improve operational efficiency. In fact, these methods are characteristic of any highly efficient system. The first method is maintenance of excess capacity within a system to maintain its scheduling flexibility to keep lead time low. This concept was discussed in Chapter 5 in the context of queuing analysis and is shown in Table 5.12. Also, improvements in quality, maintenance, and training reduce process breakdowns, which require that work be redone. The application of these methods will directly improve workflow efficiency. The creation of product family processes based on similar product or service design features or characteristics allows the design of similar workflows. This reduces the number of setups and increases scheduling efficiency. Additional benefits associated with fewer setups include higher yields and lower cycle times. Higher yields result from the fact that scrap and rework associated with starting up a job are eliminated through fewer setups. The use of multifunctional equipment also increases system flexibility. This is because equipment can be used to produce more than one type of job. As discussed above, the measurement of key process workflow metrics related to lead time, quality, and uptime is also important. The

Table 6.4 10 Key Methods to Improve Workflow Efficiency

1. Maintain excess capacity in the system.
2. Improve quality, maintenance, and training.
3. Create product family processes (collapse MRP).
4. Use multifunction equipment.
5. Measure lead time, quality, and uptime.
6. Simplify processes.
7. Use multiskilled workers.
8. Only accept orders you can complete.
9. Make to order with no excess.
10. Partner and share demand data with a few suppliers.

sixth method, process simplification, is a major topic of this chapter using value stream mapping (VSM). The seventh method, multiskilled workers, has the effect of increasing system flexibility because direct labor can be matched more closely to production schedules. Method 8 suggests that an organization should only commit to orders it knows it can efficiently produce on time, rather than make promises that cannot be kept. Making such promises results in scheduling problems because other orders must be reprioritized for production. This wastes capacity and other system resources. Products should be made with no excess unless this is a strategic decision based on external or internal factors. Making an excessive amount of a product wastes capacity and resources. Finally, contractual obligations should also be standardized and consistent across the supply chain to ensure an uninterrupted supply of materials or services.

Mapping and Analyzing Customer Value

Value stream mapping is one of the most useful and productive process improvement methods available in modern operations management. It is also called brown paper mapping because the maps are sometimes created on top of brown paper taped to a wall. The specific operations of a process are represented by sticky notes on a VMS. Visual information, regarding process metrics and opportunities for improvement, is attached to each of the process's operations. A simple VSM is shown in Figure 6.1 along with notes and a description of how metrics are added to each operation. The process mapping symbols created by the improvement team and shown in Figure 6.1 vary depending on the industry. In manufacturing, there

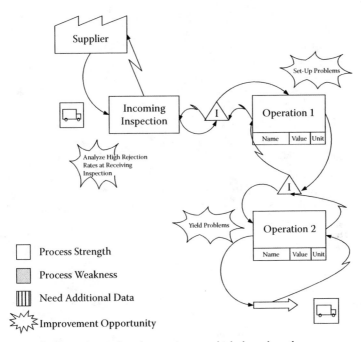

Process Strength
Process Weakness
Need Additional Data
Improvement Opportunity

Attach information to the value stream map which shows how the process is managed such as management reports, inspection and data collection forms, quality reports including scrap and rework. Maintenance reports showing machine breakdowns and any other information useful in analyzing the process.

Figure 6.1   Brown paper mapping at a supply chain or major work stream level.

are usually symbols depicting factories, trucks, and operations, but in service industries, the symbols are more representative of informational flow through the process. Below the VSM, additional information is attached to show how the process is managed at a workflow level. This information includes management reports, inspection and data collection forms, quality reports, including scrap and rework, maintenance reports showing machine breakdowns, and any other information that may be useful in analyzing the process workflow. An important characteristic of a VSM is that it is visual and built by the people doing the work operation by operation throughout a process, and it is also broken out by its major workflows or work streams. Another important characteristic of a VSM is that it is quantified relative to key operational metrics. Figure 6.2 shows a slightly different VSM that is more representative of service industries. Also, at the bottom of Figure 6.2 is a list of operational metrics that are gathered for each operation during construction of a VSM. A VSM can also be used to represent an entire supply chain or just one facility within a supply chain. However, the mapping becomes more detailed as the VSM team begins to focus on each major workflow.

Value Stream Mapping

Process:_____ Date: _____ Name:_____

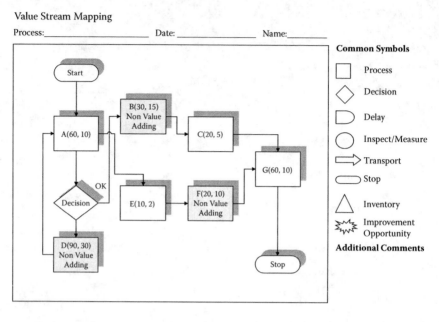

Figure 6.2   **Key forms and templates to value stream map a process.**

Operation Number:	Baseline:
1. VA/NVA/BVA	
2. Production Rate (Units/ Minute)	
3. Scrap %	
4. Rework %	
5. Downtime %	
6. Capacity (Units/Minute)	
7. Set-Up Time (Minutes)	
8. Inventory (Units)	
9. Floor Area	

Balancing Flow through the System

In Figure 6.3, a more detailed functional process map or workflow has been constructed as a network of connected activities. In this network, each operation has
been quantified using its cycle time average and standard deviation in seconds.
Please note that the standard deviation of cycle time is represented in parentheses.
After a map has been created, the baseline takt time and the key operational metrics
listed at the bottom of Figure 6.2 are calculated by the VSM team. In the current

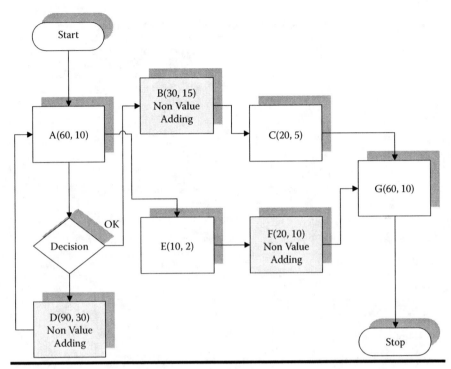

Figure 6.3 Process mapping at a product group level: current process.

discussion, Figure 6.3 has three NVA operations located at B, D, and F. Ideally, the VSM team would eliminate these NVA operations from the network. Then, over time, it would improve the efficiency of the remaining operations within the simplified network.

The takt time calculation of the current network is shown in Table 6.5. The takt time is calculated as the daily demand on the system, which is 1,000 units, divided by the available time, which is 7 hours, or 25,200 seconds, after breaks have been subtracted out of the available time. The calculated takt time for this example is 25.2 seconds per unit. In other words, every 25.2 seconds one unit is produced and exits the process workflow. In summary, a takt time is calculated by using external demand and available time per day. The next step in a VSM analysis is to add the cycle times at every operation to estimate the total time to complete one unit. In this example, it takes 290 seconds to complete one unit. Dividing the total time to complete one unit by the takt time shows the process requires 11.5 people or workstations to complete one unit with everyone working at the required takt time rate. Note that the 11.5 must be rounded up to 12 people or workstations. This would be true if every operation took exactly 25.2 seconds to complete. However, this is not usually the case because some operations take longer or less than 25.2 seconds. Referring to Table 6.5, we see that the cycle times of the various operations range

Table 6.5 Calculating Takt Time and Minimum Workstations (People)

Operation	Expected Time	Standard Deviation	Variance
A	60.0	10.0	100.0
B	30.0	15.0	225.0
C	20.0	5.0	25.0
D	90.0	30.0	900.0
E	10.0	2.0	4.0
F	20.0	10.0	100.0
G	60.0	10.0	100.0
Total	**290.0**		**1,454.0**
Demand per shift	1,000.0		
Allowed time (breaks)	3,600.0		
Available time	25,200.0		
Takt time (seconds per unit)	**25.2**		
Theoretical minimum operations or stations:			
Time to produce one unit	290.0		
Takt time	25.2		
Number of people	**11.5**		
(or a minimum of 12)			

between 10 and 90 seconds. This means we must balance the work tasks within each operation across the 12 people so that no person is allocated work whose completion time exceeds 25.2 seconds. But this may not be possible because of the spatial relationships among operations, as well as the time lost in setting up portions of different operations. This situation results in a more typical calculation, shown in Figure 6.4. In Figure 6.4, we see that some operations cannot be combined and additional people must be assigned to operations such as D, resulting in unavoidable idle time at some operations. But after initial balancing, all operations are at or below the takt time of 25.2 seconds.

The calculated efficiency of the current operational balance is just 70.7 percent of the calculated optimum because we must use 17 versus the originally calculated 12 people. At this point, the VSM team would begin analysis of the process workflow to remove all NVA operations and work tasks, deploy projects to reduce

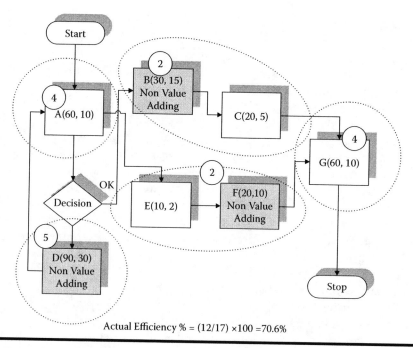

Actual Efficiency % = (12/17) ×100 =70.6%

Figure 6.4   Operation balancing.

scrap and rework, fix maintenance issues, standardize the process, apply mistake-proofing to the process, and, in summary, apply all the process improvement tools characteristic of the various operational initiatives discussed in Chapter 5. Process improvement efforts begin once the takt time has been calculated unless there are obvious forms of operational waste that can be quickly eliminated from the process. These combined improvement activities will create a "leaned out" process that is able to consistently maintain the required time of 25.2 seconds, but with lower resources requirements.

Improving Operational Efficiency

As a VSM team continues to analyze its process workflows, various "red-flag conditions" may be identified by the team. Red-flag conditions take the form of frequent changes to a job, overly complex processes, operations lacking work and inspection standards, poor measurement systems, lack of employee training, and long cycle times for a job. Additional red-flag conditions include poor environmental conditions related to lighting, cleanliness, visual perception, noise, poor employee morale, and, in situations in which capacity is constrained, equipment and people pushed to their operational limits. In situations in which order-to-delivery cycle time is long or jobs are infrequently produced, special causes of variation may also act on a process. Each of these red-flag conditions or process breakdowns may exist within a process workflow from time to time, but when a VSM team systematically documents a process using a VSM map, their combined impact on a process workflow will become apparent. The VSM process will also provide significant financial justification for process improvement efforts.

At an operational or metric level, red-flag conditions may be evident as long lead times, high per unit costs, and low quality. As an example, a VSM team will usually see high inventory levels due to queuing (waiting) of components, inefficient or unnecessary movement of materials or information, many NVA operations and work tasks, batching of work, excessive and redundant controls on a process, and long or inefficient machine or job setups. Additional process issues may include ambiguous goals or poorly designed work and inspection instructions, outdated technology, a lack of useful information relative to how to execute work tasks, poor communication between workers and supervisors, limited and poor coordination between resources and operations, ineffective training, especially with respect to employee cross-functional skills, and an overall high degree of workflow complexity, reflecting an ad hoc approach to product or service design.

There are many proven tools and methods to identify the types of required process improvements necessary to eliminate the conditions mentioned above. Several of the major ones are listed in Table 6.6, which also summarizes some of the information contained in Table 6.2 to Table 6.4. As an example, proper capacity planning is

Table 6.6 10 Key Tools and Methods of a Lean Program

1. Capacity planning (resources to meet demand)
2. Process mapping and simplification (operational spatial relationship)
3. Takt time calculation (production per time)
4. Standardization of work (used to balance flow)
5. Mistake-proofing (stabilize takt time)
6. Preventive maintenance
7. Maintaining high quality in product and process design (do it right the first time)
8. Constantly reducing lead time through application of Single Minute Exchange of Dies (SMED), transfer batching, mixed-model scheduling, and other methods (reduce lead time)
9. Continually cross-train employees and empower them within their local work groups
10. Performance measurements and visual controls (constant improvement)

a major way to ensure operations operate at their designed efficiencies. In Table 5.12, capacity was analyzed using a queuing analysis in which waiting time was analyzed versus percentage utilization of the server (person or machine). It was shown that waiting time increased nonlinearly as the utilization rate increased for the server. Of course, optimum utilization rates differ by industry. As an example, utilization rates within process industries such as paper manufacturing and oil and gasoline refining are designed to operate at a 95 percent or greater utilization, but their throughput rates have been designed to be processed at these high utilization efficiencies, i.e., continuous batches. Call centers are another example in which the servers or agents have high utilization rates. Their utilization rates often exceed 95 percent. However, incoming demand can be rerouted electronically to other call centers that are part of the same network, but currently at a lower utilization level. Unfortunately, high utilization is not often the preferred operating condition for discrete manufacturing. However, despite this fact, discrete parts manufacturers routinely load their system at high utilization rates. This has the effect of significantly increasing waiting time. This was shown in previous queuing analyses. Exacerbating these situations is the fact that high utilization rates will usually push equipment and workers to a point where quality problems begin to occur. This situation further degrades available system capacity because products or services may have to be scrapped or reworked, and others added to the schedule, to meet customer requirements.

Understanding how a process or workflow functions can also be a major positive contributor to an organization's productivity and quality. We will now discuss several specific methods that will help simplify processes and directly reduce their lead time. Figure 6.5 shows how lead time is significantly reduced by identification and

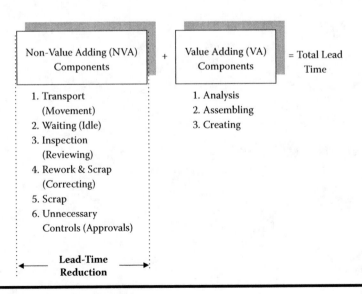

Figure 6.5　Simplifying the process.

elimination of NVA operations within a process workflow. Once a VSM has been created and quantified, its NVA operations are easily identified and can be eliminated from the workflow. Then, the modified system's takt time can be calculated as shown in Table 6.5, and the operations within the workflow can be balanced to achieve the required takt time. After process simplification and operational balancing, work tasks can be standardized and mistake-proofed to ensure that the system's takt time is stable. The result of this preliminary improvement phase of a Lean deployment is a simplified process that may still have difficulty maintaining its takt time day to day.

The next phase of a Lean improvement deployment is to manage the system's bottleneck and capacity constrained resources in a way to achieve the required takt time based on expected demand on the workflow and its variation. However, these actions will not ensure consistent performance because there will still be process breakdowns due to quality and other issues. Figure 6.6 shows the concept

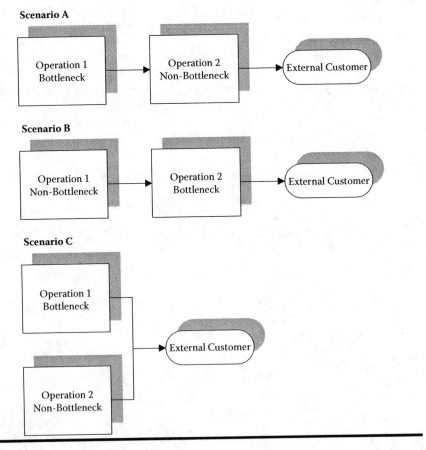

Figure 6.6 Bottleneck management.

of a bottleneck. There are three scenarios shown in Figure 6.6. In scenario A, a bottleneck resource is feeding a nonbottleneck resource. The implication is that the bottleneck has a lower throughput rate than the nonbottleneck resource. To ensure inventory remains low in the type of system represented by scenario A, downstream operation 2 must be utilized at a lower rate than the upstream operation or bottleneck resource. In scenario B, the bottleneck resource is downstream from the nonbottleneck resource, but the utilization rate of the nonbottleneck resource must match that of the bottleneck. The same utilization strategy is applied in scenario C, except two operations are feeding the bottleneck resource. In a similar manner, their throughput rates must be balanced relative to the bottleneck resource. There is a final configuration, not shown in Figure 6.6, in which a bottleneck resource feeds several nonbottleneck resources. Ensuring that the bottleneck resource is fully utilized will reduce lead time and increase the throughput of the process workflow.

Transfer batches are an important strategy that can be used to reduce lead time. In a transfer batch system, as opposed to one that uses a process batch, units are moved to a downstream work operation as soon as the required work on them has been completed by the upstream operation. Depending on the number of operations within a batch, lead time reductions of 50 percent or more are attainable using this method. The transfer batch concept is shown in Figure 6.7. Figure 6.7 shows that each unit requires one minute of work at each of the four operations, and 100 units are moved through each operation as a batch of 100 units. The total lead time, through the four sequential operations, using a process batch system, is 400 minutes, or 100 minutes + 100 minutes + 100 minutes + 100 minutes. However, using a transfer batch system, in which each unit is transferred to the downstream operation as soon as it is completed, results in a total lead time of just 100 minutes + 1 minute + 1 minute + 1 minute = 103 minutes through the four operations. This method reduces the lead time through the four operations by approximately 74 percent. Another advantage of using a transfer batch system is that quality levels will generally be higher than those of a process batch system because upstream defects are found immediately by the next downstream operation, which prevents excessive amounts of scrap or rework.

A third major method used to reduce lead time is quick response manufacturing (QRM). QRM is used to reduce lead time in master production schedule (MPS) and materials requirements planning II (MRPII) environments in which lower-level operations can react dynamically to demand or scheduling changes by matching available resources to meet demand on work cells. QRM is a modified version of MRPII systems in that local control is enabled at a work cell level. This is in contrast to an MRPII system, which pushes out customer demand based on the MPS. This MPS/MRPII demand–push environment is based on a high-level external product forecast transferred via the MPS, which is offset by the MRPII system using a product's bill of material (BOM) and related statistics, such as cumulative lead time. However, operational problems may occur if demand or capacity change within a product's cumulative lead time or frozen time fence. This may

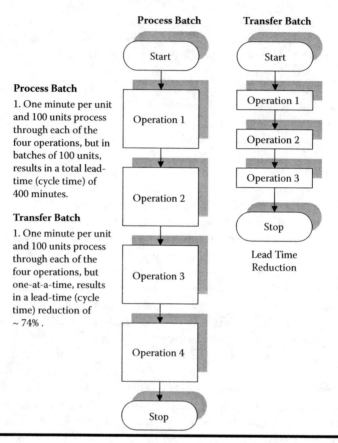

Process Batch

1. One minute per unit and 100 units process through each of the four operations, but in batches of 100 units, results in a total lead-time (cycle time) of 400 minutes.

Transfer Batch

1. One minute per unit and 100 units process through each of the four operations, but one-at-a-time, results in a lead-time (cycle time) reduction of ~ 74% .

Figure 6.7   Transfer versus process batches.

create a situation in which jobs are left uncompleted due to a lack of materials or components because materials were never ordered for production. This may cause high work-in-process (WIP) inventory levels and other process breakdowns. MPS and MRPII systems will be discussed in more detail in Chapters 12 and 13, respectively. Figure 6.8 shows a high-level view of a local work cell application of QRM in which local work cells communicate with each other using a type of Kanban system that signals upstream work cells to manufacture components for the work center immediately downstream. This communication system is enabled by collapsing the BOM so that the MRPII system is placing demand only at higher levels of the BOM. This operational change, allowing local work cells to dynamically react to schedule changes, will result in a more stable manufacturing schedule in an environment having schedule changes or unexpected process breakdowns. Other features of a QRM system include application of design-for-manufacturing (DFM) methods to simplify and modularize designs to eliminate entire portions of a BOM and outsource component manufacturing where possible. But the major advantage

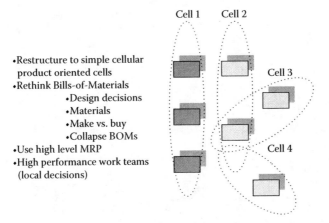

•Restructure to simple cellular
    product oriented cells
•Rethink Bills-of-Materials
        •Design decisions
        •Materials
        •Make vs. buy
        •Collapse BOMs
•Use high level MRP
•High performance work teams
    (local decisions)

Cell 1   Cell 2

Cell 3

Cell 4

*How Do Changes in System Status Inputs (MPS/MRPII Changes) at
Cells 2, 3 & 4 Impact Capacity and Flow?*

Figure 6.8   Quick response manufacturing (QRM).

of QRM is enabling and empowering high-performance work teams to make operational decisions at a local cell level based on the current workflow status relative to scheduling, available resources, and capacity. QRM, as a scheduling method, will be discussed in Chapter 13.

A mixed-model scheduling system is another useful method to reduce lead time. However, this system is very difficult to implement because its success depends on significant design changes to products or services and their process workflows. In these systems, product differentiation is made at higher levels of product assembly rather than at lower levels. The concept behind mixed-model scheduling is that if products or services have a high degree of design commonality, then their setup times will be reduced, allowing more setups at a constant cost level. This will economically allow more frequent job setups, and this will directly reduce the lead time to produce products and services. As an example, Figure 6.9 shows a manufacturing sequence (schedule) of three products, A, B, and C. In the baseline scenario, each product is produced every four weeks versus the mixed-model schedule of every two weeks. The advantage of a mixed-model schedule is that if external customer demand patterns change, the system can react to meet the revised schedule because lead time has been reduced. As an example, the lead time in the mixed-model scheduling scenario shown in Figure 6.9 is 50 percent less than that in the baseline scenario. Inventory investment is also reduced for a process workflow using a mixed-model scheduling system because it is directly proportional to the lead time of the operations with a workflow. Mixed-model scheduling systems will be discussed in more detail in Chapter 12.

Preventive and corrective maintenance systems are also deployed in Lean systems to ensure that equipment availability is at its target service level. Preventive

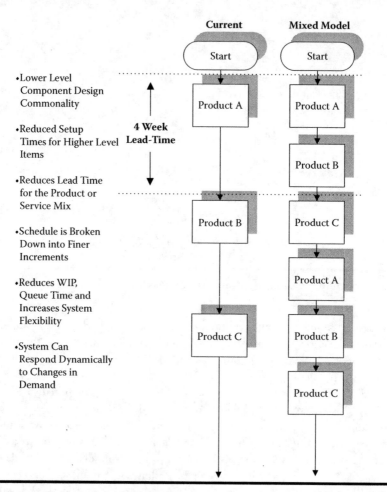

Figure 6.9   Mixed-model scheduling.

and corrective maintenance programs rely on purchasing reliable equipment and developing strategies for optimum combinations of preventive and corrective maintenance of each piece of equipment within a workflow. This ensures equipment will be available for operational usage and contributes toward takt time stabilization. Table 6.7 shows that the goal of a maintenance program is to ensure equipment availability to a target level of performance. This requires planning relative to unscheduled (corrective) versus scheduled (preventive) maintenance activities. Planning activities are accomplished by establishing equipment classifications, identifying their failure probabilities, and managing information related to economic usage of equipment. This information is used to assign maintenance responsibilities and budgets to each equipment classification to ensure their economical maintenance. Additional planning includes development of maintenance strategies based on equipment design, systems to monitor, and scheduled maintenance activities, and

Table 6.7 Key Concepts to Implementing a Maintenance Program

Availability = Reliability + Maintainability
Maintainability = (Preventive + Corrective) Maintenance

Corrective Maintenance	Preventive Maintenance
1. Diagnose problem 2. Remove failed components. 3. Order components for repair (if not in stock). 4. Repair or replace failure and correct it at that point. 5. Verify quality of the repairs.	1. System has a failure rate that increases over time and is predictable (follows a known failures distribution). 2. Cost of prevention is less than the cost of allowing the components that failed.

I.   Develop the goals and objectives for the maintenance program relative to unscheduled (corrective) versus scheduled (preventive) maintenance activities to ensure equipment availability.

II. Determine equipment classifications, failure probabilities, and other economics of maintenance by equipment classification.

III. Assign responsibilities and budgets to each equipment classification.

IV. Develop maintenance strategies based on equipment design.

V.   Develop systems to monitor and schedule maintenance activities with reporting relative to system performance and costs.

VI. Train people in use of the system.

VII. Periodically review the system performance and make adjustments as necessary to the system.

developing reporting procedures to track equipment performance and costs against their targets. Finally, people using the maintenance system must be trained in its usage, and the system must be periodically reviewed to make improvements.

Single Minute Exchange of Dies (SMED) contributes to takt time stabilization and lead time reduction by reducing setup times. This is accomplished using a combination of tools and methods. Table 6.8 list ten key steps that are necessary to successfully implement a SMED program. The first step is to identify individual work tasks related to the setup. This is done using diagrams of the local work area and identifying the sequence of work tasks necessary to do the setup work. Videos and current work and inspection instructions are very useful in SMED. After this preliminary baseline analysis of the setup work tasks and their time durations, the SMED team separates internal or online setup work tasks from those that can be completed externally or offline. In parallel, all work tasks, both internal and external, are simplified to the greatest extent possible. After the setup process has

Table 6.8 10 Key Steps to Implement Single Minute Exchange of Dies (SMED)

1. Identify individual work tasks of setup using process maps, videos, and work and inspection instructions.
2. Separate internal from external work tasks associated with setup activities.
3. Move internal work tasks to external setup work tasks.
4. Simplify all work tasks associated with internal and external setups.
5. Design equipment to unload and load dies and align tools as necessary.
6. Mistake-proof remaining setup work tasks to eliminate manual adjustments.
7. Standardize new setup procedures.
8. Apply 5-S methods to the setup areas to ensure efficient and accurate setups.
9. Train employees on the use of the new procedures.
10. Continually improve the setup process over time.

been simplified using SMED, equipment, fixtures, and other tools may be designed or purchased to help quickly unload and load dies required to complete the setups. These help to align tools as quickly as necessary. The modified setup process is then mistake-proofed to eliminate manual adjustments from the process workflow. The improved setup process is then standardized, and work and inspection procedures are developed to ensure everyone does the work required by the modified process. Integral to these SMED improvement activities is the application of 5-S methods to ensure standardization of the work and mistake-proofing. Continuous improvements are also made to the setup process over time.

Integrated with a Lean deployment may be other initiatives, such as total quality or Six Sigma. These initiatives improve process yields. They were discussed briefly in Chapter 2 and will be discussed in detail in Chapter 16. Cross-training employees and empowering them to control the quality of their work is an integral part of an effective Lean system. Performance measurements and visual controls also foster constant process improvement. Figure 6.10 shows the deployment of visual controls as a sequential process requiring 5-S as its foundation. Also, visual displays in either electronic or physical form increase the ability of the local workflow team to actively control their process workflows.

The net result of effectively deploying the Lean tools and methods listed in Table 6.6 will be a system having lower cycle times, lower per unit cost, and higher quality. Also, inventory investment will be lower because the system's operations

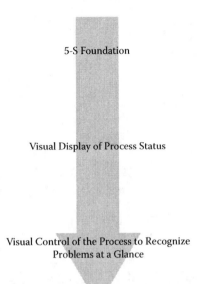

5-S Foundation

Visual Display of Process Status

Visual Control of the Process to Recognize
Problems at a Glance

Figure 6.10   Key steps to implement a visual system.

are balanced with the required takt time. This reduces WIP inventory. Now that we discussed the tools and methods listed in Table 6.6, let us return to our previous takt time example, now shown as a modified and improved version in Figure 6.11. The required resource inputs into the process have dramatically reduced over the initial baseline example, which was shown in Figure 6.3. This situation would occur when a VSM team eliminates NVA work tasks from a workflow. This is shown in Table 6.9, in which only 50 percent of the original people or workstations are now required to maintain the workflow takt time. However, Figure 6.12 only shows a reduction of just 41 percent in direct labor in the modified workflow due to balancing constraints. Additional reductions in resource levels can be obtained by applying the Lean tools and methods discussed in this chapter and summarized in Table 6.6.

Summary

Numerous organizations have attempted to deploy Lean initiatives. However, in many deployments the resultant business benefits are low, questionable, or non-existent. It is not that Lean tools, methods, and concepts do not work, but rather that they are often applied in an ad hoc manner and only sporadically within an organization. In marginal deployments, Lean tools, methods, and concepts have

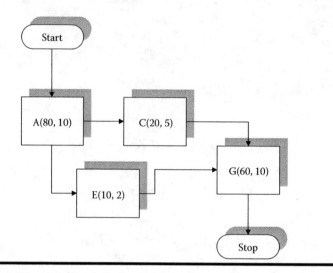

Figure 6.11   NVA operations eliminated from the process.

Table 6.9   Recalculating Takt Time and Minimum Workstations (People)

Operation	Expected Time	Standard Deviation	Variance
A	60.0	10.0	100.0
C	20.0	5.0	25.0
E	10.0	2.0	4.0
G	60.0	10.0	100.0
Total	**150.0**		**229.0**
Demand per shift	1,000.0		
Allowed time (breaks)	3,600.0		
Available time	25,200.0		
Takt time (seconds per unit)	**25.2**		
Theoretical minimum operations or stations:			
Time to produce one unit	150.0		
Takt time	25.2		
Number of people	**6.0**		

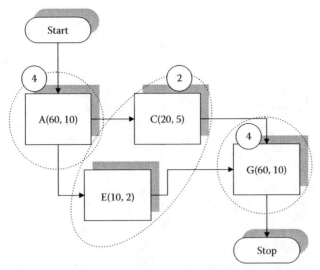

(A) Resource Reduction Over Baseline % = [(10–17)/17] × 100 = 41.2%
(B) Current Actual Efficiency % = (6/10) × 100 = 50%
   (Implement Operational Improvements on VA and BVA Operations)

Figure 6.12   Operation balancing after NVA elimination.

a minor impact on an organization. However, there are numerous case studies in which organizations have applied Lean tools and methods with great success. These are the successes that inspire others to deploy a Lean initiative within their organization. Table 6.10 listed several key concepts associated with a successful Lean deployment. They included establishing metrics to measure operational improvements to better customer on-time delivery (schedule attainment), increasing the percentage of value added (VA) time to total time, increasing the throughput of materials or information through process workflows, enabling faster machine or job changeovers (especially at bottleneck resource), increasing machine uptime (available time), improving the quality of work (reductions in scrap, rework, warranty, and returns), using less floor space through process simplification and changes to workflows, lowering system inventory levels to expose operational problems, improving supplier on-time delivery, and lowering overall system cost. These benefits are achieved because Lean tools, methods, and concepts help simplify and standardize process workflows. In addition to process simplification, there are several components that must be sequentially implemented to deploy a Lean system. These include establishing a takt time to create a baseline from which waste can be systematically eliminated from a process, and applying five key tools or methods to increase operational efficiency. These tools and methods, in addition to process simplification, include process standardization, bottleneck management, transfer batching, and mixed-model scheduling.

Table 6.10 Key Concepts of Lean Systems

1. Establish operational metrics to measure improvements relative to higher customer on-time delivery (schedule attainment), higher value added time/total time, higher throughput of materials or information, faster machine or job changeover (especially at bottleneck resource), higher machine uptime (available time), higher quality of work (scrap/rework/warranty/returns), less floor space utilized, lower system inventory, higher supplier on-time delivery, and lower overall system cost.
2. Lean tools, methods, and concepts help simplify and standardize a process.
3. There are several critical components that must be sequentially implemented to deploy a Lean system.
4. Establishing a takt time is important to create a baseline from which waste can be systematically eliminated from a process.
5. There are five key tools that will greatly increase operational efficiency: process simplification, process standardization, bottleneck management, transfer batches, and mixed-model scheduling.

Suggested Reading

Eliyahu M. Goldratt and Jeff Cox. (1986). *The Goal*, 2nd ed. North River Press, Great Barrington, MA.

Peter Hines, Richard Lamming, Dan Jones, Paul Cousins, and Nick Rich. (2000). *Value Stream Management*. Prentice Hall, Englewood Cliffs, NJ.

Rajan Suri. (1998). *Quick Response Manufacturing: A Companywide Approach to Reducing Lead Times*. Productivity Press, Portland, OR.

James P. Womack and Daniel T. Jones. (1996). *Lean Thinking: Banish Waste and Create Wealth in Your Organization*. Simon & Schuster, New York.

Chapter 7

Measuring and Improving Productivity

Competitive solution 7: Manage operational activities and improve financial performance by developing integrated financial and operational metric reporting systems.

Overview

Highly competitive organizations focus on increasing productivity and shareholder economic value added (EVA). They align organizational resources to achieve their strategies in the context of a highly competitive global environment. They always ask questions that bring them closer to their competitive goals and objectives. Invariably, their behavior is driven by metric analysis. The key to the identification of operational improvement opportunities is the analysis of financial and operational metrics. Metrics provide a focus for resource alignment and ensure an organization works on things that will increase its competitive position over time. However, there are probably thousands of metric variations across organizations and industries. These can be either aggregated into higher level classifications, such as time, money, or quality, or condensed into basic lists that almost every organization uses to manage their business. In this chapter we will present the 20 key metrics listed in Table 1.4 as typical in operations management. However, the effectiveness and efficiency of deploying these 20 lower-level metrics, in an aggregated and integrated manner, are better reflected using higher-level measures of organizational performance, such as those listed in Table 7.1. These include shareholder EVA and

Table 7.1   Metrics of Competitive Organizations: Productivity

1. Market value added (MVA)
2. Economic value added (EVA)
3. Return on equity (ROE) using an average cost of debt and equity capital
4. Productivity measured year to year
5. Net operating profit after taxes (NOPAT)

productivity metrics that are the subject of this chapter. Our goal is to show how these higher-level metrics are calculated and then disaggregated to identify and strategically align improvement projects that will enhance operational performance for your organization. In other words, our goal will be to ensure that an organization's resource allocations will be more effective (doing the right things) and efficient (doing them well).

Some of the ideas originally put forth by Stan Davis and Christopher Meyer in their book entitled *Blur: The Speed of Change in the Connected Economy*, mentioned in Chapter 1, included "make speed your mindset," "connect everything with everything," "grow your intangibles faster than your tangibles," "be able to do anything, anyplace," "put your offer on-line," "make your offer interactive," and "customize every offer." In all, they listed 50 ways an organization can blur its business. Over the past few decades, many of the new entrants into the global marketplace have effectively blurred their marketing and operational strategies to become the dominant players within their market space and niches. The ability to think outside the box to understand what is really important for an organization is difficult. But best-in-class organizations and new market entrants exhibit this unique ability. In fact, they often create entirely new markets. This enables them to gain significant market share over competitors. Shareholder value and productivity are increased in organizations that have the right strategic direction and can execute their strategies well at a tactical level. Effectiveness and efficiency also contribute to higher organizational productivity because an organization's resources are more effectively allocated and efficiently utilized to produce products or services. We will discuss several common financial measures to ensure that operations are aligned, effective, and efficient to enable year-over-year improvements in productivity and shareholder EVA.

Productivity targets should be created when an organization creates its annual operations plan. The operations plan is based on the strategic goals and objectives of an organization and is developed from the perspective of creating tactical projects to implement organizational strategy. In this complicated translation process it is extremely important that an organization create strategies to achieve its marketing, financial, and operational goals and objectives. It is also important that it actually does achieve its objectives according to schedule. But to do this, projects must be identified, linked to strategic goals, and executed on schedule. These projects must be realistic and practical to be successfully deployed and implemented on schedule. In fact, project linkage is where many organizations lose their momentum. However, rigorous financial and operational analysis can create the strategic and tactical linkages necessary to execute strategic goals and objectives. It should be noted that the execution phase of this deployment process is impacted either positively or negatively by cultural and leadership factors. These were discussed in Chapters 1 and 2. As a result, it is a fact that some organizational cultures execute well and some do not. In the latter case, there is usually a lack of accountability within an organization. Larry Bossidy and Ram Charan describe several important characteristics of a strategic plan, as well as how to effectively execute it to improve an organization's productivity and shareholder value. In an organization having poor strategic direction, even an excellent operational strategy and its execution will be hard-pressed to significantly increase productivity. As a simple example, if marketing's strategic plans are wrong, an organization may build products or services very efficiently, but be unable to sell them at expected margins, or perhaps not at all. A goal of an effective operational strategy is to ensure that all actions taken at a local operational level are consistent with higher-level goals and objectives. This chapter discusses how to link higher-level financial goals and objectives to improvement projects to increase productivity. The figures and tables in this chapter are designed to show the interrelationships between financial and operational metrics to reinforce these concepts.

Organizational productivity can be calculated as an efficient utilization of labor, materials, and capital versus the revenue received by their conversion and sale. It is calculated by taking a ratio of outputs to inputs based on inflation and economical adjustments, as shown in Figure 7.1. Figure 7.1 also shows that productivity is calculated as a year-to-year index. Pricing adjustments and changes in international currency exchange rates are also incorporated into a productivity index to ensure that production efficiencies are accurately estimated net of the impact due to external factors beyond an organization's immediate control. Figure 7.1 also shows that higher productivity results from simultaneously increasing sales and lowering costs. Net operating income after taxes (NOPAT) is another useful measure

$$\text{Productivity} = \frac{\text{Current Year Index}}{\text{Previous Year Index}} - 1$$

$$\text{Previous Year's Index} = \frac{\text{Previous Year's Sales} - \text{Adjustments}}{\text{Previous Year's Operating Costs} - \text{Adjustments}}$$

$$\text{This Year's Index} = \frac{\text{Previous Year's Sales -Adjustments} - \text{Pricing-Exchange Rates}}{\text{Previous Year's OperatingCosts} - \text{Adjustments-Exchange Rates}}$$

Figure 7.1 Calculating productivity.

of organizational efficiency unless an organization is highly leveraged financially. Higher net operating income drives higher cash flow and increases shareholders' return on equity (ROE). In fact, evaluating NOPAT relative to the capital invested to create it allows estimation of economic value added. EVA is a measure of how well assets were managed to create the NOPAT metric. It also shows the ROE that shareholders received through an organization's operational effectiveness and efficiency. Productivity can be seen as being directly correlated to ROE and EVA because it is an aggregate measure of how well an organization manages its assets in support of sales. However, like ROE, it can be distorted by how investments are financed and their assets valued by an organization. These financial metrics and others will be discussed in the context of project selection later in this chapter.

Creating Shareholder Value

ROE is influenced by the manner in which assets are financed and valued, as well as how expenses are accrued for acquisitions and some overhead components such as research and development. In other words, the full cost of these assets may not be accounted for by an organization, resulting in distortions of corporate financial performance and, by implication, its operational performance and productivity estimates. Also, ROE favors use of debt rather than cash financing relative to the acquisition of capital. For this reason, it is often recommended that ROE be estimated using an average cost of debt and equity capital to provide insight relative to shareholder equity. On the other hand, EVA measures the rate of return on total capital. EVA is estimated by dividing net operating profits after taxes (NOPAT) by the total capital used to sustain operations. These concepts are shown in Figure 7.2. Capital is calculated as all the cash invested in net assets over their useful life without adjusting for their financing. However, the cumulative depreciation expense of assets is subtracted from their investment because their value decreases over their useful life. EVA can be increased by increasing profits with the same capital (e.g., inventory, accounts receivable, cash, plants, equipment), by maintaining the same level of profit using less capital resources, or by using a strategy that combines both approaches. EVA is useful in measuring organizational performance because it focuses attention on growing sales, reducing costs, and better managing assets. These actions increase shareholder value by ensuring an investment's rate of return on invested capital is higher than the cost of that capital. This concept is used to ensure capital is not assigned to projects or investments that provide a low return on invested capital. An analogy would be to invest $100 in a bank that provides 10 percent interest rather than one that provides just 5 percent. The higher interest rate is more attractive to an investor. This is where the money should be invested. This is the basic concept behind EVA. As a side note, G. Bennett Stewart III of Stern Stewart & Company, describes a modification of the EVA concept in which an organization's value creation is based on its market value or market value added

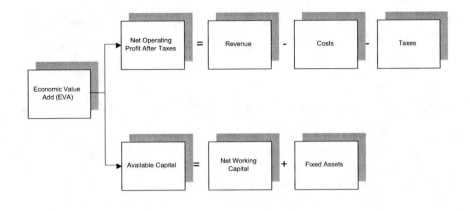

EVA = (Rate-of-Return −Cost-of-Capital) x Capital Invested

EVA = NOPAT- (Cost-of-Capital x Capital Invested)

Figure 7.2   Increasing economic value added (EVA).

(MVA). The MVA is calculated by subtracting the costs of capital from an organization's market value. MVA information on 1,000 corporations is embodied in the Stern Stewart Performance 1,000 report. However, the MVA method might be impacted by external economic factors such as stock speculation. These could bias an MVA analysis. An argument could also be made that an organization's stock is usually fairly valued by the market, based on an expected return on equity to stockholders. In either situation, MVA is outside our discussion because we are focused at an operational level.

In summary, there is a hierarchy of financial performance measurements or metrics that show how well an organization performs relative to increasing sales, reducing costs, and managing its assets. These are *market value added* (MVA), *economic value added* (EVA), *net operating income after taxes* (NOPAT), and *return on equity* (ROE). But ROE should be properly calculated using a weighted cost of capital. Productivity indices measure income received versus the costs necessary to attain that income. Income and costs should be adjusted for external economic conditions and estimated using a weighted cost of capital. These performance measures do not guarantee that an organization's future operational performance will be competitive. However, used with an understanding of the external market forces that are impacting an organization, MVA, EVA, NOPAT, ROE, and productivity indices will help an organization improve its operational performance by ensuring its resources are properly allocated and its production activities are effective and efficient. The interrelationships between financial and operational performance measurements also require that an organization work with financial analysts to ensure its improvement projects are aligned with available capital and its cost. The balance of this chapter will discuss various aspects of financial analysis and its impact at an operational level to identify improvement projects that will increase productivity and shareholder value.

Aligning Performance Metrics with Strategic Objectives

The return on equity (ROE) financial model shown in Figure 7.3 will be used in our next discussion of the measurement of operational performance. This model has been described by many authors and is also called the DuPont financial model. An assumption is that an average cost of debt and equity capital is used in the analysis. This discussion will apply to the production of both products and services, including their related functions, such as manufacturing, purchasing, accounting, and other process workflows. It should also be noted that the financial amounts and ratios shown in Figure 7.3 have been simplified and are not related to the other examples discussed in this chapter. The model is very useful at an operational level because it identifies many of the operational drivers of ROE and allows analysts to change the levels of these drivers to determine their impact on ROE. As an example, to improve an organization's profit margin percentage, sales could be increased at current pricing levels (but adjusted for inflation and other economic factors), the cost of goods sold (COGS) could be decreased (through cost reduction projects), or a combination of both strategies could be employed. Of course, this is a well-known fact, but the usefulness of a financial model occurs when we need to improve profit margins but do not know exactly where to focus our operational improvement efforts. Alternatively, there might be several competing cost reduction projects that must be evaluated and prioritized. Using a financial model will ensure alignment of resources to projects that increase ROE and, by implication, productivity. Information relative to alternative project selection and its impact on ROE and productivity can also be easily obtained by varying the model's inputs, i.e., COGS, depreciation expense, selling, and general and administrative (G&A) expenses, or perhaps by increasing sales levels or pricing to evaluate the impact of these changes on the model's higher-level financial and productivity ratios. This systematic evaluation of an organization's revenues, costs, and asset levels helps ensure a linkage between higher-level financial goals and objectives and the process improvements necessary to execute them. From our perspective, *operations* includes all organizational activities that are components of a process workflow. In other words, in addition to production, accounting, sales, marketing, logistics, and other organizational functions are considered operational. In summary, a financial model is also useful to improve MVA, EVA, NOPAT, ROE, and productivity year to year, and to meet or exceed competitive productivity levels within an organization's industry.

Table 7.2 lists several common financial ratios that are used by organizations to quickly measure their operational efficiency. It should be noted that there may be other ratios useful in measuring an organization's financial and operational

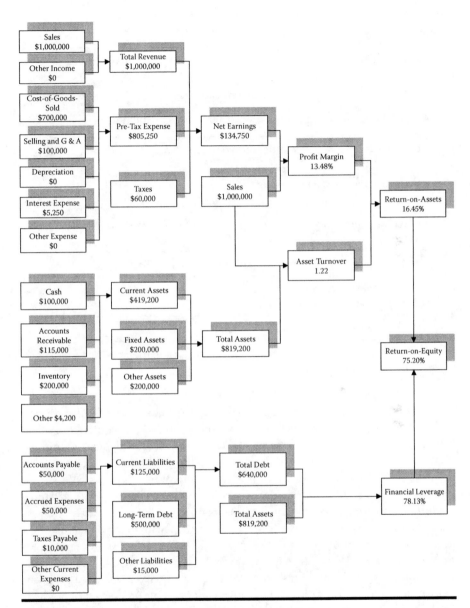

Figure 7.3   Return on equity (ROE) financial model.

performance. In fact, improvement projects can also be deployed to improve financial or operational ratios that are directly tied to EVA, ROE, NOPAT, and productivity. As an example, high liquidity implies an organization does not have to highly leverage itself through debt, but instead can self-finance its projects. An ability to self-finance investment opportunities having a high return on investment (ROI) implies an organization's ROI will be higher than if the organization was

Table 7.2   Common Financial Ratios

1. **Liquidity ratios** measure how well an organization meets its current financial obligations. ■ **Current ratio** = current assets/current liabilities ■ **Quick ratio** = (current assets – inventory)/current liabilities
2. **Activity ratios** measure the efficiency with which an organization uses its assets. ■ **Inventory turns** = cost of goods sold/average inventory ■ **Days sales outstanding** = accounts receivable/(sales/365) ■ **Asset turnover** indicates how many dollars of sales are supported by $1 of assets.
3. **Profitability ratios** measure an organization's profitability.
4. **Profit margin** shows the percent of every sales dollar the organization was able to convert into net income.
5. **Return on assets (ROA)** relates net income to total assets.
6. **Return on equity (ROE)** indicates the rate of return earned on the book value of owner's equity.

forced to borrow money. Investment opportunities include capital expenditures, increases in equipment, plant or fixed assets, and the resources required to expand into new markets or within the same market space. Also, to the extent an organization can find internal improvement projects that will generate returns higher than the cost of its invested capital, it will see improvements in its EVA, ROE, productivity, and similar metrics. Activity ratios show the efficiency with which an organization utilizes its assets. Competitive organizations have high activity ratios. As an example, inventory turns is a measure of how well an organization manages its inventory assets or investment in support of COGS or sales. As an example, for constant COGS, the lower the required inventory that is invested in raw materials, work in process (WIP), and finished-goods, the higher will be the inventory turns ratio. An inventory turns ratio can be calculated for a single product or all products produced by an organization.

How to Improve Productivity

Table 7.3 shows a dataset containing the general ledger of a hypothetical profit center for the years 2004 and 2005. This information will be used in the next several figures and tables to demonstrate the usefulness of financial analysis in the identification of productivity improvement opportunities within your operations. The first step in the analysis is to create an income statement as shown in Table 7.4 for the year 2005, including its corresponding income and expenses. The income statement is a snapshot of a company's profitability over a specified period. In this case, the period is 2005. However, it should be noted that an income statement can be impacted by the specific accounting method used to calculate its expenses. As an example, most organizations use an accrual rather than a cash accounting system. In an accrual system, revenues from sales are recorded when they are earned and expenses are recorded in anticipation of their incurrence. The accrual system is in contrast to a cash system, in which revenue and expenses are recorded as they occur without the accrual of anticipated expenses. The choice of accounting method has an impact on income for the period under consideration. The income statement shown in Table 7.4 would be used to identify projects to improve income and, by extrapolation, higher-level financial metrics. As an example, an analysis could focus on the magnitude of an expense, or perhaps a comparison of year-to-year expenditures for the same operating expense category could be made with a view toward looking for increases or decreases of the expense over its baseline year. There are many useful strategies for identifying improvement opportunities.

The second step in a financial analysis is to construct a balance sheet of an organization's profit center's assets, liabilities, and shareholder's equity using information listed in Table 7.3. Components of a balance sheet include assets, liabilities, and shareholder's equity. Assets are economic resources that are owned by a business and are expected to benefit future operations by helping to create a revenue stream that exceeds the cost of the asset and other related expenses. In fact, the evaluation of the rate of return versus the cost of capital invested in an asset is the basis of the EVA calculation as shown in Figure 7.2. Projects to improve productivity can be created to evaluate how assets are acquired, managed, and disposed of by an organization. Asset acquisition, management, and disposal require an ongoing evaluation by an organization. As an example, ongoing questions related to whether an organization should purchase or lease assets are always important. Asset conversion, through the sales or lease of current assets, frees up cash for investments that may generate higher rates of return on investment (ROI) for an organization. This occurs when assets help to increase sales or reduce operating costs. Liabilities are debts or obligations of a business to creditors. Liabilities reduce the asset value of a business and include accounts payable, loans, and other debt. Projects can be deployed to reduce liabilities relative to late fees, as well as simplification and standardization of the accounts payable workflow, or perhaps the causes for incurring these expenses. The last category of a balance sheet is shareholder's equity. It is calculated as assets minus liabilities and is a measure of a shareholder's net investment in the business. The relationship among these three balance sheet categories is defined as assets = liabilities + shareholder's equity.

Several in-depth financial analyses are usually made to correlate financial and operational performance after these basic financial statements have been created.

Table 7.3 Profit Center General Ledger

Identification	2004 Baseline (000)			
	Facility 1	Facility 2	Facility 3	Total
Cash	—	—	$85,000	$85,000
Accounts receivables	—	—	$2,500,000	$2,500,000
Inventory	—	—	$3,250,000	$3,250,000
Inventory reserve	—	—	$(45,000)	$(45,000)
Plant, property, and equipment	—	—	$8,000,000	$8,000,000
Accumulated depreciation	—	—	$(6,000,000)	$(6,000,000)
Additional assets	—	—	$1,200,000	$1,200,000
Accounts payables	—	—	$(3,250,000)	$(3,250,000)
Additional liabilities	—	—	$1,900,000	$1,900,000
Equity	—	—	**$7,640,000**	**$7,640,000**
Revenue	$(675,000)	$(450,000)	$(600,000)	$(1,725,000)
Equity income	—	—	$1,200	$1,200
Direct labor and fringe	$55,000	$20,000	—	$75,000
Indirect labor and fringe	—	—	$135,000	$135,000
Overtime premium	—	$8,000	—	$8,000
Salary and fringe	—	—	$280,000	$280,000
Inventory obsolescence	—	—	$250	$250
MRO	$9,500	$8,500	—	$18,000
Depreciation	$19,000	$9,500	$4,100	$32,600
Contracted services	$5,800	—	$4,500	$10,300
Materials to CGS	$230,000	$65,000	—	$295,000
Scrap	$900	$900	—	$1,800
Total operating cost	**$320,200**	**$111,900**	**$423,850**	**$855,950**
Volume	**3,000**	**1,000**	**2,000**	

2005 Actual (000)				Difference
Facility 1	Facility 2	Facility 3	Total	
—	—	$168,000	$168,000	$83,000
—	—	$3,100,000	$3,100,000	$600,000
—	—	$2,500,000	$2,500,000	$(750,000)
—	—	$(28,000)	$(28,000)	$17,000
—	—	$9,500,000	$9,500,000	$1,500,000
—	—	$(7,500,000)	$(7,500,000)	$(1,500,000)
—	—	$950,000	$950,000	$(250,000)
—	—	$(3,200,000)	$(3,200,000)	$50,000
—	—	$(2,100,000)	$(2,100,000)	$(4,000,000)
—	**—**	**$3,390,000**	**$3,390,000**	**$(4,250,000)**
$(700,000)	$(500,000)	$(650,000)	$(1,850,000)	$(125,000)
—	—	$1,200	$1,200	—
$61,000	$25,000	—	$86,000	$11,000
—	—	$150,800	$175,000	$40,000
$8,700	—	—	$55,000	$47,000
—	—	$302,016	$302,016	$22,016
—	—	$300	$1,500	$1,250
$9,100	$9,200	—	$18,300	$300
$29,000	$16,000	$4,300	$49,300	$16,700
$11,000	—	$5,000	$16,000	$5,700
$196,000	$66,000	—	$310,000	$15,000
$800	$1,100	—	$1,900	$100
$315,600	**$117,300**	**$462,416**	**$1,015,016**	**$159,066**
4,000	**2,000**	**3,000**		

Table 7.4   Profit Center 2005 Income Statement

Revenue	
Sales	$1,850,000
Equity income	$1,200
Operating Expenses	
Direct labor and fringe	$86,000
Indirect labor and fringe	$175,000
Overtime premium	$55,000
Salary and fringe	$302,016
Inventory obsolescence	$1,500
MRO	$18,300
Depreciation	$49,300
Contracted services	$16,000
Materials to CGS	$310,000
Scrap	$1,900
Income	**$836,184**
Taxes	—
Net income	**$836,184**

The first in-depth analysis is shown in Table 7.6. It is an evaluation of changes to pricing between 2004 and 2005. In Table 7.6, we see pricing was negative in 2005 relative to 2004 for the three facilities making up the combined profit center report, which was shown in Table 7.3. The negative pricing shown in Table 7.6 reflects the fact that there has been price erosion of the aggregate product mix manufactured by each facility. Negative pricing may be due to several factors, including competitive pressure or pricing discounts. The next step in the analysis of the erosion of selling price would be to evaluate the specific pricing of every product within the three facilities to identify the source of the pricing erosion. As an example, there could have been several reasons for the erosion of pricing, including warranty problems, external competition, and poor product forecasting that created an inventory excess, to name just a few. Analysis of the reasons for negative pricing will help to identify operational areas that need to be improved by an organization. As an example, warranty problems could have occurred due to design problems or because of process breakdowns resulting in poor quality. External competition may have increased

Table 7.5   Profit Center 2005 Balance Sheet

Assets	
Cash	$168,000
Accounts receivable	$3,100,000
Inventory	$2,500,000
Inventory reserve	$(28,000)
Plant, property, and equipment	$9,500,000
Accumulated depreciation	$(7,500,000)
Additional assets	$950,000
Total assets	**$8,690,000**
Liabilities	
Accounts payable	$3,200,000
Additional liabilities	$2,100,000
Equity	$3,390,000
Total liabilities and equity	**$8,690,000**

Table 7.6   Evaluating Price Changes

2005	Facility 1	Facility 2	Facility 3
Sales	$700,000	$500,000	$650,000
Volume	$4,000	$2,000	$3,000
Price	$175	$250	$217
2004			
Sales	$675,000	$450,000	$600,000
Volume	$3,000	$1,000	$2,000
Price	$225	$450	$300
Price change	−22%	−44%	−28%

due to product performance differentiation. Finally, in situations characterized by poor product forecasting, forecasted quantities may have exceeded actual demand and created excess inventory or product obsolescence problems. In summary, a root cause analysis is required to understand the pricing problem because there could be many reasons for price erosion. This is important because eliminating or reducing the negative impacts of pricing will have a positive impact on productivity and other higher-level financial metrics.

Table 7.7 shows how an analysis of operating income and margin can help identify where operational improvements should be made to improve productivity. Changes in operating income may be due to several factors, including those related to revenue and changes in operating expenses. Changes in revenue may be due to external economic factors such as inflation and currency valuation, increases in net allowances to customers, such as returns and warranty, or pricing changes. Changes to operating expenses, if positive, may be due to process improvements, supplier discounts, or other factors. Negative changes to operating expenses may be due to poor management of process workflows, which can be caused by myriad process breakdowns. In all cases, it is important to evaluate changes in operating income relative to the basis year under evaluation, i.e., 2004, as well as their magnitude. In situations in which the reductions in operating income cannot be easily understood or corrected at a management level, improvement projects should be created to reduce cost or increase revenue. The percentages of Table 7.7 show that sales revenue increased by 7 percent from 2004 to 2005, but, operating income

Table 7.7   Evaluating Operating Income and Margin

	2004	*2005*	*Change*	*% Change*
Revenue	$1,725,000	$1,850,000	$25,000	7%
Direct labor and fringe	$75,000	$86,000	$11,000	15%
Indirect labor and fringe	$135,000	$175,000	$40,000	30%
Overtime premium	$8,000	$55,000	$47,000	588%
Salary and fringe	$280,000	$302,016	$22,016	8%
Inventory obsolescence	$250	$1,500	$1,250	500%
MRO	$18,000	$18,300	$300	2%
Depreciation	$32,600	$49,300	$16,700	51%
Contracted services	$10,300	$16,000	$5,700	55%
Materials to CGS	$295,000	$310,000	$15,000	5%
Scrap	$1,800	$1,900	$100	6%
Operating income	$869,050	$834,984	$(34,066)	–4%
Operating margin %	50%	45%		–10%

decreased by 4 percent and operating margin decreased by 10 percent over the basis year 2004. This erosion in operating income and margin was due to increases in all the cost categories listed in Table 7.7. However, indirect labor and overtime categories had large increases in cost, and their amounts in 2005 were also large relative to 2004. Improvement projects should be deployed in areas having high percentages. As an example, the reasons for the increases in overtime and indirect labor cost should be investigated. Analysis and elimination of the root causes of high operating expenses will help improve an organization's operating income and margin as well as its productivity. An adjustment is often made to the analysis of operating income to evaluate it net of taxes and with additional income sources added to show the final income position of an organization. High income is, of course, important to an organization because the money can be used for internal investment, used to pay down debt, or given to shareholders as dividends, or shareholders' equity can be increased through stock repurchase plans.

An analysis of free cash flow is also an important concept. Reduction in the cash-to-cash cycle, as shown in Figure 7.4, helps improve productivity because an organization can reduce the amount of money it must borrow to finance its internal investments. As an example, although money can be borrowed to purchase equipment, facilities, and other assets, an organization would incur an interest expense if it borrowed money. This would tend to weaken an organization's financial position unless the cash could be put to use earning a higher rate of return than the prevailing interest rate. Analysis of the supplier-to-customer cash flow cycle allows a firm to understand how its cash is used over time and develop strategies to reduce the cash flow cycle time. This concept is analogous to increasing a system's throughput rate

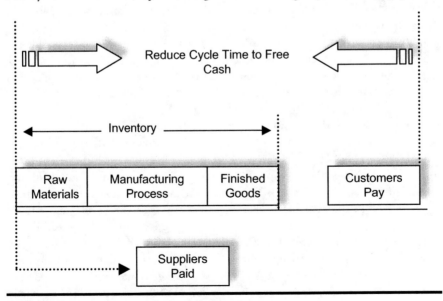

Figure 7.4   Compressing the cash flow cycle.

Table 7.8   Measuring Net Income

	2004	2005
Operating income	$869,050	$834,984
Equity income taxes	$1,200	$1,200
Measurement net income	$870,250	$836,184

or the ability to convert inputs into outputs, which are purchased at a faster rate. In best-in-class organizations, free cash flow has been optimized to a point where an organization is paid by its customers for its products or services prior to having to pay for the labor, materials, and overhead that were used to create the products or services. As an example, Dell's supply chain is famous for creating this type of system. The goal in best-in-class cash management systems is to compress the cycle time between the payment for goods and services. This is represented, in aggregate, by the COGS expense relative to receipt of payment from customers. Organizations can also utilize several strategies to compress their cash cycle. These include paying suppliers as late as possible or offering customers pricing discounts for early payment. However, best-in-class organizations compress their cash cycles by simplifying their workflows and reducing lead time throughout their process across all workflows within their supply chain. In these "leaned-out" supply chains, per unit transaction value is increased because supply chain costs are low and customers receive products and services based on compressed order-to-delivery cycle times. Table 7.9 is a cash flow analysis at a single point in time using the information contained in Table 7.3. The analysis shows cash flow increased by $1,186,184 in 2005 relative to the basis year 2004. Further analysis of Table 7.9 shows that the cash flow increase was due to reductions in inventory investment, the sale of other assets, and increases in depreciation expense, which reduced income taxes. This extra cash can be used for capital investment to increase sales revenue or to decrease operating expenses.

Table 7.10 shows four common methods that are helpful in an evaluation of how an organization should invest its free cash. These are net present value (NPV), internal rate of return (IRR) and time adjusted, payback period, and the average rate of return (ARR) methods. In the evaluation of capital expenditures or other investment decisions, the concept of the time value of money must be considered during the financial analysis. In other words, when we invest money, two facts must be considered in a financial analysis. The first is that we should evaluate the interest we would earn on the money if it were safely invested with a guaranteed rate of return because this is always a feasible and logical investment alternative to internal investments. The second is that a dollar earned in the future will be worth less than one earned today for the simple reason that we could earn interest on today's dollar, and external economic conditions such as inflation or currency exchange rates may impact the value of a future dollar. The NPV method compares the present value

Table 7.9   2005 Cash Flow Analysis

Cash Flow	2005
Measurement net income	$836,184
+Changes in working capital	
−Increase in accounts receivable	$(600,000)
+Increase in accounts payable	$(50,000)
+Net change in inventory	$750,000
+Change in other assets and liabilities	$250,000
+Depreciation	$1,500,000
−Capital expenditure paid in cash	$(1,500,000)
Cash creation	**$1,186,184**

Table 7.10   Evaluating Potential Investments

1. Net present value (NPV) is a calculation of all cash inflows, positive and negative. Investments are negative cash outflows. Project savings are treated as positive cash inflows. When evaluating multiple alternatives, select the project with the greatest NPV.

2. Internal rate of return (IRR) is the rate of return that a project earns over the period of its evaluation.

Initial investment	$20,000
Investment useful life (years)	10
Annual cash inflow	$4,000
Cost of capital	10%
Present value of annuity factor	5
The approximate IRR	16%

3. The payback method calculates the number of years required before a project recovers its initial investment. It does not discount future cash inflows.

   $$\text{Payback Period} = \frac{\text{Initial Investment}}{\text{Annual Cash Inflow}}$$

4. The average rate of return (ARR) method is the project's average cash inflows minus depreciation divided by the initial investment of the project.

   $$\text{ARR} = \frac{(\text{Cash Inflows per Year}) - (\text{Depreciation})}{\text{Initial Investment}}$$

of a project's future cash flows against the initial investment costs and relative to the minimum rate of return available from using a safe investment such as a bank account. The common rule applied is that an investment should be undertaken if its NPV is positive or its return is higher than that which would be obtained from a safe investment. However, it is also important to accurately determine a project's expected cash inflows to ensure its NPV reflects actual project risks throughout the life of the project. As an example, in some projects, the cash inflows occur early, while in other projects, they occur toward the end. Cash flows derived from the latter scenario will have more risk because external and negative factors have a greater period over which to influence a project. The IRR method evaluates the NPV of a project's cash inflows and outflows. If the IRR is equal to or greater than the minimum required rate of return of a project, then it should be undertaken. The minimum required rate of return depends on project risk versus the availability of other investment alternatives. The payback method calculates a simple ratio of the initial investment divided by the project's annual cash inflow. It does not consider the time value of money, but it does provide a quick estimate of the project's benefit. The ARR method is calculated by dividing the project's cash inflows minus depreciation by the initial investment. The investment alterative having the highest ARR is selected. However, the time value of money is ignored in the ARR analysis, and income rather than cash flow data is used in its calculation. On a positive side, ARR considers the full useful life of the asset's investment and is directly related to an organization's financial statements.

Figure 7.5 shows how productivity can be calculated using some of the key information contained in Table 7.3. The productivity improvement is shown to be 6.9 percent in 2005 over 2004. These are the types of analyses your organization may want to use to identify and measure its operational improvements. The other higher-level metrics shown in Table 7.3 could also have been improved in the 2005 versus 2004 scenarios. The resultant productivity improvement was assumed to have occurred through numerous process improvements that positively impacted revenue, cost reductions, and more efficient asset utilizations. Also, the productivity

$$\text{Productivity} = \frac{2.16}{2.02} - 1 = .069$$

$$\text{Previous Year's Index} = \frac{1,725,000}{855,950} = 2.02$$

$$\text{ThisYear's Index} = \frac{1,850,000 + 185,000}{1,015,016 - 11,000 - 40,000 - 22,016} = 2.16$$

Pricing Impact = $1,850,000*10% = 185,000
Direct Labor Increase = $11,000
Indirect Labor Increase = $40,000
Salary Increase = $22,016

Figure 7.5   Productivity analysis for 2005.

index was impacted to some extent by external factors. This implies that an organization must develop strategies to minimize external risks that may negatively impact productivity. Another interesting observation derived from the analysis is that productivity must be improved throughout an organization, rather than only within its production operations. It makes no sense to optimize production operations only to waste the resultant cost savings on inefficient front office operations.

Aligning Operational Improvements with Strategy

An organization's productivity and financial performance are directly related to its operational effectiveness and efficiency. In turn, operational effectiveness and efficiency are directly related to how an organization's products or services are designed and the production processes that were created to produce them. Also important to operational effectiveness and efficiency are the day-to-day management decisions that may impact the yield, availability, and cycle time of an operational system. Figure 7.6 shows that once a production process has been created, it should be managed to execute an organization's strategic goals and objectives. At an operational level, the goal will always be to select a mix of projects, tools, and methods to systematically improve process yields, increase system availability or capacity, and lower operational cycle times within the limitations of the design of its products or services. Specific tools and methods are required to improve productivity at a local workflow level based on productivity opportunities. As an example, to improve yield, Six Sigma tools and methods are applied to identify the root causes for the low yields. On the other hand, increasing system availability or capacity and reducing its operational cycle times requires the application of Lean tools and methods. Reduction in operational cycle time implies that the non-value-added work content of a process can be systematically reduced to enable periodic rebalancing of work across an organization's process workflows. This will help an organization meet demand, but with fewer resources. These activities reduce operating expenses and improve productivity.

An organization must systematically identify and prioritize the operational projects that are required to achieve its strategic goals and objectives. This is done using financial and operational data to identify productivity opportunities down to a workflow level of detail. Figure 7.7 shows how this identification process is achieved, in practice, using a strategic flow-down model. The flow-down analysis could start at any level of Figure 7.7, but when it is completed, the lower-level projects must be linearly aligned with higher levels of Figure 7.7. As an example, we could start the project identification analysis at a business enterprise level, then successively break down high-level goals and objectives to a project level. Alternatively, we could start the analysis bottom-up using a major process breakdown to create improvement projects. The ultimate goal of this analysis and the subsequent deployment of improvement projects is to correlate performance gaps and their financial impact on an organization to the root causes of the performance gaps at an operational level. As

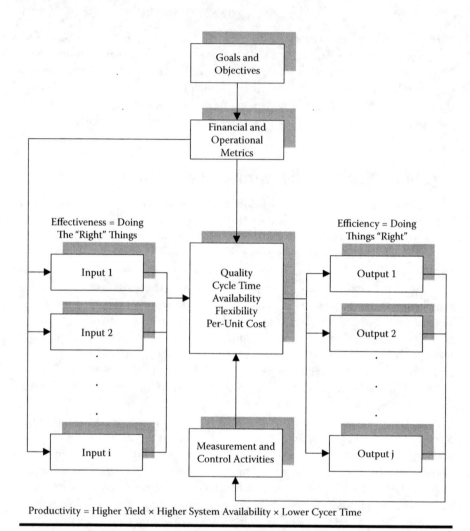

Figure 7.6 Evaluating productivity at an operational level.

an example, in Figure 7.7, the high-level financial goal is improvement of cash flow. Two areas have been identified as impacting cash flow, and thus provide an opportunity to improve it. These are reductions in assets, such as inventory and fixed assets. The next step of the analysis is to break down the inventory investment category and its turns ratio for each facility within an organization. Recall that an inventory turns ratio is defined as the cost of goods sold divided by the average inventory investment necessary to maintain the COGS level. The lower the inventory investment at constant COGS, the higher will be its turns ratio. Taking the analysis down another level, the two major drivers of inventory are identified as lead time and demand variation. The longer the process lead time, the more raw materials, work in process (WIP), or finished-goods inventory that will be required to cover the time necessary

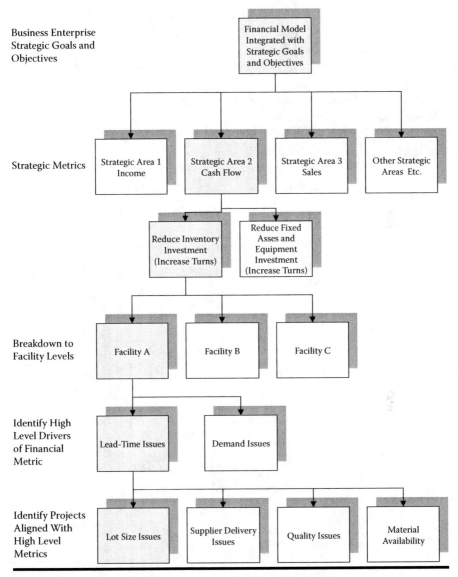

Figure 7.7   Aligning operational improvements with strategy.

to meet expected customer demand. Also, the higher the variation in demand or its forecasted value, the higher the safety stock inventory required to meet demand at the targeted per unit service level. Finally, working down through lead time, any operational problems that increase an operation's cycle time are potential improvement projects once their percentage contributions to the inventory investment problem and turns ratio have been identified by an improvement team. Figure 7.7 also shows that the category "lead time issues" can be broken into subcategories, such as lot size, supplier delivery, quality, and material availability. Lean or Six Sigma projects can be formed around any of these issues to reduce inventory and improve cash flow, and ultimately productivity.

Figure 7.8 shows there are several other methods that may be useful to identify and classify operational projects.

Often, one or more of these methods can be used to fully characterize and identify performance gaps. As an example, cultural surveys may identify areas in which a workflow is breaking down, but a subsequent financial and operational analysis may be required to quantify the magnitude of the process breakdown. Cultural surveys include one-on-one interviews at all organizational levels to identify opportunities for process improvement. In addition to one-on-one interviews, online surveys can

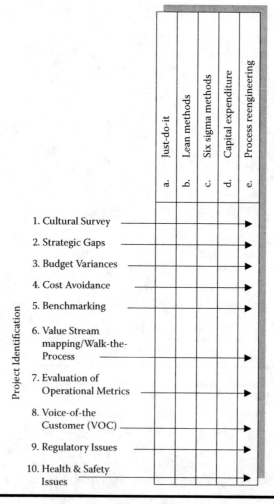

Figure 7.8   Project selection versus process improvement strategy.

also be conducted to ask questions of selected groups of employees, suppliers, or customers to follow up on previously asked questions. The identification of strategic performance gaps has already been discussed as the process of determining the relationship between higher- and lower-level financial and operational metrics. Budget variances can be used in the analysis of performance gaps, but it is important to ensure that the budget was accurately set in the first place, and the budget variance is a chronic problem, before deploying improvement projects. Cost avoidance projects may also be useful if their basis can be rigorously verified by financial analysts. An example of a cost avoidance project would include a situation in which current materials must be replaced with safer materials, perhaps due to regulatory requirements, and a failure to replace them in a timely manner may result in future fines to an organization. Benchmarking is another useful analytical tool that can be used to identify improvement projects. In benchmarking, similar processes either within or external to an organization are evaluated, and their performance metrics compared to those of the organization benchmarked. Organizational differences between metric levels may indicate opportunities to create projects to close identified gaps in performance. Because many aspects of an operation are not captured in management reports, it is always useful to "walk the process" to identify the process waste associated with non-value-adding operations, including their rework loops. Value stream mapping (VSM) and other Lean tools and methods are useful tools in these analyses. The direct evaluation of performance gaps associated with operational metrics will also show where improvement projects can be deployed within an organization. But these opportunities must also be evaluated relative to their strategic alignment. Listening to the VOC through marketing research, complaints, one-to-one interviews, surveys, and on-site visits will also often yield many potential areas for process improvement. Finally, process breakdowns causing regulatory, health, safety, or environmental problems can serve as good sources for improvement projects.

Figure 7.8 also shows there are several strategies or toolsets that can be employed to execute a project. These include just-do-it projects, Lean methods, Six Sigma methods, capital expenditures, and process reengineering. Many projects have a known solution. In these types of projects, the root causes for the problem should be eliminated as soon as possible without extensive analysis. On the other hand, Lean methods, including 5-S (sorting, simplifying, sweeping, standardization, and sustaining), mistake-proofing, and process simplification, should be applied if a root cause analysis is known and its elimination lends itself to the application of well-known Lean tools and methods. However, in more complex situations in which extensive data analysis is required of the problem, Six Sigma tools and methods may be more appropriate for the identification and elimination of root causes. Solutions to process breakdowns might also be related to inefficient product or process designs. In these situations, capital expenditures may be required to automate or significantly change the design of the product or process using design for Six Sigma (DFSS). Finally, reengineering may be required to extensively change a process workflow design. Often, reengineering is associated with across-the-board cuts in direct labor. However, across-the-board cuts in resources, including direct labor, without process analysis, often cause as many problems as they eliminate. When properly executed, however, reengineering will include a root cause analysis of a process workflow using one or more tools and methods associated with initiatives such as Lean, Six Sigma, and others, with a goal of improving productivity based on fact-based improvement actions.

The operational goal is to always link deployment of improvement projects with relevant toolsets and methods to improve financial performance and organizational productivity. This concept is shown in Table 7.11, in which several projects are correlated to the initiative most likely to be useful to their solution, as well as the operational and financial metrics that will most likely be impacted by subsequent process changes. As an example, increased line rates will increase material or information flow by reducing cycle time within the various operations throughout a process. Of course, reduction in cycle time or increases in line rates must be tied to a system's takt time. However, a project's benefits will include direct labor savings and increases in capacity at an operation or workstation level. The direct labor savings are due to the fact that as operations become more efficient, there will be a point reached at which they can be combined into fewer workstations. These concepts were discussed in Chapter 6. But as a simple review, if two workstations were originally matched to a hypothetical takt time of one unit every 60 seconds, and their cycle time is reduced by 50 percent, they can be combined into just one station. This would save one full-time-equivalent person across both of the original workstations. Using another example from Table 7.11, increasing manufacturing

Table 7.11   Linking Projects to Achieve Productivity and Value Targets

Project Focus	Initiative Toolset	Key Productivity Enabler	Financial Statement Impact
Increase line rate	Deploy Lean projects	Increase throughput	Labor and increase available capacity
Increase inventory turns/reduce investment	Lean projects to reduce lead time	Reduce average inventory levels to increase turns	Reduce holding costs and material handling expenses
Increase manufacturing yield	Deploy Six Sigma projects	Reduce scrap and rework	Reduce material and labor expense
Reduce unscheduled maintenance	Total Productive Maintenance (TPM)	Increase equipment availability and reduce downtime expense	Reduce direct labor cost and increase capacity

yields directly reduces the direct labor and materials required by a production process. This is because scrap and rework require material and labor over the predetermined work standards. There are many other relevant examples throughout various industries, and even functions within a given industry. But a common theme of Table 7.11 is that metric linkage must be established for every project to ensure organizational alignment and optimum resource allocation to increase productivity year to year.

Once project improvement opportunities have been identified, they are incorporated into a project charter, as shown in Figure 7.9. A project charter contains several sections, used to describe the process workflow in which the problem occurs, the extent of the problem, its impact on the organization, and the anticipated business and customer benefits obtained by eliminating it from the process workflow.

Administrative Information

Project Name: Date:

Business Unit:

Champion: Process Owner:

Project Timeline:

Project Definition Information

Problem Statement:

Project Objective:

Project Metric (s):

Resource Requirements

Team Members:

Project/Team Leader:

Financial Information	Margin Revenue	Cost Reduction	Cost Avoidance	Other
One Time Cost Savings				
Project Costs				
Total Benefit				

Figure 7.9   Common elements of a project charter.

Also included are the resources required to investigate and eliminate the problem, as well as a detailed financial analysis of the project's cash inflows, outflows, required investment, applicable financial ratios, such as payback and internal rate of return (IRR), and their combined effect on a project's productivity impact. Project charters are also communication vehicles enabling an improvement team to gain organizational support for its project. Finally, charters are useful when aggregating many projects across an organization to show senior management how strategic goals and objectives will be executed at an operational level.

Summary

The major concepts of this chapter are summarized in Table 7.12. The first major concept that is important to organizational competitiveness is the measurement and improvement of EVA for shareholders. This should be a major goal of any commercial organization. Increasing productivity will enable an organization to increase EVA and become more competitive. However, increasing productivity is a methodical process that requires implementing financial systems to measure year-to-year productivity. Financial systems also help identify projects that improve productivity to ensure organizational competitiveness. It is important to align projects at an operational level with strategic goals and objectives to ensure optimum resource allocation. Another important project deployment consideration is that projects should be balanced relative to all initiatives. Every project should also be documented using project charters. This will enhance communication across an organization and enable easy summarization of an organization's productivity efforts.

Table 7.12　Key Concepts to Improve Productivity

1. Measure and improve economic value added (EVA) for shareholders. This will focus attention on improving productivity.
2. Measure year-to-year productivity and identify projects that will improve productivity to ensure your organization is competitive.
3. Align projects at an operational level with strategic goals and objectives.
4. Deploy projects throughout the organization to achieve organizational productivity goals and objectives.
5. Ensure the deployed projects are balanced relative to the initiative they will use and the resources necessary to implement the improvements.
6. Use project charters to document and communicate all projects.
7. Measure all project benefits and take corrective action if the benefits are not achieved on schedule.

Suggested Reading

Larry Bossidy and Ram Charan. (2002). *Execution: The Discipline of Getting Things Done.* Crown Business.

John Donovan, Richard Tully, and Brent Wortman. (1997). *The Value Enterprise: Strategies for Building a Value Based Organization.* McGraw-Hill, New York.

Robert S. Kaplan, Ed. (1990). *Measures of Manufacturing Excellence.* Harvard Business School Press, Boston.

James M. McTaggart, Peter W. Kontes, and Michael C. Mankins. (1994). *The Value Imperative: Managing Superior Shareholder Returns.* Free Press.

Jae K. Shim and Joel G. Siegel. (2001). *Handbook of Financial Analysis, Forecasting and Modeling,* 2nd ed. Prentice Hall, Englewood Cliffs, NJ.

G. Bennett Stewart III. (1990). *The Quest for Value.* Harper Business.

OPERATIONS PLANNING, MANAGEMENT, AND CONTROL

3

Chapter 8

Capturing Customer Demand

Competitive solution 8: Manage customer demand using best-in-class tools, methods, and concepts to increase sales revenue, lower operational costs, and prevent lost sales and stock-outs.

Overview

Managing demand estimates to ensure they are accurate and timely is a challenging task for an organization. It requires an understanding of customers' needs at specific points in time and geographical locations across a supply chain. This is an increasingly challenging task, on the one hand, because consumer markets have become fragmented and culturally diverse, but also easier because information technology can be deployed to immediately measure customer demand when and where it occurs. In this chapter, we will discuss demand management with a focus on the actual mechanics of forecasting. In later chapters we will discuss the migration toward developing more effective demand management systems that rely on customer relationships as well as the collection of real-time demand information. *Real-time* implies that demand information can be made available to an organization through its information technology (IT) systems, point-of-sale (POS) data collection and analysis, as well as electronic Kanban, and other advanced IT applications that help to manage and control the process workflows of a system. The major purpose of this chapter is to disuses the wide range of quantitative tools and methods that comprise demand management. These range from forecasting models

Table 8.1   Competitive World Metrics: Demand Management

1. Month-over-month forecasting accuracy by product group and product by location
2. Month-over-month percentage of products whose demand is certain by product group and customer
3. Month-over-month percentage of forecasted products on a minimum/maximum system by product group
4. Month-over-month number of products managed by forecasting analysts
5. Expenses directly attributable to poor demand management practices by their category and reason

using simple time series estimates of future demand to more advanced econometric models that use several independent variables to help predict future sales. Relative to econometric models, independent variables, including leading, lagging, and coincident economic indicators, as well as other variables, are used to construct these models. Although many industries rely on forecasting models, an ultimate goal of an organization should be to build closer customer relationships to better understand its customers' demand patterns. Closer customer relationships will minimize the necessity of developing formal mathematical forecasting models. In the last part of this chapter, nonmathematical tools and methods will be discussed relative to demand management. Table 8.1 lists key metrics that reinforce a philosophy that organizations should move to the greatest extent possible away from mathematical forecasting. However, if it must be done, then it should be done well. This means that forecasting accuracy should be measured and improved over time. Also, process breakdowns that are attributable to poor demand management practices should be measured and their root causes eliminated from an organization.

Organizations use a combination of methods, both qualitative and quantitative, to predict product demand. Qualitative methods include simply obtaining opinions of key managers, bringing people together who are knowledgeable of a customer segment in the form of a "jury of executive opinion," and polling an organization's sales force using one or more survey methods. This is called obtaining a sales force composite. Quantitative methods fall under the general categories of time series analysis and econometric models. In time series analysis, a forecasting model is built using lagged values of a dependent variable to predict its future demand. An example would be predicting sales next month based on sales this month. In contrast, econometric models forecast sales in future periods using lagged values of a dependent variable, as well as one or more independent variables. Leading variables in particular allow an organization to economically model and predict future demand based on current values of one or more important variables that are known to predict future demand.

Forecasts are also required by many diverse functions within an organization to plan their operations. As an example, marketing uses forecasts to plan its marketing, advertising, and sales promotional activities, including product pricing and promotion for various distribution channels. These forecasts are usually made at a product group level on a monthly basis as well as into the future. Sales uses forecasts to measure their operational performance against sales targets and objectives. Sales forecasts are usually made by product group and region on a monthly basis and out into the future for 12 months. Logistics requires forecasts to determine where, when, and how much inventory is required to satisfy customer demand, as well as where to make capital expenditures to move materials more efficiently through their supply chain. These types of forecasts are usually required at an item and warehouse stocking location level on a monthly basis and out into the future for 12 months. Manufacturing or operations requires that forecasts be made for purchased materials and components or dependent demand items, as well as to set up its manufacturing schedules. Forecasts are also required by manufacturing or operations at an item and facility level on a monthly basis and 12 months out into the future. Finally, finance requires that accurate forecasts be made to properly set sales, costs, profit, and cash flow projections for an organization at corporate, divisional, and product line levels on a monthly basis and out into the future 12 months. Selection of a forecasting time horizon is an important characteristic of all types of forecasting methods. The forecasting time horizon is the period over which a forecast is estimated and used by an organization. Another important concept in developing a forecast is the forecasting time interval. This is the actual unit of time on which the forecasting model is based, i.e., month or other convenient time intervals.

Statistically based forecasting models require various degrees of analytical sophistication. The simpler time series models characterized by moving average or exponential smoothing models require little skill. In fact, they can be automated by an organization. If seasonality is modeled, then 36 to 60 months of data is required to accurately estimate the seasonal indices month over month. However, if seasonality estimates are not required, then 12 to 24 months of demand data is required to build a model. However, more complex econometric models require advanced analytical skills. The data required to build these types of models is usually a minimum of 10 observations or time periods per estimated parameter in the model. As an example, if a model has two or three parameters, then more than 36 months of demand data may be required to build the model. In conclusion, statistically based forecasting models, although useful in estimating future demand, may have accuracy issues and require advanced analytical skills, and the required length of the required historical demand pattern may span several years. However, because of technological advances and an improved capability to acquire real-time customer demand information, organizations are moving away from these statistically based models to the greatest extent possible, but they are also learning to more effectively build and analyze forecasting models to the extent they must be used within their organization.

An effective and efficient use of demand management tools and methods is critical to an organization. However, few organizations systematically work to improve their demand management capabilities. This results in a heavy reliance on statistically based forecasting models with their associated high error rates. Forecasting error rates may also increase over time. As the time horizon becomes longer. In other words, forecasts made at a lead time of 90 days, or on a quarterly basis, will be more accurate than those made at a lead time of 1 year, or on an annual basis, all other things equal. Forecasts are also more accurate in aggregate at higher levels, such as a product group, than at lower levels, such as an item and location. As an example, industry forecasts tend to be more accurate than those made at a business entity level. Also, business unit-level forecasts tend to be more accurate than those at the product group level. Studies by John Mentzer and Carol Bienstock have shown that at the business-unit level, statistical forecasting can be successfully applied to forecast product demand with error rates in the 5 to 25 percent range under typical conditions that impact demand estimates. As an example, at an item and location level, forecasting error rates can easily exceed 25 percent on a month-to-month basis. In summary, forecasting error rates are difficult to reduce. This requires that an organization develop demand management strategies that do not rely exclusively on statistically based forecasting models. Also, to the extent forecasting models are used by an organization, they should be systematically reduced over time.

The application of forecasting models relative to an estimation of future demand requires that their demand pattern be nonrandom. In other words, it should have an underlying structure that is manifested in identifiable demand patterns, such as trends and periodicity, seasonality, or cycles. These underlying patterns should also be relatively stable or predictable from one time interval or period to another. Also, to build forecasting models having a maximum degree of accuracy, it is important that demand patterns repeat several times over the same time interval. Thus, to build a seasonal forecasting model requires several month-over-month historical demand observations. This means that several years' worth of historical data is required to build a seasonal model using a time period of one month to estimate the monthly seasonal indices. Also, econometric models may also require incorporating future-looking information such as leading economic indicators or an extensive historical record if long cycles at a macroeconomic level are present. It should also be noted that there are many situations in which standard forecasting methods cannot be used to build a model. These include unusual events such a loss of market share, recessions, and similar unexpected events that impact customer demand patterns. Forecasting models will also not be effective in situations such as one-off events, in which there are no underlying patterns within the historical record. Examples of such events include the creation of unforeseeable technology that becomes a competitive threat and adversely impacts future sales, and customer bankruptcies that lower expected sales.

What Is Demand Management?

Demand management is a combination of estimating, planning, and scheduling activities that are used to accurately estimate customer demand across a supply chain period to period into the future. This information is used to ensure that adequate capacity and resources are available to meet forecasted demand. Initially, forecasts are strategically deployed through an organization, as shown in Figure 8.1. Then they are pushed down to lower organizational levels. This ensures future demand is efficiently allocated across an organization's business units and production facilities at a product group level for each period over the forecast time horizon. At a facility level, manufacturing schedules are created, by a master requirements planning (MRPII) system, for dependent demand items, which include the materials and components making up a product. At this point in a manufacturing schedule, demand is firm or "frozen" based on the cumulative lead time required to assemble all components into the final product or independent demand item. Figure 8.2 shows how demand is aggregated and forecast from several perspectives to enable

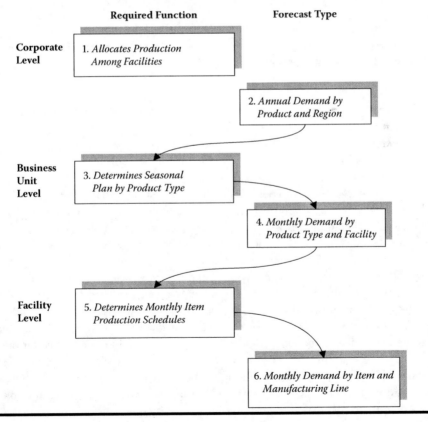

Figure 8.1   Strategic forecasts.

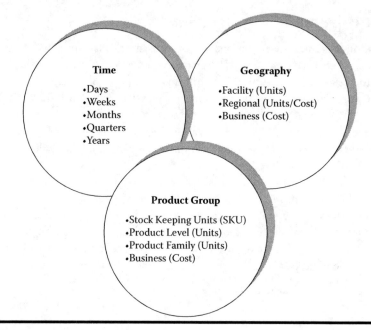

Figure 8.2 Demand aggregation.

more effective management and control of capacity across an organization's supply chain.

Demand is estimated or forecast for independent demand items or end items, where the final products are actually sold to customers. This hierarchal concept is shown in Figure 8.3. A product consists of subassemblies that are made of components or parts. In turn, components are made up of various materials. Once demand has been estimated for independent demand items, it is fed into a master production scheduling (MPS) system. The MPS contains the higher-level manufacturing schedule for an organization's products in an aggregated form by facility and offset by the time at which a product should be manufactured to meet its schedule. An MPS aggregates several sources of demand within an organization and transfers this aggregated information to a material requirements planning (MRPII) system. An MRPII system, using a bill-of-material (BOM) as well as on-hand inventory information, creates schedules for the receipt of raw materials, components, and similar dependent demand items. This is done by item and location based on their lead time offsets. This information is made available to the supply chain for planning and execution purposes, including the purchase or manufacture of dependent demand items. This process is shown in Figure 8.4, in which firm orders are combined with forecasts based on uncertain demand using historical demand patterns of many customers. This information is aggregated and used by an MPS along with

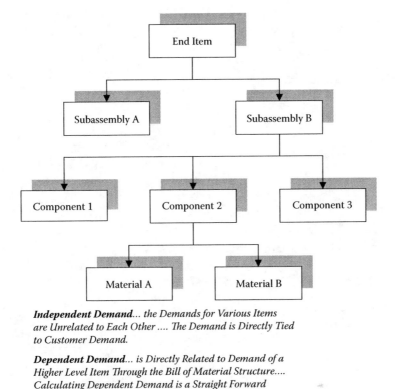

Independent Demand... the Demands for Various Items are Unrelated to Each Other .... The Demand is Directly Tied to Customer Demand.

Dependent Demand... is Directly Related to Demand of a Higher Level Item Through the Bill of Material Structure.... Calculating Dependent Demand is a Straight Forward Computational Problem.

Figure 8.3   Independent and dependent demand.

rough-cut capacity requirements and transferred to an MRPII system. An MRPII system uses a product's BOM and on-hand inventory status and the aggregated demand of product by quantity, location, and required due date to schedule the time-phased manufacture of all dependent demand items throughout a supply chain. The system is planned and controlled by an MPS system as shown in Figure 8.4. As a product's schedule arrives at its cumulative lead time or "time fence," it becomes firm, or frozen, and orders are placed for its dependent demand items based on their cumulative lead time. Also, demand forecasts past a product's cumulative lead time are not fixed because they can be modified as shown in Figure 8.5. This discussion will continue, at a more detailed level, in Chapters 11 to 13.

Figure 8.6 is a more detailed perspective of the basic elements of a forecasting system than that shown in Figure 8.4. In Figure 8.6, the sources of demand are aggregated by a demand management module within a foresting system and used to build the forecasting models. These models can be of varying types. Two common forecasting models include time series, using exponential smoothing algorithms,

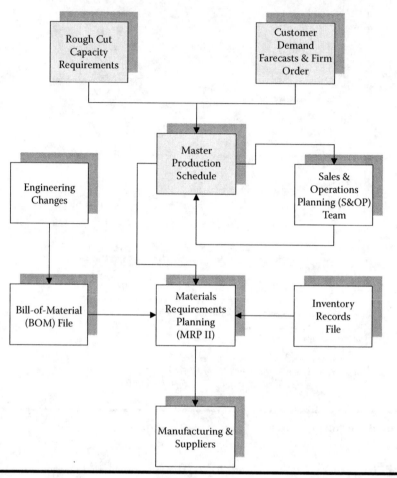

Figure 8.4   Forecasting system overview.

and multiple linear regression (MLR). Exponential smoothing models are built using historical demand information, and smoothing parameters to fit the model to the historical pattern, as well as by modifying the length of the historical demand record. The final form of a forecasting model depends on its position within its life cycle. As an example, models of new products are usually built using exponential growth curves because their demand is rapidly increasing over time, whereas mature products may exhibit no trend because their month-to-month demand is constant or flat. A forecasting system also creates management reports of various types. These break forecasts down by time period, geographical location, organizational level, and product group. The forecasts are also made on a unit basis, but are converted into monetary units using standard cost data. Forecasting accuracy metrics are created by these systems to aid in continuous improvement efforts.

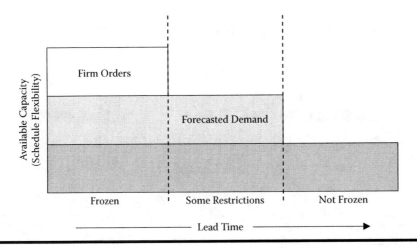

Figure 8.5   Time fence.

Table 8.2 lists ten key characteristics of an effective foresting system. These enable creation of efficient and useful forecasts for an organization. Reviewing the list, we see it is important to use a product's actual historical demand to develop forecasting models. As an example, some organizations use a product's shipment history to forecast demand, but this is a serious error because shipment history reflects what was actually available to ship to the customer at the time of filling the order. At the time of order filling, a product may not have been available. Basing forecasts on shipment histories will create a chronic backorder situation for a product once it becomes unavailable. Basing forecasts on actual customer demand is the proper method to build a forecasting model because if items are not available for shipment, the forecast will still be based on original customer demand, and the product's target inventory level will be maintained by the system. However, it is very useful to simultaneously record a product's shipment history and actual and forecasted demand. This will enable an organization to analyze and eliminate ordering discrepancies from its system. Also, time series that exhibit periodic patterns such as seasonality require at least three to four years of month-over-month observations to ensure monthly seasonal indices are accurately estimated by a model. Another important characteristic of a good forecasting system is that its time horizon goes out at least as far as the organization's annual operating plan to enable it to plan capacity. It is also important that forecasting accuracy be very high at a product's cumulative lead time, based on the time fence concept shown in Figure 8.5. This ensures its manufacturing schedule is estimated accurately and will remain stable. In addition, time series periodicity, caused by anticipated product promotions or other atypical demand patterns, must be analyzed and incorporated into a product's forecast. Forecasting analysts should also be able to specify the periodicity of a forecasting model to truncate a time series' historical basis if there have been

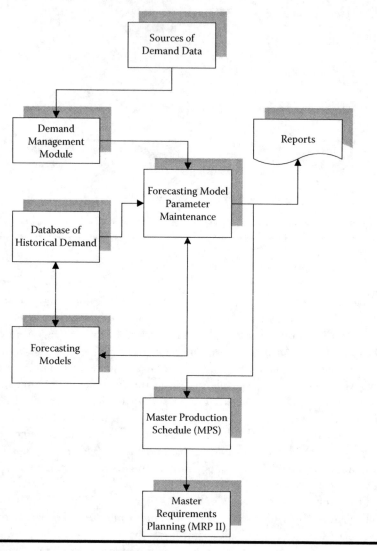

Figure 8.6   Forecasting modeling system.

significant and recent changes to its underlying demand pattern. This might occur if a product is at the end of its life cycle and its demand exhibits irregular patterns. In this situation, analysts may want to use only the most recent demand history to ensure the forecast model represents current demand patterns. Additional information required to build a forecasting model may include underlying macroeconomic trends such as recessions or expansionary cycles. Effective forecasting systems should also have the capability to automatically create and track product forecasts.

Table 8.2   10 Key Characteristics of an Effective Forecasting System

1. Use actual demand by item and location
2. In addition, records demand by orders and shipments by item/location
3. Three or more seasons (years)
4. Forecast horizon at 12 months for all items
5. User-specified periodicity
6. Allows subjective adjustments by management
7. Trend, seasonal, and other models
8. Tracking and automatic parameter estimation
9. Ability to change forecast at group level
10. Allows for continuous improvement of the system

This is extremely useful to organizations that sell thousands of products to their customers. Automatic tracking of a forecast model enables analysts to focus their attention on products that have unusual demand patterns or are more critical to an organization. Advanced forecasting systems also allow aggregation and desegregation of product forecasts up to the product group level, as well as down to an item location level. Finally, a forecasting system should enable continuous improvement to its models over time by providing accuracy metrics for each model.

In addition to improving forecasting accuracy, the overall strategy of an effective demand management system is to make an increasingly larger proportion of its product demand firm while simultaneously decreasing the percentage of products that must be forecast. An effective way to achieve this objective is to develop relationships with customers to obtain accurate demand information at its source. This is very important in industries that sell expensive items such as capital equipment. Alternatively, in some industries, the application of advanced technology can be used to measure customer demand at its point-of-sale (POS). If POS information is available to a manufacturing organization, it will be able to update manufacturing schedules based on actual customer demand, rather than rely exclusively on forecasting models. This concept is qualitatively shown in Figure 8.7. A demand management strategy also enables analysts to concentrate their attention on developing forecasts of products that have complicated demand patterns, but are important to an organization. This concept is shown in Figure 8.8. In Figure 8.8, products or items are stratified by their demand variation and other important characteristics, such as volume. Figure 8.8 also shows that it may be possible to place low-volume products having low demand variation on a minimum/maximum (min/max)

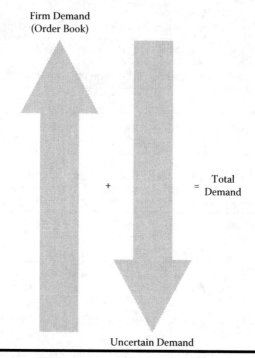

Figure 8.7   **Managing demand.**

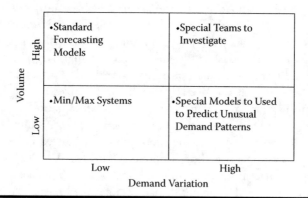

Figure 8.8   **Stratified item forecasts.**

system within an MRPII system. This allows an MRPII system to order inventory when it is needed, as measured by its reorder point, without a formal forecast of a product's demand. Reorder points will be discussed in Chapter 14. This stratification strategy enables forecasting analysts to focus on high-volume or critical products having high demand variation. On the other hand, high-volume products

Table 8.3   Forecast Reconciliation

1. The business should have a single high-level financial forecast goal for the organization.
2. This financial goal should be broken down by each product group.
3. The financial forecast should be developed for each product group.
4. This forecast should be linearly adjusted by item and location.
5. The financial and converted unit forecast should be reconciled at the S&OP meeting.
6. Based on the S&OP discussions, a consensus forecast should be developed for every product group.

having low demand variation can be automatically forecast by a system using time series models. Finally, products having low volume but high demand variation may require special forecasting methods to estimate their future demand.

An integral part of a forecasting process is reconciliation of demand across various organizational functions to ensure an organization plans and schedules its manufacturing to a one-number consensus forecast for its various aggregated demand levels throughout the organization. Table 8.3 shows the basic steps required to ensure a consensus forecast is developed based on an organization's strategic forecast. A first step requires that a high-level strategic forecast be made for an organization. This process will be discussed in Chapter 12 and is shown in Figure 12.3. These higher-level strategic forecasts are eventually reconciled by a sales and operational planning (S&OP) process based on a group consensus. This reconciliation is developed as marketing and sales plans are broken down to a product group level and forecasts are applied to each group. This allocation is applied on a linear basis down to an item and location level. Plans are developed to resolve issues related to capital, labor, and available capacity to meet manufacturing schedules. Finally, updated forecasted quantities are aggregated upwards through an organization. The updated consensus forecasts are also represented in several forms, including unit quantities and extended costs.

Forecasting errors are calculated after actual demand has been realized and compared to the original forecasted quantity for each forecasted period. Although there are several forecasting error statistics, two are commonly used by most organizations (shown in Figure 8.9). The first metric is percentage error (PE). This statistic is calculated by subtracting actual demand from its forecast and dividing by actual demand. Because a percentage error is volume adjusted, it is useful in comparing error rates across different products and volumes. A modification of a PE statistic is the mean absolute percentage error (MAPE) statistic. It is calculated as the average

	January	February	March	April
Original Forecast	200	180	210	190
Actual Demand	190	200	220	200
Error	10	(20)	(10)	(10)

$$\text{Mean Absolute Percentage Error (MAPE)} = \frac{\sum\limits_{t=1}^{n} \left| \frac{\text{Forecast}_t - \text{Actual}_t}{\text{Actual}_t} \times 100 \right|}{n}$$

$$\text{Root Mean Squared Error (RMSE)} = \sqrt{\frac{\sum\limits_{t=1}^{n} (\text{Forecast}_t - \text{Actual}_t)^2}{n}}$$

Figure 8.9   Calculating forecasting error.

of absolute percentage errors over several periods. The root mean square error or deviation (RMSE or RMSD), shown in Figure 8.9, is another useful error statistic. It is calculated on a per unit rather than percentage basis. This allows it to be substituted for a unit standard deviation in safety-stock calculations. As an example, if a forecast is very accurate, as measured by its RMSD, the required safety-stock inventory quantity will be less if an RMSD is used in the safety-stock calculation, rather than a standard deviation. Forecasting accuracy or error statistics are a basis for continuous improvement of a forecasting system. Table 8.4 lists several of the most common process breakdowns caused by poor forecasting accuracy in manufacturing and service systems. Some of the major organizational functions impacted include customer service, manufacturing or operations, finance, transportation, marketing and sales, inventory management, logistics and facility management. The resultant process breakdowns increase a product's per unit transaction cost and a supply chain's cycle time, and lower customer satisfaction.

In summary, Table 8.5 and Table 8.6 compare and contrast characteristics of poor versus good demand management practices. In good systems, there is a consensus forecast by a sales and operations planning (S&OP) team. In good forecasting systems, products should be stratified based on their inherent demand variation. Also, in progressive demand management systems, analysts are well trained in statistical procedures and model building, as well as modern demand management practices. Modern demand management relies on real-time customer relationship building as well as obtaining information using information technology (IT) systems to capture product POS or similar information. In addition to basic product forecasts based on simple exponential smoothing models, an organization must also estimate industry trends by market segment. This information is incorporated

Table 8.4 Examples of the Impact of Poor Forecasting Accuracy

Manufacturing Operations	Service Operations
Customer Service	**Customer Service**
Poor line item availability	Customer complaints
Backorders	
Customer complaints	
Manufacturing	**Operations**
Schedule changes	Schedule changes
Overtime expense	Overtime expense
Finance	**Finance**
Increased inventory carrying expense	Increased labor expense
Lower cash flow	Lower cash flow
Transportation	**Transportation**
Unnecessary product transfer	Unnecessary information transfer
Higher premium freight expense	Higher premium freight expense
Marketing	**Marketing**
Excess and obsolete inventory	Excess and obsolete promotional materials
Inventory Management	**Inventory Management**
Lower inventory turns	Lower transaction expense
Higher inventory obsolescence	Employee skill obsolescence
Logistics	**Facility**
Excess warehousing space and expense	Excess warehousing space and expense
Damaged product expense	

into macroeconomic models that help predict product demand based on external business conditions. An overriding theme in demand management is that progressive organizations should manage demand rather than "push" forecasts. This concept, if applied in practice, will improve operational efficiencies and increase customer satisfaction.

Table 8.5   10 Characteristics of Poor Demand Management Practices

1. Top-down forecast based only on profit rather than operational efficiency considerations
2. Several different forecast estimates rather than one-number forecast for the organization
3. Forecasts dominated by department, such as finance, marketing, or operations
4. Interfunctional conflict over demand estimates
5. Forecasts based on corrupted demand streams, such as shipments and one-time events
6. Little forecast stratification or focus on an item and location level of detail
7. Lack of training of forecast analysts and other critical resources to manage forecast
8. Accuracy of forecasts is not consistently measured to focus improvement activities
9. Forecasts not reconciled bottom-up through organization to verify accuracy
10. Lack of real-time customer information

How to Build Quantitative Forecasting Models

Figure 8.10 shows four common classes of forecasting models. These include judgmental methods; several time series methods, including autoregressive integrated moving average (ARIMA) models; multiple linear regression models; and various specialized models, such as nonlinear regression, the Cochran–Orcutt method, and logistic regression. Judgmental methods are qualitative and cannot provide a statistically based forecast, whereas the other three classes are quantitative. Quantitative forecasting models differ relative to the type of data they require to build a forecasting model, the length of the required historical record, and their analytical sophistication. These models also provide different types of information to an analyst. However, there is commonality among the methods relative to how a sales forecast is created at a basic level. Table 8.7 lists the key steps required to create sales forecasts using any one of these methods. However, regression-based and ARIMA models may require additional analysis after a model is built. The first step in creating a forecasting model is to identify the market segments and sales drivers of each segment because different customer segments may be expected to have differing

Table 8.6   10 Characteristics of Good Demand Management Practices

1. One-number top-down and bottom-up forecasts through sales and operations planning team
2. Forecast stratification based on demand variation
3. Forecasting accuracy measured and continually improved over time
4. Forecasting analysts trained in statistics, forecasting modeling, and modern demand management methods
5. Demand models built using leading, lagging, and coincident indicator variables
6. Electronic Data Interchange (EDI)/Advanced Shipping Notification (ASN) technology and client/server architecture deployed to capture demand as it occurs
7. Demand management rather than statistical modeling focus
8. Demand management driven by point-of-sale data or other real-time data
9. Integration of demand management across the supply chain
10. Integrated metrics deployed across the supply chain to measure and improve demand management practices

demand patterns. Next, forecasting models are created by market segment using historical demand information and other relevant data in a manner similar to that described in Chapter 3. As an example, Chapter 3 showed that market potential, purchase intent, and expected product usage rates should be carefully estimated to create forecasting models.

Time Series Models

Time series are a major class of forecasting models used by almost every major corporation to estimate future demand. Table 8.8 shows they consist of several components that describe an average level, a trend if present, seasonal variation if present, and longer-term cyclical patterns. These demand components can be modeled using one of several time series models that we will discuss in this chapter. Time series models forecast demand into the future at time periods $t + 1$ using actual demand from a current and previous time period's t, $t - 1$, $t - 2$, $t - 3$, etc., where t is a time period whose interval is usually expressed in months. These terms are called lagged dependent variables. As an example, sales next month can be estimated in terms of sales this month and last month. In this simple example, sales this month and last month lag the forecasted sales of the dependent variable "sales next month." Time

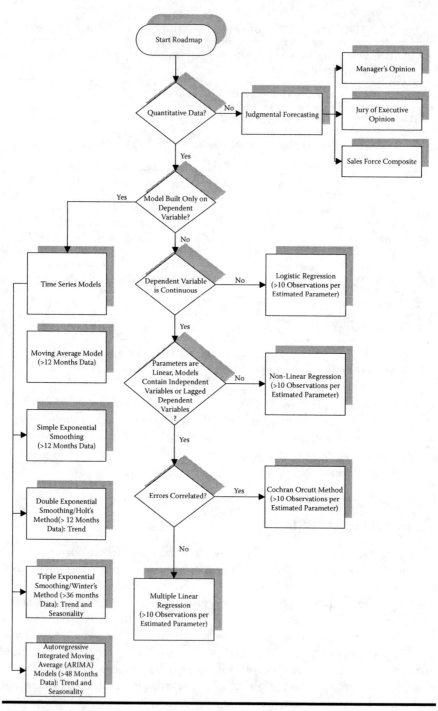

Figure 8.10   Road map of important forecasting methods.

Table 8.7   Creating Sales Forecasts

1. Identify market segments and the demographic factors that drive sales.
2. Collect and analyze data.
3. Estimate market share.
4. Use this information to develop models to forecast sales.
5. Forecast sales.
6. Update forecasting sales models as new information becomes available.

Table 8.8   Time Series Components

1. Level of the time series
2. Time series trend
3. Seasonal patterns within the time series
4. Major cycles
5. Irregular pattern

series models also use smoothing parameters to weight the impact of various lagged dependent variable terms on a dependent variable. This has an effect of making a model more or less representative of more recent demand. In other words, more recent portions of historical demand are emphasized or deemphasized by using smoothing parameters. Table 8.9 summarizes several time series models and their applications. We will discuss these models using a single example, introduced in Figure 8.11. Multiple linear regression models will be discussed separately.

In Figure 8.11, monthly sales data was collected over 11 years. A simple graphical plot of this sales data by its time order or sequence shows that monthly demand exhibits a periodic pattern and upward trend. We will use this sales data to show key characteristics of each of the time series models listed in Table 8.9. It will be obvious that some time models fit the pattern of historical sales better than others, as measured by their mean absolute percentage error. In other words, some of the time series models will be an obviously poor choice for this dataset. Determining the accuracy of a time series model (or alternatively, its error) requires fitting a model to historical data and measuring the deviations of forecasted to actual values at every period. This was shown in Figure 8.9. As a side note, when statisticians compare a new forecasting method against older ones, they use a standardized database of several hundred time series, and error metrics to compare the different time series methods. In these evaluations, forecasting models are compared

Table 8.9   Major Time Series Models

Trend plot	Plots time series data versus time without creating mathematical model.
Time series decomposition	Breaks a time series into its level, trend, seasonal, and irregular components. It models both trend and seasonal patterns using constants calculated from the decomposition.
Moving average models	A time series model created by taking the average of observations from the time series to smooth out seasonal or other data patterns.
Simple exponential smoothing	Models a level (stationary) time series, i.e., no trend or seasonality, using one smoothing parameter.
Double exponential smoothing (Holt's method)	Models a level (stationary) time series with a trend but no seasonality using two smoothing parameters.
Triple exponential smoothing (Winter's method)	Models a level (stationary) time series with a trend and seasonality using three smoothing parameters.
Autoregressive integrated moving average (ARIMA) models	Statistically based time series models that model level, trend, and seasonal components of a time series.

•Monthly Sales(000) have been Collected for the Past 132 Months (11 years) ... these Sales have been Increasing on Average Each Month... also the Month-to-Month Variation has been Increasing... Management Would Like to Develop a Forecasting Model to Predict Sales Through Time ...

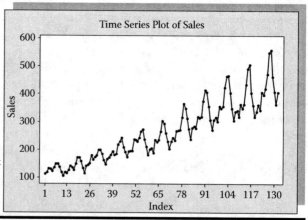

Figure 8.11   Simple plot of monthly sales.

by fitting them to earlier portions (historical basis) of each reference dataset and forecasting demand out over the later portion of the dataset (hold-out period), then comparing the forecast to the actual data contained in the hold-out period of each reference time series. This enables an analysis of a forecasting method against other methods for the same time series by comparing their forecasting error statistics. We will summarize the comparative analysis of each time series in Table 8.11.

Trend Plot

If a time series of monthly sales data has a trend and a periodic pattern, the trend plot will not adequately model the historical sales pattern because it cannot estimate the periodicity of the time series. Looking at Figure 8.12, it is obvious the model fits the data at an average level through historical sales approximately equidistant between the seasonal highs and lows. The corresponding forecast is a simple extrapolation of the fitted line 12 months out into the future, but without a periodic pattern. The resultant mean absolute percentage error is 11.95 percent. Reviewing the summarization shown in Table 8.11, this is the worst of any of the time series models and is an obvious poor choice because it does not incorporate information relative to the seasonality or periodicity of the time series.

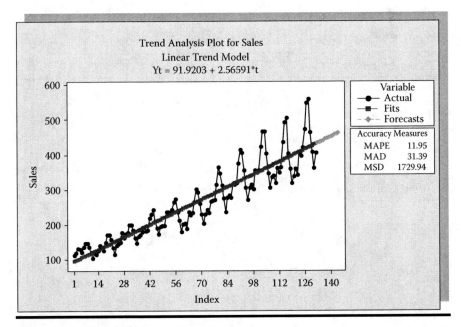

Figure 8.12   Trend plot.

Decomposition Models

The decomposition method breaks down a time series pattern into its component parts. These are shown in Figure 8.13 and Figure 8.14 and Table 8.10. Figure 8.16 shows that the underlying time series structure could be additive, multiplicative, or mixed, based on how a model's terms are combined to build it. A multiplicative

Table 8.10 Time Series Decomposition

1. Start with a time series.
2. Time series = trend + cycle + seasonality + irregular
3. Calculate a new time series using a moving average model having the same order as the seasonality of the time series to create (A).
4. (A) Time series = trend + cycle
5. Determine the seasonal indices. De-seasonalize the original time series to create (B).
6. (B) Time series = trend + cycle + irregular
7. Subtract (A) from (B) to obtain the irregular component to identify outliers that may be adjusted.

Table 8.11 Summary of Time Series Analyses

Trend /Quarterly Data	11.95%
Decomposition Model	5.11% (rounded)
Moving Average Model	10.58%
Simple Exponential Smoothing	8.65% (rounded)
Double Exponential Smoothing Model (Holt's Method)	8.83% (rounded)
Triple Exponential Smoothing Model (Winter's Method)	4.00% (rounded)

$X_t = T_t + S_t + I_t$ Additive Components Model

$X_t = T_t{}^* S_t{}^* I_t$ Multiplicative Components Model

$X_t = (T_t + I_t) S_t$ Mixed

Figure 8.13 Underlying structure of the time series model.

1. $T_{\text{Original Time Series}} =$ Trend + Cycle + Seasonal + Irregular

2. $T_{\text{Deseasonalized Time Series}} =$ Trend + Cycle +   + Irregular

3. $T_{\text{Trend and Cycle Only}} =$ Trend + Cycle

4. $T_{\text{Irregular Component}} =$ + Irregular

Figure 8.14   **Summary of the decomposition method.**

A 95% Confidence Interval is Estimated for the Irregular Component. Outliers are Adjusted to +/− 1.96 Standard Deviations... then the Analysis is Repeated to Obtain a Better Model...

$$\left[\frac{\sum\limits_{t=k}^{n} I_t^2}{\hat{n}} \right]^{1/2}$$

Figure 8.15   **Time series decomposition: irregular component.**

model is the correct choice if demand variation increases over time, which is evident in our time series. Building a decomposition algorithm is a straightforward process. Referring to Table 8.10 and Figure 8.14, the first step in time series decomposition is to fit a moving average model to a time series having the same order as the periodicity of the time series. In other words, if the times series has a periodicity on a quarterly basis, then the moving average model is built using four periods as its basis. In the current example, the periodicity is 12, so the model is centered to ensure the forecast is at an integer time period rather than between two periods. Creating a moving average model eliminates seasonality from the original time series. Also, when a moving average time series is subtracted from the original time series, it is possible to calculate the seasonal indices of each time period. Thus, if data is quarterly, then there will be four seasonal indices. This decomposition process continues until all components have been isolated as shown in Figure 8.14. In Figure 8.15, an irregular component is also calculated as part of the decomposition algorithm. The irregular component is the variation of sales for which the model cannot account. Reviewing Figure 8.16, we see that the decomposition model is a very good fit to the historical data. The resultant forecast also exhibits a periodic pattern coincident with the original monthly sales data. The mean absolute percent error (MAPE) is 5.11 percent (rounded). Minitab software also displays the decomposition analysis from the several perspectives shown in Figure 8.17 and Figure 8.18. As an example, in Figure 8.17, the original data is de-trended showing the periodicity of the time series. On the other hand, when the historical data has been seasonally adjusted, an upward trend is evident. Finally, when the trend and seasonality impacts are removed from the original data, the irregular components become evident. Figure 8.18 shows seasonal indices for each month as well as the variation in monthly sales.

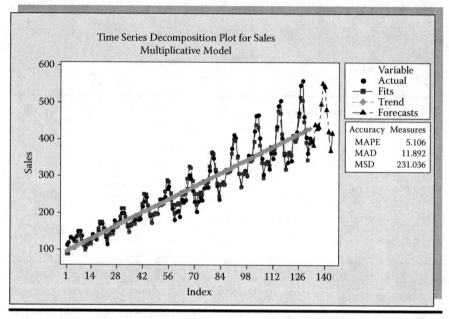

Figure 8.16   Decomposition model.

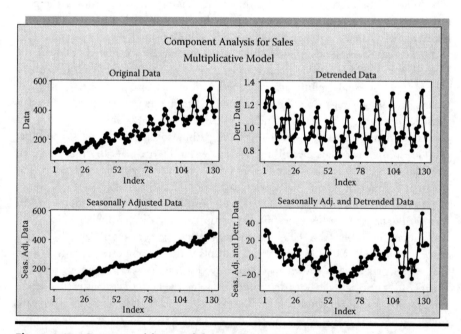

Figure 8.17   Decomposition model: complete decomposition.

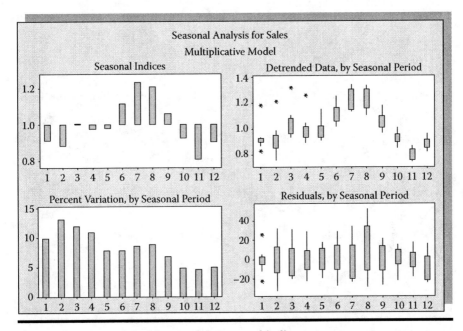

Figure 8.18   Decomposition model: seasonal indices.

Moving Average Models

Moving average models are very good at matching the average level of the time series period by period. A moving average model will follow the upward or downward movement of a time series. But the resultant forecast will be level, as shown in Figure 8.19. In this example, the moving average forecast also has a higher MAPE error rate, i.e., 10.58 percent, relative to some of the other models shown in Table 8.11. This implies that a moving average model would not be a good choice relative to the models that incorporate the periodicity of the time series under discussion.

Simple Exponential Smoothing

Simple exponential smoothing models build a forecast model as a composite of previous sales weighted by a smoothing parameter α. The higher the value of α, the more heavily recent sales will be weighted in a forecast. If the time series is changing rapidly, i.e., new sales, α should be set at a high level. In the example shown in Figure 8.20, the forecast error of the simple exponential smoothing model is 8.65 percent. This is higher than the decomposition method and is a poorer

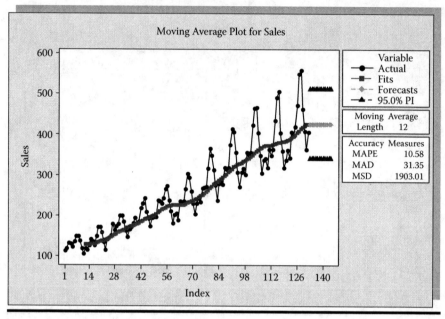

Figure 8.19   Moving average models.

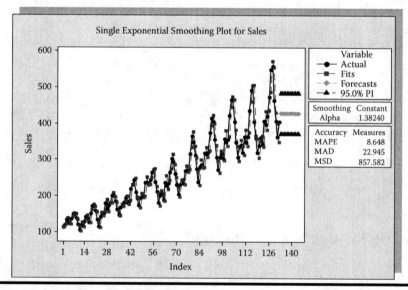

Figure 8.20   Simple exponential smoothing.

model choice as a result. The reason for poorer model fit is that a simple exponential smoothing model is not designed to forecast time series having either a trend or seasonal components.

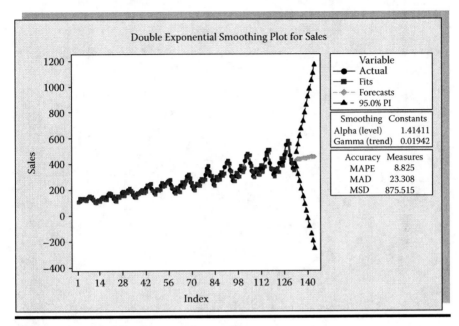

Figure 8.21   Double exponential smoothing.

Double Exponential Smoothing (Holt's Method)

Double exponential smoothing (Holt's) models build a forecasting model using a trend component, but not a seasonal component. Figure 8.21 shows a double exponential smoothing model fit to the monthly sales data. The error rate of 8.825 percent is higher than the decomposition method. Also, the 95 percent confidence interval around the forecast significantly diverges. This means the resultant forecast has a high degree of uncertainty. The reason is that a double exponential smoothing model predicts a trend line going out from the historical basis of the sales data. It does not incorporate seasonal information into a forecasting model. A double exponential smoothing model uses two smoothing parameters, α and β, to estimate the level and trend components of a time series, respectively.

Triple Exponential Smoothing (Winter's Method)

Winter's method is designed to model time series level, trend, and seasonal components using three smoothing parameters, α, β, and γ. Reviewing Figure 8.22, we see the model fits very well and has a forecast error of only 4.00 percent (rounded). Also, the resultant forecast has a seasonal pattern that matches the historical basis of the time series quite well. A summary of the MAPE statistics is shown in Table 8.11. The most accurate models appear to be Winter's and the decomposition

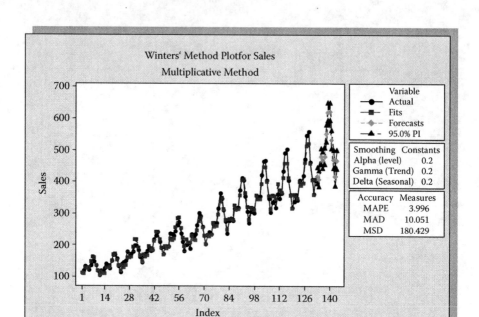

Figure 8.22 Winter's method.

methods. This is not surprising because the example we used contained a noticeable trend and seasonality.

Autoregressive Integrated Moving Average (ARIMA) Models, or Box-Jenkins Methodology

Because the ARIMA modeling technique is complicated, most organizations do not use it to forecast their product sales. In fact, exponential smoothing models are preferred because their accuracy rates and ease of use make them superior to the ARIMA techniques in situations in which thousands of product forecasts must be made on a frequent basis. Interestingly, exponential smoothing models are a subset of ARIMA models. As an example, the simple exponential smoothing model is a (0, 1, 1) ARIMA model, and the double exponential smoothing model is a (0, 2, 2) ARIMA model. However, ARIMA models provide advantages when augmented as transfer or intervention models. In these situations, other time series are added to the model to provide independent information to increase forecasting accuracy. In fact, augmented ARIMA models are very useful in incorporating the impact of special events such as natural disasters, strikes, or other adverse or positive business conditions into the forecasting model. Given the complexity of ARIMA models, we will discuss the monthly sales example, but now we will show all the modeling assumptions and calculations inherent in an ARIMA model for the current sales example.

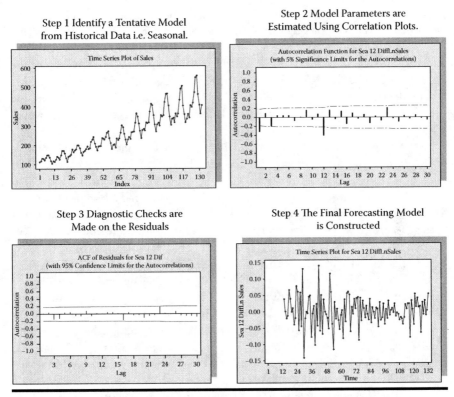

Figure 8.23   Autoregressive integrated moving average (ARIMA) models.

A first step in building an ARIMA or any model is to simply plot the historical data as shown in Step 1 of Figure 8.23. Reviewing the plot of monthly sales, we note, as discussed previously, that the time series contains both a trend and seasonal variation. The construction of an ARIMA model requires that a time series be stationary with respect to its mean and variance. In other words, the mean should not be increasing (no trend) and the variance should be constant over the entire range of the historical data. However, in the current time series, neither the mean nor variance are stationary. To make the variance stationary, we will take a natural logarithm of the monthly sales demand. Thus, the model will be built using the working time series, Z_t, or $\ln Y_t$, where Y_t is the actual monthly sales demand. In addition to making the variance stationary, we must also eliminate the trend from the data by taking a difference of the actual monthly sales. We will thus create a working time series $Z_t = \ln Y_t - \ln Y_{t-1}$ with which to build the forecasting model. However, given that we also have seasonality in the data, we must also take a seasonal difference of 12 and build the model off the seasonally differenced natural logarithm of the actual monthly sales. Rather than visually examine a time series plot such as the actual monthly sales demand, we will use a sample autocorrelation

(SAC) plot of the time series to determine if it is stationary with respect to its mean and variance. This is done by using the SAC to evaluate, in sequence, the actual monthly sales demand, Y_t, then the working time series, Z_t, i.e., the seasonally differenced working time series using the ln Y_t transformation. The SAC shows the transformed and differenced working time series to be completely stationary. This will be the time series used to build the ARIMA forecasting model. But after the model is built, it must be "untransformed" and "undifferenced" to predict actual sales.

Once a time series has been made stationary, one or more ARIMA models can be built using the stationary time series. These ARIMA models can contain pure moving average, pure autoregressive, or mixed terms. In Figure 8.23, the SAC shows periodicity of the working time series, Z_t, at lags 12 and 24 (multiples of 12). The pattern in the SAC indicates an ARIMA model can be built based on moving average terms (these are the forecasting errors, a_t, from previous time periods, i.e., $a_t = Y_{\text{forecast at time= t}} - Y_{\text{actual sales at time=t}}$. It will be shown that the patterns in the SAC help build ARIMA models with moving average terms, and the sample partial autocorrelation (SPAC) function can help build autoregressive models with lagged dependent variable terms and of the form $Z_t = Y_{t-1} + Y_{t-2} + Y_{t-3} + \dots$. We will discuss how to actually do the ARIMA calculations in the next several paragraphs. Referring to Steps 3 and 4 in Figure 8.23, an ARIMA model is built using the working time series, Z_t, which is the seasonally differenced transformation ln Y_t. Diagnostic checks are also made on an ARIMA model. If the model is acceptable (to be discussed), then it can be used to predict future sales.

Figure 8.24 shows how monthly sales demand, used in this example, is checked using the SAC. The resultant SAC pattern confirms that the time series is not stationary and must be transformed and differenced to make it stationary. The SAC of the final working time series is shown in Figure 8.25. It can be seen to be stationary, and as discussed above, an ARIMA model can be fit to the working time series using moving average terms based on the SAC pattern. In addition, Figure 8.26 shows that the SPAC of the working time series is stationary and an autoregressive-based ARIMA model can be fit to the working time series. Figure 8.27 shows the basic logic of a generalized ARIMA model of order (p, P, q, Q), where p is the nonseasonal autoregressive terms, P is the seasonal autoregressive terms, q is the nonseasonal moving average terms, and Q is the seasonal moving average terms. There are three possible classes of ARIMA models that can be built using the underlying structure of the current working time series. These are a pure moving average model, a pure autoregressive model, or a mixed model. This concept is shown in a generalized form in Figure 8.28. The generalized model becomes a specific model of the working time series once we examine the SAC and SPAC functions. The location of the spikes relative to the lags (time periods) indicates the number and order of each term in the model. As an example, Figure 8.29 shows that we can build a pure moving average ARIMA model and the SAC function has two spikes, i.e., one nonseasonal spike at lag 1 and one seasonal at lag 12. Multiplying the terms provides

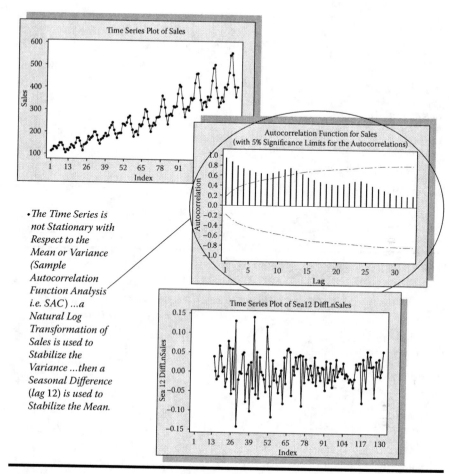

Figure 8.24 Preliminary analysis.

the intermediate equation shown in Figure 8.29. Using Minitab, we can build the specific ARIMA model of the working time series using the shortened form $Z_t = \delta + a_t - \theta_1 a_{t-1} - \theta_{1,12} a_{t-12} + \theta_1 \theta_{1,12} a_{t-13}$. The resultant final parameter estimates are shown in Table 8.12. Examining the probability values associated with the coefficients of the reduced model, we see that they are statistically significant (<0.05). It should be noted that in the initial ARIMA model the constant of the equation was eliminated from the analysis because it was not statistically significant. Also, a diagnostic evaluation of the model's residuals (errors) also shown in Table 8.12 and Figure 8.30 indicates the residuals are not statistically significant. Residuals (errors) are the moving average terms or forecasting errors shown in Figure 8.31. Forecasting errors are calculated at every time period as actual sales at time period t minus forecasted sales at time period t. The statistical analysis indicates we have an adequate ARIMA model of the working time series, Z_t. Additional information is

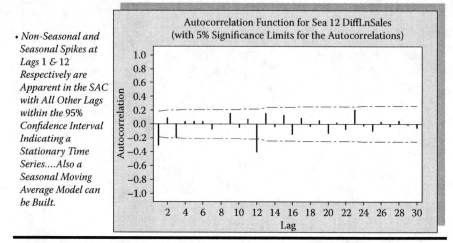

• Non-Seasonal and Seasonal Spikes at Lags 1 & 12 Respectively are Apparent in the SAC with All Other Lags within the 95% Confidence Interval Indicating a Stationary Time Series....Also a Seasonal Moving Average Model can be Built.

Figure 8.25   Is the time series stationary?

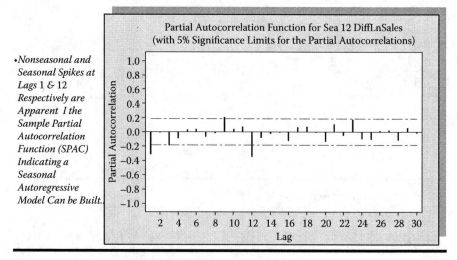

•Nonseasonal and Seasonal Spikes at Lags 1 & 12 Respectively are Apparent I the Sample Partial Autocorrelation Function (SPAC) Indicating a Seasonal Autoregressive Model Can be Built.

Figure 8.26   Analysis of the SPAC.

provided by Figure 8.32 for the working time series, Z_t, forecast, and by Table 8.13, which shows the actual forecasted values of the working time series, Z_t. Figure 8.33 shows how the ARIMA forecast at time period t = 133 was calculated. However, to obtain a forecast in terms of the original monthly sales, the working time series, Z_t, must be untransformed and undifferenced. The calculations required to transform Z_t back into original monthly sales are shown in Figure 8.34. The originally transformed time series was seasonally differenced using a backward shift operator, shown in Figure 8.35 and Figure 8.36. Now the working time series is transformed back into the original monthly sales units, as shown in Figure 8.34, by

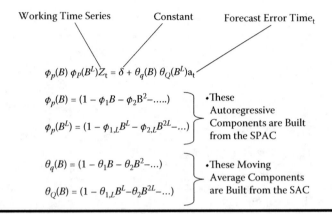

Figure 8.27   General box-Jenkins model of order (p, P, q, Q).

Moving Average Model ...

$$Z = \delta + \theta_q(B)\,\theta_Q(B^L)a_t$$

Autoregressive Model ...

$$\phi_p(B)\,\phi_P(B^L)Z_t = \delta$$

Mixed Model...

$$\phi_p(B)\,\phi_P(B^L)Z_t = \delta + \theta_q(B)\,\theta_Q(B^L)a_t$$

$$Z_t = \delta + (1 - \theta_1 B^1)(1 - \theta_{1,12}B^{12})a_t$$

$$Z_t = \delta + (1 - \theta_1 B^1 - \theta_{1,12}B^{12} + \theta_1\,\theta_{1,12}B^{13})a_t$$

$$Z_t = \delta + a_t - \theta_1 a_{t-1} - \theta_{1,12}a_{t-12} + \theta_1\,\theta_{1,12}a_{t-13}$$

Figure 8.28   What types of models could we build?

Figure 8.29   What is the specific seasonal moving average model?

undifferencing the transformed monthly sales and finally raising the undifferenced transformed sales (which are still in natural logarithm format) to the power e = 2.718, as shown in Figure 8.34. As mentioned earlier, this is a complicated method that requires a high degree of analytical sophistication.

Regression Models

Multiple linear regression (MLR) models explain the variation of a dependent variable by using a least squares (LS) algorithm to fit a linear model through a dataset. The LS algorithm fits an equation or line through a dataset in a way in which the sum of squared deviations from every data point to the fitted line is a minimum relative to any other line that could be fit through the same dataset. Over the past several decades, many important statistical tests have been developed to analyze and improve the fit of a linear equation to a dataset. Figure 8.37 shows some common regression-based models many of which do not use an LS algorithm to fit a linear equation to a dataset. In this chapter, we will discuss MLR models as they apply to the monthly sales example we have been using throughout this chapter, except several independent variables will be added to the analysis.

Table 8.12 Final Parameter Estimates

We estimate the coefficients of the model using the working time series Z_t and nonseasonal and seasonal moving average components, as well as a constant.

Final estimates of parameters					Parameters are statistically significant and invertibility conditions are satisfied.
Type	Coefficient	Standard Deviation	T	P	
MA 1	0.3540	0.0864	4.10	0.000	
SMA 12	0.6258	0.0768	8.15	0.000	

Number of observations: 119 Residuals: SS = 0.152361 (backforecasts excluded) MS = 0.001302, DF = 117	■ 132 – 1 – 12 = 119 Lost observations because of differencing

Modified box-Pierce (Ljung-box) chi-square statistic					■ The residuals are not statistically significant; we extracted all the important information from the dataset.
Lag	12	24	36	48	
Chi-square	7.1	19.2	29.3	37.4	
DF	10	22	34	46	
P value	0.716	0.634	0.698	0.814	

Correlation matrix of the estimated parameters: 1 2 –0.039	■ No statistically significant correlation between the parameters

MLR requires parameters of a model be linear so they can be estimated by an LS algorithm. Referring to Figure 8.37, we see there are several additional assumptions that must be met by the model. These are that its residuals are normally and independently distributed around zero with constant variance. Recall that a residual is the difference between the model's fitted value Y_{fitted} and its observed value $Y_{observed}$ for each experiment or observation of a dataset. An experimental observation consists of a Y, or dependent variable, i.e., monthly sales quantity, as well as the levels or values of each independent variable, i.e., X, which are used to build a predictive MLR equation represented as $Y = f(X) = \beta_0 + \beta_1 X_1 + \beta_2 X_2 + \ldots + \beta_k X_k$. As an example, if an MLR model estimates a monthly sale's quantity as $100,000, but the actual observed value of monthly sales was $90,000, then the residual would be $10,000. It is obvious that the larger the magnitude of a residual,

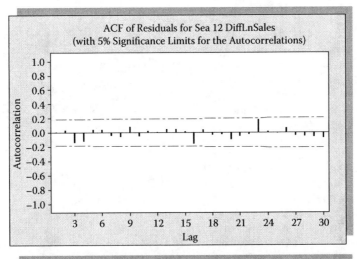

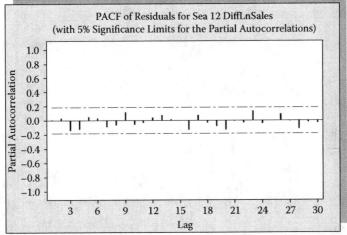

Figure 8.30   Residual analysis.

the poorer the fit of an MLR equation. We will discuss this topic in more detail in the next few paragraphs.

In addition to the basic MLR model, there are several specialized regression models used in specific analytical situations. Several of these are shown in Figure 8.37. In the MLR model shown in Figure 8.38, it is apparent that its parameters or coefficients are linearly related to a dependent variable, Y, although the form of the independent variables can be quadratic, i.e., x^2, or contain higher-order terms. However, there are other types of regression models that can be used to explain the variation of a dependent variable, or Y, when the assumptions required for the use of an MLR model cannot be met in practice. As an example, nonlinear regression can be used when the estimated parameters of the equation are not a

t	z_t	a_t	y_{actual}
Period	**Y**	**RESI1**	**FITS1**
119	0.007742	0.006599	0.0011435
120	−0.038768	−0.058387	0.0196196
121	0.054187	0.023687	0.0304999
122	0.015601	0.001457	0.0141438
123	0.041950	0.025781	0.0161688
124	0.014503	0.011143	0.0033594
125	0.016640	0.039177	−0.0225365
126	−0.064219	−0.032245	−0.0319741
127	0.028198	0.025961	0.0022371
128	−0.008240	0.024271	−0.0325111
129	0.034721	−0.014922	0.0496432
130	−0.010821	−0.002151	−0.0086706
131	0.004102	0.008528	−0.0044255
132	0.054211	0.019232	0.0349794

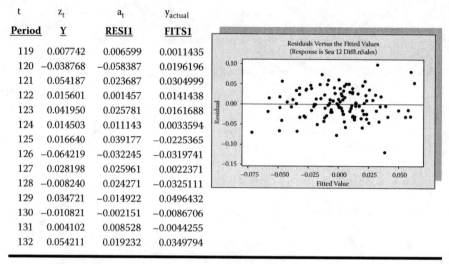

Figure 8.31   Residual analysis continued.

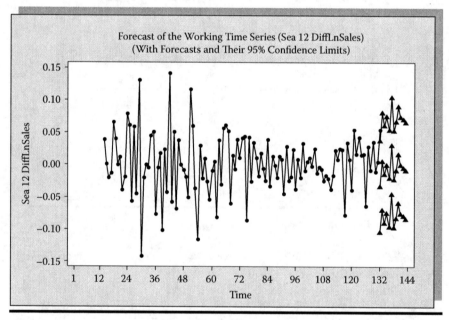

Figure 8.32   Forecasted values of Z_t (working time series).

linear function of the dependent variable. An example would be if the parameters were in the form of an exponential function such as $Y = \beta_0 + \beta_1 e^{\beta_2 x_1}$, in which β_2 is raised as a power of e. In this situation, a transformation of the nonlinear equation could be used to build a linear relationship of $Y = f(X)$, but this may not always be possible. The Cochran–Orcutt method is another example wherein the MLR

Table 8.13 Forecasts of Period 132 (95% Confidence Level)

$Z_t = a_t - .3540_1 a_{t-1} - .6258 a_{t-12} + .2215 a_{t-13}$			
Period	Forecast	Lower	Upper
133	−0.034564	−0.105308	0.036180
134	0.004335	−0.070710	0.079381
135	−0.015810	−0.090855	0.059236
136	−0.001262	−0.076308	0.073783
137	−0.022047	−0.097092	0.052999
138	0.028856	−0.046190	0.103901
139	−0.023388	−0.098434	0.051657
140	−0.009437	−0.084483	0.065608
141	0.014714	−0.060332	0.089759
142	−0.001960	−0.077005	0.073086
143	−0.005813	−0.080858	0.069233
144	−0.010146	−0.085191	0.064900
145	0.004260	−0.082869	0.091390
146	0.000000	−0.088527	0.088527
147	0.000000	−0.088527	0.088527
148	0.000000	−0.088527	0.088527
149	0.000000	−0.088527	0.088527
150	0.000000	−0.088527	0.088527
151	0.000000	−0.088527	0.088527
152	0.000000	−0.088527	0.088527
153	0.000000	−0.088527	0.088527
154	0.000000	−0.088527	0.088527
155	0.000000	−0.088527	0.088527
156	0.000000	−0.088527	0.088527

Table 8.14 Key Concepts to Manage Demand More Effectively

1. Ensure your organization's forecasts are strategically aligned at all levels of the organization.
2. Migrate your demand management systems to obtain direct demand information from customers or through point-of-sale (POS) information.
3. To the extent forecasts are necessary, use accurate demand data by market segment and the appropriate forecasting model.
4. Stratify your products to place some of them on automatic forecast by the system so analytical resources can be focused on products having higher demand variation or unusual demand patterns.
5. Measure and continually improve forecasting accuracy.

$$Z_{133} = a_{133}^{\;\;0} - .3540\, a_{132} - .658\, a_{121} + .2215\, a_{120}$$

$$Z_{133} = (-.3540^*.019232) - (.6258^*.023687) + (.2215^* - .058387)$$

$$Z_{133} = -.006809128 - .01423324 - .01293272 = \mathbf{-0.034564}$$

Figure 8.33 How does the model work?

$$Z_{133} = (1 - B^{12})^1 (1 - B^1)^1 y_t^* = f(X)$$

$$Z_{133} = Y_t^* - Y_{t-1}^* - Y_{t-12}^* + Y_{t-13}^* = -.034564$$

$$Y_{133}^* = f(x) + Y_{t-1}^* + Y_{t-12}^* - Y_{t-13}^*$$

$$\ln Y_{133} = f(x) + Y_{132}^* + Y_{121}^* - Y_{120}^*$$

$$\ln Y_{133} = -.034564 + 6.00389 + .588610 - 5.82008 = 6.035346$$

$$Y_{133} = e^{6.035346} = 417.94$$

Forested Sales in Time Period$_{133}$ = \$417,940

Figure 8.34 Creating the forecast.

assumptions are not satisfied by the specific analysis. In this situation, the residuals are correlated by time and are not independent. This requires that the serial correlation information contained in the residual pattern be incorporated into an MLR to more adequately explain the variation in the dependent variable. This is where the Cochran–Orcutt method is useful. As another example, if independent variables are correlated to each other (as determined using the variance inflation factor (VIF)), ridge regression can be used to build an MLR equation. Also, the robust regression method can be used when MLR assumptions are not met due to

Working Time Series

$$Z_t = \bigvee_L^D \bigvee^d y_t^* = (1-B^L)^D (1-B)^d y_t^*$$

Where d = Degree of Non-Seasonal Differencing and D = Degree of Seasonal Differencing

Example of the Backward Shift Operator ...

$$By_t = y_{t-1} ... By_{10} = y_9 \text{ and } B^k y_t = y_{t-k}$$

$$\bigvee = 1-B \qquad\qquad \bigvee^L = 1-B^L$$

Figure 8.35   General stationary transformation.

Constant Term

Where μ is the True Mean of the Stationary Time Series

$$\delta = (\mu) \; (\phi_p(B)) \; (\phi_P(B^L))$$

Forecast Errors

$$a_t = y_t - \hat{y}_t \text{ but in Our Case } a_t = Z_t - \hat{Z}_t$$

Figure 8.36   Other terms.

severe outliers in a dataset. Finally, if a dependent variable is discrete or not continuous, logistical regression can be used to build a model. There are three major types of logistic regression models. These are categorized as binary (pass/fail), ordinal (1, 2, 3, 4, etc.), and nominal (red, white, blue, etc.), depending on how the data of the dependent variable is structured.

Several statistics are associated with an MLR model. Our goal will be to discuss some of the more important ones and then apply the various concepts to the monthly sales example we have been using in this chapter, but using several independent variables in the analysis. Figure 8.39 shows an R^2 statistic and its modified or adjusted version, $R^2_{adjusted}$. These statistics are measures of the percentage of variation of the dependent variable explained by an MLR equation. As an example, an R^2 statistic of 0.9 implies that 90 percent of the variation in Y is explained by an MLR equation. An R^2 value of 0.5 implies that just 50 percent of the variation in Y is explained by an MLR equation. It is apparent that high R^2 statistics imply a good model fit of an equation to a dataset. $R^2_{adjusted}$ adjusts R^2 downward to account for the number of independent variables incorporated into the MLR model relative to the sample size used to build the model. This is because R^2 can be increased by simply adding variables to the MLR model even if they do not explain changes in Y.

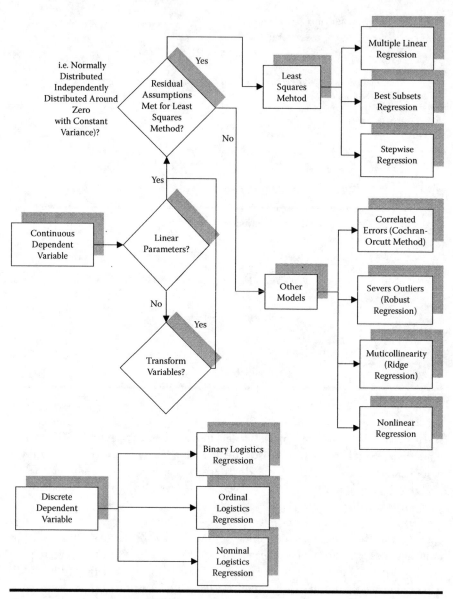

Figure 8.37 Regression models.

A second important test statistic is the Durbin–Watson (DW) statistic, which measures serial correlation of the model's residuals (assuming data is ordered by time), as shown in Figure 8.40. An important assumption of an MLR model is that its residuals are not serially correlated over time. Figure 8.40 shows that it is possible to have positive or negative serial correlation in a fitted model. In actual practice, the calculated DW test statistic is compared to critical values in a statistical table.

Explains Relationships between the Response (Y) and
Predictor Variables (Xs)...Coefficientsare Linear; but,
Terms may be Quadratic or Higher...

$$Y = b_0 + b_1 X_1 + b_2 X_2 + ... + b_k X_k + e$$

$$Y = b_0 + b_1 X_1 + b_2 X_2^2 + ... + b_k X_k^k + e$$

Figure 8.38   Linear regression.

$$R^2 = 1 - \frac{SSE}{SST}$$

$$R^2_{adj} = 1 - \frac{SSE / (n-k-1)}{SST / (n-1)}$$

$$SEE = \sum_{i=1}^{n} (y_i - \hat{y})^2$$

$$STT = \sum_{i=1}^{n} (y_i - \bar{y})^2$$

Where k = number of independent variables in the

regression model; n= sample size; y_i =actual data value;

$\hat{y}$ =model fit; and y =average of all actual data values.

Figure 8.39   What is R² adjusted?

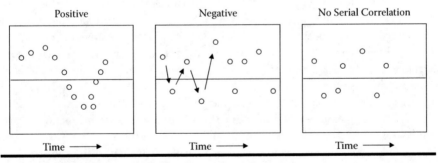

| Positive | Negative | No Serial Correlation |

Time ⟶   Time ⟶   Time ⟶

Figure 8.40   Durbin–Watson test for serial correlation.

These critical values are determined using sample size, the number of independent
variables in a model, and the desired type I error level required by the test. As a
rough rule, an ideal range of the DW test statistic as being between 1.5 and 2.5,
but this range, as mentioned above, will vary in practice. The presence of serial correlation requires that the observations associated with it be removed from the MLR
model, or that additional terms be incorporated into the MLR model to account for

Regression Model	No Correlated Residuals (Errors)	Correlated Residuals (Errors)
Simple Linear Regression	Use Least Squares Method	Least Squares Parameters Estimates are Inefficient; use Cochran-Orcutt Method.
← Use Durbin-Watson Test to Detect Serial Correlation →		
Models Having Lagged Dependent Variables	Use Least Squares Method	Least Squares Parameter Estimates are Inconsistent; Use Nonlinear Regression.
← Use Durbin-h Test to Detect Serial Correlation →		

Inefficient: *Produces a Larger Variance of the Parameter Estimate and a Larger Sample Size is Required to Reject the Null Hypothesis : Parameter = 0.*

Inconsistent: *The Estimated Values of the Parameter will not Correspond to the True Value.*

Figure 8.41 Correlated errors.

the serial correlation of the residuals. Alternatively, the Cochran–Orcutt method can be used to build the MLR model. Figure 8.41 summarizes various MLR regression models using a lagged dependent variable in the presence or absence of serially correlated residuals. It should be noted that serially correlated residuals can result in either an inefficient model (without lagged dependent variable terms in the model) or an inconsistent model (with lagged dependent variable terms in the model). Inefficient means the estimated coefficients of the model are accurate on average; they have a large variance, i.e., a larger sample will be required to precisely estimate them. Inconsistent means the estimated parameters are incorrect. A third useful statistic is the variance inflation factor (VIF). The VIF statistic is shown in Figure 8.42. It measures the degree of correlation between two independent variables. Highly correlated independent variables, if left in the final model, will result in inefficient estimates of the independent variable coefficients. This will require a larger than necessary sample to precisely estimate them.

Figure 8.43 is a useful tool to evaluate how well an MLR model fits a dataset based on its R^2 value and residual pattern. Figure 8.39 shows the R^2 statistic in terms of the sums of squares associated with the model's error SS_{Error} or SSE, i.e., $1 - (SS_{Error}/SS_{Total})$. SS_{Error} is the variation of the dependent variable not explained by the MLR models or the squared differences between each datapoint (y_i) and the fit of the models ($\hat{y}_i$). SS_{Total} is all of the variations of the dataset as measured by the squared differences between each datapoint (y_i) and the average of all datapoints ($\bar{y}$).

The Variance Inflation Factor (VIF) is Used to Detect
Linear Relationships Between the Independent Variables.

$$VIF_{(i)} = 1/(1 - R^2_{(i)})$$

Where: R (i) is the R Value Resulting from
Regressing Xi on the Other Independent Variables
in the Prediction Equation. A $VIF_{(i)}$ Factor Less
than 5 Indicates Low Multicollinearity.

Figure 8.42   Variance inflation factor (VIF).

Level of R^2	Small Random Variation	Large Random Variation	Non-Random Pattern
R^2 Low	N/A	•Poor Model •Incorrect X's •Measurement Accuracy	•Poor Model Add Terms to Model •Transform X's, Y's or Both
R^2 High	•Good Model •Correct X's	N/A	•Good Model •Add Terms? •Transform?

Figure 8.43   Interpreting model residuals and $R^2_{adjusted}$.

The importance of making this point is that the higher the SSE term of the model, the poorer the MLR model fit, and vice versa. Thus, if the model fits the dataset poorly, we need to analyze its residual pattern, reflected by the SSE term, to look for clues as to how to modify the model to make it fit more exactly, i.e., explain more of the variation of the dependent variable. As an example, in Figure 8.43, when R^2 is low, i.e., less than 0.90, the magnitude of a model's residuals will be large. As Figure 8.43 shows, there could be many reasons for this situation, including not having all important independent variables in an MLR model, or there could be measurement errors associated with the methodology of data collection. On the other hand, if there is a nonrandom pattern in the residuals, it may be possible to transform the dependent or independent variables to obtain a more exact MLR model fit to the dataset. Another option might be to add an additional term to the MLR model. As an example, if a quadratic pattern was observed in the residual pattern, it might make sense to add an X_i^2 term to an MLR model. This discussion has assumed that serial correlation was eliminated from the model and the independent variables are not collinear, i.e., their VIFs are equal to or close to 1.

The forecasting models discussed earlier in this chapter were built on previous values of a time series. In other words, they were built using lagged dependent variable terms, i.e., previous values of monthly sales demand. The fit of the decomposition and Winter's models, as represented by their absolute errors (MAPE), was quite good at 5.11 and 4.00 percent, respectively. However, in many situations, dependent variables are better explained by combinations of lagged dependent variables and independent variables that contribute independent information useful in predicting variation of the dependent variable. Some of the independent variables may even be leading indicators of the dependent variable. That is, they may correlate to future values of a dependent variable in that a change of a leading variable in the current time period predicts with high probability changes in a dependent variable in future time periods. In Figure 8.44, we augmented the original monthly sales example to include the three new independent variables of Income, Month, and Region. It should be noted that the variable Income is continuous, but Month and Region are discrete. To incorporate them into a model, discrete variables must be transformed into indicator or dummy variables, as shown in Figure 8.44. Figure 8.44 shows that there are four regions, called A, B, C, and D.

Monthly Sales Analysis: Data Representation Using
Indicator Variables

Income	Month	Region
76000	1	A
49274	2	B
55305	3	C
53492	4	D
65000	5	A
57266	6	B
55000	7	C
60311	8	D

Region A	Region B	Region C	Region D	Jan	Feb	Mar
1	0	0	0	1	0	0
0	1	0	0	0	1	0
0	0	1	0	0	0	1
0	0	0	1	0	0	0
1	0	0	0	0	0	0
0	1	0	0	0	0	0
0	0	1	0	0	0	0
0	0	0	1	0	0	0

Figure 8.44　Building econometric models: part 1.

The Region variable is broken into four indicator variables to prevent a bias or offset in the MLR's constant. As an example, Region A is represent by the pattern 1 0 0 0 across the four indicator columns Region A, Region B, Region C, and Region D. Region B would be represented as 0 1 0 0. The discrete variable Month would be transformed in a similar manner using 12 columns of indicator variables to uniquely represent each month. Once the discrete variables have been transformed into indicator variables, the MLR model can be built and evaluated.

Figure 8.45 shows the results of the MLR analysis using stepwise regression. Stepwise regression is a type of automated version of MLR. In Figure 8.45, the analysis went through four iterations and stopped at step 4, which is highlighted in

Monthly Sales Analysis: Stepwise Regression

Response is Sales on 17 Predictors, with N = 132				
Step	1	2	3	4
Constant	2.773	7.182	5.145	3.000
Income	0.00243	0.00248	0.00246	0.00243
T-Value	27.94	30.86	31.75	32.75
P-Value	0.000	0.000	0.000	0.000
Region A		−38.1	−33.4	−27.9
T-Value		−5.07	−4.56	−3.91
P-Value		0.000	0.000	0.000
Aug			40	45
T-Value			3.48	4.12
P-Value			0.001	0.000
July				41
T-Value				3.75
P-Value				0.000
S	40.5	37.1	35.6	33.9
R-Sq	85.72	88.09	89.12	90.21
R-Sq(adj)	85.61	87.91	88.86	89.90

Figure 8.45   Building econometric models: part 2.

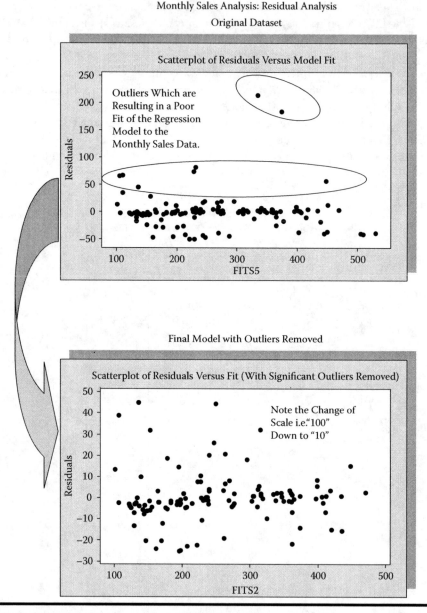

Figure 8.46   Building econometric models: part 3.

Figure 8.45. The $R^2_{adjusted}$ statistic for the final model is 89.90 percent. The important variables are Income, Region A, August, and July. These variables explain 89.90 percent of the variation in monthly sales. An analysis of the model's residual pattern, shown in Figure 8.46, indicates the presence of outliers and severe serial

Monthly Sales Analysis: Multiple Linear Regression

The Regression Equation is:

Sales = 0.00239 Income

Predictor	Coef	SE Coef	T	F
No Constant				
Income	0.00239467	0.00001583	151.27	0.00

S = 19.4301

Analysis of Variance

Source	DF	SS	MS	F	F
Regression	1	8638321	8638321	22881.23	0.00
Residual Error	118	44548	378		
Total	1	8682869			

Durbin-Watson Statistic = 2.18102 R^2 adjusted = 99.4

Figure 8.47   Building econometric models: part 4.

correlation, i.e., the Durbin–Watson test statistic was 1.1 (previous MLS analysis), which indicted that the residuals were positively correlated with each other. After the outliers were successively removed from the MLR, a better MLR model was obtained, as shown in Figure 8.47. The final model shown in Figure 8.47 has an $R^2_{adjusted}$ statistic equal to 99.4 percent (SSM/SST) and Durbin–Watson statistic of 2.18, which indicates no serial correlation of the residuals of the reduced model (outliers removed) from the dataset. In the final MLR model, sales depend only on the variable Income. The final residual pattern is shown in the bottom portion of Figure 8.46. In summary, MLR and similar methods are very useful in developing forecasting models because they allow inclusion of one or more independent variables that contribute information useful in explaining variation of a dependent variable.

Summary

Accurate demand management drives an organization's supply planning activities. Problems in demand estimation result in misalignment of scarce resources and significant process breakdowns throughout a supply chain. These situations can result in significant productivity erosion. It is important that an organization's forecasts are strategically aligned at all levels and a consensus forecast is developed by an

S&OP team. To the extent forecasts are necessary, an organization should use accurate demand data that is broken into market segments and apply an appropriate forecasting model. A useful approach is to stratify products and place as many as possible on an automatic forecast system so analytical resources can be focused on products having higher demand variation or unusual demand patterns. It is also important to measure and continually improve forecasting accuracy. However, best-in-class organizations emphasize customer relationships and develop systems to provide visibility to demand across their supply chains through point-of-sale (POS) and similar technologies. Depending on the industry and supply chain, visual control methods such as Kanban may also be excellent systems to match supply to demand and avoid heavy reliance on forecasting models. These systems will be discussed in later chapters of this book.

Suggested Reading

Bruce L. Bowerman and Richard T. O'Connell. (1993). *Forecasting and Time Series: An Applied Approach*, 3rd ed. Duxbury Press, Belmont, CA.

John T. Mentzer and Carol C. Bienstock. (1998). *Sales Forecasting Management*. Sage Publications, Newbury Park, CA.

J. Holton Wilson and Barry Keating. (1998). *Business Forecasting*, 3rd ed. McGraw-Hill, New York.

Chapter 9

Expanding Global Capacity

Competitive solution 9: Satisfy customer demand anytime and anywhere in the world by creating inexpensive and flexible systems with sufficient capacity.

Overview

There was a time when capacity was measured by the number of production facilities, pieces of equipment, and the number of people within an organization. In this environment, large and well-capitalized organizations dominated national and international markets. Also, these markets were relatively uniform, which enabled economies of scale to dominate the competitive landscape. Market entry was difficult in this environment because the barriers to competition were significant. In fact, to become competitive, an organization would have to invest significantly in an infrastructure necessary to provide sufficient capacity to satisfy expected customer demand. However, in today's world, capacity is dynamic because markets have become highly segmented based on changes in customer needs and value requirements, as well as an expansion of localized markets across the world and technology has evolved. However, the historical definitions, tools, and methods of capacity management still apply relative to the creation and utilization of capacity, but the concepts related to capacity management have evolved due to globalization and virtualization of supply chains over the past few decades. This environment has dramatically changed the competitive landscape and the strategies and tactics by which organizations compete. *Insourcing, outsourcing, offshoring, supply chaining, informing,* and *workflow structure* are the terms that were defined and discussed by Thomas L. Friedman and others over the past several years. These authors have described how organizations are managing capacity in today's world. In this chapter, our discussion will be from a viewpoint that organizations should develop capacity sufficient to satisfy expected demand anywhere in the world with minimum investment cost and risk. This discussion is facilitated by the fact that information availability, technology deployment, global teams, and new process workflow structures have become critical components of capacity across the world in recent years. In these new systems, capacity has some physical presence, but also an increasingly higher virtual content. *Virtual* implies that capacity can be created using technology deployed within process workflows through efficient management of resources. It is also integrated throughout a supply chain through negotiation, agreements, contracts, and other informational means that result in joint ventures, partnerships, the sales of noncore workflows, the sharing of information and resources, and related organizational and functional structures. These organizational and supply-chain designs are able to increase available supply-chain capacity without large capital outlays to build redundant infrastructure by participants within the supply chain. As a result, supply chains become more flexible and are able to easily match capacity to changing customer demand patterns. Customer demand changes for many reasons, including evolving needs and perceived values of products and services. This enables best-in-class global supply chains to quickly dominate niche markets very efficiently at a low per unit transaction cost.

Capacity is the dynamic measure of the ability of a system to produce or transform inputs, represented by materials, labor, machines, information, energy, and other types, into outputs, represented by products, services, or information. Capacity is measured on a per unit time or throughput basis under specified system conditions related to system availability, as well as the demand placed on a system. As an example, we know that available capacity changes as the demand on a system varies. This concept was discussed in Chapter 5 under the subject of queuing analysis and was shown in Table 5.12. Capacity can also be broken into components of labor, capital, and the effectiveness and efficiency of its utilization. In other words, although a system may have a certain predefined capacity at a specified demand level, its actual capacity may be less than the available capacity due to process breakdowns and inefficiencies related to the inefficient utilization of a system's inputs. Capacity can also exist in several forms, including currently available, temporarily stored, or made available at some future date through planning activities. Process workflows can be designed to have each of the three forms of capacity in various ratios. As an example, in older systems, 100 percent of the capacity was on site and available. In other systems, capacity can be made available as needed by an organization based on business relationships. In the latter system, we should think along the lines of supplier agreements, leasing equipment or labor, self-service systems, and related strategies that exist to create capacity based on actual demand placed on a system. In this chapter, we will discuss how process workflows can be created to change the ratios of the three types of capacity using the concepts listed in Table 9.1, as well as several others.

Table 9.1 Competitive Metrics: Managing Capacity

1. Performance gaps among design, available, and actual capacity by process workflow
2. Asset utilization efficiencies by workflow
3. Per unit cost versus workflow volume
4. Rate of organizational learning by workflow
5. Percentage of noncore work outsourced or core work insourced by workflow

Table 9.2 How Should Capacity Be Defined?

Design capacity	The throughput rate the system has been designed to achieve with all operations working at standard levels
Available capacity	Design capacity minus calculated losses in efficiency due to time lost for setups, inspection, processing, transport of materials, and waiting for processing
Actual capacity	Available capacity minus time lost due to interactions between system inputs and processing efficiencies

Capacity is the ability of a transformation system to produce goods or services according to a schedule at an agreed upon time, location, and quantity. A system's capacity is also dynamic and changes. In other words, a system's efficiency varies based on the inputs, their processing status, and the mix of products or services flowing through a process workflow or system at a particular point in time. Variations in the efficient use of labor and capital or the impact of external factors are the reason for dynamic fluctuations in available capacity within a system. Table 9.2 shows a system's capacity can be defined quantitatively in at least three ways: a system's design capacity, available capacity, and actual capacity. Design capacity is the throughput rate of a system when all labor and capital are working at their optimum levels. Available capacity is defined as the system's design capacity minus expected or planned losses in operational efficiency. These losses are usually caused by known variations in time lost due to setups, inspection of work, processing of work, the transport of materials, and waiting for processing. A system's actual capacity is defined as the available capacity minus time lost due to unexpected interactions among the components of the system that negatively impact the throughput rate of the system. Actual capacity is caused by lower than expected production efficiencies due to various types of process breakdowns, including higher than expected scrap or rework, schedule variations, and lack of resources.

Operational schedules are made based on a system's expected available capacity. However, process variation may result in an inability of a system to meet operational schedules. This has an effect of further lowering available capacity as jobs are introduced into the workflow. This is because these jobs increase the overall number of setups, and therefore the overall setup time for a system. An increase in setup time is subtracted from the available capacity of the system. If there are breakdowns in the workflows of the process, then improvement projects may be required to increase the level of actual capacity to that of the available capacity. This implies that the workflows of a process should be designed in ways that reduce the probability that they will fail, because their failure reduces the available capacity of a system. The information contained in Chapters 3 to 6 is particularly important in the design of efficient workflows. As an example, it was shown that there is a limiting physical fact concerning systems: because a system's throughput or capacity is only as high as its bottleneck resource, and depending on operational variation within the system, its capacity constrained resources may periodically become system bottlenecks. In other words, to increase available or actual capacity, we must increase the capacity at a system's bottleneck resource. This concept was discussed in Chapter 6 and shown in Figure 6.6. Available and actual capacity can also be increased by a deployment of several Lean tools and methods. These were discussed in Chapter 6 and consisted of establishing a takt time to utilize capacity only when required to satisfy external customer demand, and operational balancing of work tasks across a system's processes and their workflows. Other ways to increase available and actual capacity are the use of transfer batches, the application of mixed-model scheduling, waste elimination to reduce rework and scrap, and deployment of pull systems. Additional ways to increase system capacity include the implementation of quick response manufacturing (QRM) as applied to the efficient use of master production scheduling (MPS) and materials requirements planning (MRPII) systems. Quality improvement tools and methods, such as Six Sigma or design for Six Sigma (DFSS), can also be used to reduce process breakdown incident rates to improve yields. These tools and methods, as well as others, will be discussed in the next several chapters.

Another important consideration in expanding a system's capacity is the economy-of-scale concept. It is known that many systems have a minimum per unit cost at a specific capacity utilization level corresponding to their available capacity. This is called the economy-of-scale or capacity utilization–cost model and is shown in Figure 9.1. Using this capacity utilization–cost model, it can be shown that if a system is utilized at a level below its available capacity level, then indirect costs must be allocated across a smaller throughput volume, resulting in a higher per unit transaction cost than if throughput volumes had been higher. On the other hand, as a system's throughput volume increases, its per unit cost decreases to its minimum level, after which it begins to increase due to operational inefficiencies. As an example, it has been found that as production volumes increase, there are fewer required job setups and changeovers from one product or service to another. This

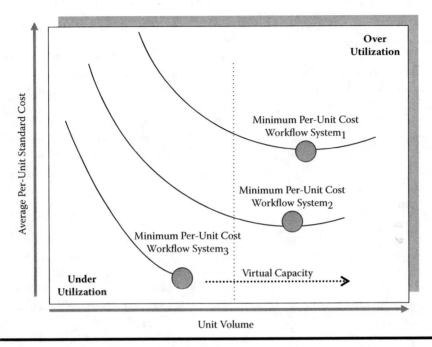

Figure 9.1   Historical relationships between economy of scale and cost.

allows a higher level of standardization of production equipment and methods, and by implication, the system's utilization level increases. Also, indirect or overhead costs can be allocated over larger production volumes, which reduces per unit cost. However, it is also known that as a system's utilization increases past its minimum per unit cost due to increasing throughput rates, operational inefficiencies increase within the system. This is because labor and capital resources are pushed past their designed utilization rates. This situation causes higher rework and scrap and other operational breakdowns.

At this point in our discussion, we should distinguish between the utilization and activation of a resource. This is best understood in the context of the bottleneck resource discussion of Chapter 6. In Chapter 6, it was stated that upstream resources should be activated only when a system's downstream bottleneck resource needs material or information. In other words, it was shown that material or information flow through a non-bottleneck resource must be balanced with that of the system's bottleneck. Thus, the utilization levels of nonbottleneck resources should match their required activation levels, as determined by a system's bottleneck, and very likely should not be utilized 100 percent of the time. In fact, if their utilization exceeds their required activation level, then work-in-process (WIP) inventory will be created in the system. A complicating factor in this scenario is that other products may be starved for materials and components if a production schedule changes especially at a bottleneck resource. An example of this phenomenon was shown in in Table 5.12: when a system's capacity was increased past its design level, waiting times for processing significantly increased and the throughput of the system was significantly reduced below its available capacity level. The analysis shown in Table 5.12 suggests that even if a system has been correctly designed to provide a particular capacity or throughput rate, operational performance as measured by lead time will deteriorate as a production volume increases past the design capacity or throughput rate of a system. Available capacity will also decrease due to poor quality, misinformation, and other mistakes made within a system. Based on these facts, we should evaluate capacity from several operational perspectives. Also, we should clearly state our capacity definition as well as its target level relative to a system's conditions and rules.

This economy-of-scale concept shown in Figure 9.1 has been modified to show that as the percentage of virtual capacity in a system increases, the minimum cost curve shifts down, reflecting a decreasing per unit transaction cost even at lower throughput system volumes. How is this possible? As mentioned earlier in this chapter, historically, an expensive infrastructure was required to create capacity sufficient to gain access to customer markets. But as markets have become segmented and fragmented into niche markets across the world, it has become increasingly difficult to gain economies of scale to directly reduce per unit costs of products or services. This has resulted in the creation of workflow structures that can be activated on demand and are characterized by low per unit cost and flexible capacity levels. Relative to services, several trends have enabled these types of systems to evolve. The first is technology deployment, which enables an increasingly higher percentage of virtual and informational components within products and services. This allows their creation almost instantaneously anywhere in the world and eliminates the need for building hardware and infrastructure to use these products and services. A second evolving trend is that the actual work of processing information can be shifted across the world to low per unit labor cost regions using the World Wide Web or Internet. This capability also lowers per unit transaction costs and creates supply chains in which capacity can be inexpensively increased or decreased based on the demand placed on a system. These and other global trends have also blurred the concept of under- or overutilization of a system because labor and capital resources can be activated only as necessary. On the other hand, in industries that produce tangible products requiring manufacturing processes and workflows, the impact of economies of scale has also been minimized relative to its historical basis using the tools, methods, and concepts of mass customization. Mass customization was discussed in Chapter 4 and Table 4.16. Many of the tools and methods described in Table 4.16 are derived from design-for-manufacturing (DFM) methods discussed in Chapter 4 or Lean methods discussed in Chapters 5 and 6. These new concepts also apply to industries characterized as infrastructure intensive, such as telecommunications. In the telecommunications industry, technology has shifted the economy-of-scale model to lower minimum per unit transaction costs based on system throughput rates. As an example, new cell phone technologies enabled many regions of the world, without having a major telecommunications

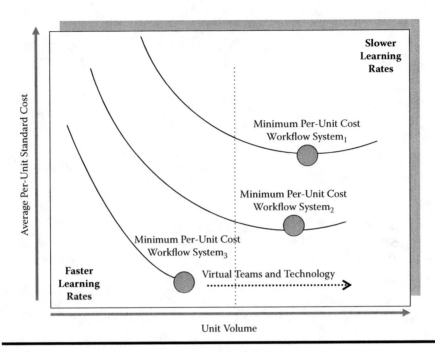

Figure 9.2   Experience increases capacity (learning curve theory).

infrastructure, to quickly connect using satellite technology, rather than creating an entirely new infrastructure by laying cable across their countries.

In addition to economies of scale, learning curve theory shows that capacity also increases as experience is gained in producing a product or service. This concept is shown in Figure 9.2, but modified for our discussion. Learning curve theory assumes that an improved understanding of system structure and dynamics, gained through experience with a process workflow, contributes to higher operational efficiencies. These in turn contribute to higher available system capacity as experience is gained through a careful study of the major process workflows comprising a system. Learning occurs as people work with supporting equipment, tools, and methods that are used to produce products and services. In addition to learning efficiencies, process workflows are also continually improved and standardized over time. This also increases the available capacity of systems because people can learn how to operate them at a faster rate. Standardization is also increased by the application of new tools, methods, and other technologies that help eliminate process waste associated with non-value-adding work tasks. As an example, in Figure 9.3 (a modified version of Figure 7.6), we see that every part of a system is subject to variations in the levels of its input and processing variables. In addition, the demand placed on a system could also fluctuate. This may negatively impact the operational efficiency of process workflows and their associated work tasks. Finally, measurement and control activities also introduce variation as we evaluate system

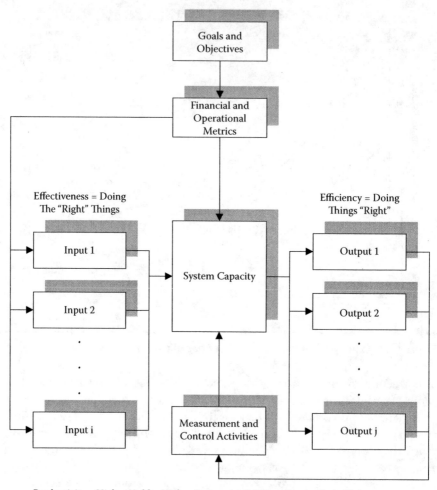

Productivity = Higher Yield × Higher System Availability × Lower Cycle Time

Figure 9.3 System capacity is dynamic.

performance. In addition to the major impacts caused by process variation, it is important that a system's workflows are effective and efficient. Effective and efficient utilization of system resources increases the available capacity of a system as well as its productivity, as we do the right things more efficiently.

In summary, a system's design capacity is determined up front when a product or service is designed, as described in Chapter 4. Recall that design engineering always has an opportunity to create simple and efficient designs that production operations will find easier to produce in a standardized and efficient manner. In other words, a process design, and its available capacity, is constrained by the product or service it must produce. It was also shown in Chapter 4 that simple and easy-to-produce

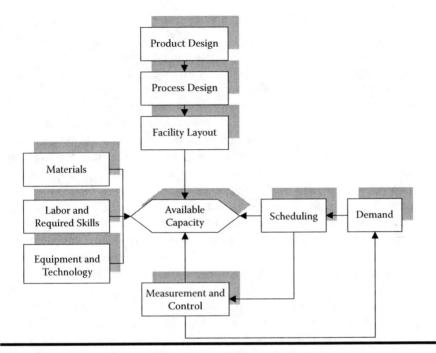

Figure 9.4 Critical factors impacting available capacity.

products and services enable a system to maintain stable and high capacity levels and respond dynamically to changes in customer demand. This concept is shown in Figure 9.4, in which available and actual capacity are determined by interacting process variables, as well as changing demand patterns.

Several major operational components of the system shown in Figure 9.4 include those driven by product or service design as well as the production process. In addition, incoming materials, labor, information, equipment, and many other inputs impact a system's available and actual capacity. This is especially true if there are breakdowns in the system's workflows that supply the inputs into the process. The production process itself also has numerous variables that impact available and actual capacity. Finally, the management tools and methods used to control a system's workflows impact its efficiency, throughput rates, and available and actual capacity. However, sufficient capacity will be available to meet production schedules if a system has been designed correctly based on expected demand.

How to Plan Capacity Based on System Forecasts

In Chapter 8, capacity was discussed in the context of strategic and operational forecasts. Strategic forecasts are made at long time horizons to ensure sufficient capacity is available to produce products or services in the future. Strategic forecasts may also show that there will be a future need for a new facility or new process workflow, or that current locations and facilities must be relocated for various reasons. These changes might be regional, national, or global and either temporary or permanent in nature. Strategic capacity planning is important to an organization because a failure to adequately plan future capacity will result in significantly higher supply-chain costs and longer lead times across a supply chain.

Strategic capacity planning supports an organization's expansion into new markets for products or services. Important components of this planning process require estimation of facility size and location, required equipment, materials, and the hiring and training of employees to build capacity to meet forecasted demand. Available capacity is estimated based on strategic demand forecasts period by period, over the forecasting time horizon, for each location within a supply chain. It is based on the expected throughput rate of the system. Allowances are also made by process engineering, which reduces the design capacity or maximum available throughput rates to a calculated available capacity for the system. Actual capacity is a reduction of available capacity due to unexpected process breakdowns. Figure 9.5 shows that a system's capacity is estimated at first at an aggregated business unit level, by quarter and month, to ensure labor and capital are at least at their right locations and in amounts sufficient to satisfy forecasted demand by location and time period. Business unit forecasts are made by year and broken into quarters and months by facility. At a facility level, forecasts are broken into months and weeks by product group. Capacity is planned on an aggregated basis accordingly by each facility. Finally, at a local work cell level, capacity is planned on a monthly, weekly, and daily basis as required by a particular product or service. In Chapters 5 and 6 we began a discussion of how to organize process workflows to increase a system's throughput rate and operational efficiencies. These concepts will help a system achieve or expand its available capacity.

Organizational productivity is tied in large part to its system design and how well it utilizes its resources to meet capacity and system throughput rates to meet external customer demand. In other words, productivity depends on how well a system matches its supply and demand across its supply chain. There are basic and proven ways to accomplish supply and demand matching. In fact, many organizations have found very creative ways to match supply and demand that have drastically reduced supply-chain cost and increased its capacity, in a flexible manner. This is the focus for the balance of this and subsequent chapters. In fact, many of today's competitive organizations have found creative ways to expand their global capacity at levels of investment below those of competitors by not having to deploy similar infrastructures.

Creating Virtual Capacity

Virtual capacity is an ability of a system to efficiently satisfy customer demand, without large investments in infrastructure, using information technology to

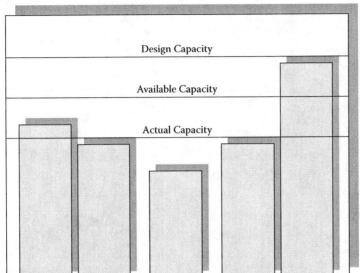

Utilization = Actual Capacity/Design Capacity

•Finite Loading: Load the System so Capacity is not Exceeded.
•Infinite Loading: Load the System without Regard for Capacity Constraints.

Business Unit Level:	Quarter 1	Quarter 2	Quarter 3	Quarter 4	Quarter 5
Facility Level:	January	February	March	April	May
Local Work Cell Level:	Monday AM PM	Tuesday AM PM	Wednesday AM PM	Thursday AM PM	Friday AM PM

Figure 9.5   Measuring capacity.

match supply and demand across a supply chain at high activation levels. System utilization might be high or low depending on the invested capital of an organization and the demand patterns acting on the system. This concept is qualitatively shown in Figure 9.6 and Figure 9.7, in which all system components are connected by information technology and systems. In Figure 9.6, if a schedule is pushed out through the system. This may overload the available capacity of each facility within the system. In this scenario, unmet demand is carried over to future time periods and capacity is lost, which leaves some facilities idle due to fluctuations in demand placed on the system. In contrast, in systems that have been designed to pull demand through a network of facilities, demand is level loaded based on facility availability. In some systems, utilization rates may exceed 98 percent. In combination with low-cost labor, which is available throughout the world, available capacity of a system can be varied to match almost any demand pattern by creating

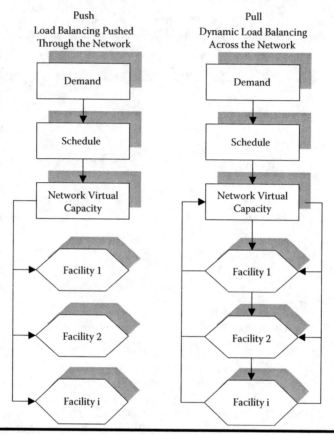

Figure 9.6   Load balancing across a network.

a pull system. This is a simple example in which information system technology deployment as well as Lean tools, methods, and concepts can be easily applied to diverse industries and systems to increase their available capacity. Figure 9.7 also shows that the throughput of a system can be increased by adding capacity at its bottleneck resource. Pull systems will be discussed in Chapter 12.

As an example, many organizations have call centers spread geographically across the world. If properly designed, these systems can transfer incoming and outgoing calls from call centers at which demand exceeds available capacity to other call centers that may currently have excess capacity. In reality, the calls are transferred automatically in seconds. Given the large investment required to build a call center, this type of system design is an efficient way to ensure utilization rates are very high across the system by matching activation to utilization rates based on required employee skills and service levels. However, organizations do not have to actually build their call centers. Many corporations increase their available capacity at a very low per unit transaction cost by outsourcing their call center work

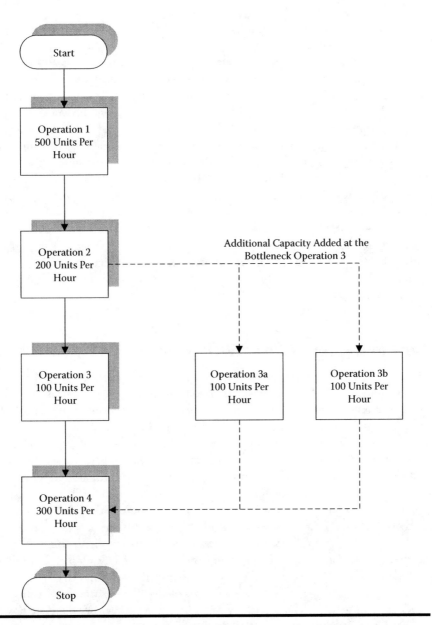

Figure 9.7   Improving capacity at bottlenecks.

internationally to countries such as India. This virtual capacity is enabled through contract, information technology, and the transfer of operational and proprietary information to the organization providing the outsourced services. This situation enables an organization having a virtual supply chain to reduce its investment and operational costs as well as expand and contract its capacity based on demand.

This flexibility enables these organizations to easily enter and leave markets without high business costs. In other words, an organization can increase its available capacity past the system's original design capacity, but at a very low cost. In effect, technology, information, collaboration, and new organizational systems are replacing physical facilities and objects, by increasing the total global utilization rates for supply chains that link their organizations and facilities across the world. In fact, any organization can benefit from developing similar virtual capacity scenarios, although admittedly those systems that must produce physical objects or provide services that are geographically or culturally isolated may require unique tools and methods to create similar virtual systems. These systems may not be as efficient as those created in industries that are information intensive, such as call centers and electronic publishing. However, the more a supply chain can substitute materials and physical objects for information, the greater will be its ability to convert its system to a virtual analogue. The tools, methods, and concepts discussed in the earlier chapters of this book relative to product or service design, as well as process design, and the application of Lean principles can also be applied to virtual systems to expand their capacity.

How to Improve Capacity Utilization

Once a system has been designed to achieve an available capacity level and throughput rate under specified operational conditions, there are several additional operational tools, methods, and concepts that will ensure capacity remains at its available level. In fact, it may be possible to exceed this level if process improvements are made to the system's workflows. Table 9.3 lists 25 recommendations to increase system capacity using tools, methods, and concepts discussed in this book. In many cases, an ability to implement a particular recommendation will depend on several other system components. The first method listed in Table 9.3 is efficiently matching available resources to demand through effective forecasting and scheduling methods. This will ensure the system is not idle or producing the wrong products, services, or information. However, this recommendation is complicated and relies on the implementation of several system components. As an example, scheduling should be managed relative to the system's bottleneck resource, and all other system resources, at an operational level, must be balanced to the bottleneck. In turn, the bottleneck must be matched to the system's takt time; otherwise, the system will build up excess work-in-process (WIP) inventory. Several other methods to increase scheduling flexibility were discussed in Chapter 6 using mixed-model scheduling to enable a system to respond dynamically to variations in external demand. This increases actual or available capacity. Chapter 6 also discussed the concept of transfer batches and the advantages of moving a system from a process batch to one piece or unit flow using transfer batches. Strategies to improve demand management

Table 9.3   25 Ways to Increase Capacity for Manufacturing or Service Organizations

1. Match resources to demand through effective demand management.
2. Work with customers to level load demand.
3. Use price and promotional policies to level load demand.
4. Enable customers to self-service their needs.
5. Hire temporary or part-time workers.
6. Use overtime to handle demand.
7. Overlap work shifts.
8. Lease facilities.
9. Lease equipment.
10. Modify product design.
11. Modify process design.
12. Modify the facility layout.
13. Move to mixed-model production strategies.
14. Use transfer batch processing.
15. Change the service discipline and type, i.e., self-servicing.
16. Improve quality.
17. Reduce operational cycle time.
18. Increase equipment and worker availability.
19. Use Single Minute Exchange of Dies (SMED) to reduce setup time.
20. Transfer lessons learned across the supply chain.
21. Increase the flexibility of workers through cross-training.
22. Deploy simple and standardized redundant equipment that can be utilized at different rates or levels.
23. Create virtual capacity using information technology.
24. Outsource noncore operations.
25. Insource core operations.

were discussed in Chapter 8. As another example, recommendations 10 and 11 in Table 9.3 suggest that capacity can be increased by making simple modifications to the design of a product or service and their workflows to simplify, standardize, and mistake-proof them. These actions will ensure high process yields, which increases available capacity because scrap and rework are reduced. Although design improvements may be difficult, it is possible to increase design capacity by modifying product and service designs and their production processes. These concepts were discussed in Chapters 4 and 5.

Relative to recommendation 12, in Chapter 12 and Figure 12.5 we will discuss the fact that some facility layouts are more efficient than others in bringing labor, equipment, and materials closer together to enable unit flow through a system. In these highly efficient layouts, lead time and cost are reduced and quality is increased over less efficient layouts. This increases the available capacity of a system. In Chapter 12, we will also show that the rules we use to schedule products or services through a system impacts its throughput rates. Table 9.3 also recommends several other ways to increase available capacity. These include the application of Lean, Six Sigma, and maintenance tools to reduce process waste. Also, because direct labor is a major component of available capacity in most systems, the more highly cross-trained the workforce, the better a system can match its resources to meet customer demand. The same concept applies to the selection of equipment. The more we can deploy multipurpose and simple machines, the greater a system's operational flexibility will be. Finally, we can work with other organizations to plan and allocate capacity across a global supply chain through a strategy of outsourcing and insourcing of work to improve asset utilization efficiencies and productivity. In summary, many of the concepts, tools, and methods presented in this book are designed to improve available capacity, system throughput rates, and productivity, as shown in Table 9.3 as well as other sections of this book.

Managing Capacity with Insourcing and Outsourcing

Organizations have been outsourcing and insourcing their work for many years. In many ways, these types of activities have not changed in several decades. In fact, the tools and methods associated with outsourcing and insourcing are still very applicable in today's world. But given the extent of globalization and the sophistication of available technology, as well as the ease of creating virtual teams across the world, new outsourcing and insourcing options have become available in recent years. These enable organizations to inexpensively increase their capacity. As an example, historically, organizations have vertically or horizontally integrated their workflows. However, in today's world, outsourcing and insourcing work is not simply sending it out and bringing it back into an organization, but it is a combined set of activities that determine where and how work should be done, by whom, and under which circumstances to increase the value-added content of a product or service. In other words, the concept of what an organization *is* and *does* is now under constant review and revision across global supply chains. As a result, outsourcing and insourcing have grown to be more than the sum of the work moved around the world. This has meant that organizations may become involved in work that may appear to be outside their core competency, but it actually contributes to the overall value-added content of a product or service, as well as an organization's productivity. As an example, a manufacturer might insource some work activities that reduce the customer order-to-receipt cycle to gain sales or reduce operational cost. Or perhaps an organization wants to increase customer satisfaction and its revenue by expanding its current product and service offerings based on new customer needs. However, contrary to the old way of outsourcing noncore works, insourcing or outsourcing decisions are now made from an entire supply-chain viewpoint. In other words, outsourcing and insourcing decisions are justified at a business level to increase organizational productivity and economic value added (EVA) for shareholders. Thus, competitive organizations in today's word take a holistic view of their supply chain and look for ways to continuously increase its value-added content in unique ways.

Table 9.4 lists ten reasons why organizations outsource or insource their work. Increasing capacity is the most obvious reason. However, the fact that some

Table 9.4   10 Key Reasons to Outsource and Insource Products and Services

Reason	Outsourcing	Insourcing
1. Increase capacity	Expand current labor and equipment capacity at low cost and risk	Increase utilization of current capacity using labor and equipment having similar skills and capabilities as insourced work
2. Obtain new technology	Avoid the cost and risks of developing new technologies fully, especially those that are not aligned with core technology	Purchase or license new technology that has been developed by another organization to reduce cost and lead time and ensure quality targets are met
3. Reduce financial and market risks	Allocate financial resources to core processes and current marketing activities	Bring in work that external organizations cannot do at the cost, lead time, and quality levels required

Table 9.4 (continued)   10 Key Reasons to Outsource and Insource Products and Services

Reason	Outsourcing	Insourcing
4. Reduce supply-chain lead time	Move supply activities closer to markets to reduce lead time and cost	Bring in work which will reduce supply-chain lead time; do not send work all the way across the supply chain
5. Focus on core processes	Outsource noncore processes and insource core activities important to drive sales growth	Outsource noncore processes to focus organizational resources on core process work to improve volume efficiencies
6. Expand into new markets	Partner with organizations in other markets to expand market share and reduce risk and cost	Bring in work that is not currently done, but uses common labor skills and equipment
7. Improve operational efficiency and reduce cost	Work with external organizations that have a competitive labor or capital cost advantage	Bring in work that will increase volume and level load schedules
8. Satisfy country rules, regulations, and laws	Work with organizations having a favored regulatory position within their country, such as licenses or permits	Bring in work that cannot be outsourced due to country rules, regulations, and laws
9. Obtain cultural expertise relative to market segmentation	Work with organizations to obtain design and marketing expertise relative to cultural norms and behavior	Bring in design and marketing experts from other countries to create new products and markets
10. Environmentally challenging operations	Work with organizations to deploy challenging operations that can only de done in certain regions of the world, i.e., dry, wet, hot, or cold	Bring in work that requires special handling equipment or skills

organizations are increasingly insourcing completely different types of work to increase the value added by their core competency is a relatively new concept. This insourcing is not a simple extension of an organization's current workflows, but rather, creates ancillary workflows within an organization. However, organizations must be careful to insource only value-adding work aligned with their core competency. Insourcing extraneous work into a process workflow that is not designed to do the work will result in operational inefficiencies. In fact, these types of process breakdowns are classic, in the sense that many organizations mix high-technology with low-technology operations with the result that quality problems occur in the high-technology operations and high per unit costs occur in the lower-technology operations. The historical solution to these process breakdowns is to separate diverse operations at a local level. However, if the insourced work can add value to an organization's core competency, and it is properly designed into a process workflow, there should not be process breakdowns.

A second reason for outsourcing or insourcing work is to obtain new and unique technology. In the case of outsourcing work, it might be more efficient to let other organizations that have advanced technology to do portions of the work that an organization cannot or will not do. However, the proper contractual and other controls must be in place to ensure the technology remains available over time at specified cost and lead time targets. Relative to insourcing, organizations can also license advanced technology from other organizations. A third reason for outsourcing or insourcing work is to minimize financial risk to an organization or allocate scarce resources to an organization's core activities. On the other hand, to the extent suppliers or partners cannot meet their financial obligations or are at risk financially, insourcing could be the only option for an organization. Other reasons for outsourcing and insourcing are listed in detail in Table 9.4. These include:

Table 9.5 shows several strategies that can be used to create new relationships to outsource or insource work across a supply chain. These apply to the management of intangible and tangible assets, including fixed assets, facilities, equipment, and labor. These structural strategies span a range of options, from the outright sale of a business or its workflows, including core or noncore operations, to the licensing of new technology and methods or the sharing of information on an informal basis. Regardless of the organizational relationships within a supply chain, it is important that an organization understand its strategic goals and objectives when making its outsourcing and insourcing evaluations. It is also important that strategic evaluations of outsourcing and insourcing be objectively made based on predetermined decision criteria in advance of fact-finding and data collection activities. These evaluations should also be conducted relative to cultural, demographic, economic, and political considerations. Risk analyses must also be made for every aspect of a proposed outsourcing and insourcing arrangement, as well as its combined impact on

Table 9.5   Outsourcing and Insourcing Strategies

Strategy	Intangible Assets and Intellectual Property	Fixed Assets and Facilities	Equipment	Labor
Sale of core business	✓	✓	✓	✓
Sale of noncore business	✓	✓	✓	✓
Joint venture	✓	✓	✓	✓
Partnership	✓	✓	✓	✓
Licensee relationship	✓	✓	✓	✓
Share information	✓	✓	✓	✓
Share resources	✓	✓	✓	✓
Supplier relationship	✓	✓	✓	✓
Contractor relationship	✓	✓	✓	✓

Note: Anything can be outsourced or insourced under the right circumstances.

an organization. Table 9.6 provides a listing of 20 key factors that will help an organization evaluate the feasibility of outsourcing or insourcing between one or more alternative organizations and locations. The list has been marked up to show how an outsourcing or insourcing team might use it to evaluate a particular scenario. This listing can be expanded for your organization's particular needs and requirements. In addition to ranking the relative importance of each factor, one must establish the methods necessary to collect and analyze data for each factor and build an overall model for every combination of factor levels to systematically evaluate the outsourcing and insourcing decisions. The risk analysis tools and methods presented in Chapter 4 and Figure 4.8 are also very useful in these types of decisions. In the next chapter we will discuss facility location and continue our discussion of the 20 factors listed in Table 9.6, but from a project risk perspective.

The discussion of capacity at a local facility or work cell level will be continued in Chapter 13. Chapter 13 will show how an adjusted MPS schedule is broken down, using master requirements planning (MRPII) and other systems, into supplier orders for raw materials and components using a bill-of-material (BOM).

Table 9.6 20 Key Cultural, Demographic, Economic, and Political Factors Impacting Outsourcing and Insourcing Decisions

Category	Evaluation Factor	Importance Low 1	Medium 2	Medium 3	High 4	High 5
Cultural	1. Cultural norms		x			
	2. Cultural values		x			
Demographic	3. Population size			x		
	4. Population density			x		
	5. Age distribution			x		
	6. Education and skills			x		
	7. Language			x		
	8. Religious tolerance		x			
Economic	9. Economic stability				x	
	10. Available infrastructure			x		
	11. Available capital				x	
	12. Available equipment				x	
	13. Available labor				x	
	14. Available suppliers				x	
	15. Available customers			x		
Political	16. Legal system		x			
	17. Regulatory system		x			
	18. Taxation policies		x			
	19. Internal political stability		x			
	20. Geopolitical stability	x				

The sales and operational planning (S&OP), MPS, and MRPII systems will be discussed in more detail in Chapters 11 to 13, respectively. In these chapters, our discussion will focus on an intermediate time horizon in which a system forecast is incorporated into the MPS and adjusted to the S&OP team's consensus forecast.

Table 9.7   Key Concepts to Effectively Manage Capacity

1. There are different levels of capacity, including design, available and actual. Improvements should be undertaken to increase actual capacity to the design capacity.
2. Economy-of-scale models show that capacity can be increased by application of technology, information sharing, and other factors that allow minimum per unit cost at lower unit volumes than historically feasible.
3. Experience curve models show that capacity can be increased through higher learning rates.
4. System capacity is dynamic and must be managed dynamically.
5. Lean principles are very useful in increasing available capacity.
6. The design of product and services has a significant impact on system capacity.
7. Insourcing and outsourcing of work can dramatically increase system capacity.

Summary

The efficient use of capacity is critical to increasing organizational productivity and its competitiveness. This chapter discussed the management of capacity from several perspectives, as shown in Table 9.7. My opinion is that organizations must think "outside the box" to create systems in which the percentage of virtual capacity is maximized for their particular industry and workflow design. Investment in costly infrastructure should be made based on strategic reasons and only as a last resort, because customer demand patterns are rapidly changing and access to sources of supply also migrates over time. Process improvements should also be undertaken to increase a system's actual capacity to closely match or exceed its available capacity.

It was also shown that the application, information sharing, and other technologies enables a low per unit cost and at lower unit volumes than historically feasible. Organizational learning rates are also accelerating in global supply chains. This is important because experience curve models show that capacity can be increased through higher learning rates. The challenge for today's organizations is to accelerate their organizational learning to increase operational efficiencies. Additional ways to increase capacity include the application of Lean principles and the design of products and services. Finally, insourcing and outsourcing of work can dramatically increase system capacity. In Chapters 10 to 14 we will discuss facility location, sales and operations planning, scheduling systems, materials requirements planning, and inventory control, respectively. These tools, methods, and concepts will provide additional ideas to help increase global supply-chain capacity.

Suggested Reading

Richard B. Chase, F. Robert Jacobs, and Nicholas J. Aquilano. (2006). *Operations Management for Competitive Advantage*, 11th ed. McGraw-Hill, New York.

Thomas L. Friedman. (2005). *The World Is Flat*. Farrar, Straus, and Giroux.

Chapter 10

Using Hybrid Decentralization to Increase Productivity

Competitive solution 10: Locate and manage facilities using best-in-class tools and methods to reduce supply-chain cost and lead time.

Overview

Organizations locate facilities for many reasons. Some of these include lower production costs, to obtain technological advantages not available locally, to minimize risk, to expand system capacity and increase operational flexibility, to reduce supply-chain lead times, to be near suppliers or customers, as well as others. When an organization decides to locate a new facility or close an existing facility, an analysis should be conducted to consider all relevant factors involved in the decision. To some people, relocation decisions should also be based on productivity considerations and the needs of various organizational stakeholders, such as employees, customers, suppliers, and the surrounding community. However, business organizations are open systems versus closed systems, such as countries. An open system is not necessarily accountable for its actions as they impact other societal groups. As an example, without laws and regulations, a corporation might be able to pollute at will, fire workers indiscriminately, and heavily use public infrastructure without incurring additional cost. But a closed system, such as a country, cannot do these things without incurring costs. As a result, society has a vested interest in ensuring its environment remains clean, workers have access to jobs, and its infrastructure is created and maintained for its citizens. In contrast, if a business organization closes a facility, its employees must find other work within the surrounding community. A business organization has little obligation to help employees find work unless it has voluntary internal policies regarding such situations, or local laws and regulations require notification or place other responsibilities upon the organization. However, being a closed system, society must provide displaced employees with unemployment, health, and related types of insurance as part of its social safety net. But this varies by society. Recognizing these facts, society places boundaries on business behavior as it impacts other societal groups. This forces business organizations to follow local laws and regulations, restricting their actions, to avoid sanctions and penalties by government. Using this logic, facility location is a set of economic activities by an organization to increase its productivity and shareholder economic value added (EVA). Political, demographic, cultural, technical, and other factors are considered relevant only to the extent they constrain an organization's economic activities or other business interests. As a result, from an organizational viewpoint, an organization must fully consider the costs of entering and leaving global markets over the useful life of its relocation investment and in the context of local laws, regulations, and cultural norms. As an example, several years ago I consulted with a very well established New England manufacturer of capital equipment. This company had been in business for over 100 years when it made a poor decision regarding facility location due to the purchase of another company in Southern Europe. After it expanded into this country, it found that productivity rates were low and profits were negative. As a result, it closed its Southern European facilities. Unfortunately, it was required to pay its employees several years' worth of salary due to local laws. As a result, the company went bankrupt and was sold to a competitor within two years. This is an example where a facility location decision was not well thought out. The project team did not do the necessary work to fully evaluate all project risks. In summary, facility location decisions should be based on a full understanding of productivity opportunities and project risks over the useful life of an investment.

Our goal in this chapter is to review several important factors that impact facility location decisions in today's competitive world. Table 10.1 shows that a team which is assigned a facility location project must analyze the project from several

Table 10.1   Competitive Metrics: Facility Location and Management

1. Financial metrics relative to return on investment (ROI), cash flow, and payback met according to schedule
2. Asset utilization efficiencies by workflow and the entire facility
3. Capacity, throughput rates, and per unit transaction cost and other operational benefits assumed by the original project

perspectives using financial and operational metrics. These include return on investment (ROI), cash flow, payback time, asset utilization efficiencies, capacity, throughput rates, and per unit transaction costs, as well as other business benefits. In this chapter our discussion will be from a risk perspective, using evaluation tools and methods such as a Pugh matrix, linear programming, regression analysis and decision tree analysis. However, the complexity of facility location decisions will vary by organization. The information contained within this chapter should be considered a minimum level of detail required for facility location decisions. We will build on the information presented in Chapters 4 to 8 relative to the use of risk analysis and operations research tools and methods.

Prior to locating a facility, a project team should ask relevant questions such as: Why do we need to locate these facilities? Why do we need facilities at these particular locations? What products or services will be allocated to these facilities? How should the new facilities be designed? How long will we need the new facility? If circumstances change, how will we use the new facilities? How easy will it be to close these facilities in the future? What are the relevant laws, regulations, customs, and cultural norms of the country or region? What will be the environmental impact of locating a facility at this particular location? What are the relevant factors in selecting a facility location? Depending on the organization, there may be many other questions relevant to facility location decisions. In summary, an organization should begin its facility location discussions with a full review of the questions necessary to ensure it is making a correct investment decision. There are many tools, methods, and templates that can be employed in an analysis of facility location. We will discuss elements of these tools, templates, and methods in this chapter in an attempt to show why they are useful in an overall analysis of global facility location decisions.

Applying Hybrid Decentralization to Facility Location

Integral to a discussion of facility location are the concepts of where work should be performed, by whom, and why. These discussions are an ongoing and dynamic process in which competitive organizations continually engage. In competitive organizations, as business needs change, work is moved to where it is done best to improve productivity. A continual review of the work performed within a global supply chain results in the centralization, decentralization, disaggregation, and aggregation of work as required by an organization to increase the value content of the entire supply chain. These activities are sometimes described as hybrid decentralization (HD). Hybrid decentralization evolved as information technology provided organizations with an ability to easily reconfigure and relocate process workflows. This capability has resulted in increasingly higher productivity across global supply chains. However, rationalization of work always results in friction at both an organizational and local community level because work may be lost to other locations.

However, in order for an organization and its supply chain to remain competitive in today's world, its value content must be increased year over year and customer needs must be satisfied as they migrate over time. However, this natural competitive process may be inhibited by political, cultural, or organizational factors or special interest groups. In our discussion, we will focus on organizational factors that impact facility location decisions, but it should be remembered that facility location decisions do not occur in a political or cultural vacuum. In many situations, political and cultural considerations far outweigh economic factors. As an example, it would make no sense to locate a facility within a country that has a high probability of nationalizing the organization's assets, no matter how low the operational costs or favorable the local market opportunities might become. Organizations that are blindsided and suffer economic losses due to political or cultural factors have most likely not done their homework relative to the risk associated with facility location decisions. Also, many organizations simply will not modify their workflow to integrate them in local cultures. They either have not built the necessary capability or will not consider reconfiguration and relocation of their process workflows. As a result, their relative competitive position, internal productivity, and shareholder economic value added (EVA) performance are lower than they might otherwise be if they had made these modifications.

I first saw the advantage of hybrid decentralization when working for Allied-Signal (now Honeywell) in the 1990s. At AlliedSignal, workflows were systematically migrated to locations where they could be done with a higher level of productivity. As an example, for the entire corporation, recruiting activities were performed in one location, intellectual property activities were performed in another location, and employee benefits were handled in still another location. This was also true for forecasting and invoicing workflows. Hybrid decentralization is a very common practice across modern global supply chains, requiring an ongoing analysis of where work should be performed to increase organizational productivity and economic value added (EVA). HD is an important concept of this chapter because it is a major driver of facility relocation decisions.

How to Locate Facilities across the World

In Chapter 9 we discussed ways to increase system capacity. Increases in capacity can be considered from at least two perspectives. The first is expansion of current available capacity through the addition of facilities or capital improvements, and the second is increasing the actual capacity to the available capacity of the system though process improvement projects. In Table 9.4 to Table 9.6 we discussed capacity expansion in the context of global factors related to local culture, demographics, economics, and political environment. In this chapter, we will discuss several tools and methods useful in facility location decisions. Figure 10.1 is a modification

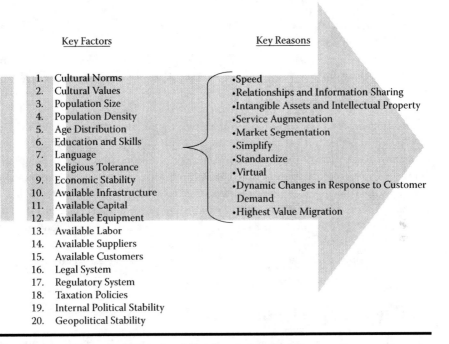

Key Factors	Key Reasons
1. Cultural Norms	•Speed
2. Cultural Values	•Relationships and Information Sharing
3. Population Size	•Intangible Assets and Intellectual Property
4. Population Density	•Service Augmentation
5. Age Distribution	•Market Segmentation
6. Education and Skills	•Simplify
7. Language	•Standardize
8. Religious Tolerance	•Virtual
9. Economic Stability	•Dynamic Changes in Response to Customer Demand
10. Available Infrastructure	•Highest Value Migration
11. Available Capital	
12. Available Equipment	
13. Available Labor	
14. Available Suppliers	
15. Available Customers	
16. Legal System	
17. Regulatory System	
18. Taxation Policies	
19. Internal Political Stability	
20. Geopolitical Stability	

Figure 10.1   Where facilities should be located and why.

of Table 9.6. In Figure 10.1, our discussion focuses on several key criteria or reasons that must be considered in facility location decisions. It should also be noted that every industry and organization will use modifications of the 20 key factors impacting outsourcing or insourcing decisions shown in Table 9.6, as well as the evaluation criteria or key reasons shown in Figure 10.1.

The key reasons in Figure 10.1, including the 20 key factors, would most likely be broken down further and reprioritized based on an organization's specific facility location analysis. Another important consideration in this type of analysis is that a facility location decision should also consider risks associated with the anticipated financial benefits expected over the useful life of an investment. A second component of Figure 10.1 relates to how the facility location decision will improve an organization's relative competitive position, productivity, or economic value added (EVA). Improvement will be expected to relate to reductions in speed or cycle time, an increased ability to share information and collaborate across a supply chain, entry into new markets, simplification and standardization of process workflows, and improvements to the value content of a product or service. As an example, if we need to locate a facility in another country, perhaps our first response would be to construct a building and hire a local workforce. However, creation of fixed assets, at any location, is the last option an organization should use to expand its capacity, and only if the gains in productivity and EVA justify the addition of fixed assets. Instead of an outright purchase of fixed assets, perhaps a cooperative agreement can be reached with a local organization to do the work, or other working relationships, such as those listed in Table 9.5, could be implemented by an organization. Or perhaps the work could be redefined in a way that would negate the necessity of building a new facility. There are many variations on this approach, but the common theme is that a facility location team should fully discuss all aspects of a facility location decision. In this decision-making process, they should keep in mind organizational goals, including competitiveness, productivity, and EVA, when they deliberate. Regardless of the final facility location decision, an organization's products and services should be simplified and standardized and migrate dynamically with customer needs and value expectations over time. Also, to the extent that a product or service can be made more virtual in nature and self-service in form, its useful life will be extended and its required investment will be lower compared to products and services not having these characteristics. Using these concepts, facility location decisions will be much easier and contain less risk to an organization.

Facility Location Using Simple Rating Methods

After a review of the 20 key factors impacting facility location decisions and the reasons or potential benefits to an organization, the team could use one of several ranking tools and methods to evaluate the benefits of various location alternatives. Figure 10.2 shows an ad hoc ranking method in which three alternative locations, 1, 2, and 4, are compared to a baseline location, 3, and rated against the 20 key factors shown in Figure 10.1. Recall that an organization's list might be modified and more extensive. Also recall that in Table 9.6, a rating scale of 1 to 5 was used to rank the relative importance of each factor. In this rating system, a 1 was considered to be low in importance and a 5 was considered to be high in importance to an organization. This importance rating will be used as an input in more quantitative facility location evaluation methods, such as the Pugh matrix, which is shown in Figure 10.3. The difference between Table 9.6 and Figure 10.2 is that instead of prioritizing or ranking the 20 factors directly, the team uses the matrix shown in Figure 10.2 to rank one potential location against another, but using all 20 factors in a calculation of the total ranking for an alternative. As an example, relative to the factor Available Infrastructure, location 4 has a rating of 2 and is ranked lower than the current baseline location, which has a rating of 4. If we look at the total rating for each location alternative, we see that location 4, with a rating of 62, has a higher total rating than the other two locations and the current baseline location. The result is that it is ranked as the most favorable location. This example assumes that the 20 evaluation factors are equally weighted, but the weighting by factor can be unequal, which would result in a weighted total rating for each location alternative.

Category	Evaluation Factor	Location 1	Location 2	Baseline Location 3	Location 4
Cultural	Cultural Norms	2	3	2	4
Cultural	Cultural Values	1	2	1	3
Demographic	Population Size	4	4	3	2
Demographic	Population Density	4	4	3	5
Demographic	Age Distribution	2	4	2	2
Demographic	Education and Skills	4	4	3	1
Demographic	Language	3	2	2	4
Demographic	Religious Tolerance	3	2	2	4
Economic	Economic Stability	3	2	4	5
Economic	Available Infrastructure	4	3	4	2
Economic	Available Capital	4	3	4	2
Economic	Available Equipment	4	3	4	3
Economic	Available Labor	4	3	4	3
Economic	Available Suppliers	1	2	2	3
Economic	Available Customers	2	4	3	4
Political	Legal System	2	2	3	3
Political	Regulatory System	2	4	3	2
Political	Taxation Policies	4	4	4	4
Political	Internal Political Stability	4	2	4	4
Political	Geopolitical Stability	1	4	2	2
	Total Rating	58	61	59	62

Low = 1
Medium = 2
High = 5

Figure 10.2   Ad hoc algorithms to locate facilities.

A more useful tool to evaluate several alternative scenarios is the Pugh matrix, which is shown in Table 10.3. Recall that the Pugh matrix was discussed in Figure 4.7 and was used to evaluate several alternative design concepts. In this chapter we will use this method to evaluate several alternative locations relative to a current baseline location, as well as the factor importance ratings developed in Chapter 9 and shown in Table 9.6. The ratings calculated by the Pugh matrix method are weighted based on the relative importance of each of the 20 factors relative to the team's judgment of the comparative advantage of each location alternative against the current baseline location for each of the 20 factors. In this analysis, location 4 is favored over the baseline location, and location 1 is rated as the worst alternative location. The Pugh matrix is also useful in evaluating the best characteristics of the alternatives not selected as the final solution. As an example, location 1 had higher ratings for the factors Available Infrastructure, Capital, Equipment, and Labor than the baseline scenario. This information may allow an organization to negotiate for better terms relative to actually building or renting a facility at location 4.

Category	Evaluation Factor	Location 1	Location 2	Baseline Location 3	Location 4	Table 9-6 Importance Rating
Cultural	Cultural Norms	−1	0	B	1	3
Cultural	Cultural Values	−2	−1	B	0	3
Demographic	Population Size	1	1	B	−1	4
Demographic	Population Density	1	1	B	2	4
Demographic	Age Distribution	−1	1	B	−1	4
Demographic	Education and Skills	1	1	B	−2	4
Demographic	Language	0	−1	B	1	4
Demographic	Religious Tolerance	0	−1	B	1	3
Economic	Economic Stability	0	−1	B	2	5
Economic	Available Infrastructure	1	0	B	−1	5
Economic	Available Capital	1	0	B	−1	5
Economic	Available Equipment	1	0	B	0	5
Economic	Available Labor	1	0	B	0	5
Economic	Available Suppliers	−2	−1	B	0	5
Economic	Available Customers	−1	1	B	1	4
Political	Legal System	−1	−1	B	0	3
Political	Regulatory System	−1	1	B	−1	3
Political	Taxation Policies	1	1	B	1	3
Political	Internal Political Stability	−1	−1	B	1	4
Political	Geopolitical Stability	−2	1	B	−1	2
	Weighted Total	**−12**	**3**	**0**	**6**	

Figure 10.3   Pugh matrix analysis of facility location ratings.

Facility Location Using Linear Programming

At a more advanced level, linear programming (LP) can be used to build models to evaluate the many factors and constraints that impact facility location decisions. Table 10.2 lists several applications of linear programming that have been applied to facility location decisions. In fact, the LP literature contains an extensive number of LP applications to facility location problems. These applications range from minimizing distance and cost between located facilities and their demand points to determining how to locate facilities that are offensive to their demand points. These include waste dumps and prisons. LP models range from a relatively small number of discrete sources of supply and demand points to very complex models in which service facilities are located based on many characteristics of the calling population, including buying preferences, the required types of services or products, travel distances, and related economic considerations, as well as consumer demographic factors. Recall from Chapter 5, Table 5.14, Figure 5.14, and Figure 5.15, that LP models have an objective function that is minimized or maximized subject to one or more system constraints. In this chapter we will discuss at a very high level some simple facility location examples using LP methods. The discussion will be completed when we cover evaluation of facility location decisions using a

Table 10.2 Applications of Linear Programming to Facility Location Problems

1. Warehousing and distribution centers
2. Manufacturing facilities
3. Public service centers
4. Medical clinics
5. Fire services
6. Police services
7. Distribution hubs
8. Schools
9. Restaurant chains
10. Service facilities
11. Call centers
12. Banks and financial services
13. Hospitals
14. Government services

regression-based model. Recall the regression analysis was discussed in detail at the end of Chapter 8.

Table 10.3 lists the common types of LP facility location models. Additional details describing these models would be available through a literature search. In every LP model listed in Table 10.3, the goal is to minimize or maximize an objective function, but the particular objective function varies in each model. The suffix M after a model implies the model attempts to minimize or maximum distance between sources of supply or facility locations and aggregated demand points or nodes. The suffix A after a model implies it attempts to minimize or maximize an average distance between sources of supply and demand points. The LP models range in complexity and are designed to answer specific questions relative to the systems they were designed to model. A simple modification of the transportation problem is shown in Figure 10.4. Recall a similar transportation example was shown in Figure 5.15. However, Figure 10.4 shows a modified version of the model in which there is an excess of supply for locations 2 and 4 of 5,000 and 60,000 units, respectively. The advantage of using an LP approach to facility location analysis is that many location alternatives can be evaluated relative to an objective function and several system constraints. In the current solution, each of the four alternative

Table 10.3   Common Linear Programming Models for Facility Location

Set covering location models (M)	The goal is to develop a minimum set of locations that will cover all the demand points. The objective is to minimize the number of facilities (total fixed cost).
Maximal covering location models (M)	The goal is to locate a target number of facilities to maximize the number of demand points covered given cost constraints. The objective is to maximize total demand points covered.
Fixed charge location models (A)	The goal is to minimize fixed facility location and transportation costs between locations and demand points. The objective is to minimize transportation and fixed facility location costs.
P-hub location models (A)	The goal is to reduce transportation costs between nonhub and hubs. The objective is to minimize transportation costs between nonhub and hubs. These models are complex.
Multi-objective location models	The goal is to identify locations that will maximize the weighting of several stakeholder preferences. Another version of the method optimizes one objective, then optimizes a secondary objective once the optimum solution to the primary objective has been found. These models are complex.
Dynamic location models	The goal of these models is to bring time into the analysis to model the migration of a facility location life cycle based on a parameter such as changes in demand. These models are complex.
Maximum location models (A)	The goal is to maximize the distance between locations and demand points. Normally, the locations are not desirable to the demand points. The objective is to maximize distance subject to demand points assigned to the most remotely located facilities.
P-center location models (M)	The goal is to minimize the maximum distance between a given facility location and an associated demand point. The objective is to minimize the maximum distance between each location and the closest demand point.
p-Median location models (A)	The goal is to determine the locations necessary to minimize the total distance between demand points and the locations assigned to service them. The objective is to minimize total distance traveled through the system.
P-dispersion location models (M)	The goal is to minimize distance between locations and demand points. The objective is to maximize the minimum distance between pair-wise facility comparisons.

Solution Obtained Using a Transportation Algorithm

From/To		Region A	Region B	Region C	Region D	Supply
	Location 1	$ 1	$ 1	$ 10	$ 10	10,000
	Location 2	$ 5	$ 15	$ 20	$ 30	20,000
	Location 3	$ 3	$ 5	$ 20	$ 5	30,000
	Location 4	$ 5	$ 8	$ 10	$ 20	100,000
	Required Demand	15,000	30,000	40,000	10,000	

Candidate Solution					Shipped
Location 1	0	10,000	0	0	10,000
Location 2	15,000	0	0	0	15,000
Location 3	0	20,000	0	10,000	30,000
Location 4	0	0	40,000	0	40,000
Supplied	15,000	30,000	40,000	10,000	

Cost						
	Location 1	$ -	$ 10,000	$ -	$ -	$ 10,000
	Location 2	$ 75,000	$ -	$ -	$ -	$ 75,000
	Location 3	$ -	$ 100,000	$ -	$ 50,0000	$ 150,000
	Location 4	$ -	$ -	$ 400,000	$ -	$ 400,000
	Total Distribution Cost	$ 75,000	$ 110,000	$ 400,000	$ 50,000	$ 635,000

Excess Supply

Location 2	5,000
Location 4	60,000

Figure 10.4   Application of transportation model to locate facilities.

facilities would ship products or provide services to the four regions under analysis. However, a next step in the analysis would be to evaluate the profit of the current solution against the required investment for the four facilities. It might make sense to combine one or more facilities and increase transportation cost to lower overall investment and operational costs for the new system.

Facility Location Using Regression Models

Facility location as discussed in the preceding paragraphs involves evaluation of one or more location scenarios based on criteria known to be relevant to the location decision, including the 20 factors shown in Figure 10.1. Given that these factors are usually important to most discrete facility location analyses, it makes sense to use them as well as other factors that would help ensure an optimum decision. However, the key factors that influence a facility location decision may not be known in advance of a decision. A facility location team may have to first determine the relevant and significant factors impacting the facility location decision prior to developing quantitative models of the relevant factors and system constraints. In these analyses, regression-based methods have been found useful. In multiple linear regression (MLR) analysis, the contribution of every independent variable in explaining the variation of the dependent variable is quantitatively determined using historical or experimental data. These models include information of the independent contribution of each variable, and may also include variable interactions if the data collection had been executed as an experimental design in which the variables were verified as independent or orthogonal to each other. This allows the variable interactions to be estimated without multicollinearity problems, as described in Chapter 8. In addition, a linear regression model may contain quadratic terms. It should be noted that nonlinear regression models may also be useful, as well as several variants of the regression modeling approach. Several of these modeling variants were discussed in Chapter 8. We will use the information contained in Chapter 8 to expand our discussion of regression analysis to the evaluation of statistically significant factors that may impact facility location decisions. In particular, we will be using dependent variables such as productivity, operating margin or cost, and other relevant business metrics that an organization would want to build into its facility location decision.

In an analysis of several alternative facility locations, databases of alternative facilities are built to include demographic, operational, financial, and other relevant information by location. This information is used to develop a facility location model to estimate the factors having the most impact on the dependent variables or system outputs of interest, such as productivity, operating margin, sales, or operational metrics such as time, distance, and cost. The goal of a regression analysis is to develop a list of factors that will help the facility location team evaluate alternative locations and select a location that will minimize, achieve a target, or maximize the outputs of interest to an organization. As an example, in Figure 10.5 a regression model is used to identify several factors that are important in predicting annual store-to-store sales. Six independent factors or variables were analyzed relative to their impact on annual store-to-store sales for 125 stores. The independent variables are listed in Figure 10.5. The stepwise regression selected Disposable Income and Population as the important variables explaining 97.16 percent of the variation of annualized store-to-store sales based on the $R^2_{adjusted}$ statistic. Recall this statistic was described in Figure 8.39 and discussed in Chapter 8. The higher the $R^2_{adjusted}$ statistic, the greater the percentage of variation of the dependent variable that is explained by a model. A facility location team could use this information in its evaluation of location alternatives. A next step in a facility location analysis would be to evaluate the specific characteristics of several alternative sites within a particular geographical area using a list such as that shown in Figure 10.1, and perhaps the Pugh matrix, shown in Figure 10.3.

In summary, facility location decisions are very complex and depend on a multitude of factors. Some factors are qualitative and others quantitative. Qualitative factors can be evaluated using one of several methods to estimate future scenarios occurring. However, this may be difficult. Examples would be estimates of political unrest or changes in regional demand patterns for a location. On the other

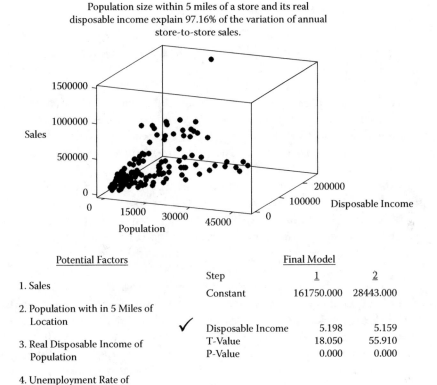

Population size within 5 miles of a store and its real disposable income explain 97.16% of the variation of annual store-to-store sales.

Potential Factors	Final Model		
	Step	1	2
1. Sales	Constant	161750.000	28443.000
2. Population with in 5 Miles of Location			
✓	Disposable Income	5.198	5.159
	T-Value	18.050	55.910
3. Real Disposable Income of Population	P-Value	0.000	0.000
4. Unemployment Rate of Population			
✓	Population		10.680
	T-Value		32.800
5. Floor Space of Store	P-Value		0.000
6. Number of Employees Per Store			
7. Number of Competitors with in 5 Miles of Store	S	124222.000	39807.000
	R-Sq	72.600	97.210
	R-Sq(adj)	72.380	97.160

Figure 10.5 Identification of factors important to facility location.

hand, certain evaluation variables or factors can be estimated with a high degree of certainty. These may include local infrastructure, capital, labor skills, and equipment. Quantitative factors such as transportation cost and the maximum number of locations required to satisfy expected demand points would benefit from using quantitative models, and in particular LP models. After the factors relevant to the facility location decision have been identified and quantified, analytical tools such as the Pugh matrix can be used to evaluate trade-offs between alternative locations. A facility location team will be in a good position to combine the best characteristics of all location alternatives to make their facility location decision if they used fact-based tools and methods.

Managing Facility Location Risk

Risk management is an important set of activities every project team must use to ensure their project's deliverables are met according to schedule. However, in addition to risks, which have an inherent occurrence probability as well as an impact on a facility location project, projects have issues, which must also be managed by the team. An issue has a 100 percent occurrence probability and an impact on the project's performance, including its cost, schedule, and deliverables. Facility location teams need to manage risks and issues to ensure a project's success. As an example, when investments are made in anticipation of future earnings, there is always a risk that a project's net present value (NPV) of expected earnings, the return on investment (ROI), or payback will not be realized according to the project's plan. As a result, the project may not meet organizational objectives. There are many different types of project risk, and some may be very difficult to quantify. However, a facility location team must review project risks and concerns and make the necessary contingency plans to minimize or eliminate identified risks and concerns from the facility location project.

Several tools and methods can help your team manage facility location risk. The most effective method is to ensure everyone on the team agrees on the specific risk factors that may impact a project. Then a team should objectively rate a project's risk relative to its occurrence probabilities and impact to a project. Figure 10.6 shows a modified version of Figure 4.8, in which the risks associated with the 20 factors relevant to facility location decisions are listed and evaluated against their occurrence probabilities and project impacts. The rating scale ranges between 0 and 9. A high rating indicates significant project risk or impact for a factor, which must be managed by a team. It is obvious that several factors will most likely exhibit little risk once properly defined. As an example, Education and Skills, once properly defined, will probably have little risk to a project unless there are certain requirements regarding education and skills, such as skills enhancements, that a team must manage to ensure a project's success. As an example, perhaps local education and skills are known to be low and must be improved prior to a facility's opening. This situation would be defined as a project issue rather than a risk, which can be eliminated through training. In other words, it is a certainty that must be managed, or it will be a problem. On the other hand, there may be pending taxing legislation that, if enacted, would significantly impact a project's ROI. In this case, because enacting the legislation is not a 100 percent certainty, this factor or situation is a project risk that requires contingency plans be created to manage the risk if it occurs. Reviewing the risks associated with the factors shown in Figure 10.6, we see that several of the factor risks are probably not applicable for a given project, and others may be issues that must be managed by a team, with the balance being actual risks having varying occurrence probabilities and impacts to a project. This type of simple rating tool is very useful to ensure a full discussion by the facility location team regarding the project risks that may impact their facility location decision.

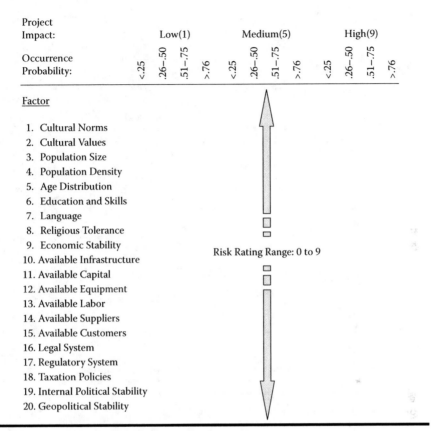

Project Impact:	Low(1)				Medium(5)				High(9)			
Occurrence Probability:	<.25	.26–.50	.51–.75	>.76	<.25	.26–.50	.51–.75	>.76	<.25	.26–.50	.51–.75	>.76

Factor

1. Cultural Norms
2. Cultural Values
3. Population Size
4. Population Density
5. Age Distribution
6. Education and Skills
7. Language
8. Religious Tolerance
9. Economic Stability
10. Available Infrastructure
11. Available Capital
12. Available Equipment
13. Available Labor
14. Available Suppliers
15. Available Customers
16. Legal System
17. Regulatory System
18. Taxation Policies
19. Internal Political Stability
20. Geopolitical Stability

Risk Rating Range: 0 to 9

Figure 10.6   Evaluating facility location decisions using risk models.

In addition to rating models and methods similar to the one shown in Figure 10.6, quantitative evaluation methods can be used by a team to analyze project risk. As an example, a decision tree analysis is shown in Figure 10.7. A decision tree analysis evaluates all possible alternatives relative to their occurrence probabilities and expected payoffs. In Figure 10.7 it can be seen that the highest expected payoff is obtained by investing in location 3, although its initial investment is higher than those of the alternative locations, 1 and 2. In the example shown in Figure 10.7, two major factors are evaluated in the analysis. The first is the economic condition, which has three states: weak, moderate, and strong economic growth. The probabilities of each economic state vary by location, with location 3 having a higher probability of moderate to strong economic growth. The second factor evaluated in this example is political stability. Figure 10.7 shows that political stability varies for each location, as well as the state of economic growth. Every possible combination of economic and political factor levels has a payoff amount shown at the far right of Figure 10.7. The expected payoff of location 3 over all possible states is $147,817. The decision tree analysis can also be expanded to include several other

Alternative	Profit 1st Year	Sales		Political Environment		Revenue
				$ 100,000 More Stable	10%	$ 1,000,000
		$ 215,000 Strong Growth	25%	$ 720,000 Status Quo	80%	$ 900,000
				$ 40,000 Unstable	10%	$ 400,000
				$ 80,000 More Stable	10%	$ 800,000
Location 1 $ 95,000	$ 295,000 Moderate Growth	50%	$ 480,000 Status Quo	80%	$ 600,000
$ (100,000)				$ 30,000 Unstable	10%	$ 300,000
				$ 50,000 More Stable	10%	$ 500,000
		$ 75,000 Weak Growth	25%	$ 240,000 Status Quo	80%	$ 300,000
				$ 10,000 Unstable	10%	$ 100,000
				$ 47,500 More Stable	5%	$ 950,000
		$ 148,750 Strong Growth	20%	$ 640,000 Status Quo	80%	$ 800,000
				$ 56,250 Unstable	15%	$ 375,000
				$ 75,000 More Stable	10%	$ 750,000
Location 2 $ 83,517	$ 217,000 Moderate Growth	40%	$ 440,000 Status Quo	80%	$ 550,000
$ (75,000)				$ 27,500 Unstable	10%	$ 275,000
				$ 45,000 More Stable	10%	$ 450,000
		$ 109,800 Weak Growth	40%	$ 220,000 Status Quo	80%	$ 275,000
				$ 9,500 Unstable	10%	$ 95,000
				$ 75,000 More Stable	5%	$ 1,500,000
		$ 585,000 Strong Growth	50%	$ 960,000 Status Quo	80%	$ 1,200,000
				$ 135,000 Unstable	15%	$ 900,000
				$ 120,000 More Stable	10%	$ 1,200,000
Location 3 $ 147,817	$ 356,000 Moderate Growth	40%	$ 720,000 Status Quo	80%	$ 900,000
$ (175,000)				$ 50,000 Unstable	10%	$ 500,000
				$ 45,000 More Stable	10%	$ 450,000
		$ 27,450 Weak Growth	10%	$ 220,000 Status Quo	80%	$ 275,000
				$ 9,500 Unstable	10%	$ 95,000

Figure 10.7   Analyzing risk using decision trees.

factors and analyzed using off-the-shelf software. An NPV analysis should also be conducted if the project's investment versus financial benefits extends over multiple years. Finally, because facility location projects require significant investment and have internal and external risks, it is important to fully analyze all alternative investment scenarios to ensure an organization receives a maximum return from its investment. This requires a cross-functional team that understands the basis of facility location, including all the potential benefits, risks, and issues associated with such projects.

How to Manage Facilities to Ensure Availability

Availability implies that a system has sufficient labor, equipment, and material and other resources to meet its schedule. The management of labor, including development of work standards and equipment availability, was discussed in Chapter 5. In this section we will discuss 10 major functional areas that are considered part of facility management. These are shown in Table 10.4 and include electrical, water,

Table 10.4   10 Key Areas Important in Managing Facilities

1. Electricity, including lighting and power
2. Water management
3. Heating, air conditioning, refrigeration, and ventilation
4. Compressed air
5. Building and grounds maintenance
6. Waste disposal
7. Material handling and other equipment
8. Process control systems
9. Telephone and communication systems
10. Information technology and equipment

grounds, and equipment and building maintenance, as well as the other areas listed in Table 10.4. These functional areas are critical in managing a system's available capacity as well as its cost. It should be noted that the tools and methods associated with each area are specialized by trade. As an example, electrical systems are maintained by electricians. Water systems are maintained by plumbers, etc. Facility maintenance is very important, but unfortunately many organizations do not professionally manage their facilities. Recently, I consulted with a large process organization. During the several months I worked with them, they experienced several facility shutdowns across the United States. These unplanned shutdowns lowered the organization's available capacity. To make matters worse, they were in a sold-out market. In other words, when a plant shut down, it was a 100 percent gross margin loss on sales to the organization. Once a facility has been successfully modified, expanded, or located, it is important to professionally manage it.

Summary

Facility location decisions are important to enable organizations to access global markets, obtain access to sources of supply, and ensure sufficient capacity to meet customer demand over time, as well as other reasons. The major concepts associated with facility location decisions are listed in Table 10.5. One of the first steps is determining which factors are relevant in an analysis for each alternative location. Next, a team should consider the project risks associated with each alternative location using quantitative models to understand the relationships between relevant factors and business goals and objectives. After an analysis has been finalized by a

Table 10.5   Key Concepts of Facility Location and Management

1. Determine the factors that are relevant to the facility location decision for each alternative location.
2. Determine the risks associated with each factor by location.
3. Use quantitative models to understand the relationships between the factors and outputs of interest.
4. Select the best location based on a full consideration of all relevant factors, risks, and business benefits, as well as forward-looking strategic goals and objectives.
5. Consider deploying best-in-class facility management tools and methods when designing and managing the new facility to ensure it meets the original assumptions of the facility location project.

team, the best location is selected using a full consideration of all relevant factors, risks, and business benefits, as well as future strategic goals and objectives. Finally, a team should consider how to deploy best-in-class facility management tools and methods when designing and managing a new facility to ensure that it meets the original assumptions of the facility location project.

Suggested Reading

Richard B. Chase, F. Robert Jacobs, and Nicholas J. Aquilano. (2006). *Operations Management for Competitive Advantage*, 11th ed. McGraw-Hill, New York.

Fredrick S. Hillier and Gerald J. Lieberman. (2005). *Introduction to Operations Research*, 8th ed. McGraw-Hill, New York.

Chapter 11

Integrating Demand and Supply through Sales and Operations Planning

---

Competitive solution 11: Create a sales and operations planning (S&OP) team to integrate supply and demand across the supply chain.

Overview

Competitive organizations deploy information technology and other systems to coordinate, manage, and improve the diverse process workflows within their supply chain. However, even in workflow environments that rely heavily on information technology (IT), interpersonal and interfunctional communication is critical in creating and maintaining efficient workflows. In contrast, noncompetitive supply chains are characterized by functional silos. These silos inhibit the flow of material and information through their system. The reason for this situation is that in process workflows having functional silos, there are numerous handoffs at functional interfaces between silos, which contributes to process breakdowns. A system structured as a series of functional silos pushes materials or information from one functional silo to another without regard to the status of downstream operations. It is also characterized by little or no feedback to upstream operations regarding the status of downstream resources. The flow of materials or information is also inhibited, at interfunctional interfaces, if the functions within each silo have contradictory goals

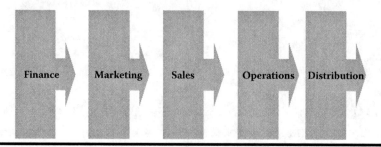

Figure 11.1 Functional silos contribute to process breakdowns.

and objectives. Unfortunately, this is usually the situation in large organizations. The result is suboptimization of process workflows across the functional silos. Typical operational characteristics of functional silos are long order-to-delivery cycles and higher per unit transaction costs. These concepts are qualitatively shown in Figure 11.1.

Although some supply chains are heavily automated, through deployment of information technology (IT), their infrastructure may contribute little to the efficient management of materials and information through major process workflows. In most systems, automation sets in stone the functional silo infrastructure, making it difficult to change an organization's process workflows. Also, some supply chains may require a high degree of automation given the number and complexity of products or services they produce. In these environments, competitive organizations use a sales and operating planning (S&OP) team to manage variations in demand and supply as they dynamically change with their supply chain. A list of key performance metrics that are useful in measuring the effectiveness and efficiency of typical S&OP processes is given in Table 11.1. The S&OP team will manage these metrics at a minimum, and usually several others. The metrics listed

Table 11.1 Competitive Metrics: Aggregate Sales and Operations Planning

1. Asset utilization efficiencies
2. Percentage forecasting accuracy at several levels
3. Percentage MPS changes to total orders
4. Percentage accuracy of MRPII parameters and constants
5. Customer order-to-delivery cycle time
6. Percentage of supplier on-time delivery by supplier and item
7. Per unit transaction costs at each step of the supply chain by workflow

in Table 11.1 include asset utilization efficiencies for inventory and other invested capital, forecasting accuracy at several levels within an organization, master production schedule (MPS) changes to total orders, the accuracy of materials requirements planning (MRPII) parameters and constants, customer order-to-delivery cycle time, the percentage of supplier on-time delivery by supplier, and per unit transaction costs at each step of a supply chain. In most situations, an S&OP team can navigate and negotiate across functional silos to improve its process workflows. In summary, initiating an S&OP process across functional silos is an effective and efficient way to coordinate complicated and constantly changing demand and supply information within a supply chain.

At any point in time, there are also usually several pressing issues surrounding the management of demand and supply. The S&OP team coordinates and manages the resolution of these issues for the organization. Common examples include the loss or gain of major customers, management of seasonal or promotional demand patterns, and increasing inventory levels in anticipation of work stoppages. Many other risks and concerns may impact an organization's supply chain. Varying demand may also create imbalances in a supply chain, making it difficult to match supply to demand. Relative to the supply side of a system, resources such as inventory, equipment, labor, and related inputs of a process workflow impact an organization's available capacity. A major advantage of using an S&OP approach to the management and coordination of supply-chain workflows is that the S&OP team represents the views of an organization's various functions and, if properly structured, will have the authority to make operational changes to portions of the supply chain if they become necessary.

How the S&OP Team Integrates Strategy with Operations

Table 11.2 lists several sequential activities a sales and operations planning team works through to ensure demand and supply are balanced to meet an organization's strategic operational plan. The most important step in planning an organization's supply operations is that they be fact based relative to matching demand forecasts. This means there will be sufficient capacity to meet demand. In the first step of Table 11.2, an organization develops a three- to five-year strategic plan that estimates demand and supply geographically and temporally across its supply chain. The strategic plan is broken down, by product group, into annual operating plans that are used to deploy an organization's goals and objectives at a business unit or facility level. Once the deployment plan of aligned objectives is completed, operational plans are executed, at a local level, to meet annual operational objectives. The specific tools and methods used to execute an annual operating plan may vary depending on the specific productivity goals and objectives. Some goals may require lead time reductions using Lean tools and methods. Others may require

Table 11.2 S&OP Integration Strategy

Executive goals and objectives = strategy + fact-based methods
1. Three- to five-year strategic plan
2. Commit to realistic strategic goals and objectives
3. Annual plan and aligned objectives
4. Deployment of aligned objectives throughout the organization
5. Execution of plan to meet annual objectives
6. Use data-based problem-solving tools
7. Quarterly review of actual performance to plan
8. Adjustment of plan as necessary
9. Learn and adjust next year's plan
10. Organization migrates to an execution culture

yield improvements and Six Sigma tools and methods. Still other goals may require capital expenditures or reengineering. Monthly or quarterly reviews should also be held to ensure all levels of an organization are meeting their annual operations plan. Adjustments, including recovery plans and risk containment, should be made to the annual operating plan as necessary. As an organization works through its annual operating plan during the year, all lessons learned regarding what has worked or not worked should be incorporated into the next year's plan. This will enable the organization to develop more of an execution-style culture. An execution-style culture is one in which goals and objectives are consistently met regardless of external factors impacting the organization. This subject was discussed in Chapter 1 relative to the book *Execution: The Discipline of Getting Things Done*, by Larry Bossidy and Ram Charan, in which the authors discuss the importance of strategic execution.

Key Success Characteristics of a Successful S&OP Process

At a business unit level, an S&OP team manages supply, demand, and new product planning to achieve an organization's financial goals and objectives. The planning and coordination activities are done at various forecasting time horizons, geographical locations throughout the supply chain, and its various product families or groups. Figure 11.2 shows the key characteristics of a successful S&OP process. If the combined activities of the S&OP team are successful, then key financial

S&OP Focus on Time, Geography and Product Group

1. Clear Direction and Commitment to Realistic Goals and means at All levels.

2. Sales, Cashflow and Budgets are to Plan 100%.

3. Master Production Schedule (*MPS*) is Equal to Shipments and the Original Production Plan.

4. There are no Schedule Changes within Lead-Time (Time Fence).

5. MRPII data is Accurate and Material Availability is 100%.

6. Supplier On-Time Delivery is 100%.

7. S&OP Participants are Empowered to Make Decisions Regarding Supply and Demand at the Product and Family Level.

8. Customer Service Targets are Met 100%.

9. Plans Continuously Improved Throughout Implementation and Feed into Next Year's Plan.

10. Organizational Capability to Achieve and Sustain Operational Breakthroughs is Enhanced.

Figure 11.2   Key characteristics of a successful S&OP process.

and operational metrics should meet the annual plan's objectives. In other words, revenue from product sales and cash flow targets and operational budgets should be at their planned levels or close to levels that approach 100 percent of annual operating plan objectives. A failure to achieve an annual operating plan's goals and objectives necessitates a root cause analysis of the reasons for poor performance. Also, contingency plans need to be developed by an S&OP team to achieve an organization's goals and objectives.

Another indicator of an effective S&OP process is that the master production schedule (MPS) and actual shipments to customers should balance each other relative to the original operation's plan. In other words, an organization delivers on schedule without having to process backorders. Backorders result in longer order-to-deliver cycle times and higher per unit transaction costs due to missed shipments and deliveries. In situations in which schedules or shipments are missed, the reasons should be investigated and corrective actions taken to ensure their root causes are eliminated from the process workflow. Another important characteristic of an effective S&OP process is that no schedule changes should occur within a product's lead time or frozen time fence. Production schedules should also be accurate and realistic. This means that process workflows should be standardized, mistake-proofed, and available when needed for production. In other words, published and agreed-upon work schedules should not be changed except on very rare occasions, if at all. MRPII and other system data should also be reliable in order to efficiently manage all sources of demand and supply.

The accuracy of supply and demand data should be reviewed on a continuing basis because decisions regarding the efficient allocation of supply require accuracy. As an example, if forecasting accuracy is low, then demand will be poorly estimated, resulting in too much or not enough of a product. Alternatively, a product may be produced in the wrong location. A metric that is useful to monitor, manage, and improve forecasting accuracy is percentage accuracy. Alternatively, its opposite, percentage forecasting error, can be used to estimate process performance. Two common forecasting error metrics were discussed in Chapter 8, and their calculation was shown in Figure 8.9. On the supply side, lot sizes, lead time, and other system parameters and constants directly impact supply decisions. These decisions will directly impact an organization's internal production or supplier schedules. Material availability, supplier on-time deliveries, and customer service targets should also be at their planned levels. If they are not, then production schedules will be adversely impacted, resulting in workflow disruptions. These problems will result in longer order-to-delivery cycle time and higher per unit transaction costs within a supply chain. S&OP participants must also be empowered to make decisions regarding supply and demand at a product family or lower levels. This is to ensure a fast response to changing supply-chain conditions that impact the sources of demand and supply. Finally, an organization's annual operating plan should be continuously improved throughout its implementation cycle to continuously improve the S&OP process.

Although an S&OP process should be effective and efficient, and execute its responsibilities well, this may not always be true. In fact, there may be several indications that an S&OP process is not working properly. Table 11.3 lists 10 key process breakdowns that show if this situation is occurring. As an example, if product forecasts are not based on an S&OP consensus, the result may be differing demand estimates within a supply chain. In this scenario, there will be several demand estimates floating around an organization. This situation will create an imbalance between demand and supply as people start to second-guess each other, resulting in suboptimization of a supply. There may be several reasons for this type of situation. In one scenario, senior management may be forcing an S&OP team to plan its supply using unrealistic forecasts. This may be due to external pressures to meet certain levels of sales revenue. This poor practice can seriously reduce operational effectiveness and efficiencies because building products to satisfy nonexistent orders will increase inventory levels throughout a supply chain. Over time, the inventory pipeline of a supply chain may be filled with products that will not sell in the

Table 11.3   10 Process Breakdowns Prevented by the S&OP Team

1. Forecast not based on consensus
2. Building of nonexistent orders
3. Excess inventory levels
4. Filling of the pipeline with excess product
5. Incorrect product mix
6. Capacity deterioration
7. Arbitrary reduction of inventory
8. Excessively long lead times
9. Missed schedules
10. Deterioration of customer service levels

immediate future. This situation occurs when, after a period of time, customers will not accept additional inventory, even with pricing discounts. The result is an inversion of sales. Once a sales inversion occurs, it becomes apparent that an organization never had the originally claimed sales volume. This may result in a temporary suspension of internal production operations or supplier deliveries because there will be no demand for the products until the inventories within its supply chain are worked off by customers over time. Another indication of a poorly performing S&OP process is excess inventory for some products or not enough inventories for others. There may be several reasons for these situations, including new products that could not be sold or ordering in lot sizes that are multiples of lead time. Inventory is a barometer of successful supply-chain practices relative to the management of demand and supply. The S&OP team should continually monitor its inventory investment levels and take corrective action to prevent an increase of excess and obsolete inventory. We will discuss inventory in more detail in Chapter 14. The buildup of excess and obsolete inventory may indicate that a consensus forecast was never reached by an S&OP team regarding its demand forecasts. Another indication of a poorly performing S&OP process is capacity deterioration. Capacity deterioration can occur for several reasons. Many of these reasons were discussed in Chapter 9. But building products that cannot be sold is the most egregious waste of available capacity. However, not achieving target operational efficiencies also wastes available capacity. Additionally, an arbitrary reduction of inventory at the end of the year to meet cash flow and investment objectives is an indication that too much inventory was built during the year. Arbitrarily reducing inventory results in lower order-fill rates and operational inefficiencies early in the next fiscal year because internal production levels must be increased to meet expected demand, which cannot be satisfied due to low inventory levels. Excessively long lead times are another indication of breakdowns in the S&OP process. Reducing lead times has a dramatic impact on a supply chain because it can respond dynamically to changes in customer demand. As a final comment, missed production or shipment schedules and a deterioration of customer service levels are also characteristics of a dysfunctional S&OP process.

Key Activities of the S&OP Team

Fifty key activities of an S&OP team are listed in Table 11.4 and Table 11.5. The 50 activities are listed by organizational function. The finance function of an S&OP team is particularly concerned that revenue, cash flow, and budgetary targets are achieved to execute the goals and objectives of the organization's annual operating plan. Variations to the annual operating plan require that an S&OP team make adjustments in its demand or supply planning. At the very least, an S&OP team manages supply to meet demand forecasts across its supply chain. However, when the financial numbers are not at planned levels, intervention must be taken to improve operational performance to meet financial goals and objectives.

A financial forecast is one of several versions of a forecast that may exist within an organization. A financial forecast is allocated linearly across a supply chain, down through to the product group level and, finally, to an individual item and location level. It is also converted to a unit forecast using an item's standard cost. Initially, marketing and sales may have different forecast estimates based on the information they obtain from customers and their sales force. The differences between what finance has forecast and forecasting estimates by the marketing and sales organizations must be reconciled by an S&OP team. This reconciliation process should have also occurred within the strategic planning process at a higher level. At the strategic planning level, forecast variations between finance and marketing and sales are eliminated through promotional and sales activities that are designed to create demand to meet organizational financial objectives. However, at an S&OP level, the adjustments to financial plans would be expected to be minor. In summary, the major function of the S&OP team is to reconcile financial, sales, and marketing forecasts to obtain a consensus forecast, or one number for their organization. This may require additional promotional and sales effort, but it is important that the forecast on which the strategic goals and objectives of the annual operating plan were based be achieved at a product group level and executed according to plan. Supply is then matched to demand by the S&OP team.

Key marketing activities include the introduction of new products, expansion of current markets, and development of new markets and customers. In this work,

Table 11.4   50 Topics of Interest to the S&OP Team: Part 1

Finance	1. Revenue
	2. Cash flow
	3. Budget
Marketing	4. New product sales
	5. New markets and customers
Sales	6. Current product sales
	7. Gross margin on sales
	8. Returned product
Design	9. New product development
Engineering	10. Design revisions
	11. Bill-of-material issues (BOM)
	12. Warranty issues related to design
Procurement	13. Acquisition cost management
	14. Supplier delivery (lead time)
	15. New product launch (lead time)
	16. Sourcing strategy
	17. IT integration
	18. Supplier development (productivity/quality)
	19. Inventory levels
	20. Expediting/premium freight costs
	21. Study new sourcing opportunities and identify benchmarks
	22. Consolidate supply sources where possible
	23. Relocate offshore suppliers closer to your operations
	24. Standardize designs and components
	25. Consolidate procurement across the business

Table 11.5   50 Topics of Interest to the S&OP Team: Part 2

Manufacturing/ production operations	26. Capacity requirements
	27. Scheduling issues
	28. Quality issues
	29. Throughput rates
	30. New product requirements
	31. Process design issues
	32. Supplier issues
Materials	33. Maintenance of customer fill rates/service levels
	34. Lead times by product class and inventory type
	35. Improve forecast accuracy
	36. Balance inventory levels/improve turns
	37. Reduce unplanned orders/MPS schedule changes
	38. Manage order backlog
	39. Ensure material availability/data accuracy
	40. Eliminate excess/obsolete inventory
	41. Manage labor expense/overtime
Distribution	42. Ensure orders are shipped on time
	43. Order accuracy
	44. Inventory/data accuracy
	45. Eliminate damaged product
	46. Eliminate emergency orders
	47. Eliminate order redeployment
	48. Eliminate backorders
	49. Optimize inventory transfer
	50. Reduce order lead time

it is very important that marketing use statistically based market research tools, methods, and concepts to develop forecasts of new product sales because they will feed an organization's sales plan and directly impact its supply chain. Chapter 3 discussed the key steps necessary to develop market research plans for new products. In this context, new product forecasts should be very carefully created by marketing and evaluated by the S&OP team. Miscalculations can significantly increase excess and obsolete inventory investment within the organization's supply chain. This is why the proper use of market research and segmentation methods is important. Also, assigning the cost of the excess and obsolete inventory a marketing's budget is an effective way to ensure marketing is not creating problems for its organization. If demand is estimated using methods such as those discussed in Chapter 3, there will be a higher probability that new product forecasts will be close to actual sales. New product forecast accuracy is especially important in industries in which they are the basis for revenue growth and profit. As an example, it was stated in Chapters 3 and 4 that in high-technology industries the first company to arrive to market with a product often retains a sizable market share, even after competitors enter the same market. Marketing decisions also impact the degree of design obsolescence if they change product packaging and other features of products and services. If the changes are not properly time-phased into a supply chain, through the S&OP team, the result may be that products or services become obsolete, but inventory must be written off an organization's balance sheet, incurring a financial loss.

The sales function is concerned with revenue and gross margin on current product sales as well as product returns and other adjustments to sales due to customer complaints. A failure to meet the planned sales forecasts will create a situation in which an organization fails to achieve its revenue and other financial goals and objectives for the year. The information obtained from the sales force is critical to estimating demand at a product group level. Also, because sales personnel are in close contact with customers, they routinely obtain valuable information that can help an S&OP team more efficiently manage supply to meet demand. Unfortunately, many organizations use ad hoc or informal methods to obtain information from their sales force. This practice may result in missed opportunities to effectively manage supply and demand within their supply chain. In fact, in some organizations the sales forecasting process is so broken that an organization can be put out of business due to numerous breakdowns in its process workflows.

Design engineering responsibilities to the S&OP teams include management of issues surrounding new product development, design revisions to current products or services, bill-of-material (BOM) issues, and warranty claims. Problems in these areas will delay the time to market of new products, increase their standard, and may have negative impacts on product quality. These issues directly impact sales forecasts for new products and the supply of current products. BOM and warranty issues may also negatively impact an organization's operational costs. In Chapter 4, several characteristics of an organization's design function were discussed relative to product cost, quality, and impact on production lead times. It was shown that product design and marketing drive the life cycle cost of the production and distribution of products and services. In fact, the more complex a product or service, the more difficult it is for the S&OP team to manage its supply and demand across its supply chain. In addition, the greater the number of mistakes found in a product or service design, after its release to production, the greater the number of required changes that must be made to eliminate the mistakes. This situation increases the levels of returned goods, warranty costs, production costs, and inventory investment.

Procurement is responsible for the purchase of raw materials, components, and other resources that are necessary to produce products or services. Key procurement activities include acquisition cost management, management of supplier delivery (lead time), new product launch (lead time), strategies related to sourcing materials, and IT integration across the purchasing systems used to control material flows. In some organizations, procurement may also manage the master production schedule (MPS) and master requirements planning (MRPII) systems. Otherwise, these systems are managed by materials planning or manufacturing. In addition, procurement is concerned with developing suppliers, optimizing inventory levels, reducing order expediting and premium freight costs, studying new sourcing opportunities, consolidating supply sources where possible, and insourcing or outsourcing activities. Finally, procurement works with design engineering to standardize product and service designs as well as their purchased components. As part of the S&OP team, procurement is responsible for decisions impacting major portions of an organization's supply chain.

The operations or manufacturing function is responsible for creating and managing available capacity to meet production schedules. In addition, manufacturing also resolves production scheduling issues, quality issues, material throughput issues, new product requirements, and process design issues, as well as supplier issues that impact production operations. It is important that operations be provided with the resources and information required to successfully produce an organization's products or services. The representatives of manufacturing or operations have major responsibilities on the S&OP team.

The materials group may be separate from or part of procurement or operations. In Table 11.5, several key activities are listed that fall under the control of a procurement group. These include the maintenance of customer fill rates to meet service levels, management of lead times by product class with procurement and suppliers, management of inventory investment for each inventory classification, and improvements to forecast accuracy with the forecasting group, which may reside within the marketing or material group. Additional responsibilities may include managing unplanned orders and master requirements planning (MPS) and materials requirements planning (MRPII) changes with production activity control (PAC), managing order backlogs, ensuring materials are available to manufacturing, and ensuring the MRPII and MPS system data is accurate.

Distribution is concerned with the maintenance of customer fill rates and distribution inventory service levels, lead times by product class and inventory type and the balancing of inventory levels within distribution centers to improve inventory turns. In addition, distribution works to reduce unplanned orders for service parts. Additional responsibilities include management of labor expenses and overtime and ensuring that orders are shipped on time and are accurate, products are not damaged and emergenc orders and back orders are eliminated.

Additional concerns are the efficient transfer of materials among distribution centers and the reduction of order-to-cycle lead times. These are key distribution activities that are integral to an S&OP process.

Summary

The S&OP team is critical to ensure demand and supply remain balanced within a supply chain as conditions dynamically change over time. The key concepts of the chapter are listed in Table 11.6. Creating value stream maps (VSMs) of the process workflows related to the 50 key S&OP activities is also useful in fully understanding how these workflows work, their interrelationships, and identifying ways to simplify and standardize the S&OP process over time.

Table 11.6 Key Concepts to Increase S&OP Effectiveness

1. Create an S&OP team to manage demand and supply within your organization.
2. Eliminate functional silos within your supply chain to increase its material and information throughput rates.
3. Create demand and supply metrics that measure supply-chain performance and provide the basis for continual improvement over time.
4. Eliminate workflow conditions that contribute to S&OP process breakdowns.
5. Value stream map (VSM) the workflows of the 50 key S&OP activities to understand how they are related and to simplify and standardize them over time.

Suggested Reading

Joseph L. Cavinato and Ralph G. Kauffman, Eds. (2000). *The Purchasing Handbook: A Guide for the Purchasing and Supply Professional.* McGraw-Hill, New York.

Harvard Business Review on Supply Chain Management. (2006). Harvard Business School Press, Boston.

James W. Martin. (2007). *Lean Six Sigma for Supply Chain Management: The 10-Step Improvement Process.* McGraw-Hill, New York.

Chapter 12

Lean Scheduling Methods

Competitive solution 12: Apply efficient scheduling tools and methods to reduce process workflow lead time and optimize available capacity.

Overview

Ideally, products and services should be available when and where they are required by customers. In Chapter 9 we discussed a system's capacity and, in particular, its available capacity. Also, in Chapter 9 and Figure 9.1 we discussed the historical relationship between the concept of economy of scale and minimum per unit cost based on production volume. In this discusson it was also mentioned that former productive systems relied on large unit volumes to standardize product or service production. This enabled dedicated process workflows, based on the technology that was available at that time, to operate at a minimum cost. Production paradigms have changed over the past several decades due to the development of new tools, methods, and concepts that have enabled jobs to be run at a lower cost, and hence more often. This has effectively reduced the production volumes required to achieve a minimum per unit cost. As a result, system flexibility has been increased, allowing production schedules to change more quickly in response to demand variations. In fact, some production systems have moved closer to a concept of self-service or service on demand to satisfy niche markets based on changing customer needs and values. For example, customers "help themselves" to electronic products or services, such as online movies, or self-order when they check in at an airport or check out products at Home Depot or grocery stores. In these situations, customers schedule their services based on a system's queuing characteristics and service design. As technology becomes more sophisticated, systems that schedule the production of complex products and services will continue to evolve in ways that are similar to those found in leading-edge service industries, in which customers "pull" products or services as needed from the system. However, most organizations use push scheduling systems in which products are scheduled at a cumulative lead time. At an extreme, are those organizations that use either extremely flexible or a self-service scheduling strategy. The question we will attempt to answer in this chapter is: How can current scheduling tools, methods, and strategies be applied to increase an organization's competitiveness?

Scheduling requires understanding a system's available capacity and lead time as it changes over time relative to expected demand. A system's available capacity should be evaluated based on a maximum quantity per unit of material or information that can be moved through a system at its lead time or throughput rate. It can be defined as the cumulative lead time of every operation in a workflow. At an operational level, within a process workflow, lead time can be broken into several smaller time components. These include time queuing or waiting time, setup time, processing time, inspection of the work, and transporting work to the next operation. In this context, work can be either material or informational in form.

Other important considerations relative to the scheduling of work include an evaluation of the underlying design of a product or service, as well as its required service discipline. As an example, the greater the degree of design commonality that products and services have, the greater the ability to bundle or aggregate products and services into similar groups and schedule them together. This practice enables an organization to move toward a mixed-model scheduling system, as described in Chapter 6 and in Figure 6.9. The beneficial impacts of using a mixed-model scheduling system result from setup time reductions. But these are enabled by product and service design commonality. Chapters 4 to 6 discussed how design commonality can be created within an organization through the application of design-for-manufacturing (DFM) and Lean tools, methods, and concepts. The ability to set up a job quickly to produce a product or service results in reduced lead time through a system, which reduces cost and increases quality.

In addition to a commonality of product or service design, the selection of a system's service discipline is also useful to schedule work and reduce lead time. As an example, in Chapter 5 we discussed several service disciplines in the context of queuing theory and process design. These included first-in-first-out (FIFO), last-in-last-out (LILO), service in random order (SIRO), prioritization of service (POS), and a general service discipline (GSD). It can be shown that the lead time of a system varies depending on the service discipline that is used to schedule the production its products or services. It should also be noted that, depending on a system's workflow design, there may be other possible service disciplines. As an example, it was also shown in Chapter 5 that a scheduling system depends on the arrival pattern of customers or demand on a system (per unit time), as well as a system's service pattern. This includes the design of the service system relative to the number of service channels or parallel servers in a system, as well as its phases or the number of sequential steps within a channel.

Operations Scheduling

The three key metrics listed in Table 12.1 are good indicators of how well a scheduling system is performing. Our goal in this chapter will be to discuss scheduling tools and methods to help manage and improve these three metrics. But first we will discuss operations scheduling from a classical operations perspective. Operations scheduling includes ten major steps. These are shown in Table 12.2. The first step requires allocation of capacity (rough-cut capacity planning) to meet an organization's strategic forecast. A strategic forecast estimates demand over three to five years by product group and location. This ensures that there will be sufficient capacity in the form of fixed assets, equipment, labor, and materials to satisfy forecasted demand. Available capacity must also be strategically planned based on considerations such as demand patterns by location and the required resources necessary to satisfy demand over the forecasted time horizon. It should be noted that available capacity may need to be increased by purchasing new facilities and equipment. Also, that to maintain available capacity, employees and suppliers must be sequenced into a supply chain at specific locations and times. At an intermediate forecast time horizon, typically between 6 and 18 months, a master production schedule (MPS) is loaded based on product forecasts and firm demand for products. The MPS uses this demand information and aggregates all demand streams for a product by time period. Figure 12.1 shows that the aggregated demand will be downloaded into an MRPII system after a consensus forecast has been reached by the sales and operational planning (S&OP) team, in Step 3 of Table 12.2. MRPII performance and related information will be discussed in Chapter 13.

The scheduling of production through an S&OP process is shown in Table 12.3. Reviewing Table 12.3, we see that a system forecast is adjusted based on senior management's financial goals and objectives. In the calculations shown in Table 12.3, a forecast, for the current year, is increased by 5 percent. Using this strategic target,

Table 12.1   Competitive Metrics: Operations Scheduling

1. Percentage adherence to schedule
2. Scheduling cost per unit or transaction
3. Percentage adjustments to schedule

Table 12.2   10 Key Steps to Schedule Products in a Manufacturing System

1. Allocate capacity (rough-cut capacity planning) to meet strategic forecast.
2. Develop the master production schedule (MPS) based on intermediate demand.
3. Review the S&OP and adjust the MPS to create a consensus forecast.
4. Load the consensus forecast into the MRPII system.
5. Determine available local capacity and resources at a facility level.
6. Integrate consensus forecast into the scheduling system based on its design, i.e., push, pull, transfer batching, mixed-model scheduling, quick response manufacturing, or self-service.
7. Determine scheduling discipline by product group, including prioritization requirements.
8. Develop and apply scheduling algorithms as well as decision support systems to dynamically schedule flow through the system.
9. Actively manage dynamic changes in system status through the decision support system and production activity control (PAC).
10. Modify the scheduling system as required to maintain material flow through the system.

the S&OP team develops a consensus forecast as shown in Step 3 of Table 12.3. This consensus forecast is based on current facts available to an S&OP team, including available resources, expected changes in demand due to the loss or gain of customer orders, and other relevant factors, such as potential facility shutdowns. The final MPS quantities, by product group, are estimated using a consensus forecast created by the S&OP team, current inventory levels, and the required ending inventory investment. These MPS calculations are shown in Table 12.3 using Steps 1 through 7. Table 12.3 also describes the actual calculations necessary to complete Steps 3 through 5 of Table 12.2. Once the required products and their associated quantities have been determined and time phased by the MPS, this information is used to build local production schedules. In addition, an organization may use combinations of several systems. These systems include "push" scheduling systems characterized by MPS and MRPII; "pull" systems that use visual controls, such as Kanban; transfer batching, which enables unit flow in the context of a scheduling system; mixed-model scheduling based on product grouping; quick response manufacturing (QRM), which increases the flexibly of MPS and MRPII; and self-service systems.

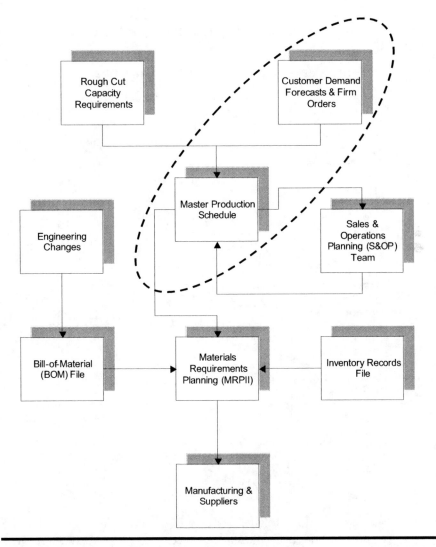

Figure 12.1   Overview of an MPS scheduling system.

Push scheduling systems use MPS and MRPII systems to translate independent demand via a bill-of-material (BOM) into schedules for dependent demand items based on net requirements for components and materials (after on-hand inventory has been subtracted from the scheduled quantities). Table 12.4 describes backward and forward push systems, but the process control problems are similar for both systems. Forward scheduling systems use a BOM to estimate the cumulative lead time necessary to build an end item or final product. Backward scheduling works backwards from the cumulative lead time to set the schedules for the dependent demand items, such as components and materials. The problem with push systems

Table 12.3 Sales and Operational Planning Review and Adjustment of the MPS

		Quarter 1	Quarter 2	Quarter 3	Quarter 4	Total
Master Production Schedule for Product						
Step 2	Strategic plan (+5%)	998	3,804	2,993	2,205	9,999
Step 1	System forecast	950	4,000	2,850	2,000	9,800
Step 3	Consensus forecast	1,000	2,000	3,000	4,000	10,000
	MPS (production)	1,000	2,100	3,100	4,100	10,300
Step 4	Beginning inventory	200	300	200	500	1,200
Step 7	MPS (production)	1,000	2,100	3,100	4,100	10,300
Step 6	Available to ship	1,200	2,400	3,300	4,600	11,500
	Consensus forecast	1,000	2,000	3,000	4,000	10,000
Step 5	Ending inventory	200	400	300	600	1,500

is that they tend to be inflexible if demand or resource availability changes during a product's cumulative lead time or frozen time fence. Changes in demand or resource availability within a product's lead time have the effect of creating large amounts of partially completed products or work-in-process (WIP) inventory. Also, setup costs increase in these systems because manufacturing must convert from one product to another due to resource constraints when a schedule unexpectedly changes. Quick response manufacturing strategies were developed to flatten a BOM, with push scheduling applied only to higher-level items. In a QRM system, scheduling is under the control of local work cells using a form of Kanban, but only among critical work cells. However, regardless of the scheduling system used in a production environment, transfer batching, as described in Chapter 6, is a useful tool to reduce operational lead times within a process workflow. Similarly, mixed-model scheduling is a good method to reduce lead time regardless of whether a scheduling system

Table 12.4   Determining the Scheduling Discipline

At a Facility Level
1. Backward scheduling using MRP to establish order completion dates based on MPS demand quantities offset by lead time
2. Forward scheduling starting with first operation, then building the estimate of the order completion time
3. Flow control using visual signals (Kanban) to balance and smooth material flow
At a Local Level
1. First-in-first-out (FIFO)
2. Last-in-last-out (LIFO)
3. Service in random order (SIRO)
4. Prioritization of service (POS)
5. General service discipline (GSD)

has a push or pull design. However, as discussed in Chapter 6, mixed-model scheduling requires there be commonality of design so the size of economic setups can be minimized for similarly designed products or services. In contrast, pull systems use a calculated takt time, based on external customer demand, to set a manufacturing schedule. An ideal combination of scheduling strategies uses a pull system, visual controls, and Lean tools applied in combination with a Kanban system set and maintain a takt time. Lean tools and methods were discussed in Chapter 6. The Kanban method will be discussed later in this chapter. We will continue our review of Table 12.4 by discussing rules for scheduling prioritization later in this chapter. This discussion will be an extension of several concepts introduced in Chapter 5 relative to establishing service disciplines to optimize scheduling prioritization. In addition, scheduling algorithms will be discussed from a perspective of resource optimization. In this context, linear programming (LP) and other algorithms will be reviewed as well as software and decision support systems useful to dynamically schedule material or information through a system.

Table 12.5 shows another perspective of the basic steps necessary for translating a strategic forecast into a production schedule. The methodology is analogous to scheduling systems within service industries. As an example, the two key concepts of efficient capacity allocation to meet a strategic forecast and having an operations review to adjust a service schedule to create a consensus labor forecast are common activities for both systems. Also, Lean concepts, methods, and philosophies are analogous with those of demand pull scheduling systems in an environment using

Table 12.5   10 Key Steps to Schedule Resources on a Service System

1. Allocate capacity to meet strategic forecast.
2. Develop a schedule and required capacity based on intermediate demand.
3. Review operations and adjust the schedule to create a consensus forecast.
4. Load the consensus forecast into the scheduling system.
5. Determine available local capacity and resources at a facility or process level.
6. Integrate consensus forecast into the scheduling system based on system design, i.e., push, pull, transfer batching, mixed-model scheduling, quick response manufacturing, or self-service.
7. Determine scheduling discipline by product group, including prioritization requirements.
8. Develop and apply scheduling algorithms as well as decision support systems to dynamically schedule flow through the system.
9. Actively manage dynamic changes in system status through the decision support system and management.
10. Modify the scheduling system as required to maintain information flow through the system.

a combination of calculated takt time, transfer batching, mixed-model scheduling, quick response manufacturing methods, and self-service systems. As an example, in a financial service organization, customers receive information in virtual format, but also as printed materials, such as brochures, financial statements, and other literature, and manage their schedules using Lean tools and methods. In both manufacturing and service systems, information and materials are transferred from upstream to downstream operations within a process's workflow. Additionally, in both production environments, the production schedule is actively managed by a local work group, in response to dynamic changes in system status and resources using decision support systems. In manufacturing, this is a production activity control (PAC) function, in which PAC modifies a production schedule to maintain material flow through a manufacturing system. In service systems this is usually a local work team.

Scheduling Algorithms

Organizations usually employ scheduling systems using Windows-based software and decision support systems. Later in this chapter, we will discuss ten key characteristics of these off-the-shelf scheduling systems. However, to understand the logic behind these more sophisticated software packages, it may be useful to first review some of the simpler ad hoc scheduling models as well as the more advanced linear programming (LP) models that are the logic behind many of those systems. It should be noted that over the past several decades, LP models have supplanted many of the original ad hoc scheduling methods.

In Table 12.6, two scheduling models are presented that differ only in their scheduling rules. The first model uses a first-come-first-served (FCFS) scheduling rule, and the second a minimum processing time (MPT) rule. Working through the calculations shown in Table 12.6, it is easy to see that, for this example, a software system using an MPT scheduling rule reduces both the number of late jobs and the cycle time for all ten jobs to flow through the system, i.e., 156 versus 115 days, respectively. In this simple example, the scheduling rules we selected had a major impact on a system's cycle time. This is a simple example showing that scheduling prioritization rules can have a significant impact on the overall cycle time of a process workflow. The conclusion drawn from this example is that organizations should analyze their scheduling rules to understand their impact on operations to ensure they meet operational goals and objectives regarding the efficient use of resources.

The second ad hoc scheduling algorithm is shown in Table 12.7. This is an assignment model in which n jobs are assigned on exactly n work cells based on the job completion time or processing cost for every combination of job and work cell. The example shown in Table 12.7 only models the n × n situation. It should be noted that in more complex situations in which there are n jobs and m work cells, the number of alternative schedules rapidly increases according to the formula $(n!)^m$. In these more complex analyses, a solution requires an analysis using simulation methods. There are three basic steps in using the assignment algorithm shown in Table 12.7. The first step includes making row calculations in which the smallest number (time or cost) in a row is subtracted from all other numbers in the same row. The second step requires that the same calculations be made column-wise by subtracting the smallest number in every column from other numbers in the same column to create a reduced matrix. In the third step, a test is made to see if exactly n lines can cover all the 0's. In the current example, exactly n lines cover all the 0's, showing an optimal assignment of jobs to work cells. This optimum assignment recommends assigning Job 1 to Work Cell 1, Job 2 to Work Cell 3, Job 3 to Work Cell 4, and Job 4 to Work Cell 2. The total processing cost is $60 + $35 + $45 + $25 = $165.

In Table 12.8, another, more sophisticated, scheduling algorithm is used to schedule at least two days off per week per employee. In this scheduling algorithm, starting with Worker 1, the days requiring the smallest number of employees, i.e., Wednesday and Friday, are scheduled as days off for Worker 1. In the second iteration, the schedule of Worker 2 is determined by first subtracting one day from the original daily schedule, except for the days taken off by Worker 1. This is because

Table 12.6 How Scheduling Rules Impact Material Flow

Sequential Jobs	Processing Time	Days Required	Modified Sequence	FCFS Time	Days Late	
1	1	3	1	1	0	
2	3	9	2	4	0	
3	4	12	3	8	0	
4	5	15	4	13	0	
5	2	6	5	15	9	
6	3	9	6	18	9	Late
7	4	12	7	22	10	Late
8	1	3	8	23	20	Late
9	1	3	9	24	21	Late
10	4	12	10	28	16	Late
Total time:	**28**	**Flow time:**	**156**	**85**		
Process time:	**2.8**	**Mean time:**	**15.6**			
Sequential Jobs	Processing Time	Days Required	Modified Sequence	Minimum Time	Days Late	
1	1	3	1	1	0	
8	1	3	2	2	0	
9	1	3	3	3	0	
5	2	6	4	5	0	
2	3	9	5	8	0	
6	3	9	6	11	2	Late
3	4	12	7	15	3	Late
7	4	12	8	19	7	Late
10	4	12	9	23	11	Late
4	5	15	10	28	13	Late
Total time:	**28**	**Flow time:**	**115**	**36**		
Process time:	**2.8**	**Mean time:**	**11.5**			

Table 12.7 Assignment Algorithm (n_{jobs} to $n_{work\ cells}$)

Initial Table				
	Work Cell 1	*Work Cell 2*	*Work Cell 3*	*Work Cell 4*
Job 1	$60	$90	$45	$60
Job 2	$45	$85	$35	$50
Job 3	$90	$45	$60	$25
Job 4	$30	$45	$90	$60

Step 1: Row reduction (subtract smallest number from each row)

Job 1	—	$60	$15	$30
Job 2	$10	$50	—	$15
Job 3	$65	$20	$35	—
Job 4	—	$15	$60	$30

Step 2: Column reduction (subtract smallest number from each column)

Job 1	—	$45	$15	$30
Job 2	$10	$35	—	$15
Job 3	$65	$5	$35	—
Job 4	—	—	$60	$30

Step 3: Line test (number of lines required to cover all zeros)

Job 1	—	$45	$15	$30
Job 2	$10	$35	—	$15
Job 3	$65	$5	$35	—
Job 4	—	—	$60	$30

Step 4: Optimal assignment

Job 1	Job 1 = $60			
Job 2			Job 2 = $35	
Job 3				Job 3 = $25
Job 4		Job 4 = $45		

Table 12.8 Scheduling Days Off

	Monday	Tuesday	Wednesday	Thursday	Friday	Saturday	Sunday
Worker 1	3	5	2	6	2	4	3
Worker 2	3	5	2	6	2	4	3
Worker 3	2	4	2	5	2	3	2
Worker 4	2	3	2	4	1	2	1
Worker 5	1	2	1	3	1	1	1
Worker 6	0	1	0	2	1	1	0
Worker 7	0	0	0	1	0	0	0
Worker 1	Worker 1	Worker 1		Worker 1		Worker 1	Worker 1
Worker 2	Worker 3	Worker 2		Worker 2	Worker 2	Worker 2	Worker 2
Worker 3	Worker 3	Worker 3	Worker 3	Worker 3		Worker 3	
Worker 4	Worker 4	Worker 4	Worker 4	Worker 4			Worker 4
Worker 5		Worker 5		Worker 5	Worker 5	Worker 5	
Worker 6				Worker 6			
Total workers	3	5	2	6	2	4	3

Period	Time	Agents	Monthly Salary
1	8:00 AM to 12:00 PM	20	$ 2,000
2	12:00 PM to 4:00 PM	30	$ 2,000
3	4:00 PM to 8:00 PM	40	$ 2,500
4	8:00 PM to 12:00 AM	30	$ 2,500
5	4:00 AM to 8:00 AM	10	$ 3,000
6	12:00 AM to 4:00 AM	10	$ 3,000

Assumption: Each Agent Works 8 Hours with no Breaks.

$$\text{Minimize } Z = 2X_1 + 2X_2 + 2.5X_3 + 2.5X_4 + 3X_5 \qquad \text{Staffing}$$

Period 1	$1X_1$				$+ 1X5$	≥ 20	20
Period 2	$1X_1 + 1X_2$					≥ 30	30
Period 3		$1X_2 + 1X_3$				≥ 40	40
Period 4			$1X_3 + 1X_4$			≥ 30	30
Period 5				$1X_4 + 1X_5$		≥ 10	10
Period 6					$1X_5$	≥ 10	10
Agents Per Shift:	20	10	30	0	10	=	$ 165,000

Figure 12.2 Application of linear programming to scheduling.

Worker 1 will work these days, i.e., Monday, Tuesday, Thursday, Friday, and Sunday. These five days now require one less person to meet their schedule. The algorithm continues, until each day has been assigned the required number of workers, with each worker having at least two days off from work. In summary, this algorithm shows that there are more efficient and sophisticated algorithms that can be used to schedule resources.

Figure 12.2 shows an integer linear programming application of a scheduling model in which its objective is to meet all required schedules with a minimum number of agents per shift, and at a minimum cost. Recall, linear programming was discussed in Chapter 5 relative to maximization or minimization of an objective function. In this example, the objective function is to minimize monthly salary expense given that each shift has a constraint relative to the minimum number of agents assigned to it and the schedule has been broken into four-hour time increments spaced over six time periods. But this schedule could have been easily broken down into hourly increments. Because agents must work an eight-hour shift, there may be multiple shifts working during a particular four-hour period. As an

Table 12.9   10 Key Characteristics of Scheduling Software

1. Develop schedules to meet forecasted demand.
2. Develop feasible schedules based on available capacity.
3. Schedule employees and contractors by location and shift.
4. Develop detailed schedules based on required versus available skill levels.
5. Minimize schedule interruptions due to absenteeism and lateness.
6. Minimize staffing costs.
7. Support job bidding (if required).
8. Create Gantt charts of project activities (if required).
9. Create management reports, including staffing levels associated with staffing cost.
10. Use advanced systems that enable model building and simulation of the process using Windows-based software.

example, Period 1 starts at 8:00 A.M. and ends at 4:00 P.M. Between 8:00 A.M. and 12:00 P.M., 20 agents are required to answer customer calls. However, during the period 12:00 to 4:00 P.M., 30 agents are required to answer calls. This implies that 10 additional agents must be added during the period 12:00 to 4:00 P.M. However, a constraint on the staffing schedule is that an agent cannot work more than 8 hours per 24-hour day. This means that four shifts of workers must be staffed according to the solution provided at the bottom of Figure 12.2. Shift 1 should be staffed using 20 agents, Shift 2 using 10 agents, Shift 3 using 30 agents, and Shift 4 using 10 agents. This optimum solution will require 140 agents for a total monthly salary of $165,000. This is the minimum cost solution obtained using the LP algorithm.

Over the past several years, advanced software has been developed to increase the efficiency of a scheduling process. Table 12.9 lists ten key characteristics of off-the-shelf scheduling software. Many software products are based on linear programming or simulation algorithms, but also provide user-friendly schedules to meet forecasted demand on a system, at minimum time or cost, based on available system capacity as well as other user-defined system constraints. In fact, sophisticated scheduling software can also provide detailed staffing schedules based on worker skill levels by function, facility location, shift, pay rate, restrictions on their schedule, and other relevant factors. Many of these software packages will also allow users to build simulations, models, and visual representations of their process workflows.

Using Pull Scheduling to Increase Flow

Visual control systems can be deployed, at a local level, to more effectively control the flow of work through a complex system. This is particularly helpful in systems in which demand or their resource availability suddenly changes, but their status is not obvious. As an example, master production scheduling (MPS) and master requirements planning (MRPII) systems are notorious for lagging the day-to-day changes in a production system. As a result, expediting of work by production activity control (PAC) is often required to attain planned schedules. However, manual intervention would not be required if a system could be automated, to a point, where its resource status were known at operational or work task levels. As an example, in the airline industry, the status of resources such as planes and flight crews is readily apparent to its scheduling system. As a result, any changes that may occur relative to external demand or resource availability, due to conditions such as weather or mechanical problems, can be easily remodeled by their system's scheduling algorithm.

The goal of a production system should be to schedule its products or services only when they are needed by an external customer. This ensures available capacity is efficiently matched to actual customer demand to avoid situations in which too little or too much product is produced by a system. Using this logic, a production or transformation process should be aligned to external customer demand by an organization's information systems, regardless if it is electronic or manual. However, this may be a difficult task in organizations that produce thousands of products or services over extended lead times and geographically dispersed locations. In these situations, it is usually difficult to easily match available resources to changes in customer demand because available capacity is allocated at fixed periods of time across many diverse products and locations in advance. These inflexible systems are also characterized by a heavy usage of forecasting, MPS, and MRPII systems that "push" a work schedule out to a supply chain using a product's cumulative lead time offset from its production due date. The assumption, in these systems, is that allocated resources will be available to production operations, and product demand does not significantly change during its cumulative lead time or frozen time fence. A problem is that unless modified by their users to reflect actual production conditions, these systems will move materials or information through their process workflows in process batches and eventually not be in synchronization with the production system.

Lean tools, methods, and concepts must also be applied within a system, in the manner described in Chapter 6, to move a rigidly structured production system from a push system using a process batch to one in which materials or information are pulled through a system. The latter system becomes a self-scheduling system based on external demand using a calculated takt time. Organizations should also consider changing their production scheduling systems to mass customize its products

Table 12.10 Scheduling at a Local Level

	Current	*Goal*
System design	Make-to-order or stock	Mass customization
System demand	Variable	Level (takt time)
Lot size	Batch	Transfer batch
Capacity strategy	Available time	Balance to takt time
PAC strategy	Push (old paradigm)	Pull
Operations layout	Operation focus	Product focus
Queue time	High	Low

or services. This requires integrating product and process designs as discussed in Chapters 4 to 6. In Table 12.10, a summarization is made of several key characteristics of push scheduling systems versus a pull system. It should be noted that the original pull system was developed by Toyota within the automotive industry and is characterized as having a relatively few number of products. Also, external demand patterns usually exhibit a relatively small unit variation. In contrast, other industries may have to schedule in an environment in which external demand changes rapidly. Pull systems are difficult to deploy in these environments. Also, sales promotions or other actions may distort demand within a supply chain, causing discontinuities. In other systems, macroeconomic trends could have a major impact on large and customized products. In summary, although pull systems were developed for the automotive industry, they have found applicability, but to varying degrees, within other industries. As a result, there have been a wide range of very unique and effective to integrate Lean tools and methods and, in particular, concepts related to pull demand into scheduling systems. However, in every situation, commonality of product and process design will improve scheduling efficiencies.

Figure 12.3 shows several elements necessary to fully implement a pull scheduling system. Many of these concepts have been discussed in earlier chapters. As an example, in Chapter 4 we discussed the concept of developing simple, standardized, and robust designs. In Chapter 5, we discussed workflow design, simplification, and standardization. In Chapter 6, we discussed lot size reductions, mistake-proofing, Total Preventive Maintenance (TPM), standardized work, takt time, the balancing of material flow, and reducing setups. In this chapter, we will expand our discussion of Lean tools and methods.

Figure 12.3 reinforces the fact that pull systems are deployed only after a significant amount of preliminary work has been done by a Lean improvement team. This preliminary work includes the many components shown in Figure 12.3. However, physical reconfiguration of a process workflow is another useful method

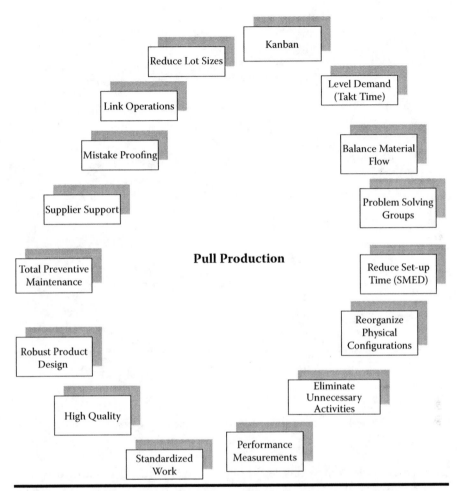

Figure 12.3   Necessary elements of a pull production system.

we have not discussed in previous chapters. It is used to configure a process work-flow, such as the one shown in Figure 12.4, which is characterized by an overly complicated flow of material or information. Figure 12.5 shows how a physical configuration such as a linear or sequential workflow may be more efficient in the sense that the distance traveled by a unit of material or information, through the workflow, is less than that of the convoluted workflow shown in Figure 12.4. However, even a linear workflow pattern may not be an optimum workflow design. As an example, the four workflow designs shown in Figure 12.5 have been well studied in diverse applications. These include a straight line or linear patterns, U-shaped patterns, L-shaped patterns, and S-shaped patterns. The correct physical configuration requires a careful analysis. In other words, prior to deploying any of the four patterns shown in Figure 12.5, a Lean improvement team should analyze

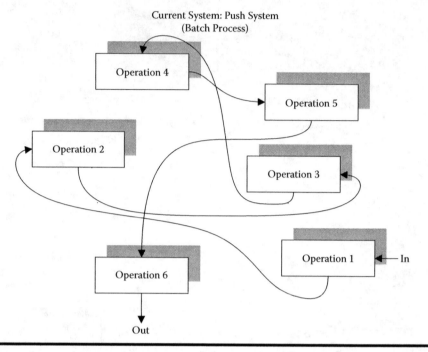

Current System: Push System
(Batch Process)

Figure 12.4   Collocation of equipment based on the build sequence: current system.

operational cycle times versus the required takt time, process waste related to scrap and rework, distance traveled, operational motions, and other relevant factors associated with each workflow configuration. However, a U-shaped work cell pattern has been often found to be very efficient from the perspective of ensuring that work entering a work cell is balanced relative to the work leaving it. Also, under certain circumstances, labor efficiency is usually improved in a U-shaped work cell because workers can be added or removed from the work cell as the takt time changes, if they have been cross-trained to perform several operations within the work cell. After the Lean tools and methods listed in Figure 12.3 have been implemented by a Lean improvement team, Kanban systems can be deployed to balance the flow of work between work cells and suppliers. The final step of a pull system and Kanban deployment is migration to a one-unit or single-piece flow. Single-piece flow is characterized by the transfer batch concept discussed in Chapter 6 and shown in Figure 6.7. According to Lean concepts, when a system contains only value-adding operations, single-piece flow will occur.

Kanbans are signals (if electronic) or physical cards (if manual) that request specific quantities of materials, services, or information per unit time. There are several types of Kanbans depending on the information conveyed to upstream and downstream operations. As an example, transport Kanbans contain information

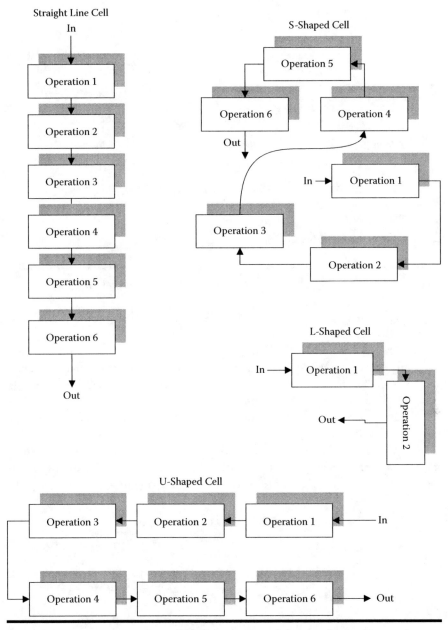

Figure 12.5 Process layouts to facilitate pull production: alternative systems.

identifying a part number, its quantity, where it was produced, and where it must be transported next. Transport Kanbans consist of supplier and withdrawal Kanbans. Supplier Kanbans signal part orders to suppliers in which parts are delivered to a

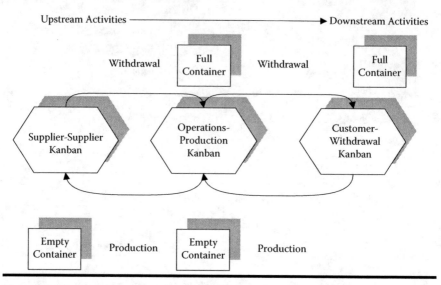

Figure 12.6   Kanban cards pull material from upstream operations.

requesting facility using "milk runs." Milk runs help establish a constant lead time for the delivered parts but, to be effective, usually require that suppliers be collocated with their customers. Withdrawal Kanbans are used internally among internal workstations or operations to signal that an operation immediately upstream should send a Kanban quantity of material to the downstream operation requesting material. Production Kanbans are used to signal an upstream operation to replace the Kanban quantity just removed by the withdrawal Kanban. These concepts are shown in Figure 12.6.

In addition to considering the general flow of Kanban cards through a system, it is also important to calculate the required number and type of Kanban cards that must be released into a system to meet its takt time. Figure 12.7 shows how the

$$\text{Kanbans} = \frac{\text{Expected Unit Demand During Lead Time} + \text{Safety Stock}}{\text{Container Size}}$$

Containers Include:	Items Pulled Include:
•Boxes	•Raw Materials
•Totes	•Parts
•Pallets	•Assemblies
•Trucks	•Products
•Any Standardized Container Volume and Type	•Lots

Figure 12.7   Kanban facts.

number of Kanban cards is calculated using the expected demand during the lead time between operations, a safety-stock factor, which is usually set at 10 percent of the expected demand, and the container size for the material or part being placed into the Kanban. As an example, if 100 parts were required per hour and the safety-stock level was set at 10 percent, the calculated quantity would be 110 parts. If a container size was 55 parts, then two containers and Kanban cards would be required to control the hourly flow of parts between operations.

As mention earlier, Toyota developed its pull system in an environment in which external customer demand was relatively smooth and detached from MPS and MRPII systems. In this environment, the material flow was relatively stable and linear, and as a result could be manually managed by local work teams. Over time, it became apparent that pull scheduling systems could not be easily applied to low-volume production processes that were controlled by MPS and MRPII systems and batching of materials. In these systems, a modification of the pull system called quick response manufacturing (QRM) was developed to provide local work cell control of the material flow in MPS and MRPII environments. QRM systems will be discussed in Chapter 13 in the context of MRPII systems and bill-of-material (BOM) hierarchy.

Summary

Efficient scheduling of products or services is an important consideration for any organization. Table 12.11 presents key concepts regarding an evaluation of scheduling systems. It was shown that some scheduling systems, prioritization rules and algorithms, are more efficient than others. For this reason, it is important that an organization determine the best scheduling rules and algorithms to manage its process workflows. These may be manual or automated systems, depending on the workflow design. Scheduling will also be easier if a workflow has been optimally configured and Lean tools and methods applied to simply and standardize its operations.

Table 12.11　Key Concepts to Improve Scheduling Effectiveness

1. Determine the best scheduling rules for your workflow to optimize resource usage while satisfying demand.
2. Deploy the best type of scheduling system for your workflow. This may be automatically or manually controlled.
3. Scheduling will be easier if the system has been optimally configured and Lean tools and methods applied to simplify and standardize its workflow.

Suggested Reading

Eliyahu M. Goldratt and Jeff Cox. (1986). *The Goal*, 2nd ed. North River Press.

Peter Hines, Richard Lamming, Dan Jones, Paul Cousins, and Nick Rich. (2000). *Value Stream Management*. Prentice Hall, Englewood Cliffs, NJ.

Rajan Suri. (1998). *Quick Response Manufacturing: A Companywide Approach to Reducing Lead Times*. Productivity Press, Portland, OR.

James P. Womack and Daniel T. Jones. (1996). *Lean Thinking: Banish Waste and Create Wealth in Your Organization*. Simon & Schuster, New York.

Chapter 13

Dynamic MRPII

Competitive solution 13: Use hybrid material requirements planning (MRPII) and quick response manufacturing (QRM) methods to create systems that can dynamically respond to variations in demand or resources in master production schedule (MPS) and MRPII environments.

Overview

Material requirements planning (MRPII) is an underutilized resource. This may be because many people believe an MRPII system simply translates the master production schedule information via the bill-of-materials (BOM) into a product's component parts. However, if MRPII users really understand how their system functions, they can provide significant value to their organizations. As an example, I have seen three dramatic uses of an MRPII system over the past few years that resulted in a significant business impact. The first effective use of an MRPII system was placing low-volume items having stable demand patterns on a minimum/maximum inventory system. This situation occurred within an organization that sold more than 50,000 products, not including their packaging variations. Prior to a minimum/maximum conversion, many of the products were forecast. In other words, models had to be built to predict sales throughout the year for every product. Given the very number of forecasted products, this created a situation in which the demand patterns of higher-volume products did not receive the attention they required from forecasting analysts. A solution was found in the stratification of the products by their volume and demand variation. This stratification resulted in four separate product groups, as shown in Figure 8.8. The quadrant characterized by low volume and stable demand variation could be automatically managed by an MRPII system using a minimum/maximum method. Minimum/maximum inventory systems use their reorder points as a signal to order additional inventory. The reorder point of a component is estimated as the expected demand over the component's lead time. This lead time is the cycle time to place and receive an order. Inventory management will be discussed in Chapter 14, and the reorder point concept is shown in Figure 14.1. A second effective use of an MRPII system occurred when a client used their MRPII system as a pull system by reassigning data fields to create an electronic Kanban that signaled the supply chain to move materials from one facility to another to meet demand requirements. This added flexibility to the supply chain dramatically reducing its inventory safety-stock levels. This is an example of a hybrid MRPII system, which will be discussed later in this chapter. In the last example, I was asked to significantly reduce inventory investment within 90 days by $10 million (10 percent of its average on-hand inventory). In this project, we worked with MRPII specialists to review investment and inventory turns ratios for every product and created a prioritized list of improvement actions, which included the elimination of excess and obsolete inventory. In addition, a more effective order management was created by the organization. These three examples demonstrate how an MRPII system can be used to significantly improve business performance if its users understand how it really works. Table 13.1 presents several key metrics which can be used to improve MRPII effectiveness and efficiency. These metrics and related bill-of-material topics will be discussed in the balance of this chapter.

The materials requirements planning (MRPII) system translates independent demand for a product (end item) from the master production schedule (MPS) through the bill-of-materials (BOM) into dependent demand for a product's components, including raw materials, parts, subassemblies, and miscellaneous supplies. In this translation process the MRPII system uses information from an engineering BOM, current on-hand inventory status, the lead time for all components, expected process yields, and other relevant information that may impact the supply of the dependent items required to meet a production schedule. The interrelationships between the MPS and MRPII, and related systems, were shown in Figure 12.1.

Table 13.1   Competitive Metrics: Materials Requirements Planning

1. Percentage MRPII accuracy
2. Percentage of bill of material (BOM) accuracy
3. Inventory investment and turns by product and location as well as other inventory classifications, such as raw materials and work-in-process (WIP) inventory
4. Percentage of products converted to a minimum/maximum inventory control using MRPII

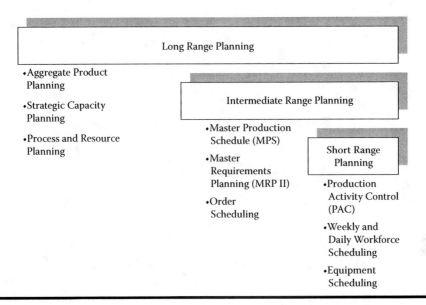

Figure 13.1 Operations planning overview.

In this chapter, we will discuss MRPII systems in greater detail, including some recent operational improvements, such as MRPII/Kanban, which enables MRPII to become a more effective management tool across a greater variety of industries, including low-volume production environments. This discussion can also be generalized to the production of services or information.

Figure 13.1 shows the demand information driving an MRPII system originates from the MPS, which in turn is driven by strategic product forecasts integrated into an organization's strategic operations plan. The strategic planning process requires estimates of product demand and its required capacity between three and five years into the future. However, in some industries this time horizon could be longer. The goal of an MRPII system is to coordinate the flow of materials throughout a supply chain to ensure that dependent demand components are available in exactly the right quantities and times to build higher-level items. These higher-level items appear in the form of assemblies or products. Resource requirements that are based on intermediate-range product forecasts, having a time horizon of 6 to 18 months, are aggregated by the MPS and allocated by the MRPII system across its supply chain. Production schedules are created, at an intermediate level, to build the necessary products based on either product forecasts or firm orders for products. Although MPS and MRPII systems are loaded with the information necessary to execute the production schedule at an intermediate level to allocate capacity, the final production schedule will be firm only at the cumulative lead time of a product. This lead time is called the time fence. The concept of a time fence was discussed in

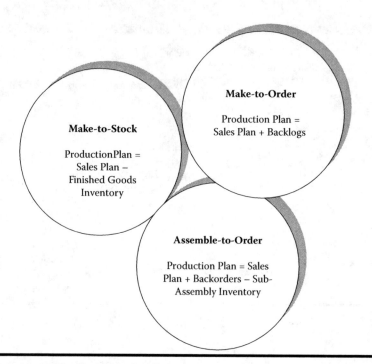

Figure 13.2   Production planning.

Chapter 8 and shown in Figure 8.5. A manufacturing schedule should be "frozen" within a product's time fence because raw materials and components may have been ordered through the MRPII and related systems. Within a product's time fence, production activity control (PAC) monitors and controls the production of a product on a weekly and daily basis, including its required equipment and work-force scheduling.

An additional complicating factor in the MPS-to-MRPII translation process is that these environments may be characterized by one of several basic workflow systems. These are shown in Figure 13.2 as make-to-stock, assemble-to-order, and make-to-order systems. In a make-to-stock system, finished products are produced and inventoried in central locations called warehouses or distribution centers for future shipment to customers. These systems are characterized by the production of numerous products that cannot be produced on demand due to capacity limitations. As an example, in manufacturing industries such as consumer products, there may be thousands of products that are sold through several distribution channels. More often than not, these products will not have common designs, thus requiring separate setups to produce every product. In service industries, an analogous situation would be creating a diverse set of services that must be inventoried because they cannot be produced simultaneously. This is common in the marketing services operations of major financial institutions. Examples include information brochures, performance reports, and product specification sheets, to name just a few. In larger organizations, the number of inventoried products could be in the thousands. In make-to-order systems, orders for products are scheduled according to firm customer demand or order book. However, in these systems, capacity is also limited because not every order can be produced at once. In other words, orders have a lead time. In these systems, demand is relatively fixed, but there is usually a backlog of orders that must be worked off over time. The decision regarding how fast orders should be worked off is made using financial models that balance the cost of additional resources versus the time value of money lost due to delayed orders and payment. In make-to-order environments, an MRPII system is used to manage the flow of components that compose its products, in a manner similar to that of other process workflow environments. Assemble-to-order systems are characterized by higher-level assemblies or systems that have been only partially manufactured for assembly, until orders arrive to complete their production. The final assembly of partially manufactured assemblies also depends on their required production sequence. In each of these three workflow systems, the production plan and its required resources depend on the amount of the product that must be manufactured versus currently available on-hand inventory, as was shown in Table 12.3.

MRPII and Bill-of-Material (BOM) Relationship

Figure 13.3 shows that the BOM is a hierarchal depiction of a product's manufacturing sequence, and higher levels of the BOM correspond to higher levels of a product's structure. The MRPII system translates independent demand for a product from the MPS and creates information that is used to generate time-phased manufacturing and purchase orders. Integral to this process is calculation of a product's cumulative lead time based on its BOM relationship, as well as the ability of either manufacturing or suppliers to produce it. Calculating when a component should be manufactured to ensure it is available for production is accomplished by working backwards from the products' shipping date and using MRPII systems' lead time constants by component. As an example, if a product must be shipped in 90 days, but the total cumulative lead time to build, receive, and assemble its components is 60 days, then the products' manufacturing schedule will be offset from the 90 days by 60 days to start 30 days from today. In addition to accessing an engineering BOM file, an MRPII system uses the inventory file to offset independent demand for a product. In other words, if demand for the product was 100 units, but there were currently 50 units in finished-goods inventory, then only 50 units would become part of the MRPII ordering and scheduling process. As an example, the BOM shown in Figure 13.3 for a table requires one top, four legs, eight screws, and paint to assemble the product. At the lowest level of the BOM, the table top and legs require 3 square meters of wood. In other words, if 10 tables are required by the

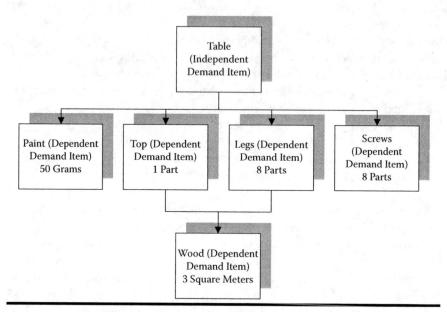

Figure 13.3 Product structure drives the MRP through the BOM.

MPS schedule, then initial MRPII requirements would be 10 table tops, 40 table legs, 80 screws, and 30 square feet of wood and paint.

Inventory status information is particularly important to an MRPII system. If inventory is on hand to satisfy MPS demand, then the production schedule will be based on a product's net requirements (with on-hand inventory netted out of the original demand). On-hand inventory is calculated as current inventory minus the safety-stock quantity assigned to a product. Table 13.2 shows that in addition to inventory levels, an MRPII system uses lot sizing rules, lead times, and yield information based on expected scrap and rework levels to estimate the net requirements of the BOM's components. The lot sizing rules shown in Figure 13.4 are extremely important considerations in an economic lot size calculation. This is because lot sizes that are larger than necessary will increase a product's inventory levels. This

Table 13.2 Important Information on Inventory Status

1. Beginning period inventory quantities
2. Current allocations of raw materials
3. Safety-stock requirements
4. Lot sizing rules (economic order or production quantities)
5. Lead times by component
6. Yield information related to scrap and rework

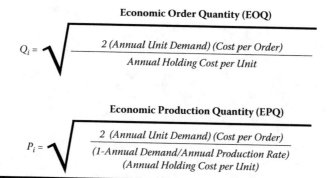

Figure 13.4 Lot sizing formulas.

has the effect of reducing the available capacity for other products within a process workflow. Figure 13.4 shows two of the most common lot sizing rules, but there are many different rules depending on the characteristics of a system. These rules are the economic order quantity (EOQ) and the economic production quantity (EPQ). The EOQ calculation balances the cost of setting up a job against the inventory holding cost of the product. In effect, without process improvements, fewer setups require larger lot sizes, which results in higher inventory holding costs. However, a product's cost per order or setup costs can be reduced using Single Minute Exchange of Dies (SMED) tools and methods to simply and standardize a setup process. This will reduce the cycle time of the setup process. SMED was discussed in Chapter 6. Alternatively, if products have common design features, then their setups can be combined with those of other products. This will have the effect of reducing the number of setups and their costs. The economic production quantity calculation works in a similar manner. There may be modifications to these lot sizing rules depending on specific applications and organizational requirements. As an example, Kanban quantities are lot sized using an EOQ formula and the component's container size, as shown in Figure 12.7. The lot sizing rule used by an MRPII system can have a major impact on an organization's inventory investment.

How an MRPII System Functions

An MRPII system integrates accounting, finance, accounts payable, design engineering, distribution, and other organizational functions into the manufacturing scheduling and inventory functions necessary to produce products. The major elements of an MRPII system include the release of planned orders based on their lead time offsets, scheduling of BOM components based on their lead time offsets, and notification to suppliers or internal operations to execute the planned orders. Additional functions include reporting open orders that require rescheduling due to capacity availability issues, helping close the loop on all open orders through

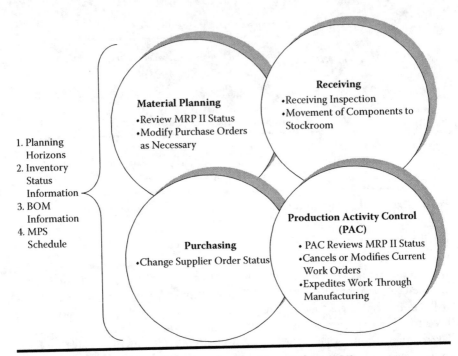

1. Planning Horizons
2. Inventory Status Information
3. BOM Information
4. MPS Schedule

Material Planning
•Review MRP II Status
•Modify Purchase Orders as Necessary

Receiving
•Receiving Inspection
•Movement of Components to Stockroom

Purchasing
•Change Supplier Order Status

Production Activity Control (PAC)
• PAC Reviews MRP II Status
•Cancels or Modifies Current Work Orders
•Expedites Work Through Manufacturing

Figure 13.5   MPS and other system changes impact the MRPII.

planning and control, and analyzing a system's parameters and metrics, and their combined impact on the resource requirements planning system. The mechanics of how these activities are accomplished will be discussed in the next several paragraphs.

The MRPII system contains a long list of data fields, constants, and parameters that help to specify how items are purchased, received, and controlled by the system. In addition, the production activity control (PAC) function is integral to coordination of the MRPII schedule on the manufacturing floor on a weekly and daily basis. PAC was discussed in Chapter 12 at a local manufacturing level. Figure 13.5 shows that MRPII, PAC, and related systems are associated with four basic functions. These include material planning, receiving of materials, ordering of materials, and PAC. Also, Figure 13.5 shows that changes in a master production schedule (MPS) impact all four systems. As an example, MPS changes require that an MRPII system send scheduling notices across a supply chain. This has the effect of modifying supplier schedules. In addition, purchasing can modify these orders based on external or internal constraints. At a local manufacturing level, PAC reviews the MRPII schedule, and depending on local production conditions, relative to capacity, materials, and labor, it may modify the original schedule. Also, if schedules are late, PAC can use the MRPII to obtain the information necessary to expedite a customer order. In this context, PAC and MRPII systems have different but complementary functions. Figure 13.6 shows these differences relative to

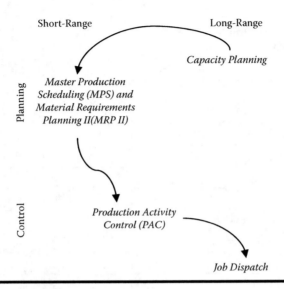

Short-Range   Long-Range

Capacity Planning

Planning

*Master Production
Scheduling (MPS) and
Material Requirements
Planning II(MRP II)*

Control

*Production Activity
Control (PAC)*

Job Dispatch

Figure 13.6   MRPII planning versus PAC.

production planning and control. Production planning activities are an ongoing process until a product has been manufactured and delivered to a customer. However, production control activities are especially important prior to the production planning phase. In summary, MRPII is a planning function driven by the MPS but modified by other systems, including the BOM file, inventory transactions file, and files that store constants and parameters used in MRPII calculations. Other functions within an organization use the MRPII system to determine lot sizing, lead time, and other important information necessary to plan production activities.

Table 13.3 shows the basic operations of an MRPII system, using the table example from Figure 13.3, but at a component level. It should be noted that although the format in which this information is represented may vary by organization, all MRPII systems use information related to lot size, on-hand inventory, lead time, required safety stock, MPS requirements, and the BOM structure with its hierarchal relationships, as well as the required quantities of each component based on a product's net requirements. Referring to Table 13.3, it is easy to see that the MPS demand for the table example is accurately represented by the MRPII schedule, as well as the subcomponents necessary to build the product. Required producton is offset by each component's on-hand inventory minus its safety-stock quantity. Orders for tables are released to production based on their required due date minus the component lead time offsets and the lead time to assemble the components. Table 13.3 also shows the labor and equipment that are required to build the tables to meet the MRPII production schedule. Recall that we discussed capacity in Chapter 9 at a strategic and organizational level. In that discussion, capacity was created and assigned at a product group level based on a forecast by facility over the relevant forecasting time horizon. However, at an MRPII and PAC

Table 13.3 Determining Capacity Requirements Based on Time-Phased Requirements

Master production schedule for tables			25	50	100	50
		Weekly Time Periods				
	−2	−1	1	2	3	4
Table Top (Lead Time 1 Week)						
Gross requirements			25	50	100	50
Scheduled receipts			0	0	0	0
Allocations			0	0	0	0
Projected on-hand inventory			25	25	25	25
Projected available inventory			0	0	0	0
Net requirements			25	50	100	50
Planned order receipts			25	50	100	50
Planned order releases		25	50	100	50	
Table Legs (Lead Time 2 Weeks)						
Gross requirements			100	200	400	200
Scheduled receipts			0	0	0	0
Allocations			0	0	0	0
Projected on-hand inventory			25	25	25	25
Projected available inventory			0	0	0	0
Net requirements			100	200	400	200
Planned order receipts			100	200	400	200
Planned order releases	100	200	400	200		
Labor Requirements						
Table top (1 hour per top)	0	25	50	100	50	0
Table legs (0.5 hour per leg)	50	100	200	100	0	0
Total labor hours required	50	125	250	200	50	0
Machine Hours						
Table top (0.25 hour per top)	0	6.25	12.5	25	12.5	0
Table legs (0.25 hour per leg)	25	50	100	50	0	0
Total machine hours required	25	56.25	112.5	75	12.5	0

level, capacity is planned on a monthly, weekly, and daily basis to meet immediate production conditions. In other words, available capacity has already been created based on strategic forecasts.

An MRPII system is a good planning tool, but a poor execution tool at an operational level. In other words, it cannot dynamically respond to process changes caused by variations in labor, machines, material, or other capacity. In fact, Kanban was designed specifically for the effective execution of manufacturing schedules to manage workflows at an operational level. Without real-time control of the process by MRPII, PAC maintains control by monitoring available resources to execute the production schedule. But this monitoring is usually after the fact, with the result that expediting of order often occurs when schedules are missed due to process breakdowns of various types. However, there are several systems that have been developed to overcome some of the disadvantages of MRPII relative to control and execution at an operational level. Two examples are Kanban and quick response manufacturing (QRM). These systems were discussed in Chapter 12. In this chapter, we will discuss elements of hybrid MRPII systems in which the MRP system is modified to act as a Kanban system using external customer demand as its pull signal.

Creating a Pull System Using Hybrid MRPII and Kanban

A key characteristic of hybrid MRPII systems is that they calculate Kanban quantities every time the MRPII system refreshes. Also, they enable simulations of projected demand versus the probability of stock-outs, as well as better capacity planning. But the most useful attribute of these systems is that they verify component availability as the resource status of a supply chain dynamically changes over time. Table 13.4 lists ten key characteristics of a hybrid MRPII system using a Kanban control system. The first important characteristic is the management of daily demand through the process workflow. This is accomplished by having an MRPII system accumulate required component quantities up to their calculated Kanban quantity, as shown in Figure 13.8. In addition, the management of daily demand is based on a component's expected demand and its lead time. Also, the on-hand and available inventory quantity versus order status must also be managed and adjustments made to the demand quantity that is used to release the Kanban to the supply chain. Other important characteristics of a hybrid MRPII system include the number of Kanbans allocated within a system, the maximum lot size of a given Kanban, and the required container size of its components. In a hybrid Kanban system, parameters are calculated for every component making up a product's BOM. The Kanban quantities are then used to calculate labor and related resource efficiencies and yields, as well as required quality inspections or other special handling considerations.

Table 13.4   10 Key Characteristics of Hybrid MRPII Systems

1. Daily demand	Demand for the component on a daily basis and location
2. Lead time	Agreed upon lead time from suppliers or manufacturing facilities
3. Order policy codes	Compare on-hand versus Kanbans on order to place orders across the supply chain
4. Containers in use	The number of Kanban containers assigned to a particular part number
5. Component containers	The number of Kanban containers assigned to a particular part number
6. Kanban lot size	The calculated Kanban lot size based on daily demand and lead time plus the safety stock
7. Kanban container size	The calculated size of the Kanban container for each part number
8. MRPII parameters	Related to direct labor requirements, efficiencies, and yields
9. Inspection requirements	If inspection of the Kanban components is required, this is noted by the MRPII system
10. Kanban codes	Assigned based on whether the components are purchased or manufactured, as well as the type of work cell they are manufactured within

Figure 13.7 graphically describes, at a high level, how a hybrid MRPII system works in practice. In hybrid MRPII systems, estimates are made for preliminary Kanban lot sizes, using MRPII information, versus current demand using a modified version of the Kanban formula shown in Figure 13.8. This formula calculates Kanban lot size equal to average demand per day times lead time plus the safety stock, which is normally set as a percentage of demand over lead time. Because this is the Kanban lot size, the MRPII requirements are aggregated day by day until they equal or exceed the Kanban lot size. At that point, they are released as an order and sent to external suppliers or internally to production operations. In parallel, direct labor and other resource requirements are calculated by the MRPII system. To ensure high customer on-time service levels are maintained according to their targets, a demand aggregation time is set as some multiple of daily MRPII demand. In Figure 13.8, the MRPII gross requirements for a component are aggregated until they are at least greater than the calculated Kanban quantity. The Kanban quantity shown in Figure 13.8 is calculated as 318 units. Because the accumulated MRPII

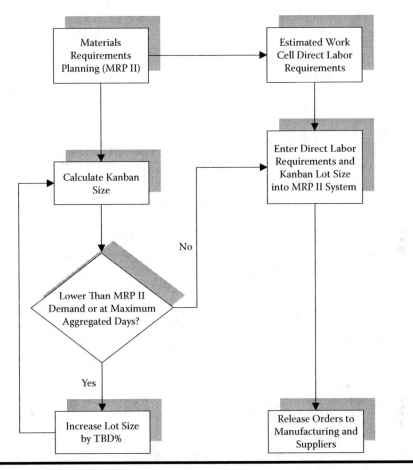

Figure 13.7   Hybrid MRPII systems using Kanban.

gross requirements exceed 318 units, a Kanban is released into the system for this component using a rounded quantity of 320 units. In summary, in hybrid MRPII systems, Kanban quantities are calculated for every component at every refresh of the MRPII system. The MRPII system compares the gross requirements of a component to its calculated Kanban quantity and creates a Kanban. Kanban information is communicated to external suppliers and internal operations by modifying MRPII field descriptions relative to Kanban container sizes, direct labor and equipment requirements, conversion efficiencies, and other information that is related to the quality and special handling requirements of BOM components.

Implementation of a hybrid MRPII Kanban system also depends on proving the feasibility of the concept on a limited and controlled basis and expanding it slowly across an organization and its supply chain. It has been found that the best implementation results are obtained by initially deploying this system with key suppliers of high-volume and high-quality components that have sophisticated MRPII and

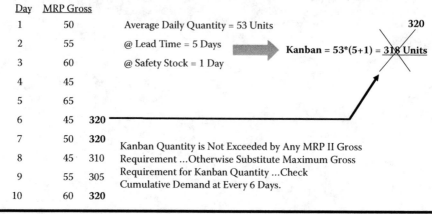

1. Kanban Lot Size = [Average Daily Demand *(Lead Time Days + Safety Stock Days)]
2. Average Daily Demand = Gross Requirements OverLead Time/Lead Time Days

Day	MRP Gross		
1	50		
2	55		
3	60		
4	45		
5	65		
6	45	320	
7	50	320	
8	45	310	
9	55	305	
10	60	320	

Average Daily Quantity = 53 Units

@ Lead Time = 5 Days

@ Safety Stock = 1 Day

Kanban = 53*(5+1) = 318 Units

320

Kanban Quantity is Not Exceeded by Any MRP II Gross Requirement ...Otherwise Substitute Maximum Gross Requirement for Kanban Quantity ...Check Cumulative Demand at Every 6 Days.

Figure 13.8   Calculating Kanban size based on MRPII gross requirements.

similar systems. Products should also have a relatively stable design to ensure the BOM does not change too frequently and demand for the component should be relatively smooth and exhibit small variation. After the suitability of a hybrid MRPII Kanban system has been proven for one product, it can be expanded to others.

Quick Response Methods to Support Hybrid MRPII

Hybrid MRPII systems can be deployed in manufacturing environments character-ized by stable demand and linearly sequenced operations. However, it is difficult to deploy a pull system in low-volume systems characterized by batch-and-queue material flow, which is scheduled by MPS and MRPII systems. However, a modi-fication of the Kanban concept was developed several years ago. In these systems, local control is given to workflows or their operations by collapsing the BOM at a subassembly level. This is called quick response manufacturing (QRM). In QRM, higher-order subassemblies are still controlled directly by an MRPII system, but lower-level components are controlled using QRM methods at a workflow or oper-ational level. QRM methods use Kanban cards to control the flow of materials between local work cells based on an MRPII pull signal from operations building higher-level subassemblies. The advantage of using a QRM system is that if the availability of resources changes, then local work cell production can be matched to the new resource levels and the required MRPII gross requirements of the higher-level BOM assemblies. This prevents waste of valuable capacity and prevents the buildup of work-in-process (WIP) inventory. QRM is implemented by designing work cells that are based on a product or subassembly's BOM structure as shown in Figure 13.9, and then collapsing and controlling the material flow at the level of

•Restructure to Simple Cellular Product Oriented Cells
•Rethink Bills-of-Materials

  •Design Decisions
  •Materials
  •Make vs. Buy
  •Collapse BOMs

•Use High Level MRP
•High Performance Work Teams (Local Decisions)
•How Do Changes in System Status Inputs (MPS/MRP Changes) at
 Cells 2, 3 & 4 Impact Capacity and Flow?

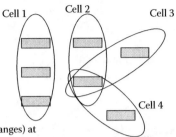

Figure 13.9   Quick response methods for hybrid MRPII.

the collapsed BOM. In addition, basic Lean methods and tools are implemented in QRM systems to increase operational stability.

Summary

MRPII systems are important in complex environments characterized by many products. Table 13.5 lists several key concepts that may help an organization improve its competitiveness. These include ensuring the MRPII calculations are correct, including lot sizing and constants such as lead time parameters. This is an important concept because decisions regarding production schedules, inventory investment, and projected shipment schedules depend on MRPII database accuracy. The second key concept is to stratify products by their current demand variation versus production volumes and place the products on a minimum/maximum inventory system. This will improve low volume and low variance forecasting accuracy of other products because forecasting analyst's attention can be focused on them. A third key concept is to investigate the feasibility of implementing hybrid MRPII within a supply chain to stabilize production schedules as resources and

Table 13.5   Key Concepts to Improve MRPII Effectiveness

1. Ensure MRPII calculations are correct, including lot sizing and constants such as lead time parameters.
2. Review the demand variation versus product volumes and stratify and place as many products on a minimum/maximum system as possible.
3. Investigate the feasibility of implementing hybrid MRPII in your supply chain.
4. Investigate the feasibility of implementing quick response manufacturing (QRM) methods in situations in which the product volumes are very low volume and are processed through many work cells.

demand changes. Hybrid MRPII systems increase operational flexibility because demand forecasts are more closely tied to actual component usage at a local work cell level. The last key concept is to investigate the feasibility of implementing quick response manufacturing (QRM) methods in environments in which the product volumes are very low and are processed through many work cells.

Suggested Reading

Richard B. Chase, F. Robert Jacobs, and Nicholas J. Aquilano. (2006). *Operations Management for Competitive Advantage*, 11th ed. McGraw-Hill, New York.

Rajan Suri. (1998). *Quick Response Manufacturing: A Companywide Approach to Reducing Lead Times*. Productivity Press, Portland, OR.

Chapter 14

Strategic Inventory Management

Competitive solution 14: Build financial models to fully understand how much inventory or other assets are required and where they should be located to achieve customer service levels at minimum cost to increase cash flow and asset utilization.

Overview

Inventory requires a significant investment and negatively impacts an organization by reducing its return on asset (ROA) utilization or inventory turns ratios. Inventory turns is a specific asset utilization metric that measures the efficient utilization of inventory and is defined as the average inventory investment necessary to support the cost of goods sold (COGS). Depending on the industry or organization, inventory investment may represent a significant proportion of its COGS (~5 to 20 percent). These situations may be caused by several factors including the type of industry, process breakdowns, and poor strategic planning. The root causes of excessive inventory levels or low inventory turns ratios also depend on a product's lead time, expected demand, and required service levels. Because of the high invesstment cost, many organizations have taken actions to significantly reduce their inventory levels using Lean and Six Sigma methods as well as advanced technology. In fact, benchmark statistics show inventory turns ratios vary across diverse industries, from 1 to 100 or higher. In summary, some organizations can manage their inventory well, but many cannot, for a variety of reasons, which will

363

Table 14.1 Competitive Metrics: Inventory

1. Order fill by distribution center
2. Line item fill by distribution center and item
3. Inventory turns and investment by item and its location
4. Excess inventory by item and its location
5. Obsolete inventory by item and its location
6. Cycle counting accuracy by item and its location
7. Unit service level by item and location
8. Lead time by item and its location
9. Demand variation by item and its location
10. Forecasting accuracy by item and its location
11. Lot size by item and location

be discussed in this chapter. Table 14.1 lists several key metrics that can help an organization measure and improve its inventory management systems and increase customer service levels.

It should be mentioned that a certain level of inventory investment may be necessary due to the state of technology of an industry. This is especially true in organizations that have a large number of diverse products and limited capacity. It was mentioned in previous chapters that when an organization produces diverse products, it may be difficult to reduce its economic production lot sizes without applying Single Minute Exchange of Dies (SMED) principles. Also, inventory management practices will vary based on the underlying system design. Recall that there are three basic system designs: make-to-order, assemble-to-order, and make-to-stock systems. Inventory investment strategies would be different in each system. As an example, make-to-order and assemble-to-order workflows will not have a large finished-goods inventory compared to make-to-stock systems. Make-to-stock systems are characterized by relatively high finished-goods inventory levels due to a diverse number of products, but only limited available capacity. However, investment in raw material and work-in-process (WIP) inventories may be higher in make-to-order and assemble-to-order systems if system throughput rates are low. In summary, organizations will have different relative inventory investment positions due their industry, as well as their internal inventory management policies. Having said this, it is important that every organization understand what is necessary to manage and reduce its inventory investment. Internal benchmarking should be conducted by an organization using inventory models. These models use lead time, expected demand, and service levels to calculate an optimum inventory quantity. This quantity is the amount of inventory an organization should have available for an item and its location to satisfy customer demand at the required service level. A model could also be used to calculate inventory investment requirements assuming reductions in lead time or demand variation or forecasting error. An analysis of this type would provide a reasonable inventory improvement target to reduce inventory investment. We will demonstrate this concept later in this chapter by discussing how to build simple inventory models using Microsoft Excel. These models will calculate an optimum inventory quantity for every item and location throughout an inventory population, including raw material, WIP, and finished-goods inventories. However, an organization may be constrained as to how it can achieve the calculated optimum inventory quantities. These process constraints may be caused by product and process designs, internal process breakdowns related to quality and other issues such as inventory management of economic order quantities. Also, there may be significant quantities of excess and obsolete (E&O) inventory within an organization from prior years due to poor operational performance. It may not be possible to immediately work off or dispose of these types of inventories. However, an organization can develop a strategic plan to eliminate chronic inventory problems by systematically reducing lead times and demand variation using Lean and Six Sigma principles.

Table 14.2 shows that an inventory investment problem can be exacerbated by where a product is positioned within its life cycle. As an example, in the introduction phase of a product, its demand forecasts may be in error. In fact, demand for some new products may not even occur, resulting in a large amount of obsolete

Table 14.2   Life Cycle Impact on Inventory

Poor forecasts for product/service result in major profitability and market share loss.		
Introduction	*Growth*	*Maturity and Decline*
Quality and performance problems	Cost control	Cost reduction
Demand difficult to predict	Competitors increase	Competitors decrease
Obsolescence/excess inventory	Product/service differentiation emphasis	Excess or obsolete inventory due to low product demand
Not enough product	Inventory increases to match demand, resulting in higher variances	
Design changes		

inventory. On the other hand, if demand for a new product is higher than expected, there may not be enough finished goods or other inventory types, such as raw materials or WIP, available to satisfy unexpected customer demand. This situation may result in lost sales. Several of these issues surrounding new product forecasting were discussed in Chapters 3 and 8. As a product enters its growth phase, there is increasing competitive pressure. As a result, higher operational efficiencies and more efficient inventory management are required to maintain profit margins. Even moderate amounts of excess or obsolete inventory may significantly reduce a product's profitability at this point in its life cycle. Differentiation of a product into several design variants also complicates inventory management. This occurs when a design has been slightly modified to satisfy different market segments. This requires that design variants must all be inventoried as separate products. A common example is packaging differences among products that are similar, but sold to different market segments or major customers. Finally, in a product's maturity and decline phases, its demand may become sporadic, resulting in a mismatch between inventory availability based on forecasting models and actual customer demand. This also will result is an increase of excess and obsolete inventory.

Measuring Inventory Value

Inventory accumulates value, at its standard cost, when it progressively works its way through a process workflow. As an example, work-in-process (WIP) inventories are valued using both their accumulated material cost and the direct labor, as well as their assigned overhead costs. Another way to look at inventory is that it is an investment an organization makes to have available capacity because it cannot produce goods or services on demand or anticipates future interruptions to its workflow. These disruptions could be caused by labor issues, plant closures, or an interruption to supply. Because inventory is an asset and has value to an organization, its value must be accurately accounted for to ensure that an organization's financial statements are correct. Also, it must be protected from damage, spoilage, and pilferage to prevent loss of its value.

Organizations control inventory using one of several basic inventory models that are incorporated into their MRPII systems. The most common is a perpetual inventory model (PIM). Applications of this model will be discussed in more detail later in this chapter. PIM systems record receipt and shipment transactions for all items as they occur in the system. However, these inventory systems may not be 100 percent accurate at a given point in time, because in many organizations the material receipt and product shipment files are separate, and the information contained within their databases may not be made available to an MRPII system until all other systems are refreshed according to their schedule. This refreshment cycle is usually twice per week in large and complex systems that use different software platforms. Another common inventory model is a periodic review model (PRM). In this model, receipts and shipments are periodically adjusted by a system. In a PRM system, there will always be a mismatch between receipts and shipments until the next review point when the system balances everything. However, both inventory management systems provide information that is useful in monitoring, managing, and improving inventory investment.

Inventory valuation also varies by organization. As an example, some organizations use a first-in-first-out (FIFO) valuation method in which the assumption is that materials are used in the order in which they are purchased for use. A FIFO valuation system follows the flow of materials through a system. The cost-of-goods-sold (COGS) calculation reflects a net calculation of beginning inventory plus purchases minus ending inventory. The last-in-first-out (LIFO) valuation method calculates the COGS based on the cost of the most recently purchased materials. Inventory valuation using a LIFO method varies, depending on whether the PIM or PRM inventory management system is used as the inventory model. A third inventory valuation method is average-cost valuation. Using this method, inventory value is calculated as the current inventory investment divided by the current inventory quantity.

Fraudulent inventory valuation practices may occur if an organization does not have the financial and operational controls necessary to ensure that receipts and shipments, as well as other inventory transactions, are accurately recorded during day-to-day operational activities. As an example, an organization can distort its financial performance by not correctly entering receipt, shipment, or inventory transaction information, or delaying their entry into the various systems that manage receipt, inventory, and shipment transactions. Process breakdowns such as these will distort an organization's estimates of its income, asset level, and cash flow. Inventory valuation problems can also occur through a variety of unintentional process breakdowns. However, these process breakdowns can be detected and eliminated using frequent cycle counting as well as Lean and Six Sigma improvement initiatives. In my book entitled *Lean Six Sigma for Supply Chain Management: The 10 Step Solution Process*, I describe in detail how to identify and eliminate process breakdowns related to inventory management practice.

Why Is Inventory Useful?

Table 14.3 lists several useful purposes of inventory. These include maintaining independence of internal operations or serving as a buffer against variations in external demand, providing flexibility in production scheduling, maintaining independence in supplier deliveries, and ensuring that economic order quantities and lot sizing targets can be met in practice. Maintaining adequate inventory levels to ensure operational independence is critical to maintaining a workflow's takt time. This is

Table 14.3 Why Inventory Is Necessary

Inventory levels are set to maintain service targets at each stage of operations.
1. Maintain independence of operations.
2. Absorb demand variation.
3. Absorb lead time variation.
4. Provide flexibility in production scheduling.
5. Store capacity to meet future demand.
6. Ensure per unit customer service level.
7. Absorb variation in supplier deliveries.
8. Maintain economic order quantities (EOQ).

particularly true at a system's bottleneck. Recall, from Chapter 6, that a bottleneck resource must be kept operating to maintain a system's takt time. Inventory quantities are created as a direct result of calculating an economic order quantity (EOQ). The EOQ formula was shown in Figure 13.4. The economic production quantity (EPQ) formula, which was similar to the EOQ, was also shown in Figure 13.4. Regardless of the reasons for inventory investment, systematic reductions in investment of a product can be made through Lean and Six Sigma projects that reduce lead time and demand variation, including forecasting error.

Each inventory classification has, by convention, its own service-level target. This is shown in Table 14.4. As an example, raw materials and WIP normally have higher service levels because the entire system depends on their availability. Finished-goods inventory service levels normally vary by a product's annual demand and gross margin. Low-volume products having a low gross margin will normally have lower per unit service levels than products having a higher annual demand and gross margin. The per unit service-level statistic may also vary by inventory classification. As an example, at a raw material and WIP level, a service target is expressed in units. But at a finished-goods level, a service target could be expressed in units, lines, or orders. It should be noted that for safety-stock calculations, units

Table 14.4 Types of Service-Level Targets

1. Customer: orders, lines, units, dollars (95–99.9%)
2. Work-in-process (WIP): units (99.9%)
3. Raw materials (RM): units (99.9%)

must be used in the calculation. Also, that a "line item" is defined as one product with an associated quantity. Orders consist of one or more line items, and each line item consists of units. Normally organizations use all three service-level metrics, depending on the context of their discussion. As an example, external customers speak in terms of order fill, logistics speaks in terms of line fill, and inventory managers speak in terms of unit fill.

As mentioned above, the service target of every product should be very carefully defined and calculated to ensure an organization can fulfill orders to customer requirements and has an optimum inventory investment level. Another important reason to carefully set per unit service targets would be if competitors are providing a higher service level to your customers. Once a service-level target has been set for each inventory classification, or specific items within a classification, inventory safety-stock calculations can be made to ensure product availability at the target per unit service-level target. "Product availability" implies that the probability of not running out of a product during its replenishment lead time, or the reorder point lead time equals its service level. In other words, if the per unit service-level target is 95 percent, the probability of not running out of a product will be 95 percent. One way to think of this concept is that for every 100 units ordered, 5 will be backordered if the per unit service level is 95 percent. However, this situation may be complicated by the fact that not every order contains the product in question, and different orders may require different quantities of a product. For this reason, order fill will usually have a lower actual service-level target. This is common in situations in which orders consist of several high-volume products that drive higher per unit fill rates of an order in spite of the fact that lower-volume products may be missing from the same order. In fact, the per unit fill rate in these situations could be 99 percent, but the order fill rate, as measured by the order being 100 percent complete or not, could be less than 50 percent. For this reason, as mentioned earlier, organizations often use three service-level metrics to measure fill rates of their products. However, inventory service-level targets are usually set on a per unit basis because to do otherwise would require conducting simulations in a manner described in Chapter 5. In these types of simulations, an order distribution, as represented by the products that make up an order, is modeled and service targets are set on individual products to ensure they will be available to fill orders 95 percent of the time. Inventory levels are then set based on an order fill rather than a per unit fill statistic.

Developing Models to Systematically Reduce Inventory

Developing inventory models provides an analyst with a better understanding of how an inventory system operates based on the analogous underlying structure and parameterization of the model. The development of simulation models to design and optimize processes was discussed in Chapter 5 under the topics of simulation,

Table 14.5 10 Key Steps in Developing Inventory Models

1. Organize a group of people who have been trained to build inventory and supply-chain models.
2. Develop a list of questions that the model's methodology can realistically answer.
3. Research and select off-the-shelf inventory modeling software or develop Excel-based versions.
4. Develop the underlying inventory model structure, including its goals and objectives, system constraints, and parameter settings.
5. Identify the inputs, outputs, and demographic data required to construct the inventory model.
6. Determine probability distributions of the parameters and metrics as well as their interrelationships.
7. Develop decision rules, including initial and final states of the inventory model.
8. Develop plans to obtain the necessary process data to test the inventory model's accuracy and precision.
9. Analyze the output of the inventory model using statistical tests to determine significance of key metrics.
10. Document and communicate the model's results and develop plans to implement solutions as practical.

queuing analysis, and linear programming. In its simplest form, a model is a representation of system's inputs and outputs, as well as descriptions of the internal operations of the process workflow. Table 14.5 lists 10 steps necessary to create inventory models. However, there are some disadvantages in using models. They may not be 100 percent accurate, and complex models may be costly to construct and interpret by an analyst. It is also important that a modeling approach be standardized because its methodology is iterative and knowledge of a system is gained through analysis of prior simulations. This implies an analyst should develop an experimental plan to systematically evaluate changes in system's inputs and their impact on its outputs. System modeling also requires parameter specification and an application of decision rules that mimic the process workflow. In particular, parameter specifications should be quantitatively linked to a system's transformation mechanisms in a probabilistic sense, in that random inputs are transformed,

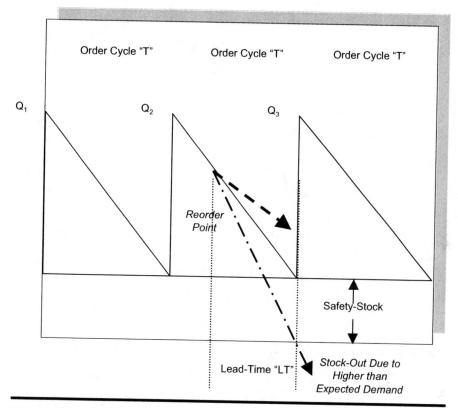

Order Cycle "T"   Order Cycle "T"   Order Cycle "T"

Q_1 Q_2 Q_3

*Reorder
Point*

Safety-Stock

Lead-Time "LT"   *Stock-Out Due to
Higher than
Expected Demand*

Figure 14.1   Perpetual inventory model (PIM).

based on their underlying probability distribution at a work task level, into an output or event of interest. In addition, a model's initial starting state and simulation time frame must be established by an analyst, as well as its ending state. Finally, throughout a modeling process, statistical tests must be conducted, by an analyst, to verify that a model accurately represents the actual process workflow.

The perpetual inventory model (PIM) is used by many inventory management systems, including MRPII, because inventory status can be monitored day to day in a perpetual manner. A common PIM is shown in Figure 14.1. At the beginning of an order cycle, T, an economic order quantity, Q_1, is ordered from a supplier. This quantity, Q_1, is expected to be linearly depleted during the order cycle, T. However, during the order cycle, the depletion rate may be higher or lower than the original forecast for an item. If demand is higher than expected, the item's reorder point quantity will be reached earlier in the order cycle, causing the MRPII system to release an order earlier than planned based on the original forecast. The reorder point quantity is calculated by multiplying the reorder point lead time, LT, by the average expected daily demand, d, and comparing the calculated quantity against

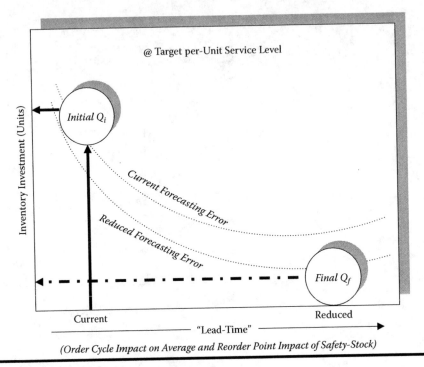

Figure 14.2   Graphical view of the PIM.

the current on-hand inventory quantity, with the safety-stock quantity netted out of the calculation. If the current inventory is equal to or less than a reorder point quantity, then another economic order quantity, Q_2, is placed by the MRPII system. Using this model, it can be seen that an optimum inventory quantity may vary during an order cycle, but its expected value is $\frac{1}{2} Q_1$ plus the safety-stock quantity, assuming a linear depletion rate proportional to forecasted demand. A qualitative depiction of a safety-stock quantity is shown in Figure 14.1.

Figure 14.2 is a generalized depiction of how an optimum inventory quantity for an item is impacted by its lead time and demand variation. In an actual inventory model, inventory quantities, their associated standard cost, and other demographic information, such as lead time, demand variation, location, supplier, and product type, can be aggregated across an entire inventory population. Once aggregated, sensitivity analyses can be conducted using an inventory model to determine where projects should be deployed to reduce lead time and demand variation. An inventory model also shows that for any given lead time and demand variation level there is an optimum inventory quantity for an item. Using this type of model, the on-hand inventory quantity of an item can be compared to its calculated optimum quantity to determine if there is excess or too little inventory relative to an item's per unit service-level target. The minimum information required to construct a PIM is shown in Table 14.6. However, additional information and conditions can

Table 14.6   10 Key Pieces of Information Required to Build an Inventory Model

1. Lead time information, including its variation
2. Demand information, including its variation
3. Unit service-level information
4. Descriptive information to allow segmenting of the database, i.e., facility, product group, customer type, supplier, etc.
5. Standard costing and pricing information, including returns and allowances
6. Related operational metrics, such as on-time delivery and inventory turns
7. Information related to forecast accuracy
8. Information related to original demand, shipments, and backorders
9. Average on-hand inventory quantities by item and location
10. Financial information related to excess and obsolete inventory

be incorporated into an inventory model to describe a specific system. Obviously, lead time is one of the most important variables to include in such a model because it is a major driver of inventory investment. Descriptive information is also essential to a model's construction because it is used to stratify an inventory analysis using factors such as product group, customer type, supplier, and facility, as well as other relevant factors, such as, forecasting accuracy, shipments, backorders, and obsolete and excess inventory quantities.

Table 14.7 shows how an inventory model's algorithm is constructed to identify an optimum inventory quantity. Using this information, it becomes obvious where additions or reductions in inventory investment are possible. Steps 1 and 2 of Table 14.7 calculate an optimum inventory quantity using a PIM assumption. Additional modeling assumptions, relative to safety-stock calculations, are shown in Figure 14.3 and Figure 14.4. Figure 14.3 shows how the total standard deviation (σ_t) is calculated using lead time and demand information. Interestingly, this safety-stock formula shows that some safety stock will always be required for an item unless the variation of lead time and demand is zero for both. Figure 14.4 defines the terms used in Table 14.7 and Figure 14.3. In Step 3 of Table 14.7, excess inventory is calculated by subtracting an optimum inventory quantity from the average on-hand inventory quantity. If the resultant number is positive, there is too much inventory for an item and its quantity should be reduced from its current level. However, there may be several complicating factors that prevent an organization from achieving a calculated optimum inventory quantity. These may include

Table 14.7   Inventory Analysis Algorithm

1. Safety stock = service constant$_k$*σ_t
2. Inventory$_{Optimum}$ = inventory$_{Average\ Demand\ during\ Order\ Cycle}$ + safety stock
3. Excess inventory = inventory$_{Actual}$ – inventory$_{Optimum}$
4. If Step 3 is positive, decrease inventory.
5. If Step 3 is negative, add inventory.
6. Excess inventory is calculated for every item and its location.
7. The excess inventory quantities are aggregated to the product and business unit levels using Excel pivot tables.
8. Extended standard cost is calculated for every item and its location.
9. Sensitivity analyses are conducted to evaluate the impact of potential lead time forecasting error reductions on inventory investment.
10. This enables customer service targets to be achieved with optimum (minimum) inventory investment, allowing strategic plans to be developed based on actual system capability, i.e., internal benchmarking.

$$\text{Total Standard Deviation } (\sigma_t) = \sqrt{\begin{array}{l}[\text{Average Lead-Time(LT)} * \text{Variation of} \\ \text{Demand}(\sigma^2_d)] + [(\text{Squared Average Demand} \\ (D^2) * \text{Variation of Lead-Time}(\sigma^2_{LT})]\end{array}}$$

Figure 14.3   Total standard deviation.

1. Total Standard Deviation (σ_t):   Combined Lead-Time and Demand Variation.
2. Average Lead-Time (LT):   The Reorder Point Lead-Time in Days.
3. Variation of Demand (σ^2_d):   Variation of Monthly Demand in Units.
4. Squared Average Demand (D^2): The Squared average Monthly Demand in Units.
5. Variation of Lead-Time (σ^2_{LT}):   Variation of the Reorder Point Lead-Time.

Figure 14.4   Variable definitions.

large lot sizes representing multiples of lead time, various operational issues, and obsolete inventory that precludes an organization from immediately reducing an item's inventory quantity. The purpose of this type of analysis is to identify items having too much inventory versus others having too little. This concept is shown in

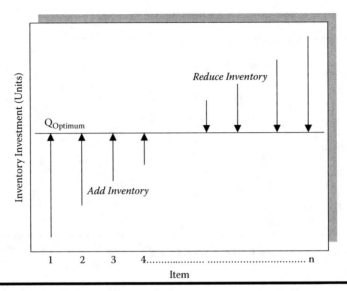

Figure 14.5   Balancing inventory quantities by item and location.

Figure 14.5, in which an item's inventory quantity is balanced relative to its optimum quantity. A particularly useful feature of the type of analysis is that optimum inventory investment can be aggregated upwards, item by item, through an organization to identify areas within an inventory population that have a significant amount of excess or obsolete inventory. This provides a financial justification to deploy Lean and Six Sigma improvement projects within these areas to reduce the drivers of high inventory investment by attacking their root causes.

Development of a useful analytical model requires that an organization build into its assumptions relevant characteristics of a system. As an example, every item in an inventory population must be described, at a minimum, by criteria such as those listed in Table 14.6 — lead time, demand variation, and relevant demographics such as product family, facility, customer, supplier, and similar descriptive factors that are important to an efficient aggregation of business benefits.

Although lead time was discussed in Chapters 5 and 6 and demand management in Chapter 8, we will expand our discussion of their impact on an item's safety-stock quantity calculation. Figure 14.6 shows two products with different demand patterns. One has a very irregular demand pattern, while the other has a periodic demand pattern that appears to be more consistent and predictable than the irregular pattern. Because the unit standard deviation of demand of a product (or item) is an important input into a safety-stock calculation, it is important to ensure it is estimated correctly. There are several ways to filter out the impact of irregular demand components. These range from statistically identifying outliers, as was shown in Figure 8.15, to truncating the time series using only observations from the most recent portion of its historical demand pattern. However, this latter

The Model Uses Monthly Standard Deviation of Unit Sales

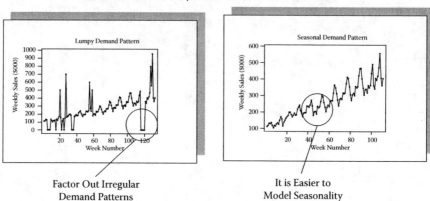

Factor Out Irregular
Demand Patterns

It is Easier to
Model Seasonality

Figure 14.6 Contrasting demand patterns.

action assumes that there is less variation in later portions of a time series. Lead time is an important input into an inventory model. As an example, Figure 14.7 shows that the MRPII system lead time is 10 days versus an actual lead time of 15 days. It is important that lead time be correctly estimated and used to calculate an item's optimum inventory quantity, as shown in Figure 14.2. Minimum lot sizes also have a significant impact on inventory investment. As an example, in Figure 14.8, the actual system lead time is 10 days. However, the minimum lot size is 20 days. The average inventory in this situation will be ½ × 20 days versus ½ × 10 days, or 10 days versus 5 days, although the reorder quantity for the item will be calculated using the actual lead time of 10 days. It is evident that a larger lot size requires an adjustment to properly calculate an optimum inventory quantity. Other adjustments may also be necessary to make an inventory model useful for analysis and improvement purposes.

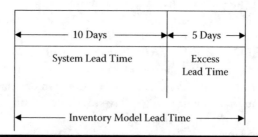

Figure 14.7 Impact of lead on the model.

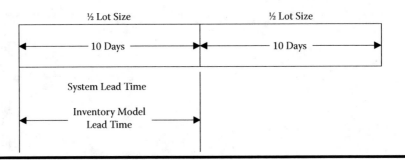

Figure 14.8   Lot size impact on inventory.

A PIM can be used in its current form, with minor adjustments, when modeling finished-goods inventories. It may also be relatively easy to apply to WIP inventories if material flows are not complicated. However, lead times must be carefully calculated based on a system's critical path and its bottleneck. However, in assembly-to-order and make-to-order (sometimes called engineer-to-order) systems, a system's network must be process mapped and its lead times carefully calculated to estimate the impact of a system's bottleneck, as well as the cash-to-cash cycle of the workflow. As an example, if a bottleneck is not managed well, WIP inventory will build up within a process workflow, or alternatively, one or more operations within a workflow may be "starved" for WIP inventory. The concept of bottleneck management was discussed in Chapter 6 and shown in Figure 6.6. Table 14.8 and Figure 14.9 expand this discussion relative to bottleneck analysis and the build-up of standard costs on inventory model accuracy. In summary, Table 14.8 shows that the lead time of the model should be considered from the viewpoint of the lead time of the system's critical path, and its demand should be based on a system's takt time. The inventory investment cost is then counted at each operation within the process workflow.

Table 14.8   Impact of Bottlenecks on the Model

1. Finished-goods inventory levels are set in anticipation of customer demand, including fixed, promotional, seasonal, trend, and random components.
2. Raw material and WIP inventories are set based on system constraints.
3. In other words, the demand is calculated from the bottleneck resource.
4. The inventory (safety stock) exists to ensure the bottleneck resource capacity is protected.
5. The bottleneck resource is tied to external customer demand.

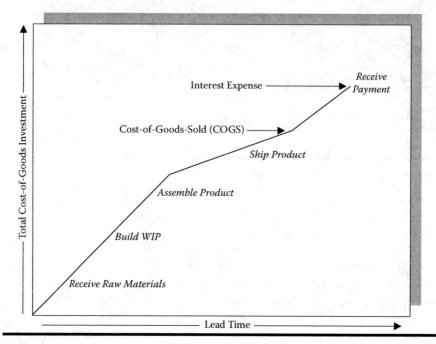

Figure 14.9   A make-to-order model.

Cycle-Counting Systems

Cycle-counting systems are used to periodically count inventory to verify that its actual to the stated book values are the same. Although there are several variations of cycle-counting systems, they have a similar purpose in understanding how materials and information flow through the inventory system. In this chapter, we will describe the basic principles and methods of cycle counting, the impact of poor inventory accuracy on investment, and the basic steps necessary to create an effective cycle-counting system. The benefits of an effective cycle counting system are listed in Table 14.9. The first benefit includes a timely detection of process

Table 14.9   Why Is Cycle Counting Important?

1. Timely detection of inventory errors enables immediate identification of the root causes for poor inventory accuracy.
2. Effective corrective action is made in a timely fashion.
3. There is minimal loss of time (avoids shutdowns).
4. System record accuracy is continuously improved.

Table 14.10   5 Reasons for Poor Inventory Accuracy

1. Poor training of employees
2. Poor document control of inventory transactions
3. Inaccurate databases or other sources of information
4. Poor physical control and identification of inventory
5. Damage, spoilage, or pilferage of inventory

breakdowns that cause inventory record errors. As an example, because an inventory auditor frequently reviews inventory accounts, there is a higher probability of finding errors. This facilitates the identification of the root causes for the inventory errors. Periodic cycle counting may also eliminate the need to shut down a facility if the audits show inventory account accuracy is high. Otherwise, external auditors may require an annual shutdown of an organization's operations to verify inventory record accuracy. Another important advantage of an effective cycle-counting program is the ability of an organization to continually improve inventory accuracy over time. There are many efficient ways to design and conduct a cycle-counting program. These will be described in the next few paragraphs.

Five major reasons for poor inventory accuracy are listed in Table 14.10. These problems can be prevented through the proper design of a cycle-counting system. Poor employee training is often real in nonstandardized processes to ensure that inventory transactions are timely and accurate. Standardization is necessary to ensure that the movement of materials and information through an inventory system is done only one way to prevent errors. In addition to standardization issues, employees must also be trained in the proper use of cycle-counting procedures. Because inventory management decisions are made using information such as on-hand inventory quantities, their locations as well as other relevant information in the databases of the warehouse management and inventory systems must be kept current and accurate. Reasons 1, 2, and 3 contribute to the poor physical control of inventory. Finally, if not properly protected, inventory may become damaged, spoiled, or stolen.

Table 14.11 list ten steps that, if taken, will improve an organization's inventory record accuracy. The first step is to process map all material and information transactions within an inventory and cycle-counting system. Figure 14.10 and Figure 14.11 show some of the common elements that are necessary to document the material and information flows through an inventory system. A second useful step in improving inventory accuracy includes developing policies and procedures that reflect the design of a new cycle-counting system. Finally, after a system has been designed and its procedures have been developed to show employees how to work within the system, the next step is to train the employees to effectively

Table 14.11   10 Steps to Improve Inventory Record Accuracy

1. Process map the system, including all transactions.
2. Develop procedures and policies.
3. Train people to work the system.
4. Determine initial inventory balances.
5. Conduct cycle counting audits to determine baseline inventory accuracy.
6. Establish the methodology (statistical sampling or other).
7. Develop cycle counting schedule.
8. Assign responsibilities.
9. Continually analyze cycle counting data to identify process breakdowns.
10. Eliminate errors and systematically improve the inventory system over time.

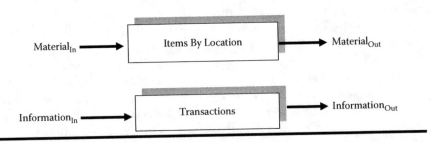

Figure 14.10   Goals of an effective cycle-counting system.

work with the new system, including its procedures, tools, and related methods. These steps and activities complete the creation of the cycle-counting system. In Step 4, the stated book values of inventoried items are verified by location and as they appear within a system. In Step 5, cycle counts are conducted to determine initial inventory accuracy for each item and location by comparing actual to stated book values. These steps and activities complete a baseline analysis of a new cycle-counting system. In Steps 7 and 8, a cycle-counting schedule and team roles and responsibilities are established. Finally, the new cycle-counting system is deployed and improvements are continuously made to increase the system's inventory record accuracy.

Table 14.12 lists several proven methods to make a cycle-counting system more efficient and accurate. "Leaning out" workflows is the most effective method to minimize or even eliminate cycle counting. This is because if there is not inventory

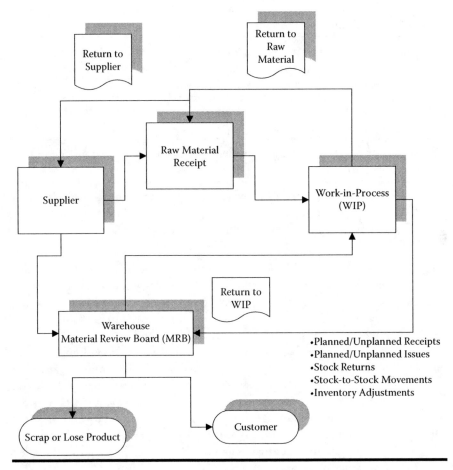

Figure 14.11   Mapping material and information flow through the system.

to count, or if it is well defined and placed within standardized containers such as Kanbans, then counting the inventory will be easy and accurate. A second efficient cycle-counting strategy is to count an item's inventory quantity when a warehouse management system (WMS) or similar system signals that an inventory location has a low quantity of inventory. If there is little or no inventory at a location, cycle counting will be simple and accurate. A third strategy is to reduce the complexity of a product's design to reduce the complexity of the product's bill-of-materials (BOM). The concept is that the fewer the items in inventory, the fewer the items that need to be part of a cycle-counting system. After applying these three strategies to reduce the overall amount of cycle counting and improve the accuracy of a cycle counting system, a next consideration is how inventoried items should be selected for the cycle counting audit. There are three common methods used to count inventoried items. The first method is to zone count the items. In this

Table 14.12   Some Cycle Counting Basics

1. The lower our inventory level, the less we have to count; i.e., lean out the system, reduce design complexity, count only when the records indicate minimum inventory is present at a given location.
2. Cycle counting assumes a representative sample is taken of the inventory. There are several ways to do this activity.
3. The major benefit is to find and systematically eliminate the root causes for inventory variation.
4. There are four basic types of cycle counting: (1) zone counting (100% audit), (2) simple random sampling, and (3) stratified sampling using an ABC classification, and (4) minimum variance stratification (optimum method).

method, all items are counted within a specified work area. The advantage of this method is that items not expected to be in the inventory will be discovered by the audit process. In effect, this is a 100 percent count of all the items within a selected zone. A second common method of cycle counting items is to randomly sample items using one of several sampling plans. A third method is to use an ABC classification into three groups based on volume or value, followed by simple random sampling within each classification. A fourth method is called minimum variance stratification (MVS). In MVS, an inventory population is arranged into several strata each having a minimum variance relative to any other stratification of the population. Minimum variance stratification is the most efficient of all the statistically based cycle-counting methods. It also results in significant resource savings, as well as providing statistical estimates and a confidence interval of the estimated inventory book value for an organization.

Excess and Obsolete Inventory Management

Unfortunately, in some organizations excess and obsolete (E&O) inventory represent a significant portion of total inventory investment. The reasons for high E&O inventory will vary, but some common reasons will be discussed in the next few paragraphs. First, organizations may have different definitions of what should be defined as excess inventory. Table 14.13 defines E&O inventory for our discussion. Also, the definition of excess inventory may vary within an organization based on annual sales volume of a product as well as its inventory turns. As an example, high-volume products may have excess inventory for a short period, but this excess can be eliminated quickly because the product is manufactured frequently. However, excess inventory associated with low-volume products can quickly become problematic if not monitored and controlled on a continuous basis. In this latter

Table 14.13   What Is Excess and Obsolete Inventory?

1. Excess Inventory is an amount of material exceeding expected sales over a specified time period. Every organization has its specific definition. A common definition is inventory amounts exceeding 12 months' supply.
2. Obsolete Inventory is material that cannot be sold at standard price. It might be sold at standard cost or lower through alternate distribution channels, or scrapped and written off the balance sheet.

Table 14.14   10 Key Reasons for Excess and Obsolete Inventory

1. Unexpected loss of major customers
2. Forecasting error due to inaccurate demand histories or poor modeling methods
3. Large lot sizes that are multiples of lead time
4. Inaccurate inventory data resulting in the ordering of excess inventory
5. Long or highly variable lead times
6. Product design changes that make obsolete previous versions of the product
7. Technology changes that make the product unnecessary
8. Undetected defects that result in the product being returned
9. Damaged and spoiled product, requiring it to be thrown out
10. Marketing package design changes that require rework or disposal of older versions of the product

situation, a common definition of excess inventory is more than 12 months' supply or some multiple of lead time. Obsolete inventory is inventory that cannot be sold at its normal selling price. In fact, it is usually sold at a very large discount from standard cost. If an inventoried item cannot be sold at any price, then it must be written off an organization's balance sheet at a loss. Some of the causes of obsolete inventory will be discussed below.

Table 14.14 lists several common reasons for excess and obsolete inventory. A common situation is one in which new products do not sell due to inaccurate marketing research or poor sales forecasting. As Chapter 3 demonstrated, it takes a rigorous and methodological approach to accurately estimate demand for a new product or improve its forecasting accuracy. This will be difficult if an organization does not apply standard marketing and forecasting tools and methods.

Organizational politics may also create E&O inventory. This situation occurs in the form of "pet" projects by management or decisions to overstate new product forecasts to "beef up" sales projections. These practices reduce operational efficiency because capacity is allocated to nonsaleable products. Cash flow is also reduced because inventory has been built but cannot be sold by an organization. Another problem occurs when forecasting error is high for new products. In summary, poor marketing research and sales forecasting practices are major contributors to E&O inventory levels. Another major contributor is the purchase of materials and components, or manufacturing them, in larger than necessary lot sizes. In theses situations, applying Lean tools and methods to "pull" materials through a system is the best way to ensure lot sizes are reduced correctly and subsequent inventory reductions will be sustainable over time. Transaction errors associated with ordering raw materials and components are another contributor to E&O inventory. These types of errors occur for a variety of reasons, including clerical mistakes and inaccuracies within an MRPII and related systems. As an example, if an MRPII system calculates inventory quantities at higher than required levels, additional inventory will be created over time. Breakdowns in cycle-counting systems also contribute to E&O inventory. A fifth major contributor to E&O inventory is very long product lead times, which become especially problematic when a product's design changes and increases the risk of inventory obsolescence due to packaging obsolescence. Inventory may also contain manufacturing defects that must be reworked or require that items be scrapped. Finally, inventory may become damaged as it moves through a system. As an example, in the food industry perishable products may become excess or obsolete when their shelf-life expires.

Figure 14.12 shows several methods that may prevent or minimize the impact of E&O inventory on an organization. The basics of these methods have been discussed in other chapters relative to reductions in lead time and demand variation and improvements in quality. Regarding any of these issues, a sales and operations planning (S&OP) team is an effective conduit through which chronic problems associated with E&O inventory can be identified and eliminated from a process.

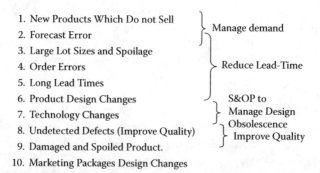

1. New Products Which Do not Sell
2. Forecast Error
3. Large Lot Sizes and Spoilage
4. Order Errors
5. Long Lead Times
6. Product Design Changes
7. Technology Changes
8. Undetected Defects (Improve Quality)
9. Damaged and Spoiled Product.
10. Marketing Packages Design Changes

Manage demand

Reduce Lead-Time

S&OP to
Manage Design
Obsolescence
Improve Quality

Figure 14.12   Prevention of excess and obsolete inventory.

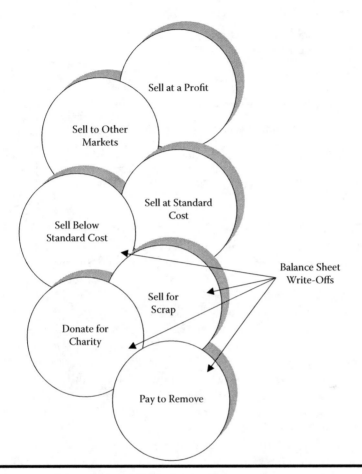

Figure 14.13 Disposal of excess and obsolete inventory.

In fact, using an S&OP team to prioritize projects to eliminate excess and obsolete inventory makes sense because the root cause of these problems usually span several organizational functions.

Figure 14.13 shows that the disposal of excess and obsolete inventory is a coordinated set of activities designed to attain the highest possible sales price for the E&O inventory. These disposal activities will also require coordination with several organizational functions, including marketing and sales, finance, materials, and logistics. The overall strategy of disposal is to first attempt to actually sell E&O product using discounts from the normal selling price if current sales will not be significantly eroded by a lower sales price. A second disposal strategy is to sell in other markets or countries. A third strategy is to sell the items at or below their standard cost. Finally, E&O material could be sold for scrap or donated to charity. The last activity shown in Figure 14.13 requires a total write-off of an inventory asset with payment for disposal. It should be noted that any sales price that is below

Table 14.15   Creating an Effective Program for E&O Management

1. Only cross-functional teams add items (S&OP)
2. Visibility to excess and obsolete inventory
3. Standard agenda item for S&OP meeting
4. Accountability by one person or team
5. Disposal program with responsibilities

an item's standard cost also requires a write-off to a balance sheet. Some methods to implement these disposal strategies include using the current sales force to sell E&O material, advertising in various industry media, or using Internet and other types of auctions to dispose of the E&O material. The ability of the excess and obsolete disposal team to sell the E&O material mitigates the E&O problem to an extent, but prevention of the problem is the best course of action for an organization.

When an organization finds that it has a problem with E&O inventory, one of its first reactions is to cut the inventory of high-volume or fast-moving items. This is because they have a large impact on inventory turns and investment. Unfortunately, most organizations fail to go to the next step and identify the root causes for the E&O inventory problem. As a result, the problem may become chronic, requiring an organization to cut supplier orders or manufacturing schedules every year. Table 14.15 shows some basic steps that would assist in reducing the incident rate of E&O inventory. A cross-functional team can be created that represents those organizational functions that either cause or are impacted by the problem. This team should have authority to take action to eliminate the root causes for an E&O inventory problem. In other words, representatives of various organizational functions must be in a position to make decisions for their respective functions. The entire population of E&O inventory must also be visible to an improvement team. Visibility is usually attained through data mining and analysis methods that are incorporated into an inventory model. An E&O team should also set a standard agenda for each meeting, and accountability should be given to one individual for each work task. This includes the responsibility to dispose of various E&O inventory items as necessary.

Unnecessary Product and Component Proliferation

Uncontrolled product proliferation is another major cause of inventory investment because the more products or services an organization provides, the larger the number of materials and components, as well as finished goods, that must be

Table 14.16   Impact of Product Proliferation on Inventory

1. Bill of material proliferation
2. Increased expediting
3. Increased material handling
4. Lower quality
5. Higher inventory

ordered, manufactured, managed, and controlled by its systems. Table 14.16 lists several negative impacts of uncontrolled product proliferation. These include bill-of-material (BOM) proliferation, resulting in a larger number of raw materials, WIP items, and products that must be managed, and thus a higher frequency of expediting, higher inventory, increased material handling, and lower overall quality due to various types of processing errors. A proven way to minimize product proliferation is to periodically review the numbers and types of product offerings. In particular, a goal should be outsourcing or discontinuing products with low profit margins. A profitability analysis should include a careful review of a product's profit and loss statement because low profitability may be due to factors related to sales adjustments or high standard cost, which can be improved. Figure 14.14 shows that this review activity should be an ongoing process. An E&O team should be appointed to continuously review product proliferation issues. In most situations, marketing

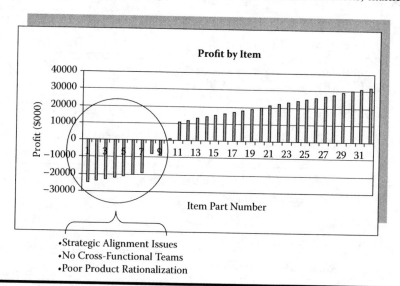

Figure 14.14   Use of profitability analysis to avoid product proliferation.

is usually a major contributor to a proliferation problem because its goal is to have a broad range of product offerings. On the other hand, at a BOM or component level, design engineering is a major contributor to proliferation problems. Product designs should be made as simple as possible using the design-for-manufacturing (DFM) methods discussed in Chapter 4.

Summary

Inventory is a major investment for an organization. However, organizations seldom work systematically to identify and eliminate the root causes of high inventory investment. This chapter presented several proven methods to help an organization to improve its inventory turns ratio and reduce its investment. Table 14.17 lists nine key concepts to more effectively manage inventory. The first includes managing products throughout their life cycle and adjusting inventory levels based on a product's life cycle position. A second is creating an inventory model to calculate optimum inventory quantities for every item in an inventory population to identify and reduce excess and obsolete (E&O) inventory. A third is identifying and eliminating the root causes for E&O inventory to enable an organization to systematically improve its inventory turns. Because inventory investment decisions require accurate data, it is also important that MRPII and other system data be well measured

Table 14.17   Key Concepts to Manage Inventory More Effectively

1. Manage a product throughout its life cycle to reduce inventory.
2. Create an inventory model to calculate optimum inventory quantities for every item in your inventory population.
3. Analyze the model to look for ways to reduce excess and obsolete inventory as well as to focus Lean and Six Sigma projects.
4. Ensure the MRPII and other system data is accurate to reduce inventory.
5. Develop effective cycle counting systems in which the materials and information flows are well standardized, mistake-proofed, and documented.
6. Count only when necessary by simplifying the system and using visual controls or when inventories are low.
7. Develop strategies to manage excess and obsolete inventory, including its prevention and efficient disposal.
8. Simplify product designs to reduce inventory.
9. Eliminate unnecessary products to reduce inventory.

by an organization. Effective cycle-counting systems should be developed to ensure that material and information flows throughout an inventory management system are standardized, mistake-proofed, and documented. Cycle-counting efficiency can be increased by only counting items when necessary through several strategies, including simplifying a system and using visual controls or counting when inventories are low. The last several recommendations listed in Table 14.17 is to attack the drivers of high inventory investment. In summary, an organization should develop strategies to manage E&O inventory by its prevention, efficient disposal of E&O, simplifying product designs, and eliminating products with low profit margins.

Suggested Reading

James W. Martin. (2007). *Lean Six Sigma for Supply Chain Management.* McGraw-Hill, New York.

Richard J. Tersine. (1994). *Principles of Inventory and Materials Management*, 4th ed. PTR Prentice Hall, Englewood Cliffs, NJ.

COLLECTING, ANALYZING, AND SHARING INFORMATION ACROSS A GLOBAL SUPPLY CHAIN

4

Chapter 15

Agile Project Management and Workflow Design

Competitive solution 15: Eliminate intermediaries from all process work-flows and share information using information technology.

Overview

The inherent capability of information technology (IT) to create and improve process workflows has dramatically increased within the past few decades. Improvements in IT capability are easily visible in reductions in cycle time from concept to market, a reduction in the number of design changes, a reduction in the percentage of rework costs to revenue, a reduction in the total customer life cycle cost, and a reduction in software design costs as a percentage of revenue. These metrics are also listed in Table 15.1. This capability has been enabled, in part, by the explosive growth of the Internet and personal computing, which have connected people to each other all over the world. These connections allow the exchange of information of all types, as well the collaboration of diverse work teams on projects spanning global supply chains. This increase in technological sophistication has evolved through the major IT areas shown in Figure 15.1. These include the business process management suite (BMPS), business process management (BPM), business process modeling and analysis (BPMA), business intelligence (BI), business activity monitoring (BAM), enterprise application integration (EAI), and workflow

Table 15.1   Competitive World Metrics: Business Process Management

1. Cycle time from concept to market
2. Number of change requests to final design
3. Percentage of rework cost to revenue
4. Total customer life cycle cost
5. Software design costs as a percentage of revenue

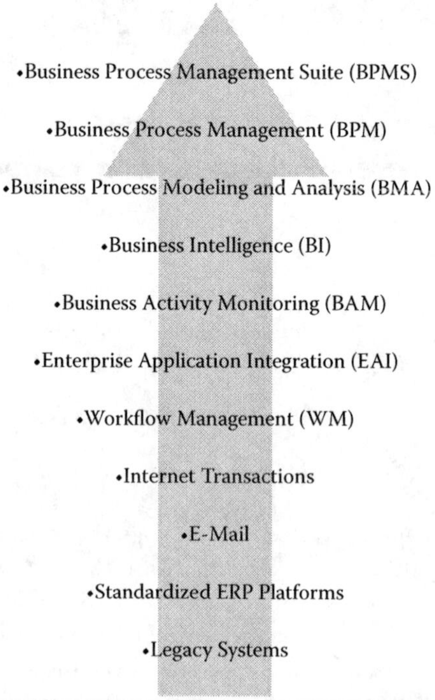

•Business Process Management Suite (BPMS)

•Business Process Management (BPM)

•Business Process Modeling and Analysis (BMA)

•Business Intelligence (BI)

•Business Activity Monitoring (BAM)

•Enterprise Application Integration (EAI)

•Workflow Management (WM)

•Internet Transactions

•E-Mail

•Standardized ERP Platforms

•Legacy Systems

Figure 15.1   Information technology (IT) increases organizational productivity.

management (WM), as well as Internet transactions, e-mail, and standardized enterprise resource planning (ERP) systems. In this chapter, our goal is to discuss these systems, including their tools, methods, and concepts, as they apply to the design and management of global supply chains.

The information technology systems shown in Figure 5.1 enable process monitoring, management, control, and improvement. As they continue to evolve over time, their focus and objective is to execute one or more of the successful IT characteristics found in Table 15.2. As an example, a direct advantage resulting

Table 15.2 10 Characteristics of Effective Information Technology (IT) Deployment

1. Automate work tasks and eliminate labor.
2. Analyze system data to enable decision making.
3. Share and leverage information across the supply chain.
4. Increase modularization.
5. Increase system configurability and flexibility.
6. Allow process monitoring.
7. Enable control of system components and work elements.
8. Integrate and coordinate globally.
9. Integrate supply-chain components.
10. Eliminate intermediaries.

from implementing IT can be seen across process workflows in the form of work task automation and elimination of labor from a workflow. In fact, this has been the justification for most IT implementations for the past several decades. However, in the past decade, the emphasis of workflow automation has shifted toward adding process workflow intelligence to the monitoring, management, and control of process workflows. This has been the impetus for the deployment of business activity monitoring (BAM), business intelligence (BI), business process modeling and analysis (BPMA), and business process management (BPM). Intelligent IT applications promote the sharing and leveraging of information across an organization's supply chain. Higher IT system modularization also enables higher system configurability and flexibility. In a different context, this was an important philosophy behind design-for-manufacturing (DFM) and Lean applications. Evolving IT has also fostered global integration and coordination as well as higher organizational productivity.

Business Process Management Suite (BPMS)

A BPMS integrates and coordinates the diverse components of an enterprise resource planning (ERP) system. Prior to BPMSs, these components were usually scattered across a supply chain. The BPMS enables users to exchange data throughout an ERP system and at several levels within the system to coordinate supply-chain management functions. These functions include the ordering, receipt, and shipment of products, their inventory transactions, customer transactions and service

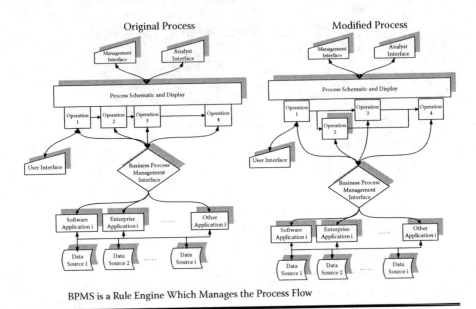

BPMS is a Rule Engine Which Manages the Process Flow

Figure 15.2 Business process management suite (BPMS).

interactions, related accounting functions, payroll functions, human resource functions, materials planning and purchasing activities, sales and marketing forecasts, and bill-of-material (BOM) control. There may also be other ERP functions that vary by specific industry. Systems configured in BPMS format can be easily reconfigured to match the modifications to the design of a process workflow as material or information flows change over time. Figure 15.2 shows a BPMS application, including its various integrative components. BPMS enables an organization to manage and dynamically change process workflow in an integrated manner rather than from a functional silo perspective. Because BPMS systems are process workflow focused, they are intimately linked to the workflows supporting customers and suppliers. However, customer and supplier interfaces remain relatively stable as internal workflows are modified by business analysts over time. An ability to modify a process workflow to satisfy changing customer needs and value perceptions, based on market segmentation, enables organizations to bypass the economy-of-scale paradigms discussed in Chapter 9 and provide products and services at lower per unit transaction costs than competitors due to their high-value content. This is shown in Figure 15.2 in the "modified process" which has been reconfigured.

Figure 15.3 shows a generic BPMS application as a hierarchal system configured to a process workflow. This includes a process workflow's rules and its design. As an example, some BPMS software is highly specific for industries such as financial services or call centers. In these applications, the software will usually be configured based on an organization's customer segmentation strategy. An allocation of organizational resources may be assigned differentially by a system based on

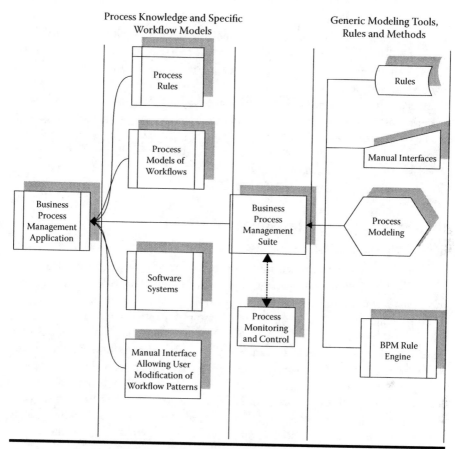

Figure 15.3 Business process management suite application.

a segmentation strategy. Based on the rules assigned to each customer segment. As an example, in financial service industries, customers may be segmented based on their net worth, they may also differ. One rule may state that highly affluent customers wait no more than 10 seconds for their telephone call to be answered versus customer segments having a small net worth and few assets. Also, the type of service that is provided may vary, with highly affluent customers being routed to call center agents who have been highly trained in the types of financial service products preferred by wealthier customers. The BPMS system can be configured to monitor and control the volume of call center traffic. Additional system capability may include product and service cross-selling or providing useful information to customers. Although, in many applications, BPMS software must be initially configured by IT, once deployed, it can be easily modified by business analysts with minimum IT support. The rules driving BPMS software can range from a few to several hundred, depending on the complexity of the process workflow monitored and controlled by a system. BPMS applications use three implementation elements. A first is manual modifications by its business users. In these situations, work lists can be modified by users to specify different process sequences of the workflow of products or services. A second implementation element could include specifically invoked software applications, such as a system forecast. Finally, a third implementation element could be one of several ERP applications. Also, the coordination and execution of BPMS software can be either internally managed or Web based and hosted by third-party providers. An important difference between BPMS and ERP software is that ERP software must be compiled and is somewhat inflexible in that its rules cannot be changed without direct IT support.

Business Process Management (BPM)

BPM is an IT management discipline allowing process workflows to be easily modified, monitored, and controlled by an organization. It provides a process-centric approach to workflow management. The business impact of BPM system implementation has been impressive, with reports of productivity increases exceeding 50 to 80 percent, a reduction in transition errors of 90 to 95 percent, and cycle time reductions exceeding 90 percent. Also, IT cost avoidance is an obvious business benefit because business analysts can reconfigure process workflows without direct IT support. BPM uses a concept called loose process coupling, which fosters reuse of low-level software components. In fact, system functionality is not 100 percent implemented in an initial application of BPM to a process, but rather, evolves over time as its applications are refined by users based on their process workflows. This characteristic of BPM applications reduces software development and maintenance costs.

Table 15.3 lists ten key functions of a BPM system. The list is hierarchal in that an initial focus of a BPM team is to capture the basic required functionality from an IT system perspective, and then work through lower levels of a system until its rules and procedures are standardized for the process workflow currently modeled by the BPM system. As a result, a BPM deployment process begins with determining business modeling specifications and the required user-specified design goals and objectives. Supporting higher-level system functionality are middleware applications, including specific system hardware, peripheral hardware components, software components, telecommunications equipment, and related system components. The system's components are integrated through language mapping, Cobra, and similar software specifications, which are used to enable dynamic scheduling and real-time modeling of a process workflow. Supporting this capability are modeling and metadata specifications using data warehousing information. Other related functionality includes structuring mechanisms for transaction management, data collection management, time management, object location, and security management. Additional features are object management group (OMG) domain specifications, which

Table 15.3   10 Key Functions of a Business Process Management (BPM) System

1. Business modeling specifications (business design goals and objectives)
2. Middleware specifications (components, software, telecommunications)
3. Language mapping specifications
4. Cobra specifications (dynamic scheduling, real-time modeling)
5. Modeling and metadata specifications (data warehousing, modeling)
6. Modernization specifications
7. Structuring mechanisms for transaction management, data collection management, time management, object location, and security management
8. Object management group (OMG) domain specification (operations by industry)
9. Embedded intelligence specifications
10. Security specifications

vary by industry, and embedded intelligence and security specifications. A BPM system provides higher-level system capabilities and flexibility through these normalized and standardized processes.

Business Process Modeling and Analyses (BPMA)

Business process modeling, including simulation, queuing, and linear programming models, has been in use for several decades. However, more recently, it has gained popularity due to an exponential growth in computing power, as well as a need for higher-process workflow productivity. Process modeling was discussed in Chapter 5, so only those topics related to BPM will be discussed in this chapter. Table 15.4 lists ten key steps that enable process models to be developed by business analysts. The first step is to create an electronic version of a process workflow. This task is similar to constructing detailed process maps of the material and information flows through the workflow being modeled by a business analyst. Once a process workflow has been analyzed, using a detailed process map of material and informational flows, workflow rules are designed to model the workflow's resources and operations, as well as their parameter distributions, levels, and initial states. Once a process workflow has been quantified, an analysis is conducted to estimate its baseline cost, time, and quality level. Also, a process workflow's operational

Table 15.4   10 Key Steps for Business Process Modeling and Analysis (BPMA)

1. Create graphical representation of the process.
2. Specify process rules to model the process flow, including its resources and their parameter distributions, levels, and initial states.
3. Develop baseline cost, time, and quality estimates related to the system's operational cycle times and capacity, as well as other specific characteristics, such as yield and uptime.
4. Specify transition state probabilities for each operation, including their frequencies and rates.
5. Analyze the output of every operation relative to its cycle time and queuing characteristics.
6. Analyze overall system performance related to bottlenecks, capacity constrained resources, system throughput rates, and operational cost.
7. Evaluate changes to the process, including elimination of non-value-adding operations.
8. Evaluate the addition of resources and modifications to the remaining value-adding operations.
9. Determine optimum solutions relative to the baseline scenario, including all optimized system parameters and their levels.
10. Document the modified process based on the organization's major quality and other standardization systems, such as ISO 9000.

cycle times, capacity, and other specific characteristics, such as yield and uptime, are estimated for use in the model. The specification of operational transition state probabilities for each operation, including frequencies and rates, is also required to construct a model. Once the model has been populated with the necessary quantitative information and its rules have been established, analysts can evaluate numerous alternative processing scenarios to determine the optimal parameter levels for each resource relative to bottlenecks, capacity constrained resources, system throughput rates, and operational cost. Additional simulations can be made to evaluate changes such as elimination of non-value-adding operations, addition of resources, and modifications to the remaining value-adding operations. Process modeling is a useful characteristic of BPM systems and provides benefits similar to those discussed in Chapter 5. Final modeling tasks include evaluation of alternative solutions, including their parameters levels. As a last activity, the modified process is formally documented based on an organization's major quality and other standardization systems, such as the International Standards Organization's (ISO) quality system document ISO 9000. These systems will be discussed in Chapter 16.

Business Intelligence (BI)

Business intelligence uses data-mining techniques and related tools and methods to search and aggregate information from diverse and disparate databases for subsequent analysis by an organization. The resultant information could be a simple listing of relevant characteristics associated with the questions prompting a search, or it could be fed into decision support software and related algorithms to analyze and provide information that can be used to answer more complex questions. BI methods rely to a great extent on meta-tags or common data strings, such as part numbers or customer numbers, and key search words and phrases. These pieces of data correlate one piece of information to another across disparate databases. Increasingly, algorithms are also being developed to text mine disparate databases without relying on meta-tags for coalescence and aggregation of data fields. An example would be typing in phrases to enable Internet searches of various specific topics. Specific BI strategies currently under development to improve the efficiency of extracting relevant data from disparate databases and sources include clustering, classification, and taxonomic-related methods. Applications of these methods include looking for data patterns that are associated with event outcomes of interest. As an example, we may find that a subset of customer service agents in a call center have high productivity and customer satisfaction ratings, but we cannot observe them either directly or in person. Using BI data extraction methods would enable us to extract key phases related to their customer interactions, which would provide clues as to what behavioral patterns are driving the higher productivity and quality levels. BI methods combined with decision support and process modeling capabilities can greatly enhance the ability of an operations manger, anywhere in the world, to optimally configure and manage his or her process workflows.

Business Activity Monitoring (BAM)

In addition to process automation and monitoring, BAM has several important business applications. These include increasing the visibility and status of a process workflow in real-time to enable real-time process control, rather than simply responding after the fact to process breakdowns occurring within various workflows within a global supply chain. Visibility implies an ability to drill down, from higher-level symptoms or poor performance, to the root causes. In these systems, an alarm event usually signals a process breakdown. In a sense, these system attributes are very similar to mistake-proofing, in which error conditions are eliminated to prevent defect occurrence. If prevention is not possible, then alarm systems are placed within a workflow to predict defect creation, based on models that incorporate process status information known to predict failures, or by detecting the creation of defects as soon as they occur. BAM is enabled through an integrated messaging system in which messages regarding workflow status are sent to all required recipients of the alarm messages. Alternatively, BAM can be used to proactively improve a process by understanding its metric levels and the reasons for their variation.

Table 15.5 lists ten key steps necessary to implement a BAM system. A primary prerequisite of a BAM implementation is development of a stable process workflow within a system. Once a workflow has been stabilized, its key metrics are identified, and used to show the status of various operations within the workflow. Decision rules and support systems are layered on top of the basic process workflow model to monitor and show process status information, including abnormal events. The software logic depends on an analysis of workflow metrics, including their patterns, dynamic thresholds, and trends. Notifications are sent to specified users with recommendations for action. Finally, BAM systems enable dynamic analysis of the reasons for system alarms, as well as an offline analysis of event occurrences.

Table 15.5   10 Key Steps to Implement Business Activity Monitoring (BAM)

1. Design workflow systems.
2. Develop lists of performance metrics, including their minimum, target, and maximum levels.
3. Develop rules to enable actionable decisions regarding process status and control actions.
4. Develop a hierarchy of process status notifications.
5. Determine response actions required of the persons notified of system status.
6. Automate manual processes related to the monitoring and control of workflows.
7. Extract operational and other business metrics from various parts of the organization.
8. Integrate metric status information using decision support systems into information related to system status with actionable recommendations.
9. Record system status changes and resultant process changes.
10. Enable drill-down analysis and reporting of process events.

Enterprise Application Integration (EAI)

EAI systems integrate the many functions of a global supply chain. These include purchasing transactions, accounts payable, accounts receivable, warehousing transactions such as order management, inventory transactions and material flow, finance applications, and production activity control (PAC), as well as other functions. Figure 15.4 shows that EAI systems coordinate the many IT system interfaces using just one interface between all systems and users versus previous configurations, which used numerous system-to-system connections. These previous systems were not able to integrate IT applications and databases to enable their information to be shared across a global supply chain. However, the high level of integrative ability in modern supply chains is due, to a large extent, to hardware and software standardization, as well as Web-enabling technologies. These IT system characteristics have been particularly effective in allowing users to access disparate systems to obtain information relevant to their business applications. The configurability and flexibility of disparate IT systems have been streamlined using EAI system integration in several application areas. These include intelligent routing of data

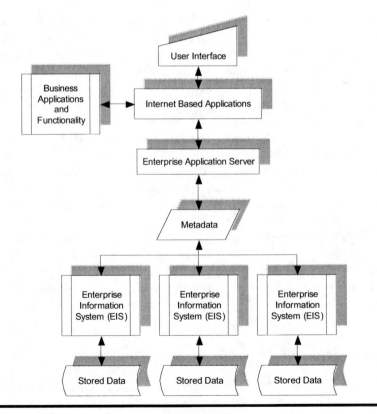

Figure 15.4   Enterprise application integration (EAI).

and instructions, middleware supporting messaging to monitor and control system applications, and an ability to manage several processes at a higher level.

However, there are several issues that inhibit full implementation of an enterprise information system (EIS). These issues are caused by lower-level incompatibilities between application programming interfaces (APIs), as well as the fact that EISs may use different programming models and client APIs. Legacy systems may also make integration difficult due to issues such as user security clearances, an inability to create new user accounts, and an inability to support new APIs. However, to the extent EAI can be deployed within a global supply chain, its benefits include workload balancing, asynchronous messaging, distributed communications, and business process application sharing, as well as the access and sharing of disparate databases. EAI systems support the business process management suite as well as business process modeling and analysis, business intelligence, business activity monitoring, and workflow management.

Workflow Management (WM)

The design and management of process workflows has dramatically evolved over the past several decades. In the first systems developed 20 to 30 years ago, a process workflow was manually represented using process maps and programmed by specifically using the process map as a representation of a process workflow. This situation inhibited users from easily changing actual workflow patterns of their processes based on updated customer or business requirements. However, in the past few decades, electronic versions of the manual process workflow systems have been created by users. These electronic process maps are easy to change in response to changing process workflow designs. This new ability has enabled users to change the design of their process workflows more frequently. In fact, in the past ten years, with increased computing power and global competition, electronic models of process workflows have been modified to enable dynamic analysis, using simulation, of system inputs and outputs. More recently, advanced adaptive systems can optimally reconfigure a system dynamically. This evolution in process workflow design and functional capability is shown in Table 15.6. In summary, the design, management, and control of process workflows has moved from highly manual systems to real-time control by the system itself. These advanced systems are characterized by an ability to reconfigure, add, delete, and modify workflow elements dynamically.

Agile Project Management (APM)

Agile Project Management (APM) has gained widespread acceptance as an important set of tools and methods that have been shown to be useful in managing

Table 15.6 Workflow Management (WM)

Capabilities	Methods	System Design
Manual workflow systems	Simple functions including calculating and checking text	Ad hoc design based on local content
Electronic versions of manual workflow systems	Standardized workflow and reporting	Workflow monitoring structure and definition, allowing systematic improvements to the workflow over time
Electronic version with modeling and analytical capability	Workflow optimization based on current or predicated data	Rapid ability to analyze workflow to create several alternative designs and optimize the best design relative to goals
Adaptive workflow systems enabling simple responses to changes in inputs	Workflow reconfiguration due to changes in system status caused by variation of input levels and external influences	The system changes the workflow design based on rules and logic programmed by its users to optimize certain critical outputs
Advanced adaptive systems that reconfigure a system dynamically to optimize several outputs	Optimization algorithms to ensure goal alignment and convergence	These advanced systems are characterized by an ability to reconfigure, add, delete, and modify workflow elements dynamically

software development projects. Many APM tools and methods have been adapted from analogous Lean tools and methods. Table 15.7 lists 20 key characteristics of APM. Many of these characteristics can be clearly seen as modified Lean concepts. As an example, some of these characteristics include aligning project goals and objectives, clearly listening to the voice of the customer (VOC), compressing software design cycles to obtain immediate customer feedback, and deploying Lean methods related to standardization and reusability of software components, as well as the visual communication of project status. Also, an APM team attempts to deliver the simplest possible workflow necessary to manage and control workflows at a local level.

Table 15.7 20 Key Characteristics of Agile Project Management

1. Ensure project goal alignment with users.
2. Ensure that communication tools and methods enable the open exchange of project status and relevant design information.
3. Use visual displays of project work tasks, activities, and milestones to manage and effectively communicate the project's status.
4. Create a rapid feedback system by using several incremental software development cycles to ensure the design functions properly in the user's environment.
5. Use feedback loops and checklists to manage the project.
6. Keep project milestone activities visible to keep project on track and within budget.
7. Communicate project information within the team and among stakeholders.
8. Clearly link design attributes with user and business benefits.
9. Clearly link team activities with specific outcomes that are aligned with the project's goals and objectives.
10. Develop as the baseline design the simplest possible workflow.
11. Minimize and eliminate unnecessary product attributes from the baseline workflow design.
12. Only add additional features as required by users.
13. Use the simplest possible software components in the software design.
14. Standardize all procedures and components of the software design.
15. Mistake-proof the software design to the extent possible.
16. Minimize the number of system components using modularization and off-the-shelf reusable software.
17. Ensure the software meets user requirements, i.e., works according to user specifications.
18. Keep next-generation requirements visible through development of multigenerational designs.
19. Identify key system management and control points to provide effective user interfaces.
20. Provide greater management and control of the final workflow design by its users at a local level.

Table 15.8   Key Concepts to Improve Workflow Management

1. Use business process management (BPM) systems to integrate your process workflow systems.
2. Apply BPM to enable market segmentation and to ensure your process workflows meet the voice of the customer (VOC).
3. Use Agile Project Management to coordinate and manage your information technology (IT) projects.

Summary

In today's competitive world, organizations should develop and deploy best-in-class business process workflow management systems to integrate their diverse supply-chain activities. Having an ability to create adaptable and flexible process workflow management systems enables an organization to satisfy customer needs even though markets are increasingly becoming segmented. Agile Project Management (APM) has been shown to be an effective methodology in coordinating and managing information technology (IT) projects. Table 15.8 summarizes key concepts that improve the management of process workflows.

Suggested Reading

Sanjiv Augustine. (2005). *Managing Agile Projects*. Prentice Hall, Englewood Cliffs, NJ.
Paul Harmon. (2003). *Business Process Change: A Manager's Guide to Improving, Redesigning, and Automating Processes*. Morgan Kaufman Publishers, San Francisco.
Ken Schwaber. (2003). *Agile Project Management with Scrum*. Microsoft Professional, Redmond, WA.

Chapter 16

Integrating Six Sigma Methods with Operational Strategy

Competitive solution 16: Measure and improve the quality of products and services to increase sales and customer satisfaction and lower operating cost.

Overview

High quality is a core competency every organization should develop to maintain high levels of customer satisfaction, retain current customers, and increase productivity. Effective quality management ensures that customer requirements and internal specifications are met by an organization in its day-to-day activities. Also, competitive quality management systems continuously improve the process capability of their process workflows to reduce failure expenses related to warranty, returned goods, scrap, and rework. Table 16.1 lists several of these systems' characteristics. In this chapter, we will discuss the roles of quality management from two perspectives. First, we will discuss quality management relative to its classic functions. This discussion will also include a very brief history of some of the more important quality initiatives that have been deployed over the last several decades. Unfortunately, much of this history will be left out of our discussion because our focus is Lean, Six Sigma, and operations management applications to global supply chains. A second

Table 16.1 Competitive World Metrics: Integrating Quality Improvements

1. Customer satisfaction and retention ratings
2. Percentage productivity increases due to quality improvements
3. Process capability of process workflows
4. Percentage of quality expenses spent on proactive versus failure activities
5. Warranty, returned goods, scrap, and rework expenses as a percentage of sales

goal of this chapter will be to discuss important quality tools and methods, from the basic to more advanced, with an emphasis on Six Sigma methodology.

Table 16.2 lists ten key quality system activities, from the identification of the voice-of-the-customer (VOC) to the development of new product or service designs. The design development process is enabled using reviews of customer requirements as specified in contacts, drawings, and specifications. In this regard, a quality assurance organization assists the product planning process and the concurrent engineering (CE) team with the development of process auditing and control procedures, as well as sign-offs of documentation related to a new product or service. These activities include inspection, the evaluation and approval of testing and measurement equipment and fixtures, inspection procedures, and training. Quality assurance also performs capability analyses and product or service performance analyses as required by a CE team.

Quality assurance has an integrative role to play in development of quality control plans based on new product designs and their process information. This role includes ensuring that failure-mode-and-effects-analysis (FMEA), specifications, testing schedules, product performance testing, and similar supporting documentation are developed on schedule by a CE team. Quality assurance also works with a CE team to verify that new products and their processes meet original customer requirements when evaluated using product and process capability analyses during preproduction trials. Quality assurance incorporates this information into an organization's quality control plans for its customers. Although these are the basic activities associated with many quality assurance organizations, they also engage in the day-to-day auditing, inspection, and management of production. Quality tools, methods, and concepts can be used as a proactive and strategic resource to dramatically improve organizational competitiveness. In fact, quality should be one of several core competencies every organization builds. These concepts will be the focus of this chapter.

Over the past 30 years, I have been involved with a number of quality initiatives. However, it has only been in the past ten years, through the Six Sigma quality initiative, that the various tools, methods, concepts, and theories of quality have coalesced

Table 16.2   10 Key Quality System Activities

1. Review customer requirements as specified in contacts, drawings, and specifications.
2. Assist the product planning process with the concurrent engineering (CE) team.
3. Assist in the development of the design and process procedures with the CE team.
4. Assist in the development of the sign-off documentation with the CE team.
5. Assist in the design and development of inspection, testing, and measurement equipment, fixtures, procedures, and training with the CE team.
6. Assist with capability analysis and similar performance analysis as required by the CE team.
7. Develop quality control plans based on design and process information, including failure mode and effects analyses (FMEAs).
8. Develop auditing procedures.
9. Assist in product and process verification with the CE team as specified by customer requirements.
10. Provide feedback to the CE team on production information and product and process capability as determined by the quality control plan.

into a coherent whole. Admittedly, many quality initiatives have used subsets of quality tools and, in particular, the simpler and graphically oriented quality tools and methods. As an example, prior to the increased popularity of Six Sigma starting in the mid-1990s, I attended seminars on control charting, quality function deployment (QFD), experimental design, failure-mode-and-effects-analysis (FMEA), quality control plans, and many other similar one-off-type seminars. The problem with all this one-off information was that it was not integrated into a coherent whole. Also, the tools and methods did not appeal to higher management levels. In this highly technical and acronym-filled environment, most organizations relegated quality assurance to their back rooms.

To complicate matters, there are many competing interests in the quality field that tended to reinforce their versions of the various improvement methods. However, in recent years, the diverse interests and approaches to quality assurance and improvement have borrowed heavily from each other and their message is becoming similar. As an example, Six Sigma became Lean Six Sigma, and the International Standards Organization (ISO,) which was originally a set of auditing activities, developed tools and methods to improve ISO-approved systems. Although there are many other examples of coalescence, the Malcolm Baldrige Award is probably the most visible. The Malcolm Baldrige process is a series of standards, policies, procedures, and philosophies to which every organization should aspire. However, to say that an organization can be competitive based on this narrow set of activities was shown to be an exaggeration. As a result, Malcolm Baldrige criteria have been modified over the past several years to make its evaluation criteria more holistic and proactive from a process workflow improvement perspective. These are all great initiatives, but the problem is that they are driven by consultants and individuals who have a vested interest in promoting narrowly focused philosophies characterized by specialized tools, methods, and concepts. In Table 16.3, we have listed some of the more common quality initiatives, along with comments of their major and unique characteristics. Entire books have been written describing each of these initiatives. Because in this chapter our intention is to promote a bias for process improvement and competitiveness, we will present the discussion from the viewpoint of Six Sigma tools, methods, and concepts. This implies that your organization has also deployed ISO, AIAG, Malcolm Baldrige, Lean, and Total Quality Management (TQM), because these are all very important quality management and improvement initiatives. Lean was discussed in Chapter 6, TQM will be discussed in this chapter, and ISO, AIAG, Malcolm Baldrige, and similar initiatives will be discussed briefly in Chapter 20.

Deploying the Six Sigma Improvement Model

The Six Sigma improvement model is designed to dramatically improve process performance over current baselines. In fact, it was originally conceived by Motorola using Dr. Joseph Juran's breakthrough performance model. In this regard, it is considered to be one of the most successful process improvement models ever conceived, because it methodically enables a systematic analysis of current process performance and provides a detailed road map to analyze and eliminate the reasons or root causes for poor process performance. The objective of Six Sigma is to improve the ability of an organization to satisfy the voice-of-the-customer (VOC) and voice-of-the-business (VOB) to increase organizational competitiveness on a consistent basis. Figure 16.1 shows that the Six Sigma strategy is to drive operational excellence across an organization from a business unit to a local process workflow level. This deployment process is generally faster than that of Total Quality Management (TQM), but it depends on a well-defined and executed project focus. Figure 16.2 shows some of the major differences between TQM and Six Sigma. However, this does not mean dramatic and fast process improvements cannot be obtained using TQM. TQM usually focuses on a small portion of a process to eliminate a problem's root causes using simple quality tools and methods. From this perspective, many TQM activities have actually migrated into the Six Sigma

Table 16.3 Current Quality Programs and Methods

Deming–Shewart	Dr. W. Edward Deming advocated that the system was the problem, not the people. Deming and Walter Shewart proposed a process improvement model called the Deming wheel, which consisted of four phases: plan, do, check, act.
Juran	Key concepts of Dr. Joseph Juran where quality improvement could be achieved using continuous improvement or breakthrough methods; quality experts need to speak the language of senior management and ensure quality is customer and business focused; and organizations should invest in preventive measures to reduce failure costs associated with quality, such as scrap, rework, and warranty expenses.
Total Quality Management (TQM)	A continuous improvement program that is designed to involve everyone in an organization to improve the process, using simple quality tools. Although the concept is good, deployments are usually targeted at isolated processes. Customer and business benefits are sporadic.
Continuous improvement	A variation of the TQM concept, but it has been recently revitalized by the toolsets contained in Lean and Six Sigma.
Kaizen events	Similar to continuous improvement, except the process analysis and improvements are focused on a small portion of a process or work stream in a short period, resulting in immediate benefits to an organization. Simple Lean and Six Sigma tools are used in Kaizen events.
Lean	A process improvement program that focuses on elimination of process waste, simplification, standardization, and mistake-proofing the process to improve quality.
Six Sigma	A phased problem-solving methodology to improve quality, characterized by five phases: define, measure, analyze, improve, and control. It was initially developed at Motorola using Juran's breakthrough method.
Malcolm Baldrige Award	A system for measuring organizational performance relative to measurement and control of processes. It measures how well procedures are followed based on a point system. Quality is improved through an auditing process that identifies process breakdowns.

(continued on next page)

Table 16.3 (continued)   Current Quality Programs and Methods

International Standards Institute (ISO)	A group of standards that are mandated, including that an organization strictly follow its procedures. It defines a minimum level of quality an organization must maintain to sell its products across the world.
Automotive Industry Action Group (AIAG)	The AIAG system consists of five sets of deliverables for designing and producing a product or service: (1) AIAG quality product planning and VOC, (2) AIAG product design and DFM, (3) AIAG process design and development, (4) AIAG product and process validation, and (5) AIAG control plan methodology.

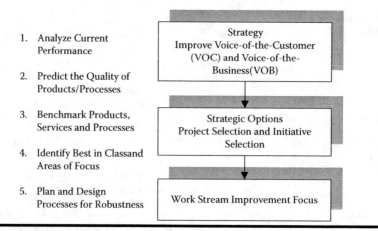

1. Analyze Current Performance

2. Predict the Quality of Products/Processes

3. Benchmark Products, Services and Processes

4. Identify Best in Classand Areas of Focus

5. Plan and Design Processes for Robustness

Strategy
Improve Voice-of-the-Customer (VOC) and Voice-of-the-Business(VOB)

Strategic Options
Project Selection and Initiative Selection

Work Stream Improvement Focus

Figure 16.1   Quality improvement model.

green belt role. However, Six Sigma offers several business advantages that were absent from TQM deployments over the past several decades. The first advantage of Six Sigma is a top-down alignment of improvement activities versus the bottom-up approach characteristic of TQM. A second advantage is the fact that Six Sigma has provided significant business benefits for organizations using its tools, methods, and concepts. As a result, TQM has been largely supplanted by Six Sigma, from a philosophical viewpoint, in the past several years in many organizations. However, Six Sigma has often been deployed as a project-based initiative and must be fully integrated within an organization's quality assurance and management systems. In fact, in organizations that do not have a formal quality organization, reliance on a Six Sigma deployment alone to improve and sustain process improvements would be risky. In the absence of formal quality systems, Six Sigma process improvements will deteriorate over time.

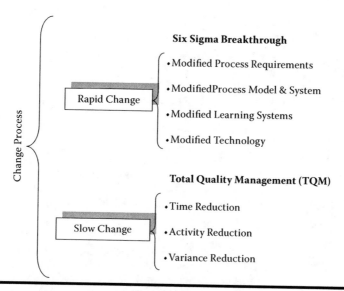

Figure 16.2   Rate of process improvement.

Transition from Tactical Problem Solving Towards Business
Process Development and Customer Excellence

Six Sigma Goals	**Six Sigma Vision**
•Understand Customer Requirements	•Integration Into Culture
•Reduce Process variation	•Maturity to "Six Sigma" Performance
•Center process on Target	•Six Sigma Skills Enable Learning Organization
•Focus on cause not Symptom	•Six Sigma Used in Developmental Training
•Ensure improvements are Sustained	

Figure 16.3   Key characteristics of Six Sigma.

As mentioned above, Six Sigma has been designed as a breakthrough initiative. The origin of the Six Sigma program was deployment at Motorola of Dr. Joseph Juran's concept of breakthrough improvements in quality, and aligning projects with goals and objectives important to senior management to secure resources for quality improvement activities. Figure 16.3 shows several important characteristics of an effective Six Sigma program. These goals are achieved using the five Six Sigma phases: define, measure, analyze, improve, and control (DMAIC). The DMAIC phases are further expanded into 10 to 12 steps (depending on the consulting organization), with each having key deliverables. Over an extended deployment, an organization may actually mature into a true Six Sigma-performing culture.

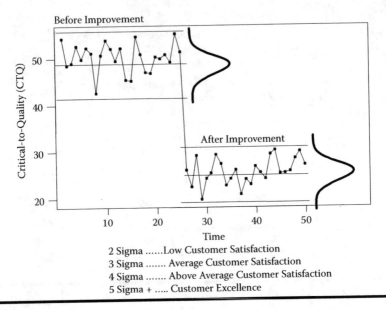

Figure 16.4   What is Six Sigma?

However, this will only occur if an organization has a quality assurance and management infrastructure that can support the daily management of a Six Sigma deployment to enable its continual improvement over time.

The DMAIC methodology is applied to improve the performance levels of critical-to-quality characteristics (CTQs). Figure 16.4 shows the breakthrough concept applied to a single CTQ. Before application of the DMAIC methodology, a CTQ or key process output variable (KPOV) exhibits variation around its average (or mean) level. There may also be periodic disruptions occurring within a process that "spike" the CTQ, causing nonrandom patterns. These are called assignable causes of process variation. In the absence of assignable causes of variation, the process exhibits common cause variation or random variation of the CTQ. The concept of assignable versus common cause variation will be discussed later in this chapter in the context of control charts. From a Six Sigma perspective, a key concept is that a process that exhibits common cause variation will remain at its current level (good or bad from a customer's viewpoint) unless the root causes of the common cause variation are investigated and eliminated through data collection and analysis. However, this is a very difficult task without deployment of focused resources and projects using the DMAIC methodology. Figure 16.4 also lists some common "Sigma" levels correlating to customer satisfaction. These Sigma levels will be discussed in more detail later in this chapter. As an example, Table 16.12 correlates Sigma levels to percentage defect levels.

The DMAIC phases are usually broken down as shown in Table 16.4 by their deliverables and the common tools and methods used in each phase. However,

Table 16.4   DMAIC Problem-Solving Methodology

Phase	Deliverables	Tools and Methods
Define	Define the problem, including its extent, occurrence frequency, customer, and business impact	Problem statement High-level process mapping Metric analysis Cost of quality (COQ) analysis
Measure	Verify the CTQ can be measured accurately and precisely, determine baseline capability of the CTQ, and develop a data collection plan on the X's, and the CTQ	Problem statement High-level process mapping Metric analysis Cause and effects (C&E) Failure mode and effects (FMEA) Measure system analysis (MSA) Basic statistics Process capability Cost of quality (COQ) analysis
Analyze	Eliminate the trivial X's and develop a short list of key process input variables (KPIVs) impacting the CTQ or key process output variable (KPOV)	Basic statistics Graphical analysis tools Hypothesis testing Contingency tables One-way ANOVA Multi-vari analysis Correlation Regression Detailed process map
Improve	Experiment with the KPIVs and KPOVs to determine their interrelationships and select the best combination of KPIV levels to optimize the KPOVs	General full factorials 2^k full factorials Fractional factorials Response surface designs
Control	Ensure the improved process will be sustainable and remain in control	SPC Mistake-proofing Measurement control Maintenance Training Validate capability Control plans Final COQ review

many of these tools and methods are used in more than one DMAIC phase. We will discuss many of the tools and methods listed in Table 16.4 relative to the questions they can answer. Important concepts shown in Table 16.4 are that a process problem must be well defined relative to its extent, occurrence, and impact on an external customer. Relative to methodology, a Six Sigma team must estimate accurate CTQ baselines using measurement system and capability analyses, and collect and analyze data related to the process problem. This is done in sequence by the DMAIC phases. In the improve and control phases of a project, a process workflow is modified based on the root cause analysis and experimentation to move the CTQ to a new performance level. Using a Six Sigma improvement model, we will discuss the tools and methods of each DMAIC phase.

Define Phase: Basic Tools

There are many tools and methods available to help clearly define the VOC and VOB. These tools and methods range from the use of financial and operational analyses and value stream mapping to the application of marketing research methods. Many of these methods were discussed in Chapters 3 to 8. In Chapter 17, we will discuss how to use the tools and concepts presented in all these chapters, as well as this chapter, to perform operational assessments to identify and refine project definitions to improve an organization's competitiveness. Our goal in this chapter is to assume a project exists and needs refinement, and should be solved using an application of the DMAIC methodology. In Table 16.5, three important tools are listed to help a team define a project more clearly from VOC and VOB perspectives. These tools are a SIPOC, a project charter, and a team. Recall from Chapter 3 and Figure 3.12 that a SIPOC is an acronym representing supplier–input boundary–process–output boundary–customer. It is used to more clearly define where projects exist and to help select team members from suppliers, customers, and others who are within the process. A project charter describes a project from several perspectives,

Table 16.5   Define: Basic Tools

SIPOC	A high-level process map showing the inputs and outputs among suppliers, the process, and customers, as well as the metrics at the input and output boundaries, i.e., supplier–inputs–process–outputs–customer.
Project charter	A formal document either electronic or in paper format that describes the project's objective, its anticipated customer and business impacts, including their timeline, the required resources, and the project's team members.
Quality improvement teams	Two or more individuals assigned to a project and having roles and responsibilities necessary to complete the project or associated work.

including the problem it must eliminate, customer and business impact, estimated business benefits, and the resources required to move it forward. Team members are another important part of a project definition process. A project's team members are selected based on where the project is focused within a process workflow, as well as their specific knowledge of the workflow under investigation. Once it is formed, an improvement team works through each of the project deliverables as specified by the DMAIC phases and key deliverables listed in Table 16.4 and Table 16.6. Project definition requires identifying customer satisfaction elements, business benefits, and their strategic alignment. Also, a project's objective should be narrowly focused to ensure that it can be executed according to the project's deployment timeline. However, the statement "narrowly focused" does not refer to business benefits, but rather, to the project's time frame and required resources. In other words, a project saving $5 million and taking four months may require the same resource commitment as one saving $1,000 and taking the same four months. The project's definition should also include a historical baseline of a project's CTQ metrics, as well as its required resources and team members. Figure 16.5 lists several operational areas in which projects have been successively deployed within organizations. In fact, wherever an existing process workflow is not achieving its entitlement or its deigned performance level, there may be an opportunity to create DMAIC improvement projects.

SIPOC

A SIPOC, if properly quantified, helps identify new or refine existing projects. This concept is shown in Figure 16.6, in which a SIPOC is used to identify several potential projects or to more clearly define a particular project relative to significant customer or business benefits. As an example, there are four business metrics listed in Figure 16.6. These metrics are broken down for each of the four operations 1, 2, 3, and 4. Depending on organizational priorities, 16 projects can be deployed within this process at this point in the analysis. These projects would reduce cycle times, defect rates, and costs, and improve yields. Using this project deployment concept, a team can be assigned to improve any one of these metrics. If a SIPOC does not currently exist, then a team can use the questions listed in Figure 16.6 to begin constructing its SIPOC and quantify it in a manner similar to that shown in Figure 16.6.

Project Charter

A project charter is a formal document that communicates to an organization the problem a team is investigating. The charter has several important components, which were discussed in Chapter 7 and shown in Figure 7.9. We will discuss a

Table 16.6 Key Deliverables of a Six Sigma Quality Project

1. Project title
2. Black belt name
3. Team picture
4. Problem statement
5. Project objective
6. Process baseline
7. High-level process map
8. C&E analysis
9. Failure mode and effects analysis (FMEA)
10. Measurement systems analysis (MSA)
11. Capability analysis
12. Business benefit verification
13. Elimination of the many trivial input variables
14. Section of the few vital variables using root cause analysis and statistical tools
15. Final solution
16. Integrated control plan
17. Mistake-proofing strategy
18. MSA control plan
19. Instructions and training plan
20. Verified business benefits
21. Next steps
22. Project translation opportunities
23. Lessons learned
24. Proof of process control

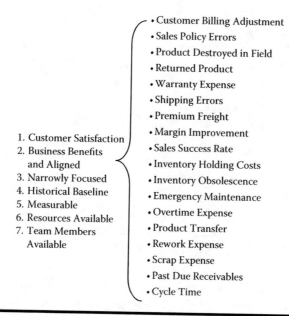

1. Customer Satisfaction
2. Business Benefits and Aligned
3. Narrowly Focused
4. Historical Baseline
5. Measurable
6. Resources Available
7. Team Members Available

- Customer Billing Adjustment
- Sales Policy Errors
- Product Destroyed in Field
- Returned Product
- Warranty Expense
- Shipping Errors
- Premium Freight
- Margin Improvement
- Sales Success Rate
- Inventory Holding Costs
- Inventory Obsolescence
- Emergency Maintenance
- Overtime Expense
- Product Transfer
- Rework Expense
- Scrap Expense
- Past Due Receivables
- Cycle Time

Figure 16.5 Project definition: how to select projects.

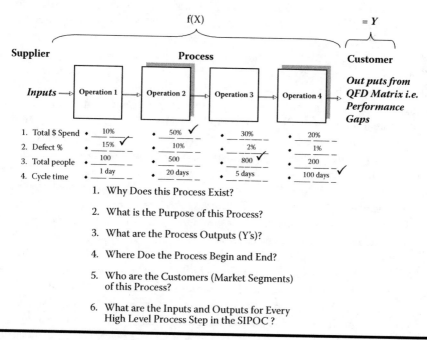

1. Why Does this Process Exist?
2. What is the Purpose of this Process?
3. What are the Process Outputs (Y's)?
4. Where Doe the Process Begin and End?
5. Who are the Customers (Market Segments) of this Process?
6. What are the Inputs and Outputs for Every High Level Process Step in the SIPOC ?

Figure 16.6 Project definition: how to build a SIPOC.

Primary Metric-A Yard Stick Used to
Measure Project Success...
Consistent with the Problem
Statement And its Objective...
Includes Two Time Series: Baseline
Performance (Average Over Past 12
Months) and Actual Performance
Versus the Project's Objective.

Business Metric
Project Metric
Financial Metric

Secondary Metric-Used to Drive
The Right Team Behavior... Tracks
Potential Negative Consequences of
the Project Improvements... More
Than One Secondary Metric May be
Required.

Figure 16.7 Project definition: business metrics.

project charter in more detail in this chapter. The first key component of a project charter describes the process in which the project will be deployed, its starting and ending dates, as well as its project leader, champion, and process owner. A second key component describes its metric definitions as well as their current performance levels. Metrics must be carefully defined and should have the characteristics shown in Figure 16.7. There are two basic categories of metrics: primary and secondary. The project team is focused on primary metrics, but it does not want to inadvertently induce a deterioration of the secondary metrics, or, as some organizations call them, the conscience metrics. A primary metric is represented by three submetrics. The first submetric is a business metric. The business metric is linear and can be aggregated across an organization. As an example, an inventory turns statistic can be calculated for every product, facility, and division of an organization. Recall that an inventory turns ratio is calculated as the cost of goods sold (COGS) divided by the average inventory investment necessary to support the associated sales level. The higher an inventory turns ratio, the lower the required inventory investment that is necessary to support sales. The financial metric is specified in terms of money. In the inventory turns example, the inventory investment would be a financial metric used to measure a project's success. However, as a team works through a root cause analysis, the reasons or root causes for low inventory turns or high investment will be identified and eventually eliminated by the team. These root causes could be due to several different operational factors, including lead time, poor forecasting, and other process breakdowns. The result of a root cause analysis may identify several projects, each having a different operational metric or project metric, which is tied to a project's business, financial, and secondary metrics. In other words, a team might focus its project on lot size reductions or other lower-level operational metrics to improve inventory turns and lower investment. In this inventory example, a

Table 16.7 Project Definition: Characteristics of Effective Problem Statements

Effective Problem Statements
1. Complete description of a problem
2. Shows current baseline performance levels of metrics
3. Describes customer requirements
4. Links to business objectives
5. Contains no solutions
6. Is quantified
7. Defines its measurement sources
Ineffective Problem Statements
1. Customer requirements not known
2. No linkage to business objectives
3. Quantification not reliable
4. Measurement sources not defined
5. Little linkage to customer metrics
6. Solutions or causes stated in advance

compensating or secondary metric would be maintenance of required customer service levels. In other words, we do not want to lower inventory investment without adequate process improvements to avoid deteriorations of customer service.

Concurrently, as a team begins refining its project's definition, it needs to create a logical statement of a project's business problem. Table 16.7 shows several characteristics of good versus poor problem statements. A good problem statement should communicate to an organization a complete description of a problem and strategically link it to senior management's goals and objectives. An effective problem statement contains no solutions to bias a root cause analysis. In Figure 16.8, additional characteristics of effective problem statements are shown. Figure 16.8 also shows how a poor problem statement can be improved through a discussion among the team members. Once a problem statement has been refined by its project team, a project's objective is refined in a similar manner. Although a problem statement communicates important information to an organization, several smaller projects may be required to significantly reduce a larger problem. As an example,

Problem Statement

1. Focus the Team on a Process Deficiency.

2. Communicate the Significance to Others.

3. Does not Contain Solutions or Causes.

4. Is as Quantified as Possible.

A Poor Problem Statement

Product Returns Are Too High And will be Reduced by Analyzing First And Second Level Pareto Charts.

A Better Problem Statement

Product Returns are 5% of Sales, Resulting in a Negative Profit of $ 5m and Reduced Market Share of 10%.

Project Objective

1. Part of the Problem Statement.

2. Address Problem Statement.

3. Quantify Performance Improvement.

4. Identify Timing.

A Poor Project Objective

Reduce Product Returns by Implementing Individual Performance Measures and Objectives.

A Better Project Objective

Reduce Returns of Product Line xyz from 5% to 2.5% of Sales by Year End to Reduce Overall Business Unit Returns by 1% and Save $ 1 MM.

Figure 16.8 Project definition: how to write a problem statement and objective.

the reasons for a high inventory investment might be due to several different root causes, as described above, with each one requiring a separate project. Each project would also have a slightly modified project objective. These project objectives would be aligned with a higher-level problem statement that is common to all the projects.

Quality Improvement Team

Members of an improvement team have different roles and responsibilities. Some of the roles are directly related to project execution, whereas others are indirect. As an example, in Table 16.8 several team roles are listed based on their contribution to an improvement team. These roles may have other names, depending on the context of the discussion. A project manager may also be called black belt, or master black belt in some situations. Referring to Table 16.8, we see that a project champion breaks barriers for a team and secures the resources necessary to move a project through an organization. The role of the process owners is to work with a DMAIC team to ensure that it remains on track. Process owners also provide resources to a team. A project manger or black belt leads a team through the DMAIC methodology. The team may also have ad hoc members from finance, information technology (IT), and other functions within an organization.

Table 16.8 Quality Improvement Teams, Including Roles and Responsibilities

Project champion	Breaks down barriers inhibiting the project
Process owners	Manage day-to-day process activities and control local resources
Project manager	Leads the team and works with the champion and process owner
Team members	Support brainstorming, data collection, data analysis, and process improvement work
Financial representative	Validates project definition, alignment, and financial benefits
Other functional experts	Provide information, advice, or specific resources, such as data extractions for the team

Measurement Phase: Basic Tools

The tools and methods of the measurement phase have been gathered from several other quality disciplines for the purpose of ensuring that the CTQ baselines and their performance gaps, relative to required targets, have been accurately identified and measured. Also, for data collection activities the team must brainstorm potential input variables, or X's, that may be impacting CTQ performance. Table 16.9 lists the common tools and methods used in the measure phase of a Six Sigma project. These include measurement systems analysis (MSA), capability analysis, cause-and-effect (C&E) diagrams, the cause-and-effect matrix, data collection activities, and statistical sampling.

Measurement Systems Analysis (MSA)

The purpose of measurement systems analysis is to verify that a CTQ can be measured accurately and with a precision sufficient to detect changes in its level as a DMAIC team implements process improvement in the improve phase of a project. Although an MSA is applied to the evaluation of a CTQ, a key process output variable (KPOV), or Y, it may also be applied to the evaluation of one or more of the input variables, or X's. Table 16.10 shows that there are at least six components of an MSA. These include its resolution, accuracy, reproducibility, repeatability, stability, and linearity. Several tools and methods can be used to evaluate each of these six components. Four of the MSA components are relatively easy to evaluate. As an

Table 16.9	Measurement: Basic Tools
Measurement systems analysis (MSA)	Determining the components of a measurement system, including its resolution, accuracy, stability, linearity, repeatability, and reproducibility.
Capability analysis	Determining how well a process output, i.e., Y, or CTQ meets customer requirements relative to its central location and variation.
Cause-and-effect (C&E) diagram	A brainstorming tool that qualitatively relates causes to their effects. It is used to identify potential X's for data collection.
Cause-and-effect matrix	A matrix that allows ranking of potential X's to several Y's or CTQs using information obtained from several C&E diagrams.
Data collection	The process of collecting data on the potential process inputs, i.e., X's, thought to impact the process outputs, i.e., Y's.
Statistical sampling	A series of efficient data collection methods that select some members of a population for data collection and analysis, but not all members. This information is used to estimate the magnitude of the population's statistical parameters with a stated level of statistical confidence.

Table 16.10   Measurement: Measurement System Analysis (MSA)

1. **Resolution**: The ability of the measurement system to discriminate changes in the characteristic measured (1/10 rule).
2. **Accuracy (bias)**: The ability to measure a characteristic and be correct on average over many samples.
3. **Reproducibility**: The ability of two or more people (or machines) to measure a characteristic with low variation between each person (machine).
4. **Repeatability**: The ability to measure a characteristic with small variation when a sample is measure several times under constant conditions.
5. **Stability**: The ability to measure a characteristic with the same person (machine) and obtain the same measurement value over time.
6. **Linearity**: The ability to measure the characteristic over its entire range with equal variation (error).

example, *resolution* implies that a measurement system should be in units smaller than the CTQ it is measuring. As an example, if we have historically measured lead time in days, but need to make process improvements in the range of hours, then our measurement system resolution needs to be in units of hours rather than days. The second component, accuracy, is easy to estimate and fix because if a measurement system consistently reads low or high, then we can adjust its level to its target value. Stability is another characteristic of a measurement system that can be managed. As an example, if we are using visual color standards to evaluate product acceptability, then inspection procedures and training must be developed to periodically replace these color standards and similar evaluation tools because they fade over time. A fourth MSA component is linearity. Our measurement tools or methods should be used within the range in which their variation remains constant. In other words, we should avoid situations in which the MSA tools and methods used to evaluate a CTQ are highly variable over a portion of their range of measurement. On the other hand, reproducibility and repeatability (R&R) are evaluated using a gauge R&R study. Reproducibility measures the consistency of two or more people to agree, on average, when measuring the same part with the same measuring tool. Repeatability is the consistency of one person measuring the same part using the same tool. Two common methods are used to conduct a gauge R&R. These differ based on the distribution of a CTQ. If a CTQ is distributed as a continuous variable, then a variable gauge R&R can be used to evaluate reproducibility and repeatability. If the CTQ is discrete, i.e., pass or fail, then an attribute agreement gauge R&R can be used to evaluate the reproducibility and repeatability components. There are also several variations of an MSA depending on the measured CTQ. Additionally, it should be recognized that not all six measurement components may be applicable with an evaluation of a given measurement system. As an example, if the measurement system is automated within a single system, without manual intervention, then its reproducibility component would not exist.

Capability

Capability analysis is a set of tools and methods designed to compare process performance of a CTQ to customer requirements. A capability analysis compares the VOC, in the form of specifications, to the voice-of-the-process (VOP), using a simple ratio of the two metrics, as shown in Figure 16.9. It is important that an improvement team be able to measure a CTQ with an accuracy and precision sufficient to determine its capability level. An ideal situation is one in which a CTQ distribution is centered on a target with a small amount of variation. In fact, if six standard deviations of a CTQ distribution can be fit on each side of a specification's lower and upper limits, then a process is called a Six Sigma process by definition. There are different versions of capability metrics, but they are related and can be converted back and forth using simple transformation equations. As an example, Motorola

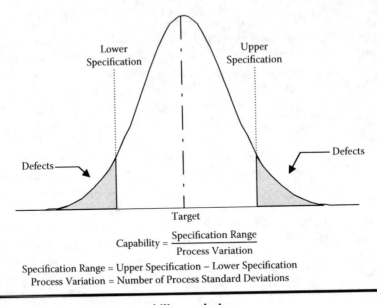

$$\text{Capability} = \frac{\text{Specification Range}}{\text{Process Variation}}$$

Specification Range = Upper Specification – Lower Specification
Process Variation = Number of Process Standard Deviations

Figure 16.9 Measurement: capability analysis.

adopted the Six Sigma capability metrics Z or Sigma, while most other organizations adopted the Automotive Industry Action Group's (AIAG) terminology of C_p, Cpk, P_p, and P_{pk}. These capability metrics are shown in Figure 16.10 with a simple transformation equation of Z_{st} = Sigma = $3 * C_p$. In other words, C_p = at Six Sigma performance = 2. This is because C_p was originally defined as a process capability of ±3 standard deviations within the upper and lower specification limits with the process centered on target, but a Six Sigma process has ±6 standard deviations.

Important in our evaluation of process capability are the yield metrics shown in Table 6.11, which are commonly used in quality programs such as Six Sigma. The most often used metrics are defect-per-unit (DPU) and parts-per-million (PPM).

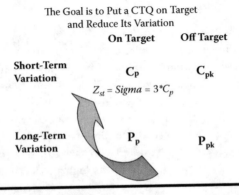

Figure 16.10 Measurement: capability metrics.

Table 16.11   Measurement: Process Yield Metrics

1. Defects-per-unit (DPU) = $\dfrac{\text{Total Defects Found in Sample}}{\text{Total Units in Sample}}$
2. Parts-per-million (PPM) = DPU × 1,000,000
3. Rolled throughput yield (RTY) = $\displaystyle\prod_{i=1} \dfrac{\text{Defect Free Units at Each Step}_i}{\text{Total Units at Each Step}_i} \times 100$
4. RTY = (Yield 1) × (Yield 2) × (Yield 3)
Over a very large number of workflow operations the RTY approximation is:
5. RTY = $e^{-DPU_{Total}}$
Opportunities = Number of workflow operations that are right or wrong:
6. Defects-per-million opportunities (DPMO) = $\dfrac{\text{PPM}}{\text{Opportunities/Unit}}$
7. Sigma = Z value from a normal table corresponding to DPMO (must be converted to short-term Z)

Although not as popular, several of the other metrics listed in Table 16.11 are also useful in specific situations. As an example, rolled throughput yield (RTY) is useful because it is a measure of the number of units that pass through each operation of process workflow defect-free. *Defect-free* means that units were not scrapped (with material made up to replace scrapped units) or reworked as they were transformed by an operation. This is also called the first-time yield (FTY) or first-pass yield (FPY), which is calculated operation-by-operation. In Six Sigma quality programs the concept of opportunity counting was introduced to allow PPMs to be aggregated for every CTQ of a product or service. Dividing a product or service's PPM number by the opportunity count of the process workflow allows calculation of a defects-per-million-opportunity (DPMO) statistic, from which the Z_{st} or Sigma of the overall process workflow is calculated. Although organizations use the differing quality metrics described in this chapter, most of them can be shown to be equivalent. We have already shown in Figure 16.10 that quality metrics can be broken into four major groups, depending on whether a CTQ is on or off target, and how its standard deviation was estimated. A target is defined as the midpoint between bilateral specifications' lower and upper limits. A standard deviation can be calculated using either a short-term or long-term historical baseline. A short-term historical baseline is calculated using data that has been collected as rational subgroups. A rational subgroup is defined as a set of observations taken from a process that represents the smallest practical amount of variation a process can produce. As an example, if the hour-to-hour variation of a process is of interest, then a rational subgroup would be an hour. This implies that there will be higher observed variation between hourly subgroups than within them. In Figure 16.10, the quality improvement strategy is to improve process capability by moving the mean of a CTQ on target, then reducing its variation around its target.

Another complication of capability estimation, within a Six Sigma program, occurs when a constant of 1.5 is arbitrarily added to a calculated Z or Sigma value. This is seen in Table 16.12, in which the classical probability calculations are shown in the long-term portion of the table and the Six Sigma calculations are shown with a 1.5 constant or Sigma shift added to the capability estimate. Most statisticians do not accept an assumption of a 1.5 Sigma shift in every process. In my opinion it is best to use long-term calculations, and use shorter-term or subgroup statistics to calculate an actual shift for your specific process. As an example, a defect percentage of 50 percent correlates to a Z value from a standard normal distribution of 0, which is its mean value by definition. However, the Six Sigma scale shifts the mean of "0" by +1.5 standard deviations. The resultant defect percentage decreases from 50 to 6.68 percent. This practice may significantly overestimate process capability. The practical way to calculate short- and long-term capability is by using actual historical process data without using an assumed 1.5 shift, although this is not what some organizations may actually practice.

Table 16.12   Measurement: Tabulated Probabilities

Short-Term		Long-Term (Actual Percent)			
Sigma	C_p	PPM	Percent	Zlt	C_{pk}
1.50	0.50	500,000	50.00%	0.00	0.00
2.00	0.67	308,549	30.85%	0.50	0.17
3.00	1.00	66,809	6.68%	1.50	0.50
4.00	1.33	6,210	0.62%	2.50	0.83
5.00	1.66	233	0.023%	3.50	1.16
6.00	2.00	3.4	0.000%	4.50	1.50
(2 parts per billion)		(3.4 parts per million)			

Note: Most statisticians do not accept an assumption of a 1.5 sigma shift in every process. In my opinion it is best to use long-term calculations and then use shorter-term or subgroup statistics to calculate an actual shift for your process.

Cause-and-Effect (C&E) Diagram and Matrix

A C&E diagram is used to identify potential inputs, or X's, that may be impacting a CTQ, or Y. The purpose of a C&E diagram is to help a DMAIC team brainstorm all possible X's to enable their prioritization for subsequent data collection. In Figure 16.11, the C&E concept is applied to a high inventory investment example. The X's are grouped in this example by their common major branches of measurements, methods, procedures, and people. However, a project team can use different categories, depending on their particular situation. The common Six Sigma categories include machine, measurements, methods, materials, people, and environment. It is important that a team work together to identify all the potentials X's that may be contributing to changes in a Y. If a team uses a C&E diagram effectively, then a root cause analysis will eventually show that one or more of the X's identified on a C&E diagram have a significant impact on Y. X's are also called key process input variables (KPIVs). In the improve phase, we will experiment by changing the levels of these X's.

The C&E matrix shown in Figure 16.12 is used to rank X's for subsequent data collection relative to several CTQs, or Y's. This situation would occur if the team has two or more C&E diagrams, each containing several common X's. The C&E matrix provides a weighting for each X relative to its correlation to each Y, as well as an overall ranking of the Y's relative to each other. In Figure 16.12, a single calculation is made for the variable Temperature relative to each of the Y's. The weighted total score for Temperature, across the Y's, is 207. After the ratings of the other X's have been calculated using the C&E matrix, the X's are prioritized, in descending order, from high to low based on their weighted totals. Data collection efforts would be focused on those X's having the highest weighted total scores.

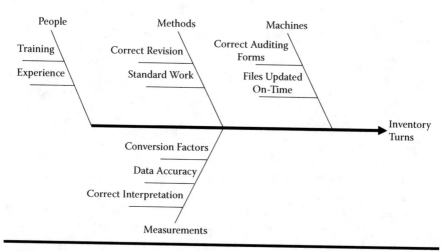

Figure 16.11   Measurement: cause-and-effect (C&E) diagram.

Rating of Importance to Customer		10	8	7	6	8	
		1	2	3	4	5	
Process Inputs		Yield%	Cost	Strength	Color	Cycle Time	Total
1	Temperature	5	1	3	8	10	207
2	Pressure						
3	Catalyst Level						
4	Material A						
5	Material B						
6	Line Speed						
7							
8							
9							
10							
Total							

Figure 16.12   Measurement: cause-and-effect matrix.

Data Collection Activities

The ten data collection activities listed in Table 16.13 are used to measure the levels of the X's, identified using a C&E diagram, and the corresponding Y's under similar process workflow conditions. This is done to identify how changing levels of each X impact the Y's. The most important data collection activity is asking the right questions, because this helps align the data collection activities that must be applied to collect data from a process workflow. In data collection activities, it is important that a team work from an initial set of questions to collect the data necessary to complete its root cause analysis. This does not mean that a team must know every question prior to data collection because data collection is an iterative methodology. In other words, an initial set of questions is answered that results in subsequent follow-up questions after data collecton activities. Table 16.13 lists several useful ideas to improve a team's data collection activities. Finally, a periodic review of a team's data collection strategy and related activities is very important for a project success.

Table 16.13 Measurement: 10 Key Data Collection Activities

1. Ask the right questions to ensure the assessment meets its goals and objectives.
2. Determine the type of information and data required to answer the assessment questions.
3. Bias the data collection efforts toward quantitative data to increase analytical sensitivity.
4. Develop a data collection plan specifying where the data will be collected, by whom, and under which conditions.
5. Review the collection plan with your team and the people who will be part of the data collection activities.
6. Develop data collection forms that are easy to use and will not be misinterpreted, and include all instructions as well as examples.
7. Remember to collect data for easy data entry into Minitab, Excel, or other software packages.
8. Ensure the team is trained in the correct procedures, tools, and methods, including measurement of the data.
9. Periodically analyze the assessment data to ensure it provides the necessary information.
10. Allow resources and time in the schedule for follow-up data collection efforts as necessary.

Statistical Sampling

Statistical sampling becomes an important consideration once a team develops its data collection plan. These activities include determining where data will be collected, by whom, and under which conditions, as well as how it will be measured, its measurement frequency, and the size of the data sample. Figure 16.13 shows that statistical sampling is conducted when an entire population cannot be counted. However, samples must be representative and of sufficient size to make inferences about a population's parameters. However, these considerations will also depend on the specific statistical tests used by an analyst. An important consideration in data collection is that the sample data be representative of its population. A second important consideration is the size of the representative sample. The size of a required sample depends on the statistical tools used, the statistical risk we assume in stating our statistical conclusions, and the distribution of the CTQ, or Y, being analyzed. Ensuring that a sample is representative implies that we have collected data from every possible factor combination of the population. As an example, if

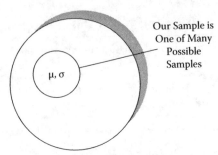

Sample: A Subset of Members Possessing the Same
Characteristics as the Universe or Entire Population.

Figure 16.13 Measurement: what is sampling?

our CTQ is the operational cycle time of four machines across three shifts, then we
need to collect data from each machine on each shift if we want to answer questions
concerning overall performance across the four machines and three shifts, or our
population. On the other hand, if a project focus is just one machine and shift, then
data would be collected for one machine and shift. In summary, a sample drawn
from a population should reflect the questions which must be answered as part of a
project's root cause analysis.

Sampling is a complex subject, but there are some simple guidelines that are
useful for common situations. Figure 16.14 shows four common sampling strategies. Simple random sampling is conducted when a population is not stratified
relative to the X's, or independent variables. In simple random sampling, a sample
of size n is randomly drawn from a population and sample statistics are calculated
relative to the sample's central location and dispersion. These sample statistics are
used to estimate the population's parameters, which are also related to central location and dispersion. However, in most sampling situations there are several variables at several levels. In these situations, a sample is stratified by the number of X's
as well as their discrete levels. Random samples are then drawn from each stratum.
The example given above, in which cycle times were analyzed over four machines
covering three shifts, is this type of situation. A third sampling methodology, if a
process is changing over time, is called systematic or rational subgroup sampling.
It can be used to collect data from a process at periodic intervals to identify relationships, between a Y and several X's, with the Y having a time dependency. If a
population consists of several naturally occurring groups, then cluster sampling can
be used to collect data.

The size of a sample depends on several considerations. These include the distribution of the dependent variable, or Y, the stated confidence levels (we will discuss this concept later in this chapter) of the statistical test used in an analysis,
the specific statistical test used, and the variation of the dependent variable, or Y.
Although sampling can be a very complex subject, some simple sampling guidelines

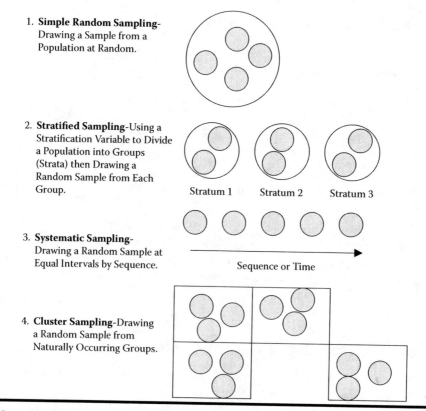

1. **Simple Random Sampling**-
Drawing a Sample from a
Population at Random.

2. **Stratified Sampling**-Using a
Stratification Variable to Divide
a Population into Groups
(Strata) then Drawing a
Random Sample from Each
Group.

Stratum 1   Stratum 2   Stratum 3

3. **Systematic Sampling**-
Drawing a Random Sample at
Equal Intervals by Sequence.

Sequence or Time

4. **Cluster Sampling**-Drawing
a Random Sample from
Naturally Occurring Groups.

Figure 16.14   Measurement: common sampling methods.

Continuous Data Measured Along a Scale Such as Temperature:

- One Sample Test ~ 20–30 Observations.
- Two Sample Test ~ 10–15 Observations Per Subgroup.
- One Way ANOVA ~ 5–10 Observations Per Subgroup.
- 2 Level Factorial Designs use 2–6 Replicates Per
  Experimental Combination.

Discrete Data Either Pass/Fail or a Set of Discrete Counts:

- One Sample Proportion Test > 100
- Two Sample Proportion Test > 100 Per Group
- Contingency Tables ~ Sample Until there are 5
  Observations per Cell Minimum.

Figure 16.15   Measurement: sampling guidelines.

are provided in Figure 16.15. These guidelines should be verified using an exact
sample size formula prior to their usage. A final consideration in sampling is when
a dependent variable, or Y, is highly skewed. The required sample size will be larger

Table 16.14 Measurement: If the Data Is Not Normally Distributed

1. Errors in the data (remove them)
2. Outliers (investigate why)
3. Measurement error (use measurement system analysis and fix the measurement method and tooling)
4. Several distributions present (analyze them separately)
5. Fitting of the data to an off-the-shelf distribution
6. Small sample size (calculate the exact sample size)

for a skewed rather than normally distributed dataset because its variance will be higher, because the distribution assumptions will not assume a normal distribution. However, several statistical methods can be applied to ensure a population distribution is correctly assumed and we use a correct or nonparametric test. These guidelines are listed in Table 16.14.

Analyze Phase: Basic Quality Tools

Once data on the Y's and the associated X's has been collected, there are several simple analytical tools that have proven useful in analysis of data relationships between variables. These simple quality tools and methods are listed in Table 16.15. Each tool and method is designed to answer a very specific question and requires that its data be in a specific format. These tools and methods include process maps, histograms, Pareto charts, box plots, scatter plots, and time series graphs.

Process Maps

There are several versions of process maps that help to graphically represent a process workflow. We have already discussed SIPOCs and value stream maps (VSMs). The discussion in this chapter will focus on functional process maps — detailed process maps that show how material and information flow through a process operation by operation, including all internal and external rework loops between operations. Functional process maps show all operational work tasks, inspection tasks, materials and information movements, and other activities taking place within a process. There are three common versions of this type of process map. The first is the current version of a process, which is often inaccurately depicted. The team must verify the accuracy of its current process map by "walking" the process. The second version of a functional process map is a "should-be" or optimum process map. The optimum

Table 16.15   Analyze: Basic Quality Tools

Process map	A detailed schematic of a process that is usually quantified relative to time, cost, yield, capacity, and the value content of every step or operation within the process. Several versions of process maps were shown in Chapter 6.
Histogram	A graph that shows the relative frequency of a continuous variable and is used to graphically show central location and dispersion of the continuous variable.
Pareto chart	A graph that shows the frequency or count of a continuously distributed characteristic relative to several different discrete variables arranged in descending order based on their occurrence frequency.
Box plot	A graph that shows the location and dispersion of a continuously distributed variable relative to one or more levels of one or more discrete variable. It is used to look for differences between central location, or dispersion between the levels of discrete variables.
Scatter plot	A graph that plots two continuous variables against each other.
Time series	A graph that plots a continuous variable sequentially by time. It is useful in identification of time-ordered patterns.

map is the version of the process as it will appear when improved by the team. In an optimum process map, all non-value-adding operations and rework loops have been removed from the original current map. This methodology is similar to that used in VSM, except there is more operational detail at a work task level in functional process maps. Many value stream maps are broken into functional process maps to study a process workflow in more detail. Table 16.16 lists 20 key steps that are useful in building a functional process map. The first is to assemble an improvement team around a project's problem statement. Process maps, in different formats, are also used throughout the DMAIC project cycle, depending on the required analytical questions which must be answered. This concept is shown in Figure 16.16, in which the different types of process maps are shown by DMAIC phase.

Histograms

Histograms are graphical summarizations of continuously distributed data. The histogram shown in Figure 16.17 shows the central location and dispersion of the number of returned goods in units by month. Notice the distribution is highly skewed right. Subsequent statistical analysis of the population's central location or

Table 16.16 Analyze: 20 Key Steps to Build Effective Process Maps

1. The project's problem statement should be well defined.
2. Include all required functions on the mapping team.
3. Brainstorm for solutions to how the team should analyze the process.
4. Interview people who are part of the process workflow.
5. Include people who perform work tasks within the process on the team.
6. Define as-is (current) and should-be (future) process maps.
7. Understand the process by walking it.
8. Have a willingness to identify process workflow shortcomings.
9. Team members should provide constructive solutions to problems.
10. Use open-ended questions when investigating the process.
11. Collect all available process information.
12. Map the process workflows.
13. Include the process boundaries using a SIPOC.
14. Analyze all metric linkages.
15. Ensure the correct level of detail in the process map.
16. Analyze the current process metrics.
17. Analyze the current process interfaces.
18. Create the as-is and should-be process maps.
19. Compare the maps.
20. Migrate the process to the should-be process map.

median will require the use of nonparametric tools and methods because the data is obviously not normally distributed in form. These nonparametric tools and methods will test the distribution's median rather than mean. The data is also required to be continuous when using these nonparametric tools. The returned goods histogram shown in Figure 16.17 could be used to represent the project's baseline prior to starting an improvement project. After a project is completed, it would be useful to compare the before versus after returned goods distributions to see if the median returned goods quantity was reduced by a project team, or if its variation was reduced over the baseline scenario.

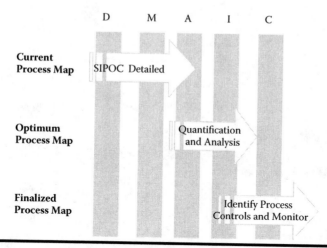

Figure 16.16   Analyze: where are process maps used?

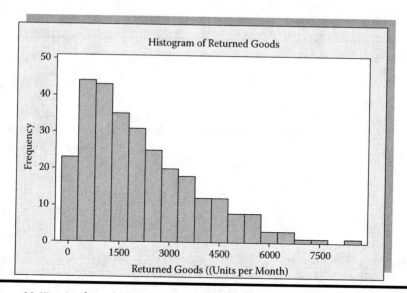

Figure 16.17   Analyze: basic quality tools/histogram.

Pareto Charts

Pareto charts are useful for ranking discrete categories by their relative count or frequency. In Figure 16.18, a second-level Pareto chart breaks inventory down for each of four machines. Notice the inventory classes having the highest observed counts by machine are placed first on the chart, in descending order. Pareto charts

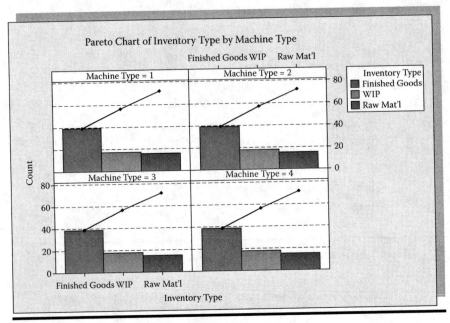

Figure 16.18   Analyze: basic quality tools/Pareto chart.

are useful in root cause analysis because they focus a team's attention on those categories making the highest contribution to the total observed count. Pareto charts are also very useful communication vehicles for the team because they are graphical. The data required to construct a Pareto chart includes several categories, with each having an observed count.

Box Plots

Box plots graphically depict the central location and range of a continuous variable for one or more of its discrete categories. Figure 16.19 shows a three-level box blot showing monthly sales ($000) for three price levels within two industries and two regions. Notice that the average monthly sales change by price level, industry, and region. The variation in monthly sales also changes for each discrete level of the three variables. The advantage of a box plot is that it depicts sample data without assuming a specific probability distribution. The ends of the whiskers of each box are calculated using the following formulas: lower limit = Q1 − 1.5 (Q3 − Q1) and upper limit = Q3 + 1.5 (Q3 − Q1). The first, second, and third quartiles are represented by horizontal bars, as shown in Figure 16.19. Box plots are useful in qualitatively comparing several variables to a dependent variable or Y.

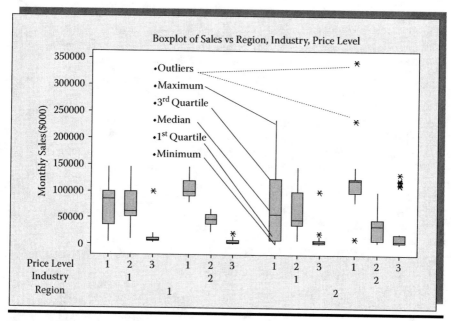

Figure 16.19   Analyze: basic quality tools/box plots.

Scatter Plots

Scatter plots show qualitative relationships between two continuous variables. In Figure 16.20, gross margin ($000) is plotted versus monthly sales. The dataset has also been stratified by price level, region, and industry. Scatter plots are useful in qualitatively evaluating how one variable changes in response to changes in the second variable, and as a preliminary analysis prior to developing quantitative relationships. As an example, if a scatter plot shows a curvilinear pattern, a subsequent higher-level mathematical analysis may show its quantitative relationship as $Y = a + b_1 X_1^2$. In the pattern shown in Figure 16.20, it appears that margin ($000) increases as monthly sales ($000) increase.

Time Series Plots

Time series plots graphically show changes in a continuous variable over time in a manner similar to that of scatter plots, except that the independent variable, or X, is sequentially arranged by its time order. In other words, the continuous variable is on the Y axis and the time index is the X axis. Figure 16.21 shows an example of a time series graph of Scrapped Units per Day for several machines in a study related to the Day of the Year arranged in sequential order. Figure 16.21 shows that

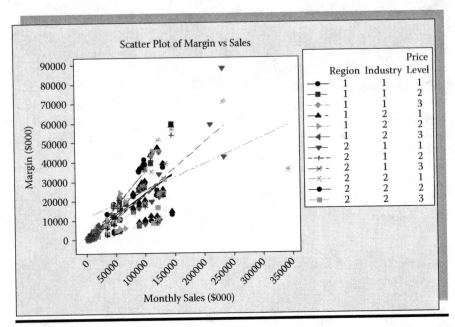

Figure 16.20   Analyze: basic quality tools/scatter plots.

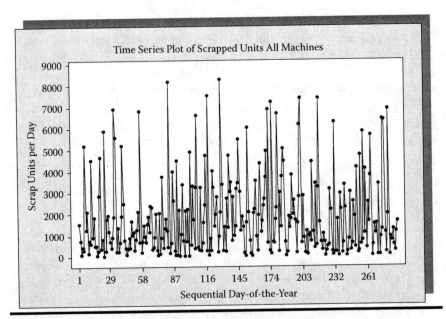

Figure 16.21   Analyze: basic quality tools/time series.

time series graphs are useful in showing time-ordered patterns within sample data. In fact, in Chapter 8 we showed that mathematical models can be fit to these data patterns using several forecasting models. Time series models will also be discussed later in this chapter from a control chart viewpoint.

Analyze Phase: Advanced Quality Tools

The root cause analysis required in most quality improvement projects necessitates the use of the simple analytical tools and methods just discussed in the preceding section. In this section, we will review more advanced tools and methods that may be useful in the root cause analysis of DMAIC projects. These tools and methods include distribution fitting because many statistical tests require a specified probability distribution and tests of means and medians for continuously distributed data. Tests of proportions, when the data is discrete or pass/fail, as well as the other advanced tools and methods are listed in Table 16.17. The assumption in this chapter is that the discussion is a review and the reader has training in the use of these advanced analytical tools and methods.

Hypothesis Testing

Hypothesis testing consists of formulating a statistical statement dependent on a practical question. The statistical statement is also associated with a specific statistical test method having certain assumptions relative to its usage. In Figure 16.22, we see nine sequential steps used to set up a statistical hypothesis. In all hypothesis tests, the null hypothesis, H_0, is a statement of equality, and the alternative hypothesis, H_a, is a statement of not equal, less than, or greater than. Also, the test method associated with the practical question has a test statistic whose magnitude is evaluated relative to its statistical significance. The larger the magnitude of the test statistic, the smaller the area to the other side of the test statistic, which is also called a probability value, p, of the test. This area is the probability of incorrectly stating that the null hypothesis is false, or it is incorrectly rejected in favor of an alternative hypothesis.

Statistical Risk

Figure 16.23 shows that the concept of statistical risk is related to a decision of correctly rejecting or failing to reject a null hypothesis. As an example, if a null hypothesis is correct, but we say it is not correct, then we have made a type I decision error. Alternatively, if a null hypothesis is actually false, but we say it is true, then we made a type II error in failing to correctly reject a null hypothesis. The concept of statistical risk originates with setting an original sample size for data

Table 16.17 Analyze: Advanced Quality Tools

Distribution fitting (normality)	The process of fitting known probability distributions to empirical data using one or more statistical methods, of which the Anderson–Darling is the most common. A probability value of less than 0.05 indicates that the assumption the empirical data represents the known distribution can be rejected with 95% confidence of not committing a type I decision error.
Tests of means and medians	Tests of central location of a continuously distributed population parameter. If the distribution is normal, the tests are on the mean. If the distribution is skewed, the tests are on the median.
Tests of proportions	Tests of proportions when the data is binomially distributed, i.e., the output is success or failure (pass or fail).
Contingency tables	A test of the independence of two discrete variables in which the output or response is counted data.
Equal variance tests	Tests that help determine if one or more samples have equal variances. In a one-sample test, the sample variance is compared to a constant value. In the balance of the analysis, two of more variances, estimated from samples, are compared to each other. If the samples or subgroups are normally distributed, the F, or Bartlett's, method is used. If the samples have a skewed distribution, Levene's test is used in the analysis.
Analysis of variance (ANOVA)	A method that compares the equivalence of several population means. The assumption is that the samples are normally distributed and have equal variances. There are also equivalent nonparametric tests.
Multi-vari charts	A graphical tool that plots the levels of several independent variables (or factors or input variables) versus the changes in a dependent variable (output variable, or Y).
Correlation	A statistical tool that measures the degree of positive or negative linear relationship between two continuous variables.
Linear regression	A set of statistical methods that explain linear relationships between one or more independent variables and a dependent variable. The dependent variable could be continuous (multiple linear regression), binary (binary logistic regression), ordinal (ordinal logistic regression), or nominal (nominal logistic regression).

Two-Sided Test

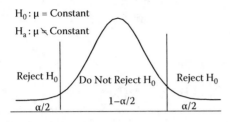

$H_0 : \mu = \text{Constant}$

$H_a : \mu \nmid \text{Constant}$

Reject H_0 Do Not Reject H_0 Reject H_0

$\alpha/2$ $1-\alpha/2$ $\alpha/2$

1. A One-Sided Test is More Sensitive than a Two-Sided Test i.e. Critical Value is Less.

2. Correctly Reject the Null Hypothesis with $1-\alpha$ Confidence i.e. when the Calculated "p" Value Corresponding to the Test Statistic is Less than 0.05 then Reject H_0.

One-Sided Test

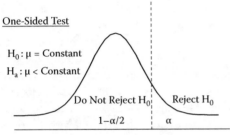

$H_0 : \mu = \text{Constant}$

$H_a : \mu < \text{Constant}$

Do Not Reject H_0 Reject H_0

$1-\alpha/2$ α

1. Set Up the Hypothesis and its Alternative
2. Set the Significance Level of the Test α and β
3. Choose a Test Statistic to Test H_0
4. Determine the Sampling Distribution of Test Statistic
5. Set Up the Critical Region where H_0 is Rejected
6. Set the Sample Size
7. Choose Random Sample and Collect Data
8. Compute Test Statistic and Look at "p" Statistic
9. Make Decision on H_0

Figure 16.22 Hypothesis testing overview.

		Your Decision	
		Reject H_0	*Accept* H_0
Reality	H_0 True	Type I Error *P (Type I Error) = α*	Correct
	H_0 False	Correct	Type II Error *P (Type II Error) = β*

Figure 16.23 Statistical risk.

collection based on an applicable statistical test, the variation of a dependent variable, Y, its distribution, and the magnitude of the difference to be detected by the test.

Distribution Fitting (Normality)

Because every statistical test is developed based on assumptions concerning the underlying probability distribution of its test statistic, we must ensure that we satisfy the assumptions of every advanced statistical test prior to using it in an analysis. As a result, as we review each advanced method, we will explain its assumptions as well as how to interpret its analytical results. A common assumption of many statistical tests is that a sample was drawn from a normal distribution. However, we prove this assumption or normality by using a goodness-of-fit test. Distribution fitting is a series of methods used to determine if sample data can be assumed to follow a specific probability distribution. This is also a form of hypothesis testing in which a null hypothesis states that sample data follows a presumed distribution. Using a normality test, a null hypothesis can be correctly rejected with $1 - p$ confidence of not making a type I error, or stating the sample data is not from a normally distributed population when in fact it is. In Figure 16.24, sample data representing monthly demand, in units, is summarized and includes an Anderson–Darling

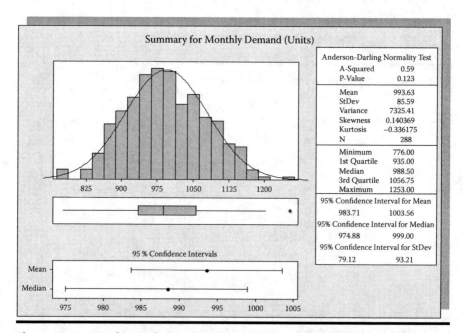

Figure 16.24 Analyze: advanced quality tools/distribution fitting.

goodness-of-fit normality test. The p value indicates that we can reject the null hypothesis correctly with only $1 - 0.123 = 87.7$ percent confidence of not making a type I error. It should be noted that by convention, we set a critical level of p to 0.05 to make $1 - p = 95$ percent. In the current example, we would assume that the sample data was drawn from a normal distribution and go on to conduct any statistical test requiring normality as its basis.

Tests of Means and Medians

Tests on means and medians are required when data is continuous and we are asking questions concerning central location. Statistical tests of means include one-sample t-tests, two-sample t-tests, and one-way analysis of variance (ANOVA) tests. The one-sample t-test answers a simple question: Is a sample mean equal to a constant? The two-sample t-test answers: Are two means equal? Figure 16.25 shows this concept using a two-sample student's t-test. The practical question shown in this example is: Are the mean monthly units that customers demand equal to the mean units shipped? In the analytical results, the calculated test statistic is shown to be 17.65, and its associated p value is very small and close to 0.000. This implies that we should reject the assumption of equal means and conclude the samples differ at a statistically significant level. A one-way ANOVA answers the question: Are these k sample means equal? In all three statistical tests, an assumption is that the subgroups are drawn from a normal distribution. The one-way ANOVA also assumes the variances of the k subgroups are equal. However, if sample distributions are continuous, but highly skewed, nonparametric tests of medians are required to compare central locations of subgroups. The one-sample Wilcoxon test compares a sample median to a test median, Mood's median test or a Mann–Whitney test compares two sample medians to each other, and a Kruskal–Wallis test compares several sample medians. In all comparative tests, when a p value associated with the calculated test statistic is less than 0.05, or 5 percent, we reject the null hypothesis of assumed equality with $1 - p = 95$ percent confidence and state that there is a difference in central location.

Tests of Proportions

Tests of proportions answer practical questions related to differences between proportions. As an example, a one-sample proportion test answers the question: Is the sample proportion equal to a known test proportion? A two-sample proportion test answers the question: Are two-sample proportions equal? The underlying assumption in proportion tests is that the variable measured and analyzed is discrete because it is measured as a success or a failure, or as pass or fail. The underlying probability distribution in these tests is binomial.

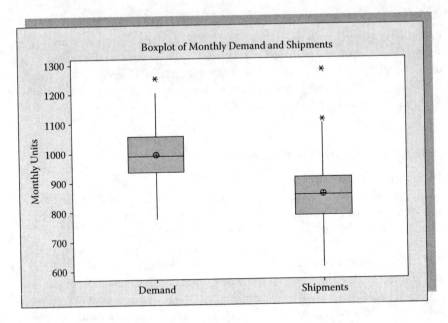

Figure 16.25 Analyze: advanced quality tools/tests of means and medians.

Contingency Tables

Contingency tables answer a practical question: Are two variables or factors related to each other based on an observed count or frequency? In Figure 16.26, the null hypothesis states that the observed counts of defective invoices are the same regardless of the type of form used or the shift using a form. The observed counts are

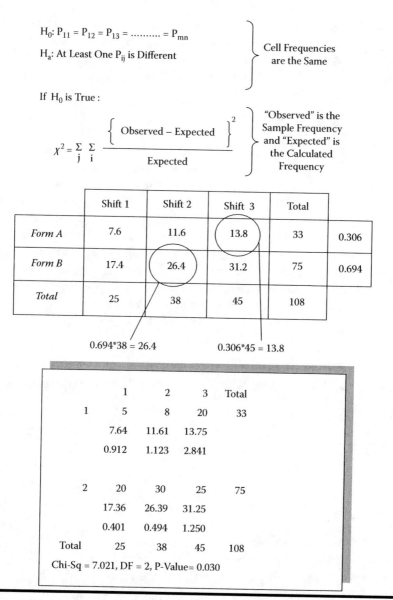

$H_0: P_{11} = P_{12} = P_{13} = \ldots\ldots = P_{mn}$

H_a: At Least One P_{ij} is Different

⎫ Cell Frequencies
⎬ are the Same
⎭

If H_0 is True :

$$\chi^2 = \sum_j \sum_i \frac{\left\{ Observed - Expected \right\}^2}{Expected}$$

⎫ "Observed" is the
⎬ Sample Frequency
⎬ and "Expected" is
⎬ the Calculated
⎭ Frequency

	Shift 1	Shift 2	Shift 3	Total	
Form A	7.6	11.6	13.8	33	0.306
Form B	17.4	26.4	31.2	75	0.694
Total	25	38	45	108	

0.694*38 = 26.4   0.306*45 = 13.8

	1	2	3	Total
1	5	8	20	33
	7.64	11.61	13.75	
	0.912	1.123	2.841	
2	20	30	25	75
	17.36	26.39	31.25	
	0.401	0.494	1.250	
Total	25	38	45	108

Chi-Sq = 7.021, DF = 2, P-Value= 0.030

Figure 16.26 Analyze: advanced quality tools/contingency tables.

shown in the table in Figure 16.26 to be 5, 8, and 20 for form type A and shifts 1, 2, and 3, respectively. The observed counts for form B were 20, 20, and 25 for shifts 1, 2, and 3, respectively. The calculated or expected counts (rounded) are shown to be 7.6, 11.6, and 13.8 for form A and shifts 1, 2, and 3, respectively. The expected counts for form B are 17.4, 26.4, and 31.2 for shifts 1, 2, and 3, respectively. Contingency tables help answer the question: Are the observed counts close enough to the expected counts to be considered a random pattern? If the p value of the calculated test statistic is less than 0.05, or 5 percent, the null hypothesis with its assumption of equality is rejected, and we conclude that the counts differ by the type of form or shift.

Equal Variance Tests

Equal variance tests answer the practical question: Are the variances of several subgroups equal? The null hypothesis is that subgroup variances are equal. If the subgroups are normally distributed, then the more sensitive Bartlett's test can be used for the analysis. However, if one or more subgroups are not normally distributed, then Levene's test should be used. In Figure 16.27, we see that the p value associated with Bartlett's test is 0.166, which exceeds 0.05. Based on this high p value, we conclude that the subgroup variances are equal. Equal variance tests are also used to determine if an assumption of equal subgroup variance is satisfied prior to using tests such as two-sample t-tests and one-way ANOVA tests.

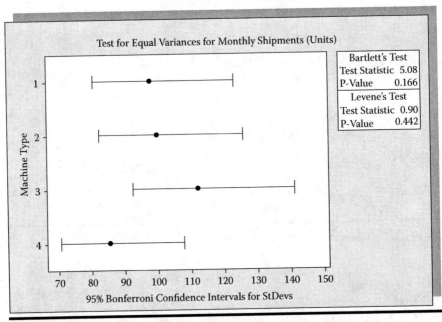

Figure 16.27   Analyze: advanced quality tools/equal variance.

One-Way Analysis of Variance (ANOVA) Tests

One-way ANOVA tests answer a practical question: Are the means of the sub-groups equal? The null hypothesis is that the sample means are equal. The assumptions necessary to use this test are that the subgroups are normally distributed and have equal variance. Figure 16.28 shows an example of a one-way ANOVA test. In the example, the mean monthly shipments of four machines are compared to each other. The null hypothesis is that the machines have the same mean number of shipments. The high p value of 0.591 indicates that we do reject the null hypothesis and conclude that the mean numbers of shipments of the machines are equal. In other words, the machines are the same relative to their monthly shipments. If the assumptions for the one-way ANOVA are not met, then a nonparametric test of sample medians can be used to test the null hypothesis that the sample medians are equal. A common nonparametric test of medians is the Kruskal–Wallis test.

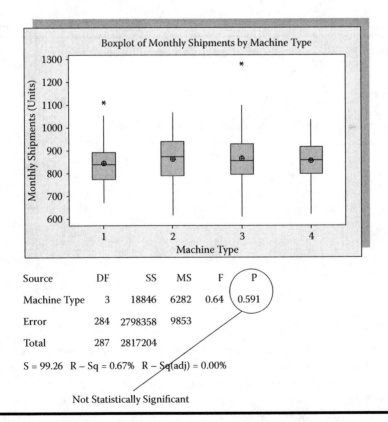

Source	DF	SS	MS	F	P
Machine Type	3	18846	6282	0.64	0.591
Error	284	2798358	9853		
Total	287	2817204			

S = 99.26 R – Sq = 0.67% R – Sq(adj) = 0.00%

Not Statistically Significant

Figure 16.28 Analyze: advanced quality tools/one-way analysis of variance (ANOVA).

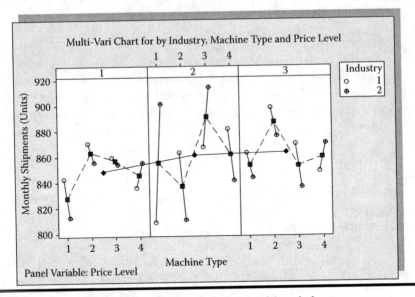

Figure 16.29 Analyze: advanced quality tools/multi-vari charts.

Multi-Vari Charts

A multi-vari chart is a sophisticated graphical method that compares up to four independent variables or factors relative to a continuous dependent variable, or Y. An example is shown in Figure 16.29, where the dependent variable is monthly shipments in units. The multi-vari chart is a graphical tool showing how the level of a dependent variable changes as the levels of several independent variables change. The independent variables shown in Figure 16.29 include machine type, price level, and industry. The greatest variation in machine shipments appears to be due to industry. Multi-vari charts are very useful in displaying the interrelationships among variables. This information may not be easily seen using a one-way ANOVA.

Correlation

Whereas a scatter plot graphically compares relationships between two continuous variables, a correlation analysis compares a linear relationship between two independent and continuous variables, but provides information that shows if the linear relationship is statistically significant based on the sample size. In a correlation analysis, the r, or simple correlation coefficient, varies between −1 and +1. A −1 indicates a perfect negative correlation in which, as one variable increases, a second variable decreases. A +1 indicates a positive correlation in which, as one variable increases, a second variable also increases. In Figure 16.30, several continuous

	Margin%	Percent Error	Warranty	Returned Goods
Percent Error	0.005			
	0.934			
Warranty	0.099	0.032		
	0.094	0.591		
Returned Goods	0.099	0.032	1.000	
	0.094	0.591	*	
Scrap	0.031	0.060	0.629	0.629
	0.600	0.311	0.000	0.000
Rework	0.031	0.060	0.629	0.629
	0.600	0.311	0.000	0.000

Not Statistically Significant   Statistically Significant

Figure 16.30   Analyze: advanced quality tools/correlation.

variables are pair-wise compared to each other, and their simple linear correlation coefficients are estimated for every pair-wise comparison. A p value is also calculated relative to the null hypothesis that there is no linear correlation between the variables. As an example, the correlation between Warranty and Rework is 0.629, or weakly positively correlated, but the associated p value is 0.000, which is lower than our standard value of 0.05, or 5 percent. As a result, we reject the null hypothesis of no correlation and conclude that the variables are linearly correlated to each other with at least 95 percent confidence of not making a type I decision error. On the other hand, Warranty and Margin % have a correlation coefficient of 0.99 and a p value of 0.094, indicating no statistically significant linear correlation at a 95 percent confidence level.

Simple Linear Regression

Multiple linear regression (MLR) analysis was discussed in Chapter 8 to build forecasting models. In this section, we will discuss simple linear regression as an analytical tool used in the analysis phase of the DMAIC methodology. Figure 16.31 shows a simple example of monthly warranty units versus the number of reworked units by month. The assumption is that as the number of reworked units increases, there will be leakage to customers. Based on the analysis shown in Figure 16.31, we see that there appears to be positive correlation between the numbers of reworked versus warranty units. However, there is a lot of noise in the analysis, as reflected in

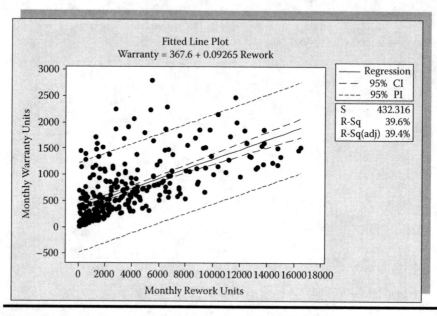

Figure 16.31   Analyze: advanced quality tools/linear regression.

the fact that the $R^2_{adjusted}$ value equals just 39.9 percent versus the required 90 percent or higher. In other words, recalling from Chapter 8, this statistic implies that the current linear regression model explains just 39.9 percent of the variation of monthly warranty units using reworked units as a predictor.

Improve Phase: Advanced Quality Tools

The improve phase of the DMAIC methodology uses information gained from the analysis phase. This information includes the key process input variables (KPIVs), or X's, that have been found to be important in changing the level of the dependent variable, or Y. Recall that Y is also called the key process output variable (KPOV). Once a list of KPIVs has been determined, the team experiments with the KPIVs by changing their levels in an organized way and evaluating their impact on a KPOV. This evaluation is done using experimental designs. Several types of experimental designs are listed in Table 16.18. We will briefly discuss each of the experimental designs in the next several paragraphs. However, prior to this discussion, we will first review the information contained in Table 16.19.

The information contained in Table 16.19 shows that creating an experimental design consists of five steps: planning, selecting a design, conducting an experiment, analyzing experimental data, and improving the process workflow based on the experimental analysis. Planning an experiment is the most important step. It is

Table 16.18   Improve: Advanced Quality Tools

Full factorial designs	An experimental design in which the independent variables are studied at two or more levels and they are discrete. The dependent variable is continuous.
2^k designs	An experimental design in which the independent variables are studied at two levels relative to their linear relationship with the dependent variable. Normally used when the independent and dependent variable are continuous.
Fractional factorial designs	A 2^k experimental design in which not all factor combinations are evaluated. In fact, higher-order interactions are traded away to reduce the size of the experiment.
Screening designs	Special types of 2^k experimental designs in which the fractionation is at a very high level. A special class of screening designs called Plackett–Burman designs allows intermediate numbers of experiments versus the 2^k situation to further reduce the number of required experiments.
Response surface designs	Experimental design that allows quadratic modeling between several continuous independent variables and a continuous dependent variable.

important that a team agree to the types of information an experiment will need to provide to determine the key process input variables (KPOVs) and their combined impact on the key process output variable (KPOV). Other considerations include the distribution of KPOV, i.e., continuous versus discrete, risk mitigation planning if experiments do not go exactly as planned, and resource requirements. It should be noted that a continuously distributed KPOV requires significantly fewer experiments to detect a change in a KPOV than to detect changes in the levels of the KPIVs. Another important consideration in planning an experimental deign is selection of the types of KPIVs that will be part of the experiment, as well as the range over which they will be evaluated during an experiment. As an example, a team should ask questions such as: Is an X variable continuous or discrete? How far apart should we evaluate levels of X? Once KPIVs and the KPOV have been selected for experimentation, an experimental design can be specified by the DMAIC team. The second critical step is to carefully plan and conduct the process workflow experiments. This includes developing risk mitigation plans to ensure that everyone knows what they will be doing during the experiment. The analysis of experimental data is also relatively easy if experiments are executed well and according to plan. Finally, the DMAIC team must verify their experimental model and conduct confirmatory experiments using the optimum KPIV levels to validate their initial experimental results.

Table 16.19 Improve: Experimental Design Overview

Planning	What functions must the product/process perform?
	Experimental design objective(s)
	Time frame of the study
	Select response (outputs, i.e., Y)
	Select factors, i.e., independent variables whose levels will be varied in the experiment (sources of X's are the C&E matrix, FMEA, SIPOC, etc.)
	Determine resource requirements
Select design	Best design type (orthogonal array)
	Consideration of relationships among independent variables (interactions)
	Degree of confounding, i.e., alias structure
	Randomization of runs and factors
	Allocation of factors to the array
	Nonlinearity of effects
Conduct experiment	Making sure everyone knows about the experimental plan
	Knowing how to measure inputs and outputs
	Recording of experimental conditions
Analyze data	Developing the relationship between the dependent and independent variables, i.e., $Y = f(x)$
	Analysis of each variable independent of others (main effects)
	Analysis of variables acting together on the output (interactions)
	Understanding the optimum levels to set each of the X's to put Y on target (best factor settings)
	As the X's vary within specification, how does Y vary? (prediction interval)
	Running another experiment using the optimum levels of each X to confirm Y is on target
Put process Y or CTQ on target with reduced variation	Confirmation of original analysis

Table 16.20 Control: Advanced Quality Tools

Failure mode and effects analysis (FMEA)	A method that evaluates how a system can fail and the impact or severity of the failure mode on the external customer. Also, the causes of the failure mode are evaluated, as well as their occurrence and detection probabilities.
Risk assessment	A formal evaluation of the probability of failure and its impact to a project. A project team is concerned with risks and issues impacting the project. Concerns are situations in which there is a 100% probability of occurrence.
Control charts	Charts that enable decisions to be made between random and assignable causes of variation with statistical confidence.
Control plan	A formal document consisting of several reference documents that are used jointly to ensure the voice of the customer (VOC) is met in practice by operations.
Communication plan	A formal set of documents, procedures, and practices containing information of the project relative to its purpose and benefits, as well as its impact on the organization.

Full Factorial Designs

Full factorial experimental designs are required when all KPIVs have two or more discrete levels, such as an evaluation of yields for four machines, several lots of materials, and various process conditions that could be set (if continuous) at discrete levels. As an example, temperature, which is continuous, could be set at several discrete levels, for the purpose of evaluating its impact on a KPOV, using a full factorial experimental design. Figure 16.32 shows an example of a full factorial experimental design. It can be seen that price level is the most significant factor in predicting monthly sales. The factor plot shows large changes in monthly sales as the price level changes from level 1 to level 3, whereas the other factors in Figure 16.32 have little apparent impact on monthly sales. This is also confirmed by the ANOVA tables, in which the p value associated with price, are 0.000. This "p" value is statistically significant because it is less than 0.05, or 5 percent. Also, notice that the levels of the KPIVs, or factors, are all fixed and discrete in a full factorial experimental design.

2^k Experimental Designs

Figure 16.33 shows an example of a 2^k factorial design. In these experimental designs, all factors have just a low and high level, hence the 2 for the k factors. Also,

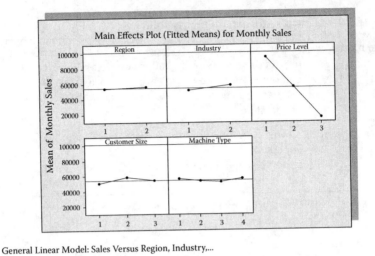

General Linear Model: Sales Versus Region, Industry,...

Factor	Type	Levels	Values
Region	Fixed	2	1, 2
Industry	Fixed	2	1, 2
Price Level	Fixed	3	1, 2, 3
Customer Size	Fixed	3	1, 2, 3
Machine Type	Fixed	4	1, 2, 3, 4

Analysis of Variance for Sales, using Adjusted SS for Tests

Source	DF	Seq SS	Adj SS	Adj MS	F	P
Region	1	540262278	540262278	540262278	0.30	0.582
Industry	1	2648573371	2648573371	2648573371	1.49	0.223
Price Level	2	3.07080E + 11	3.07080E + 11	1.53540E + 11	86.52	0.000
Customer Size	2	2736877373	2736877373	1368438687	0.77	0.463
Machine Type	3	897503568	897503568	299167856	0.17	0.918
Error	278	4.93360E + 11	4.93360E + 11	1774675039		
Total	287	8.07263E + 11				

Statistically Significant

Figure 16.32   Improve: advanced quality tools/full factorial designs.

some KPIVs may be discrete at two levels, whereas other KPIVs may be continuous at two levels. The assumption, in this design, is that the relationships between every KPIV and the KPOV are linear. An assumption of linearity requires only low- and high-level evaluations of each KPIV versus the KPOV. Once a linear regression model has been calculated from an experimental analysis, a team can interpolate between the low and high levels of the KPIVs to evaluate their linear relationship with the KPOV. The analysis of Figure 16.33 also shows that price level is a

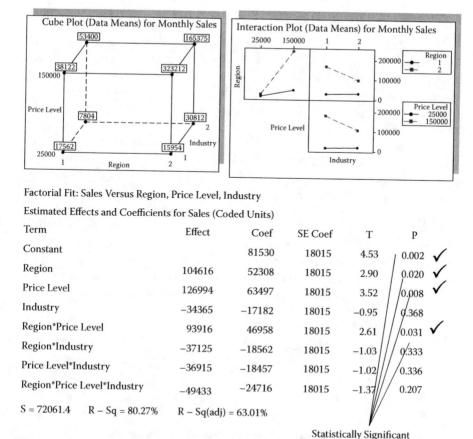

Factorial Fit: Sales Versus Region, Price Level, Industry

Estimated Effects and Coefficients for Sales (Coded Units)

Term	Effect	Coef	SE Coef	T	P
Constant		81530	18015	4.53	0.002 ✓
Region	104616	52308	18015	2.90	0.020 ✓
Price Level	126994	63497	18015	3.52	0.008 ✓
Industry	−34365	−17182	18015	−0.95	0.368
Region*Price Level	93916	46958	18015	2.61	0.031 ✓
Region*Industry	−37125	−18562	18015	−1.03	0.333
Price Level*Industry	−36915	−18457	18015	−1.02	0.336
Region*Price Level*Industry	−49433	−24716	18015	−1.37	0.207

S = 72061.4   R – Sq = 80.27%   R – Sq(adj) = 63.01%

Statistically Significant

Figure 16.33   Improve: advanced quality tools/2k designs.

significant predictor of monthly sales. In this example, the p value associated with price level is 0.008. Notice that the $R^2_{adjusted}$ value of the current model with all KPIVs and their interactions is 63 percent. This implies that the current regression model explains 63 percent of the variation of monthly sales. However, the model must be reduced by eliminating KPIVs having high p values, which imply they are not statistically significant. Regardless of the final $R^2_{adjusted}$ statistic, price level will remain an important predictor of monthly sales. The advantage of using an experimental design is that a model shows the impact of every KPIV on the KPOV independently, as well as their combined impact in the form of their interaction information. Interactions exist when certain combinations of KPIV levels cause unusual changes in the level of a KPOV. In fact, in some models the KPIVs by themselves may not be significant, but combinations of the KPIV levels may be statistically significant.

Fractional Factorial Designs

Fractional factorial designs are a special case of the 2^k experimental designs, in which not all combinations of the KPIVs are evaluated in an experiment. Fractionation can be very useful in situations in which there are many KPIVs, because the higher-order interaction information is usually not useful. This is shown in Figure 16.34, in which a 2^3 experimental design containing three KPIVs was fractionated into two parts, or a one-half fraction, in the final analysis. Whereas fractionation saves experimental resources, it also reduces the information obtained from an experiment. This is particularly true relative to interaction information. As an example, in Figure 16.34 we see that prior to fractionation, each of the KPIVs which are A, B, and C, and their interactions, AB, AC, BC, and ABC, had different patterns of +'s and −'s in the full experimental design. After fractionation, however, A and BC, B and AC, and C and AB had similar patterns. In other words, we cannot know if the change in the KPOV is due to changes in A or BC, B or AC, or C or AB. This situation is also called aliasing because some variables are indistinguishable relative to their impact on the KPOV. The situation is also called confounding because there is confusion in the experiment relative to which factors or interactions are really

Factors	2^k	Main Effect	1st	2nd	3rd	4th	5th	6th
5	32	5	10	10	5	1		
6	64	6	15	20	15	6	1	
7	128	7	21	35	35	21	7	1

1. Resolution III   Retrieves all Main Effects in a 2^k Fractional Factorial; but, Each will be Aliased with Some Two-Way Interactions.

2. Resolution IV   Retrieves all Main Effects Clear of two-way Interactions but, Some Two-Way Interactions are Aliased with Each Other.

3. Resolution V   Only Three-Way or Higher Interactions are Aliased.

Run	A	B	AB	C	AC	BC	ABC	
(1)	−	−	+	−	+	+	−	
a	+	−	−	−	−	+	+	Block 2
b	−	+	−	−	+	−	+	
ab	+	+	+	−	−	−	−	
c	−	−	+	+	−	−	+	Block 2
ac	+	−	−	+	+	−	−	
bc	−	+	−	+	−	+	−	
abc	+	+	+	+	+	+	+	Block 2

Figure 16.34   Improve: advanced quality tools/fractional designs.

impacting the KPOV. The interpretation of fractional factorial designs is similar to full factorial interpretation, except not all KPIV and interaction terms are required because they are aliased with other terms.

Response Surface Designs

The previously discussed experimental designs were linear relative to how they modeled relationships between the KPIVs and the KPOV. Response surface models explain curvilinear relationships between the KPIVs and the KPOV. Figure 16.35 shows such a relationship between Adhesion, the KPOV, and Temperature and Pressure, the KPIVs. In other words, the KPIV terms in these models are of the form X^2 as well as X. There are several versions of these models, with the central

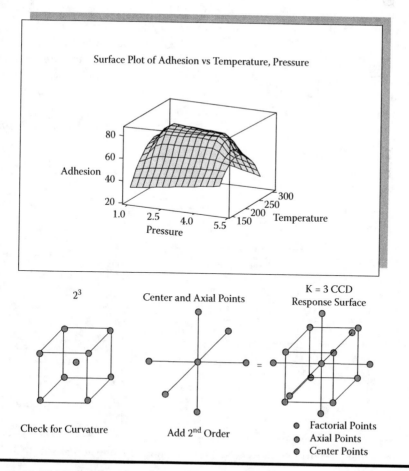

Figure 16.35 Improve: advanced quality tools/response surface methods.

composite and Box–Behnken designs being the two most popular. In addition, Figure 16.35 shows that a central composite design is useful, in particular because 2^k-level experimental designs can be augmented using axial points off the design faces if a curvilinear rather than linear relationship is discovered by a DMAIC team. To determine if a curvilinear situation exists, the team runs center points along with their two-level designs to test for curvilinear relationships.

Control Phase: Basic Quality Tools

Once a team understands the relationships between KPIVs and the KPOV, using one of several experimental designs or even much simpler methods, optimum KPIV settings are fixed and the team discussion moves to how to control the optimized process workflow. Table 16.20 shows several important control tools. There are also many other versions of these tools, which vary by organization. We have already discussed the failure-mode-and-effects-analysis (FMEA) tool in Chapter 4 and Figure 4.9. The FMEA is used in the control phase of a DMAIC project to reduce the probability that KPIVs will move from their optimized levels. The FMEA is shown again in Figure 16.36. In addition to an FMEA, a risk assessment could be conducted by a DMAIC team to evaluate the effectiveness of the current KPIV controls. Figure 16.37 is a modified version of the risk assessment tool shown in Figure 4.8. There may also be other risk analysis tools more applicable to your particular project needs.

Process or Product Name:							Prepared by:		
Responsible:							Date (Orig) ___ (Rev) ___		
Process Step/Part Number	Potential Failure Mode	Potential Failure Effects	S E V	Potential Causes	O C C	Current Controls	D E T	R P N

Figure 16.36   Control: advanced quality tools/failure mode and effects analysis.

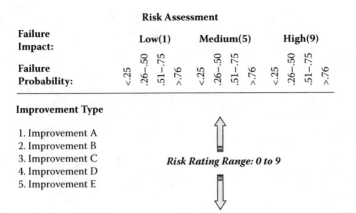

Figure 16.37 Control: advanced quality tools/risk assessment.

Control Charts

Control charts are time series charts that have been modified using control limits to aid in evaluation of the patterns of the variable being charted. Control limits are calculated as ±3 standard deviations from a mean value of a reference distribution to encompass 99.73 percent of the variation. Figure 16.38 lists ten key characteristics of control charts and shows an example of an X-bar and R chart. As Figure 16.38 shows, control charts are useful in evaluation of common versus assignable cause variation. This is possible because an original sample from the process was used as a reference distribution to set up the control chart. The control chart concept is that subsequent samples taken from a process should match the reference distribution if the process has not changed over time. This is the general basis of control chart theory and applications. Common cause variation remains within a control chart's upper and lower control limits with a high probability without exhibiting nonrandom patterns, whereas special cause variation exhibits nonrandom patterns. These may include outliers beyond the control limits, as well as trends and cycles. Control charts are constructed by taking sequential samples of size n from a process workflow. Over time, additional samples are taken from the same process workflow of size n and compared to the reference distribution. If the process workflow has not changed, relative to its mean or variation, then the more recent patterns should be similar to the historical pattern.

There are many different types of control charts that have as their basis different underlying assumptions and practical uses. The most common difference is relative to the distribution of the variable being charted. As an example, if a variable is continuously distributed and subgroups are taken from a process, then the resultant distribution of subgroups will most likely be normally distributed (central limit theorem). This is the basis of the X-bar and R control charts shown in Figure 16.38. However,

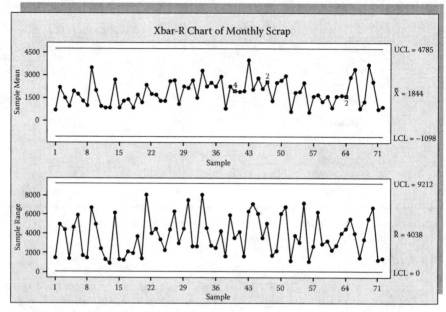

1. If the Process is Stable, its Behavior can be Predicted
2. Statistical Conclusions can be Drawn from the System
3. The Process Operates with Less Variability
4. Allows Identification and Removal of Special Causes
5. Prevents Excessive Tweaking of the Process
6. Applied to Analysis of Process Variation
7. Variation Due to Common Causes
8. Variation Due to Special Causes
9. Monitors Common Cause Variation if Present
10. Distinguishes Common from Special Cause Variation

Figure 16.38 Control: advanced quality tools/control charts.

if a variable is measured as pass or fail, then the resultant probability distribution will be binomially distributed, and discrete control charts such as p or np charts will be constructed by a team. Finally, another common type of control chart can be constructed if the variable is simply counted. An example would be counting the number of defects on an automobile. In this situation, a control chart will be based on the Poisson distribution, and the charts will be C or U. There are also many other types of control charts that have been developed for special process control situations.

Quality Control Plan

A quality control plan is a formal document with supporting information that shows a process owner and local work team the important variables, or KPIVs, that

1. What Process?
2. What Action?
3. How will Action (s) be Accomplished?
4. Who is Accountable?
5. When will Improvement Activity Start/be Completed?
6. How will be Know when the Action (s) are Successful?

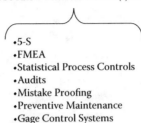

- •5-S
- •FMEA
- •Statistical Process Controls
- •Audits
- •Mistake Proofing
- •Preventive Maintenance
- •Gage Control Systems
- •Training

Figure 16.39   Control: advanced quality tools/control plan.

impact a process workflow relative to its outputs, or KPOVs. It also shows how to control the KPIV levels so KPOV stays on target with minimum variation. In addition, reaction plans must be created and incorporated within a control plan to enable a local work team to bring a process back into control if KPIV levels dramatically change. There are many other types of control tools used to keep KPIVs at their optimized levels. Many of these were discussed in Chapters 5 and 6 under the topic of Lean. Several of these Lean tools and methods are listed in Figure 16.39. The list includes 5-S (sorting, simplifying, sweeping, standardization, and sustaining), mistake-proofing, preventive maintenance, and measurement system controls as examples. It is important that a set of control tools reflect the countermeasures required to maintain the KPIVs at their optimized levels. Finally, all information and control strategies, tools, and methods must be incorporated into an organization's quality control systems, including ISO or related systems. Figure 16.40 shows a high-level viewpoint of how various control systems are overlaid on a system. The integration of quality improvement activities will be discussed in Chapter 20 under the general subject of system integration.

Summary

Quality management and improvement are critical to improving an organization's competitiveness in today's world. Table 16.21 lists five key concepts that will improve an organization's quality systems. First, it is important to align quality assurance and control activities with the concurrent engineering team's goals and objectives. It is also important to ensure that products and services are designed using the voice-of-the-customer (VOC) and have high capability to meet customer

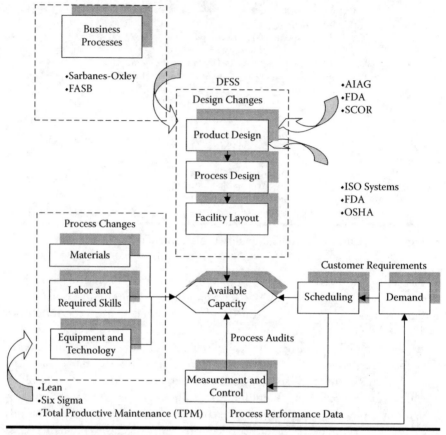

Figure 16.40 Control: integrating process improvements.

Table 16.21 Key Concepts to Improve Quality System Effectiveness

1. Ensure quality assurance and control activities are aligned with the concurrent engineering team's goals and objectives.
2. Ensure your quality program has elements of continuous improvement as well as breakthrough.
3. Use a rigorous problem-solving methodology, such as Six Sigma's DMAIC.
4. Understand the tools, methods, and concepts of quality management to improve your process capability.
5. Integrate your quality management systems to increase organizational productivity.

requirements under a variety of usage conditions. A quality program should also have elements of continuous as well as breakthrough improvement. Everyone should be trained in basic quality tools, methods, and concepts to continuously improve their process workflows. Once process breakdowns become apparent, it is important to use a rigorous problem-solving methodology such as Six Sigma's DMAIC to quickly eliminate the problems from a process workflow. It is also important that an organization understand the tools, methods, and concepts of quality management. Finally, it is important that all quality tools and methods be fully integrated within your quality management systems to increase organizational productivity.

Suggested Reading

Davis R. Bothe. (1997). *Measuring Process Capability*. McGraw-Hill, New York.

Charles R. Hicks and Kenneth V. Turner, Jr. (1999). *Fundamental Concepts in the Design of Experiments*, 5th ed. Oxford University Press, Oxford.

J.M. Juran and Frank M. Gryna. (1993). *Quality Planning and Analysis*. McGraw-Hill, New York.

Douglas C. Montgomery. (1997). *Introduction to Statistical Quality Control*, 3rd ed. John Wiley & Sons, New York.

Chapter 17

Identifying Productivity Opportunities with Operational Assessments

---

Competitive solution 17: Use ongoing operational assessments to identify projects to increase productivity and shareholder economic value added (EVA).

Overview

Operational assessments are structured activities used to identify improvement projects in an initiative. Although operational assessments require a significant commitment of time and resources from an organization, Table 17.1 shows that they can be used to increase an organization's productivity. A well-done assessment will provide documented business benefits to an organization if its projects are integrated and strategically aligned with the organization's business goals and objectives. Prior to an assessment, a thorough preparation is important, to ensure it will be focused on chronic process breakdowns. These breakdowns occur throughout all organizational workflows. This is important because productivity should be improved across an organization and its supply chain, rather than in just a few operational areas, such as manufacturing and distribution. This will also ensure resources and capital are efficiently allocated, rather than overloaded in one area. Assessment preparation includes conducting cultural surveys, gathering operational

Table 17.1 Competitive World Metrics: Operational Assessments

1. Productivity increase over the current baseline by future time period
2. Total business benefits by category, i.e., expense reduction, revenue increase, cost avoidance, and others, by future time period and net of investment
3. Assessment return on investment (ROI), i.e., assessment benefits versus expense

and financial data of important process workflows, and developing an assessment plan to analyze an organization's major process workflows using value stream maps (VSMs). These data-gathering activities will eventually focus an assessment on those areas of an organization that require improvement and offer the highest productivity opportunities to the organization. This is especially important in situations in which external consultants and local assessment teams are deployed across very large organizations. It is also important that assessment activities be focused within areas that offer significant productivity improvement opportunities. These opportunities should be documented by creating project charters for every potential project. Recall that project charters were discussed in Chapter 7 and shown in Figure 7.9.

Cultural surveys are a good way to begin an assessment because they include employees, at all levels of an organization, in data collection activities. Cultural survey information can also be used to augment other assessment activities, such as value stream mapping (VSM), financial analysis, and external benchmarking. As an example, cultural surveys may uncover interfunctional issues and other problems that are not generally known by senior management. Also, they may highlight opportunities to improve employee satisfaction over current levels. A cultural assessment attempts to understand an organization's strengths, weakness, opportunities, and threats (SWOT). This analysis takes into account an organization's current and future business environment, organizational goals and objectives in the context of available resources, and current and anticipated financial and operational performance. In particular, the SWOT analysis, with other relevant data, evaluates how well an organization executes its goals and objectives in its current business environment.

A cultural assessment is conducted through surveys of employees, managers, and executives. The assessment explores an organization's culture relative to its values and expectations, including its customer focus, vision and mission statements, and clarity and alignment of its goals and objectives to its strategy. In particular, an assessment attempts to quantify the degree of organizational goal alignment throughout all levels of an organization relative to its vision and mission statements. Also, an organization's market position and reputation, including its branding, are explored in relation to its competitive position in its industry. A cultural assessment also focuses on organizational structure and interfunctional behavior. Relative to its structure, the number of reporting levels and functions is analyzed, as well as how well they interact with each other. Resource availability is also explored as part of a cultural assessment, including employee education and skill levels. In addition, the motivation and commitment of employees is evaluated relative to their satisfaction with current organizational policies. A cultural assessment is the voice-of-the-organization relative to how "it thinks" it is currently performing. The actual operational assessment will validate or reinforce these opinions. The advantage of deploying a cultural survey prior to the operational assessment is that it provides unique qualitative information on how people perceive organizational performance. It also provides the assessment team with ideas of where to expand an operational assessment relative to process breakdowns that have been identified through the cultural assessment.

Another important data-gathering tool is analysis of financial and operational data for every major process workflow. Financial and operational data is gathered through interviews with key executives and process owners, as well as the analysis of management reports. This analysis identifies process workflows having high expenses or low sales, or that exhibit other types of process breakdowns relative to key performance measurements. This financial and operational information is used to internally benchmark current facility and workflow performance to identify the worst- and best-performing areas within an organization. Value stream mapping (VSM) major process workflows also helps to identify process improvement opportunities. The advantage of creating VSMs of major workflows is that the information gained through "walking a process" provides process improvement information beyond that available within higher-level management reports, including rework loops and other aspects of a hidden factory. *Hidden factory* is a term used to describe all the undocumented and nonvaluing process activities that take place within an organization. An organization is unaware of these activities.

After completing an assessment, all collected data and other information are analyzed and their business impact calculated in terms of return-on-investment (ROI), payback period, and other financial and operational metrics. Information relative to financial and operational performance issues is used to create project charters. These charters must be fully defined, financially justified, and signed off by local process owners to be considered viable improvement projects. A project charter, as shown in Figure 7.9, summarizes all the information that is known regarding poor financial and operational performance of a process workflow, as well as the resources that are required to investigate and eliminate the process breakdown within a workflow as identified by the project charter. The types of initiatives and other improvement toolsets will depend on the types of project charters created during an assessment and their cumulative productivity opportunities. As an example, process improvements are usually executed using one or several operational initiatives, including Lean, Six Sigma, Total Productive or Preventive Maintenance (TPM), and others, depending on the anticipated root cause analysis and the process workflow that must be improved to increase productivity. If an organization has not built an internal capability to deploy and execute a required initiative, then training will be required in the use of specific toolsets prior to deployment of projects identified during an assessment. A well-executed assessment will usually identify a mix of projects having productivity opportunities in the range between 0.5 and 1 percent of the cost-of-goods-sold (COGS) or a departmental budget using Lean and Six Sigma tools and methods with their operational focus. However, additional productivity opportunities will be identified during the project execution phase of a deployment. This may push productivity to a range between 0.5 and 2 percent per year. In many organizations, productivity can be pushed higher than 2 percent by deploying other methods, such as process reengineering, capital expenditures for new equipment, and savings from purchasing price negotiations. In summary, ensuring assessment activities are fully aligned across an organization, integrated with its goals and objectives, and quantified in the form of a project charter will guarantee that business benefits are identified in a systematic manner.

Aligning Operational Assessments with Strategy

In Chapter 7, we stated that the goals of an organization should be to increase productivity to increase shareholder economic value added (EVA) as well as related metrics, such as return-on-shareholder-equity (ROE) and return-on-investment (ROI). However, these high-level financial goals must be successively deployed down through an organization into lower-level financial metrics such as sales, cash flow, and operating expenses that drive the higher-level financial metrics and ratios. And finally, all financial metrics and ratios must be linked to operational initiatives to improve lower-level operational metrics. Figure 1.2 and Figure 1.3 showed this strategic alignment concept. Also, Table 1.1 and Figure 1.5 showed the concept of using linking initiatives or toolsets to identify and execute productivity opportunities at a project level within a process workflow. These concepts were also discussed in Chapter 7. The critical link between an assessment and its identified business benefits is well-defined and financially and operationally justified project charters. An organization's year-over-year productivity and relative competitiveness will increase through an effective execution of well-defined project charters and using the correct initiative. In summary, the purpose of an operational assessment is to identify projects to improve financial and operational performance to increase an organization's productivity and EVA, as well as related measures, such as ROE and ROI. Improvement opportunities are identified by finding financial or operational metrics that deviate or exhibit high variation from their targets. As a result, one major measure of the success of an operational assessment is the number of project charters clearly defined relative to business opportunity.

Preparing for an Operational Assessment

An operational assessment involves and impacts many organizational functions, including their people and external resources. It may also include key customers and suppliers. For this reason, it must be well organized to ensure that it is efficient and provides information useful to creating actionable project charters. In the early stages of an assessment, two critical activities are necessary to initiate assessment activities. The first activity includes training and working with an organization's executives to document their strategic goals and objectives. This will help to align an assessment throughout an organization. The alignment of strategic goals and objectives was discussed in Chapters 1 and 7. The second major activity of an assessment is quantitative analysis of financial and operational data as well as process workflow analysis using VSMs. Through these important activities, higher-level financial and operational metrics can be successively delayed down to a level of detail required to create a project charter.

Table 17.2 lists ten key steps that will ensure that adequate preparation has been made to conduct an assessment. In addition to organizational goal alignment, the assessment deliverables, including their financial and operational objectives, must be calculated by each facility and its major process workflows. As a rough rule, the financial or productivity goal of an assessment should be to identify projects having a cost savings of approximately 0.5 to 1 percent of budget or COGS. Of course, there may be other business benefits, such as improvements in sales margin, revenue increases, cost avoidances, and improved customer satisfaction. Achieving this level of productivity should be a major assessment goal. However, from my experience, smaller organizations usually have a lower percentage of potential productivity.

Table 17.2   10 Key Steps for Assessment Planning

1. Identification of assessment goals, objectives, and deliverables
2. Identification of resource requirements
3. Identification of assessment schedule and communication plan
4. Identification of assessment team
5. Identification of key client contacts
6. Organizational charts
7. Maps of major process workflows
8. Current work and inspection procedures for major workflows
9. Key metrics for each workflow
10. Project ideas by major workflow

Resource requirements and assessment timelines can be established once the financial goals or productivity targets have been established by location and major process workflows. Assessment teams should be deployed across an organization using these expected productivity opportunities. A simple way to think about this concept is that larger facilities would be allocated a larger percentage of assessment resources or assessors. In parallel, information is brought together by an organization's leaders to enable an assessment team to quickly learn about the locations or facilities it will be visiting. This information usually includes key client contacts, organizational charts, operational and financial data, and a list of major process workflows. A major assessment goal will be to begin interviewing the local management team, at each facility, and successively working down through the organization to a process workflow and process owner level of detail. At a process owner level, assessment teams will be formed around the major workflows to begin VSM and other data collection activities. These local workflow teams will consist of people who do the work within the process workflow and consultants or facilitators. The deliverables for each workflow team will be fully defined project charters that have supporting financial and operational data.

Prior to the deployment of the assessment teams at a facility level, executive training is usually conducted as a one-day hands-on workshop. In this workshop, the agenda is designed and structured to lead an organization's senior management group through the overall assessment plan and obtain their feedback on how to improve the proposed plan. The executive training is really a workshop in which all key executives and their direct reports are facilitated through a discussion to identity higher-level financial and operational performance gaps. These gaps will be investigated during the assessment. The critical-to-quality (CTQ) strategic flow-down also acts as a reality check to ensure that the project charters identified during an assessment meet each executive's goals and objectives. The strategic flow-down concept was shown in Figure 17.7 and will be discussed in the context of Figure 17.2. It is also important to ensure that all identified projects are incremental to a senior executive's current operational plans. In other words, it is important that an assessment not "double count" productivity opportunities and focus within areas not under active review and whose solution is currently known by an organization. It is also important not to focus an assessment within process workflows that may be divested or radically redesigned in the future. This is particularly important in the case of potential capital equipment expenditures that may change the design of a process workflow. Local management and process owners should also be trained in assessment specifics and provided the technical tools and methods necessary to participate in an assessment prior to initiation of these activities. At the end of the local facility training (which is sometimes called project champion training), the consultants and managers deploy out across a facility to begin data collection within major process workflows. The next step of an assessment will be an analysis of the collected data and creation of project charters.

Conducting an Operational Assessment

The key assessment activities or deliverables, at a local facility level, are listed in Table 17.3. The first important activity requires that once an assessment team arrives on site at a facility, a meeting is scheduled with local management to review the assessment's objectives, activities, and deliverables. One-on-one interviews follow an initial meeting with the facility's leadership team. In these interviews, the business unit level critical-to-quality (CTQ) flow-downs, which were constructed during the senior management training sessions, are augmented and expanded based on additional information supplied by local facility management. The goal, at this point in an assessment, is to identify productivity opportunities that exceed those currently in the facility's annual operation plan (AOP). Another goal of the local interviews is to confirm perceived issues regarding breakdowns in the process workflows. This discussion also helps identify team members for local assessment activities within a specific process workflow. At the end of an assessment, a summarization of assessment findings is developed by local management and the consulting team. This information is used to construct project charters, including time-phased business benefits and required resources, which are actionable at a local level. As the assessment team finalizes its activities at a facility, it also creates a deployment schedule for the facility that is integrated with the overall organizational strategy. This information is presented at an exit meeting with local management.

Table 17.3   10 Key Assessment Deliverables

1. Local business unit and leadership meeting
2. One-on-one interviews with key process owners
3. CTQ flow-down of major goals and objectives
4. Identification of major areas of productivity opportunity
5. Site tour of major work streams
6. In-depth analysis of major works streams using financial and operational reports
7. Value stream mapping of major work streams (current and future states)
8. Development and approval of actionable project charters, including financial backup
9. Assessment summary of findings
10. Local management debriefing

Table 17.4   10 Key Requirements of an Assessment Report

1. Executive summary
2. Focus of assessment
3. Key interview themes
4. Business strategic and tactical goals and objectives
5. SWOT analysis (strengths, weaknesses, opportunities, and threats)
6. Employee opinions organized into major themes by level of the organization and functional area
7. Actual process performance of major work streams
8. Project charters by major work stream
9. Major barriers to change and productivity improvements
10. Assessment recommendations

Table 17.4 lists ten key requirements of an assessment report that ensure an assessment team remains on track and delivers relevant information to an organization. It is important that a consensus be reached relative to the types of projects that are necessary to improve a facility's productivity and shareholder value. The executive summary of an assessment report provides local management with the key assessment findings. These may include specific areas within a process workflow where productivity improvements can be made given resource constraints. A SWOT analysis is also used to aggregate key interview themes from the local assessment. This information shows local management the key issues its employees believe are impacting the major process workflows of their facility. Quantitative analyses of financial and operational reports, as well as VSM analyses of major workflows, are also integral parts of an assessment report. This information results in the creation of project charters by major process workflow within the facility, as well as their business benefits. It is important that these project charters are not ideas or abstractions, but rather, well-defined and financially justified project charters. In addition to documented business benefits, in the form of project charters, required resources and anticipated barriers to implementation are discussed in an assessment report. Finally, the recommendations of the assessment team are presented to the local leadership team. These findings include projected productivity levels, return-on-investment (ROI), and other relevant information necessary to deploy an initiative at a local facility level.

Analyzing the Assessment Findings

An operational assessment collects data and information using one or more of the methods shown in Figure 17.1. These include identification of strategic performance gaps, budget variances, cost avoidances, benchmarking, value stream mapping (VSM), evaluation of operational metrics, voice-of-the-customer (VOC) information, and regulatory and health and safety issues. In addition, information from a cultural assessment can be incorporated into the analysis. Strategic performance gaps are created when actual performance deviates from strategic goals

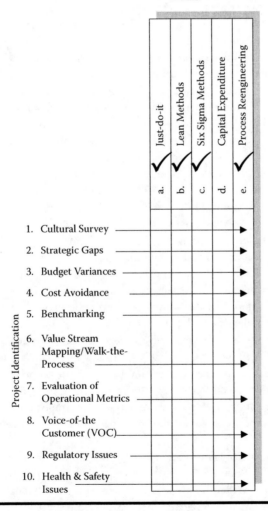

Figure 17.1 Project selection versus process improvement strategy.

and objectives. Budget variances are another area that may help to create ideas to improve process performance. But budget targets must be realistic, and their variance should be chronic and repeatable to justify a formal project. Investigation of cost avoidance ideas might also be a good source of projects, although there are no direct cost savings. However, in some situations, not making improvements such as replacing hazardous materials or taking similar actions may cost a significant amount of money in the future, necessitating an improvement project in the near term. Benchmarking is also a good source of projects if the process workflows being compared to each other are similar. It would make no sense to compare inventory investment or its turns ratio of one distribution center against that of another if their strategic inventory goals and objectives were different. As an example, if the first distribution system had as its strategic goal a policy of inventory centralization, with subsequent distribution of product as needed at a local level, but the second system had an opposite inventory policy, then their investment levels or inventory turns, would not be comparable to each other. The four project identification methods just discussed rely on data that is available in management reports. However, if data is not available in the management reports, value stream mapping may help identify rework loops and similar non-value adding activities. Also, projects may be found by analyzing VOC information. This is especially important if customers are leaving, sales revenues are decreasing, or gross margins are too low. Finally, health, safety, and environmental (HS&E) issues may be good areas in which to identify projects during the operational assessment. This is especially true if there are chronic problems due to environmental (HS&E) incidents that result in higher operating costs.

Regardless of the method used to identify productivity opportunities, all projects must be integrated with senior management's goals and objectives. This integration was discussed in Chapter 7 and shown in the CTQ flow-down of Figure 7.7. The CTQ flow-down discussion will continue using Figure 17.2. In Figure 17.2, we see that senior management's high-level goals and objectives have been deployed past the fourth level of the CTQ flow-down, to a project level of detail in which specific projects have been identified relative to incorrect setups, machine repair issues, and materials issues. These projects as well as their financial and operational improvement goals and objectives will be described in a team's project charter. The CTQ flow-down process can be used at every level of an organization, in both assessment training and project execution. It is also a very good training and communication tool because everyone in an organization can see the importance of aligning projects to improve productivity and manage the allocation of scarce resources across an organization.

In Table 17.5, we continue our discussion of project identification using a profit and loss (P/L) statement. There are several ways in which a P/L can be analyzed by an assessment team to identify projects. First, any line item that exhibits a monetary variance greater than that budgeted may be a good project if the original budget

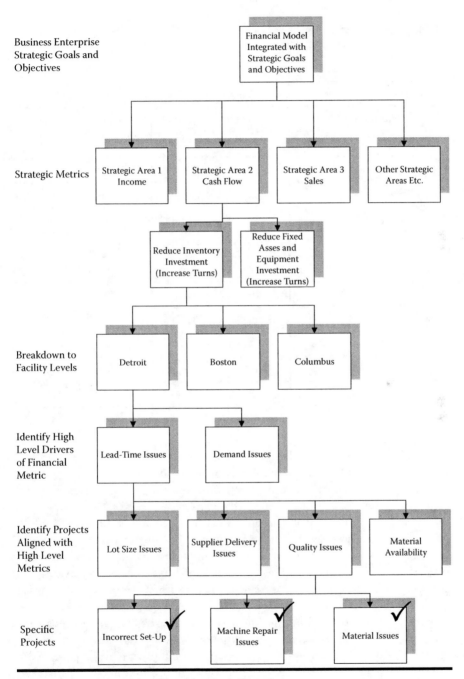

Figure 17.2   Project identification: CTQ flow-down.

Table 17.5 Project Identification: Profit and Loss Analysis

	2004	2005	Change	% Change
Revenue	$1,725,000	$1,850,000	$125,000	7%
Direct labor and fringe	$75,000	$86,000	$11,000	15%
Indirect labor and fringe	$135,000	$175,000	$40,000	30% ✓
Overtime premium	$8,000	$55,000	$47,000	588% ✓
Salary and fringe	$280,000	$302,016	$22,016	8%
Inventory obsolescence	$250	$1,500	$1,250	500% ✓
MRO	$18,000	$18,300	$300	2%
Depreciation	$32,600	$49,300	$16,700	51% ✓
Contracted services	$10,300	$16,000	$5,700	55% ✓
Materials to CGS	$295,000	$310,000	$15,000	5%
Scrap	$1,800	$1,900	$100	6%
Operating income	$869,050	$834,984	$(34,066)	–4%
Operating margin %	50%	45%	–10%	

target was correctly set. Also, changes in the magnitudes of expenses year over year may indicate a breakdown in internal processes. Analysis of a P/L is also useful because it shows operating expenses across several budget categories. This will ensure that resources are not concentrated on just a few process workflows, because this situation may tax available resources beyond their limits. In other words, a P/L analysis justifies project deployment beyond just one or two organizational functions, such as manufacturing and distribution operations. In addition to the evaluation of P/L expenses such as overtime premiums, contracted services, and other expenses, sales revenue and its adjustments such as warranty and returned goods can be analyzed. As an example, if revenue has not grown at its expected rate, projects can be deployed within the impacted areas to investigate and eliminate the reasons for lower than expected revenue growth. Also, if sales adjustments, such as returned goods and allowances, exceed those allowed by sales policies, projects can be created to mitigate or reduce their impact on an organization's P/L. It should be noted that cash flow and the balance sheet position can also be analyzed for opportunities to convert assets into cash to reduce interest expenses and increase asset utilization efficiencies.

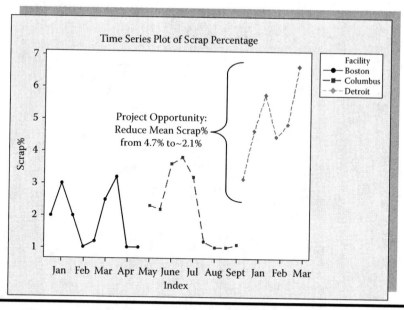

Figure 17.3   Project identification: internal benchmarking.

An assessment greatly benefits from Lean, Six Sigma, and other analytical tools and methods. An ability to compare and contrast different process workflows to identify best-in-class versus poorer-performing process workflows is also a very useful aid in project identification. As an example, in Figure 17.3 three facilities are analyzed relative to their scrap percentage. Detroit has a higher scrap percentage than Boston or Columbus. Also, Detroit's scrap percentage appears to be increasing in contrast to the stable patterns exhibited by Boston and Columbus. The performance gap between Detroit and the other two facilities may indicate areas where projects can be deployed to reduce Detroit's scrap percentage. After the Boston and Columbus workflows have been analyzed, best-in-class practices and methods may be identified that will be useful in reducing Detroit's scrap percentage. In Figure 17.4, we drill down deeper into the scrap percentages of the three facilities and find that the mean scrap percentage of Detroit is 4.8 percent versus those of Boston and Columbus, which are approximately 2.0 percent. A financial analysis can be constructed using the performance gap of approximately 2.8 percent to estimate the financial benefits of closing the performance gap of Detroit by 2.8 percent. Also, according to the one-way analysis-of-variance shown in Figure 17.4, the performance gap is statistically significant and most likely not due to chance. In Figure 17.5, we drill down within each facility to a local process workflow level. To the extent local workflows are comparable, it will be possible to internally benchmark the best-in-class to the worst-performing workflows for clues for process improvement. Finally, Figure 17.6 and Figure 17.7 show three issues that are causing the process breakdowns across all three facilities: incorrect setups,

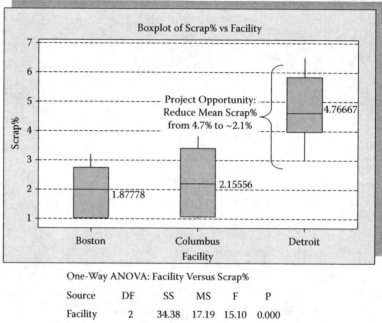

Figure 17.4 One-Way ANOVA data:

Source	DF	SS	MS	F	P
Facility	2	34.38	17.19	15.10	0.000
Error	21	23.91	1.14		
Total	23	58.29			

S = 1.067   R-Sq = 58.98%   R-Sq(adj) = 55.07%

Figure 17.4   Project identification: internal benchmarking by facilities.

machine repairs, and material issues, with the last appearing to be a major contributor to the scrap problem across all three facilities. An assessment team should use analyses like these to identify and financially justify improvement projects.

In addition to operational and financial analyses, it is important to analyze major process workflows using on-site audits and operational reviews as described in Chapter 6. In other words, an assessment team must walk the process to verify how it operates and where it breaks down. This analysis should include the causes of process breakdowns and their breakdown frequency. Figure 17.8 is a modified version of the VSM shown in Figure 6.3, in which the three non-value-adding operations have been highlighted for elimination. However, even operations adding value may contain some inefficient work tasks that adversely impact process yield, cost, cycle time, and throughput. These process breakdowns are also a good source of improvement projects. However, it is very important that the VSM method not be applied only to manufacturing or distribution operations. Major productivity improvements are also possible within front office or service-oriented processes. Once projects have been fully defined and financially justified, they can be prioritized relative to other projects for execution.

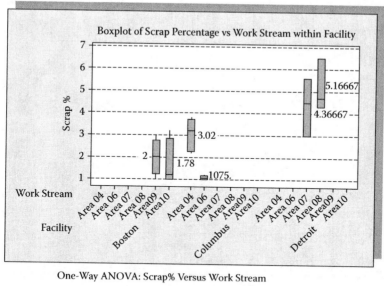

One-Way ANOVA: Scrap% Versus Work Stream

Source	DF	SS	MS	F	P
Work Stream	5	43.853	8.771	10.94	0.000
Error	18	14.437	0.802		
Total	23	58.290			

S = 0.8956   R-Sq = 75.23%   R-Sq(adj) = 68.35%

Figure 17.5   Project identification: internal benchmarking by work stream.

Project Deployment and Execution

Project deployment and execution does not just happen within an organization. It must be integrated with strategic goals and objectives. The project identification process should also work across and between organizational functions to ensure the entire organization is involved with increasing productivity in a systematic manner. Table 17.6 to Table 17.8 list common areas in which projects are identified in assessments.

Figure 17.9 shows that in addition to project identification, a prioritization of projects relative to their business impact and resource availability is critical to productivity improvements within an organization. An important point is that projects requiring significant levels of resource investment should also have a large business impact. In addition, a project deployment should include a mix of various projects, ranging from the easier "just do it" to the more difficult Lean and Six Sigma projects and, if financially justified, to those requiring a large capital investment. In summary, projects should be well defined during an assessment and deployed across an organization's major process workflows according to organizational strategy and

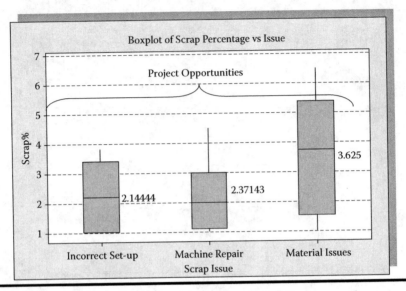

Figure 17.6 Project identification: internal benchmarking by scrap issue.

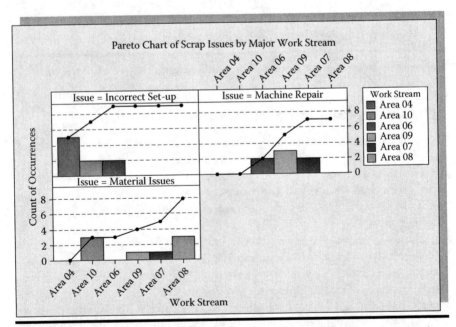

Figure 17.7 Project identification: internal benchmarking by scrap issue and major work stream.

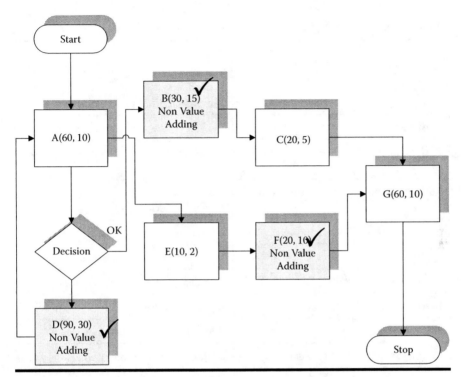

Figure 17.8   Project identification: value stream mapping.

productivity opportunity. Also, integrative initiatives such as Lean and Six Sigma with their associated toolsets are often very useful in project execution, depending on a project charter's problem statement and objective and required root cause analysis.

Summary

Table 17.9 list several key concepts that ensure an operational assessment will be successful. First, operational assessments should be used to identify productivity opportunities on a continuing basis within an organization. Second, it is important that an assessment team create well-defined and financially justified project charters across every process workflow within its organization. An assessment should be conducted using several different analytical methods to identify project opportunities, rather than rely on management reports or opinion. It is also important that once a project has been identified through an assessment, the correct toolset or initiative be used to identify the root causes for process breakdowns. It is also

Table 17.6 Typical Project Examples: Part 1

Finance	Marketing
Reduce finance charges	Increase market share
Reduce operational cycle times	Increase market penetration
Reduce auditing errors	Reduce marketing expenses
Reduce accounts receivable billing errors	Increase customer loyalty
Reduce accounts payable errors	Reduce the cycle time for market research studies
Sales	*Human Resources*
Improve quotation success rate	Increase employee retention rate
Increase sales revenue	Increase employee satisfaction
Increase sales per person	Reduce employee hiring cycle time
Reduce rework expense	Reduce hiring expenses
Increase sales quotation accuracy	Reduce termination expenses

important that all assessment activities are aligned throughout an organization. Additionally, rigorous analysis should be used to verify that productivity opportunities are real. These opportunities should be incorporated into a project charter. As a final thought, productivity opportunities should be balanced relative to available resources to prevent an overload on a just few process workflows.

Table 17.7 Typical Project Examples: Part 2

Administration	*Manufacturing/Service Operations*
Reduce facility maintenance expense	Reduce operational scrap and rework
Reduce facility energy usage per employee	Reduce operational lead time
Optimize materials and operating supplies cost per employee	Improve schedule adherence
	Reduce standard cost
	Reduce emergency maintenance
Purchasing	*Materials Planning*
Increase the accuracy of supplier quotations	Improve inventory turns based on controllable lead time and demand
Reduce the number of suppliers	Maintain materials requirements planning (MRP) accuracy
Improve supplier on-time delivery	Reduce excess and obsolete inventory
Reduce per unit purchase order expense	
Reduce purchased standard cost	

Table 17.8   Typical Project Examples: Part 3

Distribution	Freight Operations
Reduce emergency maintenance	Reduce freight classification errors
Reduce per unit transaction cost	Reduce shipment damage
Improve order accuracy	Reduce per unit freight costs
Improve order fill rate	Improve inbound and outbound on-time delivery percentage
Reduce emergency replenishment	
Information Technology (IT)	*Research and Development*
Reduce the information technology cost per person	Reduce new product cycle time
Increase the percentage of reusable software	Reduce hours per project
Decrease the percentage of software errors per line of code	Reduce engineering errors
Reduce software development cycle time	Increase the percentage of new products developed per year
Reduce waiting time for IT service	

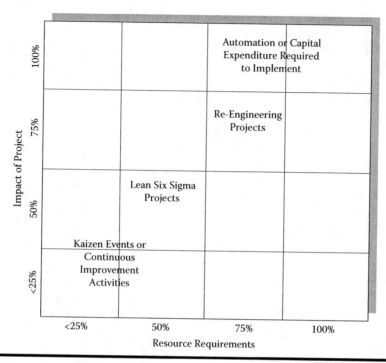

Figure 17.9 Project prioritization.

Table 17.9 Key Concepts to Improve Operational Assessments

1. Use operational assessments to identify productivity opportunities on a continuing basis.
2. Create well-defined and financially justified project charters across every process workflow within your organization.
3. Use several different analytical methods to identify projects, rather than rely on management reports or opinion.
4. Use the right toolset or initiative to identify the root causes for a process breakdown.
5. Ensure all assessment activities are aligned throughout your organization.
6. Use rigorous analysis to prove that productivity opportunities exist.
7. Balance productivity opportunities with available resources to prevent an overload on a few process workflows.

Suggested Reading

Larry Bossidy and Ram Charan with Charles Burck. (2002). *Execution: The Discipline of Getting Things Done.* Crown Business, New York.

Robert S. Kaplan, Ed. (1990). *Measures of Manufacturing Excellence.* Harvard Business School Press, Boston.

Chapter 18

Executing Projects with Multicultural Teams

Competitive solution 18: Manage projects to meet deliverables, the schedule, and cost targets.

Overview

Project management is a complicated set of activities that require the effective planning and execution of numerous interrelated activities to ensure a project achieves its goals and objectives on schedule. Table 18.1 lists several metrics that are useful in managing projects. Project management requires many diverse skills. These include forming teams, analyzing financial and operational reports to build a business case for a team's project charter, leading and facilitating a team, and ensuring that a project remains on schedule and within its budget, and accomplishes its objectives. Table 18.2 lists ten key steps that are required to ensure a project is managed for success. The first step requires that a business case for a project be justified based on financial and operational analysis of an organization's major process workflows. In addition to a financial and operational analysis, which compares current with projected performance, a good business case ensures that a project is strategically aligned with an organization's goals and objectives. The tools and methods necessary to build a business case have been discussed in previous chapters. In Chapter 2, we discussed the basics of forming and deploying high-performance work teams within an organization. Productivity analysis was discussed in Chapter 7, and the basics of conducting an operational assessment were discussed in Chapter 17. In

Table 18.1   Competitive World Metrics: Project Management

1. Working days used versus allocated for the project
2. Work tasks that must be completed within 24 hours
3. Work tasks starting within the next 10 days
4. Work tasks in progress, including percentage complete
5. Completed work tasks, including consumed resources, cost, and schedule adherence
6. Work tasks that have been started late
7. Work tasks that are not meeting schedule or cost targets
8. Actual versus resource usage to date
9. Project cash flow projections
10. Actual versus budgeted cost to date
11. Work tasks that are overbudget
12. Work tasks that can be "crashed" to reduce their expected completion time

this chapter, we will discuss the tools and methods necessary to manage projects to a successful conclusion. A second step of project management requires selecting a team. Team selection is a critical part of a project management process at several levels. First, a team must be selected based on a project charter's problem statement and objective. There are several useful tools and methods that can help scope a project into a manageable size for a team. A supplier–input–process–output–customer (SIPOC) map, such as was shown in Figure 3.12, is particularly useful in scoping projects because it clearly defines a process workflow's input and output boundaries. A SIPOC also helps to clarify how to select a project's team members. As an example, team members should be selected from suppliers to the process workflow, the people who are part of the process and people who receive materials or information from the workflow. In addition to team selection, the specific individuals who are part of a team should have the requisite skills and knowledge to help their team drive toward the root causes of a process problem. In addition to team selection, its management is critical to a successful project execution. The balance of steps listed in Table 18.2 are activities related to identifying project risks; developing project milestones, activities, and work tasks; and creating a project schedule or Gantt chart to execute the work tasks making up a project's activities and major milestones. In addition to Gantt charts, we will discuss a specific technique to calculate probabilities of the completion of a project schedule using the program evaluation

Table 18.2   10 Key Steps in Project Planning

1. Develop project justification, including the project's problem statement and objective, using a project charter.
2. Select team based on project's process boundaries as specified by its SIPOC.
3. Identify project success criteria jointly with the team.
4. Identify potential project risks and barriers to success.
5. Develop project milestones, including their activities and work tasks, and time phase them to create a project schedule.
6. Establish the linkage between work tasks to estimate the critical path through the network.
7. Estimate required resources and costs by work task.
8. Analyze the completed project schedule and network diagram (Gantt chart) using network analysis techniques (PERT), and adjust work schedules and resources as necessary.
9. Create a project reporting format and schedule updates with key organizational stakeholders.
10. Ensure work tasks are completed on schedule according to plan.

and review technique (PERT). Finally, at the end of this chapter, we will discuss key aspects of effective project status reporting.

Building Globally Diverse Teams

Teams are important, but they are seldom selected and managed according to best-in-class practices. In Chapter 2 and Table 2.3, we briefly discussed teams in the context of several common initiatives deployed by organizations. However, in this chapter, we want to discuss team formation and management in more detail. In particular, we want to discuss the actions necessary to form and manage highly diverse teams on a global basis because this is how work is done in today's competitive world. Figure 18.1, Table 18.3, and Table 18.4 show several concepts important to the selection and management of highly diverse teams. We will discuss team selection and management from these perspectives. We will also discuss the impact of the external environment, required facilitation tools and methods, team selection and management, and team member perspectives.

Prior to forming a team, an organization needs to ask the question: Is a team really needed to investigate and execute this project? Not every project requires

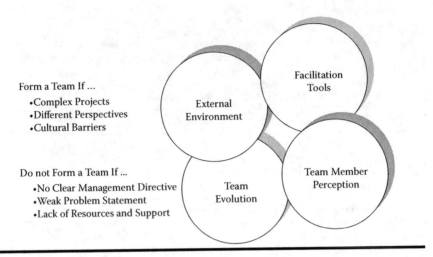

Form a Team If ...
  •Complex Projects
  •Different Perspectives
  •Cultural Barriers

Do not Form a Team If ...
  •No Clear Management Directive
  •Weak Problem Statement
  •Lack of Resources and Support

Figure 18.1 Developing high-performance work teams.

deployment of a project team. In situations in which a project is small in scope or its solution methodology obvious, a formal team may not be necessary to execute the project. On the other hand, a formal team may be required to execute a complex project that requires different team member perspectives and skills, or if there are cultural barriers to data collection, analysis, and process improvements. A project team should not be formed, or a project formally chartered by an organization, if there is no clear management directive to initiate the project, as reflected in a weak problem statement; its project objectives are not clear; or resources and other necessary support for the project do not exist. Also, once a project team has been formed around a project charter, there are several issues that every team may face to one degree or another. These common issues are shown in Figure 18.1 under the categories of external environment, facilitation tools, and team evolution and team member perceptions. A project manager must be aware of these common issues and develop plans to mitigate their impact on the team's schedule and planning activities.

The external environment can have an impact on a project team relative to project prioritization and the resources necessary to complete a project on schedule. A formal project charter is necessary to prioritize and secure organizational resources from stakeholders at an agreed-upon level. Resources include providing people who work within a process to work with a team and providing a team access to information. In addition, an external environment may pose one of several risks to a project. These may include competitive threats, technological problems, regulatory barriers, and adverse economic conditions. Competitive threats include the loss or gain of major customers, or new products and services offered by a competitor. Technological problems may also occur if a project relies on a major improvement in technology. In these situations, if a project team cannot develop new performance features for their current product or service, then the project may fail to achieve its

Table 18.3   Empowering a Multicultural Work Team

Sources of Team Conflict
1. Differences in group cultural values and psychological perceptions
2. Differences in goals and expectations based on cultural perceptions
3. Lack of understanding of cross-cultural norms
Conflict Positive Attributes (with Group Facilitation)
4. Increased solution alternatives once understanding is achieved through group facilitation
5. Communication increased through awareness of cultural and psychological differences
6. Increased motivation due to group goal alignment
Conflict Negative Attributes (without Group Facilitation)
7. Stress due to misconceptions as a result of different cultural expectations
8. Fewer solution alternatives due to an inability to agree on problem statements and data interpretation
9. Less communication due to poor facilitation
10. Lower morale due to a failure to achieve project milestones and complete required activities on schedule and according to plan
11. Decision making slowed due to a lack of clear goal and project planning agreement

objectives. Regulatory and economic conditions in different regions of the world may also have a major impact on a project's success. There are usually other external threats to a project, which will vary by industry and organization.

Facilitation tools and methods are also critical to effective team performance when its members are highly diverse. Although high-performance work teams may have been selected for their diversity and difference of perspective, diversity may result in disagreements, which must be properly facilitated to ensure all team members are respected and encouraged to contribute to a team's goals and objectives. As an example, simple facilitation tools and methods such as having a meeting agenda, ensuring that everyone on the team has a chance to speak, recording meeting minutes, and rotating team roles and responsibilities are good ways to ensure that all team members are respected and feel free to contribute their ideas to the team. An opposite situation would exist if team members are homogeneous and agree on most issues without serious discussion. This is often called groupthink. Teams

Table 18.4   10 Key Steps to Build a Globally Diverse Team

1. Objective of project team
2. Team structure, including leader, facilitator, team members, ad hoc technical experts, timekeeper, and note taker
3. Input and output boundaries as specified by the project's problem statement, objective, and SIPOC, as well as the project's internal and external customers, related organizational functions, and process owner
4. Team should include diverse viewpoints and perspectives and consist of people who are part of the process, as well as those just before and after the process
5. Current process characterization, including current process performance related to the project charter, as well as business benefits
6. Proper team facilitation tools and methods, including an agenda for each meeting, clear roles and responsibilities, and effective tools to facilitate and minimize conflict
7. Team should also use tools and methods to facilitate decision making and ensure the full participation and discussion of all team members
8. Team should obtain outside assistance and resources as necessary
9. Team should understand its strengths and weaknesses to maximize contributions by all its members, and avoid a lack of focus and dominance of the meetings by assertive personalities
10. Team should collect and analyze data to answer project questions in a fact-based manner and drive solutions based on fact, rather than team consensus

having groupthink are dysfunctional and seldom identify alternative or optimum solutions to a project's problem statement and objective. A team member perception refers to how a person perceives the world in general, as well as his or her preferred method of working problems. Although there are several psychological systems available to measure how people perceive themselves and others in their work environments, a common concept is that people should work a problem from several perspectives. In other words, a culturally diverse team having similar psychological perspectives may in fact be as dysfunctional as a more homogeneous group of people from a similar culture. One common psychological evaluation technique is the Meyers–Briggs. The Meyers–Briggs method ranks people along four dimensions: introversion to extroversion, sensing versus intuitive, thinking versus feeling, and judgmental versus perceptive. In a Meyers–Briggs system, although these four dimensions are represented as a continuum, they are often presented as 16 major discrete categories. As an example, a person may be highly introversive to highly extroversive, and anything in between the two extremes. Our purpose is not to describe the Meyers–Briggs system in detail, but only to show that it, and similar psychological evaluation systems, may help to understand team dynamics and evolution. As an example, without proper team facilitation, the extroverts on a team will dominate conversations, resulting in little contributions from the introverted members. A good facilitation method to avoid this type of problem is to ask each team member, in turn, if he or she would like to contribute an idea to the team's conversation. This ensures that everyone will get a chance to contribute to a team's meetings. Using another Meyers–Briggs dimension as an example, sensing individuals have a need to sequentially evaluate a problem, whereas intuitive people have a need to find a solution without following a sequential methodology. To the intuitive personalities, the sensing personality types move too slowly as they collect the necessary facts and information to investigate a problem. On the other hand, to the sensing personalities, the intuitive personalities type are moving along through the root cause analysis without factual justification. In these situations, everyone should agree on the required data collection plan and information, and once it is obtained and analyzed, decisions should be made based on the analytical results. These simple examples show how team members can disagree and conflict may develop without proper team facilitation.

A final category shown in Figure 18.1 is team evolution. All project teams move through four stages as they mature into a high-performance team: forming, storming, norming, and performing. A forming stage consists of team members developing initial impressions of each other. Not many serious discussions of project objectives are had during this stage of a team maturation process. But as a team begins to discuss a project's goals and objectives, disagreements may occur if team facilitation is not effective. However, if a team is well facilitated, it will pass through its storming stage very quickly and begin to develop a consensus of how to work through a project's deliverables. Over time, as team members perform their roles and responsibilities to meet schedule requirements, mutual trust develops among its members. At this point in the team maturation process, a team enters a performing stage to become a high-performance work team. Table 18.3 lists the positive and negative aspects of team conflict. Conflict by itself is a necessary precursor to the investigation of a project's problem. In fact, it increases the number of solution alternatives, and with facilitation, the team can achieve its goals. On the other hand, if a team is not properly facilitated, then conflict may result in a dysfunctional project team that cannot achieve it goals and objectives.

The key concepts necessary in forming a globally diverse project team are listed in Table 18.4. I have used these tools and methods with great success in building teams across Asia, Australia, and Europe, as well as across North America, and found that the basic principles of team formation and management do not change regardless of the cultural background of the team members. Admittedly, there are cultural differences across the world that may necessitate modifications to how teams are formed and managed in those regions. However, it is especially important in today's competitive world, because teams do not have the time to slowly adapt as they evolve and mature, to go through the team maturation stages in a matter of weeks. This is not only possible, but, in fact, occurs on a regular basis across many industries and organizations throughout the world. As an example, in my book entitled *Lean Six Sigma for Supply Chain Management*, I described how a multicultural team consisting of individuals from across the United States and India, whom I have never met in person, worked effectively together to publish a book on schedule without any issues. I have also been involved in several consulting assignments in which the process workflows were managed across several countries. This type of work is becoming the norm, not an exception. Global team coordination is accomplished using basic team facilitation tools and methods. These include establishing a work schedule, assigning roles and responsibilities, and using simple communication vehicles, including e-mail, phone calls, and faxes.

Project Planning

Project planning begins once a team has confirmed that a project's problem statement and objective are correct, or it has been modified to reflect a team's project goals and objectives. Once a problem statement and its objective are finalized by a team, they are broken into project milestones. Project milestones are used as project control points and consist of one or more aggregated work activities. In turn, work activities are disaggregated into the work tasks. A major objective of a project team is to decompose and time phase a project's high-level goals and objectives or deliverables into milestones, activities, and work tasks using a method called work breakdown structure (WBS). The WBS method creates a list of sequential and well-defined work tasks that are aggregated at an activity or operational level of detail for presentation purposes. Activities have a start and end point, specific deliverable or measurable output, defined resource requirement, and time duration.

Estimating the Critical Path Using PERT

A project Gantt chart and PERT model of a project's sequential and spatially related work tasks represented as a network is constructed using a project's WBS and its aggregated activities. Figure 18.2 shows a simple example of a project network. This network has six operations or activities spatially arranged into two parallel paths. For simplicity, we will not go deeper into the work task level, but instead quantify the model at an activity or operational level. We will use the simple example shown in Figure 18.2 to demonstrate the concepts necessary to build a network model. These include creating its work breakdown structure (WBS), building a Gantt

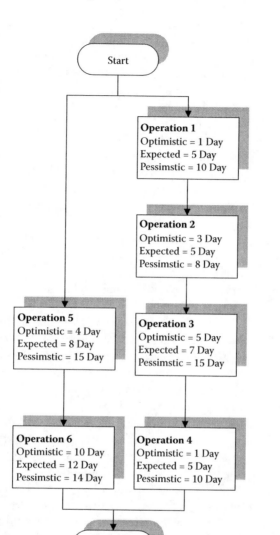

Figure 18.2   Analysis using the program evaluation and review technique (PERT).

chart, and calculating a network's critical path and the probability of completing a project on schedule along its critical path.

A project team begins its analysis by estimating the time to complete each activity or operation within a project's network. In the absence of actual historical or current cycle time data for each operation, a team estimates the most optimistic, expected, and most pessimistic times to complete each activity or operation based on a team's collective knowledge. This knowledge is based on the known work tasks and risks of completing an activity. To show how this analysis is actually conducted,

Figure 18.2 is constructed using six activities or operations. However, depending on the required level of analytical detail, activities or operations can be disaggregated into their associated work tasks, as shown in Figure 18.3, in which operation 1 is broken into several lower-level work tasks. However, in the current example, we will work at an activity or operational level of detail. Each operation of Figure 18.2 has three completion time estimates. These will be used to calculate an expected completion time for each operation, as well as a variance in completion time. The calculations for operation 1 are shown in Figure 18.3. The expected completion time of operation 1 is 5.17 days, and its variance is 2.25 days^2. Calculations for the other five operations in the project network are summarized in Table 18.6, along with several other statistics. We will discuss these statistics later in this chapter.

There are several ways to characterize the network shown in Figure 18.2. The most common is a Gantt chart, as shown in Figure 18.4. The two parallel paths of the network are clearly shown in Figure 18.4. Also, it will be demonstrated that a network's critical path is through operations 1 to 4, and that a calculated overall expected project completion time for these four operations is 23.5 days. But notice that the total time required to complete all six operations is 44.0 (rounded) days. This implies that operations 5 and 6 have slack or extra time available on their parallel path. We will discuss the concept of slack time below. It should be mentioned that software such as Microsoft Project is very useful in constructing Gantt charts and managing project resources on a daily basis. Gantt charts also help divide a network into milestones, work activities, and work tasks. The project in this example is managed at an activity or operational level.

Figure 18.5 shows the procedure used to identify and analyze a network to find the operations making up its critical path. In this procedure, several statistics must be calculated to identify operations along a project's critical path. These statistics are the earliest starting time (ES), earliest finishing time (EF), latest starting time (LS), and latest finishing time (LF) of an operation. In complicated networks, these statistics are calculated using software. A first step in the calculation is to use an expected completion time of each activity and make a forward pass through the network to estimate the ES and EF statistics of every operation. This is shown in Step 2 of Table 18.5. Once the earliest finish time has been calculated for the last operation or activity of a project network, which in this example is 23.5 days, a backward pass is made through the network. This backward pass is used to help calculate the LS and LF statistics using the relationship in Step 3 of Table 18.5. The slack time of every operation is calculated using the relation shown in Step 4 of Table 18.5. An operation having zero slack must be started and finished on time and is on the critical path of a network. In other words, it has no slack time. The statistics described in Table 18.5 are summarized in Figure 18.6 and again in Table 18.6. Once network information is summarized, it can be used to find the probability of completing a project at various target times. In Figure 18.6, a

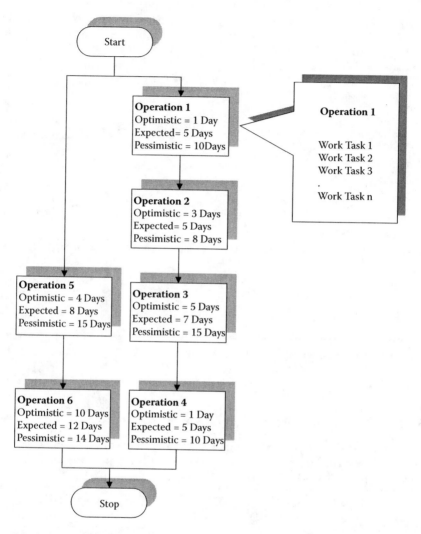

Calculations for Operation 1:

$$\text{Expected Completion Time (t)} = \frac{\text{Optimistic} + (4{*}\text{Expected}) + \text{Pessimistic}}{6} = 5.17 \text{ Days}$$

$$\text{Variance of Completion Time} = \left[\frac{\text{Pessimistic} - \text{Optimistic}}{6} \right]^2 = 2.25 \text{ Days}$$

Figure 18.3   Developing a work breakdown structure (WBS).

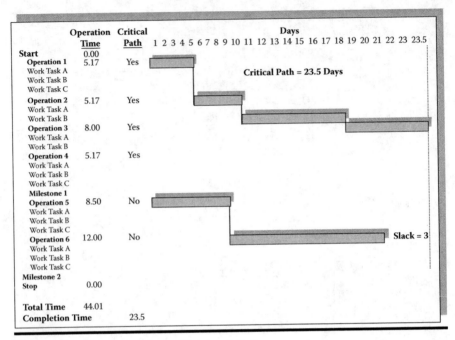

Figure 18.4   Gantt chart-prioritized task listing.

Table 18.5   Determining a Critical Path of the Network

1. A path is a linked sequence of work tasks within a network, beginning with a start node and ending with a stop node. The critical path is the longest sequence of network work tasks.

2. Earliest start time (ES) and earliest finish time (EF) for a work task are defined by the relation EF = ES + t, where t is the duration of the work task.

3. Latest start time (LS) and earliest start time (ES) for a work task are defined by the relation LS = LF – t.

4. Slack time for a work task is defined by the relation LS – ES = LF – EF.

5. Make a forward pass through the network calculating the EF and LF times for every work task.

6. Make a backward pass through the network using the total calculated completion time as the LF time.

7. The critical path is defined as the sequence of work tasks having zero slack time, as defined in Step 4.

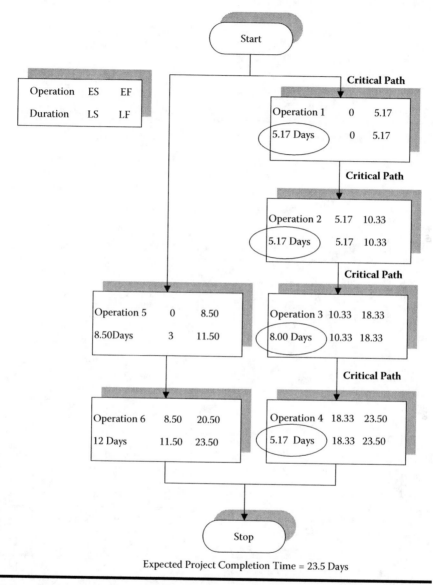

Figure 18.5 Calculation of the project's critical path.

completion probability of 34 percent was calculated based on a hypothetical target completion time of 20 days and assuming the project completion times formed a normal distribution. These calculations also assumed that the expected completion time was 23.5 days with a 7.97 day^2 variance (or 95 percent interval of 23.5 ± (1.96) (2.83 days) = 18 to 29 days).

1. Expected Completion Time (t) =
   5.17 + 5.17 + 8.00 + 5.17 = 23.5 Days

2. Variance of Completion Time =
   2.25 + 0.69 + 2.78 + 2.25 = 7.97 Days

3. Probability of Completing Project in 20 Days =
   Probability Z ≤(20 − 3.5)/7.97) = −0.41 = 34%

Figure 18.6   Summarized statistics for critical path operations.

Table 18.6   PERT and Critical Path: Summary Statistics by Operation

Operation	Optimistic Completion Time	Expected Completion Time	Pessimistic Completion Time	Average (Expected Time)	Variance	Earliest Start (ES)	Latest Start (LS)	Earliest Finish (EF)	Latest Finish (LF)	Slack	Critical Path
1	1	5	10	5.17	2.25	0	0	5.17	5.17	0	Yes
2	3	5	8	5.17	0.69	5.17	5.17	10.33	10.33	0	Yes
3	5	7	15	8.00	2.78	10.33	10.33	18.33	18.33	0	Yes
4	1	5	10	5.17	2.25	18.33	18.33	23.50	23.50	0	Yes
5	4	8	15	8.50	3.36	0	3	8.50	11.50	3	No
6	10	12	14	12.00	0.44	8.50	11.50	20.50	23.50	3	No

Calculations for Operation 1:

$$\text{Expected completion time (t)} = \frac{\text{Optimistic} + (4*\text{Expected}) + \text{Pessimistic}}{6} = 5.17 \text{ days}$$

$$\text{Variance of completion time} = \left[\frac{\text{Pessimistic} - \text{Optimistic}}{6}\right]^2 = 2.25 \text{ days}$$

Table 18.7   20 Key Project Management and Control Activities

1. Top-level project tasks
2. Critical tasks that must be done on schedule
3. Milestones that must be met on schedule and cost
4. Working days used versus allocated for the project
5. Responsibility matrix of resources to work tasks and schedule
6. Work task that must be completed within 24 hours
7. Currently overallocated resources by work task
8. Unscheduled tasks that have been or must be completed, including resource requirements and schedule
9. Work tasks starting within the next 10 days
10. Work tasks in progress, including percentage complete
11. Completed work tasks, including consumed resources, cost, and schedule adherence
12. Work tasks that have been started late
13. Work tasks that are not meeting schedule or cost targets
14. Actual versus resource usage to date
15. Project cash flow projections
16. Actual versus budgeted cost to date
17. Work tasks that are overbudget
18. Work tasks that can be "crashed" to reduce their expected completion time
19. Currently identified project risks, issues, and concerns
20. All other issues currently impacting the project schedule or cost

Project Management

Project management requires that a combination of tools and methods be applied to manage people and other resources to ensure that a project's activities remain on schedule and within budget, and a team effectively executes its deliverables or objectives. Table 18.7 lists 20 key project management and control activities that are necessary to manage projects. There are also many software packages that will provide the information listed in Table 18.7. Listing the network's activities and work tasks in Gantt chart format is an important step to managing a project because it shows when and in which sequence activities must be completed by a team. In addition to quantifying work task duration and similar cycle time information, a team must estimate the resources necessary to complete each work task. Once this project information has been gathered and summarized, it can be analyzed to find a project's critical path and create management reports as a project moves through its schedule. In fact, the information listed in Table 18.7 can be communicated and published on a continuing basis to communicate a project's status to an organization. Depending on a project's complexity, project management software may also be required to monitor and communicate a project's status.

Project management requires attention to detail. The information listed in Table 18.7 will enable a project manager to keep a project on schedule and within budget. It will also help manage a project as conditions dynamically change if project management software is used to control a project. Software enables a team to create simulations of a project's activities and analyze the impact of adding resources to operations on its critical path. Alternatively, if a project's activities are delayed, its resources can be reallocated to the delayed activities. In other words, simulations allow cost versus time trade-offs, which allow a project manager to control a project more effectively. This may be important in situations in which a project is completed ahead of schedule and incremental revenues can be obtained that more than offset the incremental resource costs necessary to move the project ahead of its original schedule.

Managing Project Risk

Projects have several associated risks. These include achieving required performance targets, financial benefits, and achieving cycle time targets. Figure 18.7 shows how project risk information can be summarized and managed by a project manager. The summarization shown in Figure 18.7 is similar to that shown in Figure 4.8. Figure 18.7 can also be modified based on the specific project management requirements. In summary, a project team must consider a project's risks, by their type, the probability of risk occurrence, their project impact, and alternatives that will eliminate or mitigate risk occurrence.

Summary

Project management is a complicated series of activities requiring specialized tools and methods. In many ways, effective project management requires attention to detail at a work task level, but also keeping the overall project schedule in view to achieve the projected time, cost, and other benefits required by the project's charter. Table 18.8 lists several key concepts that are necessary to ensure effective project

Failure Impact:	Low(1)				Medium(5)				High(9)			
Failure Probability:	<.25	.26–.50	.51–.75	>.76	<.25	.26–.50	.51–.75	>.76	<.25	.26–.50	.51–.75	>.76

Identify Risk Type:

1. Project Schedule
2. Project Cost
3. Deliverables
    1. Performance
       Benefits

    2. Financial
       Benefits

    3. Cycle Time
       Benefits

    4. Other Customer
       Requirements

    5. Health & Safety
       Requirements

    6. Regulatory
       Requirements

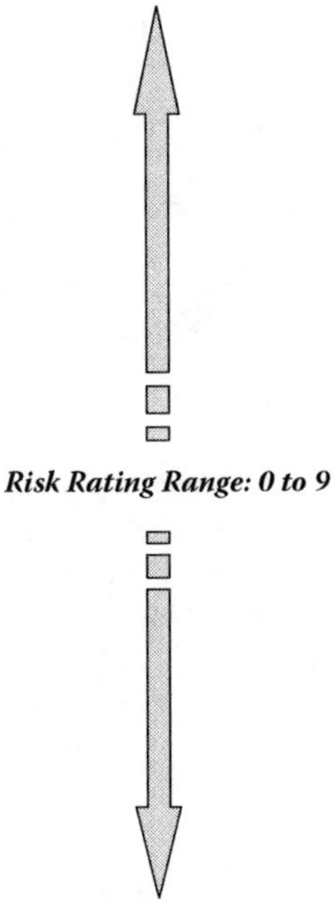

Risk Rating Range: 0 to 9

Risk Response Plan:

Figure 18.7 Management of a project's risk.

management. These include building a business case for a project, forming a multicultural and diverse project team around a project charter, using proper team facilitation methods, developing a list of project milestones, activities, and work tasks with their earliest and latest starting and finishing times, as well as required resources, developing Gantt charts and PERT models of a project's network to analyze project risks, and developing plans to reduce, eliminate, or manage that risk.

Table 18.8 Key Concepts to Improve Project Management Effectiveness

1. Build a business case for the project and form a multicultural and diverse project team around the project charter. Remember to use proper team facilitation methods.
2. Develop a list of project milestones, activities, and work tasks with their earliest and latest starting and finishing times, as well as required resources.
3. Develop Gantt charts and PERT models of the project's network to analyze the project as it moves through its schedule.
4. Analyze project risks and develop plans to reduce, eliminate, or manage the risk.

Suggested Reading

James P. Lewis. (2001). *Project Planning Scheduling and Control*, 3rd ed. McGraw-Hill, New York.

Robert K. Wysocki with contributions by Rudd McGary. (2003). *Effective Project Management*, 3rd ed. Wiley Publishing, New York.

GLOBAL SUPPLY-CHAIN MANAGEMENT INTEGRATION AND CONTROL

5

Chapter 19

Value Integration through Global Supply Chains

Competitive solution 19: Increase capacity, flexibility, and productivity by insourcing and outsourcing process workflows.

Overview

Global supply chains continue to evolve due to the increasingly competitive environments, technology, changing consumer preferences, and increased access to local markets across the world. Political and cultural changes aside, from an operations management perspective, this evolutionary process has been supported through enabling technologies and newly developed tools, methods, and concepts that increase supply-chain responsiveness and its flexibility to match supply and demand. In parallel, customers have been demanding higher quality and lower per unit transaction costs for their products and services. To satisfy these evolving customer requirements, delivery strategies and systems have been developed to transport highly differentiated products and services across the world. In addition, new types of organizations have come into existence and older ones have reinvented themselves in an effort to provide an increasingly greater variety of products and services to a global economy. In fact, many of these newer organizations have been formed around completely new products and services that did not exist several years ago. This evolutionary process continues to accelerate.

Productivity and shareholder economic value added (EVA) have been obvious drivers of supply-chain globalization. This has forced organizations to create new ways to lower their per unit transaction costs and increase international sales. As an example, the per unit transaction costs in many service industries have been dramatically reduced because the transportation costs associated with moving information are low, and its delivery infrastructure can be located anywhere in the world. This is because information in electronic format can be created, reviewed, and electronically distributed locally anywhere in the world. In this context, service businesses have gained much through supply-chain globalization and enabling information technologies. In addition to improvements in hardware and software, people have also learned to work more effectively across global supply chains. This has been accomplished using team building and project management tools and methods such as those discussed in Chapter 18 and shown in Table 18.4. As an example, a few years ago, I worked with a major corporation's project champions located in Japan, Korea, Hong Kong, and Singapore. The net result of our combined efforts was a successful Lean Six Sigma operational assessment and training that delivered many process improvement projects ahead of their schedule. The training was also conducted simultaneously in Japanese, Korean, and English using interpreters. In parallel, the project mentoring was conducted on site as I visited each country every month between training classes. At the end of the consulting assignment, the leader of the corporation's worldwide deployment told the Asian country's president that the deployment was the most successful in his business unit. In summary, this multicultural team, which was thrown together in less than 30 days and spanned 12,000 miles, was more effective than teams located within the United States that were more homogeneous, linguistically, culturally, and geographically. This was not an unusual situation because project teams deployed by many global organizations across the world are achieving similar results every day.

In addition to service businesses, manufacturers have benefited from globalization due to lower manufacturing costs and new market opportunities. In Chapter 9, we discussed ways to increase global capacity. In addition to making internal operations more effective and efficient, the insourcing of value-adding work, associated with core competencies, or outsourcing non-value-adding work, not associated with core competencies, can dramatically increase an organization's supply-chain capacity and productivity. Table 9.4 listed ten reasons driving the insourcing and outsourcing of work across global supply chains over the past several decades. In parallel, Table 9.5 showed that there are many types of business relationships that can be created to facilitate the globalization of work activities. An optimum insourcing or outsourcing strategy will depend on increasing productivity and shareholder EVA for all the participants within a supply chain over time. However, insourcing and outsourcing strategies will have risks, as shown in Table 9.6. Project teams can identify and manage these risks to achieve productivity and EVA goals. The high degree of globalization that has been created within the past few decades has been enabled by information technology using process workflow management tools, methods, and similar concepts discussed in Chapter 15. In summary, all of the operation management tools, methods, and concepts presented in this book have contributed, to various degrees, to the current state of globalization of product and service systems.

Value Integration across the Global Supply Chain

Table 19.1 lists several topics that will be important in our discussion of global supply chains. A quick review of Table 19.1 shows that best-in-class supply chains should be profitable, dominate their markets, manage assets efficiently, and continually improve their operations relative to the management of supply and demand activities. Unfortunately, many organizations cannot execute their strategic goals and objectives. Also, their supply chains are not profitable and do not dominate their markets or continuously improve productivity and EVA. This is caused, in part, by an inability to meet customer needs and value expectations. In fact, in some situations, an organization may not have formulated a consistent long-term strategic vision. As an example, some U.S. automotive organizations have become a classic and overused example of rigorous cost-cutting strategies to become competitive, rather than developing effective long-term value integration strategies through marketing research. However, admittedly, a complicating factor in this industry's noncompetitiveness is that they have been under a heavy burden of legacy costs associated with retirees and other worker entitlements. Unfortunately, competitors such a Toyota and Honda have been increasing their value content at a faster rate with a lower overall legacy cost structure. This situation started to become obvious in the mid-1980s; however, since then, the U.S. automotive industry has not been able to match the productivity increases of its Japanese competitors. The point I want to make is that organizations that use globalization as a vehicle to only lower product or service cost may not be focused entirely on the critical task of enhancing the value of their product and service offerings from an external

Table 19.1 Competitive World Metrics: Global Supply Chains

1. Profit and gross margins by process workflow
2. Market share by product group
3. Asset utilization efficiencies by process workflow
4. Gross margin return on investment (GMROI)
5. Customer service levels by process workflow
6. Lead time by process workflow
7. Forecasting accuracy by process workflow
8. Percentage of value-adding work by process workflow

customer viewpoint. In other words, customers are differentiated and do not necessary want a lowest-cost product or service. A focal point of this book has been to build adaptable and flexible operations to produce products and services of value that customers need. Operational strategies should follow business and marketing strategies, and not the other way around. Unfortunately, this is not always an easy situation when an industry has invested heavily in outdated products, services, and their process workflows. On the other hand, I have observed Holiday Inn over the past ten years. On a personal level, I have found it very interesting to see Holiday Inn significantly improve its infrastructure and differentiate its product and service offerings. I believe they offer real value to their customers. Marriott is another example where there is a fair value exchange between all parties. The list of great organizations is long.

In Figure 19.1, the concept of a global supply chain is abstracted to show its three major components of environment, organizational strategy, and tactical competencies used to execute higher-level strategies in a competitive environment. This competitive environment includes competitive threats, various forms of govern-

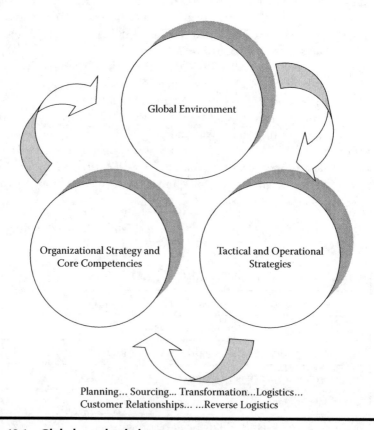

Planning... Sourcing... Transformation...Logistics...
Customer Relationships... ...Reverse Logistics

Figure 19.1 Global supply-chain components.

mental regulations, incentives and sanctions, various levels of regional political stability, and myriad other factors that impact international organizations. Many of these environmental factors are also listed in Table 9.6. High-level global supply-chain activities associated with Figure 19.1 include planning, sourcing, transformation, logistical management, customer relationships, and reverse logistical activities combined with the production of products or services. We will discuss the components of these higher-level supply-chain activities within this chapter in more detail.

Figure 19.2 breaks down higher-level global supply-chain activities from a value perspective. This value perspective emphasizes process integration using the voice of the customer (VOC) to pull value through a global supply chain. This concept is especially important as customer needs and value expectations have migrated. In fact, order fulfillment process workflows have become more sophisticated through the use of information technology to enhance operational flexibility. Also, Lean methodologies and concepts have significantly increased supply-chain flexibility through process simplification, standardization, and mistake-proofing strategies. In fact, within the demand management side of a supply chain, the acquisition of point-of-sale (POS) and similar real-time demand information has minimized the use of forecasting models with their notoriously poor accuracy. In parallel, electronic commerce increasingly enables the capture of customer demand based on local purchasing preferences. Enabling technologies also help to smooth out aggregated product and service demand patterns and increase the number of supply points to more evenly match demand. eBay is a good example in which demand for a variety of goods is supplied by numerous suppliers and is matched literally one to one. This negates the need for high capital or inventory investment, except for the logistical systems that transport the purchased products to eBay customers.

Table 19.2 lists ten important characteristics of successful global supply chains. These include high collaboration among all participants, a high multicultural presence, adherence to global operational standards, high product availability, low per unit transaction costs, low order-to-delivery cycle times, a high transaction accuracy,

←——————————— Value Chain Integration ———————————→

Demand Management	Supply Base Capability	Order Fulfillment	Voice-of-the-Customer (VOC)
•Account Management •Electronic Commerce •Product Growth •Marketing Activities	•Lean Production •Short Lead Times •Small Lot Sizes	•Direct Source to Customer Shipments •Merge inTransit •Distribution Focused on Consolidation Vs Inventory	•On Time, Accurate, Consistent Delivery of Quality Products at Competitive Prices and Differentiated Products Supplied on Demand Through Vendor Managed Inventory (VMI)

——————————————————————————————————→ Pull

Figure 19.2   Global supply chains integrate value.

Table 19.2 10 Key Characteristics of a Global Supply Chain

1. High collaboration	Improve communication and develop joint ventures and partnerships to insource and outsource work and to share supply-chain risks.
2. High multicultural presence	Develop workforces reflecting local demographics and supplier and customer networks within the supply chain.
3. Adherence to global operational standards	Adhere to standards to improve communication and help to simplify product and process designs, lowering cost and cycle time. Quality is also improved through standardization.
4. High product availability	Deploy effective demand management strategies, including customer contracts (order book), point-of-sale (POS) information, and other real-time-enabled demand collection systems.
5. Low per unit transaction cost	Drive low cost at all levels of the supply chain through improved quality, reduced cycle time, and more efficient product and process designs.
6. Low order cycle time	Eliminate intermediaries throughout the supply chain, as well as all non-value-adding operations, using Lean methods.
7. High transaction accuracy	Deploy continuous quality improvement tools, methods, and concepts through Six Sigma, TQM, and other initiatives to improve quality.
8. High asset availability and flexibility	Deploy Lean, Total Productive Maintenance (TPM), and Six Sigma to improve availably and flexibility.
9. High asset utilization efficiency	Increase asset utilization and efficiency metrics, as seen by improved return on assets and inventory turns to "Lean-out" the supply chain.
10. High process standardization	Standardize and mistake-proof all work using Lean tools, methods, and concepts to improve quality and reduce cycle time and cost.

and high asset availability and flexibility. Achievement of high collaboration is enabled by a supply chain's communication systems. High collaboration helps identify where assets should be positioned within a supply chain to increase their return-on-assets (ROA) targets. Chapter 18 showed that it is also important to develop project teams that reflect local demographics and supplier networks. Another characteristic of a successful global supply chain is its adherence to commonly accepted design and operational standards. This ensures that its products and services consistently meet customer requirements across diverse regions and cultures. Standards also help simplify product and service designs. Product and service simplification, in turn, helps lower supply chain per unit transaction costs and cycle time. The tools, methods, and concepts necessary to design and produce products and services, with a view toward standardization and simplification, were discussed in Chapters 4 and 5. High product availability is another important characteristic of successful global supply chains. *Availability* implies demand has been efficiently matched to its supply. Along this line of thought, it is important to deploy demand management strategies that ensure demand accuracy. In other words, demand management systems should move away from a heavy reliance on forecasting models toward the use of customer contracts (order book), point-of-sale (POS) information, and similar systems that accurately capture customer demand in real-time or by contract. Important tools, methods, and concepts related to demand management were discussed in Chapter 8. Many of the methods discussed in this book will enable a global supply chain to increase its operational performance. Integral to improving supply-chain productivity is an elimination of intermediaries using design-for-manufacturing (DFM), mass customization, and similar design methods to simplify products and services. In parallel, Total Productive or Preventive Maintenance (TPM) and Six Sigma should also be deployed to improve a supply chain's availability and flexibility. Finally, standardization, mistake-proofing, and similar Lean tools, methods, and concepts can help to improve supply-chain productivity and reduce its cycle time. The overall business benefits using these combined initiatives results in higher asset utilization and efficiency.

Table 19.3 lists ten strategic objectives of a global supply chain. These include the development of global strategic partnerships or other business relationships as specified by their incremental value to all parties, high margins, highly differentiated products and services to increase supply-chain competitiveness in its local markets, an ongoing rationalization of asset utilization and efficiency, and technology deployment as described in Chapter 15. Technology deployment includes deployment of a business process management suite (BPMS), business process management (BPM), business modeling and analysis (BMA), business intelligence (BI), business activity monitoring (BAM), enterprise application integration (EAI), workflow management (WM), and enterprise resource planning (ERP) systems. Additional strategic objectives include an ongoing rationalization of transportation modes and their relative efficiencies, ongoing insourcing and outsourcing rationalization activities, an effective matching of supply to its demand through global capacity planning activities, and development of process-driven operations having a high value content and a high degree of global standardization with local differentiation.

Strategic partnerships can also help expand a supply chain's available capacity and new marketing opportunities. In this context, every organization within a supply chain must be able to extract a level of value higher through its participation

Table 19.3 10 Strategic Objectives of Global Supply Chains

1. Global strategic partnerships	Strategic partnerships can expand a global supply chain's resource base and demand space. However, all parties must be able to extract value incremental to other forms of association.
2. High margins across the supply chain	Margins should be at their entitlement level. Entitlement means every part of the supply chain extracts a margin reflective of its capital investment and risk given its competitive environment.
3. Highly differentiated products to increase competitiveness in local markets	Products and services must be designed to reflect local culture and consumer needs and value expectations, but be designed in a way that allows mass customization principles to be used effectively and efficiently.
4. Ongoing rationalization of asset utilization and efficiency across the supply chain	Questions surrounding what assets are required, where they should be located, and who should own them are an ongoing series of analyses designed to ensure all parts of the supply chain have high asset utilization efficiencies.
5. Technology deployment through BPMS, BPM, BMA, BI, BAM, EAI, WM, and ERP	Integration of the flow of materials and information through the supply chain is an ongoing integrative process that uses a hierarchy of information technology platforms, tools, and methods to create useful information to manage workflows.
6. Ongoing rationalization of transportation modes	The development of optimum routing sequences is a series of ongoing network evaluations using operations research tools and methods designed to reduce cycle time along a network's cricitcal path and reduce cost by evaluating constraints related to demand and supply and other relevant information.
7. Insourcing and outsourcing rationalization	The analysis and decision regarding where work should be performed within the supply chain are ongoing activities based on where the most value can be added to reduce overall supply-chain cycle time and cost.
8. Match supply and demand	The ability to determine item demand by location and time enables an efficient matching of supply to demand. Demand estimation is enabled using real-time point-of-sale (POS) data that is obtained from the customers regarding actual sales of products or services.

Table 19.3 (continued)   10 Strategic Objectives of Global Supply Chains

9. Process-driven operations having high value content	Processes should be designed around major work streams having similar output requirements related to time, cost, and quality, as well as similar product or service designs.
10. High operational standardization	High standardization is required to ensure that operations are completed in a minimum amount of time without error. However, a system should be easily reconfigurable, with its resultant standards reflecting the newly configured system.

than without it. In fact, a goal of an efficient supply-chain should focus on which organizations may participate, but on a differentiated basis, depending on their strategic goals and objectives. This was discussed in Chapter 9 and shown in Table 9.5. Regardless of the eventual business relationships, a best-in-class global supply chain, at an operational level, should exhibit high operating margins and similar successful performance characteristics for its participants. As an example, operating margins should be at an entitlement level, in the sense that every part of a supply chain should extract a profit margin, reflective of its capital investment and risk given its local competitive environment. Products and services should be designed to reflect local culture and consumer needs and value expectations, and designed in a way that enables mass customization principles to be implemented effectively and efficiently. Best-in-class supply chains also optimally manage assets and determine where they should be located and who should own them. This is an evolving series of analyses that are designed to ensure that all organizations within the supply chain have high asset utilization efficiencies. Effectively integrating the flow of materials and information through a supply chain is also an ongoing evaluative process that uses a hierarchy of information technology platforms, tools, and methods to create useful information to manage a supply chain's process workflows. The development of optimum routing across process workflows is also important. These activities require a continual evaluation of a supply chain's demand and supply constraints using operations research tools and methods to improve productivity. Decisions regarding where and how work should be performed within a supply chain are an ongoing set of activities to evaluate where the highest value can be added to reduce overall order-to-delivery cycle time and per unit cost. This concept was discussed in Chapter 5 and shown in Table 5.15 as a simple linear programming model.

It is also important that organizations accurately estimate demand for their products by stocking location to minimize high inventory investment. Point-of-sale (POS) data, obtained from customers using actual sales of products or services, can greatly enhance efficiency of demand management in these environments.

Also, the design of process workflows should be similar to the greatest extent possible. Finally, a major objective of best-in-class global supply chains should be a high degree of process workflow standardization to ensure operational work tasks are efficiently completed without error. However, although highly standardized, a supply chain should also be easily reconfigurable and its operational standards automatically updated to reflect newly reconfigured systems. As an example, many years ago, when I worked at United Parcel Service (UPS), I noticed that its network could easily be expanded or contracted by more than 50 percent based on seasonal variations of daily package volume. This operational capability was enabled by a high degree of process standardization and technology.

Several Important Supply-Chain Functions

Supply chains contain thousands of different work tasks that can be aggregated into the basic functions shown in Figure 19.3. This format is also called a SIPOC (supplier–input boundary–process–output boundary–customer) high-level map. Recall that a SIPOC is a high-level graphical representation of a process and was discussed in Chapter 3 and shown in Figure 3.12. On the supplier side of a SIPOC, suppliers ship products or services to one or more distribution centers within a supply chain. Important integrative systems at this point in a distribution system may include distribution requirements planning (DRP) and materials resource planning (MRPII), as well as enterprise resource planning (ERP) systems. The MRPII system is used to order materials, components, and other items that may be needed for immediate production requirements or for placement into inventory for later usage. A DRP system manages inventory throughout the distribution center network. Supporting activities include the management of purchase orders and accounts payable as well as the selection and management of suppliers and carriers. Additional information that may be necessary to manage the incoming traffic at a supply chain's input boundary may be related to the types of products it distributes. This is because product characteristics may impact freight rates, shipping modes, and how a product is transported within a supply chain. Other important activities may include the routing of shipments, governmental regulations and tariffs, carrier costs and policies, accuracy of bills-of-lading, special tracking requirements, and required sign-offs. In parallel, customer claims, returns, and fleet maintenance are usually controlled at a distribution center level within a supply chain. Distribution centers also receive and warehouse materials for shipment to customers. There may also be packaging and light assembly operations within a distribution center. Supporting activities may include developing workload forecasts, maintaining equipment, receiving inbound trucks, storing inventory, and replenishment activities and order picking, including pack-out, dock audits, and the loading of outbound trucks. Also, there may be invoicing operations within a distribution center as well as claims and returned goods operations. Each of these operations requires systems

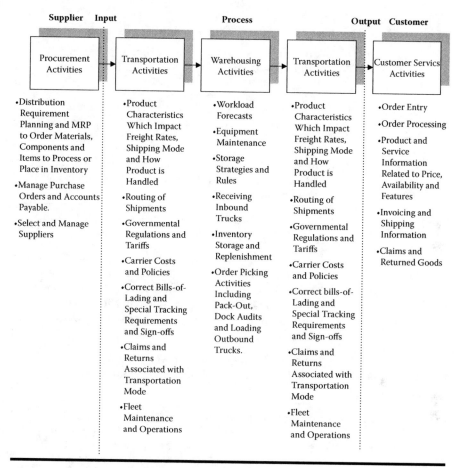

Figure 19.3   Global supply-chain overview.

to control its material and information flows. Any of these process workflows may be complicated and require unique operational tools and methods. As an example, if order entry and processing functions reside within a distribution center, then information related to products and services, including their pricing, availability, and performance features, must be made available to order entry people to provide customers with the information necessary to place their orders.

Table 19.4 views supply-chain operations at a more detailed level. Imports and exports from one country to another require specialized process workflows to ensure that orders are put together quickly using the most efficient means of transportation for shipment to customers. Supply chains also rely on many different types of software systems that enable information systems in disparate locations to communicate with each other. In addition to these tools and methods, the best routings and modes of transportation for products in a supply chain must be determined. At

Table 19.4   15 Important Global Supply-Chain Functions

1. Import/export	Imports and exports from one country to another require specialized processes and training, at which global supply chains excel.
2. Electronic Data Interchange (EDI)	Software systems that allow information systems in disparate locations to communicate with each other.
3. Transportation analysis	The tools and methods used to determine the best routing and mode of transportation for products in the supply chain.
4. Carrier management	The tools and methods used to select, negotiate, and monitor organizations that move products within a supply chain.
5. Load optimization	The tools and methods used to ensure products are loaded correctly relative to weight, volume, and quality, to ensure that they arrive without damage, and that target per unit costs relative to labor and transportation are achieved.
6. Fleet management/ maintenance	The tools and methods used to ensure that the supply chain has the correct number and types of equipment, and it is available for use on demand.
7. Traffic routing	The tools and methods used to direct the flow of products through different transportation modes and networks to achieve the lowest cycle time and cost.
8. Claims management	The tools and methods used to identify, manage, and reduce customer claims relative to errors, high cost, or longer than expected cycle times.
9. Distribution requirements planning (DRP)	A system of tools and methods that matches supply with demand across a supply chain and inventory investment levels by item and location.
10. Network analysis	The tools and methods used to describe a supply chain, including all operations, as well as their spatial relationships quantified relative to time, costs, and other information.
11. Materials handling	The tools and methods used to move materials within distribution centers and various modes of transportation.

Table 19.4 (continued)   15 Important Global Supply-Chain Functions

12. Packaging	Operations within a distribution center that remove items from stock and insert them into protective packaging for either direct shipment to customers or storage as inventory.
13. Inventory management	The tools and methods used by organizations to ensure that inventory is available to satisfy customer demand, by maintaining inventory at an optimum level as determined by lead time, expected demand, and target per unit service levels.
14. Light assembly	Operations within a distribution center that involve work other than packaging by bringing together items.
15. Workload management	The tools and methods used to ensure that sufficient labor, material, and capital capacity exist to meet work schedules.

an operational level, products must be loaded onto trucks or containers in sequence and according to their weight and volume to ensure they arrive without damage at customer locations. It is also important that a supply chain has the correct numbers and types of equipment available upon demand. Finally, the balance of Table 19.4 describes the tools and methods used to manage and control the flow of products through different transportation modes and networks to achieve the lowest order-to-delivery cycle time and per unit cost. In summary, it is important that adequate tools and methods are available to ensure that sufficient labor and material capacity exist within a supply chain, and that they are efficiently utilized to move materials and information through the system.

Important Financial and Operational Metrics

Table 19.5 lists ten important financial metrics and ratios that are useful measurements of effectiveness and efficiency of a global supply chain. In addition, Table 19.6 lists ten key operational metrics that are also used for the same purpose. Relative to the financial metrics, a profit and loss (P/L) statement summarizes an organization's revenues and expenses for a specific period. Expenses on the P/L represent costs incurred in the course of business operations. An asset's value, such as inventory, is recorded on a balance sheet. Inventory investment is the amount of money invested in inventory by the various organizations within a supply chain. Inventory investment must be evaluated in conjunction with an inventory turns ratio. Excess

Table 19.5   10 Key Global Supply-Chain Financial Metrics

1. Profit/loss	A profit and loss statement summarizes an organization's revenues and expenses for a specific period. Expenses on the P/L are costs incurred in the course of business operations.
2. Inventory investment	Inventory investment is the amount of money invested in inventory.
3. Excess and inventory	Excess inventory is calculated based on multiples of lead time. A correlating metric is days of supply (DOS). If DOS exceeds either the demand quantity expected over the order cycle (or lead time in some situations) or the required lot size, there may be excess inventory in the system.
4. NOPAT	Net operating profit after taxes is calculated by dividing income after taxes by total revenue. Higher NOPAT levels are better than lower ones, but NOPAT tracks industry averages, so it is difficult to compare performance across different supply chains. As a result, NOPAT should be evaluated against direct competitors.
5. Asset efficiency	Asset efficiency (or turnover) is calculated by dividing total sales revenue by the total asset investment necessary to obtain these sales for the time period under analysis. Asset efficiency is an important metric to measure the degree of supply-chain "leanness." Lean supply chains have high asset efficiencies relative to their competitors'.
6. Fixed-asset efficiency	Fixed-asset efficiency (turns) = sales/(average property + plant + equipment)
7. Receivables efficiency	Receivables efficiency (turns) = net credit sales/average accounts receivables
8. Profit margin	Profit margin = gross profit/sales
9. ROA	Return on assets (ROA) = net profit margin × asset efficiency
10. GMROI	Gross margin return on investment (GMROI) = gross margin/average inventory investment at cost

Table 19.6   10 Key Supply-Chain Operational Metrics

1. Customer service target	Service-level targets can be expressed in unit fill, line fill, order fill, and financial terms. Service-level targets can also be defined from several perspectives, such as on-time delivery or delivery-to-promise and manufacturing schedule attainment, as well as other processes that touch the customer.
2. On-time supplier delivery	Supplier on-time delivery performance is calculated based on an agreed-upon versus actual delivery time. There could be several variations of the metric.
3. Overdue backlogs	Overdue order backlogs occur for many reasons. In most cases, available capacity may not exist (for a variety of reasons) or the backlog represents industry practice based on technology constraints, i.e., make-to-order systems.
4. Inventory efficiency (turns)	The number of times that an inventory "turns over" during a year is calculated as the ratio of annualized cost-of-goods-sold (COGS) divided by monthly average inventory investment.
5. Unplanned orders	There are many reasons for unplanned orders. These include poor demand forecasts by customers, internal process breakdowns, or failure to adhere to standard operating procedures regarding lead time and capacity requirements.
6. Schedule changes	Schedule changes are different from unplanned orders in the sense that they are caused by process changes or unforeseen circumstances.
7. Data accuracy	Data inaccuracies existing within a supply chain often impact one or more functions within an organization, as well as several organizations. Because decisions regarding how much product to make and which subcomponents to order, as well as their quantities, depend on accurate data within supply-chain systems, it is important to understand the degree of measurement error in supply-chain information technology (IT) systems.
8. Material availability	Lack of available material also drives up inventory investment because raw material and work-in-process (WIP) inventories remain unutilized due to missed manufacturing schedules.

(continued on next page)

Table 19.6 (continued)   10 Key Supply-Chain Operational Metrics

9. Forecast accuracy	Poor forecasting accuracy results in too much or too little inventory. There are many reasons for poor accuracy.
10. Lead time	Lead time is the time required to perform a single operation or series of operations in a network. Individual components of lead time include order preparation time, queue or waiting time, operational processing time, movement or transportation time, and time to inspect the work or a process.

inventory is another important financial metric tied to inventory management. It is usually calculated based on multiples of lead time. A correlating metric is days of supply (DOS). If DOS exceeds either the demand quantity expected over the order cycle (or lead time in some situations) or the required lot size, there may be excess inventory for a product in a system. Net operating profit after taxes (NOPAT) is calculated by dividing income after taxes by total revenue. Higher NOPAT levels are better than lower ones. But NOPAT tracks industry averages, so it is difficult to compare performance across different supply chains. Asset efficiency or turnover is calculated by dividing total sales revenue by the total asset investment necessary to obtain these sales for the period under analysis. Asset efficiency is an important metric used to measure the degree of supply-chain "leanness." Lean supply chains have higher asset efficiencies than their competitors. The other financial metrics represent key efficiency ratios.

Several of these metrics were discussed in Chapter 7 in the context of improving an organization's productivity level.

Ten key operational metrics are listed in Table 19.6. These will be discussed in the context of supply-chain operations. The first operational metric is service-level targets. These can be expressed in unit fill, line fill, and order fill. However, service-level targets can also be defined from several perspectives, such as on-time delivery, or delivery-to-promise and manufacturing schedule attainment. A second metric, supplier on-time delivery performance, is calculated based on an agreed-upon versus actual delivery date. There could also be several variations of an on-time delivery metric, depending on the organization and industry. A third metric, overdue order backlogs, can occur for many reasons. In most situations, available capacity may not exist for a variety of reasons, or an order backlog may be due to technology constraints, such as those found in make-to-order systems. A fourth metric, inventory efficiency (turns), is calculated as the ratio of annualized cost-of-goods-sold (COGS) to monthly average inventory investment. Inventory turns was discussed in Chapter 14. A fifth operational metric is unplanned orders. There are many reasons for an unplanned order, including poor demand forecasts by customers, internal process breakdowns, or a failure to adhere to standard operating procedures regarding lead time and capacity requirements. Schedule changes are different from unplanned orders in the sense that they are caused by process changes due to unforeseen circumstances that result in products not being produced as originally planned. The seventh operational metric, data accuracy, can have a significant impact on a supply chain because decisions regarding how much to manufacture and where to locate products depend on accurate data. For this reason, it is important to understand the extent, types, and locations of measurement errors across a supply chain existing within information technology (IT) systems. A lack of material required for production, the eighth metric, drives up inventory investment because raw materials and work-in-process (WIP) inventories remain unutilized due to missed manufacturing schedules. The ninth key operational metric is forecasting accuracy. Poor forecasting accuracy may result in too little or too much inventory or wasted capacity. Many of the reasons for poor forecasting accuracy were discussed in Chapter 8. The tenth operational metric, lead time, is adversely impacted by many various forms of process breakdowns. Lead time can be defined from several perspectives. In one context, it is the time required to perform a single operation with a process workflow. In another context, it may be the time to go through an entire process workflow. Individual components of lead time include order preparation time, queue or waiting time, operational processing time, movement or transportation time, and the time to inspect the work of a process. Lead time analysis and reduction were discussed in Chapters 5 and 6.

E-Supply-Chain Evolution

The extraordinarily high productivity and operational capability of today's global supply chains have been facilitated by rapidly evolving information technology (IT) systems, as discussed in Chapter 15. The evolution of IT systems and their impact on supply chains over the past several decades are shown in Figure 19.4 and Table 19.7. Modern IT systems enable information from across a global supply chain to be collected, analyzed, and used to change a process workflow based on software rules and algorithms, such as those that control workflow scheduling. As an example, workflow scheduling algorithms enable immediate changes in a production sequence based on changes to a system. This reduces lead time and increases customer service levels. Scheduling rules and algorithms were discussed in Chapter 12. Additional characteristics of e-supply and related IT systems allow coordination of process workflows and their work tasks as well as an elimination of intermediaries from a system. These supply-chain improvements result in process simplification, a deployment of differentiating processes, efficient asset allocation throughout the supply chain, and the establishment of rules for sharing information and intellectual assets across the world.

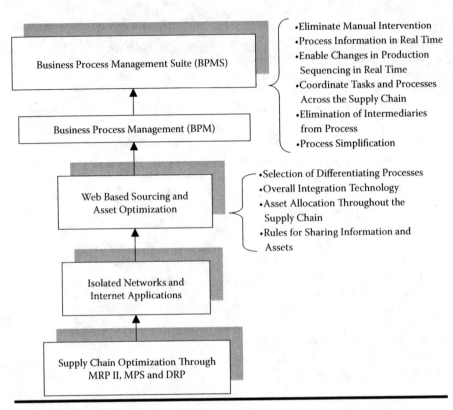

Figure 19.4 E-supply-chain evolution.

Business process management systems were discussed in Chapter 15 as higher-level systems that integrate the access and transfer of data from ERP and other supply-chain IT systems. Table 19.7 lists ten key systems used by supply chains to monitor and control their flow of materials and information. These systems include enterprise resource planning (ERP), materials requirements planning II (MRPII), materials requirements planning (MRP), distribution requirements planning (DRP), master production scheduling (MPS), the forecasting system, capacity requirements planning (CRP), the Manufacturing Automation Protocol (MAP) systems, the warehouse management systems (WMS), including auxiliary software systems, and advanced shipping notification (ASN) systems, which are used to control material flow between suppliers and their customers. An ERP system is a more sophisticated version of an MRPII system and includes accounting-related information as well as the resources needed to plan, manufacture, and ship customer orders. ERP systems may also be characterized by graphical user interfaces. MRPII was an earlier version of ERP in that it had higher functionality than the

Table 19.7   10 Key Supply-Chain Software Systems

1. Enterprise resource planning (ERP)	A more sophisticated version of an MRPII system that includes accounting-related information as well as the resources needed to plan, manufacture, and ship customer orders. These systems are also characterized by graphical user interfaces.
2. Material requirements planning II (MRPII)	A system with higher functionality than MRP. It includes operational and financial data conversion and allows business planning. It integrates functions related to sales and operations planning, master production planning, material requirements planning, and capacity planning.
3. Material requirements planning (MRP)	A system that uses bill-of-material (BOM), inventory, and master production schedule (MPS) information to calculate net requirements for materials and components for manufacturing and suppliers. The requirements are offset by material and component lead times.
4. Distribution requirements planning (DRP)	A system that replenishes inventory at branch locations throughout a distribution network using a time-phased order point or other logic for every item and location to translate planned orders via MRPII to suppliers.
5. Master production schedule (MPS)	A system that uses the sales forecast, order book demand, gross capacity, and on-hand inventory manufacturing planning to develop a netted manufacturing schedule.
6. Forecasting system	A system that uses historical demand and time series algorithms to predict future demand by forecasting time intervals over the forecasting time horizon.
7. Capacity requirements planning (CRP)	A system that uses MRPII information related to open and current manufacturing orders, as well as routings and time standards, to estimate required labor and machine time across facilities.
8. Manufacturing Automation Protocol (MAP)	A system based on the International Standards Organization (ISO) that allows communication among systems from different organizations. It depends on ISO's Open Systems Interconnection (OSI) standards.

(continued on next page)

Table 19.7 (continued)   10 Key Supply-Chain Software Systems

9. Warehouse management system (WMS)	A system that dynamically manages received materials and components, and assigns an inventory storage location. More advanced versions of these systems enable efficient order fulfillment and cycle-counting activities.
10. Advanced shipping notification (ASN)	An integrated system that allows customers and suppliers to know all the items making up an order by their pallet and vehicle using bar code scanning. A prerequisite is a supplier certification program and deployment of information technology.

original MRP. MRPII functionality includes operational and financial data conversion, which allows business planning. It also integrates functions related to sales and operations planning, master production planning, materials requirements planning, and capacity planning. The original MRP systems used bill-of-material (BOM), inventory, and MPS information to calculate net requirements for materials and components required for manufacturing and supplier orders. These net requirements were offset by material and component lead times. MRP and MRPII functions, including the BOM, were discussed in Chapter 13. A simple BOM was shown in Figure 13.3. Distribution requirements planning (DRP) is a system that replenishes inventory at branch locations throughout a distribution network. It uses time-phased order points or similar logic to translate planned orders via MRPII to suppliers for every item throughout a distribution system. The MPS was discussed in Chapter 13. It is a system that uses sales forecasts as well as order book or firm demand, estimated gross capacity, on-hand inventory levels, and other manufacturing planning information to develop a "netted" manufacturing schedule. This calculation process was discussed in Chapter 12 and shown in Table 12.3. The forecasting system uses historical demand and time series algorithms to predict future demand over a forecasting time horizon. A capacity requirements planning (CRP) system uses MRPII information related to open and current manufacturing orders, as well as product routings and time standards, to estimate the required labor and equipment at a local process workflow level. The Manufacturing Automation Protocol (MAP) system is based on the International Standards Organization (ISO) Open Systems Interconnection (OSI) standards, which allow communication among systems from different organizations. Warehouse management systems enable distribution centers to dynamically manage their materials and component receipts, and assign inventory storage locations. Advanced versions of these systems enable efficient order fulfillment and cycle-counting activities. Advanced shipment notification (ASN) systems provide customers and suppliers with visibility relative to the items making up their orders, by pallet and vehicle, and using bar code scanning systems. However, a prerequisite to deployment of an ASN system is a supplier certification program and deployment of information technology to ship and receive orders.

Common Process Breakdowns in Supply Chains

Supply chains experience process breakdowns because of their inherent complexity. Table 19.8 lists several major categories of process breakdowns. Breakdowns associated with poor line item availability result in unfilled orders, higher transaction costs, and lower customer satisfaction. A line is one product and its associated quantity. An order can consist of one or more line items. If products are not available to fill customer orders, the line item availability is less than 100 percent. The second category listed in Table 19.8 is backorders. A backorder is created when a product is not shipped to a customer as part of the original order. This type of process breakdown requires a product be shipped at a later date, resulting in incremental order handling and shipment costs. There may be several reasons for backorders. Customer complaints can occur whenever 100 percent of an order does not arrive on time and in a defect-free condition. Schedule changes may occur when products or services are ordered within their published lead time. This may result in a situation in which a regularly scheduled order is displaced from an established schedule, resulting in degradation of operational efficiency. Although schedule changes can occur due to unforeseen circumstances, chronic rescheduling should be investigated and its root causes eliminated from a process. The root causes for unplanned overtime expense should also be investigated and eliminated. Typical reasons for overtime may include unplanned orders, schedule changes, poor process yields, and similar process breakdowns. High inventory levels result in significant operational inefficiencies, as discussed in Chapter 14. Low inventory turns and their associated higher inventory carrying costs are a barometer indicating that there may be problems relative to long lead times, poor forecasting, or other process breakdowns. High inventory levels should be investigated and their causes eliminated from a process. A seventh category, low cash flow, can be caused by several factors, including long internal lead times, quality issues, internal billing errors, and customer payment policies. Incremental transaction costs related to labor and transportation also increase when materials or information is moved unnecessarily within the supply chain. Typical examples occur when materials are moved between distribution centers, instead of being initially placed at their correct location. This excludes inventory that has been strategically located at a central location. Low inventory turns are the result of high levels of current inventory relative to a product's cost of goods sold (COGS) and excess and obsolete inventory. Finally, product can also be damaged because of poor packaging, poor handling, or environmental conditions. Chronic damage problems should be investigated and their internal and external causes eliminated from a process workflow.

Table 19.8 10 Common Process Breakdowns in Global Supply Chains

1. Poor line item availability	A line is one product and its associated quantity. An order can consist of one or more line items. When product is not available to fill customer orders, the line item availability is less than 100%.
2. Backorders	A backorder is created when a product is not shipped to a customer as part of the original order. This situation requires the product be shipped at a later date, resulting in incremental handling and shipment costs.
3. Customer complaints	Customer complaints occur whenever 100% of an order does not arrive on time, defect-free, and at the agreed-upon cost.
4. Schedule changes	Schedules for products or services should not be changed within their lead time unless circumstances have changed because materials have been ordered and system capacity has been reserved to produce the product or service. Although schedule changes occur, chronic problems should be investigated and their internal and external causes eliminated from the process.
5. Unplanned overtime	Chronic problems causing unplanned overtime expenses should be investigated and their causes eliminated from the process. Typical reasons include unplanned orders, schedule changes, and poor process yields.
6. Unplanned inventory carrying costs	Chronic problems causing high inventory carrying costs should be investigated and their causes eliminated from the process. Theses causes will fall into the general categories of demand and lead time management.
7. Low cash flow	Low cash flow can be caused by several factors, including long internal lead times, quality issues, internal billing errors, and customer payment policies.
8. High product transfer costs and premium freight	When materials or information is moved unnecessarily between parts of the supply chain and, in particular, between distribution centers, incremental transaction costs related to labor and transportation increase.

Table 19.8 (continued)   10 Common Process Breakdowns in Global Supply Chains

9. Low inventory turns, excess and obsolete inventory	Low inventory turns can be caused by high levels of current inventory as well as excess and obsolete inventory. High inventory levels are caused by long. The causes of these problems should be investigated and their internal and external causes eliminated from the process.
10. Damaged product	Product can be damaged due to poor packaging, poor handling, or environmental conditions. Chronic damage problems should be investigated and their internal and external causes eliminated from the process.

Summary

The development of an effective and efficient global supply chain having workflows that are adaptable and flexible and contain high value content is very difficult. It requires that an organization create a long-term strategic vision of how it will expand its supply-chain capacity over time, including an ongoing evaluation of where work should be done and by whom. Table 19.9 presents several important concepts to build a best-in-class global supply chain. The first important concept is that an organization must develop the right types of strategic relationships in a manner described by Table 9.5. Organizations must also continually rationalize their asset utilization,

Table 19.9   Key Concepts to Improve Global Supply-Chain Effectiveness

1. Develop global strategic relationships.
2. Continually rationalize asset utilization and efficiencies.
3. Continually rationalize transportation modes.
4. Continually rationalize insourcing and outsourcing.
5. Ensure that supply and demand are matched across the supply chain.
6. Continually increase the percentage of value-adding work within process workflows.
7. Highly standardize and mistake-proof process workflows, but design in adaptability and flexibility.

transportation modes, and insourcing and outsourcing strategies. These combined actions will help to ensure that supply and demand are matched across an organization's supply chain. In addition, an organization must continually increase the percentage of value-adding work tasks within its process workflows, and standardize and mistake-proof the remaining work tasks. Finally, an organization must design its process workflows so that they are adaptable and easily reconfigurable, to ensure they evolve over time to meet customer needs and values expectations.

Suggested Reading

Joseph L. Cavinato and Ralph G. Kauffman, Eds. (2000). *The Purchasing Handbook*, 6th ed. McGraw-Hill, New York.

James W. Martin. (2007). *Lean Six Sigma for Supply Chain Management: The 10 Step Solution Process*. McGraw-Hill, New York.

James A. Tompkins and Dale Harmelink, Eds. (1994). *The Distribution Handbook*. McGraw-Hill, New York.

Chapter 20

Increasing Organizational Competitiveness through Standardization

Competitive solution 20: Integrate local standards into products and services to dominate local marketing niches across the world.

Overview

In order for an organization to be competitive in today's world, its design teams should understand, and help create, the standards that control how their products and services are designed, produced, and sold to customers. Standards form the basis of the rules and evaluation criteria organizations must jointly use, as an industry, to regulate their product and service performance. Standards also impact suppliers, customers, and a local society. As a result, standards of various types have been created for almost every product and service produced in the world today. An advantage of using industry standards is that they are usually well written by volunteers from the various stakeholder organizations within an industry based on many years of experience. Also, they contain very useful information regarding a consensus of the best practices of how a product or service should be designed, measured, and produced. This information enables a new entrant into an industry to quickly obtain information on how to efficiently develop and test its products and services to compete. However, organizations must also investigate and develop proprietary

Table 20.1 Competitive World Metrics: System Integration

1. Percentage of standards committee leadership positions for standards organizations relevant to an organization's industry
2. Level of metric dashboard integration within process workflows, i.e., level I, II, or III
3. Percentage of financially and operationally modeled process workflows

information that is relevant to their specific needs. Internal standards that exceed those minimally required by an industry group may also help an organization differentiate its performance from that of its competitors. Also, to the extent an organization satisfies local standards relative to its competitors, its products and services will be attractive to customers. This is especially true in competitive environments in which local markets are characterized by a high level of cultural and demographic diversity. Table 20.1 recommends that an organization attain leadership positions within the standards committees impacting its industry.

Figure 20.1 provides a partial listing of organizations that are actively involved in creating standards across the world. First, it should be mentioned that every country has its own unique standards. In fact, within a single industry there may be several organizations that create, update, and train participants on standard usage, although not the same standards. However, in an absence of political influence, there is a general tendency for mutual cooperation in standards development by organizations. Second, there are international standards organizations that act as umbrella organizations to facilitate global commercial activities. Global supply chains must simultaneously satisfy diverse types of standards to successfully operate their businesses across the world. To the right of the standards listing in Figure 20.1 is a hierarchal listing. This listing shows that product and service designs must often satisfy several stakeholder groups, and at several levels of conformance to a standard. These levels include governmental regulatory requirements, industry standards, specific customer performance requirements, and basic design standards, tools, methods, and concepts. Understanding and meeting or exceeding relevant standards may help an organization increase its relative competitive position.

Supply-Chain Operations Reference (SCOR) Model

The first standard or reference model we will discuss is the Supply-Chain Operations Reference Model (SCOR®). SCOR is a trademark of the Supply Chain Council. We will only present the model at a very high level based on publicly available information. Table 20.2 shows that the SCOR model breaks a supply chain into five components or process workflows: demand and supply planning; its sourcing

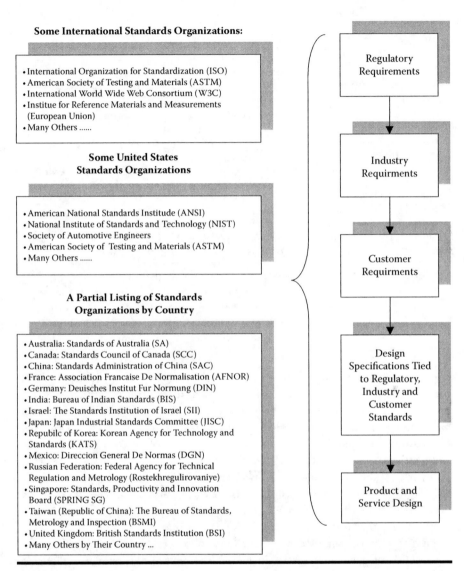

Some International Standards Organizations:

- International Organization for Standardization (ISO)
- American Society of Testing and Materials (ASTM)
- International World Wide Web Consortium (W3C)
- Institue for Reference Materials and Measurements (European Union)
- Many Others ......

Some United States Standards Organizations

- American National Standards Institude (ANSI)
- National Institute of Standards and Technology (NIST)
- Society of Automotive Engineers
- American Society of Testing and Materials (ASTM)
- Many Others ......

A Partial Listing of Standards Organizations by Country

- Australia: Standards of Australia (SA)
- Canada: Standards Council of Canada (SCC)
- China: Standards Administration of China (SAC)
- France: Association Francaise De Normalisation (AFNOR)
- Germany: Deuisches Institut Fur Normung (DIN)
- India: Bureau of Indian Standards (BIS)
- Israel: The Standards Institution of Israel (SII)
- Japan: Japan Industrial Standards Committee (JISC)
- Repubilc of Korea: Korean Agency for Technology and Standards (KATS)
- Mexico: Direccion General De Normas (DGN)
- Russian Federation: Federal Agency for Technical Regulation and Metrology (Rostekhregulirovaniye)
- Singapore: Standards, Productivity and Innovation Board (SPRING SG)
- Taiwan (Republic of China): The Bureau of Standards, Metrology and Inspection (BSMI)
- United Kingdom: British Standards Institution (BSI)
- Many Others by Their Country ...

Regulatory Requirements

Industry Requirments

Customer Requirments

Design Specifications Tied to Regulatory, Industry and Customer Standards

Product and Service Design

Figure 20.1 Organizations that create standards.

strategies; the transformation process, which varies by industry and includes systems such as make to stock, make to order, assemble to order, and engineer to order; the warehousing and delivery of products; and the reverse logistical functions necessary to process returned products. Each of these five major components is broken down by the SCOR model into specific operations. Standards have been developed for each of the operations and their associated work tasks. The goals of the SCOR model are to value stream map (VSM) a process workflow, relative to its major

Table 20.2 Supply-Chain Operations

Major Component	Partial Attribute List
Demand and supply planning	Align strategic and tactical operational and financial planning systems. Establish supply chain rules, metrics, and performance goals and objectives.
Source materials, components, and services	Identify and select supply sources, manage deliveries, pay suppliers, and manage inventory.
Make to stock, make to order, or engineer to order	Manage work-in-process (WIP) inventory and schedule production activities.
Warehouse and deliver product	Manage the warehousing, receiving, shipping of products, and invoicing processes.
Returns	Manage the reverse logistical processes involving the return of defective products, including all associated activities; the return, repair, and reconditioning of products; returns for such services.

components, and analyze all operations within each major component to compare their actual to the model's best-in-class performance benchmarks. The SCOR model provides operational definitions, expected performance metrics by operation, and best-in-class tools, methods, and systems for its members to use for their process workflow modifications. This allows the users of SCOR to adapt its tools and methods to their process workflow systems to the greatest extent possible. Typical metrics of the SCOR model include perfect order fulfillment, order fulfillment cycle time, system flexibility, cash-to-cash cycle time, and similar metrics that have been shown to be predictors of best-in-class global supply-chain performance.

An interesting feature of the SCOR model is that it uses a generic modeling technique to fit any supply chain, but allows subsequent modifications to the five components of the generic model, including its supply and demand, warehousing, and related supply-chain workflows. The SCOR modeling approach also applies specific standards to describe key supply-chain operations. As an example, in the sourcing component, S_1 is source stocked product, S_2 is source make-to-order products, and S_3 is source engineer to order. Using these basic operations, every part of a global supply chain can be integrated into the SCOR model workflow-by-workflow. In the SCOR model, the material flows connecting sources of supply and demand, as well as warehousing workflows across a global supply chain, are identified using heavy lines on the SCOR value stream map (VSM). On the other hand, the supply chain and planning processes within a supply chain are identified using dashed lines. The SCOR model is also broken into specific operational work tasks. As an example, S_1, or source stocked product, is broken into operational tasks as $S_{1.1}$, or schedule product deliveries; $S_{1.2}$, or receive product; $S_{1.3}$, or verify product; and S_4, or authorize supplier payment. Each of these operational work tasks also has a best practice standard. The SCOR model is an example of a very well thought out and proactive standardization model that is highly flexible and adaptable, as well as useful in improving supply-chain performance.

The International Standards Organization (ISO)

The International Standards Organization (ISO) has become a benchmark against which manufacturing organizations are compared and evaluated across the world. Table 20.3 describes the three basic ISO standards relating to quality systems management. It should be noted that there are many other ISO standards that apply to various industries and functions within a given industry. ISO 9000 was created to provide a mutual understanding of basic quality system requirements and systems that every organization should use as a minimum. Associated with ISO 9000 are six standards that help document basic quality system requirements in more detail. These include document control, control of records, internal quality audits, nonconforming material control and disposition, and corrective and preventive action systems. ISO 9001 was developed so organizations could demonstrate that they meet customers' contractual requirements. When an organization claims it is ISO certified, this usually means that the organization has attained ISO 9001

Table 20.3 International Standards Organization (ISO) ISO 9000 and ISO 9001

ISO 9000: *Quality Management System — Fundamental Requirements and Vocabulary* ■ Document control ■ Control of records ■ Internal audits ■ Nonconforming material control ■ Corrective action ■ Preventive action	Used to develop a mutual understanding of quality requirements and the fundamentals of a quality management system
ISO 9001: *Quality Management System — Formal Requirements for Certification*	Used to demonstrate the ability of organizations to meet customer and regulatory requirements
ISO 9004: *Quality Management System — Guidelines for Performance Improvement*	Used to demonstrate the potential for process improvement within an organization

certification status. However, a criticism of the ISO 9001 system is that it is not proactive in helping to improve quality systems, but rather, is more of an auditing and status quo-type system. In response to these criticisms, the ISO organization developed ISO 9004. ISO 9004 is used to demonstrate the potential for process improvement within an organization. Strict adherence to agreed-upon ISO standards is critical to being able to sell products and some services across the world. As mentioned above, there are numerous ISO standards in use today.

Financial Accounting Standards

Standards to control the accuracy and reporting of financial information have existed for many years. In fact, every country has its own financial accounting standards organization. The financial accounting standards used in different countries will vary from those used within the United States. In the United Sates, the Financial Accounting Foundation (FAF), and its governing board of trustees, is responsible for guiding the Financial Accounting Standards Board (FASB) and the Governmental Accounting Standards Board (GASB). These three organizational entities are supported by constituencies including accountants, audited organizations, governmental agencies, and other interested stakeholders. Figure 20.2 shows

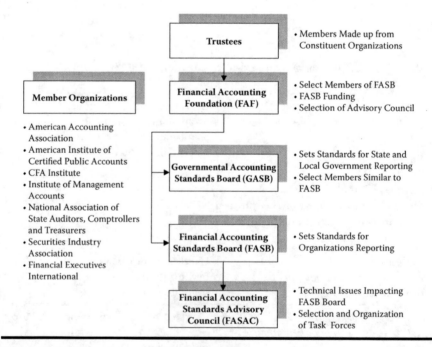

Figure 20.2   Financial accounting standards.

the basic elements of these organizations' relationships. FASB and its associated organizations develop accounting standards and procedures that are very helpful in the collection, analysis, and management of financial information within United States. In a manner similar to that of SCOR and ISO, FASB helps standardize service operations related to accounting and finance within the United States. The objectives of the FAF are to ensure that all its standards are fair and neutral, so as not to harm any of its stakeholders. These stakeholders include the accounting and financial industry, governmental institutions, and the general public. Also, the cost-to-benefit ratio of newly developed standards is an important consideration by FAF because it does not want to unfairly burden its stakeholders.

Sarbanes–Oxley Act of 2002

The Sarbanes–Oxley Act of 2002 was enacted by the U.S. Congress because of process breakdowns in accounting and financial audits in many organizations due to several factors. The most important factor was a conflict of interest between an organization and its auditors. These conflicts of interest took many degenerate forms. This act now forces the CEOs of organizations to guarantee their financial disclosure statements. Table 20.4 lists the 11 key titles of the Sarbanes–Oxley Act of 2002. The common theme running through the 11 titles is accuracy and independence of financial reporting, as well as severe criminal penalties for people falsifying financial records. Specifically, the act creates various oversight boards, regulations and enforcement guidelines. Auditing of financial reporting workflow models has been updated to take into consideration the Sarbanes–Oxley Act of 2002. This act provides an excellent basis on which to design accounting and financial control systems and their process workflows.

Occupational Safety and Health Administration (OSHA)

The Occupational Safety and Health Administration (OSHA) standards within a workplace environment require reporting of incidents related to worker injuries and elimination of their root causes. OSHA standards are extensive and cover all known materials and situations that can harm workers within the United States. In this chapter we will only describe OSHA standards at a high level. The six major categories of OSHA standards include hazardous communication, emergency action planning, fire safety, exit route planning, ensuring that all walking and working surfaces are safely maintained by an organization, and making certain that medical and first aid requirements are met in anticipation of expected incidents. These six major categories attempt to ensure that workers understand the materials and conditions they work within and all actions they must take to prevent accidents and injuries, as well as reporting requirements and prevention.

Table 20.4 Sarbanes–Oxley Act of 2002

Section of Act	Partial Description
Title I: Public Company Accounting Oversight Board	Sets registration with board; auditing and quality control and independence standards and rules
Title II: Auditor Independence	Services outside scope of auditor practice and conflicts of interest
Title III: Corporate Responsibility	Corporate responsibilities; rules for professional attorneys and improper audit influence
Title IV: Enhanced Financial Disclosure	Transaction involving management and major stockholders and disclosure of auditing committee financial expert
Title V: Analysts' Conflict of Interest	Treatment of security analysts by registered securities associations
Title VI: Commission Resource and Authority	Authorization of appropriations and federal court authority
Title VII: Studies and Reports	General Accounting Office (GAO) of public accounting firms and enforcement actions
Title VIII: Corporate and Criminal Fraud Accountability	Criminal penalties for altering documents or defrauding stockholders
Title IX: White-Collar Crime Penalty Enhancements	Criminal penalties for mail and wire fraud
Title X: Corporate Tax Returns	Signing of corporate tax returns by chief executive officers
Title XI: Corporate Fraud and Accountability	Increased criminal penalties for tampering with records

Food and Drug Administration (FDA)

The standards developed, disseminated, and maintained by the Food and Drug Administration (FDA) are extensive and specific to various industries and their related products that impact the health of U.S. citizens. In Table 20.6 we focus, by way of an example, on a small subset of FDA regulations as they apply to the manufacturing and sale of medical devices. The regulations surrounding medical device manufacturing ensure that organizations employ good manufacturing practices to develop and manufacture their products. In addition, FDA regulations require the

Table 20.5   Occupational Safety and Health Administration (OSHA) Standards: General Industry

1. Hazard communication	Understand hazardous chemicals in the workplace, including standards and material fact sheets
2. Emergency action plan	Description of actions employees must take in situations involving fire or other emergencies
3. Fire safety	Requires employers to have a fire prevention plan and standards
4. Exit routes	Requires employers to have exit routes and standards
5. Walking/working surfaces	Standards on the use of stairways, ladders, and other surfaces
6. Medical and first aid	Requirements to provide medical treatment and first aid based on expected workplace hazards

Table 20.6   Federal Drug Administration (FDA): Medical Devices

1. Preinspection activity
2. Good manufacturing practice (GMP) inspection strategy
3. Directed device inspection
4. Comprehensive device inspection
5. Preapproval device inspection
6. Sterile devices
7. The small manufacturer
8. Written procedures

approval of an organization's products based on their performance data, various trial evaluations, and process audits.

Automotive Industry Action Group (AIAG)

The Automotive Industry Action Group (AIAG) develops standards for the design, manufacture, and quality requirements of automotive products. AIAG standards help suppliers and customers design, performance test, and manufacture their products using best-in-class tools and methods. The AIAG methodology also provides

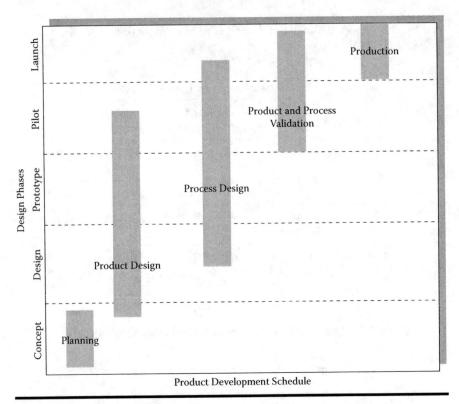

Figure 20.3 Automotive Industry Action Group (AIAG).

forms, checklists, and templates that ensure all information necessary to produce a product is available to suppliers, customers, and other supply-chain stakeholders. Figure 20.3 shows a generic version of an AIAG process. It consists of a phased methodology in which a new product design is successively moved through its concept phase, the product and process design phases, the product validation phase, and, finally, into full-scale production. In parallel, quality assurance systems monitor product and process performance and provide tools and methods to continually improve the new product design and its manufacturing process. It should be noted that the specific tools and methods of the AIAG methodology must be used in sequence, and that a successful completion of one phase leads to a subsequent next phase.

Planning Phase

Inputs to the AIAG planning phase include gathering the voice-of-the-customer (VOC) and analyzing available marketing strategy and all available product and process data from similar designs, including product reliability information. VOC, marketing strategy, and similar tools and methods were discussed in Chapter 3. The output of the planning phase includes the design team's goals and objectives, a preliminary bill-of-material (BOM), a preliminary process flowchart, and a list of special product features and related characteristics that a design team uses to create a new product design and build a preliminary product quality assurance plan. To the extent there are similar products in production, it is always useful to review their past and current performance and look for potential weaknesses in the proposed design. A design failure-mode-and-effects-analysis (DFMEA) is a useful method to look for potential weaknesses in a new product design and was discussed in Chapter 4. In addition, it is important that a team have for its use a preliminary BOM, a process flowchart, and similar documentation to help it design a new product or service. However, this documentation may change as a team begins to evaluate alternative designs.

Product Design Phase

The inputs into a product design phase are the outputs from the planning phase. In the product design and development phase, the team builds prototypes and develops documentation relative to what the design looks like, including its product drawings and performance specifications based on extensive testing and a preliminary quality control plan. This documentation should reflect all current knowledge of the new product or service design. The outputs of this phase include the final design FMEA, manufacturing recommendations, verification of performance specifications, prototypes, engineering drawings and specifications, finalization of new equipment and testing requirements, special product characteristic lists, and a quality control plan finalized relative to design requirements. Design reviews are held throughout the product design phase.

Process Design Phase

The outputs from a product design phase become inputs to the process design phase. The process design team works concurrently with other functions shortly after the design project is initiated by the organization. Packaging standards and specifications, process flowcharts and equipment layouts, process instructions including testing and auditing procedures, measurement systems analysis, preliminary capability studies, and the process FMEA are developed during the process design phase. Many of these tools, methods, and concepts were discussed in Chapter 5. The next phase of the AIAG methodology will slowly scale up the manufacturing volume of the new product to ensure that all required work tasks have been completed according to their original project plan.

Product and Process Validation Phase

It is at this point in a product development process that all customer requirements are tested and verified as having met the original VOC and other business requirements. The outputs of the product and process validation phase include a production trial under actual production conditions using all specified materials, components, and procedures and measurement systems. These outputs include a preliminary process capability study, production part approval from the customer, production validation testing, packaging evaluations, the production control plan, and the quality planning sign-off and management report.

Production Phase, Feedback, and Assessment

Once a new product has been qualified through the AIAG development phases, it matures and goes through the classic product life cycle described in Chapter 3 and Figure 3.7. During all the development phases of a new product, the goal is to reduce process variation and improve customer satisfaction, delivery, and service. The tools, methods, and techniques necessary to systematically improve the performance of a new product or service have been the focus of this book.

Malcolm Baldrige Award

The Malcolm Baldrige Quality Award was originally developed as an incentive for U.S. organizations to improve their quality performance. The first step in this process is a self-assessment against seven major categories of performance criteria. These categories are listed in Table 20.7. The first category is leadership. Some of the critical evaluation characteristics of the leadership category include fiscal accountability and auditor independence, as well as an organization's strategic plans to increase its productivity. Category II requires an evaluation of strategic planning, tactical linkage, and execution of an organization's strategy, including its resource allocation and key performance measures, which are indicative of its success. Category III includes a customer and market evaluation as measured by gathering and analyzing the VOC, as well as activities related to customer relationship-building and retention statistics. Measurement, analysis, and knowledge management are the evaluation criteria of category IV. The goals of category IV are to ensure data is effectively collected and managed within an organization, including its relevance to anticipated financial and operational performance. Also, the ability of an organization to monitor, control, and improve its process performance is evaluated by the criteria of category IV. In category V, an organization is evaluated relative to employee hiring and promotion, work organization and management, and employee training and development. Category VI requires that an organization identify the core processes associated with its value creation. These include operational planning and

Table 20.7   Malcolm Baldrige Award

Category	Partial Criterion Listing
Category I: Leadership	Fiscal accountability and auditor independence Strategic plans to increase productivity
Category II: Strategic planning	Tactical linkage and execution of strategy Resource allocation Key performance measures to indicate success
Category III: Customer and market focus	Determining voice of the customer (VOC) Customer relationship building Customer retention
Category IV: Measurement, analysis, and knowledge management	How data is collected and managed within an organization Data relevance and accuracy Using the data to monitor, control, and improve process performance
Category V: Human resources focus	How employees are hired and promoted over time How work is organized and managed How employees are trained and developed
Category VI: Process management	Identification of the core processes associated with value creation Operational planning and resource allocation Key performance measures How costs are reduced and productivity increased
Category VII: Results	Important metrics that indicate customer satisfaction Financial and market share results indicating performance

resource allocation, as well as key performance measures. This information is used to understand how an organization reduces cost and improves productivity. Finally, in category VII, important metrics indicative of customer satisfaction, financial performance, and market share are evaluated by self-assessment. However, a self-assessment is just the first step of a Malcolm Baldrige evaluation process. After an organization calculates its score relative to the seven evaluation criteria, it has the option to ask for a formal assessment by Malcolm Baldrige auditors. In this evaluation process, independent auditors use detailed criteria and checklists to evaluate an organization. Improvement recommendations are also provided by these independent auditors to help an organization improve its quality system and operational performance.

Creating Metric Dashboards

At any point in time, there is a lot of information within an organization. This information comes from numerous internal and external sources. Unfortunately, much of this information may not be useful to manage and control a business because it has not been analyzed to provide relevance and use. In recent years, the concept of metric dashboards has been used to bring together disparate data sources and provide useful information to a business. These types of systems are usually automated using business process management (BPM) tools and methods, including business process modeling and analysis (BPMA), business intelligence (BI), and business activity monitoring (BAM). There are also many different software platforms and algorithms that can aid in the creation of metric dashboards. If properly designed, metrics dashboards are useful in answering questions relative to identifying important process workflow data, analyzing it to provide useful information, and displaying for it for easy interpretation.

Table 20.8 presents a list of ten key steps necessary to develop a metric dashboard. A first step is to ask the right questions. These questions should be aligned and be

Table 20.8   10 Key Steps to Develop a Metric Dashboard

1. Develop questions, goals, and objectives to meet organization strategy.
2. Determine the information required to answer questions and meet goals and objectives.
3. Develop metric listing and definitions.
4. Determine specific tools, methods, and algorithms required to measure, monitor, and control metric performance.
5. Develop workflow diagrams and key operations.
6. Cross-reference metric control points to workflow diagrams.
7. Develop metric dashboard to provide metric information — level I.
8. Expand metric dashboard to provide user-recommended actions — level II.
9. Expand metric dashboard to enable real-time control of required metrics — level III.
10. Develop the system incrementally using Agile Project Management.

consistent with an organization's goals and objectives. A next step is to determine the information required to answer the questions. A third step is to develop a metric listing with definitions. This is an important task that requires that a team work together to ensure its process workflow metrics are properly defined and supporting data is available to enable a root cause analysis of metric patterns. A generic metric dashboard is shown in Figure 20.4 in which inventory investment, its turns ratio, and demand and service levels are displayed for a hypothetical product. A second level below this information would provide information relative to lead time, forecasting error, and other relevant operational data that would be useful in managing and controlling inventory turns and investment. After higher-level system requirements and metrics have been identified and defined by a team, it must determine the specific tools, methods, and algorithms required to measure, monitor, and control

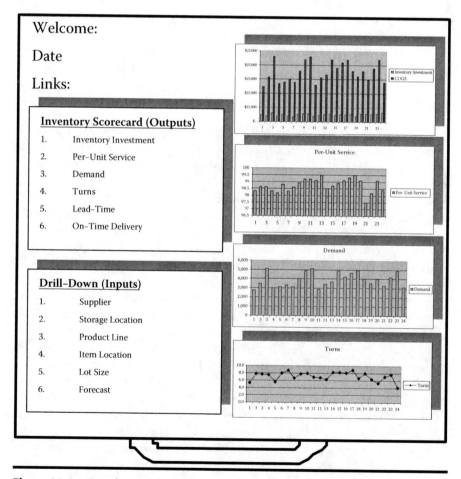

Figure 20.4   Creating, analyzing, and interpreting metric dashboards.

metric performance. The development team then analyzes its process workflows to determine how the new metric dashboard should be used to retrieve, analyze, and take action on the displayed information. Cross-reference control points are created on electronic process workflow diagrams, and the metric dashboards are overlaid onto these business process workflow management systems.

It should also be noted that metric dashboards may differ in their relative sophistication. The most basic metric dashboard provides only metric status information (level I) without intelligence. However, in the next level of dashboard sophistication, the metric dashboard is expanded to provide user-recommended actions (level II). Finally, in advanced dashboard systems, the dashboard is designed to enable real-time process control of required metrics (level III). Process industries have used level III metric dashboards for many years. These advanced monitoring and control technologies have also been modified for discrete parts manufacturing and service systems using a business process management suite (BPMS) approach. The development of a metric dashboard is most effectively managed using the Agile Project Management (APM) techniques described in Chapter 15.

Implementing Effective Process Controls

It has been shown that there are many standards organizations across the world. Organizations must simultaneously meet the requirements of several standard systems and, in parallel, deploy improvement initiatives to increase their productivity and shareholder economic value added (EVA). To ensure an efficient allocation of organizational resources, it is critical that all activities within an organization be strategically aligned and prioritized, as discussed in several chapters of this book. Figure 20.5 attempts to capture these diverse concepts in a coherent whole. How a particular organization decides to integrate these disparate programs is dependent on its industry and local requirements. Suffice it to say that every organization must develop effective and efficient process workflows having high value content. Also, these workflow systems must be integrated throughout an organization's supply chain. Many of the tools, methods, and concepts discussed in this book will show operations managers and process improvement experts how to improve organizational productivity and shareholder EVA, as well as increase customer satisfaction through the design of products and services using efficient transformation systems to capture and translate the VOC through global supply chain. Figure 20.5 also captures a major theme of this book: improving the value content of a global supply chain requires understanding many diverse tools, methods, and concepts and their relationships. Also, competitive organizations in today's world manage their assets and systems at very high efficiency levels and exhibit higher productivity and shareholder EVA than competitors. The basis for superior performance is a thorough understanding of an organization's financial and operational systems.

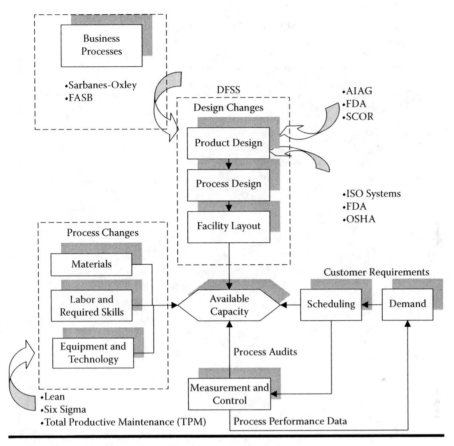

Figure 20.5   Implementing effective controls.

Summary

Table 20.9 provides a summarization of the key concepts of this chapter, which also reflect those listed in Table 20.1. System integration is critical to increasing an organization's productivity and competitiveness in today's world. However, to develop integrated systems, an organization must understand financial and operational components and how they interact with each other. This implies that an organization should be able to create models of its major process workflows. Another major concept of the chapter is that metric dashboards are necessary to enable a root cause analysis of process breakdowns, as well as enable an organization to efficiently eliminate them. But this implies that an organization understands the complex interrelationships among its supply-chain components. This knowledge requires a long-term and continuing analysis of process workflows by an organization.

**Table 20.9   Key Concepts to Improve the Effectiveness
of System Integration**

1. Work with international and national organizations to create standards, then develop products and services to meet or exceed those standards.
2. Develop metric dashboards to monitor, control, and improve your process workflows.
3. Develop financial and operational models of your process workflows and learn how they work to improve organizational productivity and shareholder economic valued added (EVA).

Suggested Reading

Paul Harmon. (2003). *Business Process Change: A Manager's Guide to Improving, Redesigning, and Automating Processes*. Morgan Kaufman Publishers, San Francisco.

Andrew P. Sage. (1992). *Systems Engineering*. John Wiley Publishing, New York.

Peter Weill and Marianne Broadbent. (1998). *Leveraging the New Infrastructure*. Harvard Business Press, Boston.

Conclusion

The purpose of this book was to present a broad and useful set of tools, methods, and concepts to improve operational efficiency in today's world. It is my experience that organizations, in diverse industries across the world, can improve productivity and shareholder value using currently available tools, methods, and techniques found in operations management, including Lean and Six Sigma methods. As a result, a major goal of this book has been alignment of operational strategy across diverse industries such as manufacturing and financial services. The 20 chapters presented the latest tools, methods, and concepts currently used in the fields of operations management, operations research, Lean manufacturing, Six Sigma programs, product and service design, and supply-chain management. These leading-edge tools, methods, and concepts will enable an organization to immediately identify and execute improvement projects within its process workflows to improve productivity and shareholder economic value added (EVA).

A major premise of this book has been that organizations neglect basic principles of marketing research, design engineering, process engineering, and operations management, as well as other fundamental business competencies. These situations contribute to their noncompetitive position in today's world. In other words, lost market share is not caused solely by low wages and similar economic factors, but also by an organization's inability to develop its strategies and execute them at an operational level. It is our opinion that an organization can improve its relative competitive position by implementing currently available operational tools, methods, and concepts. Also, because we live in a highly competitive world, an organization should identify its core competencies and create process workflows that add value from an external customer's perspective. Organizational boundaries between suppliers and customers should be torn down and replaced with flexible process workflows that are tied to the voice-of-the-customer (VOC) and properly designed and managed to increase their value content.

Organizations often struggle with questions of where and how to add value, from both customer and shareholder perspectives. A strategic goal of any organization should be to allocate its work in a way in which per unit value is maximized to improve organizational productivity. There are many ways in which organizations can improve productivity by leveling or flattening their competitive playing field. This may not be an easy task because there are often differential competitive advantages between organizations, especially in different regions of the world. As an example, organizations may have different competitive advantages due to such factors as low-cost labor, laws and regulations that either inhibit or accelerate value creation, and large and efficient infrastructures that facilitate commerce. In fact, organizations within the same industry may have differential competitive strengths and weaknesses due to both internal and external factors impacting their productivity. However, there are "flattening" or compensating factors that organizations can use to increase their relative competitiveness. These include deploying technology, effectively using capital and other resources, taking an active role in the regulatory environment, and using best-in-class organizational design and workforce management methods. These tools, methods, and concepts were the focus of this book.

My objective in writing this book was to discuss strategies to improve organizational competitiveness and productivity through five areas of focus: adapting strategies for global competitiveness; translating customer value elements into products and services and their workflow systems; planning, managing, and controlling operations; collecting, analyzing, and sharing information; and managing, integrating, and controlling global supply chains. An important goal of the section entitled "Adapting Strategies for Global Competitiveness," which included Chapters 1 to 3, was to explain how organizations must develop operational strategies that promote and augment their core competencies. Also, understanding the VOC was shown as a major competitive advantage in a global economy. In particular, an ability to mass customize products and services to satisfy local customer needs and value expectations is a major competitive strength for an organization. This allows small companies to dominate their market space or niche and compete with larger and more established organizations. In these situations, economy-of-scale and costly infrastructure may not be significant competitive factors. Thus, to provide a firm foundation on which to discuss the more technical aspects of operations management, we had to understand how to translate the VOC through our products, services, and process workflow systems. This discussion included key concepts such as mapping strategic goals and objectives through an organization down to a project level to ensure that every project was defined relative to four major metric classifications: business, financial, compensating, and project or operational metrics. In addition, it was shown that understanding how metrics were linked, including their underlying relationships, was useful. In fact, creating process models to understand how metrics dynamically change was shown to be useful for identifying productivity opportunities across an organization. It was also shown that once financial and operational performance gaps were identified, a business case for process improvement could be made. There were several other key concepts discussed in Chapters 1 to 3, which included deploying initiatives as well as aligning reward and recognition systems to organizational goals and objectives. Chapter 3 closed the first section of the book by discussing a need for using modern marketing research tools and methods and developing internal systems to gather and quantitatively analyze VOC information to translate it through product and service designs. These concepts provided a firm foundation on which to design an organization's products and services and their operational systems.

In the section entitled "Translating Customer Value Elements into Products, Services, and Workflow Systems," which included Chapters 4 to 7, we discussed VOC translation into the design of products and services using best-in-class design methods. Several important design methods were discussed in Chapter 4. These included concurrent engineering (CE), design-for-manufacturing (DFM), and the tools, methods, and concepts used to create, design, prototype, pilot, and launch new products and services. Expanding on the DFM concepts, mass customization was discussed from a perspective of increasing operational flexibility and productivity. Chapter 5 discussed various analytical tools and methods that are useful in creating service systems. These included process modeling and simulation, queuing analysis, linear programming, improving the work environment, and simplifying and standardizing work tasks. In Chapter 6, Lean topics were discussed, including value stream mapping and bottleneck analysis. Chapter 7 discussed the measurement of productivity and EVA. Productivity improvement is the basis on which operational effectiveness and efficiency was measured in subsequent chapters of this book.

Other key concepts presented within the second section included applying design for Six Sigma (DFSS) methods to minimize variation of products and services, designing to global standards to expand marketing and sales opportunities, outsourcing work that could be done more efficiently elsewhere to increase its value content, and quantitatively modeling process workflows to understand their dynamic relationships. Also discussed was the importance of work standardization, employee training, and establishing operational metrics to measure process improvements. Final comments of the second section were that the types of projects that an organization deploys should be balanced relative to the resources necessary to implement them. Project charters should be used to document and communicate all projects, and project benefits should be measured by an organization.

The third section of the book, "Operations Planning, Management, and Control," included Chapters 8 to 14. The discussion in this section focused on demand management, capacity allocation, the scheduling of work, and inventory management. In Chapter 8, demand management was discussed relative to the various forecasting models used to estimate demand. In Chapter 9, capacity allocation was discussed, including insourcing and outsourcing of process workflows. Chapter 10 discussed facility location and management, including relevant factors such as population demographics, a region's underlying political and economic infrastructure, and several other important facility location criteria. In addition, several quantitative methods were used to evaluate facility location decisions. The balance of the third section discussed sales and operations planning (S&OP) functions, as well as mathematical scheduling methods and rules to increase the efficiency of the flow of materials and information through a system. Specific workflow systems were discussed, including master requirements planning (MRPII), master production scheduling (MPS), and incorporation of various elements of pull scheduling, production activity control (PAC), and inventory management.

The key concepts presented in this section also included ensuring that an organization's forecasts were strategically aligned at all levels of the organization. Also, an organization should obtain demand information directly from customers using point-of-sale (POS) technology and similar methods, rather than rely exclusively on mathematical forecasting. Other key concepts discussed in this section included developing product forecasts by market segment strategies and measuring their accuracy. Key concepts presented in Chapter 9 included analyzing supply-chain capacity from several different perspectives, including design, and available and actual capacity of a process workflow. It was also mentioned that an economy-of-scale model is less useful in today's world due to the application of technology, information sharing, and other factors that enable minimum per unit cost, at lower unit volumes than previously possible. This is because many products and services are in a virtual format.

Another key concept discussed in this section was that system capacity can be expanded through the efficient design of products and services, as well as the application of Lean principles. The expansion of capacity using insourcing and outsourcing was also discussed, including the risks associated with facility location decisions. The goal was to select the best facility location based on a full consideration of all relevant factors, risks, and business benefits. Once capacity of various types was made available, then its efficient utilization was discussed in the context of creating a sales and operations planning (S&OP) team to manage demand and supply. Also, the discussion of scheduling systems continued into Chapter 12, in which algorithms useful for determining the best scheduling rules were covered in the context of resource optimization. It was also mentioned that scheduling is easier if a system has been optimally configured, and Lean tools and methods have been applied to simplify and standardize process workflows. The balance of this third section discussed MRPII and inventory management systems, in Chapters 13 and 14. Several key concepts were presented to more effectively manage inventory.

The fourth section of the book, "Collecting, Analyzing, and Sharing Information across a Global Supply Chain," included Chapters 15 to 18. These chapters discussed the deployment of major information technology (IT) systems and their impact on the design of workflow management (WM) systems in manufacturing and service industries. These IT systems included business process management (BPM), business process modeling and analysis (BPMA), business intelligence (BI), business activity monitoring (BAM), enterprise application integration (EAI), and Agile Project Management (APM). Chapter 16 presented quality management and improvement systems from a Six Sigma perspective using the Six Sigma define, measure, analyze, improve, and control (DMAIC) problem-solving methodology. The tools and methods of Chapter 16 ranged between basic and advanced levels.

The philosophy was to use the right tool set or initiative to identify the root causes for process breakdowns. In Chapter 17, we discussed using operational assessments to improve organizational productivity. Important concepts included ensuring that all assessment activities are aligned throughout an organization, and using rigorous analysis to prove that productivity opportunities exist in order to build a business case for a project. In Chapter 18, we discussed project management methods, including the evaluation of project milestones, activities, and work tasks to develop Gantt charts and program evaluation and review technique (PERT) models to manage projects according to their schedule. The project management chapter also included a discussion of project analysis and risk management.

The last major section of this book, "Global Supply-Chain Management Integration and Control," included Chapters 19 and 20. In Chapter 19, important supply-chain functions and key operational and financial metrics were discussed as they applied to global supply-chain management. In Chapter 20, various standardization and control systems were discussed, as well as the creation of metric dashboards to manage and control processes. Key concepts of the fifth section included developing strategic relationships, continually rationalizing asset utilizations and efficiencies, effectively selecting transportation modes, and insourcing and outsourcing to ensure that the percentage of value-adding work within process workflows continuously increases over time. Another important concept in Chapter 20 included working with international and national organizations to create standards, and develop products and services to meet or exceed those standards. Finally, development of metric dashboards was shown to be useful to monitor, control, and improve process workflows to improve organizational productivity and shareholder EVA.

This book was intended to provide operations managers, process improvement specialists, Lean specialists, and Six Sigma belts, champions, and consultants with information useful for analyzing and improving process workflows. I attempted to bring together into one place practical information that I have used over the past 30 years as the basis for both my graduate classes in operations research, operations management, and economic and financial forecasting, and consulting engagements with major organizations across the world. I hope this information will be useful to your organization.

Appendix I

Competitive Solutions

1. Increase productivity and competitiveness using modern operations management tools, methods, and concepts.
2. Create an adaptable organizational culture by deploying initiatives to improve core competencies.
3. Translate customer needs and values into new product and service designs.
4. Design products and services that can be manufactured anywhere in the world at low cost and high quality to meet customer needs and value expectations.
5. Ensure process workflows are easily reconfigurable to match inevitable changes in customer needs and values.
6. Align process workflows, using Lean tools and methods, to deliver customer value without wasting resources.
7. Manage operational activities and improve financial performance by developing integrated financial and operational metric reporting systems.
8. Manage customer demand using best-in-class tools, methods, and concepts to increase sales revenue, lower operational costs, and prevent lost sales and stock-outs.
9. Satisfy customer demand anytime and anywhere in the world by creating inexpensive and flexible systems with sufficient capacity.
10. Locate and manage facilities using best-in-class tools and methods to reduce supply-chain cost and lead time.
11. Create a sales and operational planning (S&OP) team to integrate supply and demand across the supply chain.
12. Apply efficient scheduling tools and methods to reduce process workflow lead time and optimize available capacity.

13. Use hybrid MRPII and quick response manufacturing (QRM) methods to create systems that can dynamically respond to variations in demand or resources in master production schedule (MPS) and master requirements planning (MRPII) environments.
14. Build financial models to fully understand how much inventory or other assets are required and where they should be located to achieve customer service levels at minimum cost, to increase cash flow and asset utilization.
15. Eliminate intermediaries from all process workflows and share information using information technology.
16. Measure and improve the quality of products and services to increase sales and customer satisfaction and lower operating cost.
17. Use ongoing operational assessments to identify projects to increase productivity and shareholder economic value added (EVA).
18. Manage projects to meet deliverables, the schedule, and cost targets.
19. Increase capacity, flexibility, and productivity by insourcing and outsourcing process workflows.
20. Integrate local standards into products and services to dominate local marketing niches across the world.

Appendix II

110 Key Concepts

Chapter 1

1. Map strategic goals and objectives through your organization to a project level to ensure alignment.
2. Every project should be defined relative to the four major metric classifications of business metrics, financial metrics, compensating metrics, and project or operational metrics.
3. Understand how metrics are linked, including the underlying relationships, and ideally be able to create process models to understand how metrics changes in response to changes in workflow inputs.
4. Internally benchmark workflows to identify productivity opportunities, then externally benchmark other organizations that are similar or completely different, but understand the goals and objectives of the benchmarking study.

Chapter 2

5. Identify financial and operational performance gaps to make a business case for process improvement.
6. Determine the required initiatives that must be deployed as well as their toolsets to close the performance gaps.
7. Form an executive steering committee to guide initiative deployments to ensure goals and objectives are met and resources are aligned to business opportunities.

8. Structure the initiative deployment at an operational level using Lean, Six Sigma, and Total Productive Maintenance (TPM) and at strategic levels through design, IT, human resources, and the customer, but prioritized and sequenced as necessary.

9. Align reward and recognition systems, including the organization's bonus and incentive systems, to achieve the initiative's goals and objectives.

10. Develop communication systems to promote change at every level of the organization.

11. Train people to use appropriate toolsets to analyze and improve process workflows at an operational and work task level.

12. Complete projects on a continuing basis and according to schedule to build momentum for change by showing business benefits.

13. Make modifications to the deployment based on new information.

Chapter 3

14. Use modern marketing research tools and methods to obtain customer information related to Kano needs and value elements by market segment.

15. Train sales people to use quantitative methods to enable them to obtain the maximum amount of information from customers during every interaction.

16. Develop internal systems to gather and quantitatively analyze VOC information, including product forecasts and other systems used to estimate demand.

17. Translate VOC information through the product or service design process.

Chapter 4

18. Use concurrent engineering (CE) to manage your design process.

19. Use design-for-manufacturing (DFM) to design products and services that are easy produce for customers.

20. Apply design for Six Sigma (DFSS) methods to minimize variation of products and services.

21. Effectively translate the VOC into design features.

22. Understand how design components interact to provide functions, dimensions, and other product features.

23. Design to global standards to expand marketing and sales opportunities.

24. Apply mass customization tools, methods, and concepts to reduce the order-to-deliver cycle time.

25. Outsource work that can be done more efficiently elsewhere.

Chapter 5

26. Use information from the CE team to design your process's workflows.
27. Quantitatively model your workflows to understand dynamic relationships.
28. Create a work environment that reinforces change and continual learning.
29. Create high-performance work teams to manage and improve your workflows.
30. Standardize work to reduce process variation.
31. Train people to properly use tools and follow work and inspection instructions.

Chapter 6

32. Establish operational metrics to measure improvements relative to higher customer on-time delivery (schedule attainment), higher value added time/ total time, higher throughput of materials or information, faster machine or job changeover (especially at bottleneck resource), higher machine uptime (available time), higher quality of work (scrap/rework/warranty/returns), less floor space utilized, lower system inventory, higher supplier on-time delivery, and lower overall system cost.
33. Lean tools, methods, and concepts help simplify and standardize a process.
34. There are several critical components that must be sequentially implemented to deploy a Lean system.
35. Establishing a takt time is important to create a baseline from which waste can be systematically eliminated from a process.
36. There are five key tools that will greatly increase your operational efficiency: process simplification, process standardization, bottleneck management, transfer batches, and mixed-model scheduling.

Chapter 7

37. Measure and improve economic value added (EVA) for shareholders. This will focus attention on improving productivity.
38. Measure year-to-year productivity and identify projects that will improve productivity to ensure your organization is competitive.
39. Align projects at an operational level with strategic goals and objectives.
40. Deploy projects throughout the organization to achieve organizational productivity goals and objectives.
41. Ensure the deployed projects are balanced relative to the initiative they will use and the resources necessary to implement the improvements.
42. Use project charters to document and communicate all projects.
43. Measures all project benefits and take corrective action if the benefits are not achieved on schedule.

Chapter 8

44. Ensure your organization's forecasts are strategically aligned at all levels of the organization.
45. Migrate your demand management systems to obtain direct customer demand information from customers or through point-of-sale (POS) information.
46. To the extent forecasts are necessary, use accurate demand data by market segment and the appropriate forecasting model.
47. Stratify your products to place some of them on automatic forecast by the system, so analytical resources can be focused on products having higher demand variation or unusual demand patterns.
48. Measure and continually improve forecasting accuracy.

Chapter 9

49. There are different levels of capacity, including design, available, and actual. Improvements should be undertaken to increase actual capacity to the design capacity.
50. Economy-of-scale models show that capacity can be increased by application of technology, information sharing, and other factors that allow minimum per unit cost at lower unit volumes than historically feasible.
51. Experience curve models show that capacity can be increased through higher learning rates.
52. System capacity is dynamic and must be managed dynamically.
53. Lean principles are very useful in increasing available capacity.
54. The design of product and services has a significant impact on system capacity.
55. Insourcing and outsourcing of work can dramatically increase system capacity.

Chapter 10

56. Determine the factors that are relevant in the facility location decision for each alternative location.
57. Determine the risks associated with each factor by location.
58. Use quantitative models to understand the relationships between the factors and outputs of interest.
59. Select the best location based on a full consideration of all relevant factors, risks, and business benefits, as well as forward-looking strategic goals and objectives.
60. Consider deploying best-in-class facility management tools and methods when designing and managing the new facility to ensure it meets the original assumptions of the facility location project.

Chapter 11

61. Create a sales and operations planning (S&OP) team to manage demand and supply within your organization.
62. Eliminate functional silos within your supply chain to increase its material and information throughput rates.
63. Create demand and supply metrics that measure supply-chain performance and provide the basis for continual improvement over time.
64. Eliminate workflow conditions that contribute to S&OP process breakdowns.
65. Value stream map (VSM) the workflows of the 50 key S&OP activities to understand how they are related and to simplify and standardize them over time.

Chapter 12

66. Determine the best scheduling rules for your workflow to optimize resource usage while satisfying demand.
67. Deploy the best type of scheduling system for your workflow. This may be automatically or manually controlled.
68. Scheduling will be easier if the system has been optimally configured and Lean tools and methods applied to simply and standardize its workflow.

Chapter 13

69. Ensure MRPII calculations are correct, including lot sizing and constants such as lead time parameters.
70. Review the demand variation versus product volumes, and stratify and place as many products on a minimum/maximum system as possible.
71. Investigate the feasibility of implementing hybrid MRPII in your supply chain.
72. Investigate the feasibility of implementing quick response manufacturing (QRM) methods in situations in which the product volumes are very low volume and are processed through many work cells.

Chapter 14

73. Manage a product throughout its life cycle to reduce inventory.
74. Create an inventory model to calculate optimum inventory quantities for every item in your inventory population.
75. Analyze the model to look for ways to reduce excess and obsolete inventory as well as to focus Lean and Six Sigma projects.

76. Ensure the MRPII and other system data is accurate to reduce inventory.
77. Develop effective cycle counting systems in which the materials and information flows are well standardized, mistake-proofed, and documented.
78. Count only when necessary by simplifying the system and using visual controls or counting when inventories are low.
79. Develop strategies to manage excess and obsolete inventory, including their prevention and efficient disposal.
80. Simplify product designs to reduce inventory.
81. Eliminate unnecessary products to reduce inventory.

Chapter 15

82. Use business process management (BPM) systems to integrate your process workflow systems.
83. Apply BPM to enable market segmentation and to ensure your process workflows meet the voice-of-the-customer (VOC).
84. Use Agile Project Management to coordinate and manage your information technology (IT) projects.

Chapter 16

85. Ensure that quality assurance and control activities are aligned with the concurrent engineering team's goals and objectives.
86. Ensure your quality program has elements of continuous improvement as well as breakthrough.
87. Use a rigorous problem-solving methodology such as Six Sigma's DMAIC.
88. Understand the tools, methods, and concepts of quality management to improve your process capability.
89. Integrate your quality management systems to increase organizational productivity.

Chapter 17

90. Use operational assessments to identify productivity opportunities on a continuing basis.
91. Create well-defined and financially justified project charters across every process workflow within your organization.
92. Use several different analytical methods to identify projects rather than rely on management reports or opinion.

93. Use the right toolset or initiative to identify the root causes for a process breakdown.
94. Ensure all assessment activities are aligned throughout your organization.
95. Use rigorous analysis to prove that productivity opportunities exist.
96. Balance productivity opportunities with available resources to prevent an overload on a few process workflows.

Chapter 18

97. Build a business case for the project and form a multicultural and diverse project team around the project charter. Remember to use proper team facilitation methods.
98. Develop a list of project milestones, activities, and work tasks with their earliest and latest starting and finishing times as well as required resources.
99. Develop Gantt charts and PERT models of the project's network to analyze the project as it moves through its schedule.
100. Analyze project risks and develop plans to reduce or eliminate or manage the risk.

Chapter 19

101. Develop global strategic relationships.
102. Continually rationalize asset utilization and efficiencies.
103. Continually rationalize transportation modes.
104. Continually rationalize insourcing and outsourcing.
105. Ensure that supply and demand are matched across the supply chain.
106. Continually increase the percentage of value-adding work within process workflows.
107. Highly standardize and mistake-proof process workflows, but design in adaptability and flexibility.

Chapter 20

108. Work with international and national organizations to create standards, and then develop products and services to meet or exceed those standards.
109. Develop metric dashboards to monitor, control, and improve your process workflows.
110. Develop financial and operational models of your process workflows and learn how they work to improve organizational productivity and shareholder economic valued added (EVA).

Appendix III

Figures and Tables

Chapter 1

Chapter 2

Chapter 3

Chapter 4

Chapter 5

Chapter 6

Chapter 7

Chapter 8

Chapter 9

Chapter 10

Chapter 11

Chapter 12

Chapter 13

Chapter 14

Chapter 15

Chapter 16

Chapter 17

Chapter 18

Chapter 19

Chapter 20

Appendix IV

Appendix IV

Crystal Ball and Other Simulation Software

Overview

A major theme of this book has been that process workflow models should be built and analyzed to improve their performance. A diverse set of modeling tools, methods, and concepts were presented in this book to increase modeling efficiency. Although many of the tools and methods discussed were presented as calculations, there are many sophisticated software-driven solutions. These software packages can help analyze process workflows under different operating assumptions. The goal of this appendix is to present a few of the more commonly used software packages related to simulation modeling and describe some of their major characteristics. It was discussed in Chapter 5 and shown in Figure 5.5 that simulation models are used to characterize real-world process workflows using parameters and decision rules to create a model of the workflow having performance features matching those of a real-world system. The modeling process includes specifying interrelationships among system components and experimentation of the model using time compression of simulated events.

Process Workflow Modeling

It is important that a team use the simplest possible model to characterize, analyze, and improve its process workflows. As an example, to build a simulation model, a team should process map their workflows. They should also quantify their maps relative to operational cycle times, costs, and yields, as well as other metrics. However, in some situations, a static, but quantified process map such as a value stream map (VSM) will be sufficient to enable a team to make the necessary process improvements. Although, when relationships between input and output variables are complicated, a simulation or other type of modeling approach, such as queuing analysis or linear programming, may be the only way to obtain a solution to a team's questions regarding how a process workflow operates.

In Figure 5.11, a simulation example was described in which three operations each had a different cycle time distribution relative to completion of each work task. As a result, the operational cycle times of the three operations could not be combined to obtain an overall cycle time estimate. In this situation, simulation was required to estimate an overall cycle time for the process. However, there are many different types of simulation problems. The problem described above was very simple. This may not be true in other analyses where there may be functional relationships among several variables, with each having a probabilistic distribution. This concept is captured in the classic Six Sigma relationship $Y = f(X)$. Using this relationship, we could set each X to its average or expected value and estimate the average value of Y. However, the levels of X will usually vary, causing Y to vary. This requires that a simulation be conducted to capture the probabilistic relationship between the independent variables, X's, and the dependent variable, Y. As an example, we could specify: profit = revenue – cost. A simulation could be used to calculate the probabilities of different profits by varying the levels of revenue and cost based on their assumed probability distributions. This type of analysis will enable an organization to plan for lower or higher profits based on a risk assessment of the revenue and cost inputs.

In this appendix, we will review a few of the common off-the-shelf simulation software packages and focus on Excel-based versions. In particular, we will discuss software offered by Real Options Valuation, Inc., which is very similar to Decision Engineering's Crystal Ball® software. The software versions we will discuss in this appendix are listed in Table A4.1. Crystal Ball and Real Options Valuation® software enable simulation of risk, using Excel as the base program, to evaluate the impact of changing X levels on a Y via a transfer function. In addition, they offer an option of selecting one of several probability distributions to represent the distribution of X, as well as an ability to build models based on the underlying Excel functionality. Once a simulation has been created and run by the software, statistical analysis of the simulation results, including forecasting models, is available to an analyst. The forecasting models includes time series and autoregressive integrated moving average (ARIMA) models.

Table A4.1   Major Process Workflow Analysis Software Available to Operation Managers

Example Workflow	Crystal Ball®	Real Options Valuation®	*Process Software* FlexSim®	Igrafx®	iRise Studio®
Major function	Risk simulation using Excel for modeling changing inputs via a transfer function	Risk simulation using Excel for modeling changing inputs via a transfer function	Three-dimensional dynamic process visualization	Two-dimensional dynamic process visualization	Two-dimensional Web design workflow application simulation
Basic options	Distribution selection; Monte Carlo simulation based on distribution assumptions; ability to build models based on Excel functionality; statistical analysis of simulation results	Distribution selection; Monte Carlo simulation based on distribution assumptions; ability to build models based on Excel functionality; statistical analysis of simulation results	Distribution selection; Monte Carlo simulation based on distribution assumptions; ability to build models based on Excel functionality; statistical analysis of simulation results	Distribution selection; Monte Carlo simulation based on distribution assumptions; ability to build models based on Excel functionality; statistical analysis of simulation results	White board to sketch process workflows and layer in text images of physical objects
Unique options	Forecasting models, including time series and autoregressive integrated moving average (ARIMA) models	Forecasting models, including time series and autoregressive integrated moving average (ARIMA) models	Simulation of actual physical layouts, including people and machines; facilitates communication and analysis	Ability to rapidly create process workflows and quantify them, relative to time, costs, and yield; facilitates easy use	Allows virtual teams anywhere in the world to collaborate on the design of process workflows having Web-based applications as their basis
Web site	www.decisionengineering.com	www.realoptionsvaluation.com	www.flexsim.com	www.igrafx.com	www.irise.com

In addition to Excel-based versions of simulation software, FlexSim, Inc., provides software called FlexSim® having three-dimensional dynamic process visualization capability This three-dimensional version provides an animated simulation of the actual physical layout of the process workflow, including its people, machines, and materials. Visualization facilitates communication within an organization. Another simulation software provider, called Igrafx®, provides two-dimensional dynamic process visualization of a process workflow. The software is relatively easy to use and enables a user to rapidly create process workflows and quantify them relative to time, cost, and yield. An ability to create two-dimensional process visualization also facilitates communication across an organization. These two software systems can be used to model most common process workflows. On the other hand, iRise® provides software targeted toward Web designers who must build Web sites that adjust their informational status dynamically as system inputs change. This software provides simulation capability, including a white board to sketch process workflows, text images of physical objects, and data entry fields to allow virtual teams anywhere in the world to collaborate on the design of Web-based process workflows. In addition to the five software packages discussed above, there are other software applications available, depending on the type of industry and process workflow. The algorithms used in these software packages could be based on simulation, linear programming, queuing, or other models.

Excel-Based Versions

Table A4.2 lists common features of Crystal Ball and Real Options Valuation simulation software.

To show how an Excel-based simulation model can be usefully applied, we will use the example described in Figure 18.3 and Figure 18.5, as well as Table 18.6. The analysis is applied to a network's critical path. Figure A4.1 shows that for operation 1, the beta distribution was selected to model the cycle time of the operation in a manner similar to that shown in Table 18.6. However, an advantage of using this Excel-based software is that one of several probability distributions can

Table A4.2 Some Basic Functions of Excel-Based Simulation Software

1. Distribution selection
2. Monte Carlo simulation based on distribution assumptions
3. Ability to build models based on Excel functionality
4. Statistical analysis of simulation results
5. Forecasting models, including time series and autoregressive integrated moving average (ARIMA) models

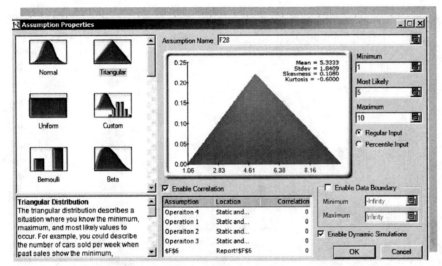

Software: Real Options Valuation, Inc. (www.realoptionsvaluation.com)

Figure A4.1   Operation 1: modeling cycle time as a beta distribution.

be used to describe a variable in addition to the simpler beta distribution. The results of the analysis are shown in Figure A4.2, in which the overall cycle time across the four operations located on the critical path is 26.52 days (rounded). This result agrees with that shown in Figure 18.6, in which a 95 percent confidence interval of the individual cycle times was 23.5 ± 16 days. The advantage of using these risk-focused software tools is that we can quickly create distributions for the input variables. The Excel basis of the software also facilitates easy modeling for workflows that are arranged in tabular format.

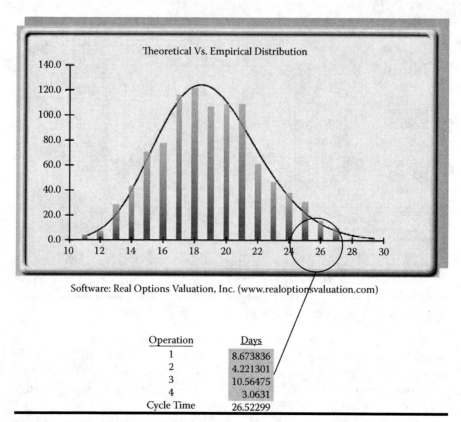

Software: Real Options Valuation, Inc. (www.realoptionsvaluation.com)

Operation	Days
1	8.673836
2	4.221301
3	10.56475
4	3.0631
Cycle Time	26.52299

Figure A4.2   Cycle time on critical path.

Glossary

2^k level design: A linear experimental design in which all variables are at their low and high levels.

5-S methodology: A set of Lean tools and methods that includes sorting, standardizing, setting in order, shining, and sustaining improvements.

5-S techniques: Lean techniques that encourage local work teams to sort, set in order, shine, standardize, and sustain improvements.

ABC inventory classification: Classification of inventory accounts based on dollar valuation.

Accounts receivable collection period: 365 days divided by accounts receivable turnover.

Accounts receivable turnover: Credit sales divided by average accounts receivable.

Accuracy: The ability to remain on target over many samples.

Activation: Using a resource only when it is needed.

Actual capacity: A capacity less than that which should be available due to unexpected process breakdowns.

Additive model: A forecasting model in which all terms are linearly additive.

Advanced shipment notification (ASN): A system in which delivery information is electronically transferred between supplier and customer.

Affinity diagram: Used to organize large amounts of data into natural groups based on a common theme.

Agile Project Management (APM): A project management system based on Lean concepts and used to develop software products.

AIAG: Automotive Industry Action Group.

Alternative hypothesis: The hypothesis mutually exclusive of the null hypothesis, which states there is a change.

Analysis of collected data: The process of applying analytical tools to understand relationships in data to obtain information.

Analytical hierarchy process (AHP): A method that allows paired comparisons between alternatives.

Analyze: The third DMAIC phase in which data is analyzed to obtain relevant information.

Analyze phase: The third phase of the Six Sigma DMAIC methodology.

Anderson–Darling test: A goodness-of-fit test that compares a sample to an assumed distribution.

Annual operating plan (AOP): A high-level financial plan that estimates revenues and costs as well as cash flow.

Annualized cost of goods sold (COGS): The total cost of materials and labor representing all units manufactured in a year.

Application programming interface (API): The software used to transfer data between different manufacturing systems.

Arrow diagram: Used to show the spatial relationships among many factors to qualitatively identify causal factors.

As-is map: A graphical depiction of a process that is usually quantified and created by "walking the process."

Assemble-to-order: The process of building product from components and subassemblies based on firm customer orders.

Assessment: A methodology for evaluation of process performance and improvement opportunities.

Assets: Equipment, facilities, and other materials that have value to an organization.

Attribute control chart: A control chart that displays a discrete variable over time, i.e., pass/fail or counts.

Automotive Industry Action Group (AIAG): A group that develops product design and production approval standards.

Autoregressive integrated moving average (ARIMA) models: An advanced time series modeling method that uses autoregressive and moving average terms.

Available capacity: Capacity less than the design capacity, with normal inefficiencies factored into its calculation.

Backorder: A situation in which not 100 percent of an order was filled, resulting in subsequent orders.

Backward scheduling: An algorithm that starts with an order's required date and works backwards to schedule its manufacturing.

Balance sheet: A financial statement that records assets and liabilities.

Basic need: One of the three types of Kano needs. Customers expect basic needs to be met by all suppliers.

Batch-and-queue system: A transformation system in which production is moved using discrete lots.

Benchmarking: Tools, methods, and techniques that compare the performance attributes of one system to another.

Bill-of-material (BOM): The document showing the hierarchal relationship of a product's components and the sequence in which it is built.

Binary logistic regression: A regression technique in which the dependent variable is binary, i.e., two states.

Bottleneck management: The process of ensuring system bottlenecks are utilized to meet the takt time without disruption.

Box plot: A graphical analysis tool showing the first, second, third, and fourth quartiles and median of the sample data.

Breakthrough improvement: Changing process performance by a discontinuous amount, i.e., a step change improvement.

Budget variance: A difference between a budgeted amount and the actual.

Business activity monitoring (BAM): A software system that monitors changes in process workflow status.

Business intelligence (BI): A software system that analyzes data and provides information useful for process workflow control.

Business metrics: A measure of operational performance used to provide information or control a process.

Business process management (BPM): A software system that integrates several other software systems to manage process workflows.

Business process management suite (BPMS): A software system that integrates data and storage among many IT platforms.

Business process modeling and analysis (BPMA): A software system that allows a process workflow to be simulated and optimizes offline.

Business value-added operations: Operations valued by external customers and obligated to meet their requirements.

Capability analysis: A set of tools, methods, and concepts that compare the voice-of-the-process (VOP) to the voice-of-the-customer (VOC).

Capability ratio: The ratio of the range of customer specification limits and the process variation measured in standard deviations.

Capacity: The amount of material or information that can be put through a system in a unit amount of time.

Capacity constrained resource: A resource that can become a bottleneck if process conditions change.

Capacity requirements: The amount of capacity required to produce a unit of material or information.

Capacity requirements planning (CRP): Planning material, labor, equipment, and facilities necessary to produce products and services.

Capacity utilization: The process of using capacity regardless of whether it is necessary.

Cash flow statement: A financial statement that estimates the amount of free or available cash by time period.

Cash investment: The amount of cash required to maintain capacity in a system.

Cash-to-cash cycle: The cycle time between paying for material, labor, and other expenses and receipt of payment from the customer.

Cause-and-effect (C&E) diagram: A graphical tool that shows qualitative relationships between causes (X's) and their effect (Y).

Cause-and-effect matrix (or C&E matrix): A matrix used to prioritize several inputs X's for data collection across several outputs, or Y's.

C chart: A control chart that monitors count data based on a Poisson distribution with equal subgroup sample size over time.

Champion: A person who removes project barriers.

Channel: The number of parallel servers in a system.

Closed system: A system responsible for its outputs.

Cluster sampling: Drawing a sample based on natural grouping of the population, i.e., by geography.

Cochran–Orcutt method: A statistical method that builds a linear regression model in the presence of correlated errors (residuals).

Coincident variable: An independent variable of the same time period as the dependent variable.

Common sampling methods: The four basic ways in which a random sample can be drawn from a population.

Computer-aided design (CAD): A software system that allows models of a product to be created on a computer.

Computer-aided manufacturing (CAM): A software system that uses CAD models of a product to manufacture the actual product using machines.

Concept phase: The first phase of the AIAG system in which the product or service design is defined.

Concurrent engineering (CE): A project management system in which organizational functions work together to design products or services.

Confidence interval: The amount of uncertainty present in estimating the expected value of a statistical parameter.

Conscience metric: A metric used to ensure other project metrics do not adversely impact a project.

Consignment inventory: Supplier inventory that has been assigned to a customer.

Constraint: A mathematical relationship that must be satisfied to obtain a solution in linear programming models.

Contingency table: A statistical method used to determine the independence between two discrete variables based on count data.

Continuous flow environment: A process workflow where there are no discrete units, such as oil refining.

Continuous improvement: Process improvement activities deployed over an extended time.

Control: The fifth DMAIC phase, in which process improvements are transitioned back to the process owner.

Control chart: A time series chart used to distinguish between common and special cause variation.

Control phase: The fifth Six Sigma phase, in which key process input variables (KPIVs) are controlled.

Control strategies: Combining various control tools to ensure process improvements are sustained over time.

Corrective maintenance: A set of tools and methods that attempt to prevent unexpected equipment failures.

Correlation: A statistical method used to determine the strength of a linear relationship between two variables.

Cost avoidance: A potential cost to an organization that will occur if not prevented.

Cost-of-goods-sold (COGS): The standard cost of goods and services sold.

Cp: The process capability when the process is on target and estimated using short-term variation.

Cpk: The process capability when the process is off target and estimated using short-term variation.

Critical to quality (CTQ): A product or service feature that is important to an external customer.

Cultural change: A situation in which an organization begins to practice one or more new behaviors.

Cultural survey: A method that asks employees their opinion of an organization's strengths, weaknesses, external threats, and opportunities.

Current map: A graphical representation of the process as it currently exists.

Current ratio: Current assets divided by current liabilities.

Customer value: Cost, time, function, utility, and importance of a product or service as perceived by a customer.

Cycle counting: The process of conducting physical audits to estimate inventory value.

Cycle-counting system design: The process of designing inventory audits to provide information using labor, data, and materials in combination.

Data accuracy: The requirement data not biased from its true average level.

Data analysis: Various tools and methods designed to create information to answer questions from data.

Data collection: The process of bringing people and systems together to obtain information.

Days of supply (DOS): The inventory quantity on hand divided by average daily demand in units.

Decision tree: A mathematical method to assign probabilities and expected payoffs to several alternative decisions.

Decomposition model: A forecasting method that breaks a time series into level, trend, and seasonal components.

Defect: A nonconformance relative to a specific customer requirement.

Defects-per-million-opportunities (DPMO): A normalized quality metric calculated by multiplying DPU by 1,000,000 and dividing by the opportunity count.

Defects-per-unit (DPU): The ratio of total defects in a sample to total units sampled.

Define phase: The first DMAIC phase, in which a project is defined relative to business benefits and customer requirements.

Demand aggregation: The process of combining unit demand for several items and locations by time period (usually one month).

Demand forecast: The process of estimating demand in the future by time period (usually one month).

Demand history worksheet: The Excel worksheet containing actual customer demand history.

Demand management: The process of estimating future demand based on a combination of mathematical models and real-time demand information.

Demand pull: The scheduling process in which actual customer demand is used to schedule upstream operations.

Demand push: The scheduling process in which forecasted demand is used to schedule operations.

Dependent demand: Demand related to independent demand through a bill-of-materials (BOM).

Dependent variable: A variable that is explained by one or more other variables (independent).

Descriptive statistics: Summarized information relative to the central location and dispersion of a sample.

Design capacity: The maximum capacity a system can attain at 100 percent efficiency.

Design excellence: An initiative that uses customer requirements and best-in-class design practices to create products and services.

Design failure-mode-and-effects-analysis (DFMEA): A tool and related methods used to identify how a design can fail to meet requirements and the causes of its failures.

Design-for-manufacturing (DFM): A design methodology using several rules and techniques that attempts to simplify and modularize designs.

Design for Six Sigma (DFSS): A set of tools, methods, and concepts used to ensure that designs meet customer requirement at a Six Sigma performance level.

Design standards: Information used to ensure that designs meet minimum accepted standards related to fit, form, and function.

DFSS scorecard: A summarization of a design's capability relative to all its components, performance, and other attributes.

Differenced time series: A time series in which observations have been subtracted from other observations to eliminate trends.

Direct labor: An expense component on the profit and loss statement representing the cost of hourly labor.

Disaggregating: The process of breaking a larger workflow system into components for insourcing or outsourcing.

Display board: A board placed in areas to show key metrics and other information useful to improve and control processes.

Distribution fitting: The process of fitting empirical data to a known distribution.

Distribution requirements planning (DRP): Inventory controlled in a distribution network based on demand placed on each distribution center.

Diverse team: A group of people brought together to work a project and having diverse viewpoints, skills, or demographics.

DMAIC: The Six Sigma five-phase problem-solving methodology: define, measure, analyze, improve, and control.

Double exponential smoothing: A mathematical method that builds a forecasting model using a level component and trend line.

DPMO: Defects-per-million-opportunities.

Durbin–Watson (DW) test: A statistical test that analyzes residual patterns for the presence of positive or negative serial correlation.

Econometric model: A regression model explaining the changes in a dependent variable using independent and lagged variables.

Economic order quantity (EOQ): An optimally calculated quantity that balances inventory ordering cost versus inventory holding cost.

Economic value added (EVA): The income shareholders receive for their investment in an organization.

Economy-of-scale: A situation in which the variable cost of a product decreases as its sales volume increases.

Effectiveness: A situation in which the right things are done.

Electronic data interchange (EDI): An electronic system that allows IT systems to exchange information among organizations.

Enabler initiative: An initiative used to execute improvement projects.

Engineer-to-order: A system in which unique products and services are designed and built for a customer.

Enterprise application integration (EAI): A software system that manages and controls information among several legacy systems.

Enterprise information system (EIS): Separate software system that manages specific portions of a supply chain.

Enterprise resource planning (ERP): A software system managing supply, demand, and customer and financial transactions in a supply chain.

Entitlement analysis: An analysis showing the best process performance, i.e., an on-target process having short-term variation.

Equal variance tests: A statistical test that compares the equivalence of two variances.

E-supply: Electronic supply-chain processes between supplier and customers.

Excess inventory: Inventory quantities exceeding expected demand during their order cycle.

Excitement need: One of the three types of Kano needs in which customers are delighted by a design characteristic.

Experimental designs: An analysis of the impact on a dependent variable of changing levels of one or more independent variables.

Exponential smoothing: A type of forecasting method in which one or more parameters are used to build a model using historical data.

Extrapolation: The process of predicting the level of a dependent variable outside the range in which the dependent variable was previously studied.

Facility location: The process of building or moving operations from one location to another.

FAF: Financial Accounting Foundation.

Failure-mode-and-effects-analysis (FMEA): An analytical tool showing the relationship of failure modes to causes and evaluating their risk levels.

FDA: Food and Drug Administration.

Feasible solution: One of several solutions that satisfy linear programming constraints.

FIFO inventory valuation: First-in-first-out inventory management.

Financial justification: The process of developing financial estimates of improvement project benefits.

Financial metric: A project metric that shows its cost savings, revenue increases, or cash flow increases if successful.

Finished-goods inventory: Inventory that has been completely built and packaged and is ready to ship to the external customer.

Finite loading: Scheduling a product with consideration for demand on its work center (available capacity).

First-come-first-serve (FCFS): A prioritization system used in queuing models.

First-in-first-out (FIFO): A prioritization system used in inventory valuation systems that value materials as they are received.

First-pass yield: The number of units meeting requirements at a single operation, excluding rework and scrap.

First quartile: The point at which 25 percent of the observations from a sample are below.

Fixed-asset efficiency (turns): Sales divided by the amount invested in fixed assets.

Flat world: A phrase by Thomas L. Friedman suggesting distance does not protect organizations from global competition.

Force field analysis: A method used to analyze technological, organizational, and other barriers to countermeasures necessary to eliminate root causes of process breakdowns.

Forecast: A set of quantitative and qualitative methods used to predict future events.

Forecast holdout period: A portion of a time series not incorporated into the model and used to test its accuracy.

Forecasting accuracy: The degree to which the actual quantity demanded by the customer matches that which was forecast by time period (usually one month).

Forecasting benchmarks: Forecasting accuracy percentages characteristic of best-in-class systems.

Forecasting error: The quantity over or under that demanded by the customer versus that which was forecast by time period (usually one month).

Forecasting model: A quantitative relationship predicting future events based on lagged dependent or independent variables.

Forecasting new products: The process of estimating demand for new products by time period (one month).

Forecasting products: The process of estimating demand for current products by time period (one month).

Forecasting reconciliation: The process of smoothing out the forecast based on factors external to the forecasting model to ensure one number.

Forecasting road map: A map of how a forecast is developed within most organizations.

Forecasting stratification: The process of categorizing items and locations by their demand variation and volume to focus attention on them.

Forecasting system: A system of people, software, and tools used to estimate future demand based on historical demand patterns.

Forecasting time horizon: The time period into the future for which a forecast is made.

Forming stage: The first stage in a team maturation process.

Forward scheduling: A scheduling method that uses a forecast to schedule manufacture of a product.

Fractional factorial design: A highly efficient two-level factorial design in which information on high-order interactions is traded for fewer experiments.

Free cash flow: The amount of money an organization has available to invest according to its needs.

Full factorial design: A two-level factorial design in which a model is built using every factor interaction.

Functional interface: The handoff between organization functions.

Functional process map: A detailed process map showing all process workflow operations by function and time sequence.

Functional silos: Different departments or work areas within an organization having different responsibilities and work tasks.

Functionality: How a product or service functions.

Gantt chart: A chart that shows the start and finish time of work tasks in a project.

Globalization: The process in which organizations establish their presence across the world.

Green belt: A process improvement specialist within the Six Sigma program who works within a function.

Gross margin: The profit before taxes, calculated by subtracting cost of goods sold from revenue minus adjustments.

Gross margin return on investment (GMROI): A product's gross margin divided by its average inventory investment.

Groupthink: A situation in which team members consistently agree with each other even if their decision is incorrect.

High-performance work team: A diverse team that has been through all four maturation stages and consistently achieves its objectives.

Histogram: A statistical method that graphically summarizes continuous data to show its central location and dispersion.

Historical demand: Actual customer demand over time.

Holt's method: A forecasting method that models level and trend components of a time series (double exponential smoothing).

House-of-quality (HOQ): A graphical method used to show quality function deployment information.

Hybrid decentralization: A system that locates work where it is performed best at lower cost and cycle time and higher quality.

Hypothesis testing: A statistical method that compares a population parameter to a constant or other levels of the parameter.

Identify phase: The first design for Six Sigma (DFSS) phase, which identifies customer requirements.

Improve phase: The fourth Six Sigma phase, in which key process input variable (KPIV), or X, levels are changed to optimize Y.

Income statement: A financial statement that records income and expenses by time period.

Incorporate phase: The fifth design for Six Sigma (DFSS) phase, which verifies that customer requirements are met in a new design.

Independent demand: Customer demand for products or services.

Indicator variables: Variables used to model discrete levels of a variable.

Indirect labor: Labor not part of actually making a product or providing a service to the customer, i.e., not hourly labor.

Individual control chart: A time series chart that separates common cause from special cause variation for nonsubgrouped continuous data.

Infinite loading: Scheduling a product without consideration for demand on the work center (available capacity).

Information disaggregating: Taking information associated with producing a product or service and sending it to different locations for processing.

Information technology excellence: A set of best-in-class management and operational practices in the area of information technology.

Input–output matrices: Matrices that correlate input variables relative to output variables.

Insourcing: A practice of bringing work into an organization to improve its productivity.

Integrated supply chains: A supply chain linked by information technology to provide system status in real-time.

Interaction: A mathematical term usually calculated by multiplying coded factor coefficients in an experimental design.

International Standards Organization (ISO): An organization that sets standards to enable commerce between organizations across the world.

Interpolation: Calculating a dependent variable by setting the levels of the independent variables within its range of study.

Interrelationship diagram: Used to show the spatial relationships between many factors to qualitatively identify causal factors.

Inventory age: 365 days divided by inventory turnover.

Inventory analysis algorithm: An algorithm that uses lead time, demand variation, and service level to estimate the optimum inventory quantity.

Inventory balance: An analysis of an optimum versus the actual inventory quantity to determine excess and insufficient quantities.

Inventory improvement plan: A plan to reduce inventory investment or improve customer service based on data analysis.

Inventory investment: The amount of money required to maintain inventory in anticipation of demand to meet target service levels.

Inventory make-to-stock model: A model that calculates required finished-goods inventory quantities by item and location.

Inventory turnover: Cost-of-goods-sold divided by average inventory investment.

Inventory turns: A ratio calculated by dividing cost of goods sold (COGS) by the average on-hand inventory investment.

Irregular component: The variation in a time series not predicted by a model.

ISO 9000: International Standards Organization standard describing basic quality system requirements.

ISO 9001: International Standards Organization standard describing system elements needed to meet customer requirements.

ISO 9004: International Standards Organization standard describing system improvement potential.

JIT system: Just-in-time supply of materials or information dependent on several underlying systems for success.

Job shop: A type of production process characterized by low volumes and high product diversity.

Judgmental forecasting: A set of qualitative forecasting methods that rely on nonquantitative information to predict future events.

Just-in-time (JIT): A Lean system in which material or information arrives when needed and in the required quantity.

Kanban: A Kanban is a physical or electronic sign attached to inventory to show order status. There are transport, production, and signal Kanbans.

Kanban calculation: Sets the WIP inventory based on lead time, demand, and service level.

Kano needs: A system that classifies customer needs into basic, performance, and excitement.

Kendall notation: A descriptive system that describes queuing models.

Key process input variable (KPIV): Independent variables that have a significant impact on key process output variables (KPOVs).

Key process output variable (KPOV): Dependent variables that are directly correlated to the voice of the customer (VOC).

Kitting: The process of bringing together components for use in service kits, replacement parts, and other applications.

Kruskal–Wallis test: A nonparametric test used to compare equality of several medians.

L-shaped work cell: A work cell layout arranged as an L.

Lagging variable: Dependent variable from previous time periods used to explain variation of the same dependent variable in current or future time periods.

Launch phase: Commercialization phase of product.

Lead time: The time to complete all work tasks.

Lead time analysis: The process of decomposing lead time into its time components.

Lead time components: Lead time can be broken into transportation, setup, waiting, processing, inspection, and idle time.

Lead time reduction: The process of reducing time within a process.

Lead time variation: The variation of task completion times within a process.

Leading variable: Independent variable used to explain future variation of a dependent variable.

Lean: A system designed to create simple, standardized, and mistake-proofed processes based on customer value.

Lean enterprise: An organization that exhibits Lean principles.

Lean performance measurements: A series of operational and financial metrics that can be used to evaluate the effectiveness of a Lean deployment.

Lean supply chain: A supply chain that uses Lean methods to improve its performance.

Least squares algorithm: A mathematical algorithm used in regression to build an equation to explain the variation of a dependent variable.

LIFO inventory valuation: Last-in-first-out inventory valuation.

Linear programming (LP): A mathematical algorithm that maximizes or minimizes an objective function subject to constraints.

Linear regression: A statistical technique used to develop a linear relationship between several independent variables and a dependent variable.

Linearity: A measurement device having a constant variation throughout its measurement range.

Logistic regression: A mathematical method to build an equation to explain the variation in a discrete dependent variable.

Long-term variation: The variation that impacts a process over a long period.

Lower specification limit (LSL): Lower level of a customer specification.

Make to order: A production system that produces products or services based on firm customer orders.

Make to stock: A manufacturing system that makes products for inventory storage.

Malcolm Baldrige Award: An award presented to organizations having best-in-class quality systems.

Market penetration: A calculation of the potential number of buyers of a product or service.

Market segment: Potential buyers of a product or service who have been stratified using a stratification rule.

Mass customization: A system of production recommending lower-level design and process commonality, but higher-level product diversity.

Master production schedule (MPS): System that aggregates demand for the MRPII system.

Materials requirements planning (MRPII): System that uses demand from the MPS and explodes it through the MRPII system.

Mean: A central location statistic calculated by summing all observations and dividing by their number.

Mean absolute percentage error (MAPE): A forecasting error statistic useful in comparing the forecasting error of different time series.

Measure phase: The second Six Sigma phase, in which the ability to measure a metric and its capability is established.

Measurement systems analysis (MSA): A series of methods used to verify accuracy, linearity, stability, resolution and identify sources of measurement variation.

Median: A central location statistic that measures the number separating 50 percent of observations on each side of the number.

Metric: A characteristic that can be measured as either a discrete or continuous variable.

Metric dashboard: A tool used to collect information on several related metrics to provide information on process status.

Metric scorecard: A matrix used to record and track process metrics by metric type and other characteristics necessary to control a process.

Meyers–Briggs system: A psychological profiling system useful in understanding individual perceptions and behavior.

Micromotion studies: Analysis using cameras that break down work into its smallest motions to set work time standards.

Milk run: A delivery system in which suppliers are located near customers and supply them based on scheduled Kanban quantities.

Min/max inventory system: An inventory system that reorders based on an item's reorder point.

Mistake-proofing: A system of tools and methods that prevent or detect errors and their defects.

Mixed-model scheduling: A scheduling system in which product lot sizes are small due to low cost setups enabling more frequent scheduling of products or services.

Monte Carlo simulation: A mathematical technique in which randomly generated numbers are transformed into a reference distribution.

Mood's median test: A nonparametric statistical test that compares the equality of two or more medians.

Moving average model: A forecasting model that predicts future values by averaging past values of a time series.

MRPII-driven Kanban: A system in which the MRPII system lot size is used as a Kanban system to control flow through the system.

Multiple linear regression: A mathematical technique used to develop a linear relationship between a dependent and several independent variables.

Multiplicative model: A forecasting model that is built by multiplying its terms.

Multi-vari chart: A graphical method used to analyze the impact of changing levels of independent variables on a dependent variable.

Nominal logistic regression: A logistic regression model in which a dependent variable has several discrete labels.

Nonlinear regression: A method that builds a non-linear relationship between a dependent and one or more independent variables.

Non-value-adding (NVA) operations: Operations within a process workflow that customers do not want.

Normality test: A goodness-of-fit test that compares a sample to an assumed normal distribution.

Norming stage: The third stage of team maturation, in which team members begin to agree on team objectives.

np chart: A control chart for binomially distributed data in which the subgroups must be constant.

Null hypothesis: A hypothesis stating that a population parameter is equal to a constant or another level of the parameter.

Objective function: A function in linear programming that must be minimized or maximized.

Obsolete inventory: Inventory that cannot be used to produce products or provide services for sale at current pricing.

One-sample proportion test: A statistical test of one proportion to a constant proportion.

One-sample Wilcoxon test: A nonparametric test used to compare equality of one median to the test median.

One-sample t-test: A statistical test that compares the equivalence of one mean to a constant.

One-way analysis of variance (ANOVA): A statistical test that compares the equivalence of several means to each other.

On-time delivery: When a supplier's shipment quantity is received at the agree-upon lead time without process defects.

Open system: A system in which the consequences of its actions or outputs are not necessarily relevant to its decisions.

Operational balancing: When every operation in a system contributes the material or information flow necessary to maintain the takt time.

Operational efficiency: How well a system functions relative to a target of 100 percent.

Operational excellence: An umbrella initiative including Lean, Six Sigma, and Total Productive or Preventive Maintenance (TPM).

Operational linkage: Ensuring operational metrics are consistent across functional boundaries.

Operational metrics: Metrics other than financial ones that indicate process status relative to time, performance, or quality.

Operational planning overview: A group of cross-functional people who meet to determine the best mix of supply necessary to meet demand.

Operational strategy: The high-level operational goals and objectives that must be achieved to meet financial goals and objectives.

Operations management: A field of study that includes tools and methods used to transform process inputs into outputs.

Operations research: A field of study that includes tools and methods used to mathematically model process inputs into outputs and outputs under variations assumptions.

Opportunity: A product or service characteristic that can be either a pass or fail state.

Optimize phase: The third phase of the design for Six Sigma (DFSS), which sets the levels of the X's to optimize Y.

Optimum map: A process map containing only value-adding operational work tasks.

Order book: Firm demand based on customer orders.

Order cycle (T): The time-to-time interval between sequential incoming order quantities from suppliers.

Ordinal logistic regression: A logistic regression model in which a discrete dependent variable is arranged in a low to high order.

OSHA: Occupational Health and Safety Administration (OSHA).

Outlier: A data point that exceeds more than two or three standard deviations from the central mean location or of a dataset.

Outsourcing: A process of sending work to other organizations to increase productivity.

Overdue backlog: Quantity of product that could not be manufactured according to customer demand due to capacity constraints.

P chart: A control chart for binomially distributed data in which the subgroups are either equal or not equal.

Paired comparison test: A statistical test of the differences between dependent observations before and after a treatment or experiment.

Parallel servers: A system in which there are two or more servers, each servicing the same calling population.

Pareto chart: A graphical analysis tool in which discrete categories are arranged in descending order by their counts.

Parts-per-million (PPM): A metric that adjusts a fraction in terms of 1 million, i.e., 10 percent × 1,000,000 = 100,000 PPM.

Payback: The number of years required to recover an initial investment.

Percent error: The number of defects found in a sample divided by the total sample and multiplied by 100.

Performance gap: The difference between a target and actual performance.

Performance measurements: Metrics used to measure process changes.

Performance need: A Kano need that helps differentiate one supplier from another.

Performing stage: The fourth stage in a team maturation process, in which a team works toward common goals and objectives.

Periodic review inventory system: A model that checks inventory at specific times and orders quantities to bring inventory up to a target level.

Perpetual inventory model (PIM): A model in which inventory is continually monitored and orders are released at a reorder point.

PERT: Program evaluation and review technique.

Pilot of solution: A test of a proposed process change within an actual process, but under controlled conditions.

Pilot phase: A phase in product development in which a design concept is tested under carefully controlled conditions.

Plan, do, check, act: Deming cycle used for problem solving.

Plan execution: The ability to make a plan and ensure it is completed on time and within budget, and meets all goals and objectives.

Point-of-sale (POS): A system that collects sales data as it occurs and provides it to suppliers to plan production.

Pp: The process capability when the process is on target and estimated using long-term variation.

Ppk: The process capability when the process is off target and estimated using long-term variation.

PPM: Parts-per-million.

Precision: A measurement of variation, i.e., high precision implies low variation.

Preventive maintenance: A system of tools, methods, and concepts designed to ensure systems are available for use.

Primary metric: A metric, including financial, business, or project, that must be improved for a project to be successful.

Prioritization matrices: Used to prioritize decisions based on various weighting rules.

Proactive data: Data actively collected by an organization.

Problem statement: A verbal description of the operational problem that must be solved by a project.

Process batch: A system that transfers materials or information to subsequent operations when all units have been processed.

Process capability: A method used to compare process performance against customer specifications.

Process failure-mode-and-effects-analysis (PFMEA): A method that analyzes how a process can fail to correctly build a product or provide a service.

Process improvement projects: Projects used to close performance gaps.

Process mapping: A method used to show the movement of materials and information through the system.

Product group: A collection of products having similar characteristics.

Product life cycle: The demand phases a product goes through over time, including its introduction, growth, maturity, and decline.

Product proliferation: When an organization allows products having little demand or margin contribution to remain active in their systems.

Production activity control (PAC): A manufacturing function on the shop floor used to schedule work through work centers.

Production Kanban: A quantity of material or information used in operations to signal an operation to process another Kanban quantity.

Productivity: A year-over-year measure of outputs divided by inputs, usually expressed in financial terms.

Profit and loss (P/L): A key financial statement that shows income and costs to show whether profit has been made by an organization.

Profitability index: The ratio of present value of cash inflows to present value of cash outflows.

Project activity: A major set of project work tasks that has been assigned a time duration and starting and ending dates.

Project charter: A document in either electronic or paper format that provides justification for the project.

Project evaluation and review technique (PERT): A project probabilistic scheduling methodology used to find a network's critical path.

Project identification: A process of identifying projects to increase organizational productivity or stakeholder satisfaction.

Project management: A set of tools and techniques used to manage project deployments.

Project metric: An operational metric used to measure project success and correlate it to financial and business metrics.

Project milestone: A major set of project activities used to monitor project schedule completion.

Project objective: A section of the project charter that states the specific business benefit of the project.

Project plan: A combination of work tasks, budgets, schedules, and resources brought together to complete a project.

Project planning: The process of scheduling the various work tasks and elements necessary to complete the project.

Project resources: Materials, labor, money, and information necessary to complete the project.

Project selection: The process of identifying work to benefit the business and customer according to strategic goals and objectives.

Prototype phase: A phase in product development in which samples or prototypes are created for test and evaluation.

Pugh matrix: A tool that enables several alternatives to be compared against a baseline scenario.

Pull scheduling system: A visual scheduling system in which the manufacturing system produces according to external customer demand.

Push scheduling system: A manufacturing scheduling system that uses a forecast through the master production schedule to schedule.

Quality control plan: A combination of documentation indicating important product features that must be controlled.

Quality function deployment (QFD): A system of tools and methods used to translate the VOC into internal specifications.

Quantitative forecasts: Forecasts that rely on mathematical models to predict future demand.

Queuing analysis: A mathematical technique used to analyze the probabilistic relationships between customer arrival and service.

Quick ratio: Cash plus marketable securities plus accounts receivable divided by current liabilities.

Quick response manufacturing (QRM): A system that provides local control of resource scheduling in an MRPII environment.

Random sampling: A sample drawn from a population without bias.

Range chart: A control chart of ranges in which a range equals the maximum minus the minimum values of each subgroup.

Rapid prototyping: A method to create prototyping using computer-aided technology.

Rational subgroup sampling: A sampling method that collects data in subgroups from a process at time intervals smaller than those that must analyzed.

Raw material inventory: Inventory that has been received from an external supplier and has had no work done on it.

Reactive data: Information that customers volunteer in the form of complaints, warranty charges, and returned goods.

Reclamation center: A system designed to receive returned product and process it according to organizational policies.

Reorder point (ROP): A quantity of inventory based on the lead time to receive an order multiplied by the expected daily usage over the lead time.

Repeatability: The ability of one person to measure the same thing consistently and obtain the same measured value.

Reproducibility: The ability of two or more people to measure the same thing and agree on its measured value.

Residual: The difference between a model's fitted versus actual value.

Resolution: The unit of scale of a measuring device versus what it is measuring. A 1/10th resolution is normally recommended.

Response surface design: An experimental design that models curvilinear relationships using squared terms of the independent variables.

Response variable: The dependent variable, which is also called a key process output variable.

Return on investment (ROI): Net income divided by available total assets.

Reverse logistics: Operations associated with receipt of customer returns.

Rework: A situation occurring when something must be done more than once due to defects.

Ridge regression: A type of regression method used in the presence of high multicollinearity.

Robust regression: A type of regression method used in the presence of severe outliers.

Rolled throughput yield (RTY): Calculated as the multiplicand of the first-pass yields at every operation.

Root mean square deviation (RMSD): A forecasting error statistic calculated as the square root of the mean summed differences of forecast to actual.

Rough-cut capacity planning: An estimate of capacity needed at a future time for a process workflow.

R^2: A statistic calculated by dividing the variation of Y explained by a model by the total variation of the dataset.

R^2 adjusted: An adjusted R^2 value to account for the number of parameters in a model versus the sample size.

Run charts: A time series chart used to analyze time-dependent data.

S-shaped work cell: A work cell layout arranged as an S.

Safety stock: An inventory quantity that is required to protect against demand or lead time variation.

Safety-stock calculation: Inventory quantity calculated as service factor times standard deviation of demand and the square root of the lead time.

Sales and operational planning: The process of coordinating demand and supply based on system constraints.

Sample mean: Calculated as the sum of the observations divided by their number.

Sample standard deviation: The square root of the variation around the mean.

Sample variance: The variation around the mean.

Sampling: The process of obtaining sample from a larger population.

Sarbanes–Oxley Act: A series of governmentally mandated requirements for disclosure and accuracy of financial data.

Scatter plot: A graphical analysis tool that plots two continuous variables against each other to identify patterns.

Scheduling algorithms: Mathematical models that help schedule resources or events.

Seasonal component: A time series component that models periodic patterns.

Seasonal differencing: A method used to factor out periodic patterns in a time series.

Seasonal index: A constant used to increase or decrease the level of a time series based on the seasonal variation or index.

Second quartile: The point at which 50 percent of the observations from a sample are below.

Secondary metric: A project metric used to prevent negative consequences of changes in the project's primary metric.

Service level: A percentage of time, units, or orders the customer will receive their order when expressed in units, time, or orders.

Short-term variation: Variation acting on a process for a limited amount of time.

Should-be map: A graphical depiction of a process with non-value-adding operations removed.

Sigma level: The short-term capability of a metric.

Simple linear regression: A method using one independent variable to build an equation explaining variation of a dependent variable.

Simple random sampling: A sampling method that draws a random sample from a stable population.

Simulation: A mathematical technique using a reference distribution and random numbers to recreate observations from the original distribution.

Single exponential smoothing: A forecasting method that uses one smoothing parameter to forecast the level component of a time series.

Single Minute Exchange of Dies (SMED): A set of techniques to reduce job changeovers.

SIPOC: Acronym for supplier–input boundary–process–output boundary–customer.

Six Sigma: A process improvement program characterized by five phases: define, measure, analyze, improve, and control.

SMED: Acronym for Single Minute Exchange of Dies.

Stability: The ability of a measurement system to measure the same thing over time and obtain the same measured value.

Standard normal distribution (SND): A probability distribution that is symmetrical or bell shaped.

Standard operating procedures (SOP): Procedures that are determined to be the current best way to do a work task.

Statistical inference: A set of mathematical techniques that allow population parameters to be estimated with predetermined confidence.

Statistical risk: Stating the null hypothesis is false when it is true (type I error), or stating it is true when false (type II error).

Statistical sampling: A set of methods that specify how observations are to be drawn from a population.

Statistical tolerance analysis: A statistical method used to evaluate the impact of varying the levels of X's to improve the capability of Y to optimumly set the level of X.

Stocking location: A specific place where an item is stored.

Storming stage: The second stage of the team maturation process, in which a team may disagree on a project's goals and objectives or other information.

Strategic flow-down: A method used to ensure alignment of strategic goals and objectives throughout an organization.

Strategic project selection: The process of ensuring that projects are selected to align with senior management's goals and objectives.

Stratified sampling: A type of sampling technique in which the population is broken into subgroups having minimal variation within each.

SWOT analysis: Strengths, weaknesses, opportunities, and threats to an organization.

System model map: A quantified process map showing input and output metrics.

Systematic sampling: A sampling method in which every nth observation is taken from the subgroup.

Takt time: The time in which one unit must be produced to meet customer schedules.

Takt time calculation: A calculation that determines how many time units it takes to manufacture one unit.

Target costing: Determining the price at which a product or service will sell and subtracting out the desired profit margin.

Theory of inventive problem solving (TRIZ): A structured brainstorming technique used to apply analogous and previously discovered solutions to new problems.

Third-party logistics: Outsourcing one or more functions to external organizations.

Third quartile: The point at which 75 percent of the observations from a sample are below.

Throughput: The cycle time between paying for material, labor, and other expenses and receipt of payment from the customer.

Time fence: The cumulative lead time to build a product.

Time series: A data series sequentially arranged by time order.

Time series graph: A graphical analysis tool that shows how a variable changes over time.

Total Productive or Preventive Maintenance (TPM): A set of methods that ensure a system is maintained and available at a predetermined percentage of the time.

Transfer batch: A system that moves units of production immediately to downstream operations.

Tree diagram: Used to map higher- to lower-level relationships.

Trend component: A time series component showing the average change of a time series over time.

Triple exponential smoothing: A forecasting method that models level, trend, and seasonal components (also called Winter's method).

Two-sample Mann–Whitney test: A nonparametric test that compares the equality of two medians.

Two-sample proportion test: A statistical test comparing the equality of two proportions.

Two-sample t-test: A statistical test comparing the equivalence of two means.

Type I error: A statement that the null hypothesis is false and should be rejected when it is true.

Type II error: A statement that the null hypothesis is true and should not be rejected when it is false.

U-shaped work cell: A work cell layout arranged as a U.

U chart: A control chart for a Poisson distributed variable in which sample size can vary.

Unidentified task: Goals and objectives that do not currently have projects assigned to ensure their solution.

Unplanned orders: Orders put into the schedule without regard for the product's lead time or time fence.

Upper specification limit (USL): The customer's upper level for the product characteristic.

Utility: A customer value element describing the usefulness of a product feature.

Validate phase: A fourth design for Six Sigma (DFSS) phase used to evaluate design specification capability levels.

Value-adding operations (VA): Operations that a customer desires in a product or service.

Value elements: Time, price, utility, function, and relative importance to a customer.

Value stream mapping (VSM): A process of mapping material and information flows through a process.

Variable control chart: A group of control charts used to evaluate continuously distributed variables.

Variance inflation factor (VIF): A statistic that calculates the degree of collinearity between independent variables.

Virtual capacity: Having available capacity when needed, but not owning or having to pay for its existence when not being used.

Visual controls: A system in which process status can be easily seen at a glance.

Visual displays: Graphics used to convey system status.

Visual workplace: A workplace in which system status can be determined immediately by looking at visual metric displays.

Voice-of-the-business (VOB): Financial and operational goals and objectives that must be considered in process improvements.

Voice-of-the-customer (VOC): Customer requirements that are translated into specifications.

Voice-of-the-process (VOP): Characteristic-by-characteristic central location and dispersion (variation) measured within a process.

Waiting line models: Mathematical models that show relationships between resources available and arriving customers.

Winter's method: A forecasting method that models level, trend, and seasonal time series components (triple exponential smoothing).

Working capital: Current assets minus current liabilities.

Work-in-process inventory: Inventory that is within a process and acts as a buffer against disruptions in material flow between operations.

X's: Independent variables that have a significant impact on key process output variables (KPOVs).

Y's: Dependent variables.

Index